Axes I and II Categories and Codes

Neurotic Disorders: *These are included in Affective, Anxiety, Somatoform, Dissociative, and Psychosexual Disorders. In order to facilitate the identification of the categories that in DSM-II were grouped together in the class of Neuroses, the DSM-II terms are included separately in parentheses after the corresponding categories.*

Affective Disorders

Major affective disorders

Code major depressive episode in fifth digit: 6 = in remission, 4 = with psychotic features, 3 = with melancholia, 2 = without melancholia, 0 = unspecified.

Code manic or mixed episode in fifth digit: 6 = in remission, 4 = with psychotic features, 2 = without psychotic features, 0 = unspecified.

Bipolar disorder,
296.6x mixed
296.4x manic
296.5x depressed

Major depression,
296.2x single episode
296.3x recurrent

Other specific affective disorders

301.13 Cyclothymic disorder
300.40 Dysthymic disorder (or Depressive neurosis)

Atypical affective disorders

296.70 Atypical bipolar disorder
296.82 Atypical depression

Anxiety Disorders

Phobic disorders (or Phobic neuroses)
300.21 Agoraphobia with panic attacks
300.22 Agoraphobia without panic attacks
300.23 Social phobia
300.29 Simple phobia

Anxiety states (or Anxiety neuroses)
300.01 Panic disorder
300.02 Generalized anxiety disorder
300.30 Obsessive-compulsive disorder (or Obsessive-compulsive neurosis)

Posttraumatic stress disorder
308.30 acute
309.81 chronic or delayed
300.00 Atypical anxiety disorder

Somatoform Disorders

300.81 Somatization disorder
300.11 Conversion disorder (or Hysterical neurosis, conversion type)
307.80 Psychogenic pain disorder
300.70 Hypochondriasis (or Hypochondriacal neurosis)
300.70 Atypical somatoform disorder

Dissociative Disorders (or Hysterical Neuroses, Dissociative Type)

300.12 Psychogenic amnesia
300.13 Psychogenic fugue
300.14 Multiple personality
300.60 Depersonalization disorder (or Depersonalization neurosis)
300.15 Atypical dissociative disorder

Psychosexual Disorders

Gender identity disorders

Indicate sexual history in the fifth digit of Transsexualism code: 1 = asexual, 2 = homosexual, 3 = heterosexual, 0 = unspecified.

302.5x Transsexualism
302.60 Gender identity disorder of childhood
302.85 Atypical gender identity disorder

Paraphilias

302.81 Fetishism
302.30 Transvestism
302.10 Zoophilia
302.20 Pedophilia
302.40 Exhibitionism
302.82 Voyeurism
302.83 Sexual masochism
302.84 Sexual sadism
302.90 Atypical paraphilia

Psychosexual dysfunctions

302.71 Inhibited sexual desire
302.72 Inhibited sexual excitement
302.73 Inhibited female orgasm
302.74 Inhibited male orgasm
302.75 Premature ejaculation
320.76 Functional dyspareunia
306.51 Functional vaginismus
302.70 Atypical psychosexual dysfunction

Other psychosexual disorders

302.00 Ego-dystonic homosexuality
302.89 Psychosexual disorder not elsewhere classified

Factitious Disorders

300.16 Factitious disorder with psychological symptoms
301.51 Chronic factitious disorder with physical symptoms
300.19 Atypical factitious disorder with physical symptoms

Disorders of Impulse Control Not Elsewhere Classified

312.31 Pathological gambling
312.32 Kleptomania
312.33 Pyromania
312.34 Intermittent explosive disorder
312.35 Isolated explosive disorder
312.39 Atypical impulse control disorder

Adjustment Disorder

309.00 with depressed mood
309.24 with anxious mood
309.28 with mixed emotional features
309.30 with disturbance of conduct
309.40 with mixed disturbance of emotions and conduct
309.23 with work (or academic) inhibition
309.83 with withdrawal
309.90 with atypical features

Psychological Factors Affecting Physical Condition

Specify physical condition on Axis III.
316.00 Psychological factors affec[illegible] physical condition

Personality Disorders

Note: These are coded on Axis II.

301.00 Paranoid
301.20 Schizoid
301.22 Schizotypal
301.50 Histrionic
301.81 Narcissistic
301.70 Antisocial
301.83 Borderline
301.82 Avoidant
301.60 Dependent
301.40 Compulsive
301.84 Passive-Aggressive
301.89 Atypical, mixed or other personality disorder

V Codes for Conditions Not Attributable to a Mental Disorder That Are a Focus of Attention or Treatment

V65.20 Malingering
V62.89 Borderline intellectual functioning
V71.01 Adult antisocial behavior
V71.02 Childhood or adolescent antisocial behavior
V62.30 Academic problem
V62.20 Occupational problem
V62.82 Uncomplicated bereavement
V15.81 Noncompliance with medical treatment
V62.89 Phase of life problem or other life circumstance problem
V61.10 Marital problem
V61.20 Parent-child problem
V61.80 Other specified family circumstances
V62.81 Other interpersonal problem

Additional Codes

300.90 Unspecified mental disorder (nonpsychotic)
V71.09 No diagnosis or condition on Axis I
799.90 Diagnosis or condition deferred on Axis I
V71.09 No diagnosis on Axis II
799.90 Diagnosis deferred on Axis II

Abnormal Psychology
A New Look

Abnormal Psychology

A New Look

MARSHALL P. DUKE
Emory University

STEPHEN NOWICKI, JR.
Emory University

CBS Publishing Japan Ltd.
New York Chicago San Francisco
Philadelphia Montreal Toronto
London Sydney Tokyo Mexico City
Rio de Janeiro Madrid

To Our Parents

Publisher Bob Woodbury
Acquiring Editor Susan Meyers
Project Editorial, Design, and Line Illustration Caliber Design Planning, Inc.
Production Manager Robin B. Besofsky
Photo Researcher Anthony Scaravilli

Library of Congress Cataloging-in-Publication Data

Duke, Marshall P.
Abnormal psychology.

Bibliography: p.
Includes index.
1. Psychology, Pathological.
2. Psychology, Pathological—Philosophy.
I. Nowicki, Stephen. II. Title. [DNLM:
1. Psychopathology. WM 100 D877a]
RC454.D84 1986 616.89 85-19075

ISBN 0-03-004404-9 (US College Edition)
ISBN 0-03-910712-4 (HRW International Edition)

Address correspondence to:
383 Madison Avenue
New York, N.Y. 10017

Printed in Japan, 1986

6 7 8 9 032 9 8 7 6 5 4 3 2 1

CBS COLLEGE PUBLISHING
The Dryden Press
Saunders College Publishing

Chapter Photo Credits:

Chapter 1 © Arthur Tress, 1972/Photo Researchers, Inc.
Chapter 2 Fritz Henle/Photo Researchers, Inc.
Chapter 3 Culver Pictures
Chapter 4 © 1976 Bruce Roberts/Photo Researchers, Inc.
Chapter 5 Sigmund Freud: © ARCHIV/Photo Researchers, Inc.; B. F. Skinner: National Library of Medicine; Carl Rogers: Douglas A. Land
Chapter 6 © 1985 Charles A. Scaravilli
Chapter 7 Lawrence Schiller © 1976 The New Ingot Co./Photo Researchers, Inc.
Chapter 8 Michael Weisbrot and Family
Chapter 9 Arthur Tress
Chapter 10 © 1985 Charles A. Scaravilli
Chapter 11 Arthur Tress
Chapter 12 © 1985 Peter Norem
Chapter 13 Michael Weisbrot and Family
Chapter 14 © 1981 Susan Rosenberg/Photo Researchers, Inc.
Chapter 15 © R. Ellis/Photo Researchers, Inc.
Chapter 16 © 1985 Peter Norem
Chapter 17 Michael Weisbrot and Family
Chapter 18 Ellen G. Chiemiego
Chapter 19 © Bob Combs/Photo Researchers, Inc.

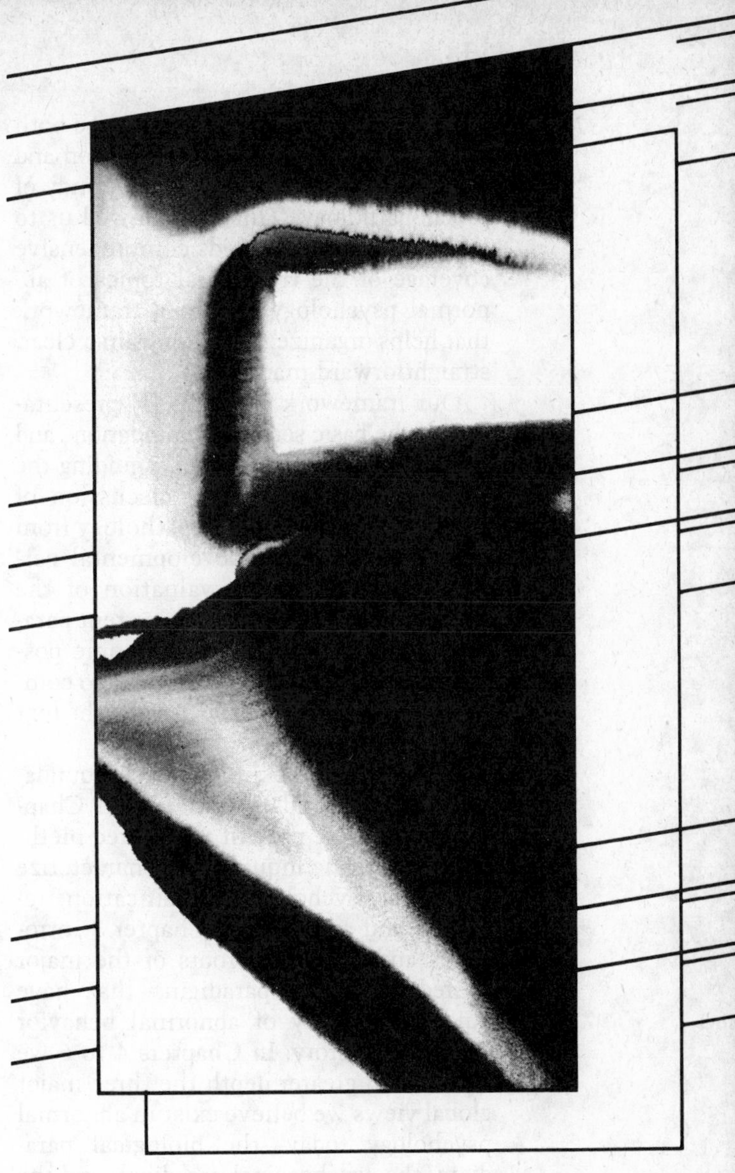

Preface

In preparing this second edition of our textbook, we sought to present the science of abnormal psychology in an organized, balanced, and integrated manner. We searched for an organizing framework that would not only guide us in our choice of topics, but also in the ways in which we might discuss these topics in as clear, understandable, and meaningful a fashion as possible. We believe that we found such an organizing framework in the writings of philosopher of science, Thomas Kuhn. Briefly, Kuhn assumes that a science is marked by (1) a set of accepted methods for approaching the problems addressed by that science and (2) one or more sets of global views of the world (paradigms) which guide researchers in their efforts to understand the phenomena they study. Befitting its status as a science, abnormal psychology also can be characterized in this manner. In our survey of the field, we have delineated what we believe are both the accepted methods of investigation and the major paradigms guiding the study of psychopathology. This has allowed us to write a book that embeds comprehensive coverage of the traditional topics of abnormal psychology within a framework that helps organize these topics in a clear, straightforward manner.

Our framework includes (1) presentation of the basic scientific foundations and the major paradigms currently guiding the study of abnormality; (2) discussion of various patterns of psychopathology from both traditional and developmental perspectives; and (3) an evaluation of the strengths and weaknesses of current paradigms and an examination of some possible emerging future paradigms. To complete these tasks, we have divided the text into four parts.

In Part I, we look at the basic foundations of abnormal psychology. In Chapters 1 and 2, we present the shared methods of scientific inquiry that characterize abnormal psychology—classification, research, and assessment. Chapter 3 introduces and traces the roots of the major shared beliefs or paradigms that have guided the study of abnormal behavior during its history. In Chapters 4 to 6 we examine in greater depth the three major global views we believe exist in abnormal psychology today—the biological paradigm, the psychosocial paradigm, and the systems paradigm. In describing each, we note the ways in which each global view spawns specific types of theories and how these theories have led to specific therapeutic efforts. Organizing the presentations of theories and therapies around the paradigms out of which they both emerge allows students to see most clearly the systematic and goal-directed quality of abnormal psychology.

In Part II we examine the patterns of psychopathology delineated by the DSM-III. Because of the basic "grounding" in the paradigmatic framework, however, our descriptions of the various patterns of disordered behavior can be accompanied by discussions of the impact of each of the three major paradigms on the study of those patterns. In many instances, these discussions reveal particular paradigmatic strengths or weaknesses. Where appropriate, we present those attempts to introduce new paradigmatic approaches to disorders. We begin the presentation of specific patterns of psychopathology with the most severe disorders—the schizophrenias and the affective disturbances. In Chapter 7 we describe the characteristics of schizophrenia and the various attempts at creating a reliable classification system. In Chapter 8, we survey the historical and modern theories and treatments for the schizophrenias from the biological, psychosocial, and systems perspectives. Recent research evidence is emphasized. We continue our coverage of the severe disturbances with an examination of the affective disorders and suicide in Chapter 9. The extensive coverage of suicide from the first edition has been updated and streamlined with special topics of age-related suicide mentioned elsewhere in the book. In our coverage, we recognize the special contributions of the biological paradigm in the understanding of both schizophrenia and mood disturbances.

In Chapter 10, we turn our attention to the anxiety states, somatoform and dissociative disorders—patterns that previously were gathered under the nominal umbrella of neurosis. We focus on each group of disorders separately, noting the special effectiveness of the psychosocial paradigm with regard to these patterns. Since the study of these disorders has led to the development of most of the present-day psychotherapies, they are described and evaluated here. In Chapters 11 to 13, our emphasis shifts to disorders that have some clear organic component. In Chapter 11, we discuss physical conditions affected by psychological factors, the psychophysiological disorders. Here, our coverage includes cardiovascular, gastrointestinal and respiratory disorders, and headaches. In Chapter 12, the possible results of damage to the central nervous system as a function of injury, disease, or age are described. The various classes of mental retardation are also discussed, and the relative importance of the biological and systems paradigms are delineated. In Chapter 13, we focus on the organic mental disorders that result specifically from the abuse of chemical substances.

Chapters 14 and 15 deal with the sexual dysfunctions and disorders, and personality disorders. These patterns of psychopathology seem to reflect less on the ongoing "disease" process than they do on the problematic aspects of personality development and environmental exigencies. Some important work concerning these disorders derive from the psychosocial and systems paradigmatic views.

Throughout Part II, the critical evaluation of the three major paradigms finds them differentially effective. In his analysis of the scientific process, Kuhn notes that paradigmatic shortcomings are normal and expected occurrences. He suggests that failures of paradigms can spur an orderly process of change in any science. In this process newer paradigms are tried out because traditional ones begin to have increasing trouble in explaining things. Within the field of abnormal psychology, it is our belief that a developmental paradigm may be an example of just such a "new" evolving global view of behavior.

Part III begins with three chapters in which we apply a developmental paradigm to the study of abnormality. An essential aspect of this developmental view is that psychopathology is not only related to biological, psychosocial, and systems factors but to age factors as well. In Chapters 16 to 18 we present disorders organized according to age or developmental level. In Chapter 16, we examine the special problems of children and adolescents; our emphases here are on developmental deviations and pervasive developmental disorders. Chapter 17, dealing with college students, remains unique to our text. In this edition we have added a special section on eating disorders, a clearly age-related pattern. Finally, in Chapter 18, we examine the special disorders not only of the elderly, but of those at other stages of adulthood, especially midlife.

We conclude our book with an epilogue, Chapter 19, in which we look at the current status of the paradigms guiding the science of abnormal psychology and speculate about its future. We describe two "emerging" paradigms, perspectives which may eventually replace or embellish the biological, psychosocial, and systems views which have been used for decades.

We have tried to organize our text to be an integrated overview of the current status of abnormal psychology. However, while the integration of our presentation was a major goal, most of the 19 chapters have also been organized in such a way that they can stand alone and/or be presented in other sequences should instructors prefer to do so. The only chapters which would best be presented together are Chapters 1 to 3 which provide the scientific foundation for abnormal psychology, and Chapters 7 and 8 which form a unit on the schizophrenias. Depending on their preferences, instructors can choose any order of presentation of the three major paradigms. Similarly, for those instructors who wish to precede discussion of the psychoses with the study of the more moderate forms of psychopathology, Chapters 10 to 15 may be presented in a variety of orders prior to the reading of Chapters 7 to 9 on the psychoses.

In addition to the flexibility available within our integrated view of the science of abnormal psychology, we have maintained many of the more popular features of our first edition, especially the "personal experiences" and "case histories." We have attempted to keep the material and writing style "user-friendly" but not simplistic. There are also "boxes" in which we have tried to present a limited number of interesting "asides" designed to embellish, but not distract from, our more formal presentation. To further help the reader, at the end of each chapter, we again have "concluding comments" that introduce pertinent topical facts and ideas and "summary charts" that concisely describe the chapter's salient points.

Compared with the first edition, there are nearly 50 percent more references and the percentage of those references within 5 years of publication is nearly 60 percent. The latest data on incidence and prevalence of disorders have been gathered from the NIMH catchment area study published in late 1984. Within the last 5 years the problem of eating disorders on the college campuses has increased dramatically; the latest work here has also been cited. While all material throughout the text has been updated, special emphasis has been placed on schizophrenia, pervasive childhood disorders, adulthood disorders, and sexual disorders.

A project such as this text is not completed without the help, support, and encouragement of many other people. We would like to thank the following individuals for their thoughtful and helpful reviews of earlier versions of the manuscript: Arthur Skibbe, Appalachian State University, M. Fazel, Indiana University-Purdue University, Leon Vande Creek, Indiana University, PA, Donald A. Gordon, Ohio University, James E. Johnson, Loyola University of Chicago, P. Leslie Herold, California State University, Kent Miller, Florida State University, Wolfgang Bringman, University of South Alabama, Maria Krasnec, University of Idaho, Arnold LeUnes, Texas A&M University.

Our sincere thanks also to the many graduate students at Emory who spent time on the project. They are Andrea Bergman, Eileen Cooley, Robynne Diller, Rene Elliot, Lisa Groth-Hinshaw, Mark Hartigan, Jeff Jones, Kim Krinsky, Susan Manheim, Susan McGovern, Jane Nofer, and David Sampson. A special thank you to Randy Mendelson for his work on the test bank. Our deep appreciation to Rosemary Richter, Theresa Barnes, Katie Gregory, Mary Campbell, and Barbara Hearon for their help in the typing of the manuscript.

We are grateful to Robin B. Besofsky, our production manager at Holt, Rinehart and Winston, who worked behind the scenes to coordinate editorial and production while keeping the book on schedule. Special mention must be made of Donna Conte and the staff at Caliber Design Planning, Inc., who are not only talented, creative professionals but wonderfully nice people to work with and know. We also are grateful for the involvement and efforts of David de Campo and Anthony Scaravilli at Holt, Rinehart and Winston. We consider ourselves fortunate indeed for the opportunity to know and work with Susan Meyers, our editor. With a few well-timed corn muffins, and incessant optimism and professionalism, she was able to help us maintain our faith in ourselves and in the quality of our text. We cannot thank her enough.

Lastly, we wish to thank our children, Sharon, Noah, Jon, and Andy, and our wives Sara and Kaaren. They have all been very patient and understanding through the many nights and weekends during which we were absorbed in writing.

We hope that other instructors find the framework of our text as effective in their courses as we have in ours. We also hope that our readers, the students of abnormal psychology, find it a stimulating and useful introduction to the study of psychopathology. We have learned a great deal during the writing of the text; we hope others share that experience through its use.

Contents in Brief

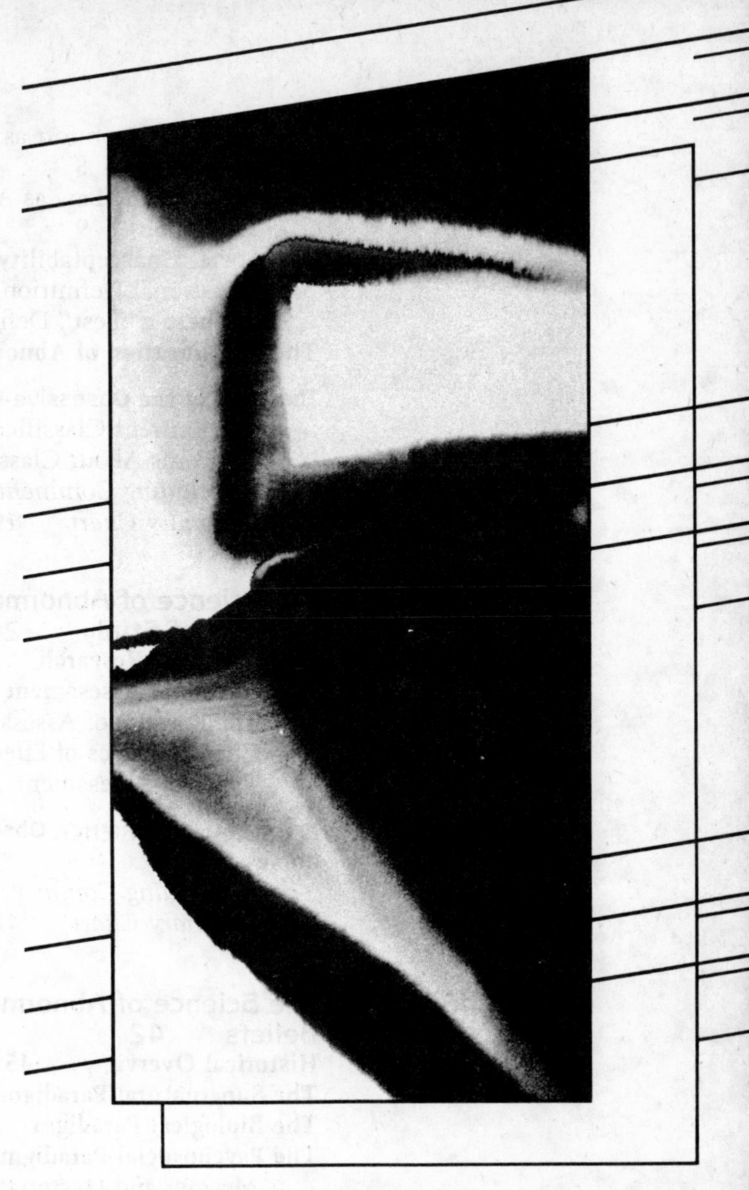

Contents

PART III Application of the Developmental Paradigm: Disorders of Childhood, Adolescence, Late Adolescence (College Students), and Adulthood 413

I

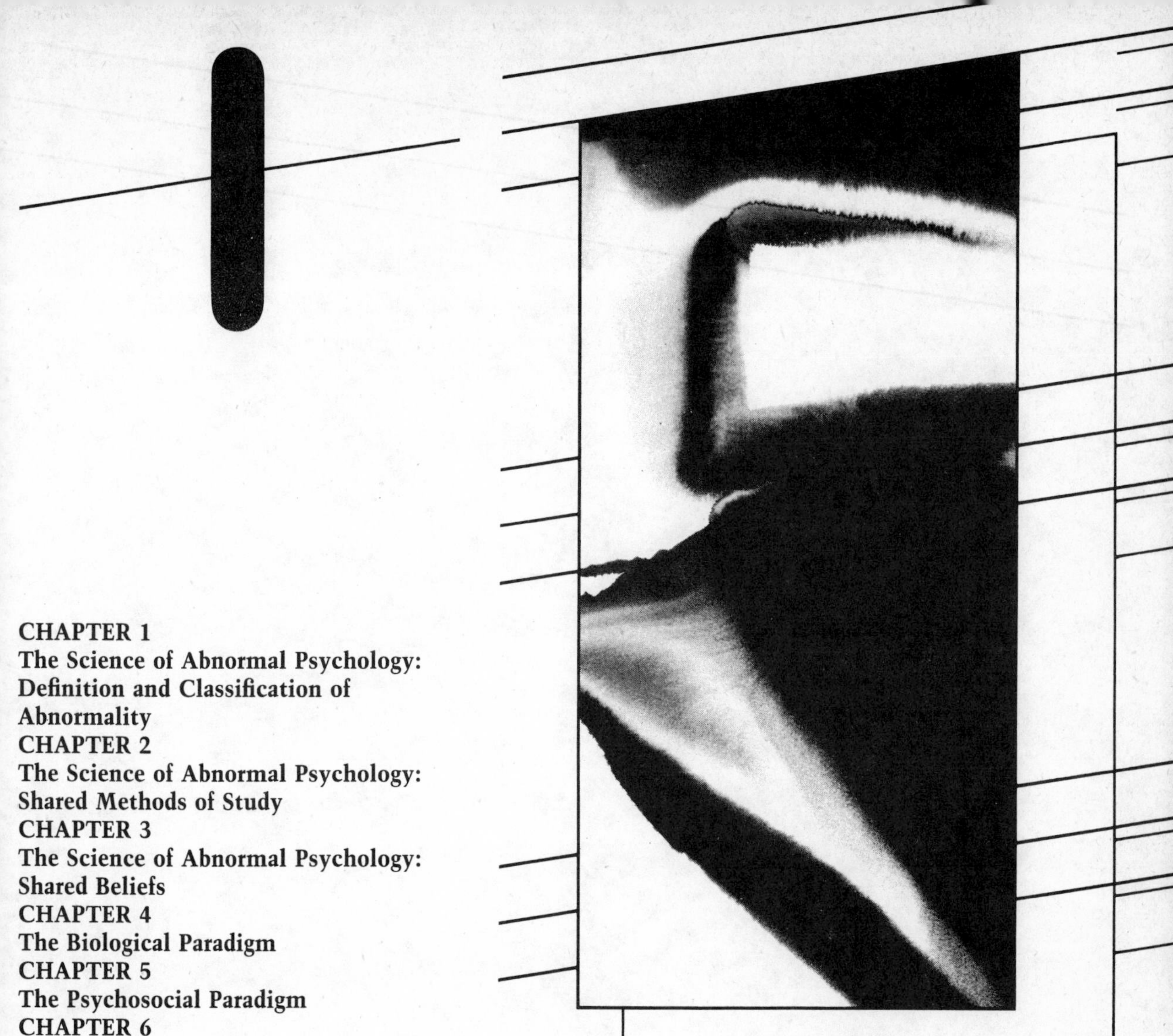

CHAPTER 1
The Science of Abnormal Psychology: Definition and Classification of Abnormality
CHAPTER 2
The Science of Abnormal Psychology: Shared Methods of Study
CHAPTER 3
The Science of Abnormal Psychology: Shared Beliefs
CHAPTER 4
The Biological Paradigm
CHAPTER 5
The Psychosocial Paradigm
CHAPTER 6
The Systems Paradigm

Foundations of Abnormal Psychology

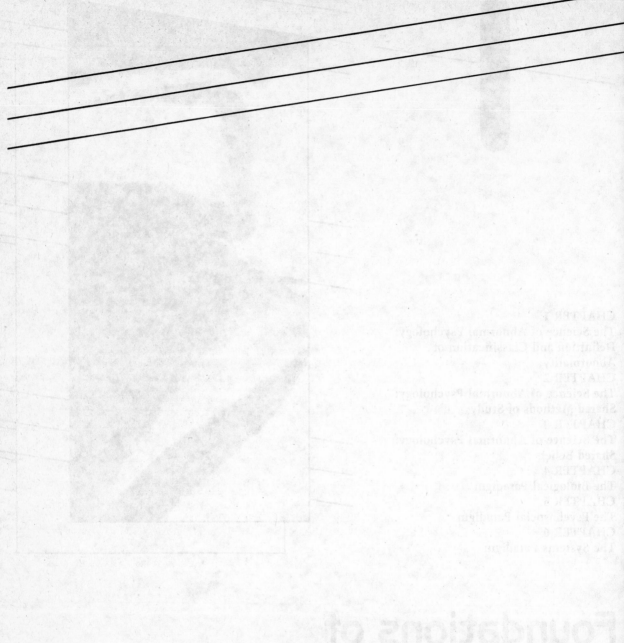

According to philosopher of science Thomas Kuhn, there are two main foundations upon which any science is built. The first of these foundations is a set of accepted systematic methods used by scientists in their pursuit of knowledge. The second foundation is the existence of one or more global views of the world—global views which are embraced by significant numbers of scientists and which guide their efforts. Like any other science, abnormal psychology may be known by the kinds of requirements described by Kuhn. In Chapters 1 to 3, we will examine these scientific foundations so that we may begin the study of abnormal psychology with an understanding of its basic definitions and methods, and with an awareness of the sources of the major global views which guide it. In Chapters 4 to 6, we will describe in greater detail the three major global views or paradigms currently impacting upon abnormal psychology and will demonstrate the ways in which these paradigms lead to theories of and interventions for psychopathology.

CHAPTER 1

The Science of Abnormal Psychology: Definition and Classification of Abnormality

The Case of Cliff

Cliff was born into a middle-class family. His parents, like most middle-class parents, had high hopes that their children would be well educated and successful. During his childhood, Cliff compiled a good if not spectacular academic record. Although he was bright, he had to work hard for the good grades he received. In school and at home, Cliff was quiet and retiring. His childhood was not especially happy but neither did it seem much different from that of his peers. Although schoolwork and tests made him nervous, his feelings did not interfere with his ability to deal with the academic work or to interact with peers. Even during his freshman year at college when many of his classmates were having difficulties with the new experience of higher education, Cliff seemed to make a satisfactory adjustment.

However, during his sophomore year in college, things began to change and Cliff began to experience intense feelings of stress and tension. Though his grades remained satisfactory at first, completing his work became more and more difficult. His feelings of anxiety increased to the point that Cliff's hands shook when he tried to write and his voice trembled when he was required to speak in front of the class. These embarrassing experiences served to create and maintain a vicious circle of increasing anxiety leading to greater difficulty in interacting with peers that in turn created more anxiety. Cliff became more frightened and depressed. Friends tried to help Cliff see the unreasonableness of his fears and when that failed, they advised him to talk to his professors or counselors. Cliff refused their offers of support, deciding instead that he could handle the situation himself—thereby isolating himself even more.

Cliff barely made it through his senior year and although he did manage to graduate, by the time of graduation his grades had suffered and he had few friends. During the years following his graduation, Cliff's emotional problems intensified. Although he managed to find and keep a job, his work efficiency was impaired by increasingly frequent feelings of depression. Three years after he graduated, Cliff's torment drove him to attempt suicide by jumping from a fourth floor apartment. Although he broke both of his legs, the attempt to end his life failed.

In the months following his suicide attempt, Cliff's condition worsened. He began to experience hallucinations. He felt wind in his face when there was none, smelled sulfur when flowers were placed next to him, and saw swarms of butterflies and large, gorgeous moths. These hallucinations were accompanied by delusions (mistaken beliefs) that people hated him so much that they wanted to kill him. This delusion expanded to include friends as well as strangers. For example, in the fall when it was suggested to Cliff that he return to college for the homecoming football game, he refused because he believed that his peers "would take him, drag him to the lawn, and there tear him limb from limb." Needless to say, with such a belief, Cliff did not go to homecoming. Instead, he stayed at home and became more withdrawn and isolated until his emotional decline finally reached a point that he could no longer be taken care of by friends and family. For his own safety he was hospitalized.

Cliff is severely disturbed. His behavior and feelings make him miserable and unhappy, worry those who know him, and require the intervention of professional helpers. While Cliff's experiences are not common, they are also not as unique as you might expect. Recent statistics (Regier et al., 1984; Freedman, 1984) indicate that one out of every five Americans has had psychological difficulties severe enough to require professional intervention. For the past decade, those difficulties subsumed under the rubric of "mental illness" have been America's costliest health problem (Ramsey, 1974, p. 168). Severe difficulties such as those experienced by Cliff affect nearly 4 million Americans, and though fewer now than 10 years ago, mental patients still occupy more hospital beds than any other single group of disorders.

Abnormal behavior such as that seen in Cliff intrigues lay people as well as professionals. To the everyday person it can be a confusing, frightening event in one's self or loved ones. To professionals, it can represent a puzzle whose solution continues to be elusive. People have endeavored to understand, prevent, and alter abnormal behavior for thousands of years, but only within the past 150 years or so has this task become a controlled scientific process. This *process of inquiry*, the *science of abnormal psychology*, is the topic of this text. It is a process whereby scientists have tried to uncover the secrets of abnormal behavior and subsequently to ease the lives of those people deemed abnormal. This text is an effort to describe the process of abnormal psychology as it has been, as it is now, and as it may be in the future. It is an effort to describe for you, our readers, the nature of abnormal psychology today and to give you a sense of its successes, its failures, and its direction. We shall begin our study of abnormal psychology with a consideration of its most basic tasks, the definition of abnormality and its classification.

Defining Abnormality

There is no one widely accepted definition of abnormality. Rather, disordered behavior has been characterized in a number of different ways. While no one of these ways is totally correct, each is valuable in that it provides *some* sense of what demarcates aberrant ways of acting or feeling. We will describe several different definitions and examine them as they apply to the problems presented by Cliff.

Infrequency as Abnormality: The Statistical Definition

In the statistical definition, abnormality is basically equated with infrequency of behavior. The frequency of any particular characteristic can be determined numerically and represented by means of a graph such as that shown in Figure 1-1, which is a representation of the heights of adult males in the United States. In such a curve we find heights greater or lesser than the "average" height of 5 feet, 8 inches. The greater the difference from the average, the more infrequent the occurrence of that deviant height. Thus, for example, heights of 6 feet, 8 inches, are rare, as are those of 4 feet, 8 inches. Heights that occur with such low frequency may be classified as abnormal (away from the norm) and may be given special labels differentiating them from the majority of heights encompassed by the normal curve. For instance, very tall people may be called giants; very short people may be termed midgets.

Extending the statistical model in height to the case of Cliff may help you to see how it can be applied to determine who should be labeled different or disordered. Cliff's behavior may be considered abnormal from the statistical perspective because it does not occur with great frequency in our society. It is unusual for a person to have delusions and hallucinations. Further, few of us become depressed enough to contemplate attempting suicide. Cliff was exhibiting some infrequent behavior and therefore might be considered abnormal on that basis alone.

However, using statistical infrequency as a basis to classify Cliff as abnormal does have some difficulties. Some behaviors exhibit a frequency that does not follow the normal curve; masturbation as a function of age is one such behavior. Some people may consider masturbation abnormal at any age, irrespective of the frequency of its occurrence; others may consider its frequency as a function of age to

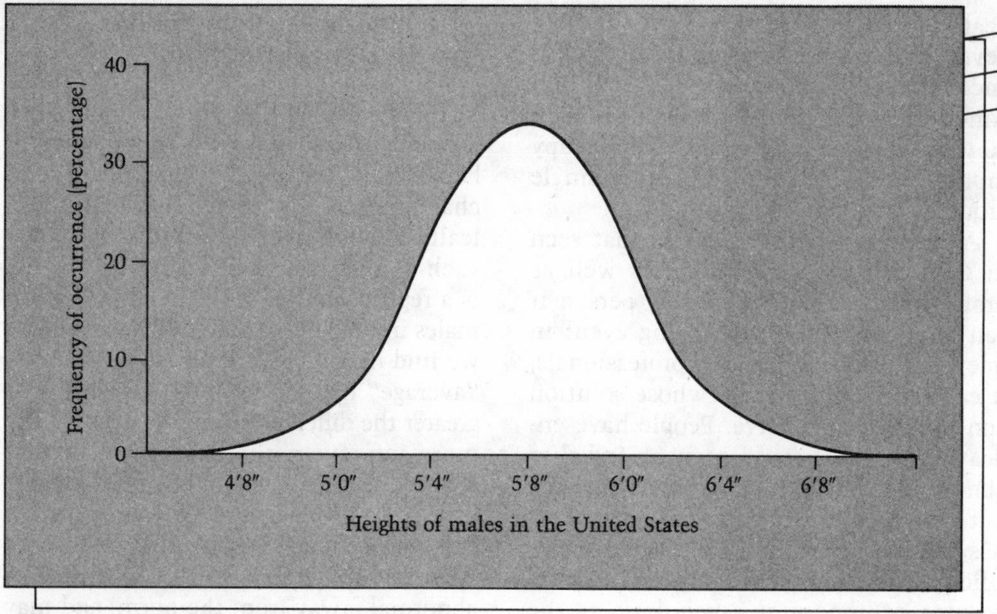

Figure 1-1 A normal curve.

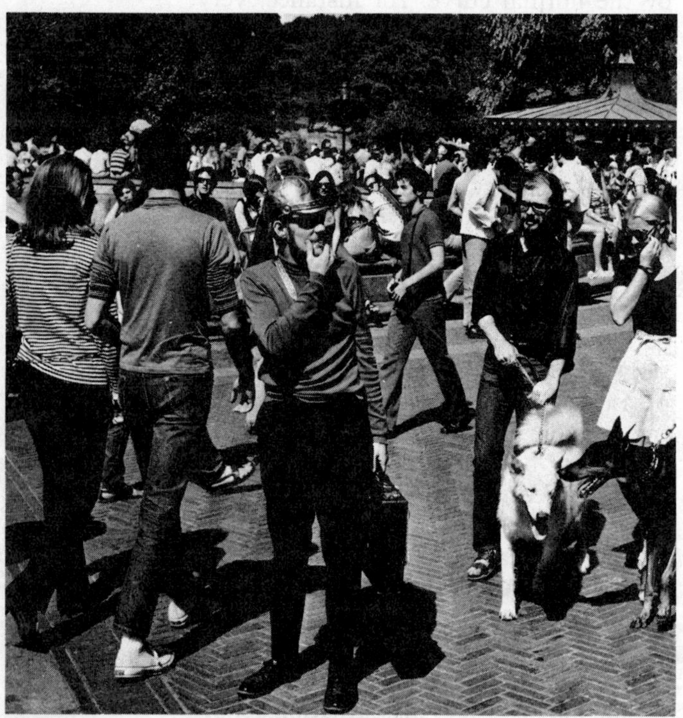

In terms of the statistical definition from the text, the man in this picture may be a prime candidate for abnormality. (*Don Morgan/Photo Researchers, Inc.*)

be normal, even though it does not describe a normal curve.

Besides not being able to fit all behaviors into a distribution such as that in Figure 1-1, the statistical definition also fails to discriminate between what groups of people or cultures might deem "good" and "bad" behavior. For example, a common normal curve is that describing the frequency of intelligence test scores. Here, those who fall very far below the average may be considered mentally inferior and may even be labeled "mentally retarded." As rare as retarded persons, however, are those at the other extreme, people with very high IQ scores, who may be called "geniuses" and are usually positively valued. For reasons like these, the statistical definitions seem insufficient to fully describe abnormality.

Feeling Discomfort as Abnormality: The Experiential Definition

Rather than some numerical limit, the experiential definition requires that abnormality be defined primarily by a person's subjective experience of emotional discomfort. In this case, a person must feel abnormal to be abnormal. As in the case of some physical illnesses, the experiential definition proposes that some "pain" must be present for there to be a disorder. Thus anxiety and depression are "true" signs of abnormality. In this view, abnormality evidenced by statistical means, but not felt by the individual, might not be considered true abnormality.

From the perspective of the experiential definition, Cliff probably would be considered abnormal because he feels so uncomfortable. He feels anxious, depressed, and very alone. Cliff is not experiencing the usual emotional ups and downs that most people do. Rather he feels intensely miserable and would qualify as abnormal from the experiential perspective.

In our opinion, feelings of discomfort probably are an important component in any definition of abnormality, but they are not sufficient to describe all disordered behavior. We know that certain patterns of abnormality are not accompanied by uncomfortable feelings. For example, in some disorders, paralyses may occur about which the affected individual is relatively unconcerned. Somewhat different, but still difficult for the experiential definition to handle, are those varieties of disorders that may not be stressful to the individual but probably are disturbing to others. Examples of such patterns are antisocial personality and sexual deviations.

Breaking the Law as Abnormality: The Legal Definition

Along with mental health professionals, legal theorists have struggled to arrive at a satisfactory definition of abnormality. After all, "insanity" is a legal term, and for over 200 years the legal system has attempted to develop proper criteria for making this judgment. A plea frequently used as a defense in trials for major crimes is "not guilty by reason of insanity." Sirhan Sirhan, the convicted murderer of Robert Kennedy, and Arthur Bremer, the assailant of George Wallace, are examples of defendants who attempted to use this plea.

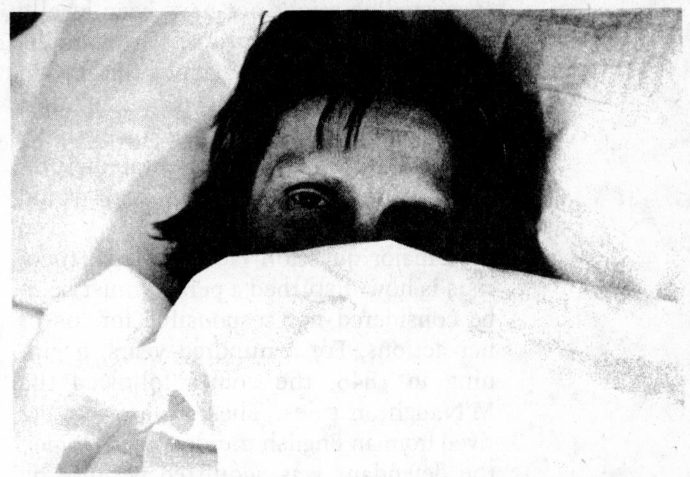

As well as having its statistical, cultural, and legal aspects, abnormality is also a personal experience. (© *Mary Ellen Mark/ Archive Pictures, Inc.*)

In Cliff's case, he might have been considered abnormal because his behavior

Personal discomfort and emotional upset combine to describe one criterion of abnormality. (© *1981 Cliff Moore/Taurus Photos*)

suggested he might not have been legally responsible for his actions. For example, attempting suicide is against the law in many states and Cliff may have been taken into custody for his actions. However, because of his history of mental disturbance, Cliff's violations of the law would probably be excused.

A major question faced by legal theorists is how disturbed a person must be to be considered not responsible for his or her actions. For a hundred years, beginning in 1843, the courts followed the M'Naughton rules. These rules were derived from an English murder case in which the defendant was acquitted because he was adjudged insane and thus unable to know right from wrong. Further, to be considered legally insane, individuals must have some mental disease that rendered them *incapable of knowing* what they were doing at the time of the crime; or if defendants were aware of their actions, their mental disorder must have prevented them from *knowing* that the actions were wrong.

Sirhan, Sirhan, convicted assassin of Robert F. Kennedy, pleaded innocent by reason of insanity. (*AP Wirephoto*)

Beginning in 1954 with the Durham decision, there was an attempt to liberalize the criteria for judging someone as insane. The Durham rules stated simply that defendants were not considered criminally responsible if their unlawful acts were a product of mental disease. Thus, defendants could be required to undergo treatment for their disorder but might not be sentenced or imprisoned.

Applying the Durham guidelines has sometimes been very difficult. For example, on whose testimony should the courts rely? Candidates could include a variety of expert witnesses and professionals. The danger of misapplying the Durham rules is exemplified by the case of Frederick Lynch. He was convicted of passing bad checks. Although he asserted that he was mentally responsible for his actions, the court found him not guilty by reason of insanity and sent him to a mental hospital for an indeterminate amount of time. Whereas he might have received a maximum sentence of 12 months in prison, his stay at the mental institution had no such limitation. "Harassed, branded, and tired, Lynch committed suicide" (Kittrie, 1971, p. 22).

In 1972, the Brawner rule (named for the defendant in the case) was developed. It stated that, "A person is not responsible for criminal conduct if at the time of such conduct, as a result of mental disease or defect, he lacks the substantial capacity to appreciate the wrongfulness of his conduct or to conform his conduct to the requirements of the law" (Gerard, 1973, pp. 39–40). The practical result of the Brawner rule is to reduce the power of expert witnesses (psychiatrists and psychologists) by allowing them to be cross-examined and by requiring them to provide support other than their own personal opinion for their contentions.

More recently, probably as a direct result of the John Hinckley case, a new choice was created in an attempt to balance fairness with justice. Hinckley attempted to assassinate President Reagan outside of a Washington, D.C., hotel. He was found innocent by reason of insanity. This verdict infuriated many people who saw Hinckley as escaping from just punishment. A new verdict, guilty but mentally ill, was proposed to fill the large space between guilty and not guilty by reason of insanity. With such a verdict the defendant would receive treatment until he or she had recovered and then would face the appropriate punishment for the crime. This verdict is appropriate when defendants know what they are doing is wrong but also have a mental disease of some sort.

The complexities of the legal definition make it difficult to apply to many cases of abnormal behavior. For example, what about the person who is constantly miserable but doesn't do anything illegal, or the person whose behavior bothers others but isn't criminal? Such people would be seen as abnormal from other definitions but probably would not be judged insane and committed to a mental hospital as a result of the legal definition of abnormality.

Social Unacceptability as Abnormality: The Cultural-Situational Definition

According to the cultural-situational definition it is not statistical infrequency, personal discomfort, or the legal system, but society that defines abnormality. From this perspective, specific behaviors may not in themselves be considered abnormal, but they are judged so on the basis of the situation in which they occur and/or the cultural rules of the people around whom they occur. For example, eating a hot dog or wearing a fur coat may not be abnormal in themselves, yet a person wearing a fur coat and eating a hot dog in St. Patrick's Cathedral during a high mass in July would most likely be considered abnormal due to the *situational inappropriateness* of the behaviors involved. Applying the situational definition to Cliff would suggest that his depressed feelings would not have been abnormal had they been in response to the death of one of his parents or some similar tragedy. However, in that his intensive feelings of depression seemed to have no apparent objective cause resulted in his behavior being judged as abnormal.

One of the primary bases upon which situation-appropriateness is judged is the culture of the group in which the behavior occurs. Termed *cultural relativism* by Benedict (1934; Wilson, 1974), the effect of culture is such that behaviors considered highly abnormal by one cultural group might be considered perfectly normal (or even desirable) by another. For example,

The boy in this picture may have defined himself as abnormal by his dress according to the cultural-situational definition of abnormality. (*Michael Weisbrot and Family*)

in American culture, talking to one's self and hallucinating are considered serious signs of disturbance; in certain Polynesian groups, however, such experiences are seen as indications of special status among deities. In another instance, many people in South America think nothing of munching on a large crunchy beetle for a snack; were a person to do such a thing in a McDonald's restaurant in the Midwest, he or she would surely be considered abnormal!

The cultural-situational definition avoids some of the difficulties of the other perspectives. For example, this view can deal with situations in which high-frequency behavior may be deemed abnormal and low-frequency behavior may be considered perfectly acceptable or desirable. In the United States, for instance, many people are fearful of speaking in front of groups. Such a fear is considered a problem by most of these people despite that it is a very frequent behavior. On the other hand, although statistically very rare, 7 foot 2 inch males are not necessarily considered abnormal, especially if they can throw a large round ball through a hoop mounted on a glass board 10 feet off the ground.

One especially productive application of the cultural-situational perspective is that of Scheff (1970). Scheff proposes that behavior which is deemed abnormal by a culture is behavior which violates what he terms *residual rules.* A definition of a residual rule is that it is a rule that is only noticed when it is broken. For example, no one ever says directly, "Always stand facing the front of an elevator." If someone gets on an elevator and stands facing us as we face forward, we become immediately aware of a "violation" and we see the person as abnormal. According to Scheff, any behavior which represents a violation of a residual rule is abnormal, and the specific residual rules in existence vary from culture to culture and from group to group.

Is There a "Best" Definition for Abnormality?

Our consideration of some of the many definitions for abnormality suggests that while each view helps to some degree, no one perspective is completely acceptable. Abnormality might best be considered a *process* rather than a state of affairs. Rather than being a quality of a particular behavior, abnormality might best be seen as a result of the interaction of many factors. Among these factors are the behavior per se, the age, sex, race, physical condition, appearance, and so forth, of the person emitting the behavior, the situation in which the behavior is emitted, and the cultural context in which the situation is occurring. Although nearly impossible to delineate at any one moment, all these factors seem to contribute to a belief that a behavior is abnormal. At some level we as people process all this information and, in many instances, we agree on what is normal and what is abnormal. Once we know that a behavior is abnormal, however, our task is only partially complete. The next step is to know what type of abnormality we are faced with. This process is called *classification.*

The Classification of Abnormality

Although psychologists studying abnormal behavior are not in full agreement as to a concise definition for abnormality, there is more general agreement that in order to understand and alter disordered thoughts and actions we must be able to identify and classify the varying forms they may take. This approach to dealing with disorders is certainly not unique to abnormal psychology. Diagnosis and classification in physical medicine traditionally have been preconditions for successful treatment. In order to know what to do, physicians need to know what disease they are dealing with; diagnosis guides treatment. Similarly, mental health professionals like psychologists, psychiatrists, and psychiatric social workers have also sought to classify the disorders they focus upon. Accurate diagnosis is important to research scientists in that they wish and need to be sure of the kind of disorders they are studying. It is important to applied mental health professionals who wish and need to guide their treatment efforts appropriately. As we shall see, however, accurate classification can be a challenging and difficult task.

Were they to be asked to help in the diagnosis of Cliff, few people would disagree that he was thinking and behaving abnormally. While lay people might call him "crazy," professionals would probably classify him as having a "bipolar affective psychotic disorder." Although their labels may differ, both groups probably are basing their judgments on the same data—Cliff's feelings of depression and anxiety and his hallucinations of sound and sight. In any case, while professional workers may use more refined terms than lay people, they probably would agree that Cliff was severely disturbed. Since Cliff was disturbed to the point of being hospitalized and could not live independently, it would probably be relatively easy to classify him. However, the diagnostic process may not be so easy when less severe varieties of abnormal behavior are considered, as in the following case of Ronald Lewis.

The Case of the Obsessive-Compulsive Personality

Ronald Lewis is a 32-year-old accountant who is "having trouble holding on to a woman." He does not understand why, but the reasons become very clear as he tells his story. Mr. Lewis is a remarkably neat and well-organized man who tends to regard others as an interference to the otherwise mechanically perfect progression of his life. For many years he has maintained an almost inviolate schedule. On weekdays he arises at 6:47, has two eggs soft-boiled for 2 minutes, 45 seconds, and is at his desk at 8:15. Lunch is at 12:00, dinner at 6:00, bedtime at 11:00. He has separate Saturday and Sunday schedules, the latter characterized by a methodical and thorough trip through *The New York Times*. Any change in schedule causes him to feel varying degrees of anxiety, annoyance, and a sense that he is doing something wrong and wasting time.

Orderliness pervades Mr. Lewis's life. His apartment is immaculately clean and meticulously arranged. His extensive collections of books, records, and stamps are all carefully cataloged, and each item is reassuringly always in the right and familiar place. Mr. Lewis is highly valued by his company because his attention to detail has, at times, saved the company considerable embarrassment. He is often asked to look over final drafts of documents to ensure that nothing has been overlooked. His perfectionism also presents something of a problem, however. He is the slowest worker in the office and probably the least productive. He gets the details right but may fail to put them in perspective. His relationships to co-workers are cordial but formal. He is on a "Mr." and "Ms." basis with people he has known for years in an office that generally favors first names.

Mr. Lewis's major problems are with women, and they follow the same repetitive pattern. At first things go well. Mr. Lewis is tall and handsome, and his courtly respect is something women initially find endearing. His sexual technique is somewhat studied but effective, and he has no trouble getting women interested in him. Soon, however, he begins to resent the intrusion upon his schedule a woman inevitably causes. This is most strongly illustrated in the bedtime arrangement. Mr. Lewis is a light and nervous sleeper with a rather elaborate routine preceding his going to bed. He must spray his sinuses, take two aspirins, straighten up the apartment, do 35 sit-ups, and read two pages of the dictionary. The sheets must be of just the right crispness and temperature, and the room must be noiseless. Obviously, a woman sleeping over interferes with his inner sanctum and, after sex, Mr. Lewis tries either to have the woman go home or sleep in the living room. No woman has put up with this for very long.

Mr. Lewis's emotional life shows a paradox. He can feel things deeply—he cries at movies or while reading a novel—and he maintains close ties to his parents and to two old friends. On the other hand, in most relationships he seems constricted, unspontaneous, and aloof. He wavers in how he regards himself. At times he believes that he is the last bastion of sanity and good sense in an otherwise poorly organized world. At other times, he accepts the criticism one woman made of him—that he is "uptight and should learn to loosen up."

Mr. Lewis comes from a lower-middle-class background with an ambitious and fastidious mother and a "sloppy Joe" father whom both he and his mother looked down upon. . . In the early grades of parochial school he developed a reputation as a raconteur of "dirty jokes" until he was caught by a nun and severely reprimanded. He then became a model student who never used dirty words. (Spitzer et al., 1983)

Although Mr. Lewis has emotional problems and perhaps may be *too* organized, he is in contact with reality and working and living independently. It might be hard for lay people to classify him as "crazy." Part of the difficulty could arise from the fact that some of us probably share some of Mr. Lewis's characteristics, such as his need to be organized, and like him, we may want to be praised for them. Indeed, compared with Cliff, Mr. Lewis is a more difficult case to classify.

The task of formally classifying the vast array of abnormal behaviors has challenged behavioral scientists for years. Yet, it is probably fair to conclude that there still is not a completely satisfactory classification system. This is less a reflection on the workers in the field of abnormal psychology than on the tremendous complexities presented by abnormal behavior. However, the scientific search for the causes and treatments for behavioral disorders requires a clear system of classification. It is very difficult to study abnormality and develop effective interventions when we do not know for certain what is abnormal and what is not.

The Current Classification System

The present-day classification system had its beginnings in the diagnostic structure of the Association of Medical Superintendents of American Institutions for the Insane (1914). However, this early diagnostic system did not include many important disorders and the categories used were not easy to agree upon. Efforts to develop a more comprehensive and reliable system continued throughout the twentieth century. In 1939, the World Health Organization (WHO) developed a diagnostic system that was revised in 1948 and again in 1978. Partly because of differences of opinion regarding certain diagnostic classifications such as homosexuality, the WHO system has not been widely used in the United States.

In 1952, the American Psychiatric Association published its first *Diagnostic and Statistical Manual* (DSM-I). Though it was one of the first systems to be accepted among most mental health disciplines, it was flawed. The authors had difficulty agreeing on the system's central organizing principles, and this resulted in a hodgepodge of classification that was often applied inconsistently.

DSM-II (1968) represented an attempt to respond to the shortcomings of DSM-I by using symptoms as the central organizing factors in the determination of diagnostic categories. Its authors sought to delineate "clusters" of symptoms in hopes of making diagnosis more reliable. However, because the system depended heavily on human judgment to identify the symptoms, there continued to be a low level of agreement among psychiatric diagnosticians (Spitzer & Wilson, 1975). Further, there was little attempt to deal with how the disorders came about (etiology) so that unlike physical disorder diagnoses which direct treatments, the DSM-II diagnoses often did not provide clear therapeutic guidance.

Replacing DSM-II in 1979, DSM-III has increased the reliability and comprehensiveness of diagnosis, but it still does not provide explanations for how most psychiatric disorders develop (those with an obvious organic basis are the exceptions). Increased reliability has resulted from the inclusion of concrete criteria for diagnosing disorders. For example, let's return to our opening case of Cliff. Based on the information given in that case description, a possible DSM-III diagnosis would be bipolar affective disorder. The actual DSM-III criteria are presented in Table 1-1. While it can be seen that Cliff meets the concrete criteria subsumed under A, B, and C, the hallucinations and delusions he experienced might also be part of another severe disorder called schizophrenia. Further information might be needed to eliminate the possibility that Cliff might actually be more appropriately diagnosed as schizophrenic. In any case, because the criteria are clear and give numerical limits, they should and do make it easier for people to agree on a diagnosis (Webb et al., 1981).

DSM-III presents a total of 16 major diagnostic classes with a total of 187 specific diagnostic categories (Kaplan et al., 1980). (*An outline-form presentation of DSM-III is provided on the inside front cover of the text.*) As compared with the so-called single dimension or axis diagnoses of DSM-II, the *multiaxial* classification system of DSM-III provides for assessment on five distinct axes or dimensions. Thus diagnosticians can communicate simultaneously details of existent adjustment and personality disorders (Axes I and II), relevant physical disorders or conditions (Axis III), severity of psychosocial stressors (Axis IV) and the highest level of adaptive functioning during the past year (Axis V). The assessment on Axes IV and V can be especially useful in indicating the *prognosis* or the chance of recovery from the diagnosed disorder. For example, if we could trace the development of Cliff's disorder to an identified "stressor," the prognosis might be more favorable than if the disorder developed slowly over a long period of time. A rating of 1 refers to no apparent psychosocial stressor, a rating of 4 reflects a moderate degree of stress such as found in a new career, death of a close friend, or pregnancy, and a rating of 7 indicates catastrophic stress such as a concentration camp experience. Likewise, Cliff would have a favorable prognosis on Axis V if his adjustment over the year prior to his "breakdown" could be judged good, very good, or superior in the areas of social relations, occupational functioning, and use of leisure time. However, his prognosis would be considerably poorer should his previous adjustment be rated as fair, poor, very poor, or grossly impaired. Based on the description of Cliff's problems, he would probably be rated as having little or no apparent stress on Axis IV and a fair premorbid (predisturbance) adjustment on Axis V.

DSM-III is a significant improvement over its predecessors. Since it is used by most mental health professionals, we generally follow its broad outlines in our presentation of patterns of abnormal behavior. However, we will not always adhere to this system. We will depart from DSM-III when another system might lead to a clearer description of subject matter, or when we present disorders not yet included within the DSM-III framework.

Table 1-1 An Example of the Multiaxial Diagnostic System in DSM-III

Axis I: *Clinical psychiatric syndromes and other conditions,* such as depressive disorder.

Axis II: *Personality disorders in adults and specific developmental disorders in children,* such as compulsive personality disorder.

Axis III: *Nonmental medical disorders that are potentially relevant,* such as diabetes in a child with a specific developmental disorder such as bed-wetting.

Axis IV: *Severity of psychosocial stressors.* Permits diagnostician to judge severity of stress that has contributed to an episode of a disorder. Can range from code 1 (none) through code 5 (severe, such as marital separation) and code 7 (catastrophe—multiple family deaths and the like).

Axis V: *Highest level of adaptive functioning.* Axis V allows diagnosticians to record the degree of adjustment or impairment during the year prior to the diagnosis. Prognosis (chance of recovery) can be based on such information. Can range from code 1 (superior) through code 4 (fair adjustment—generally functioning adequately, but some impairment in at least one area) and code 7 (grossly impaired).

Criteria for an Episode of Depressive Disorder as Experienced by Cliff

A. Dysphoric mood or pervasive loss of interest or pleasure. The disturbance is characterized by symptoms such as the following: depressed, sad, blue, hopeless, low, down in the dumps, "don't care anymore," irritable, worried. The disturbance must be prominent and relatively persistent but not necessarily the most dominant symptom. It does not include momentary shifts from one dysphoric mood to another dysphoric mood, e.g., anxiety to depression to anger, such as are seen in states of acute psychotic turmoil.

B. At least four of the following symptoms:
   1. Poor appetite or weight loss or increased appetite or weight gain (change of 1 lb a week or 10 lb a year when not dieting).
   2. Sleep difficulty or sleeping too much.
   3. Loss of energy, fatigability, or tiredness.
   4. Psychomotor agitation or retardation (but not mere subjective feelings of restlessness or being slowed down).
   5. Loss of interest or pleasure in usual activities, or decrease in sexual drive (do not include if limited to a period when delusional or hallucinating).
   6. Feelings of self-reproach or excessive or inappropriate guilt (either may be delusional).
   7. Complaints or evidence of diminished ability to think or concentrate such as slow thinking, or indecisiveness (do not include if associated with obvious formal thought disorder).
   8. Recurrent thoughts of death or suicide, or any suicidal behavior, including thoughts of wishing to be dead.

C. The period of illness has had a duration of at least 1 week from the time of the first noticeable change in the patient's usual condition.

D. None of the following which suggests schizophrenia is present.
   1. Delusions of being controlled or thought broadcasting, insertion, or withdrawal.
   2. Hallucinations of any type throughout the day for several days or intermittently throughout a 1-week period unless all of the content is clearly related to depression or elation.
   3. Auditory hallucinations in which either a voice keeps up a running commentary on the patient's behaviors or thoughts as they occur, or two or more voices converse with each other.
   4. At some time during the period of illness had delusions or hallucinations for more than 1 month in the absence of prominent affective (manic or depressive) symptoms (although typical depressive delusions, such as delusions of guilt, sin, poverty, nihilism, or self-deprecation, or hallucinations of similar content are permitted).
   5. Preoccupation with a delusion or hallucination to the relative exclusion of other symptoms or concerns (other than delusions of guilt, sin, poverty, nihilism, or self-deprecation, or hallucinations with similar content).
   6. Marked formal thought disorder if accompanied by either blunted or inappropriate effect, delusions or hallucinations of any type, or grossly disorganized behavior.

Concerns About Classification

By any measure, DSM-III is the most thorough and comprehensive system ever introduced in the United States. However, the process of diagnosing individuals, is not without its difficulties and potential dangers. Psychiatric writer Thomas Szasz (1961, 1976, 1980), for example, believes that behavioral disturbances should not be diagnosed *at all* because they are not "illnesses." According to Szasz, only those mental deviations whose source is clearly defined physically or neurologically (such as head injuries) should be seen legitimately as "disease" and treated as such. However, those disorders with no clear biological bases (as in the case of Mr. Lewis) would be better understood as "problems in living." Such problems are more likely caused by people's awareness of themselves and their world and the unreasonable demands a complex society makes on them than by some disease process. Szasz believes that people must be responsible for themselves. He contends that by diagnosing problems in living as "diseases," mental health professionals may

Rosenhan's pseudopatients faced mental hospital staffs that accepted them as mentally ill and offered them the same impersonal treatment they offered other patients. (*Mimi Forsyth/ Monkmeyer Press Photo Service*)

do more harm than good because those so diagnosed may be relieved of their responsibilities and may not need to learn to cope with the complexities of everyday life. Seen in this light, diagnoses can prevent people from adjusting and functioning in an effective and realistic fashion.

Though Szasz theorizes that diagnoses might be harmful, Rosenhan (1973) has gathered actual evidence to support that conclusion. Rosenhan had normal people gain admission to mental hospitals with the complaint that they could hear voices. All were admitted to the hospital and all but one were diagnosed as schizophrenic. Soon after being admitted, these pseudopatients stopped showing their abnormal symptoms. They were held up to 51 days and none of the staff was able to see through their charade. (Interestingly, many of the actual patients did recognize these pseudopatients for what they were.) Upon discharge, Rosenhan's assistants were typically diagnosed as "schizophrenic, in remission." That is, once applied, the label of schizophrenia was not removed but only modified. No pseudopatient was ever reclassified as normal; if they hadn't taken the precaution of using pseudonyms, they might have left the hospitals with records of mental disorder that could have remained with them for the rest of their lives.

Rosenhan's conclusions did not go uncontested. Spitzer (1976) pointed out that the hospital was forced to use the information they were given by the "patients" to make a judgment. In the absence of other data, for staff to disregard a severe symptom such as hallucinations would not be very professional. Even the diagnosis of "schizophrenia in remission," an infrequently applied category, reflected the staff's recognition of the unusual nature of these "patients."

Controversy and criticism reflect continuing efforts of scientists to improve the way we classify abnormal behavior. However, due to the number of possible ways to define abnormality and the rich variety of behavior to be classified, there probably will continue to be criticisms in the future. Controversy, however, should not detract from the positive features of DSM-III or from the fact that "the DSM-III is a reality—a tangible, if flawed, guideline to clinical diagnosis" (Millon, 1983, p. 804; see also Williams, 1985a, 1985b).

Concluding Comments

In this first chapter of our text we have tried to introduce you to modern concepts of abnormality and classification. Throughout, we have applied these concepts to the case of Cliff, the depressed and suicidal college student. However, at this point we must tell you that Cliff is over 115 years old and is actually Clifford Beers, a very famous figure in the history

Clifford Beers wrote of his experiences in mental hospitals in a book called *A Mind That Found Itself.* He was instrumental in founding the Mental Hygiene Association. (*National Library of Medicine*)

of abnormal psychology. The problems he had are not dissimilar from many experienced in modern times, and many of the questions before abnormal psychology now are not significantly different from those asked over a century ago. Perhaps a bit more information about Beers may help you appreciate his importance to the science of abnormal psychology.

Clifford Beers spent a significant portion of his adult life in mental institutions. However, he recovered from his ordeal to write a book about his experiences entitled, "A Mind that Found Itself" (1931). He dedicated his life to the energetic pursuit of improving treatment of severely disturbed people, partially through the Mental Hygiene Association that he founded. Positive ripples of his impact can still be felt in the field of abnormal psychology today. But it also is true that the difficulties experienced by Beers at the turn of the century still present great challenges for modern professional workers.

In many ways, Clifford Beers' case stands at a major crossroad in the field of abnormal psychology, for it was during his lifetime that the study of abnormal behavior seems to have emerged as a true science. Prior to Beers' time there certainly were efforts to understand and alter abnormal behavior, but it was not until the late nineteenth century that the controlled, systematic, paradigmatic science of abnormal psychology actually appeared. It is to the methodologies and conceptual foundations of that science that we will turn our attention in Chapter 2.

Summary Chart

We began our study of the science of abnormal psychology with an examination of various definitions of abnormality:

Infrequency as abnormality
Feeling uncomfortable as abnormality
Breaking the law as abnormality
Social unacceptability as abnormality

We then turned to a consideration of the DSM-III, the official system for classifying behavior which is deemed abnormal.

A multiaxial system
More reliable than previous systems
Concerns about DSM-III and diagnosis

CHAPTER 2

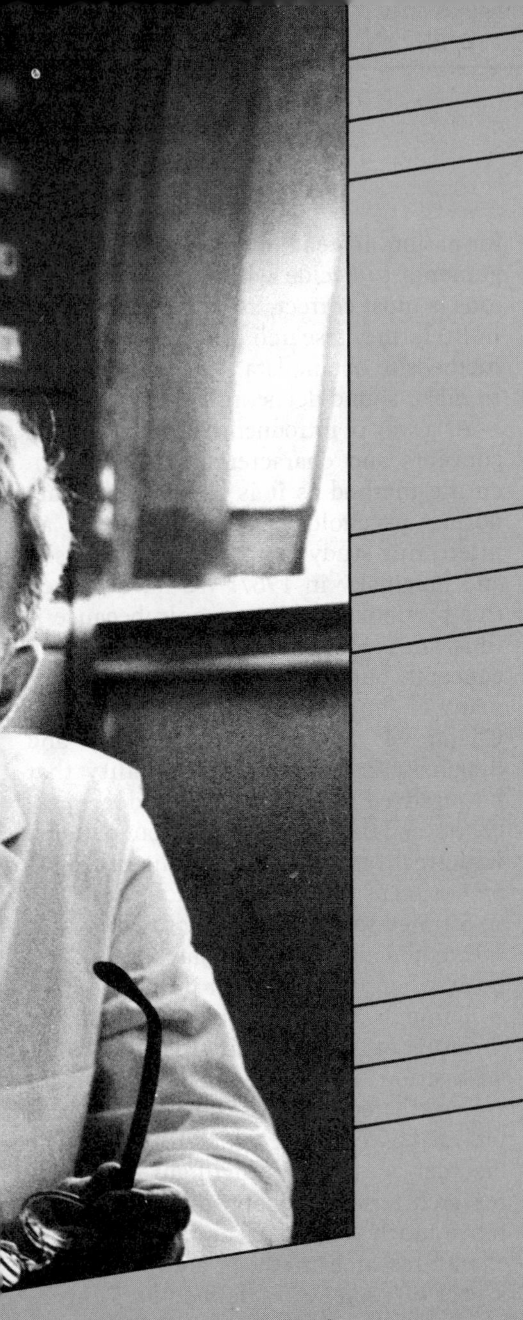

The Science of Abnormal Psychology: Shared Methods of Study

In his analysis of the nature of science, Kuhn (1962, 1981; Hacking, 1981) proposed that a true science may be characterized by the presence of two types of *paradigms* or ways in which the problems of the particular science are approached or thought about. The first type of paradigm, may be most easily thought of (and will be termed in this text) as a *set of shared and agreed-upon methods* for the gathering of information needed to solve problems. In psychology, it was not until Clifford Beers' time near the end of the nineteenth century that such shared methods were widely used to study problems scientifically. The second type of Kuhnian paradigm refers to "sets-of-shared-beliefs" of scientists regarding the nature of the world. Although such sets of beliefs about the nature of abnormality have existed for centuries, they are not sufficient in themselves for a definition of a science. Only when shared beliefs are used to guide the choice of accepted systematic methods does Kuhn conclude that a true science exists. Further, rather than being a static phenomenon, a science like abnormal psychology must be seen as an ongoing process—a process which we will attempt to describe throughout this text. In this chapter, we will consider the processes of research and assessment, the two shared methods characterizing the science of abnormal psychology. In Chapter 3, we will trace the major paradigms as sets of shared beliefs that guide its course.

The Process of Research

The research process, or "scientific method," differs from commonsense speculation in that it is a set of agreed-upon rules for the gathering of useful information. Instead of using subjective arguments to decide which of many opinions is most correct, as would be the case in literature, research offers investigators methods to obtain data that can help them to make sound decisions.

As a way of introducing to you the main concepts and characteristics of the scientific method as it is often used in abnormal psychology, we will describe an interesting study performed by Braginsky and Braginsky in 1967. We have chosen this particular study not only because it illustrates some of the major research concepts but also because it relates to many of the issues of diagnosis raised in Chapter 1. Specifically, Braginsky and Braginsky examined the possibility that hospitalized patients diagnosed as psychotic, and thus assumed to be out of touch with reality, were not as disturbed as professionals concluded. In fact, they were so attuned to the demands of reality that they could actually "role play" their diagnosis when it suited their purposes.

Through the following detailed description of Braginsky and Braginsky's investigation, by discussing how the data were gathered to assess the ability of hospitalized psychotic people to role play their disorder, we want to highlight the major research terms and concepts that characterize much psychological research. These shared research methods are a necessary aspect of a science as defined by Kuhn.

Like most researchers Braginsky and Braginsky began with an *hypothesis* or a tentatively accepted supposition to explain certain facts about the behavior of psychotic patients in a mental hospital. Their working hypothesis, or supposition, was that psychotic patients could effectively control the impressions they make on the professional hospital staff if such impressions were important to what might happen to them. They argued that patients who had been hospitalized for several years would have a strong desire to remain in the security of the hospital and therefore would change their behavior to assure staying there. Further, if they were allowed to stay in the hospital, psychotic patients would behave in ways to assure their being placed on the best ward.

Rather than attempting to prove or disprove the hypothesis by debate and logic, Braginsky and Braginsky set up an *experiment* or set of procedures to test whether hospitalized mental patients could change their behavior to manage the impressions they made on others. In this experiment, there were two *experimental* groups and one *control* group of hospitalized psychiatric patients.

Experimental groups characteristically receive differential experiences to examine how these affect the behavior the researcher is studying. Called *independent variables*, these differential experiences in the present study refer to the different reasons offered to the hospitalized patients for their being interviewed by a hospital staff member. For example, in the Braginsky and Braginsky study, one experimental group of patients was told that they were being interviewed to assess whether they would be discharged. In the other experimental group, the patients were told they were being interviewed to see whether they would be placed on an open ward with privileges or would remain on a closed ward. The behavior under investigation in an experiment is called the *dependent variable.* In the Braginsky and Braginsky research, the dependent variable was the behavior shown by the hospitalized patients during and after their interview.

To assure that changes in the dependent variable are due primarily to the effects of the independent variable (in this study the different reasons offered to the patients for being interviewed), researchers will sometimes include a control group that is similar to the other groups but is not exposed to the experimental procedures. Control groups allow researchers to more accurately assess whether changes in the dependent variable are due to the effects of the experimental procedures or to other extraneous factors such as the passage of time. Braginsky and Braginsky, for example, included a control group in which patients were told they were going to take a routine mental status exam. The mental status exam is usually a brief interview during which patients are asked questions about their present state of mind. Questions might include name, age, time of day, day of the week, adding two numbers, and the like. Most of the patients had been through previous mental status exams and thus would not ordinarily see it as threatening.

When experimental and control groups are *matched* on important characteristics that might affect the behaviors being studied, experimenters have greater confidence that changes in the dependent variable are due to their experimental manipulation and not to those extraneous factors. For example, in the Braginskys' study, the hospitalized patient samples were matched on such characteristics as age, educational level, length of stay in the hospital, and type of diagnosis. If these characteristics were not matched across the groups, they could have differentially affected the dependent variable behavior. For instance, if more manic people were part of one of the groups than the others, than their extreme talkativeness and positive moods, rather than different reactions to their interviews, might have created the differences in their interview behavior (dependent variable). While matching of subjects on important characteristics in experiments is highly desirable, sometimes it is not possible. In these instances, experimenters may use *random* samples in which all subjects are given equal chances of being assigned to any group. With random samples, it is as-

Even though psychiatric patients may appear out of touch with reality, Braginsky and Braginsky believed that they could change their behavior if it was advantageous to do so. (*Mimi Forsyth/Monkmeyer Press Photo Service*)

sumed that extraneous factors affect all groups equally and nonexperimental biasing will "even out."

In Braginsky and Braginsky's study, the hospitalized patients were interviewed. Recordings of these interviews were then rated by psychiatrists who had no knowledge of which group the patients were in. Based on these ratings, it was found that, as hypothesized, patients *could* present themselves as "healthy" when they thought they were being evaluated for being placed in the more desired open ward. As well, patients could present themselves as more disturbed when they believed it would mean they could stay in the safety of the hospital.

By applying research methods shared with other scientists, Braginsky and Braginsky were able to find support for their view (hypothesis) that far from being insensitive to other people and the outside world, long-term hospitalized psychiatric patients can process information and can use such information to change their behavior and control some aspects of their own lives. The results can be more confidently accepted because Braginsky and Braginsky used matched groups to control factors that might have affected the dependent variable. They also used procedures to eliminate the impact of *experimenter bias*, or the ability of the researcher to influence the behavior of the subject consistent with the researcher's beliefs. By having the interviewers unaware of the hypothesis of the study and the psychiatrists unaware of the specific instructions given to the psychiatric patients whose interviews they rated, Braginsky and Braginsky helped reduce the possibility of experimenter bias affecting the behavior of the patients.

A hypothesis like that proposed by Braginsky and Braginsky might not always be investigated by experimental manipulation. Another possible way to evaluate a hypothesis is through the means of *cor-*

relational procedures. In this approach, rather than manipulating the behavior of hospitalized patients, researchers could have investigated how age, medication history, and socioeconomic status of the patients were related to their ability to show normal, appropriate behavior. By using a statistical procedure that yields a correlation coefficient, the relationship of any of these patient characteristics to the patients' ward behavior could be found. The correlation coefficient reflects the extent to which two variables vary with one another. For example, if older patients also show more disturbed ward behavior and younger patients less, then the correlation coefficient would be high.

A major shortcoming of this kind of research approach, however, concerns its inability to reveal the true "cause" of relationships. If older patients are more likely to show inappropriate ward behavior, it still is not known what causes what. Does being older in and of itself "cause" the disturbed ward behavior, or does disturbed ward behavior cause someone to remain on wards longer? Or is it also possible that some unknown third factor, such as amount of education or intelligence, might be affecting both factors? In spite of this shortcoming, correlational approaches can help professionals to make sense out of masses of data and provide evidence to support or refute hypotheses.

While there are other accepted research methods available, such as case studies and surveys, the experimental and correlational procedures presented above are probably the most often used ones in the science of abnormal psychology.

The Process of Assessment

As is true of research, clinical assessment, or the systematic evaluation of behavior patterns, also has its own set of widely accepted procedures that must be followed in order to gather accurate information. However, as will become clear, there are a number of difficulties that must be overcome before assessment procedures can be used successfully within the area of abnormal psychology. In the sections to follow, we will present the nature and purpose for assessment, the characteristics of acceptable assessment, the types of assessment, and the special issues that assessment presents. We begin with the purpose of assessment.

The Purpose of Assessment

With some consideration, the necessity of assessment seems obvious. Before anyone tries to solve a problem, he or she must determine the character of the difficulty. Whether the problem solver is a plumber, tree surgeon, or clinical psychologist, the nature of the problem to be solved must be clarified. The capacity to solve problems is directly related to our ability to define them accurately. This is the case in abnormal psychology. The major purpose of the clinical assessor is to clearly describe aspects of people that are related to their psychological functioning. With clear descriptions, the psychological assessor is in a better position to accomplish two additional goals, prediction and decision making (Phares, 1979). Assessors attempt to predict future behavior on the basis of data gathered in the present. What are the chances of children of mentally ill parents developing psychological disturbances? Will children who are abused grow up to be abusing parents? Is this person I am talking with in contact with reality?

Questions such as these require information that can be used to predict future behaviors. In fact, many psychological theories are attempts to predict what behavior will be shown in present and future situations. The research techniques we described earlier and the assessment devices we will describe below are the major shared methods used by scientists to evaluate the worth of these theories.

The practical application of prediction is decision making. Generally, people are assessed because some decision concerning them needs to be made. For many clinical professionals the decision may be into which diagnostic category to place a person. Diagnosis is most useful, however, when correct placement also leads to effective treatment. A correct diagnosis of depression, for example, would lead to the use of particular types of antidepressive drugs or psychological therapies.

Other decisions also may have to be made. It may have to be decided what to do with patient A who attempted suicide. Should she be returned home? Perhaps she needs to be hospitalized for a few weeks of therapy. Or would it be helpful if the patient were placed in a halfway house away from home rather than in a hospital where she might become too dependent? There is a critical need to collect the kind of information that will help make the correct decision. An incorrect decision in this case might cost a life. While not always dealing with life and death issues, clinical assessors are constantly faced with making decisions about people. The assessors have a number of useful but potentially fallible procedures through which they can gather the information to help them make accurate decisions. In the next section the characteristics necessary for effective assessment procedures will be discussed.

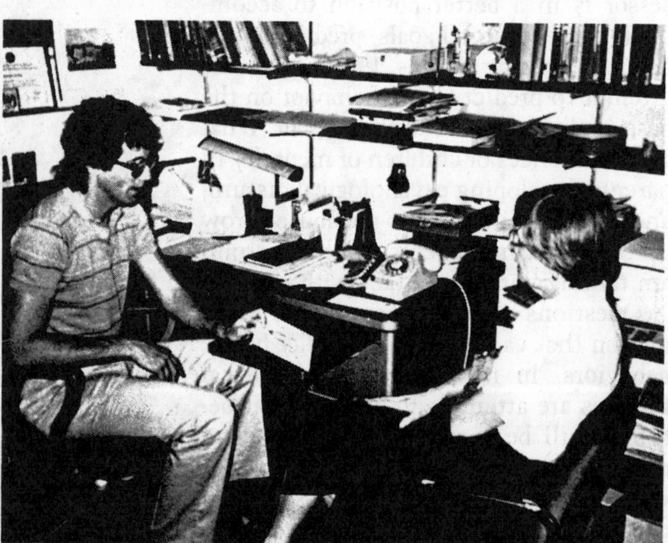

Standardized psychological testing is one of the assessor's basic tools.

Characteristics of Effective Assessment

To be useful to the clinical evaluator, assessment procedures should possess certain attributes: *validity, reliability, standardization, and norms.* These aspects are described in the "Standards for Educational and Psychological Tests," published by a joint committee of the American Psychological Association, the American Educational Research Association, and the National Council on Measurement in Education in 1974. The first and foremost attribute of an assessment procedure established by the joint commission is its validity.

Validity

If an assessment procedure measures what it is supposed to, it is said to be valid. For example, for the Scholastic Aptitude Test (SAT), a test purporting to measure knowledge necessary for college achievement, to be valid, students who do well on the SAT should also do well in college. If this correlation occurs, then the SAT is said to possess some amount of *predictive validity.* Predictive validity is also important in the area of abnormal behavior. Often professionals are asked to predict the future behavior of their patients. Known as "making the prognosis," such predictions are usually based on information obtained from a variety of assessment procedures. The more accurate the predictions, the higher the predictive validity.

Another practical application of predictive validity comes from the area of personality research. Friedman and Rosenman (1974) have identified two personality types, A and B. These two types are assessed by a *standardized stress interview* in which a number of questions are asked from the areas of ambition, competitiveness, sense of time urgency, and feelings of hostility. Based on these interviews, type A personalities who are driven, competitive, hostile individuals can be differentiated from type B personalities who are calmer, less competitive, and friendly. In a clear example of predictive validity, Friedman and Rosenman (1959) have found that type A personalities are more prone to develop heart disease than type B. In this instance because the procedures have predictive validity, interventions can be undertaken to help those type A individuals to change their present life-style to reduce the likelihood of future heart disease.

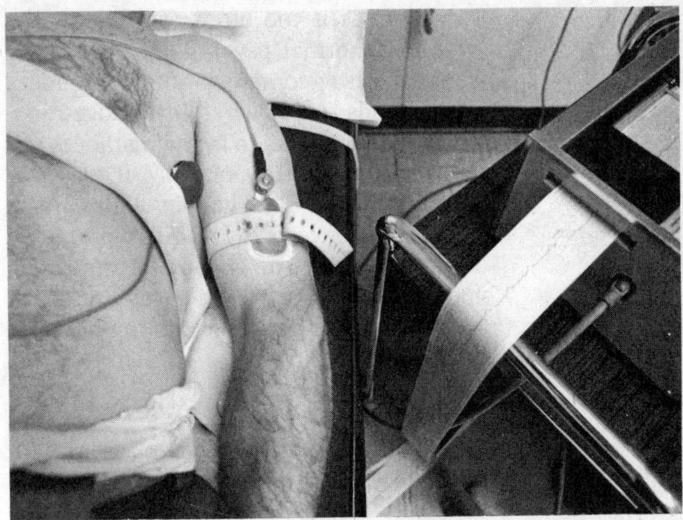

Sometimes basic stress levels are obtained through heart rate to assess a person's psychological state. (© *1983 Larry Racioppo*)

Reliability

If an assessment procedure measures something in a consistent fashion, it possesses reliability. It is possible for an assessment procedure to measure some characteristic consistently but still not be valid because the characteristic may not be what the test is supposed to measure. For example, if a test of anxiety has items that are so obviously related to anxiety that, rather than admit to anxiety, people consistently answer items to put themselves in a "good light," the test would be reliable but not valid. Perhaps the best way to describe the relationship between reliability and validity is to say that reliability is a necessary but not sufficient attribute of an assessment procedure, but validity is essential.

There are two major kinds of reliability that are of great interest to students of abnormal psychology: *test-retest and interjudge reliabilities.* Test-retest reliability is assessed by calculating how similar results are when administering the same assessment procedure twice. The more similar the results, the higher the test-retest reliability. It is important for an assessor to know that an assessment procedure will produce somewhat the same result now as it will tomorrow or next week. For example, if an assessor administers an IQ test to a client today and finds a score that indicates an average level of intelligence, he or she wants to be assured that should that test be given again in a week that the client will again score in the average range. Without such assurances of test-retest reliability, the assessor would not be able to make predictions about future behavior of the client.

While test-retest reliability refers to consistency over tests and time, interjudge reliability refers to consistency of opinions among judges. There are many times in the study of abnormal behavior when people are asked to judge the behavior of others. Nowhere is the process more important than when judges are asked to decide whether or not someone belongs in a particular diagnostic category. Should two or more people observe the behavior of a patient and be asked to diagnose that patient, interjudge reliability would be high if all judges agree on a particular diagnosis.

However, as is too often the case in the field of abnormal psychology, there may be some disagreement among the judges which leads to a lowered interjudge reliability. For example, in many instances the interjudge reliability of DSM-II was low (Blashfield, 1973). The development of operational criteria in DSM-III was one attempt to increase diagnostic interjudge reliability, and data presented by Spitzer et al., (1979) suggest that the attempt has been successful.

Standardization

The concept of standardizing assessment procedures is an intuitively obvious one. It simply means making sure that all materials and instructions given to the test takers are identical so that all administrations of the assessment procedure are the same for all subjects. Without standardization, results between various administrations of the assessment procedure are not comparable.

Norms

In addition to assessment procedures being valid, reliable, and standardized, they need to have acceptable norms. Scores obtained as a result of an assessment procedure receive their meaning by being compared with *normative groups.* Normative groups help to answer such questions as: "Is a person's score higher or lower than average?" To know that a person's score on a test of anxiety is, for example, 60, is virtually meaningless until it is also known that the average score of a group of people possessing similar characteristics to that of the test taker is 40. If it also known that only 2 people out of 100 in the normative group scored 60 or above, then the subject's score of 60 suggests strongly that he or she may be quite anxious.

The composition of the normative group is critical to making generalizations about test scores. For example, if the person being assessed is very different from those people composing the normative group, then inferences made about the subject's score are limited. If the subject is a 21-year-old white female from New York City, and members of the normative population are primarily males between the ages of 50 and 70 from small towns in the Midwest, then her scores would be difficult to relate to this normative population. However, if the normative group were made up of comparably aged peers from urban areas, then the young woman's score could be related and interpretations made about its meaning. Although they are difficult to obtain, representative norms are very important to the development of adequate assessment procedures.

Types of Assessment

Having established the required attributes of assessment procedures, we now present the major types of assessment procedures used in the study of abnormal psychology. We begin with tests of personality and follow with descriptions of tests of cognitive functioning, interviewing, and controlled observations.

Assessment of Personality

"Personality" is one of those terms that everyone uses but is actually very hard to define. By personality we mean "those relatively enduring traits and dispositions of the individual that have, over time, jelled into a pattern that distinguishes him (or her) from other individuals" (Sarnoff, 1962). Personality aspects are important when the goal is to evaluate the person's level of psychological functioning. Disturbed individuals may be described as showing "personality disintegration" or as having a "rigid personality." Because of its importance in the assessment of disordered behavior, hundreds of tests of personality have been developed since the introduction of the first personality scale, the Woodworth Personality Inventory in 1920 (Buros, 1979). There are two major ways that have been used to assess personality: *the self-report test and the pro-*

jective test. Both kinds of personality testing are popular with clinical psychologists. The frequency of use of all tests is reported in Table 2-1. Both self-report and projective tests of personality are among the most frequently used.

Table 2-1 Ten Most Frequently Used Psychological Tests

1. Wechsler Adult Intelligence Scale
2. Minnesota Multiphasic Personality Inventory
3. Bender-Gestalt Visual Motor Test
4. Rorschach
5. Thematic Apperception Test
6. Wechsler Intelligence Scale for Children
7. Peabody Picture Vocabulary Test
8. Sentence Completion Test
9. House-Tree-Person
10. Draw-A-Person

Source: Adapted from Lubin et al. (1985).

Self-Report Tests In a self-report questionnaire individuals are asked to respond in the same consistent way, usually "true" or "false" to a list of statements (Kaplan & Saccuzzo, 1982). According to the data reported in Table 2-1, the most frequently used self-report personality test is the Minnesota Multiphasic Personality Inventory (MMPI) (Hathaway & McKinley, 1943). In fact, the MMPI has been the focus of over 3500 referenced studies (Anastasi, 1982) and has become a model for numerous other self-report tests of personality.

Originally, the MMPI's major purpose was to help distinguish abnormal from normal people. In completing the MMPI people answer "true," "false," or "cannot say" to 566 statements about themselves, their attitudes, and their experiences. Items were gleaned from interviews, reports, textbooks, and other tests. Examples of MMPI types of items are, "I feel tight about the forehead" and "I read all the editorials in the newspaper every night." Items are organized into 4 validity scales and 10 clinical scales reflecting such characteristics as depression, suspiciousness, physical concerns, and anxiety (see Figure 2-1 for a sample MMPI profile and Table 2-2 for a listing of general meanings of each scale).

The validity scales reflect how individuals approach answering the test items. The first validity scale, the lie scale, measures the degree to which subjects "fake good" or portray themselves as better than they really are. A typical L scale item would be to answer "true" to the statement, "Angry, obnoxious people don't bother me."

Another one of the validity scales, the K scale, also measures the degree to which subjects portray themselves in a favorable light. However, K scale items are more subtly stated than those of the L scale and thus more difficult to fake.

In contrast to the L and K validity scales which reflect a tendency to "fake good," the F scale reflects subjects' attempts to "fake bad" or portray themselves as worse than they really are. A typical F scale item would be to answer "true" to the statement: "I often see and smell weird things."

The fourth and final validity scale is the "cannot say" scale. It consists of simply counting the number of items that were not answered. If the number of items left unanswered is very high, then the entire scale could be declared invalid.

Originally, the 10 clinical scales were named after the disorders they were supposed to identify, that is, depression, paranoia, and schizophrenia (see Table 2-2). Investigation of the scales soon revealed that individuals diagnosed as one of the disorders supposedly indicated on the MMPI scales did not necessarily score high on that scale and low on the others. In fact, at times the scale named after the disorder was among the lowest scale scores.

After these failures, clinicians looked to see if they could develop rules to predict what scale scores would be associated with certain diagnoses (Gilberstadt & Duker, 1965). This approach, however, also proved to be a failure. Making diagnoses by using rules to indicate what pattern of scores should be associated with a

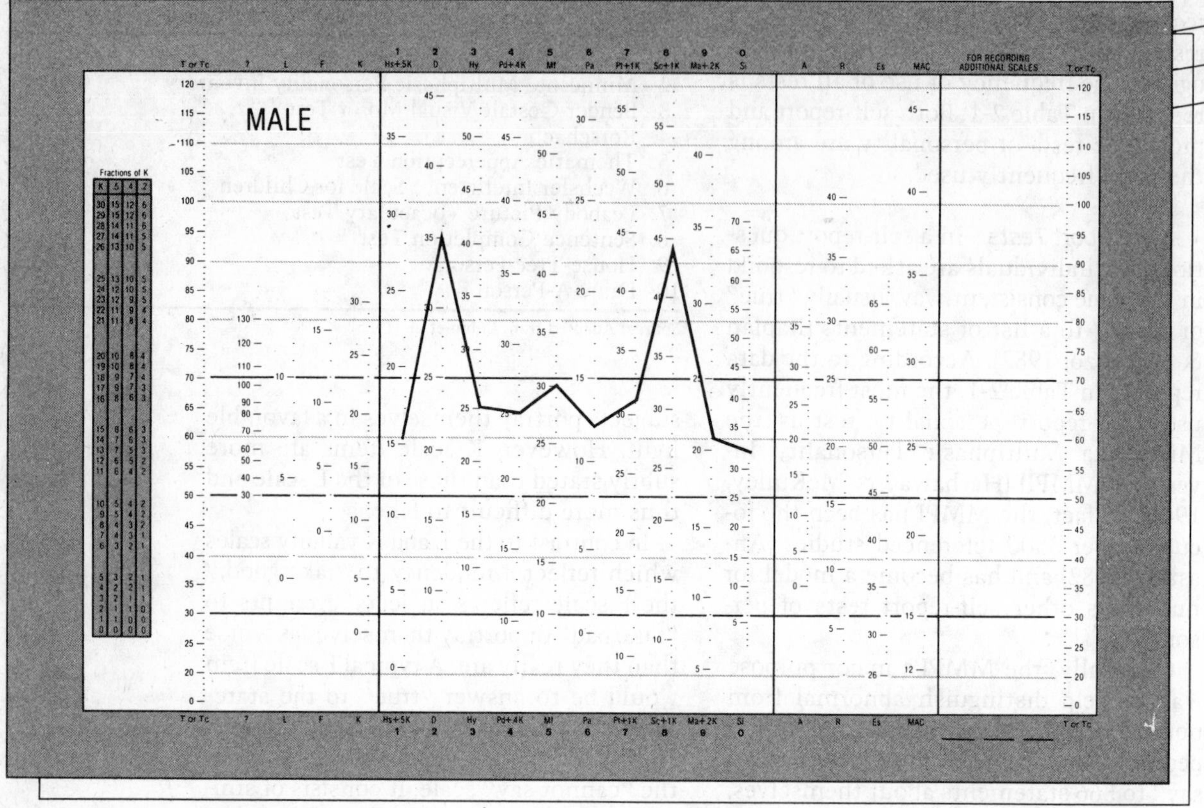

Figure 2-1 A sample Minnesota Multiphasic Personality Inventory Profile showing a 2,8 high-point scale pairing. *Source: Copyright © The University of Minnesota Press, 1982. Reprinted by permission.*

particular disorder were no more accurate than those made by untrained nonprofessionals (Gilberstadt & Duker, 1965; Meehl & Rosen, 1955).

Professionals next turned to a set of procedures that is used to the present day; they focused on the highest two scale scores on any profile. Those people who shared the same two scale score high points were examined to reveal particular common personality and behavioral attributes. For instance, those people who score high on the depression scale 2 and the schizophrenia scale 8 have been found to be viewed by others as being "odd," unconventional, and uncommunicative (Dahlstrom et al., 1975). Literally hundreds of studies have been undertaken using this approach, and manuals have been developed reporting characteristics associated with various two-point scale codes.

The MMPI is the most frequently used self-report inventory in spite of some psychometric shortcomings like relatively poor reliability and unequal proportions of true and false answers. The MMPI's popularity probably stems from the fact that data from thousands of studies have been summarized and made easily available to clinicians as an aid in diagnoses. It has become an integral part of a general assessment battery given by clinicians, and with experience clinicians have become more comfortable in interpreting what

Table 2-2 MMPI Clinical Scales

Clinical Scales	*Simulated Items (Answered True)*
Hypochondriasis (Hs). (Abnormal concern with bodily functions)	"At times I get strong cramps in my intestines."
Depression (D). (Pessimism, hopelessness, slowing of action and thought)	"I am often very tense on the job."
Conversion Hysteria (Hy). (Unconscious use of physical and mental problems to avoid conflicts or responsibility)	"Sometimes there is a feeling like something is pressing in on my head."
Psychopathic Deviate (Pd). (Disregard of social custom, shallow emotions, inability to profit from experience)	"I wish I could do over some of the things I have done."
Masculinity-Femininity (Mf). (Items differentiating between men and women)	"I used to like to do the dances in gym class."
Paranoia (Pa). (Abnormal suspiciousness, delusions of grandeur or persecution)	"It distresses me that people have the wrong ideas about me."
Psychasthenia (Pt). (Obsessions, compulsiveness, fears, guilt, indecisiveness)	"The things that run through my head sometimes are horrible."
Schizophrenia (Sc). (Bizarre, unusual thoughts of behavior, withdrawal, hallucinations, delusions)	"There are those out there who want to get me."
Hypomania (Ma). (Emotional excitement, flight of ideas, overactivity)	"Sometimes I think so fast I can't keep up."
Social Introversion (Si). (Shyness, disinterest in others, insecurity)	"I give up too easily when discussing things with others."

Source: Reproduced by permission. Copyright 1943, renewed 1967 by the University of Minnesota. Published by The Psychological Corporation, New York. All rights reserved.

MMPI scales scores mean. However, because it is a self-report personality device, the MMPI is subject to a number of potential shortcomings and its results should be used cautiously and in combination with results from other testing procedures. First, the language of self-report inventories can be misinterpreted. The word "nervous" in a self-report test item may mean "panic-stricken" to one person and "slightly tense" to another. Second, people differ in their degree of self-knowledge, and some people may not be able to accurately answer all the questions about themselves. Finally, to present themselves in an unrealistically good light (such as when applying for a job), some people may simply lie in responding to items. Because of these potential problems, other methods of assessing personality, such as projective procedures, are often used in conjunction with the self-report tests.

Projective Techniques Unlike self-report tests of personality that generally consist of straightforward verbal statements that require a fixed kind of response, projective techniques consist of ambiguous stimuli to which a person can reply in limitless ways. The projective approach is based on the belief that, if people are given amorphous stimuli such as inkblots (see Figure 2-2) or vague pictures to look at, they will tend to project onto these amorphous stimuli their inner feelings, drives, and needs. Leonardo da Vinci reportedly used images seen in clouds and fireplace ashes to test the creativity of his students and to gain some insight into their personalities (Exner, 1976). Projective techniques can be less susceptible to "faking" than self-report inventories. Test takers usually have a difficult time figuring out how their responses will be scored, thus making it difficult for them to make

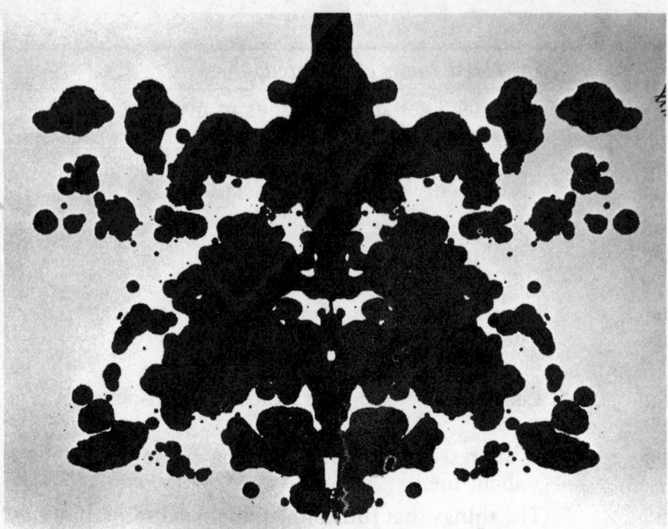

Figure 2-2 Illustration of inkblot similar to those on the Rorschach.

the test "come out" in any certain way. For instance, what does it mean to see fog in an inkblot? Does it suggest anxiety, depression, or perhaps something else?

Developed by Herman Rorschach (1942), the Rorschach Inkblot Test is today's most popular projective testing technique. In the administration of the Rorschach, subjects are handed 10 inkblot cards one at a time and instructed to tell the examiner what the inkblot looks like to them. Test takers are free to give as many responses as they wish. The examiner writes down these responses (percepts) without comment. However, after 10 cards have been administered, the examiner then returns to the first response, reads it back to the subject, and questions the subject as to where the percept was seen and what made it look that way. Each response is taken in turn until all are covered. The ability of these inkblot stimuli to elicit many different responses is shown by the wide variety of percepts given by 100 college students to a card similar to the one presented in Figure 2-2 (see Table 2-3).

The complex scoring techniques developed for interpreting the Rorschach have not yielded consistently satisfactory reliability or validity data (Anastasi, 1982). Defenders of the Rorschach say that conventional means of establishing reliability may be inappropriate because it is so much more sensitive to the day-to-day fluctuations of emotions than are self-report tests. As well, some clinicians suggest that the Rorschach's most important use is as a "hypothesis generator." That is, the contents of clients' responses to the inkblots and the manner in which they present them may give the clinician some insights into the client's personality that might not be obtainable from other assessment sources. Since the generated hypotheses are actually guesses about what is going on within a person, they must be verified by information from other sources. However, interpretation of Rorschach responses may help give direction to further information-gathering procedures. The following vignette may help to clarify this point.

One of the authors, when a graduate student, participated unknowingly in a simple experiment that showed how the Rorschach can at times be more useful in assessing personality than more structured techniques. Through a one-way mirror, our graduate class watched the assessment of a man, supposedly from the state mental hospital. On the basis of our observation of his interview and test responses, our task was to decide whether he was retarded, dangerous, or normal. As the man completed the interview and some intelligence tests as well, we were almost all certain that he was dangerous and probably retarded. Then came the Rorschach, and as the man gave his responses to the inkblots, it appeared to us that his responses were not consistent with the test behaviors we had previously observed. Instead of responses that were short and simple, he "saw" things that were more complex and integrated, certainly not what would be expected from a man who was supposed to be retarded. After the testing session was completed and we discussed the test results, everyone seemed to share the same uneasy feeling that this man was not what he had first seemed. Our uneasiness stemmed, for the most part, from the manner in which he had responded to the Rorschach. Our professor then let us know what he had done. The man interviewed was actually a professional actor who had spent the better part of 2 years playing the role of Lenny, the retarded, well-meaning, but potentially violent character in John Steinbeck's play *Of Mice and Men.* Our instructor asked him to play Lenny during the testing session. He played the role most convincingly, except for the way in which he responded to the Rorschach. In discussing his experience afterward, the actor confessed that the Rorschach made it very difficult for him to stay in his role; he did not know how Lenny would perceive these nebulous blots.

This anecdote may help to explain why the Rorschach is still one of the most frequently used tests in spite of the lack of conventional psychometric support. However, as mentioned previously, it should always be used carefully and always in combination with other tests to assess personality.

Because it contains a variety of pictures and not inkblots, the Thematic Apperception Test (TAT) is considered to be a more structured projective test than the Rorschach. Ranking just behind the Rorschach in frequency of usage by clinicians (see Table 2-1), the TAT also attempts to assess unconscious needs and conflicts, but through a series of real-life pictures varying in ambiguity for subjects to project upon (Murray, 1938). Test takers are assumed to draw upon their own feelings, motives, and needs when they are asked to produce stories in response to a given picture. Although more structured than the Rorschach, TAT cards also can elicit an impressive array of responses (see Figure 2-3 for an example of a TAT-like stimulus). Table 2-4 presents stories given about a TAT card picturing a boy seemingly staring at his violin.

Table 2-3 Responses of College Students to an Inkblot Stimulus

Inkblot Responses	*Percentage of Students Giving the Response*
Bats	18
Wolf, werewolf, coyote	15
Bird	7
Fox, fox face	7
Two animals back to back	5
Birds, dogs, wolves	5
Emblem, AMA symbol	5
Monster, devil, evil face	5
Halloween mask, pumpkin	4
Pelvis, hip bones	3
Owl	2
An inkblot	2
Valley with mountains	2
Angry animal (cat)	2
Two witches	1
Two horseheads	1
Animal skull	1
Vertebra of human spine	1
Two bears dancing	1
Shadow of a bear	1
Rabbit	1
Animal configuration (birds, wolf)	1
Two baby elephants kissing	1
Siamese twins	1
Two people protecting a child	1
Dance formation, woman in middle	1
Two cherubs and a drinking fountain	1
Angel with spread wings	1
Trees reflecting on a lake	1
Pagoda	1
Cover of "Yes" album	1
Boat with oarsmen splashing	1
Motorcycle with two girls in burlesque costumes	1

Although projective personality tests are difficult to fake, may allow for the assessment of unique characteristics, and can be used to generate hypotheses, they have failed at times to relate reliably to diagnosis. The very richness of reponses that projective tests produce sometimes makes them difficult to score and use in any standardized fashion.

Figure 2-3 In the Thematic Apperception Test (TAT) subjects are asked to create stories about ambiguous situations such as the one depicted above.

Cognitive and Neuropsychological Assessment

Focusing on a different aspect of human functioning than the personality assessment procedures, cognitive testing provides valuable information regarding intellectual ability and brain functioning. While important in terms of an overall evaluation of a person's functioning, data from these tests are especially helpful in the diagnosing of faulty thinking found in some forms of psychoses and organic brain damage.

The first scientifically developed individual intelligence test was published by Binet in 1905. His test grew out of an attempt to identify within a group of low-achieving children those who probably could benefit from public school education. Binet believed that intelligence was best defined as a global ability to make accurate practical judgments. Once the most popular way to assess intelligence, the Binet scales have gradually been replaced by the Wechsler series of intelligence scales (Matarazzo, 1980).

Wechsler believed that intelligence was a composite of several separate abilities, not one unitary trait as Binet assumed. Consistent with his belief, Wechsler constructed intelligence tests that were composed of a number of different subtests of different abilities. Eventually three separate intelligence scales were constructed to test individuals in three age groupings. The Wechsler Pre-school and Primary Intelligence scale (WPPSI) is for children from 4 to 6½ years of age, the Wechsler Intelligence Scale for Children—Revised (WISC-R) for children from 6 to 16 years of age, and the Wechsler Adult Intelligence Scale—Revised (WAIS-R) for adults over the age of 16. Each test includes a number of subtests whose procedures may vary from having subjects answer questions of general information (e.g., What is the population of Canada?) to having them place blocks together to correspond to presented designs. Table 2-5 presents a description of subtests included in Wechsler's Adult Intelligence Scale—Revised (WAIS-R, 1980).

Intelligence tests can give some indication of potential brain damage, since they assess performance in the areas of memory, spatial perception, abstraction, and concept formation—abilities usually affected by brain dysfunction (Anastasi, 1982; Benton, 1980). One of the most frequently used specialized tests for brain damage (see Table 2-1) is the Bender Visual Motor Gestalt Test (Bender, 1938). The test consists of nine designs that the subject is to look at and copy one at a time onto a sheet of paper. Scoring systems for children (Koppitz, 1975) and adults (Pascal & Sutell, 1951) have been developed to help clinicians discriminate those people who may have an organic brain disorder from those who may not. It is assumed that by age 12 everyone should be able to copy these designs without mistakes. If there are significant distortions in designs, such as those depicted in Figure 2-4, the likelihood of the presence of brain damage is increased because deficits in

Table 2-4 Responses of College Students to a TAT Picture

1. What we have here is a frustrated little boy who has had his parents pushing him to learn to build things, eat properly, and play the violin. Their intentions are good because they want him to be a success and an object they can display and be proud of. At the present moment, he is too young to appreciate and desire these admirable talents and lacks inner motivation. The end result may be that he rebels against those pressures and heads in other directions when he may have enjoyed acquiring talents had he not been forced at such a young age. A common problem of today's youth.
2. The child has just recently started to take violin lessons. His parents wanted him to take the lessons so now he is satisfying their wishes. The child must practice quite a bit but he really doesn't want to. He would rather be outside playing with his friends. He doesn't even like the violin. Well, he is debating when to start. As we all know, he will start in a few minutes and then run outside to play.
3. A child is being punished for not practicing his violin. He is very sad. He is commanded to play but he will not. He is waiting in the corner for his father to get home.
4. This little guy (Billy) is angry at his dog because he just gathered up all kinds of odds and ends (sitting on table) and he was going to make his dog a birthday present. But before he could begin construction of the not-yet-decided-upon-present, his dog came up to little Billy and bit him on the leg. Billy became angry and strangled his little Pekingese. This picture doesn't show the dog lying at his feet—dead.
5. Within the damp setting of the little wooden house, Ray sat at his little desk composing his assignment for school. His mind keeps drifting off the subject, because he is faced with a problem which is worrying him more. Ray finally decides that he will talk to his father the next day after school about his misfortune. Then he closes his books, and retires for the night.
6. Little Tommy Scott was looking in his attic one day when he came upon a strange kind of instrument. What the heck is this, he is saying to himself. As he sat staring in amazement at the strange instrument, it leaped up into his hands and starting ringing out a slow ballad. He ran outside and told all his friends about the strange happening but everyone laughed.
7. Joey wanted to be a famous musician but he also wanted to be a baseball star and see his picture on bubble gum cards. He had started his violin lessons and was exceptionally good. His teacher said that he had a fine potential. Joey was very happy. Just yesterday he came home from school, bubbling with excitement. "Mom, guess what, they're starting a baseball league at school next week." His mother was also excited but it soon became apparent that his lessons for violin and softball practice were on the same day. He now had a tough decision. What should he do? He is very depressed because he doesn't know what to do.
8. A small boy sitting by himself drowning in his sorrows. His mother has punished him for a reason he doesn't understand very well. All he can do now is moan since his favorite possession and pastime was taken away and he knows he has to just sit and wait until next week when he can once again play his violin with joy and happiness.

visual memory are known to be related to brain injury. At times examiners will increase the difficulty of the Bender Gestalt task by allowing the examinee to look at the design for a certain time, but then take the design card away making the examinee reproduce the design completely from memory.

While the Bender Gestalt Test has been a standard assessment tool for many years, it is rarely used by itself. Rather it is typically part of a group of tests which examine a number of different cognitive skills (see Table 2-6). One such group of tests devoted entirely to the assessment of brain damage is the Halstead-Reitan

Table 2-5 A Description of the Subtests of the Wechsler Adult Intelligence Scale—Revised

Subtest	Description
1. Information	29 questions to test the subject's range of general information. Example: What is the population of Canada?
2. Comprehension	12 items that measure the subject's practical judgment ability. Example: Why are banking laws needed?
3. Arithmetic	A timed subtest made up of 11 items that measure arithmetic ability. Example: How much is $7 and $4?
4. Similarities	13 items that ask the subject to state how things are the same. It measures the ability to abstract verbally. Example: In what way are trees and bushes alike?
5. Memory for digits	Measures the ability to concentrate and repeat numbers verbally administered. Example: Repeat these numbers: 8—4—6—2.
6. Vocabulary	40 words that the subject is to define. Example: What is a scissors?
7. Digit symbol	A timed subtest in which the subject copies symbols below appropriate numbers.
8. Picture completion	21 items in which the subject is to point out what is wrong with a picture. Measures ability to note small detail.
9. Block design	A timed task in which the subject must put blocks together to correspond to a design picture.
10. Picture arrangement	A timed task in which the subject is asked to put in correct order cards that are in the wrong order. This measures logical reasoning and attention to detail.
11. Object assembly	A timed task in which the subject is to put together four puzzles to make a picture of a real-life item.

Source: Adapted from D. Wechsler, *Manual for the Wechsler Adult Intelligence Scale.* Copyright © 1980, The Psychological Corporation.

Battery. Composed of a number of subtests in much the same way as the Wechsler scales of intelligence, the Halstead-Reitan is a "comprehensive neuropsychologic battery consisting of tests of general intelligence, concept formation, expressive and receptive language, auditory perception, time perception, verbal and non-verbal memory, perceptual motor speed, tactile performance, spatial relations, finger sensitivity,. . .and personality" (Strub & Black, 1981, p. 67). Through assessment of these many areas in which brain dysfunction may be manifested, the Halstead-Reitan Battery affords an excellent, systematic look at an individual's cognitive functioning.

Table 2-6 Components of Most Neuropsychological Evaluations

1. Behavior, attention, and feelings
2. All forms of intelligence, verbal and nonverbal forms
3. Language, such as word and sentence comprehension, auditory discrimination, and expressive language
4. All forms of memory—long- and short-term
5. Verbal and nonverbal abstracting ability
6. Ability to construct and reproduce
7. Geographic orientation
8. Arithmetic, spelling, and reading achievement
9. Perceptual motor speed
10. Motor strength and coordination
11. The personality structure

Source: After Heilman and Valenstein, 1985.

The full battery can take literally an entire day to administer. Of the number of subtests one of the most useful is the immediate recall of verbal stories. In this assessment method, examinees are asked to listen to a story and then to repeat everything they remember about it. An example of such a story is the following:

> A cowboy/from Arizona/went to San Francisco/with his dog/which he left/with a friend/while he purchased/a new suit

of clothes./Dressed finely,/he went back to the dog,/whistled to him,/called him by name,/and patted him./But the dog would have nothing to do with him,/in his new hat/and coat,/but gave a mournful howl./ (Strub & Black, 1981, p. 58)

As demarcated by slashes, the above story has 17 separate items of information. The greater degree of brain damage, the fewer the number of items will be remembered. It should be noted, however, that few neurologically intact individuals could remember all of them. As in the case of any test, a subject's performance must be compared with some norms in order for her score to be meaningfully interpreted.

In addition to memory, neuropsychological assessment also functions on higher mental processes such as abstract reasoning and problem solving. In the measurement of these abilities, people might be asked to discuss the abstract meanings of some proverbs or to solve mathematical problems mentally. Some examples of commonly used proverbs are: "A new broom sweeps clean"; "People in glass houses shouldn't throw stones"; and "Rome wasn't built in a day." Some mental arithmetic tasks are "Count backward from 100 by 3s" and "If I have 38 newspapers and sell 22 for 15 cents each, how many more will I need to sell in order to earn $4.50?"

Always an important part of assessment, neuropsychological testing has become even more popular. Those who believe that abnormal behavior may have biological causes are especially prone to use tests of cognitive functioning to help gather data necessary for diagnosis.

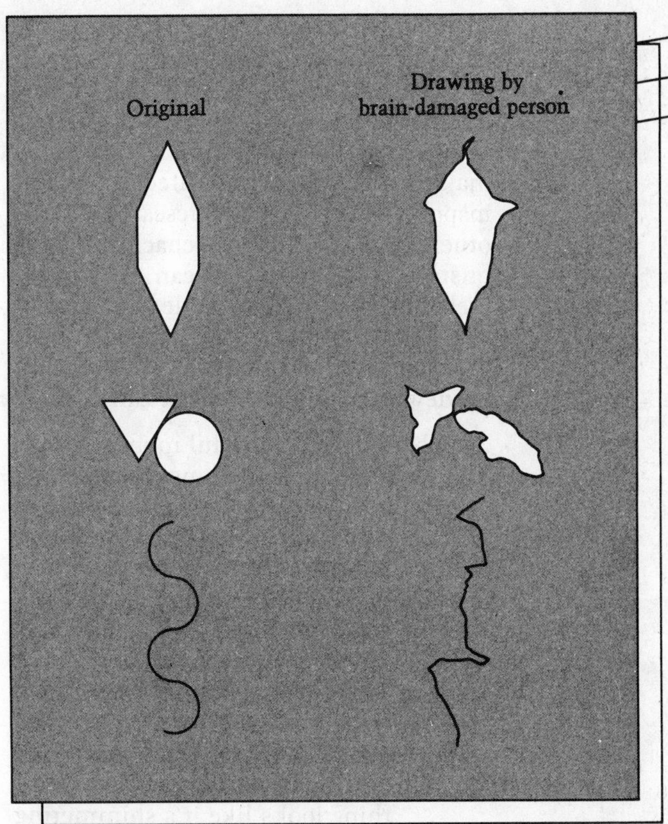

Figure 2-4 Distortion of drawings by brain-damaged persons such as might be seen with the Bender Gestalt or Benton Visual Retention Tests (diagrams are similar to those included in these tests).

Interviewing

The standardized tests of personality, cognitive abilities, and neurological functioning basically involve a subject's responding to some type of impersonal questions or tasks. By contrast, in the interview, the subject is face to face with an interviewer who asks for information that is necessary for understanding the interviewee's personality. Because information flows only in one direction, interviewing differs from everyday conversation and calls for a great deal of skill to put clients at ease, build feelings of trust, and obtain relevant information. There are many who see interviewing as the most important way that clinicians collect information about their clients (Stevenson, 1971).

Interviews can be *unstructured* or *structured*. In an unstructured verbal interaction, interviewers usually are free to cover as wide a range of topics as they desire. There are typically few constraints on what may be asked during such broad-ranging interviews. However, part of the price for this flexibility is a loss of standardization and reliability that may make the data from structured interviews inapplicable in systematic research. On the other hand, like the Rorschach inkblots, unstructured interviews can sometimes yield information that can lead to fruitful hypotheses about the basis for people's problems as is shown in the following interview with a typical client called Bob.

Bob: It's been an awful month. I can't seem to do anything. I don't know whether I'm coming or going. I'm afraid I'm going crazy or something.

Doctor: What makes you think that?

Bob: I can't concentrate. My boss tells me to do something and I start to do it, but before I've taken five steps I don't know what I started out to do. I get dizzy and I can feel my heart beating and everything looks like it's shimmering or far away from me or something—it's unbelievable.

Doctor: What thoughts come to mind when you're feeling like this?

Bob: I just think, "Oh, Christ, my heart is really beating, my head is swimming, my ears are ringing—I'm either going to die or go crazy."

Doctor: What happens then?

Bob: Well, it doesn't last more than a few seconds, I mean that intense feeling. I come back down to earth, but then I'm worrying what's the matter with me all the time, or checking my pulse to see how fast it's going, or feeling my palms to see if they're sweating.

Doctor: Can others see what you're going through?

Bob: You know, I doubt it. I hide it. I haven't been seeing my friends. You know, they say "Let's stop for a beer" or something after work and I give them some excuse—you know, like I have to do something around the house or with my car. I'm not with them when I'm with them anyway—I'm just sitting there worrying. My friend Pat said I was frowning all the time. So, anyway, I just go home and turn on the TV or pick up the sports page, but I can't really get into that either.

While unstructured interviewers usually are free to cover as wide a range of topics as they desire and in any order, structured interviewers are required to ask the same questions in the same manner to all interviewees. The structured interview is frequently used in research projects when the data from interviews need to be compared. In clinical settings probably the most common use of the highly structured interview is the *mental status exam.*

"The purpose of the Mental Status Examination is to evaluate a person suspected of neurological or emotional problems in terms of variables known to be related to those problems" (Kaplan & Saccuzzo, 1982, p. 213). In the mental status interview, the interviewer attempts to assess a person's appearance, attitudes, and general behavior. By asking a structured set of questions, the interviewer attempts to evaluate such characteristics of disordered behavior as disturbed thought processes or inappropriate emotions. Mental status examiners can assess intelligence by using brief sets of questions that require memory, judgment, and abstracting abilities to answer. Finally, the examiner wishes to see if the person can direct and focus attention onto relevant tasks. An inability to attend properly or disturbed perception usually are associated with more severe psychopathology.

The mental status exam is an integral part of the assessment process. When

Observing people in situations where they live and work can give the psychological assessor added insight into the origin of their behavior. (*Michal Heron/Monkmeyer Press Photo Service*)

properly used, it can provide essential information necessary for accurate diagnosis and effective treatment.

Like with the unstructured interview, the benefits of the structured interview come at a cost. The standardization of the interview interaction may result in a more rigid and artificial communication process that some clients may perceive as cold, unfeeling, and nontherapeutic.

The psychometric merit of interviews as assessment tools probably varies with their degree of structure (Anastasi, 1982). The more structured the interview, generally the easier it is to establish reliability. However, the unstructured interview approximates normal conversation and may facilitate freer expression of feeling. Regardless of the degree of structure, however, in the diagnostic process information gained through interviewing is usually combined with information from other assessment procedures to make decisions.

Observation

Although they are standardized and controlled procedures used in special professional settings, testing and interviewing do not give us firsthand direct data about how people behave in their home, work, or leisure settings. To obtain this kind of information, scientific practitioners turn to a systematic application of direct "observation" of human behavior.

The most direct way to find out how people behave in certain settings is to observe them in that environment. For example, in the above interview, because Bob talks about problems at his office or at playing baseball, those favoring an observational approach would suggest he be directly observed in those settings. At times, clinicians, especially those who work with children, may visit their homes to observe them in interaction with relatives in this environment (see the following personal experience).

Personal Experience: Observation of a Family at Home

Don and I get to the L______ family's house at about 6:00 p.m. Mr. L______ was sitting on the porch "playing some chickens." He told us that when he squeezed different birds they would make varying squawks and he was trying to make them sound like a song. He was good humored about this and seemed to know it was strange. He then took us inside. It was apparent that the place had been cleaned up for our arrival. We got the "grand tour" and saw where the kids and the parents slept. They all shared one big loft, the parents in a double bed behind a curtain on one side and Jill and Jim in a single bed on the other side. With both kids budding adolescents, we asked if they had any "private" space in the house and were told that they didn't. Mr. L______ made some jokes and we went down to eat. During dinner the conversation was light and careful with Mr. L______ playing jokes with the kids and Mrs. L______ apologizing to us for his behavior. It was never so clear in the office, but the family seemed like it was made up of one parent and three children. It was also apparent they all needed some private places to go to while at home. We would begin using these insights in our next session.

The great advantage of direct observation is that the behavior of interest can be viewed clearly. There is no need to ask someone about how they *would* have behaved in a particular situation; you can see clearly how they *are* behaving.

Direct observation, however, is difficult to do. People do not easily give up their privacy. Few people will allow themselves to be observed by outsiders. Schools have become less likely to allow observation of children by mental health professionals. Besides these personal and ethical concerns, there is a significant measurement problem as well. It is difficult to observe individuals without changing the natural way they behave. When the very act of observation changes how people behave, then observation (or any other assessment procedure) is said to be a *reactive* measure. Those methods of assessment that assess without changing behavior are called *nonreactive.* In order to make direct observation nonreactive, assessors may sometimes gather their information without the awareness of those being observed. Such attempts to be unobtrusive can violate the privacy of those being observed. Many believe that we all should know when we are being observed or assessed and that not being informed is an ethical violation. Suffice it to say that direct observation can provide very useful assessment information if the appropriate conditions can be developed.

Concluding Comments

In Chapter 2 we have described the shared methods of study which help to make abnormal psychology a paradigmatic science. Since these methods became a part of the process of abnormal psychology, significant progress has been made toward improved understanding of disordered behavior. The methods have become the hallmarks of the field of clinical psychology. Through experimental research and assessment, professionals have sought to identify and ameliorate abnormal behavior. However, these shared methods of study, in and of themselves, cannot make abnormal psychology a science. Clinicians and researchers using the methods also need shared sets of beliefs to guide their efforts. In Chapter 3 we will describe the major shared beliefs regarding the causes of disordered behavior. As you will see, interest in understanding and treating abnormal behavior is not a recent occurrence. Psychopathology has been a focus of study throughout the history of mankind.

Summary Chart

Noting that the study of abnormal behavior is a science characterized by shared methods of study and shared beliefs about the nature of behavior, we began in Chapter 2 to examine the methods used by professionals seeking to understand psychopathology. The first set of shared methods dealt with research:

Controlled, systematic methods of testing ideas
Hypotheses, independent variables, dependent variables, control groups, experimenter bias, statistical analysis

The second set of shared methods are the assessment techniques:

Typically used in examining individuals
Purposes of assessment
Characteristics of assessment methods: Validity, reliability, standardization, norms
Types of assessment methods: Personality assessment, cognitive and neuropsychological assessment, interviews, observation

CHAPTER 3

The Science of Abnormal Psychology: Shared Beliefs

The existence of an agreed-upon set of scientific methods is only one of two defining characteristics of a science like abnormal psychology. In addition, scientists are defined in their efforts by some *broad* view of how the things they study come about. For example, in Clifford Beers' time many professionals shared the belief that his problems were caused primarily by some disease of the brain or nervous system. Had Beers lived in the Middle Ages, on the other hand, his problems may have been ascribed to "possession" by the devil. If he were alive today, some scientists would believe that his difficulties stemmed from such causes as faulty learning, disturbed family relationships, or the stress effects of society. Such *global* views as those applied to understanding Beers' problems are termed by Kuhn "paradigms-as-sets-of-shared-beliefs," and they guide the thinking and problem-solving activities of a science. While the presence of paradigms or shared beliefs, per se is always characteristic of a science, the *specific* global views of a science are more changeable. In fact, at any point in time, one or more major beliefs may be operating. Further, existing paradigms are maintained as guides for research and theorizing only until they begin to fail to explain phenomena within the science's domain. Such unexplainable phenomena are called *anomalies,* and their very existence, according to Kuhn, produces a "state of tension" within the science. As more anomalies are encountered (i.e., as the existing view of things continues to fail), the state of tension reaches a *crisis stage* out of which eventually will emerge a new way of looking at the problems of the science. The emergence of the new perspective is called a *paradigmatic shift,* or *Gestalt switch,* and is a natural and normal part of the "life" of any science.

Some examples of paradigms or sets of shared beliefs and paradigmatic shifts in a science other than psychology may help you to understand their functions and to see why they are so important. We believe that an appreciation for these aspects of science will provide a helpful framework for your study of abnormal psychology. Let's begin with a look at some paradigms and paradigmatic shifts in biological science.

Early medical attempts to understand how disease was caused and transmitted from one person to another were guided by the *shared belief* that illnesses arose spontaneously. However, in part because this could not explain why some illnesses appeared in clusters of people, a *state of tension* arose in medical science and other paradigms for explaining the origin of disease began to emerge. One promising view was offered by Louis Pasteur. Using controlled observation, Pasteur developed the idea that disease was actually caused and transmitted by tiny living organisms called bacteria. On the basis of this perspective, such disease carriers as public drinking cups were abandoned. Further studies led to the development of vaccines for the prevention of disease and the preparation of chemicals which could kill bacteria and restore people to health.

By applying accepted methods of biological science, Pasteur and others sharing his beliefs (i.e., guided by the same paradigm) were able to show that his "germ theory" view of illness was useful. However, the progress of medicine did not stop with the wide acceptance of germ theory, for after some time there were some anomalies encountered. That is, there were some disorders for which there could not be found any bacterial involvement. With increasing numbers of such anomalies, there was a concomitant increase in a state of tension in medicine. This state of tension, in turn, motivated the search for new views of disease. Specifically, there occurred a paradigmatic shift toward a view that agents other than bacteria might be at the root of a significant number of physical diseases. The shift from a paradigm that asserted that all illnesses were caused by bacteria to one that allowed for the existence of other agents may have led the way to the discovery of viruses. Today, this particular shift has led to assessment procedures that help physicians to differentiate between bacterial and viral infections and to administer treatment more effectively. Such is the manner in which Gestalt switches can act to advance science.

Like biological science, abnormal psychology has also been characterized by a history marked by the rise and fall of differing shared beliefs. In this chapter we will examine these paradigms within their historical context in hopes of demonstrating to you the way in which each has guided the study of abnormal behavior.

By offering an explanation that differed from the then accepted belief that diseases spontaneously arise, Pasteur helped generate a paradigmatic shift in biological science. (*National Library of Medicine*)

Historical Overview

It is our belief that over the course of its history, four major paradigms have guided the science of abnormal psychology. While some authors have suggested that more than four have existed (Bootzin & Acocella, 1984; Davison & Neale, 1984), we are in agreement with the view of Marmor (1983) who, in his recent analysis of modern psychiatry, described three modern belief systems—the biological, psychological, and sociological paradigms. While we agree with Marmor's conceptualizations of the three modern paradigms, however, we believe that their names may be misleading. In light of this we have chosen to label them the *biological, psychosocial, and systems paradigms.* We bring our total to four by adding to these the now archaic, but historically important, belief in *supernatural* sources for abnormality (L. Bell, 1981; Zilboorg & Henry, 1941). Each of these four perspectives, we believe, qualifies as a paradigm because each has, for significant periods of time, guided research, theory, and practice in abnormal psychology. In the remainder of this chapter we will examine the emergence and rise of each of the four paradigms, but before we begin, we will characterize each briefly.

While the roots of all four paradigms can be traced back through many hundreds of years of history, none is more ancient than the *supernatural perspective.* Since early times, some societies have believed that people's actions were governed by "gods" or, in the case of deviant behavior, by "devils." Such beliefs significantly affected how disturbed people were treated over thousands of years with "treatment" efforts often involving torture, exorcism, or other means directed at "driving out supernatural spirits." The supernatural paradigm was most prevalent in ancient times and during the Middle Ages. It was not until the nineteenth century that this notion began to fall from favor.

Although the *biological paradigm* can trace its beginnings to Grecian times, it was not until the late nineteenth and the early twentieth centuries when research led to undeniable connections between biological functioning and some types of abnormal behavior that the belief in a physical basis for abnormality achieved major importance. Since its emergence, the biological paradigm has led to some of the most important advances in dealing with abnormal people.

Like the belief in a biological basis for disordered behavior, the *psychosocial paradigm* rose to ascendency during the late nineteenth and early twentieth centuries. The psychosocial paradigm gathers together people who believe that an understanding of abnormal behavior may be achieved through a focus on individuals and their intrapersonal and interpersonal functioning. Among those espousing this view are professionals who believe that things like learning, maturation, child rearing practices, and other such factors contribute most heavily to behavioral and mental disturbances.

Although the view that people's behavior is due primarily to the societal and familial structures they live in can actually be traced as far back as Hippocrates (circa 200 B.C.), the *systems paradigm* has only begun to rise to more formal prominence in recent years. This view is that people must be seen as embedded in systems of varying degrees of complexity ranging from families and other groups to social classes to societies and cultures (Nichols, 1984). Generally, the belief is that the success or failure of individual members of a system reflects the success or failure of the system. Normal as well as abnormal behavior is understood to arise from the reciprocal interaction of people with the systems of which they are a part. Thus, in order to understand or change the behavior of an individual, those espousing a systems view would focus their energies on understanding and altering the system in which the individual is embedded. While the systems view has been extant for centuries, it has only been in the twentieth century that it has been formally articulated (von Bertalanffy, 1981; Davidson, 1983; Nichols, 1984).

While it might be argued that other guiding perspectives for abnormal psychology may have developed over the centuries, these four seem to have had major impact on the manner in which disordered behavior has been studied, classified, explained, and modified. We will now turn to a more detailed examination of each and try to trace its emergence and historical impact.

The Supernatural Paradigm

The oldest explanation of disordered behavior and one which is rarely applied in modern abnormal psychology is the belief in spirit possession. Scientists who study primitive people by examining their paintings and artifacts have generally concluded that early humans believed spirits originating in nature were responsible for causing such irrational behavior as nightmares and hallucinations. Some anthropologists believe that, guided by their explanatory notions, certain prehistoric peoples may have attempted to "cure" these kinds of disordered behavior by boring a hole into the heads of those afflicted to allow the evil spirits to escape. Skulls with such holes, or *trephines,* have been found at archaeological sites in many parts of the world.

Spirit possession seems also to have been a major view of disordered behavior in the great ancient cultures of Egypt, Israel, Greece, and Rome, as well as among Europeans during the Middle Ages (Zilboorg & Henry, 1941). In some instances, the notion of spirit possession was expanded to include the existence of both good and bad spirits, with positive personal characteristics attributed to effects of the former and deviant behavior attributed to the latter. In a belief system based on spirit possession, the major assessors and treaters of disordered behavior were most often members of religious professions. Although there were great medical men, such as Hippocrates, Cicero, and Galen, who espoused somewhat different general views of disordered behavior, spirit possession remained the major explanation for disordered behavior throughout ancient times.

Although it had faded to some degree during the first millenium A.D., the popularity of the spirit-possession explanation rose to its peak in the Middle Ages in Europe. During these dark days, the belief in spirits flourished. Since people showing deviant behavior were usually assumed to be possessed by spirits and devils, responsibility for assessing and caring for these unfortunate individuals most often fell to the clergy. At first most clergymen, many guided by pronouncements from the papacy, perceived disordered people as innocent victims of the devil and dealt kindly with them. For example, the possessed person might first be prayed over or sprinkled with holy water. If these measures failed, however, more intense procedures were sometimes used. These sterner measures included *exorcism* for eradicating the spirits and ranged from having the person drink a mixture made of blood and sheep dung to physically beating the disordered individual. Though severe from the perspective of the 1980s, these distasteful treatment procedures were similar to ones used by the priests on themselves to deal with the devil. Given the prevailing view of abnormality, in fact, exorcism may have been the most appropriate and humane treatment the times could offer.

However, afflicted people did not receive such "favored" treatment for long. The clergy, who at first spent significant amounts of time attempting to assess who were innocent victims of the devil and those who were in league with Satan, apparently abandoned this classificatory effort in the fourteenth and fifteenth centuries. In turn, this had a significant impact on the assessment and treatment process of the times. In fact, most disordered people came to be thought of as being in league with the devil and many were tortured, maimed, or burned. The prevailing shared belief seemed to be that while Satan could take over one's body, one's soul always belonged to God. Hence, to torture or destroy a person's body would either drive out the devil or free the soul to return to heaven.

In 1487, a small group of powerful clergy organized an attempt to deal with disordered behavior that they thought was running out of control. Disturbed people were more formally seen as possessed by Satan and, as such, were deemed to be *witches.* Even such influential leaders as Martin Luther shared this view:

> The greatest punishment God can inflict on the wicked . . . is to deliver them over to Satan who with God's permission, kills them or makes them to undergo great calamities. Many devils are in woods, water, wildernesses, etc., ready to hurt and prejudice people. When these things happen, then the philosophers and physicians say it is natural, ascribing it to the planets.
>
> In cases of melancholy . . . I conclude it is merely the work of the devil. Men are possessed by the devil in two ways,

> corporally or spiritually. Those whom he possesses corporally as mad people, he has permission from God to vex and agitate, but he has no power over their souls. (Colloquia Mensalia)

Martin Luther was not the only religious leader to apply the supernatural paradigm to understanding mental illness. In 1484, Pope Innocent VIII issued a papal bull in which he called upon the clergy to join together to beat down the forces of Satan as they were manifested in withcraft. In response to the papal directive, two monks named Kramer and Spraenger wrote a book on how to detect and deal with witches entitled *Malleus Maleficarum*, or *The Witch's Hammer*. The *Malleus Maleficarum* was one of the most thorough attempts to classify abnormal behavior for that time. From the vantage point of the present, we suggest that this manual and the motivation for its publication came from a small group of people guided by the supernatural paradigm, who seem to have wanted a way of explaining what appeared to be anomalies from the perspective of the then poorly developed science of medicine.

Spirit or Satanic possession seems to have been held accountable for a wide range of bizarre activity during the Middle Ages. For example, many people believed in such things as *lycanthropy* (evil spirits changing a man into a wolf at the time of the full moon), *vampirism* (a person being changed into a vampire who lives on the blood of others), and *tarantism* (in which people supposedly bitten by a spider begin dancing out of control). Tarantism is graphically described in the following excerpt from Sigerist (1943):

> The disease occurred at the height of the summer heat. . . . People, asleep or awake, would suddenly jump up, feeling an acute pain like the sting of a bee. Some saw the spider, others did not, but they knew that it must be the tarantula. They ran out of the house into the street, to the market place, dancing in great excitement. Soon they were joined by others who like them had been bitten or by people who had been stung in previous years. . . .
>
> Thus groups of patients would gather, dancing wildly in the queerest attire. . . . Others would tear their clothes and show their nakedness, losing all sense of modesty. . . . Some called for swords and acted like fencers, others for whips and beat each other. . . . Some of them had still stranger fancies, liked to be tossed in the air, dug holes in the ground, and rolled themselves into the dirt like swine. They all drank wine plentifully and sang and talked like drunken people (pp. 103, 106–107).

The belief in demonic possession and evil spirits as explanations for disordered behavior remains with us today, although in a very minor way. Some religious groups still teach the doctrine of Satan as an entity in the world, and several cults of devil worship still exist. However, as a major shared belief for explaining disordered behavior, the concept of demonic possession and the supernatural paradigm from which it derived no longer seem viable.

The Biological Paradigm

Like the supernatural perspective, the biological paradigm also has its origins in antiquity. Some roots of the biological perspective can be found in the writings of Hippocrates around 400 B.C. Although most other Greeks of his time espoused other views, Hippocrates believed that actual brain pathology or body-fluid imbalance was primarily responsible for the appearance of disordered behavior. He offered one of the earliest behavioral classification systems, describing three major kinds of behavior disorders, *melancholia, mania and phrenitis,* and tying each one to some imbalance in specific body fluids. Melancholia, for example, was associated with an excess of phlegm and was probably similar to what we currently call depression, mania was believed to be caused by too much bile and seems like the modern manic states, and phrenitis was coupled with an excess of blood and may have been similar to what we now call schizophrenia. Based on his belief in a biological basis for behavior, Hippocrates also derived treatment for each of the disturbances he described. For example, for melancholia he prescribed quiet, a good diet, and abstinence from sexual interactions to make the person strong of body and brain (Zilboorg & Henry, 1941). He believed that these sorts of physical and psychological prescriptions would help rebalance the bodily fluids.

Hippocrates' views continued to be influential in Greece and Rome during the first few centuries after Christ when physicians were primarily responsible for treating disordered behavior. Unfortunately, their interpretation of the biological view did not always lead to what we might now consider to be sound treatment. For example, to correct the imbalance in black bile thought to cause melancholia, some patients were subjected to treatments in which large quantities of blood were drained from their bodies. Most people were weakened by this and some even died from it. Although the acceptance of the Hippocratic view of abnormal behavior sometimes led to such mistaken treatments, the basic shared belief that behavior was governed by the effects of certain body structures and substances foreshadowed the modern biological views of the causes of disordered behavior.

After the fourth century A.D., the biological view of abnormal behavior was weakened to some degree by its inability to explain anomalies such as lycanthropy, tarantism, and witchery. For several centuries, in fact, the supernatural paradigm was dominant. However, as the belief in spirit possession failed to lead to eradication of abnormal behavior and as the sciences of neurology and general medicine became more sophisticated in the nineteenth century, the belief in a biological paradigm rose once again.

Many Greek physicians believed that biological factors caused abnormal behaviors. (*National Library of Medicine*)

The emerging success of the biological approach may be exemplified by the study of the disorder called *general paresis.* General paresis is a symptom pattern now known to be caused by the progressive infiltration and subsequent destruction of brain tissue by the microscopic organisms called spirochetes associated with syphilis. Along with deterioration in physical abilities, affected people may hallucinate, forget recent happenings, and show wide swings in moods.

The finding of the cause and subsequent treatment for general paresis reads like a testimony to the use of the agreed-upon scientific methods described in Chapter Two. The following is a brief chronology of how the successful investigation proceeded (After Zilboorg & Henry, 1941). We have annotated the chronology so as to emphasize the utilization of a scientific approach.

1. In 1798, Haslam described the symptom complex of general paresis consisting of delusions of grandeur, dementia, and progressive paralysis. He

also described patients as having defective speech and memory as well as showing a progressive loss of control over voluntary muscle movements. (*Classification*)

2. In 1805, Esquirol, a French physician, pointed out that those patients who had this symptom complex never recovered from the disorder. They deteriorated and died. (*Observation*) With this information, investigators now had described a symptom complex with a typical progress and predictable outcome. (*Classification*)
3. Further investigation using hospital records and observations revealed that the disorder appeared three times as often in men as in women, with the time of onset somewhere between 30 and 50 years of age. (*Observation*) However, investigators were unsure as to how one got the disease. Early guesses implicated tobacco or alcohol. (*Incorrect application of the biological paradigm*) In fact, since the disease seemed to be prevalent among the elite of the community, such as government officials, doctors, writers, and the like, it led some investigators to conclude that high intelligence must be a primary cause. (*Erroneous conclusion based on incorrect use of psychosocial paradigm instead of biological paradigm*)
4. Postmortem examination of the brains and nervous systems of general paretics revealed damaged tissue. Improved microscopes helped investigators to see that the damaged tissue was accompanied by a growth of foreign-appearing connective tissue. Thus, by 1860, researchers were sure of the involvement of the brain in this psychological disorder. (*More sophisticated application of the biological paradigm using newly agreed-upon methods*)
5. In 1894, Fournier, studying the case histories of paretic patients, concluded that a syphilitic infection was involved in a significant number of paretic patients (65 percent) as compared with other mental disorders (10 percent). This led him to conclude that general paresis originated from a syphilitic infection. (*Experimental procedure comparing two matched or randomly sampled groups*)

A drawing of a man suffering from advancing stages of general paresis shows the characteristic posture and gait. (*National Library of Medicine*)

6. In 1897, Krafft-Ebing completed an experiment that confirmed the relationship between general paresis and syphilis. In the examination of case histories of paretics, he noted that there were some instances in which histories of syphilis were not obtained. (*Assessment problems*) It was Krafft-Ebing's belief that there was necessarily a syphilitic infection first that led to

general paresis. (*Hypothesis*) He reasoned that the lack of a one-to-one relationship in the case studies resulted because some patients did not want to admit to the indiscretions that led them to contract syphilis. (*Hypothesis*) To test this assumption, Krafft-Ebing took nine paretic patients who had denied any previous syphilitic symptoms and inoculated them (*Independent variable*) with fluid drawn from a syphilitic patient. None of them developed signs of syphilis. (*Dependent variable; improved method of assessment*) While it is doubtful that any present-day committee on human rights for experimental subjects would allow such a procedure, this was 1897, and it did prove beyond a doubt that those nine individuals had previously contracted syphilis. Krafft-Ebing's assumption that there had to be a syphilitic infection prior to general paresis was supported. (*Hypothesis supported*)

7. Further studies showed that the blood and cerebrospinal fluid of both syphilitic and paretic people shared common characteristics. This linked the two disorders even more closely. (*Experimental comparison of groups*)
8. In 1905, the syphilitic infectious agent, *Treponema pallidum*, was identified. (*Increasingly sophisticated methods within the biological paradigm*)
9. In 1913, Noguchi and Moore found this agent in the brain tissue of general paretics. The cause of general paresis was now directly identified; syphilis, if not treated in its early stages, caused this dread disorder. (*Continuing corroboration of findings; confirmation of a biological basis for general paresis; clear basis for prevention of the disorder*)

In the study of general paresis, the shared belief that a behavioral disorder had a physical cause had borne fruit; the etiology of a dreaded disorder was exposed and its agents of destruction identified. Buoyed by the successful application of the biological view of disordered behavior, physicians and others grew more optimistic about deriving effective treatments for other forms of abnormal behavior. As Bell (1981) pointed out:

> Medicine made tangible progress toward conquering diphtheria, cholera, tetanus, hookworm, and yellow fever; anesthesia and antiseptics made surgery more successful. These tangible achievements not only enhanced the prestige of medicine but also helped to confirm science as the new panacea for solving human problems. A widespread assumption held that the facts and methods of science could unravel any complex social issue. (p. 75).

Hopes for continued success within the field of abnormal psychology were raised when Emil Kraepelin supplied a classification of other disorders that could help guide the efforts of investigators. Kraepelin (1886), a German physician who influenced the thinking of psychiatrists from 1900 to the mid-1920s, used hospital records to classify behavior disorders in the same manner as physical disorders. By organizing these data in such a manner, Kraepelin reasoned, he could identify typical symptom complexes and describe typical patterns of onset, course, and outcome. The descriptions would prepare the way for finding the causal agents and eventually the "treatment" for disorders.

Kraepelin concluded from his work that there were two major groups of symptom complexes: "manic-depressive psychosis, characterized by swings in mood states, but with no deterioration in speech or memory," and "dementia praecox" (now known as schizophrenia), characterized by an early onset and progressive deterioration in thought processes. Since these two groups of symptoms afflicted two-thirds of mental hospital patients, it was apparent that their elimination would do much to solve the problem of disordered behavior. A believer in the biological paradigm,

Kraepelin was the first to classify manic-depression and "dementia praecox" (schizophrenia). (*National Library of Medicine*)

Kraepelin suggested that the cause of manic-depression was an irregularity in metabolism, while the basis of schizophrenia was a chemical imbalance resulting from a malfunctioning of the sex glands. Based on his biological perspective, Kraepelin and other investigators sharing his beliefs, attempted to apply the methodologies that had uncovered the origin of general paresis to finding the cause and cure of these other two major "diseases." Kraepelin's attempt to classify disordered behavior was laudable but the search for somatic causes has yet to be completed successfully.

Besides spurring new classifications of abnormal behavior, the success of the biological approach had other profound effects, not the least of which was the creation of a climate favorable for experimenting with a variety of physical treatments. Suffice it to say that many people were convulsed, shocked, and operated on, often with procedures lacking both scientific and medical justification, because of an almost faithlike belief that disordered behavior had a physical cause and could be treated by physical methods. As Bell (1981) concluded regarding physicians at the turn of the century:

> Although committed to objectivity, to scientific truth, to viewing medical science as the means for understanding and treating mental illness, they produced little evidence to support the new faith. . . . The fact that no concrete connection between brain lesions and insanity was found left physicians without a theory to justify any kind of therapy. Many resolved the dilemma with a declaration of faith, a belief that future discoveries would provide the physical evidence. (p. 41)

Because of the prevailing belief in the biological basis for disordered behavior, mental patients in Clifford Beers' time were often dealt with as if they *were* suffering from physical disease even though there were few proven, effective treatments available. Mental patients and the mental hospitals in which they were housed waited for the "cures" for the "diseases" to appear.

The Psychosocial Paradigm

Like the biological paradigm and its success with general paresis, the psychosocial paradigm also gained eminence through the study of a specific disorder, in this case *hysteria*. (Although the symptom pattern historically called hysteria is now termed a conversion disorder or hysterical neurosis, conversion type, we will use the term "hysteria" here in its historical context.) Known to the ancient Greeks and Romans, hysteria may be manifested by physical symptoms such as blindness, paralysis of body parts, and even convulsive attacks and memory dysfunctions—all without apparent physical cause.

In some cases, the paralyses make no anatomical sense, that is, they are not possible within the known structure and functioning of the nervous system. In other cases, the paralyses may shift unpredictably from one part of the body to another. Although these symptoms were once understood as signs of spirit possession from the perspective of the supernatural paradigm, investigators during the latter part of the nineteenth century no longer assumed that such events were due to a person's being in league with the devil. Hysterical symptoms were thus seen as an anomaly for the supernatural perspective and, as such, they were associated with an increase in "tension" in the science of abnormal psychology. This tension, in large measure, was responsible for the emergence of the psychosocial perspective. As with general paresis and the emergence of the biological view, there seemed to be an orderly progression of events leading to the "discovery" of a psychosocial basis for hysteria. Each step can be associated with the beliefs of particular scientists.

Mesmer and Hysteria

Although believing himself to be guided by the biological paradigm, the Austrian physician Anton Mesmer was actually among the first scientists to develop a psychosocial theory and subsequent "cure" for hysterical disorders. In the course of his university studies, he hit upon the theory of "universal magnetism" to explain human behavior. To Mesmer, the universe was made up of magnetic fluid; when it became unbalanced within people, they experienced behavioral difficulties. At first Mesmer used a specially prepared metal rod to touch others in his attempts to correct imbalances in their fluid. However, Mesmer later came to believe that he, himself, was a source of *animal magnetism* and used his own hands or objects he touched to "cure" others.

Mesmer believed that he had the ability to correct imbalances in magnetic fluids that were the source of abnormal behavior. (*National Library of Medicine*)

His techniques for correcting imbalances in fluid via animal magnetism became known as *Mesmerism,* which has been likened to *hypnotism,* a word introduced by Braid (1795–1860) to describe the trance induction process. Mesmer's spectacular and theatrical manner of practice earned him the animosity of many members of the professional community wherever he practiced, and it eventually led to his ruin.

It was in Paris that Mesmer seemed to have his greatest success and, as a result, his greatest difficulty. The difficulty involved resolution of the question, "What exactly is hypnosis?" A Parisian commission investigated his activites and concluded that while Mesmer assumed the

BOX 3-1 THE METHODS OF ANTON MESMER

The central feature of Mesmer's treatment room was the *baquet.* Considered to be the focal point for the magnetic fluid (a physical force Mesmer claimed to be able to manipulate), this contraption consisted of a large oaken tub filled with iron filings, water, and powdered glass. Its lid was pierced with holes through which jointed iron rods protruded. The baquet was said by Mesmer to have been magnetized. It was able to transmit this magnetic force through the rods to the patients. Patients sat around the baquet, linked hands, touched the rods and waited for Mesmer, the great magnetizer, to appear, wearing a fantastic lilac-colored silk robe and carrying a wand. He passed among the patients, touching some, making passes at others with his wand, and occasionally fixing patients with a stare and ordering them to sleep. Gradually the individual patients became agitated and restless until a "crisis" occurred. One patient would scream, break into a sweat, and convulse. Others soon followed suit, until hysterical convulsions had seized most of those present. After these violent episodes, tension subsided, patients felt calm and relaxed, and many experienced remission of their symptoms.

Source: From *Catharsis in Psychotherapy,* by M. Nichols and M. Zax. Copyright 1977 by Gardner Press, Inc. Reprinted by permission.

changes he wrought to be biologically based, the panel believed that the changes were due instead to "excitement of the imagination." In essence, this panel of esteemed scientists (which included Ben Franklin) proposed a psychosocial view to explain what they considered to be the biologically unexplainable effects of Mesmer's methods. Although damning to Mesmer, the commission's conclusion seemed to be helping to define a budding psychosocial perspective on disordered behavior. Perhaps the only involved party to realize this was a pupil of Mesmer's who asked: "If Mesmer had no other secret than that he was able to make the imagination exert an effective influence upon health, would he not still be a wonder worker?" (Janet, 1925, p. 161)

Charcot and Hysteria

From our present vantage point, we can conclude that Mesmer was probably most successful in dealing with what we presently call hysterical disorders. Mesmer himself commented that his "animal magnetism" appeared to work best on certain kinds of people who are descriptively similar to those classified today as hysteric. After the furor over Mesmer died down, the next significant person to become involved in the complexities of hysteria was the eminent neurologist, Jean Charcot. Once again, it was hypnosis that brought the disorder to the attention of the scientific community and set up a confrontation between the psychosocial and biological paradigms. Unknown to Charcot, some of his students, by means of hypnotism, prepared a physically healthy woman to show all the behavioral signs of hysteria. They then asked Charcot to diagnose her without telling him what they had done. Being a neurologist, Charcot was guided by a belief in a biological basis for behavior. When he had concluded after his examination that his patient was suffering from a physically caused case of hysteria, they showed Charcot how these "hysterical" symptoms could be removed by waking her from her hypnotic state. Charcot was most interested in what his students had been able to do. The idea that hysterical symptoms could be brought into existence and then

Although he was a neurologist, Charcot adopted the psychosocial paradigm in his explanation of hysteria. (*National Library of Medicine*)

made to disappear via hypnosis was an unexplainable anomaly from the perspective of the biological paradigm he then favored. This began a process of investigation of hysteria that eventually led him to join the *Gestalt switch* to the psychosocial perspective.

Janet and Hysteria

After Charcot, Pierre Janet, his student, continued studying hysteria. Consistent with the psychosocial view, however, Janet began with the assumption that there were nonphysical causes for this disorder. Specifically, Janet was most interested in the memory difficulties shown by some hysterical patients. Cases of amnesia (loss of memory) and sleepwalking showed that many hysterics had a propensity to adopt styles of thinking that departed from normal processes. His observations of other patients allowed Janet to describe not only the symptom complex known as hysteria, but also one he called *psychasthenia*, characterized by ruminations, doubts, and obsessions. By the beginning of the 1900s, Janet had helped create a rudimentary classification of disordered behavior, and he inspired others to gather data in support of the view that many abnormal disorders were caused by intrapersonal and interpersonal factors.

Breuer and Hysteria

At the same time that Charcot and Janet were studying the psychosocial causes of hysteria, Joseph Breuer was involved in what would turn out to be a new treatment for this disorder. Breuer called on a young colleague from Vienna, Sigmund

Freud, to help in the treatment of a woman called, for purposes of confidentiality, Anna O. She presented a number of hysterical symptoms varying from leg paralysis to dreamy states of consciousness during which she would mumble to herself as she walked around. Breuer hypnotized her and repeated back to her what she had said in her dreamy states. This feedback apparently acted as a stimulus to allow Anna O. to express fantasies and, in special instances, to reexperience intense emotions felt during certain past interactions. As a result of these procedures, she would wake up from her hypnotic state refreshed and symptom-free. The release of feeling, or *abreaction*, appeared to Breuer and Freud to be a key factor in successfully treating hysterical disorders. These experiences laid the groundwork for a psychosocially derived theory for the etiology of and treatment of an entire complex of symptoms. It took Freud years to expand the implications of such an approach. While we detail the development of Freudian theory in the following chapter, suffice it to say that Freud's explanations, though controversial, rose in popularity during the early decades of the twentieth century.

The Systems Paradigm

The modern biological and psychosocial paradigms arose through their success with the circumscribed disorders of general paresis and hysteria. The systems perspective, on the other hand, achieved its early status through its application to the understanding of more broadly defined and larger groups of severely disturbed and/or socially alienated individuals. Specifically, rather than seeing psychopathology as the result of some biological or psychosocial factors, those sharing the global systems perspective hold that the major sources of abnormal behaviors lie in the social structures of which people are members. These structures may be as small as *dyads* (as in the case of a married couple), but can range upwards in size from families, clubs, neighborhoods, school groups, religious and national communities or cultures to entire societies. Regardless of the specific level of analysis, however, it is the general view of those scientists espousing the systems paradigm that it is in the social structures of which people are part that may be found the causes and cures for their difficulties (Nichols, 1984).

Like the biological view of abnormal behavior, it is possible to trace the systems perspective as far back as Hippocrates' time. As we mentioned earlier, one of the components of Hippocrates' treatment for melancholia often was some quiet time in the country; apparently, even in 400 B.C. it was possible to see that the stresses of living in certain situations could cause disturbances and that spending some time in a more pleasant atmosphere could make people feel better. However, although the idea that systems in which people are immersed contribute to their problems had existed for many centuries it was not until the rise of the asylums for severely disturbed people that the systems perspective began to emerge as a modern paradigm. Although not initially developed as such, the asylums were self-contained social systems that were created not only to provide a corrective "healthy" system in which disturbed people could live, but also to meet society's need to remove disturbed people from its midst. At times, specific "treatments" offered in the asylums were influenced by views other than the systems perspective. For example, during the Middle Ages, many asylums were directed by clergy espousing a supernatural view of cause and cure. At other times and places, more biologically based beliefs were applied. Although these other views were involved to some degree, however, the concept of asylums, per se, grew from a belief in a systems paradigm in its early form.

We will turn now to an examination of the emergence of the systems view of abnormal behavior. We will trace the progressive fashion (not unlike that observed in the emergence of the biological and psychosocial views) by which the development of better and more effective asylums became intertwined with the growth of the shared belief in the systems basis for abnormal behavior.

Beginnings of the Systems Paradigm: The Middle Ages

From the perspective of the systems paradigm, the societal chaos inherent in the Middle Ages was partially responsible for the development of many mental disorders, and the supernatural paradigm was responsible for many of the "questionable" things that sometimes were done to disordered people to "help" them. However, in the midst of all this, there were some voices of caution and reason. For example, some physicians (such as Joseph Weyer) and religious figures (such as Vincent de Paul) did influence the thinking of society and, as a result, asylums were constructed, first in Spain (1409) and later in England and France, in hopes of giving better care to those less fortunate. Unhappily better care did not always follow. Instead, rather than being sanctuaries for the mentally disturbed, many of these asylums served as dumping grounds for political and social misfits. St. Mary of Bethlehem in England and the Tower of

The systems paradigm had some of its earliest applications in the asylums. (*National Library of Medicine*)

Vienna in Austria were notorious for the cruelties often inflicted on patients. The situation was no better elsewhere.

In the United States, the major institutional treatment facility available for disordered persons in the late 1700s consisted of three rooms in the basement of Pennsylvania Hospital in Philadelphia. Otherwise, these people were mainly to be found on the street or in almshouses. It was not until 1773 that the first institution in America devoted to the treatment of the mentally ill was opened.

Refinement of the Systems Approach: Humane Treatment

Although asylums were opened in many parts of the world, it was apparent that simply removing people from one unhealthy system and placing them in another served little therapeutic purpose. There needed to be something curative about the new system if the asylums were to help people overcome their problems. That curative "something" came about at La Bicetre in Paris when, in 1790, Philippe Pinel used the systems perspective to develop his humane treatment methods. As superintendent of the asylum, Pinel risked his job by suggesting that all means of unreasonable restraint be abolished and replaced by a treatment program including fresh air and activities. So long as patients agreed to hurt no one, Pinel promised them walks in the garden, beds with clean sheets, and good food. Thought by many to be mad himself, Pinel won a trial experiment for his "heretical" ideas and was soon vindicated by the spectacular improvement of many of the supposedly incurably insane. He published his ideas in a famous article called "A Treatise on Insanity." Pinel wrote that "The insane far from being delinquents to be punished, are sick people whose distressing state deserves all the care and consideration due to suffering humanity" (Zilboorg & Henry, 1941). Pinel also in-

Pinel's reforms represented one of the first major successes for the systems paradigm. (*National Library of Medicine*)

troduced clear and consistent record keeping on the progress of patients and insisted that the effectiveness of any treatment for a disorder be evaluated by comparison to gains made simply by waiting for the disorder to run its course. He was truly a significant force in obtaining reforms in institutional treatment for those suffering from mental disorders. As such, he must be seen as a pioneer in the application of the systems paradigm.

In the United States, Benjamin Rush, superintendant of a large hospital in New England, also struck off the chains of the insane at a time when this was not a very popular act. However, although adopting the systems perspective to some degree, Rush was also a firm believer in the biological paradigm. This mixed allegiance led him to allow a variety of ill-conceived treatments to take place within the "humane" settings of his asylum. For example, a middle-aged patient became distraught after a number of political setbacks.

He became violent and tore up 40 blankets. Rush prescribed bloodletting as a treatment, and the patient was given 47 bleedings that led to the loss of 400 to 500 ounces of blood. With other patients Rush used dousing with cold water, keeping the patient awake in an erect position for 24 hours, applying ice to the shaven head, and threatening the life of a patient by drowning if he or she didn't change (Bell, 1981).

Though initially trained within the biological approach, both Pinel and Rush eventually adopted a systems view and had significant impact on how society responded to those with severe abnormal behavior. However, both of these pioneers believed to some degree that the causes of mental disturbances were strongly biological. William Tuke, on the other hand, was one of the first physician–asylum administrators to develop a treatment consistent with the systems paradigm's basic assumption that disordered behavior is related to the reciprocal interaction of people with the systems of which they are part. He developed a method of treating disordered behavior that became the model for the *moral treatment* approach in the United States. Implicit in the moral treatment approach was an emphasis on "moral management" or the use of a consistent reward-punishment system to help the patients. If patients behaved well, they received rewards like visits from friends, healthful recreation, and approval from the staff. If the patients misbehaved, they would not be given rewards, would be isolated, and in extreme cases would be restrained.

In the moral treatment approach, the medical treatment methods derived from the biological paradigm were rarely used. Thus in the place of bleeding, purging, and food withholding, the moral treaters used persuasion, work, and rewards to help the patients in their care. Consistent with the systems view, patients were treated within the social milieu of the moral treatment hospital. They were given respect and instilled with the expectation that they would get better. The programs contained small numbers of patients, mostly from the middle class, who were treated by a relatively large number of highly trained and dedicated staff. Leaders of the moral treatment approach reported that nearly 70 percent of their patients were discharged as improved and maintained their progress years after release (Bell, 1981).

In spite of their success, during the nineteenth century, the actual number of moral treatment facilities diminished while the more standard, medically run asylums experienced a phenomenal growth. One reason for this growth was the tenacious belief that eventually within the setting of the mental hospital, the biological approach would lead to successful ways of treating disordered behavior. A second reason, however, was the effort of Dorothea Dix to make society live up to what she believed were its responsibilities for treating severely disturbed people.

Increased Impact of the Systems Approach: The Work of Dorothea Dix

Raised by her grandparents in a Puritan atmosphere, Dorothea Dix taught school until failing health forced her to resign. Her interest in helping the insane was intensified when she was a Sunday school teacher for female convicts at a local jail. Vowing to get every insane person who needed care into a hospital, Dix carried her crusade to nearly every state east of the Mississippi. "She recorded the haunting wails, the rattle of chains on frost-covered floors, and the stench arising from human excrement, unwashed bodies, filthy clothes and rancid food" (Bell, 1981, p. 24).

Dix believed insanity was curable. She corresponded with, and in turn was praised by, the superintendents of some of the

Saint or sinner? Dorothea Dix was very helpful in getting the homeless and untreated into state hospitals. However, her efforts sometimes led to overcrowding and custodial treatment. (*National Library of Medicine*)

better asylums. However, while her motives were most humane, in some ways she was too successful. The number of people in asylums grew from 2561 in 1840 to 29,558 in 1870 to 74,028 in 1890 (Deutsch, 1937; Bell, 1981). The dream of effectively treating insane people in the healthy atmosphere of the mental hospital was fast turning into a nightmare. Asylums were not prepared to deal with these large numbers of new patients and the emphasis shifted from milieu, moral, and biological treatment toward custodial care. For example, the head of the California state asylum complained that 227 beds had to be prepared in the hallways. Changes in state laws that required "dangerously insane" people to be hospitalized helped increase the numbers even more. By Beers' time at the turn of the twentieth century the following statement about asylums could be made.

> Contributing also to the asylum's odious image was its expanding welfare function. Though ostensibly a retreat for the mentally ill, it assumed responsibility for many types of persons who lacked the ability to sustain themselves or who needed public aid. The mentally deficient, the alcoholic, the aged, and the poverty-stricken were part of its clientele. By providing custody for these dependents, the asylum became a charity. In the public eye, the state mental institution quarantined the socially dependent and offensive as well as the potentially violent and dangerous. (Bell, 1981, p. 42)

While tied to some degree with early forms of the psychosocial and biological perspectives, the efforts of Dorothea Dix actually may be seen as being most consistent with the systems paradigm. In fact, her belief that the mentally ill could be better cared for by changing social structures, living environments, laws, and broad-based social attitudes represents a clear foreshadowing of the modern systems-paradigm-based approaches of community psychology, family therapy, and group therapy.

Concluding Comments

The history of abnormal psychology has much to tell the present-day student. For one thing, present-day approaches quite clearly have their roots in the past. For another, paradigms or shared beliefs guiding scientists have been evident for thousands of years. Further, history also shows that types of treatment, in great measure, depended on the paradigm adopted at any point in time. For example, when investigators assumed that disordered behavior was caused physically, they were more prone to look for, study, and attempt to develop a set of biologically based interventions.

At the beginning of the twentieth century the supernatural paradigm had faded and the stage had been set for the modern interplay among the biological, psychosocial, and systems perspectives. In Chapters 4 to 6 the basic theories, research, and treatment methods spawned by each of these perspectives will be described. The sheer variety of ideas generated by the paradigms is a testimony to their usefulness. However, as we shall also see, each perspective is limited to some degree in its ability to lead us to a full understanding of the wide variety of forms which abnormality may take.

Summary Chart

In Chapter 3 we continued our examination of the foundations for abnormal psychology with historical overviews of the development of its major paradigms. We noted that during its history abnormal psychology has been guided at different times by four major sets of shared beliefs.

Supernatural Paradigm
Oldest set of beliefs
Spirit possession
Exorcism
Malleus Maleficarum
Middle Ages
Witch hunts

Biological Paradigm
Focus on physical factors
Hippocrates
Greece and Rome
Aided by research on general paresis
Biological bases for schizophrenia and other disorders
Source for modern drug treatments

Psychosocial Paradigm
Focus on individual and interpersonal function
Aided by study of hysteria
Mesmer, Charcot, Breuer, Freud
Source for psychoanalysis and behavior modification

Systems Paradigm
Most recent to develop
Moral treatment
Pinel, Rush, Dix
Source for hospitalization, group and family therapies, and community psychology

Noting that the supernatural paradigm has essentially been abandoned, we closed Chapter 3 with the stage having been set for in-depth review of the three major modern paradigms guiding abnormal psychology—the biological, psychosocial, and systems perspectives.

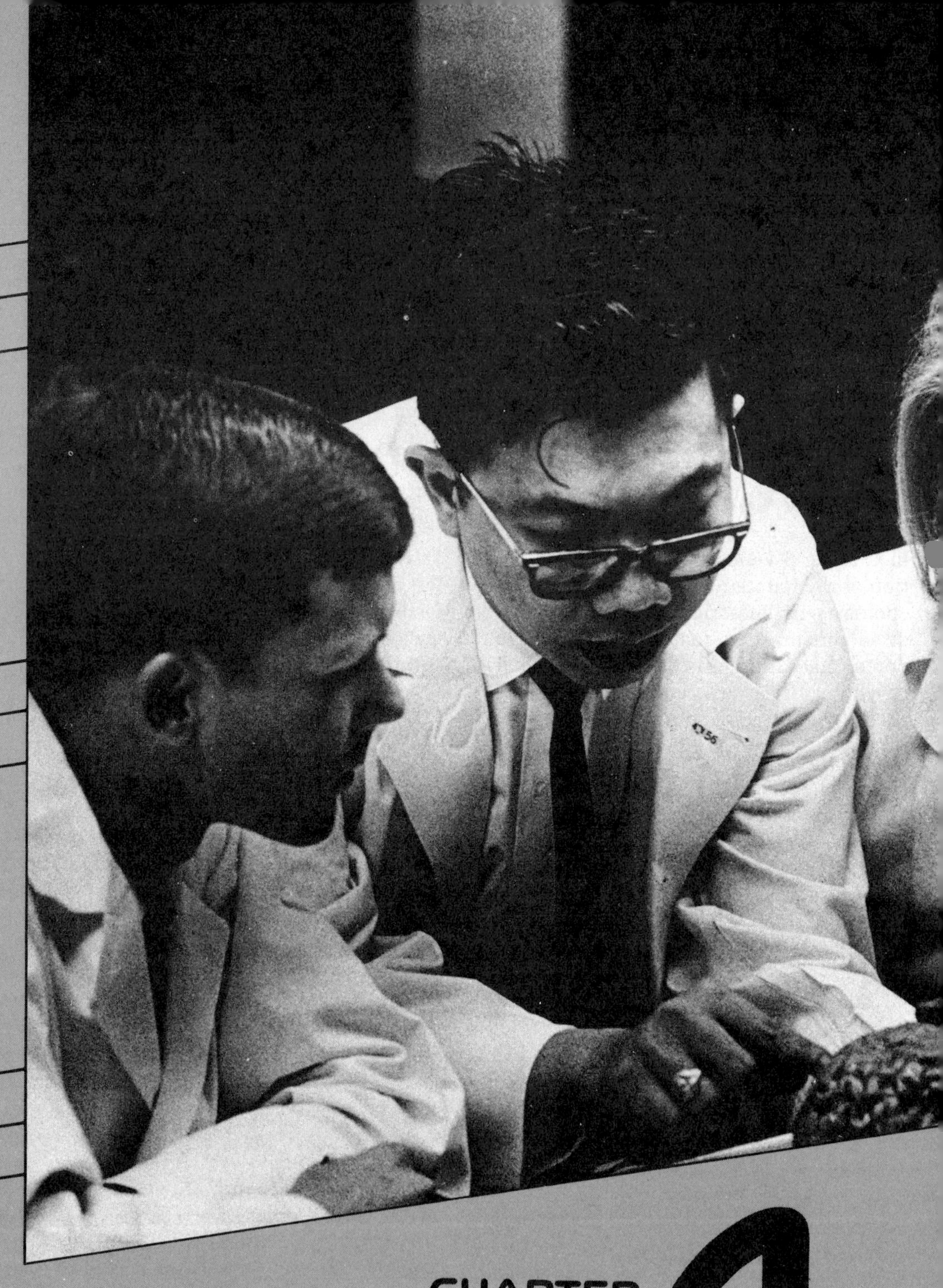

CHAPTER 4

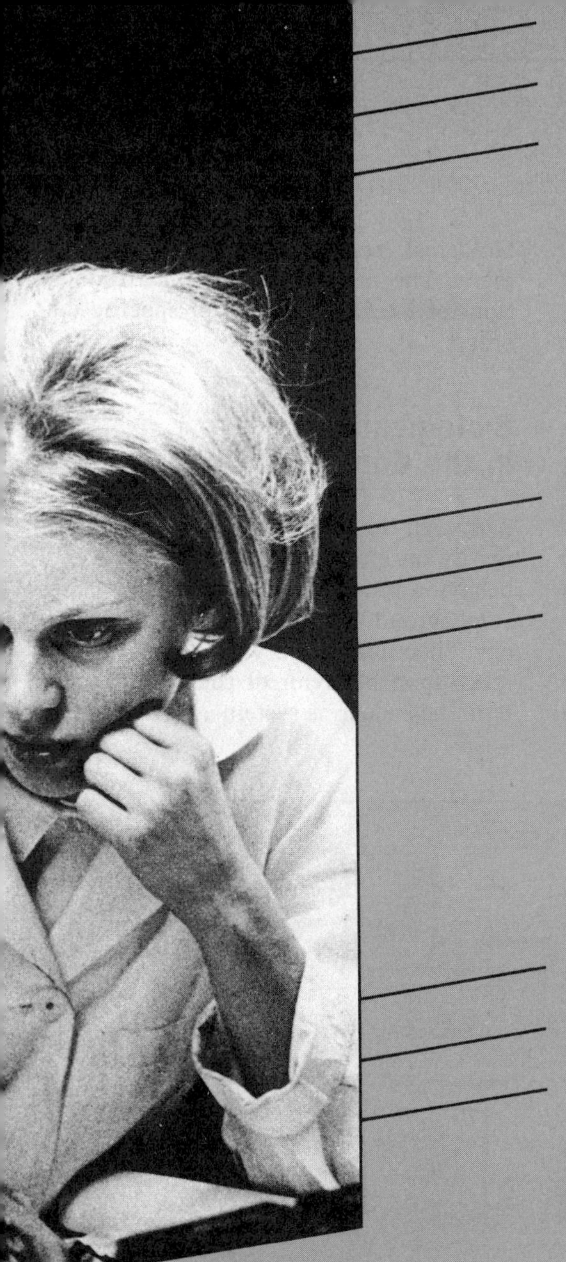

The Biological Paradigm

From the biological perspective mental disorders are seen as a result of some potentially identifiable physical dysfunction, hereditary defect, invading organism, foreign substance, or disease of the nervous system. The shared belief in a biological basis for behavior leads researchers to focus on genes, hormones, and neurotransmitters in their study of the etiology of psychopathology. This view also guides mental health professionals toward the use of biological treatments such as psychochemotherapy (drug treatment), electroconvulsive shock, and psychosurgery. In this chapter we will examine some of the developments in biological research, theory, and treatment. The material will form a foundation for later discussions of specific disorders.

Biological Factors in the Control of Behavior

Although the focus of this chapter is primarily on biological factors in *abnormal* behavior, much of our exposition requires some grounding in basic neuropsychology. Specifically, we will discuss the effects upon behavior of the nervous system, the endocrine system, and a relatively

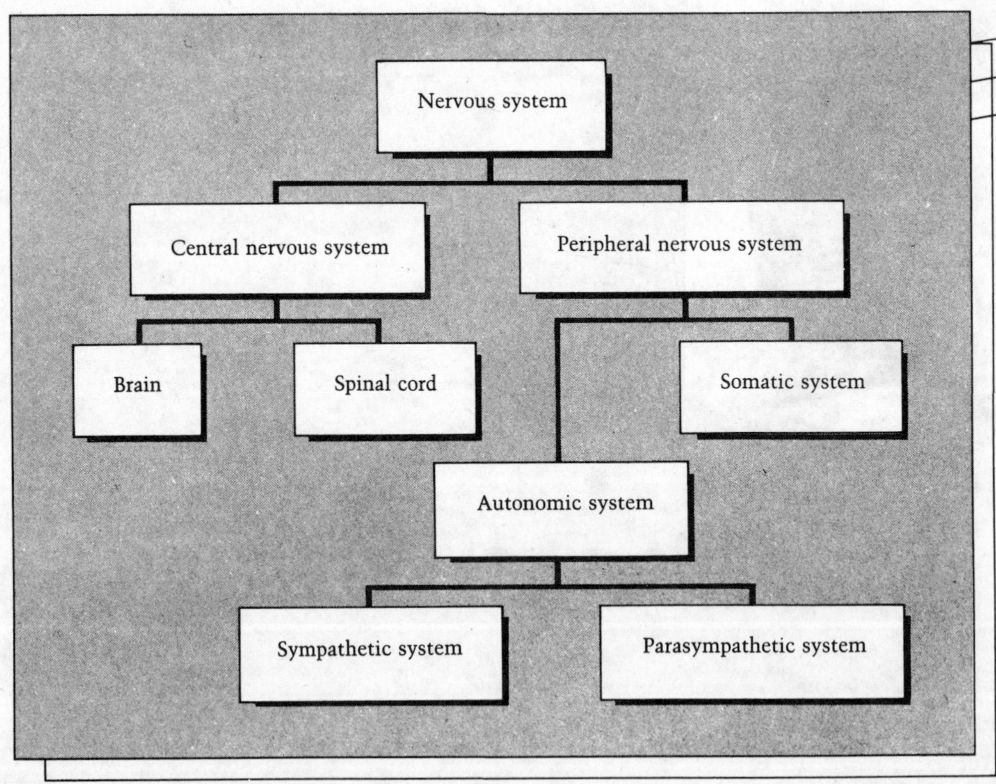

Figure 4-1 The organization of the nervous system.

recent discovery, the neuropeptide system. Given knowledge of these neuropsychological systems, it will be possible to present in a clearer way the manner in which the biological paradigm has been applied to the study of psychopathology.

The Nervous System and Behavior

The nervous system is involved in controlling and directing human behavior (see Figure 4-1) and is composed of a network of communication lines within the body that may be divided into two major parts. The first part, *the central nervous system* (CNS), is composed of the brain and spinal cord (see Figure 4-2). The second component, the *peripheral nervous system* (PNS), includes receptor nerves carrying information from the body to the CNS, effector nerves carrying messages from the CNS to the muscles, and a group of specialized nerves called the *autonomic nervous system* (ANS). The autonomic nervous system, composed of the *sympathetic* and *parasympathetic* systems, is intimately involved in emotional behavior.

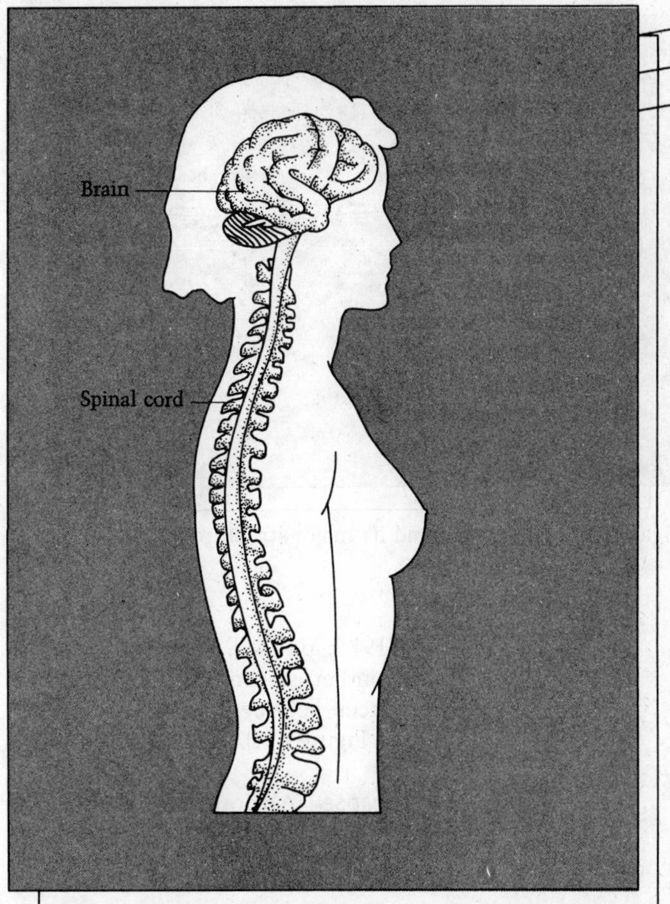

Figure 4-2 The brain and the spinal cord.

Basic Characteristics

The nervous system is responsible for a wide variety of activities. However, all these activities are carried out by the same type of specialized cells, called *neurons*, whose messages are transmitted from one cell to another by similar electrochemical means at sites called *synapses*.

Neurons Neurons are building blocks of the nervous system. As shown in Figure 4-3, a neuron is composed of a *soma*, or cell body; an *axon*, an often quite long fiber; and several shorter fibers called *dendrites* which resemble tree branches. The axon is involved primarily in carrying messages away from the cell, and the dendrites are generally "receivers." When the dendrites of a nerve cell have been sufficiently stimulated by the axons of other cells to which they are adjacent, an electrical change takes place in the soma and at the beginning of the cell's axon. This electrical change results in the production of an *action potential*, or electrical impulse, traveling down the axon until it reaches the point where the cell's excitation must be transmitted to the next cell. While it might "make sense" for there to be a simple physical connection between a given cell and adjacent cells so that the action potential could be carried in a way similar to the way wires carry electricity, this is not the case in the nervous system. Rather, "every neuron is an independent unit, having no apparent direct connection with any other neuron"

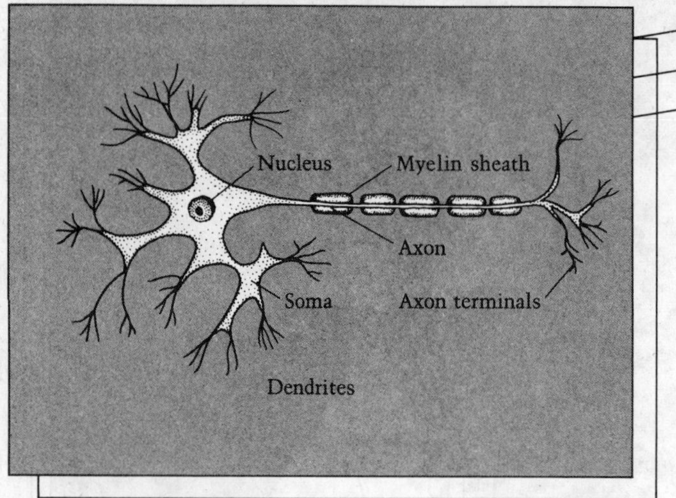

Figure 4-3 The neuron and its major structures.

(Brown, 1976, p. 246). The fact is communication between neurons must occur across spaces between them called *synapses* (see Figure 4-4).

The Synapse Although we know that there is an actual space at the point where one neuron meets another, experts once believed that transmission across this space was electrical. Even when the synaptic space between neurons was discovered, those assuming electrical transmission proposed that electrical impulses "jumped the gap" from cell to cell like a spark.

The presently accepted alternative to the electrical theory, the *neurohumoral transmission theory* (Eckstein, 1970), proposes that synaptic transmission is not primarily electrical. As seen in Figure 4-4, within the end of each axon on the transmitting neuron are small sacs (*synaptic vesicles*) of chemicals called *neurotransmitter substances.* Among these substances are biochemicals such as *serotonin, acetylcholine, norepinephrine, and dopamine.** When the vesicles containing these neurotransmitter substances are appropriately stimulated electrically by an action potential, they break open and release the neurotransmitters into the space between the neurons. These neurotransmitters then stimulate specialized receptors on the dendrites of the "receiving" cell, and an electrical impulse builds in that cell until it is sufficiently strong to produce a new action potential for within-cell transmission. Following transmission, the released neurotransmitters generally are inactivated, either by being broken down and dissipated or by being taken back up into the synaptic vesicles for reuse. As Brown (1976) states, it is known that this chemical system of neurotransmission "has profound significance for physiological psychology because it is apparently the primary

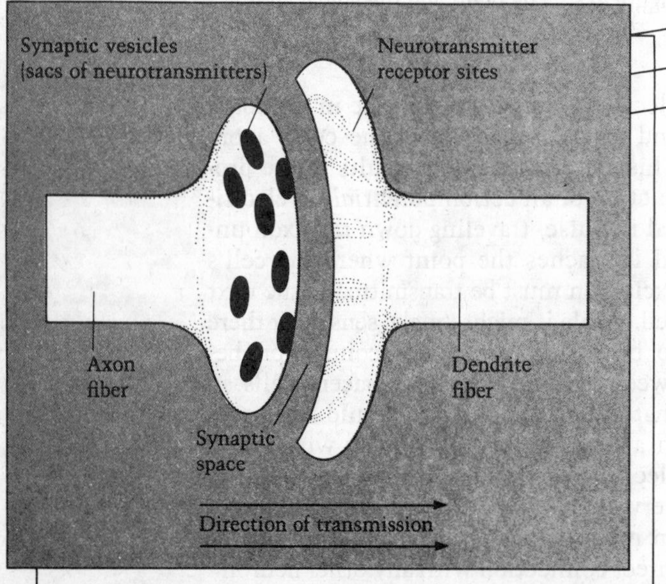

Figure 4-4 A magnified view of the structure of a synapse.

*More will be said of the variety of brain chemicals later, but in general we can say here that these substances and their variations and/or availability seem to have much to do with the occurrence of several forms of psychopathology. For example, difficulties in neurotransmission as reflected by abnormal variations in transmitters such as *norepinephrine, dopamine, acetylcholine, gamma amino butyric acid, and serotonin* have been implicated in schizophrenia and severe depression or mania (Iversen, 1980).

mechanism by which neural activity is regulated. The extent to which behavior is related to neural activity involves, in large measure, chemical actions at the synapses. In that sense the synapse has been viewed as the locus of the mind." (p. 28)

Recent developments in biochemistry and behavior have forced some reconsideration of Brown's powerful statement, for in addition to the neurotransmitter system, hormones (Haskett & Rose, 1981) and a group of biochemicals (peptides) called *endorphins* (See Bourne & Ekstrand, 1982; Craig & Stitzel, 1982) also seem to have significant effects on behavior.

The Central Nervous System (CNS) Effective neurotransmission is essential to the efficient operation of the central nervous system, the largest collection of neurons and synapses in the body. The system is composed of the brain and spinal cord and is the master controller of physical and mental functions. Composed of nearly 13 billion neurons and literally trillions of synaptic interconnections (Julien, 1981), the brain may be divided into several structures or divisions (see Figure 4-5). The majority of the human brain is composed of the *cortex*, its upper, very wrinkled looking covering. The cortex is divided into several areas called *lobes* which are associated with the control of higher mental, sensory, and physical functions (see Figure 4-6). The size of the cortex is one of the primary differences in brain structure between lower animals and primates and people.

Beneath the cortex is the mid-brain, a major part of which is the *limbic system*. The limbic system has been identified as being critically important in the regulation of emotions such as rage, fear, and sexual arousal. Once thought to represent the "seat of emotion" (Papez, 1937), the limbic system is now known to be but a part of the overall neurological system for the regulation of feelings and long-term

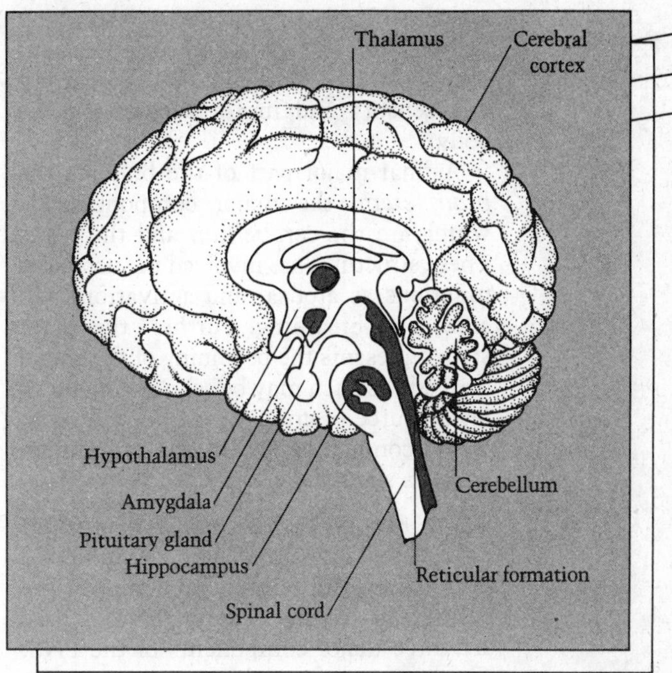

Figure 4-5 Major structures of the limbic system.

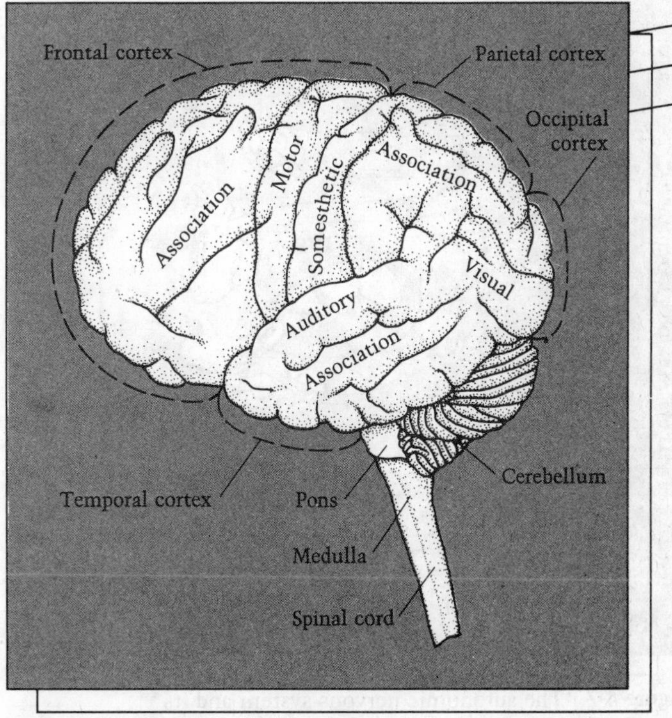

Figure 4-6 The lobes of the cerebral cortex and their functions.

memory. It also serves as a "switching station" for much of the information traveling between the brain and the peripheral sensory and motor systems of the body.

A final major part of the brain is the *brain stem,* the major components of which are the *cerebellum* and the *pons.* These structures are involved in such basic functions as arousal and activation, balance, and breathing. Further, the brain stem represents the beginning of the spinal cord and as such may be seen as the brain-level source of crucial neurological pathways connecting with the peripheral nervous system.

The Peripheral Nervous System (PNS) Parts of the nervous system not contained in the brain and spinal cord comprise the peripheral nervous system (PNS). There are three major components of the PNS: the *sensory system, the motor system, and the autonomic nervous system* (Brown, 1976; Freedman, 1982). The sensory system collects information from receptors such as the eyes, ears, and skin and sends it to the CNS for processing. The motor system carries messages from the CNS to the muscles of the body. The autonomic nervous system is involved with control of the "involuntary" systems of internal organs such as the heart, lungs, and stomach. Since the ANS is especially important for an understanding of abnormal emotional behavior, we will describe it further.

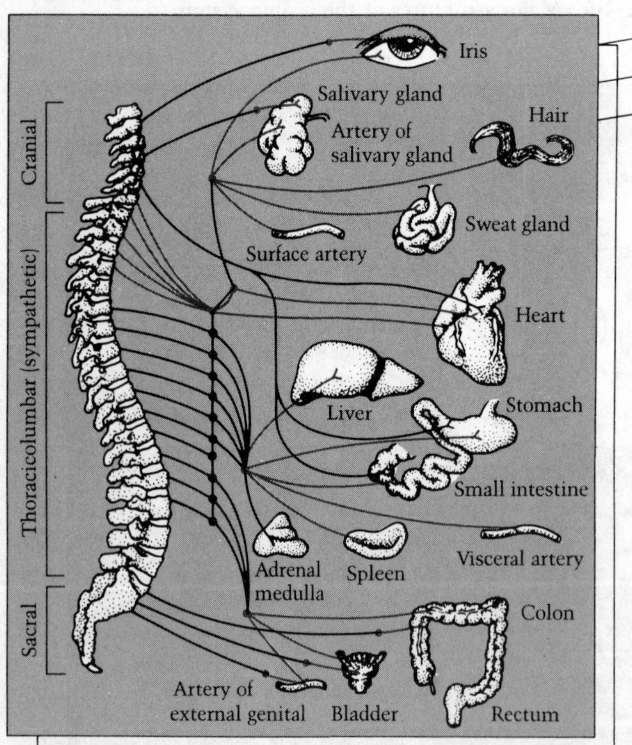

Figure 4-7 The autonomic nervous system and its connections.

Generally, the autonomic nervous system is responsible for maintaining physiological balance, or *homeostasis.* For example, when the body is hot, the ANS induces sweating and other body changes which bring cooling. Likewise, when the body is cold, the ANS may produce shivering and alteration of blood flow, which increase body heat. To aid in maintaining the safety and functioning of organisms, the ANS is further divided into two structurally and functionally distinct components, the *sympathetic nervous system* and the *parasympathetic nervous system.* As seen in Figure 4-7, each major "involuntary" organ of the body is connected to both of these systems, allowing the systems to work antagonistically to maintain homeostasis. For example, while impulses from the sympathetic system typically *speed up* the heartbeat, impulses from the parasympathetic may *slow it down.* For another example, impulses from the sympathetic system may *dilate* the pupil of the eye, while parasympathetic impulses *constrict* it.

The sympathetic system is a dominant determinant in emotional reactions such as fear and flight, while the parasympathetic tends to be more dominant in sedentary functions such as digestion. A closer look at Figure 4-7 will suggest how the sympathetic and parasympathetic systems are built to fulfill their special functions. Notice that the "switching stations," or *ganglia* (groups of neurons clumped together), for the sympathetic system are near the spinal cord and connected with one another in what is called the *sympathetic chain.* One result of this chaining is that when one of the ganglia is stimulated by the brain and spinal cord, *all* of them tend to be stimulated. This "chain reaction" of sorts yields very general and diffuse effects for the sympathetic system. Thus, when you are anxious, all organ systems affected by the sympathetic system become involved—your palms are sweaty, your heart beats faster, your digestion slows, your pupils dilate, and your kidneys work faster.

In contrast to the sympathetic system, where ganglia are near the spinal cord and interconnected, the ganglia for the parasympathetic system are located *near* the organs they control and are *not* interconnected. Since the parasympathetic system can affect only one organ at a time, it is possible for the stomach to begin digesting food without any concomitant effects on the heart, pupils, or blood pressure.

We will see in Chapter 11 that the autonomic nervous system may be involved in the development of some psychologically based physical symptoms such as migraine headaches and ulcers. Constant tension may produce extended activity of the sympathetic system, thereby shutting down some important parasympathetic functions like digestion. For example, a person who is angry and upset much of the day may not be able to digest food properly; nutritional and gastric symptoms may appear after a lengthy period of such sympathetic nervous system dominance.

The Endocrine System and Behavior

While the majority of theory and research deriving from the biological paradigm seems to have been focused on the neurotransmitters and synapses, there has been a recent increase in emphasis upon the role the endocrine system may play in mental disturbances (Haskett & Rose, 1981; Krieger & Hughes, 1980). Through blood-transported chemical secretions called *hormones* the endocrine system shares with the central and peripheral nervous systems control of a number of patterns of emotional behavior.

In contrast to the billions of neurons involved in the nervous system, there are relatively few glands in the endocrine system. However, as shown in chart form in Table 4-1, these glands can exercise through their excretions a wide range of behavioral control. The master endocrine gland, the *pituitary,* like the brain, is the primary organizer of its own behavioral control system. Since the pituitary, in turn, is regulated by a higher brain center (most likely, the hypothalamus), the endocrine system may be seen as an agent of the central nervous system (Haskett & Rose, 1981). Under normal conditions, the endocrine system significantly affects sexual behavior, maternal behavior, growth, sexual development, and stress reactions. For example, the endocrine system produces the release of adrenaline (epinephrine) that can give us a surge of energy during physically and emotionally stressful situations.

If the endocrine system functions properly, smoothly integrated activities are usually observed. However, malfunctions of the endocrine glands have been related to a variety of physical disorders with significant psychiatric concomitants. For example, reduced activity of the thyroid gland during early life may produce *cretinism.* Cretinism involves retarded growth and intelligence, distorted body features, and several psychological and emotional disabilities. Excessive activity of the thyroid, on the other hand, may result in *Basedow's disease,* usually characterized by irritability, anxiety, frequent changes of

Table 4-1 Functions of the Endocrine System

Gland	*Locus*	*Hormone*	*Target*	*Function*
Pituitary	Base of hypothalamus			
Neurohypophysis		Antidiuretic	Kidney	Stimulates reabsorption of water
		Oxytocin	Uterus	Stimulates contractions
			Mammary glands	Stimulates milk secretion
Adrenohypophysis		Somatotropic	Bone	Stimulates growth
		Thyrotropic	Thyroid gland	Activates thyroid secretion
		ACTH	Adrenal cortex	Stimulates steroid secretion
		Gonadotropic	Gonads	Stimulates secretion of estrogens and androgens
Thyroid	Neck, around pharynx	Thyroxin	Energy-expending tissues	Regulates metabolism
Parathyroid	Thyroid gland	Parathormone	Blood	Regulates calcium and phosphate levels
Adrenal Cortex	On kidneys			
		Adrenal steroids	Cell membranes	Electrolyte balance
Medulla		Epinephrine	Cardiovascular system	Increases blood flow
Pancreas	Below stomach	Insulin	Energy-expending tissues	Stimulates glucose absorption
Gonads	Sex organs	Estrogens (ovaries) Androgens (testes)	All tissues	Sex arousal, primary and secondary sex characteristics
Pineal	Third ventricle of brain	Melantonin	Gonads	Inhibits gonadal secretions

Source: From H. Brown, *Brain and Behavior: A Textbook of Physiological Psychology.* Copyright © 1976 by Oxford University Press, Inc. Reprinted by permission.

mood, and general emotional discomfort which has been likened to a severe anxiety disorder or psychotic mania (Haskett & Rose, 1981).

Abnormal variations in the secretions of other endocrines, such as the adrenals, parathyroids and gonads, may also be accompanied by abnormal behavior patterns. For example, reduced levels of adrenal corticoids (*Addison's disease*) may be related to psychological symptoms such as fear, hallucinations, irrational beliefs, and depression, as well as to physical symptoms which include muscular weakness, stomach upset, and pallor of the skin. Excess of adrenal corticoids may result in *Cushing's disease,* characterized by psychological symptoms such as crying, jitteriness, agitation, and irritability. In most instances of endocrine-based disorders,

BOX 4-1

A HORMONALLY BASED "TEST" FOR THE PRESENCE OF PSYCHOTIC DEPRESSION: A PRECURSOR OF DSM-IV?

We've noted in the main body of the text that there are several biological concomitants of emotional disturbances. While one purpose in finding such concomitants is understanding etiology, a second goal is to isolate diagnostic indicators. While we are still some distance from definitive tests for all forms of abnormality, there is one group of researchers which has developed a "laboratory test for melancholia" or endogenous depression (Carroll et al.; 1981).

Carroll et al., studied 215 patients diagnosed according to DSM-III as being severely depressed, 153 psychiatric patients with diagnoses other than depression, and 70 normals. The laboratory test for depression, the *dexamethasone suppression test* or DST, involved a procedure in which subjects were given a measured dose of dexamethasone at 11:30 in the evening and had their blood tested for plasma concentration of the drug three times over the following 24 hours. Research has shown that depressed persons tend not to process the drug in the same way as normals and thus manifest higher concentrations after 1 day.

Statistical analyses indicated that only 4 percent of the normals and nondepressed patients showed abnormal blood levels, while 95 percent of the known depressed patients showed a deviant pattern. The authors concluded that "The routine use of this simple test by internists, family practitioners and psychiatrists who treat depressed patients may help to reduce . . . diagnostic confusion" (Carroll et al., 1981, p. 22). Given the expansion of our knowledge about the biology of psychopathology, the DST may be but one of the "routine" laboratory tests in the diagnostic procedures of the future.

medical alteration of abnormal hormone levels may result in the disappearance of psychological symptoms. In fact, there is sometimes such a close relationship between certain hormone levels and particular patterns of psychopathology that some researchers have tried to use the presence of abnormal levels of certain hormones as a way of improving diagnosis of disorders like depression. (See Box 4-1 for a closer look at one of these "tests" for psychosis.)

The Endorphins (Neuropeptides) and Behavior

Thus far we have spoken of the system of neurons and of the endocrine system as if they are separate entities with nonoverlapping functions. However, it has recently become clear that there also may be a system of behavioral control which is based upon an interaction between the hypothalamus and the endocrine system (most notably the pituitary gland). In addition to its role in the neurological network of the CNS, the hypothalamus also appears to be involved in the production of a group of "behavioral modulators," or "regulators," called the *neuropeptides* (Guillemin, 1980; de Wied, 1980). First discovered in 1975 (Hollister et al., 1980), these peptides or *endorphins* are found in the brain as well as in the digestive system. While originally studied due to their opiate-like pain-reducing qualities, some researchers believe that the neuropeptides may represent a "third division of the nervous system" (Guillemin, 1980, p. 74) and may help us eventually to understand more fully the biology of behavior. Knowledge regarding the peptides is increasing at a rapid pace with the expectation being that great numbers of them will eventually be discovered. Their gen-

Table 4-2 Major Neuropeptides and Some of Their Effects

Beta-endorphin: Reduces bodily response to pain as effectively as morphine.
Enkephalins: Pain relievers similar in effect to beta-endorphin.
Bombesin: Appears to "turn on" the sympathetic nervous system.
Somatostatin; Appears to "turn off" the sympathetic nervous system.
Bradykinin: Plays a role in pain production; may be most painful substance known.
Cholecystokinin: Plays a role in "turning on" eating behavior; may be involved in obesity.
Angiotensin: Appears to "turn on" drinking behavior.
ACTH: Appears to play a role in learning and remembering new information.

Source: Based on "The peptide hit parade," *Science 81,* American Association for the Advancement of Science, 1981.

eral effects seem to be through modulation of the effects of neurotransmitters at the dendrites of neurons. Their specific effects are widely varied, as can be seen in Table 4-2.

Research relating psychopathology to neuropeptide levels has focused most heavily on the beta-endorphins and the enkephalins due to their significant concentration in key areas of the brain. One researcher is so convinced of the potential importance to psychopathology of these peptides that he has stated:

> It is clear that the endorphins and enkephalins have other functions than those suggested by their opiate-like activity and it is probable that they play some role in the functions of the brain involving mood, emotion and behavior. . . . The hypothesis remains to be proved, but since present concepts of neurophysiology and neuropsychiatry were formed without any knowledge of the existence of these substances, the elucidation of their physiology and function may well revolutionize our understanding of the mechanisms involved in the functioning of the brain. (Guillemin, 1980, p. 74)

While Guillemin's statement may seem rather expansive, there is already some evidence to support the view that knowledge of endorphins may "revolutionize" our understanding of psychopathology. For example, Hollister et al. (1980) have noted that these substances, "may play a role in schizophrenia, depression and in alcohol and drug abuse" (p. 174). Hollister et al. describe two theories of psychopathology based on endorphins. The first, the *hyperendorphinemia theory,* holds that too much endorphin can cause schizophrenic symptoms. Support for this contention comes from the work of Lindstrom, et al. (1978) who reported that administration of an endorphin blocker, naloxone, results in beneficial effects in schizophrenics. Further, Wagemaker and Cade (1977) reported improvement in schizophrenics whose blood had been filtered through hemodialysis. These researchers reported that one of the primary components of the dialysate (material filtered out) obtained from the schizophrenics was an endorphin.

A second approach takes the opposite position, that is, psychopathology is associated with *hypoendorphinemia* or abnormally low levels of brain endorphins. Early support for this approach is seen in the work of Verhoeven et al. (1979) who found that injection of a specific endorphin each day for 7 to 8 days resulted in a transitory remission of symptoms for the majority of a group of 14 schizophrenic subjects. While there is support for both perspectives regarding the role of endorphins in psychopathology, the area is so new that extensive research continues to be necessary and few comfortable conclusions can be reached at this time.

The Biological Paradigm in the Study of Psychopathology

Early applications of the biological paradigm focused on a search for some invading toxic substance or bacteria in psychopathology and were largely unsuccessful. Though such research continues in small measure, we have chosen to limit our discussion here to what we consider to be the most potentially successful derivatives of the biological paradigm—the search for a genetic basis and the search for a biochemical-neurological basis for psychopathology.

The Search for Genetic Factors in Psychopathology

Proponents of the genetic role in mental disorders believe that, to some degree, psychopathology may be hereditary (Schulsinger, 1980). We know that some physical characteristics are inherited; each of us looks somewhat like his or her parents or siblings. It was also once thought that many personality characteristics and learned skills also could be inherited, but it is clear to modern geneticists that inheritance is not so simple. Most genetic theorists now seem to have adopted the perspective that while physical characteristics are primarily controlled by the genes, such things as personality and psychopathology are probably a result of some combination of genetic endowment ("nature") and environment ("nurture"). From our perspective, this nature *plus* nurture view is probably optimal, for much research suggests that there may be both environmental as well as inherited components in such disorders as schizophrenia and the affective psychoses (Schulsinger, 1980).

Naturally Occurring Genetic Experiments: The Kallikak Family

One method of studying genetic effects on abnormal behavior is to observe naturally occurring patterns of behavior disorders within families. In 1919, psychologist Henry Goddard published a report about a family he called the Kallikaks, which had a higher proportion of mental defectives and social problems among its members than would be expected on the average. To put his study of this family in perspective, we must note that Goddard was a *social Darwinist* and, as such, believed that *eugenics*, the application of genetic knowledge to alter a species, should be used to improve the human race. In fact, Goddard was psychological advisor to a group that published such papers as "Report of the Committee to Study and to Report on the Best Practical Means of Cutting off the Defective Germ-plasm in the American Population" (1914). Specifically, Goddard studied the Kallikak family to demonstrate the manner in which this "defective germ-plasm" could pass itself from generation to generation according to known laws of genetics.

Goddard's presentation begins with Martin Kallikak (see Figure 4-8 for a sketch of the Kallikak family tree), who had seven normal children with his lawful wife. But Goddard reported that in addition to his wife, Martin also had sexual relations with a "nameless feebleminded girl." As seen in Figure 4-9, his indiscretion resulted in a feebleminded son named Martin, Jr., who married a seemingly normal woman, Rhoda, who gave birth to eight living children, five of whom deviated into sexual promiscuity, alcoholism, and feeblemindedness. Figure 4-9 shows that when one of these children, Old Sal, married a feebleminded husband, the coupling of both "defective germ-plasms" resulted in severe retardation among almost all the descendants.

After proposing that "a-sexualization" of Martin, Jr., would have prevented so much "bad blood" from entering the human race, Goddard's conclusion was as follows:

> We find on the good side of the family prominant people in all walks of life and nearly all of the 496 descendants owners of land or properties. On the bad side we find paupers, criminals, prostitutes, drunkards and all forms of social pest with which modern society is burdened. (1919, p. 116)

Goddard tended to lump deviant behavior together, without differentiating

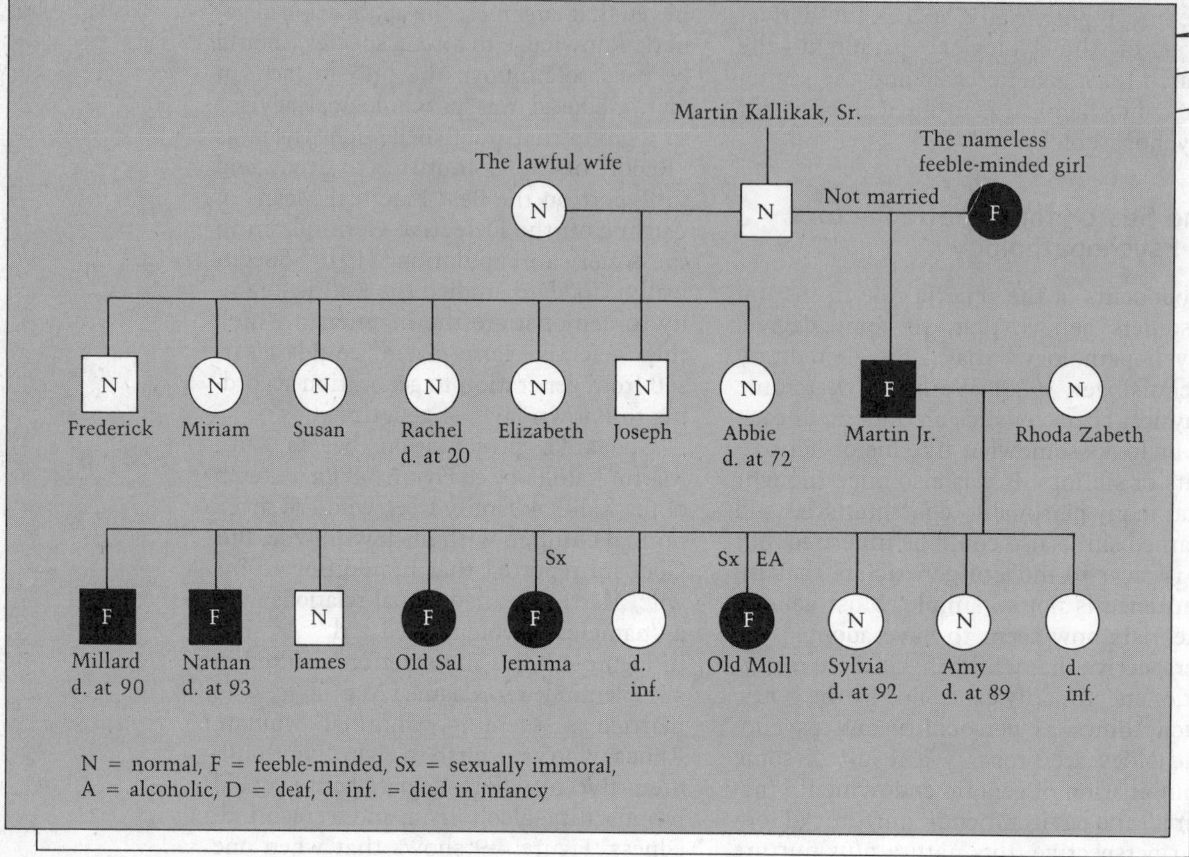

Figure 4-8 Martin Kallikak's family tree. (*From* The Kallikak Family, *by H. Goddard. Copyright © 1919 by Macmillan Publishing Co., Inc.*)

between schizophrenia and retardation or alcoholism. Although some of the data from naturally occurring "experiments" do support the notion that aberrations may occur more frequently in families, *controlled* research with animals and people provides us with a more reliable evaluation of the significance of inheritability of disordered behavior.

Planned and Controlled Genetic Experiments

The storylike manner in which Goddard presented his data may be interesting, but it lacks the scientific validity available through controlled studies of animals and people. We all know that there are different temperaments among animals. For example, in dogs, one result of breeding for "personality" is that Dobermans are more likely to be vicious than poodles. Similarly, research-based genetic explanations of abnormal behavior share the belief that people, like lower animals, inherit various emotional traits and behavioral propensities that may lead them to behave in specific ways, be these ways normal or abnormal.

Hall (1934), a pioneer in psychogenetics, studied inheritance of emotionality in rats. He used ratings to describe the emotional responsiveness of rats when they were placed in a large open area. For nine generations, those animals rated highest on emotionality were inbred, as were those with low ratings. The strain of animals

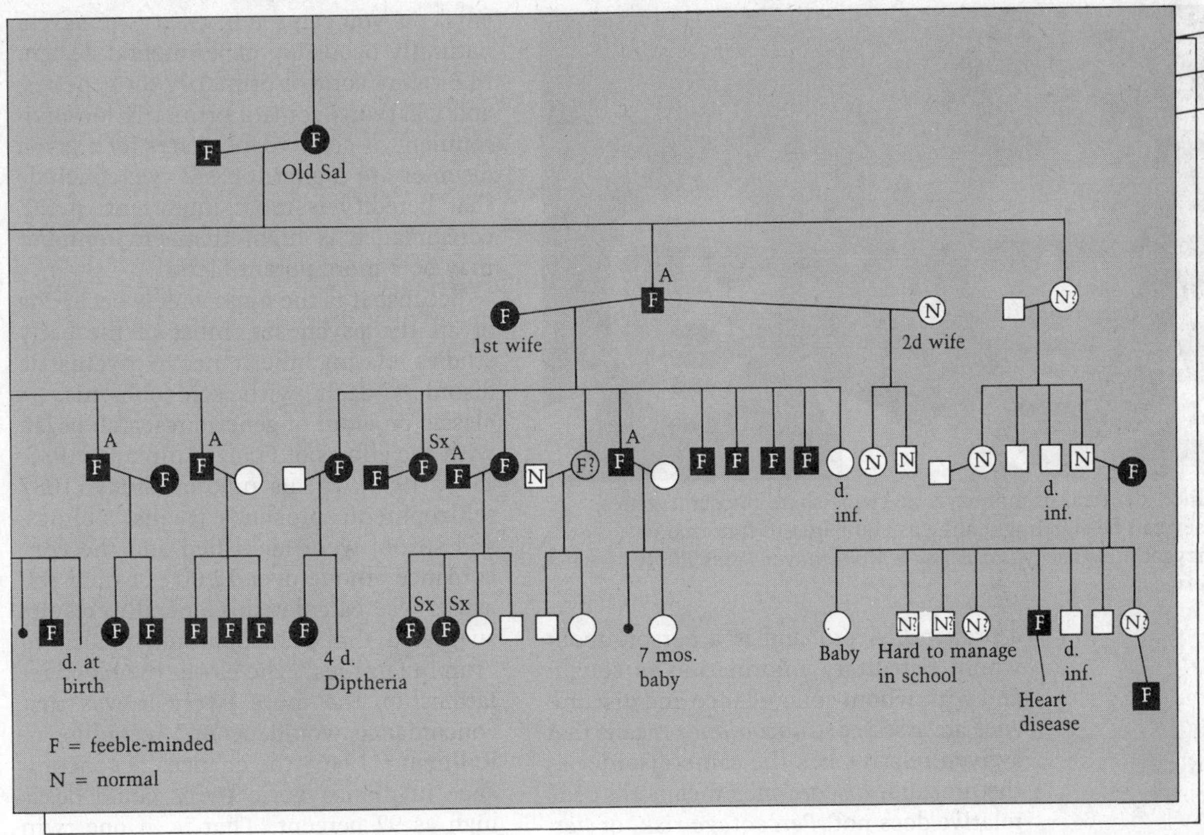

Figure 4-9 When feeble-minded marries feeble-minded. (*From* The Kallikak Family, *by H. Goddard. Copyright ©1919 by Macmillan Publishing Co., Inc.*)

rated high on emotionality became more emotional with each ensuing generation. However, the low emotional rats reached a low point of emotionality within one generation and did not reduce their levels of emotionality further with subsequent breeding. Hall concluded from these findings that, were controlled studies in humans possible, similar results would be obtained. An awareness of the number of children of professional athletes and actors who succeed in the same areas as their parents should add testimony to this conclusion.

Unfortunately, the time required to repeat Hall's study with humans is prohibitive. Within their own lifetimes, researchers cannot follow five or ten generations of people, nor can they "inbreed" people deliberately. One solution has been to use family histories of currently diagnosed people to determine what their hereditary line might have looked like. Exemplified in its early form with the Kallikaks, this retrospective methodology has recently attained a higher level of sophistication. However, before describing the results of these more recent studies, we need to provide you with some of the language necessary for understanding the data.

A case of a particular behavior disorder usually is identified by traditional diagnostic means. When the genetic background of the particular person comes under research scrutiny, the person is labeled

Since identical or monozygotic twins share the same genes, they can be startlingly alike as compared to fraternal or dizygotic twins. (*Mimi Forsyth/Monkmeyer Press Photo Service*)

a *proband.* A proband is a person about whom hereditary information is sought and with whom concordance and discordance are assessed. *Concordance* means that a given relative has the same disorder as the proband; *discordance* means that the relative does not. *Percentage risk*, or *heritability*, refers to the statistical chance that a given relative of a proband will inherit the disorder in question.

Most of the significant research relating genetics to abnormal behavior has been done with twins as the basic population. The reason for using twins may be obvious to you. Identical or *monozygotic* (MZ) twins share the exact same genetic endowment. Therefore, if a disorder is passed through the genes, one would expect that if one MZ twin is a proband, the other twin should be concordant for the aberration; that is, if one identical twin is schizophrenic, so should the other be. *Dizygotic* (DZ) or fraternal twins do *not* share the same exact genetic programming, but they do experience somewhat the same environment at the same times in their lives; genetically, they are no more similar than *full siblings* (brothers and sisters born at different times to the same parents). As you can see in twins, we have a naturally occurring experimental design: MZ twins control primarily for genetics, and DZ twins control primarily for environment. If concordance rates for a given disorder are higher for MZ, we conclude that heredity is more important; if DZ concordance is high, then environment may be a more potent factor.

Because it is the most widely occurring of all the psychoses, most of the early studies relating inheritance to psychiatric disorders dealt with schizophrenia. A classic program of genetic research began with the efforts of Franz Kallmann (1938, 1946, 1953). In his original study, 1087 schizophrenic probands (twins, siblings, and so on) were identified and the concordance among over 12,000 of their relatives was calculated. Generally, results suggested that schizophrenia tended to "run in families"; the closer the blood relationship, the more likely it was that concordance would occur. According to Kallmann (1946), the chances of concordance in monozygotic twins could be as high as 92 percent. That is, if one twin was diagnosed as schizophrenic, then 9 times out of 10 so was the other. Further, as the blood relationship became more distant, the risk of the disorder became lower.

If inheritance could explain the incidence of severe disordered behavior, then, some researchers reasoned, severe mental disorders could be prevented merely by stopping "defective" individuals from reproducing. However, closer inspection of Kallmann's data revealed some methodological problems that called for caution in applying his results to social action programs. For instance, many of the professionals who diagnosed probands and their relatives may have been using faulty data. Some patients may have been diagnosed as schizophrenic simply because the professionals knew that their relatives had been so diagnosed. Further, due to lack of reliability inherent in early diagnostic

BOX 4-2

IS THERE A RELATIONSHIP BETWEEN RIGHT VERSUS LEFT-HANDEDNESS AND SCHIZOPHRENIA?

A review of genetic research in schizophrenia indicates that concordance rates for MZ twins can be quite high. However, there is at least one researcher who has taken a closer look at the differences between MZ and DZ concordance data. Charles Boklage (1977) has shown that the *handedness* (right or left) of MZ twins appears to be related to the severity of their psychological disturbance as well as to their specific concordance pattern. Gottesman and Shields (1972) reported MZ concordance rates of approximately 45 percent and DZ concordance rates of about 15 percent. Boklage reanalyzed these concordance data by subgrouping the MZ twins into those in which both were right-handed (the "2RH" group) and those in which at least one was *not* right-handed (the "1-2NRH" group). He found that the "new" concordance rate for the 2RH group of MZ twins was 92 percent compared with only 25 percent for the 1-2NRH group! Further, 86 percent of the 2RH group were concordant for the *same subtype* of schizophrenia as compared with 0 percent of the other group. Finally, the 2RH group had a poorer prognosis and a worse premorbid history than the 1-2NRH group.

Boklage proposed that, because it reflects *brain laterality* (or *right versus left hemispheric dominance*), handedness may shed some light on our understanding of the etiology of schizophrenia. He suggests that schizophrenia may have at least two different etiologies, one reflecting a left hemispheric dysfunction, the other a problem with the right hemisphere. In support of this notion that different psychoses may be associated with damage of different sides of the brain, Boklage refers to the work of Flor-Henry (1974, 1976) who reported that "affective symptomatology was found characteristic of cases involving right hemisphere problems, schizophrenic symptomatology characterizing left hemisphere problems" (1977, p. 29).

Research continues on Boklage's contention that brain laterality is associated in some way with schizophrenia. His belief that some forms of psychosis may be caused by problems in embryonic hemispheric development may be an important part of our future understanding of the biological basis of schizophrenia and the affective psychoses.

systems, there was some question as to whether patients were being accurately classified as schizophrenic. Support for these criticisms comes from the fact that later, better-controlled studies usually failed to replicate Kallmann's high figures (for example, see Gottesman & Shields, 1972).

Even though the high degree of concordance was not easily replicated, a synthesis of a number of studies relating genetics and schizophrenia shows that in general MZ concordance *is significantly higher* than is DZ for both schizophrenia and the affective psychoses (mania and depression) (Kringlen, 1976). Since the MZ concordance rates range from 15 to 42 percent for monozygotics compared with 7 to 19 percent for dizygotics, there seems to be *some* genetic influence in these disorders. (See Box 4-2 for a closer look at a new perspective on the mechanisms of concordance.)

As well as studying twins, researchers have compared the rates of disturbance in *adopted* children with behavior problems with their biological and adoptive parents and relatives (see Schulsinger, 1980; Kessler, 1980a). The rationale for the methodology seems sound. If behavior disorders are primarily transmitted genetically, a child born of one or two disturbed biological parents would be more likely to develop a disorder even if adopted and raised by normal parents. Basically, researchers are trying to determine if a child with schizophrenic inheritance is raised by adoptive nonschizophrenic parents, are his chances less or the same for developing schizophrenia?

One example of the application of the adoption methodology is the work of Kety et al. (1968). These researchers identified a group of schizophrenics who had been adopted when they were quite young. Interviews with hundreds of both biological as well as adoptive relatives of these index cases revealed what is now known to be a stable pattern of results (Kessler, 1980b). These results were that over 20 percent of the biological relatives of the probands could be diagnosed as having some form of mental disturbance related to schizophrenia, while only about 5 percent of adoptive relatives could be similarly classified. Kety et al. interpreted their findings as suggesting that whether raised by disturbed parents or not, children who have an hereditary basis for schizophrenia are more likely to develop the disorder than children without such genetic endowment.

Shields (1973; also see Schulsinger, 1980; Kessler, 1980b) has concluded that the results from adoption studies generally support the hypothesis that "the raised incidence of schizophrenia in the families of schizophrenics is to be accounted for by shared genes and not by having been reared by a mentally ill parent" (Shields, 1973, p. 583). Considering the data on adoptees and twins, we find it difficult to deny the importance of genetics in the occurrence of abnormal behaviors like schizophrenia and the affective disorders. However, there is also mounting evidence for some genetic involvement in the etiologies of other disorders. Among those disorders are psychopathy (Schulsinger, 1972), alcoholism (Goodwin et al. 1977a, 1977b, 1985), and suicide (Schulsinger et al., 1979; Schulsinger, 1980). These studies will be described in more depth in the chapters dealing specifically with these disorders.

A Genetic-Environmental Explanation: Diathesis-Stress Theory

Although there is research support for a relationship between genes and disordered behavior, we still know relatively little about the specific mechanics of the development of behavior disorder. For example, why don't some children who are born to and raised by psychotic parents develop psychoses? Conversely, how can a person develop a psychosis when raised by parents who are not so disturbed? The occurrence of these kinds of discontinuities suggests the need to take into account *both* heredity and environment when describing how disordered behavior develops. *Diathesis-stress theory* (Rosenthal & Kety, 1968) or *vulnerability theory* (Schulsinger, 1980; Zubin & Spring, 1977) represent attempts to combine these two potential contributors to aberrant behavior.

Since concordance rates in MZ twins are never perfect for abnormal behavior, environment must play *some* role in determining the occurrence of disorders. Kallmann (1953) reported that for schizophrenia, concordance rates for MZ twins reared apart were lower than for twins reared together. Others (for example, Shields & Slater, 1961) also have reported that among discordant MZ pairs, environmental factors appear to play a significant role in whether both twins manifest the disorder. To explain these findings, the vulnerability theory (Schulsinger, 1980) makes the assumption that people are endowed genetically with a predisposition (or *diathesis*) toward developing a particular behavior disorder. Given sufficient environmental stress, the predisposition may manifest itself behaviorally. Thus, twins, both genetically predisposed to schizophrenia and both raised in the same stressful environment, should both develop the disorder. However, if they are separated early in life, the twin living in the less stressful environment may not develop the disorder.

While vulnerability theory has been refined over the years (Schulsinger, 1980; Kessler, 1980a), probably the clearest exposition of the approach may be the work of Meehl (1962). Meehl proposed that schizophrenics inherited a neural defect that he called *schizotaxia.* When the schizotaxic individual's predisposition is combined with normal learning experience during development, it could produce a *schizotypic personality structure* characterized by difficulties in handling emotion and thought. When this personality structure interacts with what Meehl termed a *schizophrenogenic environment* (especially a *schizophrenogenic mother*), the result is schizophrenia. Thus, Meehl concluded that the multiple factors contributing to the development of mental disorder were the genetic predisposition, the development of the core behavior patterns, *and* a particular kind of environment.

Diathesis-stress theory also allows us to explain why two siblings raised in the same home might be discordant for psychosis: one may be schizotaxic and the other may not. Further, the theory explains why identical twins (if one is schizotaxic, both must be) reared apart seem to have lower concordance rates: some of the twins have gone into nonschizophrenogenic environments.

The Search for a Biochemical Basis for Abnormal Behavior

As well as searching for the etiologies of behavior disorders in the genes, researchers also have looked at the role of other specific neurological and biochemical factors in behavioral dysfunctions. This has led to a focus on defects in the structures and biochemical functions involved in neural synaptic transmission as possible causes of aberrant behavior.

According to Meehl (1962), people who are born with a predisposition to develop schizophrenia may show the characteristics of this disorder when they live in an environment that is also conducive to creating schizophrenia. (*Jean-Marie Simon/Taurus Photos*)

To understand the rationale for the focus on synaptic transmission, we must look a bit more closely at the synapse itself. As depicted in Figure 4-10, successful and normal transmission of a nervous impulse involves several steps each of which may be hampered or altered in psychopathological states. The first step in the process involves the release by synaptic vesicles of a neurotransmitter substance into the synaptic cleft. These neurotransmitters must then travel across the syn-

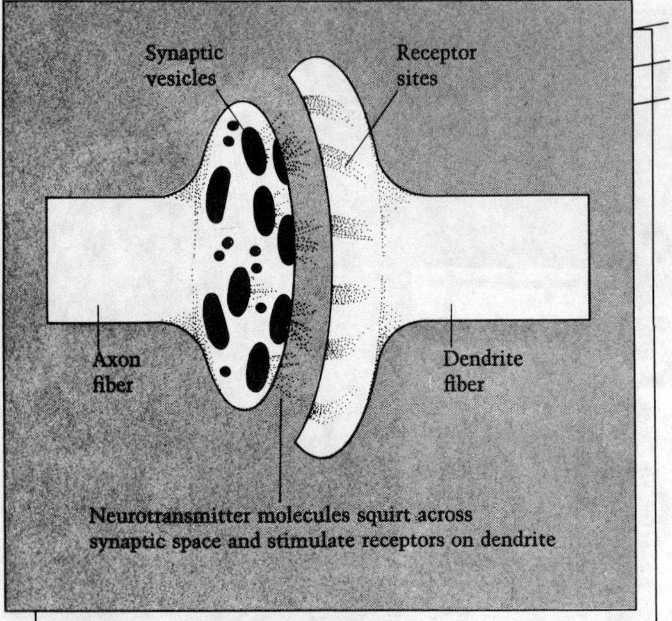

Figure 4-10 A closer look at synaptic neurotransmission.

aptic cleft, impinge on specific receptors on the dendrites of the receiving cell, and finally stimulate that receiving cell to fire. Once the impulse has been transmitted, the synaptic space must be cleared of transmitter substance so that the receiving cell's receptors do not continue to be stimulated. This "clearing" can take place in a number of ways: the sending cell may, through the process called *reuptake,* absorb the neurotransmitter substance back into the storage vesicles for reuse; or the neurotransmitters may be *metabolized* (broken down into other chemicals) via interaction with specific enzymes, thus rendering them incapable of further stimulation of receptors.

To demonstrate how the synaptic transmission process may play a role in the development of abnormal behavior, we will consider some research on the biochemistry of schizophrenia. For example, a fairly well-established finding is that in schizophrenia, the neurotransmitter, dopamine, appears to be present in excess amounts (Iversen, 1980). Further, the administration of medication that reduces dopamine levels in certain areas of the brain also alleviates symptoms like hallucinations (Colasanti, 1982a). Within the framework of our understanding of the synaptic transmission system, it is possible to identify a number of different explanations for an excess of dopamine. For example, some researchers may look for a failure in the reuptake system while others may focus on some problem with the enzymes that normally help metabolize the neurotransmitter. When we discuss schizophrenia and the affective psychoses in more detail in Chapters 7 to 9, it will become clear that each of these explanations, as well as several others, has led to an increase in our understanding of the biology of psychosis and other forms of psychopathology.

The Biological Paradigm in the Treatment of Psychopathology

Although we will be describing special treatments for a number of disorders later, we would like to introduce you here to some of the basic forms of treatment which have grown out of efforts to understand psychopathology from a biological perspective. In Chapter 3, we discussed the ways in which paradigms direct scientific efforts to understand the world. But understanding of a phenomenon is not enough especially when the object of study is a disorder which brings about unhappiness and difficulties in living. In these instances, scientists must continue beyond understanding and move toward the development of ways of changing newly understood patterns. In the case of abnormal behavior, these efforts to change patterns fall into the category of *therapy.* Since therapy grows out of theory, it appears to us that presenting both within the same chapter may help to emphasize the interplay between research and treatment.

Genetic Counseling

It is probably safe to say that there is some genetic component in many forms of psychopathology. However, treatment based upon this knowledge is not the type in which clinicians try to undo a pattern of behavior once it has developed. Rather, if we know there is a genetic component in a particular set of disorders, one option is to focus treatment efforts on *prevention.*

Preventive efforts based on genetic aspects of mental disorders involve a number of concepts. Initially, *populations at risk* for the particular disorder need to be identified. Schulsinger (1980) has noted that it is possible on the basis of biological indicators like mental health of parents (Mednick et al., 1978) to designate those children who are at high risk for a disorder. Given identifiable premorbid (before the development of observable symptoms) characteristics, Schulsinger has emphasized the therapeutic (preventive) potential of the study of populations genetically at high risk:

> Prevention of severe mental illness could, theoretically, be the result of a general change in society's attitude and policies with regard to education, nutrition, obstetrical service, and social security. But it is probably more realistic to think of primary prevention of severe mental disorders in the future as the result of intervention offered to individuals with an especially well-established high risk for the disorder in question (1980, p. 602).

In a further preventive effort couples who have an increased chance of bearing schizophrenic offspring also may be advised to reconsider their decisions to have children (Tsuang, 1978b; Kessler, 1980a). Needless to say, such counseling can be a very sensitive undertaking not only due to its eugenic overtones but also because the counselees often are suffering from severe emotional disturbance and may misinterpret or distort the information and guidance being offered (Kessler, 1980a). Nevertheless, experts believe that within the context of a trusting, therapeutic relationship genetic counseling can be an effective approach to the prevention of severe mental disturbance.

Chemical Therapies

Although prevention and genetic counseling owe their impetus to research on the genetics of abnormality, the chemical or drug therapies emanate from laboratory-based knowledge of the biochemistry and neurophysiology of abnormality. Although herbs and organic derivatives have long been used in general medicine, the massive clinical use of chemicals to control mental symptoms has been evident only since the early 1950s when tranquilizing drugs were first widely introduced (Colasanti, 1982a). Generally, the use of these drugs has been associated with a decreasing inpatient population, for with the advent of the drug therapies, patients who might otherwise have been kept in restraints or locked up in closed wards often were able to leave institutions and to function satisfactorily at home with a daily dose of psychoactive medication. Even patients who remained in hospitals often were easier to work with through drug therapies. For example, in a large hospital where one of us worked, only 2 of 32 wards were locked, and most patients were free to walk the grounds as they wished. This was a dramatic change from 10 years before, when there were 14 locked wards and very limited freedom. However, in general, drugs do not *cure,* but rather *control,* symptoms of abnormal behavior in much the same way that antihistamines merely control the symptoms of colds.

Psychoactive chemicals are not all alike in their effects. Some of them are calmative, whereas others provide energy and an emotional lift. However, in addition to their therapeutic effects, the drugs also can have adverse side effects such as those described by patients (see Box 4-3). Tradi-

BOX 4-3

WHAT'S IT LIKE TO TAKE CERTAIN PSYCHOACTIVE MEDICATION?

Sinequan: "It makes me drowsy . . . I go to sleep, and my dreams are different. I don't dream too well."
"I stopped dreaming."

Haldol: "You go from highs to lows; depending on how much you take, you can go through the floor. A little like amphetamines. When I went off it, I had a tremendous anxiety reaction. It was very scary . . . terrible withdrawal reactions."

Stelazine: "I feel groggy, fuzzy-headed. My mouth is very dry."
"When I went off it, I found myself talking a blue streak, getting very aggressive and domineering in a conversation." (This probably represents the return of symptoms.)

Thorazine: "I have respiratory problems with it, and my doctor changed to something else. It was terrible. I couldn't stay out in the sun at all. I'd get roasted. It slows you down, especially thinking."
"It made my mouth so dry that at one job I was interviewing for they thought I had a speech impediment, and they wouldn't hire me. I get hyper without it, though."

Mellaril: "I felt lowered, and I had more anxiety problems. In fact I even started to get a little paranoid."
"I get groggy, dry-mouthed . . . but it relaxes me. If I go off it, I start sweating and get tense and light-headed."

tionally, the psychoactive drugs have been categorized on the basis of their clinical effects and include the *antipsychotics,* the *antidepressants,* the *antimanics,* and the *minor tranquilizers* and *hypnotics* (Goodman & Gilman, 1980; Craig & Stitzel, 1982).

The Antipsychotic Drugs (Major Tranquilizers)

The major tranquilizers used to treat psychotic symptoms are chemicals that can reduce psychotic (especially schizophrenic) behavior such as hallucinations as well as alleviate severe anxiety and agitation. Usually the classification of the major tranquilizers is based not so much upon their antipsychotic action as on their chemical source. Among the earliest of the major tranquilizers were the phenothiazines.

According to some reviewers (Colasanti, 1982a; Jarvik, 1970), a *phenothiazine derivative* was taken by about one out of every four Americans during the decade 1955 to 1965. The most common derivative of the group, *chlorpromazine* (Thorazine), has been the most frequently used medication for the treatment of the broad range of the schizophrenias. However, the phenothiazines are not a new "miracle" drug. In fact, they were first synthesized in 1883, and as late as 1934 they were used primarily as antiworm medicine and even as an insecticide! In 1953, a French psychiatrist, Courvoisier, reported a large number of psychological and physical effects of the drug. Delay et al. (1952, cited by Jarvik, 1970) have been credited with the first use of chlorpromazine in the treatment of mental disorders. Soon after their reports of success, the drug was introduced into American psychiatry and its use expanded rapidly. Severely disturbed schizophrenics may be placed on daily dosages of up to 5000 mg of chlorpromazine. This is up to 200 times the recommended dosage for treating nau-

Table 4-3 The Major Tranquilizers, the Antidepressants, and the Antimanic Drugs

Grouping	*Trade Names*
	Major Tranquilizers
Phenothiazine derivatives	Thorazine, Largactil, Sparine, Vespirin, Prolixin, Trilafon, Compazine, Stelazine, Mellaril
Butyrophenones	Haldol
Rauwolfia alkaloids	Raudixin, Serpasil, Sandril, Moderil, Harmonyl
Thioxanthenes	Navane Taractan
Dihydroindolones	Moban
Debenzoxazepines	Loxitane
	Antidepressants
Tricyclics	Sinequan, Vivactyl, Tofranil, Pertofran, Elavil, Aventyl
Monoamine oxidase (MAO) inhibitors	Marplan, Parnate, Nardil
	Combination Drugs
	Triavil, Deprol
	Antimanic Drugs
Lithium salts	Eskalith Lithane

sea in nonpsychotic people (*Physician's Desk Reference,* 1982). The 5000 mg dose probably would produce a coma, even death, in a normal person, but in many schizophrenic patients it results in calmness and manageability.

The clinical effects of the phenothiazine derivatives are described as including "a considerable degree of tranquilization and quieting" (Colasanti 1982a, p. 507). As with many major tranquilizers, however, there may also be side effects such as drying of the mouth, nasal stuffiness, slight constipation, muscular shaking, and ejaculatory disturbances in males. These side effects can usually be controlled by simultaneous administration of other medications. The trade names for some of the most commonly used phenothiazines are listed in Table 4-3.

Like the phenothiazines, the *butyrophenones* were first developed in Europe (Colasanti, 1982a). Exemplified by haloperidol (Haldol), which was first intro-

Use of antipsychotic medications has done much to eradicate conditions like those pictured here. (*Copyright ©Jerry Cooke 1967/Photo Researchers, Inc.*)

duced in the United States in 1967, the butyrophenones seem to be just as effective as the phenothiazines in controlling psychosis and often can be used in their stead. Although haloperidol is the only butyrophenone in psychiatric use (see Table 4-3), it seems to be the chemical of choice in some rare disorders. In Gilles de la Tourette syndrome (See Chapter 16), for example, it has been reported to reduce the involuntary tics, obscene verbalizations, and explosiveness characteristic of the disorder.

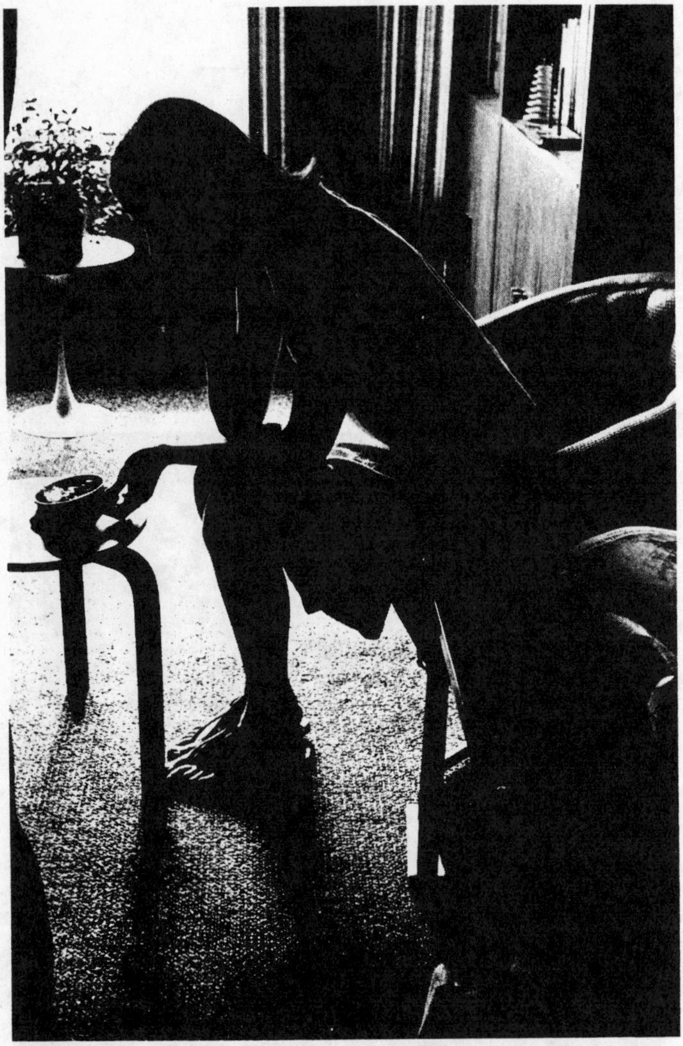

Since their introduction in the 1950s, antidepressive drugs have helped millions of people deal more effectively with their depression. (*Marion Bernstein*)

In addition to the phenothiazines and butyrophenones there are several other groupings of less widely used antipsychotics. The *rauwolfia alkaloids,* a natural drug obtained from the Indian shrub *rauwolfia serpentina,* was used to treat mental disturbances in India as early as 1931 (Jarvik, 1970). However, the drug was not used in the United States until the 1950s. *Thiothixene* and *molindone* (Ayd, 1975) are relatively newer tranquilizing agents. Similar to the phenothiazines in their effects, these drugs are often tried when the more commonly used medications do not have satisfactory effects. Used primarily in the treatment of schizophrenia, molindone is especially fast acting. Thiothixene seems to have greater mood-elevating and sedative effects than the other major tranquilizers and is therefore more widely used in the affective psychoses and the major agitated depressions. Finally, like molindone, the newest major tranquilizer, *loxadine,* also has been restricted to treating schizophrenia. In use only since 1976, loxadine appears to produce similar positive results without molindone's side effects of sedation and weight gain (Colasanti, 1982a).

The Antidepressant Drugs

When depression is the major symptom, rather than agitation, hallucinations, or social withdrawal, antidepressant chemical agents may be used. The antidepressant drugs can elevate the mood of severely depressed people. Like the antipsychotic drugs, the first effective antidepressants were introduced in the 1950s. The two main groups of antidepressant drugs, the *imipramine type* (tricyclics) and the *monoamine oxidase* (*MAO*) *inhibitors,* can have remarkable effects on the sadness and slowing associated with severe depression. Although their specific mechanism of action differs, both antidepressant groups *increase* the availability of the neurotransmitters norepinephrine and serotonin in certain areas of the brain (Colasanti, 1982b). A problem with the drugs, however, is that it can take a significant amount of time (sometimes up to 3 weeks) for them to affect depressive symptoms.

The *imipramine-type* or *tricyclic* antidepressants were first tried and used as antipsychotics (Cole & Davis, 1975). Quite by accident, it seems, when imipramine was given to tuberculosis patients to aid their breathing, the staff noticed a positive change in the mood of the hospital ward. The drug was then tried with depressed patients who showed a similar positive alteration in affect. Although at present there are several types of tricyclics in use, we will limit our discussion to imipramine, one of the most widely prescribed. In normal people, imipramine (Tofranil) typically produces only a slight sedative effect, but in severely depressed psychotics it can yield a reduction of depression within 10 days (Cole & Davis, 1975; Colasanti, 1982b). About 7 out of 10 patients given imipramine show significant mood elevation, compared with only 4 out of 10 treated with a placebo (sugar pill). Unfortunately, like most of the psychoactive drugs, imipramine can have several adverse side effects, such as dryness of the mouth, palpitations, dizziness, nausea, and constipation. The tricyclic antidepressants seem to work by inhibiting the reuptake of norepinephrine, thus increasing ease of neural transmission in the brain (Cole & Davis, 1975). However, this effect on norepinephrine levels may require up to 3 weeks before any improvement in mood is noted (Colasanti, 1982b). This delayed effect, in some instances of *severe* depression, may force a psychiatric decision to use electroconvulsive or shock therapy (see below) if the risk of suicide is great.

Increasing the availability of neurotransmitters in a different way from imipramine, *the monoamine oxidase (MAO) inhibitors* reduce the metabolism of the substances after they have been released into the synaptic space. For example, the inhibition of MAO which is involved in the breakdown of serotonin, results in the levels of serotonin not being depleted which yields a subsequent increase in the ease of neural transmission (Colasanti, 1982b). Like the tricyclics, the MAO inhibitors also require up to 3 weeks to achieve full effect and frequently produce side effects of dry mouth, fatigue, and delayed ejaculation or impotence in males. One additional note of caution: MAO inhibitors must not be taken at the same time as imipramine type drugs, for the combination can produce a sometimes fatal reaction (Colasanti, 1982b).

While the mixing of some drugs can be extremely dangerous, there are some combinations of medications which have highly beneficial effects. One of the most recent additions to the treatment of psychiatric symptoms, for example, is *combination drug therapy* in which a tricyclic antidepressant is administered simultaneously with an antianxiety drug. At first, these combinations were achieved through concurrent dosage of the different drugs, but due to the success observed in the treatment of severe depression accompanied by agitation and anxiety (such as in an extended grief reaction following the death of a loved one), several prepared combinations have been manufactured (see Table 4-3). However, along with the increase in positive effects observed with combination drug therapy, the number and variety of side effects also appear to be increased.

Antimanic Drugs: The Lithium Salts

Unlike the antidepressants, drugs to quiet manic moods have only become available relatively recently. The discovery of lithium as a treatment for mania was the result of yet another "accident" in psychochemotherapy. Its potential usefulness was first noted in 1949 by the Australian psychiatrist Cade, who reported that lithium markedly calmed excitable manic patients (Fieve, 1975). In the United States the drug was first used as a salt substitute for patients with heart trouble. However, because lithium's use wasn't controlled, abuses led to severe toxic reactions and death in some of these cardiac patients. As a result, lithium was withdrawn from use for 20 years. However, due to scientific testing and the work of Cade and others, in 1970 lithium was approved by the Food and Drug Administration for use in the specific treatment of and prevention of mania.

Lithium carbonate must be administered under careful medical supervision. Frequent blood tests are necessary so that the physician can monitor the levels of the substance in the body (Colasanti, 1982b). When administered and monitored appropriately, lithium therapy has resulted in marked reduction of manic symptoms within 5 to 10 days. The drug's primary action seems to be in its increasing the reuptake of norepinephrine and serotonin, thereby reducing the amount of neurotransmitters in the synaptic spaces at various sites in the brain (Colasanti, 1982b). Unlike the other psychoactive drugs, lithium seems to have relatively few side effects when used properly. Further, lithium carbonate can be used as a prophylactic medication, that is, to prevent future manic episodes.

The Minor Tranquilizers and Hypnotics

Unlike the "major" drugs we've discussed thus far, the minor tranquilizers and hypnotics usually are used not to treat symptoms of psychotic disorders but to alleviate mild tension and anxiety and the sleeplessness and irritability that may accompany such states. Among the most widely prescribed pharmaceuticals in the world, it has been reported that upwards of 80 to 98 *million* prescriptions per year are written for these drugs in the United States alone (Cole & Davis, 1975). Just about everyone has taken a minor tranquilizer at one time or another or knows someone who has. Not prescribed exclusively by psychiatrists, these drugs comprise the majority of the psychoactive drugs prescribed by other medical specialists (especially internists).

First used widely in 1954, the *propanediol carbamates* were among the first minor tranquilizers available. The most common of the propanediol carbamates are

Table 4-4 The Minor Tranquilizers and Hypnotics/Sedatives

Grouping	*Trade Name*
	The Minor Tranquilizers
Propanediol carbamate	Miltown, Equanil, Tybatran
Benzodiazepine compounds	Librium, Valium, Tranxene, Ativan, Serax, Centrax
	Other Minor Tranquilizers
Chlormezanone	Trancopal
Hydroxyzine	Vistaril, Atarax
	Hypnotics, Sedatives
Barbiturates	Amytal, Veronal, Butisol, Evipal, Mebaral, Nembutal Luminal, Seconal, Pentothal
Nonbarbituric acid–based drugs	Quaalude, Sopor, Optimal, Nodular, Doriden, Placidyl

meprobamate (*Miltown*) and *tybamate* (*Tybamate*) (see Table 4-4), both of which typically make people feel more relaxed, less anxious and tense, and slightly sleepy (Colasanti, 1982c). However, when these chemicals are taken in large doses over a long period of time and then stopped, a severe withdrawal syndrome—including convulsions, shaking, hallucinations, anxiety, and tremors—can result. While the neurophysiological action of the propanediol carbamates is not well understood, from their first introduction they have become one of the mainstays in biological treatment of mild anxiety.

More recently developed than the propanediol carbamates, the *benzodiazepine compounds* (see Table 4-4) also are effective in reducing mild to moderate anxiety, producing skeletal muscle relaxation, and combating alcoholism. Unlike the users of the propanediol carbamates, however, heavy users of these compounds can develop serious physical dependence (Pevnick et al., 1978; Colasanti, 1982c). Withdrawal in these cases can result in convulsions, depression, agitation, inability to sleep, and loss of appetite. Side effects of normal use of the benzodiazepines may be increase in appetite, skin rash, nausea, headache, impairment of sexual function, and lightheadedness. Valium and Librium, among the more commonly used benzodiazepine compounds, are included in many lists of the most frequently prescribed medications in the United States (Colasanti, 1982c).

The propanediol carbamates and the benzodiazepine compounds comprise the majority of minor tranquilizers in current use. However, two compounds chemically unrelated to either of these groups also have begun to enjoy some popularity. *Chlormezanone*, for example, is a drug used solely in the treatment of mild anxiety and is considered an excellent short-acting, minimal-duration tranquilizer. Similarly short-acting is *hydroxyzine* which has found special use in the reduction of preoperative anxiety in that it calms people, controls nausea and vomiting, and seems to contribute to a reduction in the amount of pain experienced in surgical patients (Colasanti, 1982c).

At times, the minor tranquilizers do not reduce tension sufficiently to allow sleep in stressed people. As a result, other classes of medications whose function it is to depress the central nervous system and induce sleep may be used. These sleep-inducing chemicals are, in general, termed the *hypnotics* or *sedatives.* They may be more specifically categorized into *barbituric acid derivatives* and *nonbarbituric acid derivatives* (see Table 4-4).

The barbituric acid–based drugs, more commonly known as the *barbiturates*, have been in use since 1903 and have been a source of both great medicinal benefit as well as significant nonmedical abuse. As a class of drugs, they have been implicated in a causative way in up to 5000 deaths per year (both homicide and suicide) (Craig, 1982). Their illegal use is included in the DSM-III classification system as a specific disorder. However, when properly used, the barbiturates can alleviate sleep difficulties that may be part of the array of symptoms associated with emotional problems such as depression, mania, schizophrenia, and anxiety disorders. Sedatives also can be used in the treatment of short-term, situational sleep disturbances such as those observed in patients prior to surgery.

In large measure due to the dangers associated with the misuse of the barbituric acid derivatives, a number of nonbarbituric acid–based hypnotics and sedatives have appeared over the past two decades. Among these are the benzodiazepines discussed above, but the nonbarbiturate sleep inducers also include *glutethimide* and *methaqualone* (see Table 4-4). However, in a clear case of the "cure being as bad as the disease," these more recently developed drugs, especially methaqualone (Quaalude), have become equally or more widely abused than their precursors (Craig, 1982).

Electroconvulsive Therapy (ECT)

Most mental health professionals would probably agree that drug therapy has had significant positive effects on the treatment of mental patients and there is widespread support for its use. Unfortunately, the same things cannot be said for *electroconvulsive therapy*. Within the mental health profession there continues to be controversy surrounding this biologically based treatment. Some practitioners, such as Breggin (1979), believe that ECT is a treatment which destroys the brain, while others such as Kalinowsky (1980) and Yudovsky (1982) hold that shock treatment can be a safe, effective mode of helping severely disturbed persons. Yudovsky (1982), for example, states, "Despite the proven benefit of antidepressant agents, comparative studies have shown ECT to be as effective or significantly more effective than drugs in the treatment of depression." (p. 392).

ECT owes its beginnings to a Hungarian physician, Von Meduna, who noticed that patients in his mental hospital often would lose their psychotic symptoms whenever they experienced a spontaneous convulsion such as that which occurs in epilepsy. He also knew from reviewing his case records that schizophrenia and epilepsy rarely occurred in the same person. Von Meduna began to experiment with various means to induce convulsions in mental patients who had not responded to other forms of treatment. He first experimented with intramuscular injection of camphor oil, but, although most patients experienced convulsions, many simply became physically sick. He then arrived at a synthetic camphor preparation, Metrazol, which produced a convulsion in a majority of patients within 30 seconds. Chemicals such as Metrazol, and later insulin, weren't widely used because they sometimes produced a variety of side effects, and even uncontrolled convulsions strong enough to cause death. To induce a convulsion more safely, Cerlitti and Bini (1938) developed electrically induced convulsions. These researchers named their technique *electroshock*, a term that is still widely used in referring to ECT.

In a typical form of ECT procedure, electrodes are attached to both temples and a current of 70 to 130 V is passed for anywhere from 0.1 to 0.5 second (Kalinowsky, 1980). One problem with early methods of electroshock was that the seizure produced by the current also resulted in rapid contraction of all skeletal muscles that sometimes caused broken bones and other injuries. To counteract this unwanted effect, in modern ECT a powerful muscle relaxant (e.g., curare) is administered prior to the shock. With the muscular system temporarily paralyzed in this way, only the central nervous system experiences the convulsion.

Supporters of modern ECT (Kalinowsky, 1980) state that the procedure causes surprisingly few complications and can be used safely even in some patients with heart disease. Kalinowsky reports that the fatality rate for 100,000 treatments over an 8-year period was 0.002. As an expert in the area of ECT, Kalinowsky believes that the procedure is safe and does not deserve the sinister reputation it still has in many professional and nonprofessional circles. However, others like Breggin (1979) warn that ECT simply "disables the brain" in order to make mental patients more tractable (less of a problem for caretakers). Breggin believes that, over time, electroshock treatments can lead to "complete neurological collapse."

Given the existing opposing views, it is hard to arrive at a sound conclusion regarding ECT. On the one hand, many patients with *severe* depressions have been helped immensely by it (Kalinowsky, 1980; Fink, 1979; Yudovsky, 1982). However, some patients have also reported rather disquieting experiences:

> Strapped to a stretcher, you are wheeled into the ECT room. The electroshock machine is in clear view. It is a solemn occasion; there is little talk. The nurse, the attendant, and the anesthetist go about their preparation methodically. Your psychiatrist enters. He seems quite matter-of-fact, businesslike—perhaps a bit rushed. "Everything is going to be just fine. I have given hundreds of these treatments. No one has ever died." You flinch inside. Why did he say that? But there is no time to dwell on it. They are ready. The electrodes are in place. The long clear plastic tube running from the bottle above ends with a needle in your vein. An injection is given. Suddenly—terrifyingly—you can no longer breathe; and then . . . You awaken in your hospital bed. There is a soreness in your legs and a bruise on your arm you can't explain. You are confused to find it so difficult to recover memories. Finally, you stop struggling in the realization that you have no memory for what has transpired.
>
> You were scheduled to have ECT, but something must have happened. Perhaps it was postponed. But the nurse keeps coming over to you and asking, "How are you feeling?" You think to yourself: "It must have been given"; but you can't remember. Confused and uncomfortable, you begin the dread return to the ECT room. You have forgotten, but something about it remains. You are frightened [Taylor, 1975].

Although Von Meduna first believed that convulsions would be helpful in the treatment of schizophrenia as well as depression, research has shown that ECT is most consistently effective in psychotic depression (Fink, 1979). Electroshock is known to be able to reduce some severe depressions after one to four treatments and, in cases of suicidal depression, may actually be preferred over the slower acting chemical antidepressants. While no one really knows for sure how ECT works, recent theories center on its effects upon the availability of neurotransmitters at the synapses in certain areas of the brain. Kety (1975), for example, has proposed that electroshock actually may increase the amounts of serotonin and norepinephrine in much the same way as the chemical antidepressants do. Regardless of why it actually works, ECT does in fact seem to help many people. When appropriately administered and monitored, it will no doubt continue to be a mainstay of psychiatric treatment.

Psychosurgery

Like ECT, the use of psychosurgery is also surrounded by controversy. In Ken Kesey's novel *One Flew Over the Cuckoo's Nest* (1962), an affable nonpsychotic criminal is placed in a mental hospital for observation. After a series of difficult experiences, he tries to kill the head nurse. The final result is that in order to control his violent behavior, an operation is performed in which certain important tracts in his brain are severed rendering him almost vegetable-like. His good friend kills him rather than let him live out his life with his personality so apparently deadened. The operation performed on Kesey's hero ostensibly was a *lobotomy* and is an example of treatment known as psychosurgery.

Psychosurgery is the term applied to a group of surgical treatments in which various parts of a patient's brain may be destroyed or made inoperative in an attempt to alter behavioral or emotional aberrations. Although there are numerous historical examples of accidental psychosurgery, it was not until 1888 that a Swiss

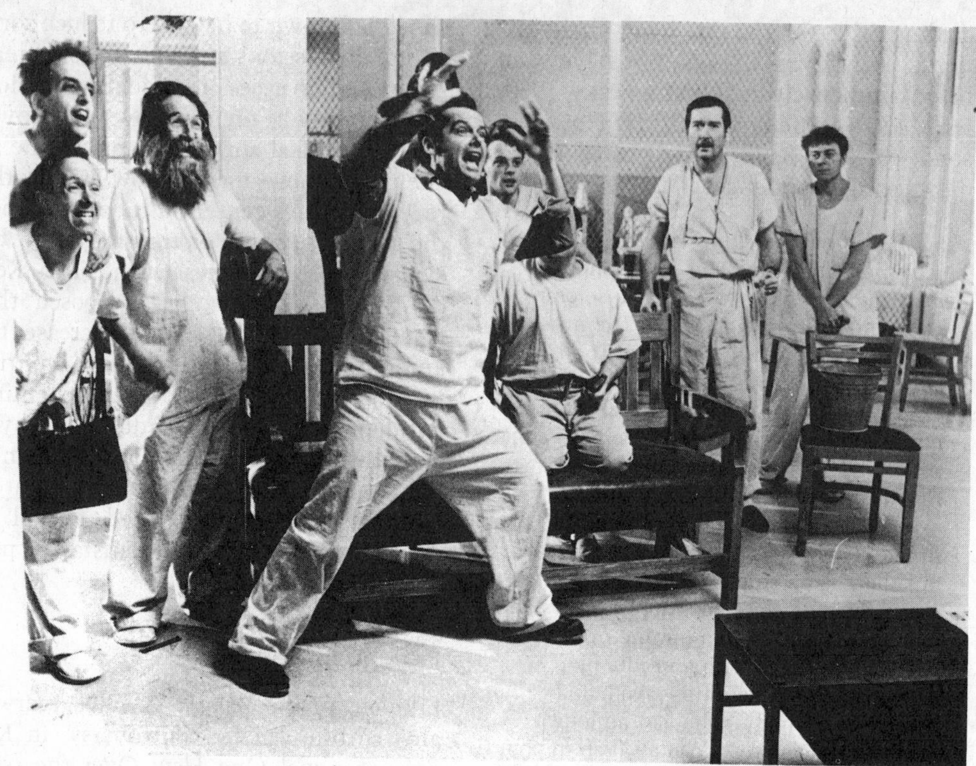

Jack Nicholson protrayed a likable, independent, gregarious, hospitalized mental patient who was changed to a sedentary, robot-like character after psychosurgery. (*The Museum of Modern Art/Film Stills Archive*)

psychiatrist, Burckhardt, reported on the purposeful destruction of part of the cerebral cortex of mental patients (Kalinowsky, 1975; Donnelly, 1980). However, Burckhardt's "discovery" soon was forgotten and it wasn't until 1936 that a Portugese physician, Moniz, proposed frontal lobe surgery as a possible treatment for schizophrenia. The operation, called a *bilateral prefrontal lobotomy,* involved surgically opening the skull and destroying various tissues connecting the frontal lobes with the rest of the brain. With time, the trend shifted toward smaller, less drastic operations, such as the *transorbital lobotomy* (Freeman & Watts, 1950). In such an operation, the central nerve tracts are severed by introducing an instrument through the eye sockets above the eye.

Unlike ECT, psychosurgery does not appear to be the treatment of choice for any particular disorder, but it has most often been used in cases of intractable psychoses. With the advent of the psychoactive drugs in the 1950s, the use of psychosurgery decreased drastically, but by then it is estimated that over 40,000 patients had been operated on (Kalinowsky, 1975). In response to such surgery, patients seemed to become insensitive to problems that previously had concerned them. For example, if a person had terribly frightening hallucinations before surgery, postsurgically she still might have the hallucinations, but might not be so frightened by them. However, after surgery some patients often required lengthy rehabilitation programs to overcome the debilitating effects of the "treatment." Psychosurgery rarely is performed today, except in cases which are deemed "completely intractable" and not amenable to *any* other mode of treatment.

When it is performed, modern psychosurgery differs significantly from its historic predecessors. Rather than drastically and inaccurately destroying brain areas, recently developed methods are much more circumscribed and selectively focus on certain brain locations, especially those in the limbic system (Valenstein, 1973; Donnelly, 1980). Such specific techniques of psychosurgery are certainly improvements over the lobotomies of the past. However, we are still left with the question as to whether a person can confidently agree to such an irreversible procedure when a future advance may make chemical or psychological treatment possible.

Biofeedback

Whereas ECT and psychosurgery are directed primarily at severe disturbances like the psychoses, *biofeedback techniques* are particularly useful in the treatment of anxiety disorders, psychophysiological

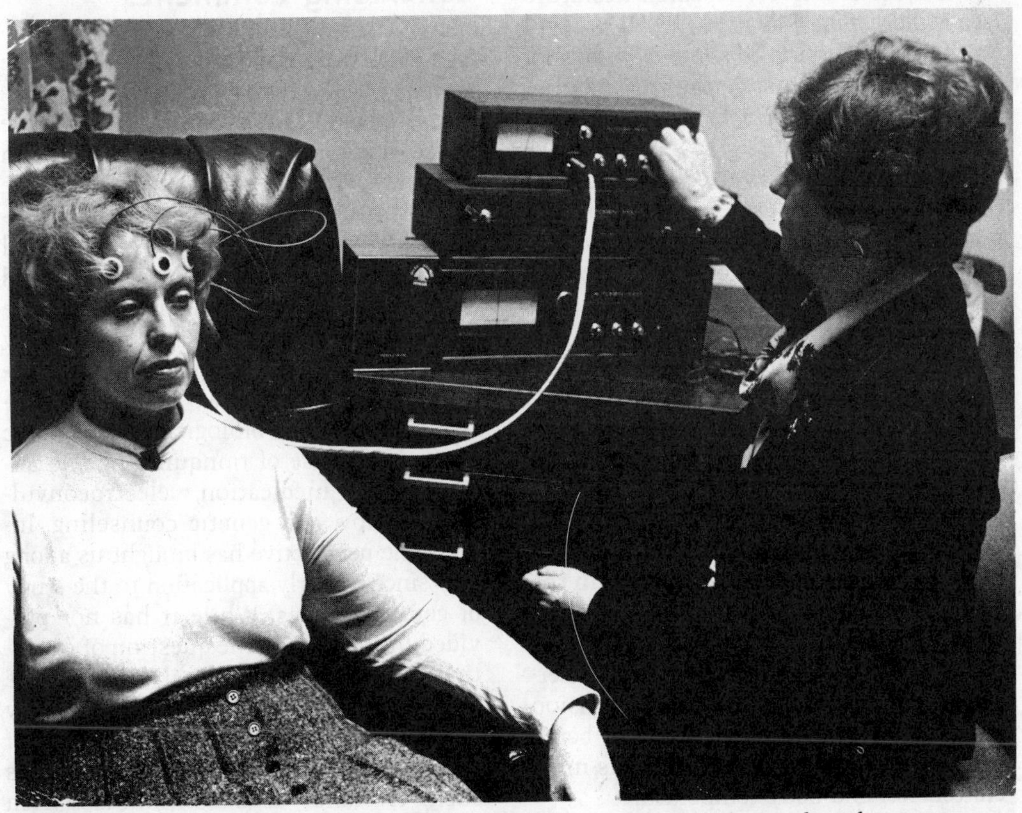

Most useful with stress-related disorders, biofeedback procedures help people to learn to control their somatic responses to events. (*Sybil Shelton/Monkmeyer Press Photo Service*)

disorders, and other patterns associated with stress. Biofeedback methods have been defined as "procedures in which an external sensor is used to provide a person with an indication of the state of a specific bodily process such as heart rate, blood pressure, skin temperature and the like" (Schwartz & Beatty, 1977, p. 1). In much the same way that watching (through an internal sensor, the eye) where our ball goes when shooting a basketball can help us to modify our muscular movement and improve our performance, the external sensors used in biofeedback help people to gain control over bodily functions once thought to be "involuntary." Although biofeedback has been applied to a variety of special problems such as epilepsy, stuttering, and asthma and is the subject of a lively research literature (see Miller, 1980; Ray et al., 1979), we will limit our discussion to some examples of its most common use in the treatment of anxiety and psychophysiological disorders.

Coursey (1975) has used feedback information about muscle tension to help patients with anxiety problems to relax. Connected to a device called an electromyograph (EMG), Coursey's subjects received continuous feedback about the amount of tension in their forehead muscles (frontalis). Coursey demonstrated that, with EMG feedback, subjects were able to reduce anxiety faster and better than with simple verbal relaxation instructions.

Just as the relaxation of the frontalis muscle of the forehead can be related to reduced tension, it can also be used in the biofeedback treatment of severe stress-related headaches. For example, Miller (1976) describes research in which 75 percent of patients with muscle tension headaches and migraine headaches benefitted from feedback about frontalis muscle tension and body temperature.

Other stress-related symptoms more serious than headaches, such as high blood pressure, cardiac arrhythmias, and asthma, can result in severe incapacity or premature death. Miller reports that biofeedback techniques have been used to teach control of blood pressure and cardiac rhythm. In fact, biofeedback treatment for cardiac arrhythmias has been called the "most convincing therapeutic application of biofeedback training to date" (Miller, 1976, p. 245). In the treatment of asthma, Rainwater and Alexander (1982) describe the use of feedback regarding body temperature to reduce significantly the symptoms of asthma in adults with life-threatening breathing difficulties which had not responded to other medical means of control.

Concluding Comments

At this point in the ongoing process of the science of abnormal psychology, the biological paradigm is clearly a perspective of major proportion. As we have seen in Chapter 4, this shared belief has led to the development of some effective and promising approaches to the study of abnormal behavior. The biological paradigm has led professionals to focus on increasingly more basic levels of analyses, even to the very chemical molecules responsible for communication between two individual neurons. From the biological view have emerged the use of tranquilizing and antipsychotic medication, electroconvulsive therapy, and genetic counseling. Indeed, the perspective has brought us a long way since its early application to the study of general paresis. While it has not provided *the* answer to the question of causation of all forms of mental disorder, the biological paradigm has been especially helpful in furthering our understanding of several types of abnormal behavior. As such, it stands as a continuously rich source of theory, research, and treatment in the science of abnormal psychology.

Summary Chart

In examining the application of the biological paradigm to the study of abnormal psychology, we began with some basic information regarding the biological bases for normal and abnormal behavior:

The neuron: Soma, axon, dendrite, action potential, synapse, chemical and electrical transmission, neurotransmitters

The central nervous sytem: Brain and spinal cord, lobes, cortex, limbic system, brainstem

The peripheral nervous system: Sensory system, motor system, and autonomic nervous system (sympathetic and parasympathetic systems)

The endocrine system: Hormones, pituitary, and other glands

The endorphins: Neuropeptides, recently discovered

Given a basic grounding in neurophysiology, we turned to several specific applications of the biological paradigm:

The search for genetic factors: Kallikaks, twin studies, adoption studies, concordance rates, heritability, diathesis-stress theory

The search for biochemical factors: Focus on neurotransmitters, problems with re-uptake, problems with metabolism

We then examined some applications of the biological paradigm to the treatment of abnormal behavior:

Genetics: Prevention, genetic counseling

Biochemical treatment: Tranquilizers, antidepressants, and other drugs

Electroconvulsive therapy

Psychosurgery

Biofeedback techniques

We closed Chapter 4 with recognition of the potential of the biological paradigm, but with a word of caution regarding too strict an adherence to it.

CHAPTER 5

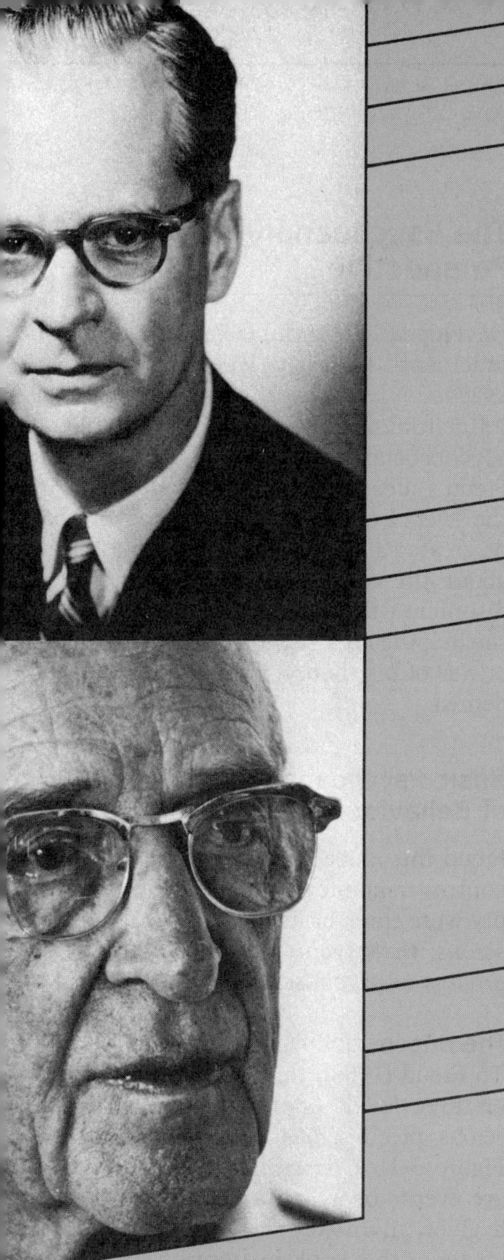

The Psychosocial Paradigm

Whereas the main focus of researchers guided by the biological paradigm is at the physical level, investigators adhering to the psychosocial perspective emphasize individual mental, emotional, and interpersonal functioning. As in the case of the biological paradigm and its multiple interpretations, there also are several models of behavior deriving from the psychosocial view. Although sharing the same basic belief that behavior is determined primarily through individual experiences, the differing models lead professional workers in varying directions. Of these directions, relatively few have attained substantial status over the years. These enduring models are the psychoanalytic, humanistic-existential, behavioral, and cognitive approaches to human behavior.

Founder of the psychoanalytic approach, Sigmund Freud had a tremendous impact on twentieth-century views of human beings. (*National Library of Medicine*)

The Psychoanalytic Perspective

Developed by Sigmund Freud in the late nineteenth and early twentieth centuries, *psychoanalytic theory* is among the most influential of all views deriving from the psychosocial paradigm. In many ways Freud's ideas represented a revolution in the science of abnormal psychology in that he created a language with which to think about the mind and brought emotional disorders within the realm of science and the helping arts. Although there are many critics of his theory, its impact cannot be denied.

Basic Psychoanalytic Concepts of Behavior

Freud introduced a number of novel and controversial ideas. At the core of his theory were three basic concepts: *the unconscious, the psychic triumvirate, and the process of psychosexual development.*

The Unconscious

To Freud (1953), thinking was composed of three levels of mental activity—conscious, preconscious, and unconscious (see Figure 5-1). *Conscious* mental activities are events of which a person is aware at a given moment. For example, you are aware of this book in front of you as you read it; perhaps you are conscious of a radio playing in the background. *Preconscious* thoughts differ from conscious mental activities in that they are ideas, feelings, or events which, though easily retrievable, are not in awareness at the given moment. Thus, if we ask you for your home address, you can state it immediately, even though you may not have been thinking about it before we asked you to do so. However, Freud's major contribution was his emphasis on the unconscious mind as the major determiner of behavior. The *unconscious mind* differs from the others in that it represents a collection of psychological events that are associated with early memories and both positive and negative intense emotions. For example, an early "long forgotten" experience of being left alone by parents may be stored in the unconscious. Rarely, if ever, will unconscious thoughts and feelings be allowed to surface at the preconscious or conscious levels, but nevertheless they are thought to be very important in the control of our behavior. For example, because Freud believed that the roots of mental disorder lay in the unconscious mind, he directed much therapeutic energy toward uncovering unconscious thoughts. He believed that these thoughts formed the basis of psychological symptomatology and represented an underlying psychological "disease."

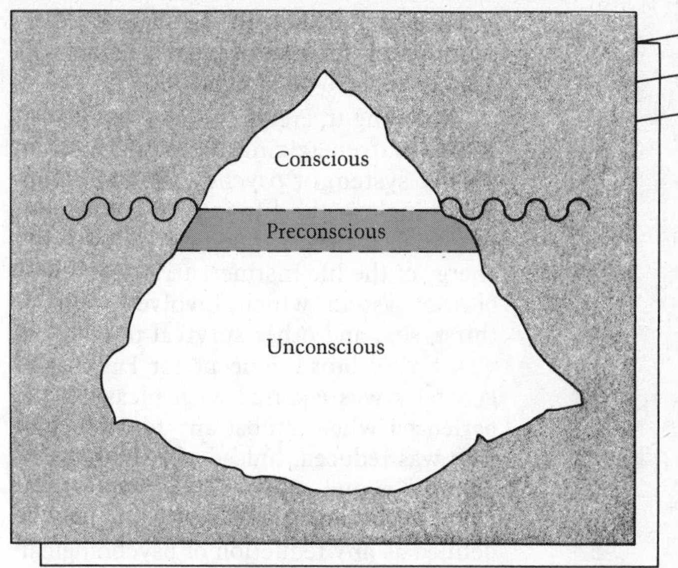

Figure 5-1 The iceberg model of the unconscious. Only a relatively small portion of one's psychological store is conscious; the vast majority, like the subsurface portion of an iceberg, is hidden from one's awareness.

The Psychic Triumvirate

While many of Freud's assumptions regarding the unconscious were gleaned from the work of earlier philosophers, it was probably his medical training that most influenced his belief that the normal personality must be understood before abnormality can be defined. In the normal "mind," Freud conceived a personality "triumvirate," or three-part governing body, composed of three major *processes* called id, ego, and superego.

The *id* may be thought of as a bubbling cauldron of inborn and instinctive needs, demands, and wishes such as hunger, thirst, and the need for comfort, security, and love. According to Freud, physiological and psychological imbalances (or needs) are uncomfortable for the id and produce tension in the psychic system. The organism moves to reduce this tension and return to a state of balance or quiescence called *homeostasis.* This drive toward tension reduction can account for much of human behavior. For example, tension

Freud believed that people's behavior was determined by unconscious motivations, thoughts, and desires. (©*Marion Bernstein*)

created by hunger will motivate the person to seek food and sexual tension will lead to social/sexual behavior.

According to Freud, the id process also gives rise to energizing forces that run the mental system or *psyche.* These psychic forces include the life instinct, *eros,* and the death instinct, *thanatos. Libido,* the energy of the life instinct, drives that part of the system which involves hunger, thirst, sex, and other survival needs. Sex was a very broad concept for Freud and generally was equated with pleasure experienced when almost any form of tension was reduced. Indeed, the id operates on what Freud called the *pleasure principle,* according to which pleasure may be defined as any reduction of psychological or physical tension. Freud developed the concept of thanatos later in his life and generally saw it as a process competing with the life force. Thanatos seemed to direct the psyche toward its own destruction, and hence ultimate quiescence and death.

Before the emergence of the superego, id impulses can cause many problems. (*Sybil Shelton/Monkmeyer Press Photo Service*)

Besides being the source of both life and death forces, the id is characterized by its own particular mode of thinking, called *primary-process thought.* Since the id cannot differentiate between what is real and what is imagined, just imagining a favorite food, for example, is the id's way of trying to satisfy the instinctual need of hunger. However, the individual would soon die if real food were not obtained. To aid in dealing with this "reality," therefore, the *ego* develops, energized by the id for its own tension reduction purposes.

Although the id can't differentiate reality from unreality, the ego can. The ego has the major task of satisfying id demands in light of reality. For example, the infant's budding ego "knows" that a loud cry will bring a parent to change a diaper or provide food. A problem solver and mediator between the id and reality, the ego usually operates on the *reality principle.* Further, ego-level thought is logical and reality-based and is termed *secondary process thinking.* While primary process thought is present at birth, secondary process typically does not appear until many months afterward.

While the id and ego are inevitable developmentally, the third member of the triumvirate, the *superego,* is not. It is formed through a process called *introjection* in which rules and regulations of parents and society are incorporated. A superego process is necessary because logical thought is not always "acceptable" thought. For example, a hungry child's ego may logically "see" food and go about reaching over and taking it. However, if that food happens to be on the plate of a younger sibling, the "logical" act of taking food when hungry will likely meet with stern parental reaction. It is between the ages of 2 and 5 that children typically are taught that certain behaviors, though logical, can be "wrong." Id needs usually cannot be met simply by considering reality; the psyche requires a process to "watch over" it to ensure that it does not violate familial, moral, and/or societal codes. The overseer is the superego which is composed of the *ego ideal* (a listing of "do's") and the *conscience* (a listing of "don'ts"). Failing to live up to the ego ideal can result in feelings of shame or lack of self-worth, while violating the precepts of the conscience can evoke feelings of guilt. Shame and guilt are uncomfortable emotional consequences that the superego may employ to "control" the choices of behavior made by the ego. According to Freud, rigidity or laxity of the superego may play a major role in the type of personality that evolves. For example, a rigid superego may produce a "frightened" person who feels guilty about "bad" thoughts or deeds. A lax or absent superego, on the other hand, might be evident in those who show little or no regard for social or moral codes and who have poor self-control.

With the development of the superego, all the components of the psychic triumvirate interact in the determination of behavior. Ideally, id needs are mediated by the ego in balance with the superego; input is obtained from each of these systems prior to any behavior being emitted.

Consider the plight of the ego, a sort of psychic traffic police officer charged with the responsibility of meeting the needs of the organism and keeping things flowing smoothly, emotionally and physically, without severe congestion or "traffic jams." Id demands and superego restrictions both must be dealt with. Reality contact must be upheld, and *most* needs fulfilled. In order to protect the individual's psychological organization, the ego evolves a set of *defense mechanisms* to help maintain its own stability. Defenses can help soften disappointments and aid a person in adjusting to everyday life stresses. As such, they may be considered a normal part of psychological functioning and development. However, when they are used to excess, they can be associated with abnormal behavior. The basic defenses outlined by Freud and some examples of ways in which they may manifest themselves are presented in Table 5-1.

Psychosexual Development

Freud's idea of the emergence of a tension reduction system was not his only developmental concept. He believed that the focus of "sexual" tensions also followed a specific sequence which he termed *psychosexual development.* He proposed a series of five stages of normal development through which people must pass on their way from birth to adulthood (See Figure 5-2 for a graphic representation of these stages). At each stage, libidinal instincts are gratified in a different way. Given proper conditions, development through the psychosexual stages progresses normally, but if conditions are not right, psychological difficulties may ensue. Freud believed that most adult psychological problems could be traced to some early (pre-age 6) problem in negotiating through a particular psychosexual stage. These problems would take the form of *fixations* in which some of a person's limited amount of libidinal energy would be left behind to deal with a developmental problem. Then, if other psychological problems occurred at a later stage of development, the fixated person was forced to deal with this new stress with a reduced amount of energy. While the presence of fixations can result in a generalized reduction in ability to cope, the site of a fixation was thought to be associated with specific personality characteristics.

The earliest psychosexual stage, the *oral phase,* is present at birth and is characterized by the focus of sexual gratification in the mouth area. *Oral dependence,* the first substage, is present during the time that the child is suckled and survives by receiving nourishment passively by the mouth. However, the mouth can give as

Table 5-1 The Ego Defense Mechanisms

1. Rationalization	Sour grapes: "I didn't want to win the game; games aren't important." Sweet lemons: "I really wanted a harder exam, because it challenged me and made me aware of my weaknesses."
2. Repression	Unconscious forgetting of painful or dangerous thoughts: "How can you remember something you never knew you forgot?"
3. Projection	Placing blame for one's problems on other people or on things: After a bad shot in a tennis match, a player looks at his or her partner or racquet.
4. Regression	Going back to an earlier developmental level with lesser requirements and lower levels of aspiration: acting like a baby under pressure.
5. Introjection	Incorporating values or characteristics of feared others so that threat from these others is reduced: POWs are often reported to act like their captors or to beat fellow prisoners in hopes that their guards won't hurt them.
6. Denial	Refusal to accept existence of a threat so that fear of it is never really felt or justified: "What are you doing about Rocky's challenge to fight you in the schoolyard?" "What challenge?"
7. Displacement	Discharging feelings on persons or things that are less threatening than the actual feared object or person: A man is angry at his boss, so he gestures at other drivers all the way home.
8. Intellectualization	Dealing with problems only with the intellect, cutting off all feeling components: "Actually I'm not deeply concerned about my current state of affairs; in a classic treatise, Plato once said that one could rise above such things."
9. Reaction formation	Avoiding dangerous thoughts by acting as if the exact opposite thoughts existed: A woman who has had a terrible time on a date says over and over what a wonderful time she had, to convince herself as well as others.

well as take and, with the appearance of teeth (at about 6 to 8 months of age), the child enters the *oral aggressive* stage. Now the infant can affect the environment orally—by biting the nipple. Freud theorized that people who were fixated at this level would be verbally aggressive, i.e., sarcastic and fond of making "biting" comments.

At approximately 1 year of age the focus of sexual gratification changes from the mouth to the anal area. Due to maturation and external pressures from parents to toilet train, the child enters the *anal phase.* The time at which toilet training actually begins depends on parent's beliefs and may range from sometime near the end of the first year of life up to 3 years or more. However, regardless of when the training actually starts, it is seen to represent a crucial step in personality development. Depending on several complex factors such as the temperament of the child, the birth order and the rigidity or laxity of the specific approach to training chosen by the parents, Freud believed that two different extreme personality types could result from fixations at the anal level. The *anal retentive* individual can be described as meticulous, compulsive, and overly controlled in contrast to the *anal expulsive,* who, typically, is very sloppy.

After the child is toilet trained, the focus of gratification shifts once again—to the genitals. The *phallic stage* occurs between the ages of 4 and 6 and is believed to play a major part in determining the child's sexual identity, thus laying the foundation for adult sexual behavior and procreation. This process differs for boys and girls.

At the onset of the phallic stage, a boy changes his sexual focus from anal activities to people around him as sexual objects. The energizing force of the id leads him to have sexual thoughts and desires about his mother. This *Oedipal phase,* however, soon creates a crisis because as the attraction to his mother intensifies, the boy's ego begins to fear that if his father finds out about his sexual motives he will cut off the boy's penis. This *castration anxiety* then becomes the primary motive for the development of a male sexual identity which is a result of the child's efforts to resolve his forbidden sexual feelings. As he grows older the normal male represses these feelings (see Table 5-1) and pushes even deeper into his unconscious the threatening mother-directed sexual thoughts. However, the repression may not be completely effective and to ensure further that these impulses will not be suspected by the father, the child carries out a special defensive maneuver called *identification with the aggressor.* He begins to behave as much like the father as possible. Through this process, he seeks to reduce his father's wrath by adopting his father's behaviors and attitudes.

Freud's theorizing about females in the phallic stage is more sketchy. He introduces the *Electra phase,* in which there is a shift from an initial attachment to the mother to a sexual love for the father, and then back again to identification with the mother's female role. Freud theorized that females feel cheated by not having a penis. The young girl supposedly blames her mother for the loss of her (the girl's) penis because she has observed that her mother "lost" her penis too. This *penis envy* leads to resentment toward the mother and a closer relationship with the father in hopes of regaining the lost penis. The Electra relationship results in the girl's beginning to fear that she will lose her mother's love. To avoid this loss of love, the young girl represses her penis envy and begins to identify with her mother. Freud saw loss of motherly love as much less drastic than loss of the penis in the Oedipal conflict. According to Freud, this difference is manifest in the fact that females typically are less strongly identified with their mothers than males are with their fathers.

Following the phallic period in which the sexual role identity has been established through repressed infantile sexuality, the child enters the *latency* stage, which lasts until the onset of puberty. Due to the extreme repression of sexual impulses in the phallic stage, boys and girls usually avoid playing with one another during latency. There may be marked animosity and mutual avoidance between the sexes.

Following the sexually dormant latency stage comes the sexually active *genital period.* Beginning at puberty and energized by physiological-hormonal changes, the repressed phallic stage sexuality resurfaces. However, the fear also reappears that if sexuality is directed at the opposite sexed parent, guilt or shame may result. To prevent these feelings, the ego usually implements the defense of *displacement,* in which the repressed sexual instincts are expressed, but are redirected toward more superego-acceptable *peers* of the opposite sex. If successful, displacement allows the child to complete his or her psychosexual development. The chain of life can then continue toward courting, marriage, and procreation.

Psychoanalytic Concepts of Psychopathology and Therapy

With the last stage of psychosexual development, there should be a smooth interaction among the id, ego, and superego; needs and wishes will generally be fulfilled directly or indirectly through defensive manipulations. However, when things go wrong inside the psychic system, abnormal behavior may develop. To Freud (1953), mental symptoms were considered "signs" that something was wrong with the workings of the psychic triumvirate.

For example, Freud believed that a severe disturbance in thoughts and perceptions marking a psychosis could be seen as an indication that unconscious impulses were so strong that the ego was overwhelmed and could not maintain its touch with reality. Thus severe emotional breakdowns typically were seen as a result of "weak ego" or "ego disintegration." In other words, the id impulses come to control the psychic system, and primary process thought replaces the rational thought of the secondary, or ego-level, process thinking. Under such pressure, people can no longer function at their present level of psychosexual development, but must regress to an earlier, simpler-to-handle stage. In this way, Freud explained many of the childlike symptoms of psychotic persons as reflecting a *regression* to infantile levels of thought and action.

In neurosis, a milder form of psychological disturbance, the ego does not disintegrate; rather, sets of rigid behaviors develop which are designed to protect the ego from continuing harm. In a sense, the defense mechanisms appear to be overused, so that threatening impulses usually are not even dealt with or consciously experienced. However, since the ego is tying up so much energy in controlling id impulses, there is less energy available for dealing effectively with new conflicts which might arise. Freud's conceptualization of psychopathology also leads to a psychoanalytic perspective on what must be done to return people to normal functioning. For Freud, the method of dealing with emotional problems was *psychoanalysis.*

In psychoanalysis, the patient (*analysand*) usually attends up to five sessions of 45 to 60 minutes each week. Initially the analyst and the analysand may speak face to face, but, after a period of time, the patient is usually asked to lie on a couch facing away from the therapist, who typically sits off to the side, out of the patient's vision. At this point, the fundamental rule of *free asssociation* is applied: The patient is asked to report, without censoring or inhibiting, all feelings, ideas, associations, and thoughts that come to mind. Classical psychoanalysis can take years. The analyst tries to provide the analysand with a blank screen onto which may be projected childhood memories, intrapsychic conflicts, and unconscious motives and emotions. The analyst listens intently and makes infrequent comments and interpretations, as seen in this excerpt from a psychoanalytic session:

Therapist: We can begin.

Patient: Last night I thought about not coming back today. I felt you were really bored with me and with what I was saying. You never seem to say anything to me, and I feel like sometimes I'm just wasting my time and money. (Pause) You see, I wait for an answer and I don't get one! I really get mad when you do that.

Therapist: Like when you were a child and you wanted your father to listen to you and take care of your troubles?

Patient: (Pause) Yes—sort of—that made me think of my father. I remember a time when we were at a lake for the summer. I was on the boat dock feeding bread to the fish and he came out and sat down beside me. He looked at me with such great love in his eyes. I feel like crying just thinking about it. He would do that when I didn't ask for it. But when I cried for help from him, he would say,

"Try to do it yourself." Why? Why?

Therapist: And I also ask you to do things yourself. And I don't even look at you with love in my eyes.

Patient: I feel alone—like a child. . . . You're right. I do wonder if you really care about me. Do you? (Pause) You won't answer me. So, DAMMIT, I get so angry with you, but I did at him, too. I miss him.

Upon entering a relationship with a psychoanalyst, the analysand often must agree to come on time, to pay the fees (even for excused absences), and to follow the analyst's guidelines for therapy. The analyst seeks to bring into awareness those intrapsychic conflicts held in the unconscious since childhood so they may be examined in the light of adult reality. To do this, the analyst focuses on *resistances* that the analysand shows to the agreed-upon rules of therapy. Examples of *direct resistances* might be refusal to pay, to talk, or to lie on the couch. *Indirect resistances* could include such things as unreasonable demands for social involvement with the therapist, excess emotionality during a session, and refusing to respond to interpretations.

The analyst interprets resistances to set the stage for the development of *insights.* Insights are new and healthier ways of looking at one's present life and feelings and represent the core of the analytic growth process (Fine, 1973; Meissner, 1980). For example, a particularly hostile person may find that the reason he hates work so much is that he unconsciously perceives his boss as being like his father whom he also feared and hated. Frequently, there will be misperception of the therapist, as well. In the process called *transference,* the patient may project thoughts and feelings about important others from the past onto the analyst. Analysts encourage the development of the process of misperception until a *transference neurosis* develops. The therapist then makes efforts to resolve this transference by instituting ego-based reality testing in the patient.

Derived from classical psychoanalysis is *analytical psychotherapy.* Analytical therapy is based on the broad tenets of psychoanalytic theory, but it does not adhere to the strict format of psychoanalysis. Due to the evolution of Freud's thinking in the minds of some of his major disciples, analytical therapies typically contain a major focus different from Freud's sexual emphasis. For example, although a disciple of Freud, Jung felt that there were other ways in which a person could become aware of his or her unconscious mind. These ways included face-to-face interactions focusing frequently on the symbolic communication of meaning in *dreams* and *fantasies* (Jung, 1964; Kaplan & Sadock, 1981).

In dream analysis, the therapist attempts to understand the dream as a metaphorical play or drama. The three parts of the dream are the *exposition,* the *crisis,* and the *solution.* In the exposition, the mood of the dream is established and the conflicts identified; in the crisis, the conflicts become salient and are faced; in the solution, either something is done about the crisis or the person awakes suddenly. By interpreting dreams, the analytical therapist directs the patient toward greater psychological health by establishing better contact between conscious and unconscious functioning.

The neo-Freudians accept many of the assumptions of psychoanalysis, but their theoretical differences led them to develop alternative explanations for human behavior. *Neoanalysts* such as Adler and Horney, for example, generally moved away from Freud's emphasis on sex as a motivator of behavior. Later the *ego-analysts* moved even further away from the intrapersonal emphasis and considered social factors to be of increasing importance to development, adjustment, and treatment. They emphasized the ego as a separate developmental entity that affected the personality. While Freud believed that the ego was subservient to the id, the ego-analysts assumed that the ego was autonomous and free to grow and change throughout people's lives (see Kaplan & Sadock, 1981). Like Freud before him, ego-analyst Erik Erikson proposed a normal sequence of personality development, deviations from which may be seen as sources of maladjustment (Kaplan & Sadock, 1981). In his book *Childhood and Society* (1963), Erikson presents eight *psychosocial stages* of development, each of which includes a *basic developmental conflict* that must be successfully resolved if the individual is to move through to more advanced stages and remain normally adjusted. Table 5-2 presents Erikson's stages and their associated goals and conflicts. Among the most important stages is that of puberty and adolescence in which the *identity crisis* (Who am I? Why do I exist?) occurs and a person moves closer to psychological and social well-being. Erikson's conflicts do not simply come and go, but are always present; certain ones emerge as more salient at different times of life. However, resolution of salient conflicts earlier in life can affect those conflicts which emerge later. For example, failure to resolve the identity crisis conflict can be a source of maladaptive behavior and may prevent an individual from successfully meeting the demands of later stages. People who are not quite sure of their identity, for example, may not be able to establish intimate long-term relationships, may eventually stagnate and cease to grow emotionally, and/or might experience despair and hopelessness later in life. On the other hand, those who emerge successfully from the adolescent ego-identity stage feel unified and can enter into deeper relationships with others.

According to Erikson, one of the basic goals of adolescence is to discover who one is. (©*Eric Kroll 1984/Taurus Photos*)

Table 5-2 Erikson's Psychosocial Stages of Development and Their Associated Nuclear Conflicts

Psychosocial Stage	*Conflict*
1. Oral-sensory	Basic trust versus mistrust
2. Muscular-anal	Autonomy versus shame and doubt
3. Locomotor-genital	Initiative versus guilt
4. Latency	Industry versus inferiority
5. Puberty and adolescence	Identity versus role confusion
6. Young adulthood	Intimacy versus isolation
7. Adulthood	Generativity versus stagnation
8. Maturity	Ego integrity versus despair

Source: Based on Erikson, 1963.

A stage theorist like Erikson, Harry Stack Sullivan's emphasis on development differed from his colleagues' in its focus on *interpersonal relationships* as the most important factor in normal and abnormal behavior. Sullivan (1953) proposed six stages of development, each representing increasing degrees of awareness of self and others and of personal integration into society. Unlike the psychosexual developmental stages, indices of successful completion of Sullivan's stages are more easily observable in that they are *interpersonal and behavioral* rather than intrapsychic and instinctual (Levy, 1970; Mullahy, 1980). Although their theoretical stages of development differ, Sullivan seemed to agree with Freud that anxiety is the core of maladjustment. But rather than the integrity of the ego, Sullivan saw the security of the *self* as all-important and in need of being maintained at all costs. To protect the self, Sullivan postulated, people develop *security operations* (similar to the defense mechanisms) which aid in avoiding interpersonal experiences leading to anxiety and threat to the self. Adjustment problems develop when security operations are imperfect and anxiety is not avoided, or when rigid dependence on unsuccessful security operations occurs. In psychosis, people's reality-oriented functioning is so severely repressed that for the most part they are no longer in contact with the outside interpersonal world. Thus, disordered behavior is usually brought about by some form of interpersonal frustrations or conflicts with which the individual has not been able to cope.

Sullivan's emphasis on interpersonal relationships has continued in the form of *interactional/interpersonal theory,* a modern school of conceptual and therapeutic thought. As characterized in the works of Leary (1957), Carson (1969), McLemore and Benjamin (1979), and Anchin and Kiesler (1982), the primary source of emotional and behavioral difficulties lies in interpersonal relationships.

The Humanistic-Existential Perspective

Similar to the neo-Freudian emphasis on interpersonal aspects of human functioning, the humanistic-existentialist interpretations of the psychosocial paradigm may be characterized by their focus on inborn goodness and innate drives toward self-actualization. The approaches may be exemplified by the ideas of Carl Rogers, Abraham Maslow, Fritz Perls, and Irvin Yalom and the therapies deriving from their points of view.

Rogers and Maslow and Self-actualization

In addition to the primary humanistic concept of people as basically good, Rogers and Maslow considered the most important part of the psychological structure to be an *actualizing tendency* acting as an initiator and motivator of behavior (Rogers, 1980). The actualizing tendency may be thought of as a driving force that directs a person toward maintaining or enhancing the self. Hence, the primary motivation of each person is not merely to survive but to grow, to develop his or her full potential, and to experience *pleasurable tension.* For Rogers, behavior seems to serve the purpose of achieving or maintaining actualization.

Normal behavior usually involves a certain sequence of events, beginning with the innate drives of actualization and con-

In Maslow's view, once basic needs are met, people will move beyond themselves to care for others. (*Michael Weisbrot and Family*)

cluding with the conscious evaluation of one's actions. In general, a person avoids negatively valued experiences and pursues those that are positively valued. If experiences result in enhancement or maintenance of the self, they are repeated; if not, they tend to disappear from the behavioral repertoire. For example, a person who experiences success and pleasure on dates is likely to continue dating; one who has difficulties may seek other social outlets. Behavior disorder is thought to occur if and when self-evaluations become distorted by inappropriate learning. In the healthy individual, learned self-evaluations and the evaluations received from others (especially parents) are in agreement. A child who receives *unconditional positive regard* from the family does not have to fight an uphill battle for acceptance and can move toward self-actualization unhampered.

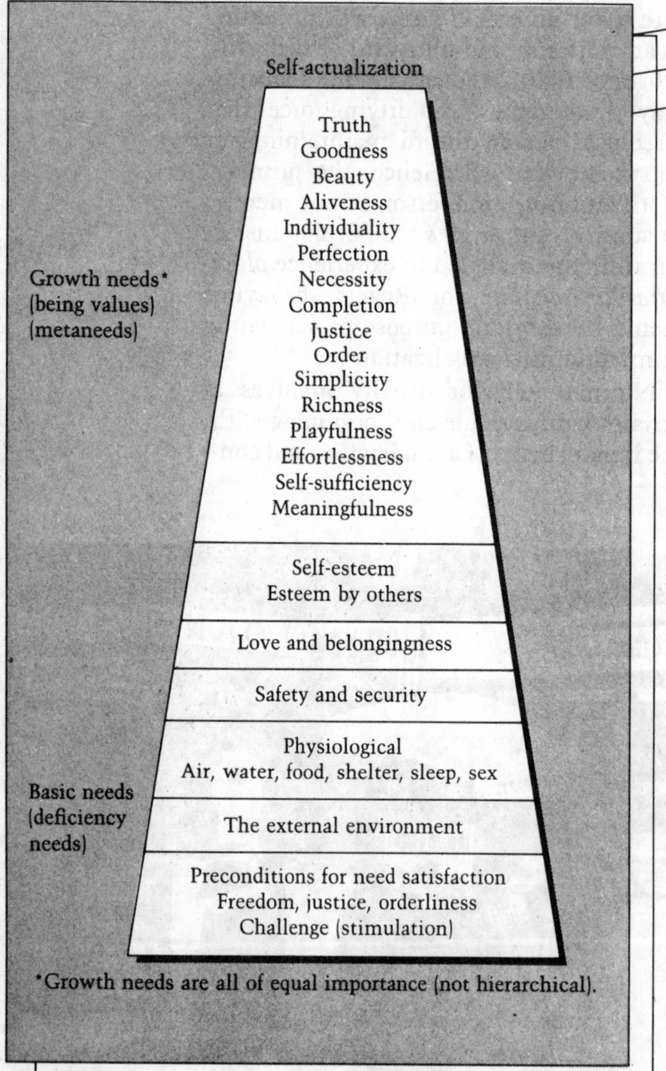

Figure 5-2 Maslow's hierarchy of human needs. (*Based on Motivation and Personality, 2nd ed., by A. H. Maslow. Copyright ©1970 by Abraham H. Maslow. Reprinted by permission of Harper & Row, Publishers, Inc.*)

Anxiety may occur when a person becomes aware of behavior that contradicts usual self-evaluations; this anxiety can be handled with one of two defenses. A person may stop experiencing anxiety either by *denial to awareness* of the anxiety-producing event (such as not paying attention to a threat) or by *distortion in awareness* (seeing a verbal threat as a friendly piece of advice). Neurotic and psychotic symptoms, respectively, can be understood as one of these two basic faulty habit patterns.

Similar to Rogers in his humanistic emphasis on inherent goodness and potential for growth and actualization, Maslow has described hierarchies of human needs and their particular effects on behavior (Maslow, 1968, 1971). As depicted in Figure 5-2, Maslow theorized that unless basic needs were met, higher ones could not be satisfied. While all people are inherently motivated to reach the self-actualized state at the top of the hierarchy, some may stop for fear of losing what they have or may have their strivings blocked by external forces beyond their control. Those who cannot continue up the hierarchy can experience deep feelings of nonfulfillment, move toward feelings of nonbeing, or experience and manifest disordered behavior.

Unlike classical Freudians who assume that people are driven by negative instincts and desires that need to be controlled, the humanists generally believe that people are basically good and if freed of the internal and external limits which they have learned, they can move toward their own actualized states. For the humanistic therapist, then, treatment typically involves the construction of situations and relationships in which innate positive growth potentials can be released. An example of such a therapeutic approach is *client-centered therapy* developed by Rogers (1942, 1980). Rogers devised client-centered therapy procedures to undo faulty self-evaluations and their deleterious effects on people's self-actualizing tendencies. The critical mechanisms of change are the therapy relationship itself and the special atmosphere produced by the therapist. The therapist must be warm and responsive and produce a receptive climate through empathy, congruence, and unconditional positive regard. By *empathy* Rogers means the ability of the therapist to understand the world as the client sees it. *Congruence* describes the high level of therapist genuineness; that is, rather than planning the next statement or topic, the therapist responds primarily only to the moment-to-moment *feelings* of the client. By *unconditional positive regard,* Rogers means the therapist's complete, total, nonjudgmental acceptance of the client and all of his or her thoughts and feelings (Rogers, 1980). In such a therapeutic atmosphere, clients are faced with a therapist who won't guide them in any way but who will make every effort to reflect accurately the feelings of the client in an absolutely accepting manner. Several of these qualities of nondirective or client-centered therapy may be seen in the following excerpt:

Client: I really feel bad today . . . just terrible.

Therapist: You're feeling *really* bad.

Client: Yeah, I'm angry and that's made me feel bad, especially when I can't do anything about it. I just have to live with it and shut up.

Therapist: You're very angry and it just seems like there's nothing you can safely do with those feelings of yours.

Client: Uh-huh . . . I mean if I scream at my wife she gets hurt. If I don't say anything to her I feel tense.

Therapist: You're between a rock and a hard place—no matter what you do, you'll wind up suffering.

Client: I mean she chews ice all day and all night. I feel stupid saying this. I know its petty. But when I sit there and try to concentrate all I hear are these slurping and crunching noises. I try not to say anything and then finally I blow up and she gets hurt.

Therapist: So you finally say something, but I guess it still doesn't solve anything and you feel even worse.

Perls, Yalom, and the Humanistic-Existentialists

Differing from Rogers and Maslow in their greater emphasis on conscious choice and awareness, the humanistic-existentialists believe that behavior is determined primarily by the manner in which people exercise their free will in perceiving and responding to life events. People are viewed as logical, feeling beings whose fate is not under the control of base forces inside or outside of them but, rather, is rationally directed. Although a number of existential theories of maladjustment and therapy exist (Binswanger, 1963; Boss, 1963; Kierkegaard, 1946; May, 1967, for example), we have chosen to describe more fully two of the currently most influential views—the Gestalt therapy of Perls and the existential approach of Yalom.

As described by Perls, *Gestalt therapy* is among the most widely used and accepted of the humanistic-existential approaches (Kaplan & Sadock, 1985; Perls, 1969a, b; Perls et al., 1958). For the Gestalt therapist, unhappy people aren't totally aware of all the elements of their here-and-now experiences. The client is responding not to the total configuration (or Gestalt) of life experiences, but rather to a limited and often distorted portion of it. Awareness may be divided into two types. *Intelligent awareness* is an experience of oneself at an intellectual here-and-now level, such that we "know" why we hurt if a flame burns our finger or we stub our toe. *Psychophysical awareness* is more subtle and often is ignored; for example, it may involve suddenly noticing that one's forehead is tense and wrinkled. Awareness is a complex phenomenon:

> We are not a happening; we are happening. At the moment we are aware and can describe what we are, we are not that at all. We are in transit, a point on a continuum, and awareness is at best capable only of immediate hindsight. To describe with awareness and seeming clarity what we are is at best a description of what we just were. What we are is describing. The experience of awareness is not precisely the same as the experience itself. Experience has no awareness. It is followed by awareness. (Kempler, 1973, p. 259)

The goal of the Gestalt therapist is to help people to coordinate intelligent awareness with psychophysical awareness so that their entire experience is congruent. Saying that you are happy, yet acting as if you are miserable, is incongruent; an awareness of your "body language" can help you to experience yourself as you really are. The Gestalt therapist works toward awareness and acceptance of psychophysical experience. Intelligent awareness can be faked and consciously controlled for social or other reasons; the same isn't true of psychophysical expression. The manner in which total awareness can be reached and genuine self-experiencing and interpersonal communication reestablished is demonstrated in the following Gestalt therapy transcript:

Client: You know, I wanted to talk today about my mother. She always was a problem for me as long as I remember. She used to. . . .

Therapist: Tell me how you feel about your mother *now*.

Client: Now? I haven't seen her in a week so I'm not too angry. When I was with her, though. . . .

Therapist: Right now, at this moment how do you feel about her?

Client: I guess I'm not too angry with her right now. When I think of some of our arguments I get a little angry.

Therapist: You say you are not angry, yet look at your hands; they're clenched into fists.

Client: So?

Therapist: Open them up. How do they feel?

Client: I feel like I want to close them again—they don't feel comfortable being open.

Therapist: Maybe acting as if you aren't angry doesn't make the anger go away. Just opening your fists doesn't make them not tense.

Client: You mean I *am* angry at her, even now?

Therapist: Your body seems to be telling us that.

The work of Perls and his followers had immense impact on therapeutic thought during the 1960s and 1970s. However, a recent spokesperson for the humanistic-existential position is Yalom (1980). In his effort to identify clearly the most basic tenets of the modern existential position, Yalom has written:

> [Modern existentialism] emphasizes a different kind of basic conflict: neither a conflict with suppressed instinctual strivings nor one with internalized

> significant adults, but *instead a conflict that flows from the individual's confrontation with the givens of existence.* And I mean by "givens" of existence certain ultimate concerns, certain intrinsic properties that are a part, and an inescapable part, of the human being's existence in the world. (1980, p. 8)

The inescapable "givens" with which we are all faced are *death, freedom, isolation, and meaninglessness.* Each of these is responsible for a *core existential conflict.* For death, the conflict is between the awareness of inevitable mortality and the wish to continue on forever. Freedom must be confronted due to a conflict between our total responsibility for ourselves and our wish to be taken care of by others. When facing isolation, we must resolve the tension between our own absolute aloneness and our wish to be part of someone or something else. The final conflict, surrounding meaninglessness, resides in our desire to find some meaning in what may in fact be a world devoid of true sense and reason.

Yalom contends that being unable to face or resolve these conflicts results in severe anxiety and that this "existential anxiety" is at the heart of psychopathology. In turn, dealing with these conflicts in a healthy and realistic manner constitutes a major aspect of existential therapy. An example of such therapy can be seen in the following transcript (Yalom, 1980, p. 237) of a person facing the core conflict dealing with freedom and responsibility:

Therapist: Ruth, you do here what you do outside the group. You wait for something to happen. How can the group possibly be useful to you if you don't use the group?

Ruth: I don't know what to do. I come here every week and nothing happens. I get nothing out of therapy.

Therapist: Of course you get nothing out of it. How can something happen until you make it happen?

Ruth: I feel "blanked out" now. I can't think of what to say.

Therapist: It seems important for you never to know what to say or do.

Ruth: (crying) Tell me what you want me to do. I don't want to be like this all my life. I went camping this weekend—all the other campers were in seventh heaven, everything was in bloom, and I spent the whole time in complete misery.

Therapist: You want me to tell you what to do even though you have a good idea of how you can work better in the group.

Ruth: If I knew, I'd do it.

Therapist: On the contrary! It seems very frightening for you to do what you can do for yourself.

The Behavioral Perspective

The behavioral interpretation of the psychosocial paradigm reflects a belief that rather than being motivated by internal or instinctual forces or being consciously or freely chosen, behavior is learned and maintained by events and forces *outside* individuals. Behavioral theorists usually conceive of abnormal behavior as being acquired by and maintained by the same rules that govern all behavior. Thus psychopathology may be viewed as faulty learning, or nonlearning, of appropriate actions or thoughts.

Basic Concepts in the Behavioral Perspective

Since learning processes are seen as being at the core of behavior problems, an understanding of some of the normally occurring rules and phenomena of learning seems to be a logical requirement. The most basic forms of learning are classical conditioning and operant conditioning.

Classical Conditioning

First investigated systematically by the Russian physiologist, Ivan Pavlov (1927), classical conditioning is considered by many psychologists to be the most basic form of learning. As diagrammed in Figure 5-3, the procedure originally involved placing in a restraining apparatus a dog in which Pavlov had implanted a salivary fistula (a tube extending from a salivary gland out through the animal's cheek and emptying into a measuring device). When some food powder was placed into the animal's mouth, the dog responded by salivating, and the amount of saliva flowing out through the tube was measured. The food powder was termed the *unconditioned stimulus*, or UCS, for without any training whatsoever, it caused a salivation response called the *unconditioned response*, or UCR. Pavlov then associated the UCS with a previously neutral stimulus such as the ringing of a bell. Time after time the bell was sounded just before the food powder was presented. After many trials, Pavlov found that when the bell was sounded *alone*—without the food powder—the animal salivated. The previously neutral stimulus was now a *conditioned stimulus* (CS) and resulted in a *conditioned response* (CR). Thus, in this most simple form of learning, a once neutral event like the sound of a bell becomes able to produce salivation.

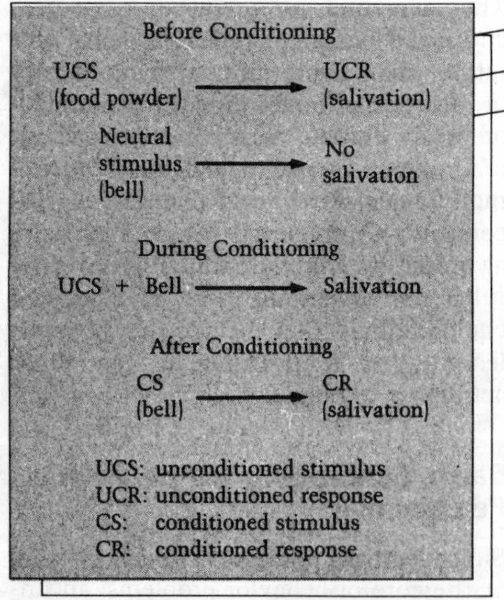

Figure 5-3 Process of classical conditioning.

Classical conditioning in humans may be demonstrated by an example. Suppose a piece of sour pickle were placed in your mouth. You would no doubt salivate heavily. Were a buzzer to be sounded just prior to each of several pickle placements, after a short time you would salivate at the sound of the buzzer alone. In this example, the pickle in the mouth is the UCS; the once neutral buzzer, the CS; the salivation response to the pickle, the UCR; and the *learned* salivation in response to the buzzer, the CR.

To understand fully the way in which classical conditioning can be used to help explain human behavior, it is necessary to understand several aspects of this form of basic learning. The sequential development of a classically conditioned response and the procedure for varying the strength of such a response are depicted in Figure 5-4. In the first phase of the sequence, called *acquisition,* the association is built between the CS and the UCS. Usually, the more repetitions (trials) of the pairing of CS and UCS and the stronger the UCS, per se, the stronger the acquired association. A second phase is *extinction,* where the CS is presented repeatedly *without* the UCS. Soon the CS no longer elicits the CR, and the conditioned response is extinguished. A last phase, *spontaneous recovery,* represents an increase in the strength of the CR after extinction is complete and a period of time has passed. Thus, in our pickle example,

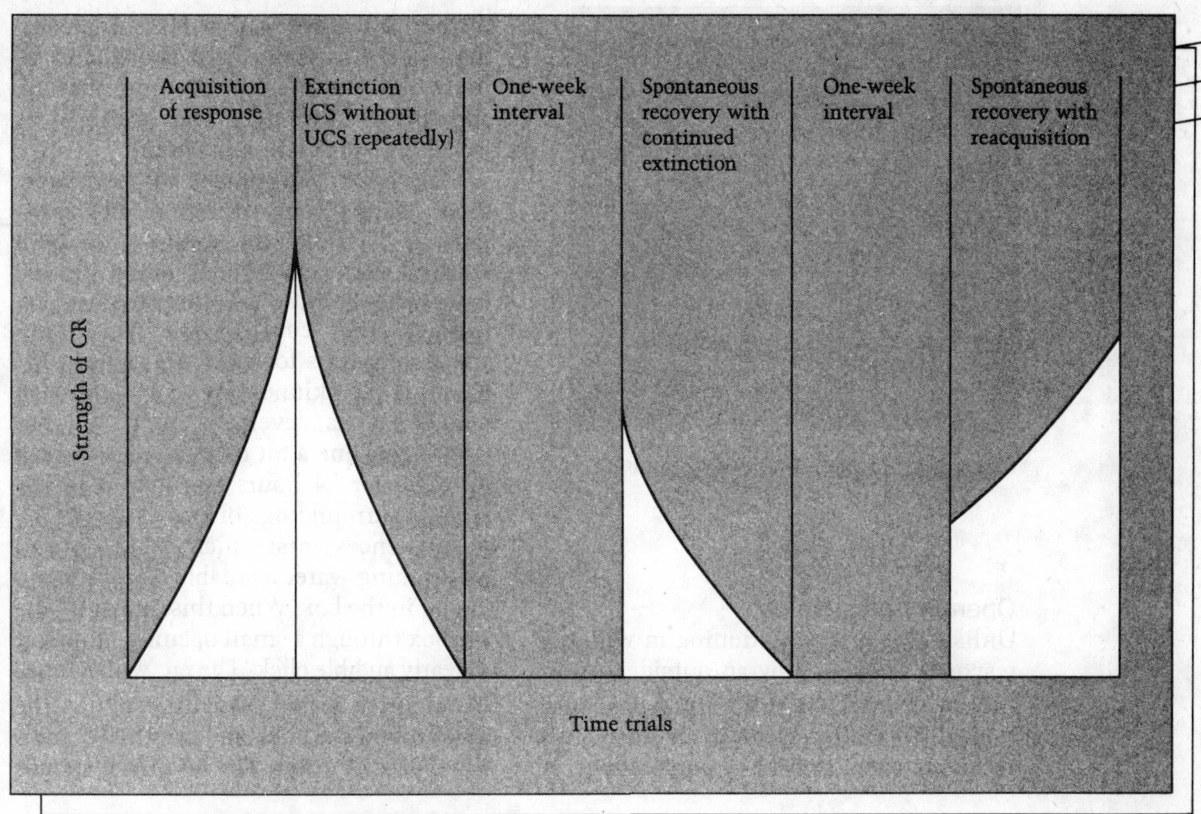

Figure 5-4 Phases of classical conditioning.

if you had stopped salivating to the CS (buzzer) following a series of extinction trials, were we to bring you back to our "experiment" after a week and sound the buzzer again, you would salivate once more. However, without the re-presentation of the UCS (pickle), extinction would recur, this time more rapidly.

In a demonstration of another classical conditioning phenomenon termed *higher-order conditioning,* Pavlov showed that another neutral stimulus such as a light could also be added to the system via pairing with the original CS (e.g., the bell; see Figure 5-5). Without ever having been associated with the original UCS (food powder), the light then could produce salivation responses on its own. To complicate matters further, CRs occurred not only to original CSs but to *similar* stimuli such as bells of different tones! This phenomenon is called *stimulus generalization* and is a very important concept in the behavioral analysis of several forms of psychopathology such as phobias and schizophrenia. Figure 5-6 provides an example of stimulus generalization.

A final important phenomenon, *stimulus discrimination,* is essentially the opposite of generalization. In stimulus discrimination, Pavlov's dogs learned to overcome the effects of generalization and to respond only to specific stimuli. An example of discrimination in humans would be learning that red lights mean stop and green lights mean go.

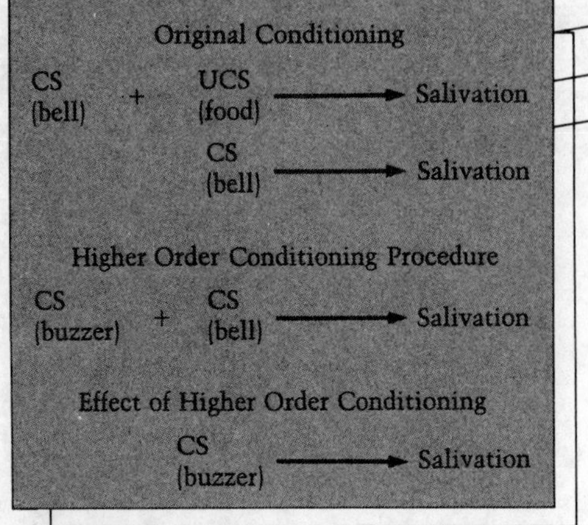

Figure 5-5 Higher-order conditioning.

Operant Conditioning

Unlike classical conditioning in which a response is elicited by an outside stimulus, in *operant conditioning* a response typically is *emitted* prior to an organism's receiving some reward or punishment. A further difference is that classical learning has traditionally been thought to be limited to the involuntary musculature, and operant learning is seen primarily as involving voluntary movement.

The basic phenomena of reinforcement, acquisition, extinction, and spontaneous recovery are common to both classical and operant conditioning, but the basic methodologies whereby responses are learned differ considerably. The traditional apparatus for studying operant behavior is the Skinner box (see Figure 5-7), named for its developer, B. F. Skinner (1938). Imagine a rat or a pigeon deprived of water for 24 hours and placed in the strange surroundings of the Skinner box. It experiences thirst which can be satiated by drinking water available from a water dipper in the box. When this dipper enters the box through a small opening, it makes a clearly audible click. The rat, which tends to orient to sound, usually explores the area around the click and eventually finds the source of water. The rat now responds

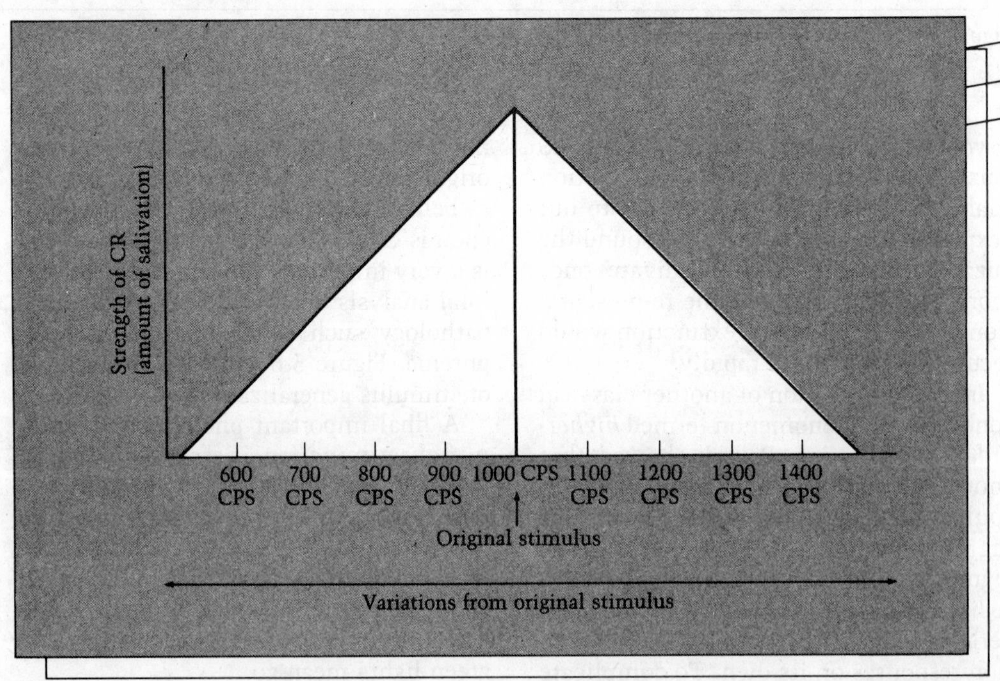

Figure 5-6 Stimulus generalization of a conditioned response of salivation to a 1000 CPS tone.

as if it "knows" where the water is in the box in that it seems to spend much of its time in that area. The experimenter now can begin a *shaping* procedure in which movements toward the goal (the experimenter's goal, that is) of pressing a metal bar for water are *selectively reinforced* by the appearance of water and the sounding of the click. In this method, called *successive approximation,* the rat at first need only face the bar to receive water; later it may have to touch the bar, then press it to obtain water. We should note here that this operant training contains a classical-conditioning component, because each time the click is sounded it is associated with water. The click becomes a CS, and after initial training it can be used to reinforce future learning. Through its association with water, a *primary reinforcer,* the click becomes a *secondary reinforcer.*

Once the bar press response is acquired, the experimenter can continue to alter the rat's behavior by manipulating various factors such as the amount of water given, the time the animal goes without water, and, most important for students of abnormal psychology due to their involvement in the maintenance of behavior patterns, the *schedules of reinforcement.* Until now we have been discussing a *continuous,* or 100 percent, schedule of reinforcement, that is, every response was reinforced with water. However, although continuous reinforcement is usually required for successful classical conditioning, it is neither necessary nor optimal in operant learning.

As an alternative to continuous reinforcement, partial or *intermittent reinforcement* was originally used by Skinner because he was tired of using up his rewards of handmade food pellets so quickly (Skinner, 1959) and decided to administer the reinforcers every few responses rather than after each response. Serendipitously he discovered the *partial reinforcement effect:* Strength and resistance to extinction of acquired

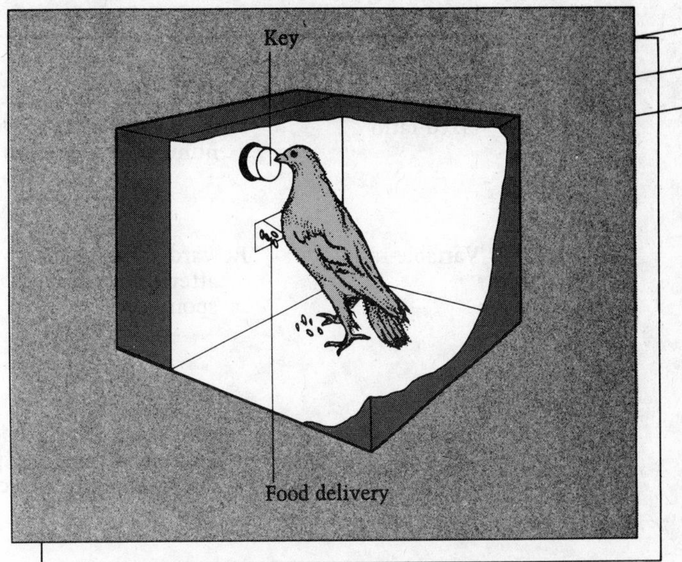

Figure 5-7 An operant conditioning situation used to investigate the effects of different schedules of partial reinforcement on behavior.

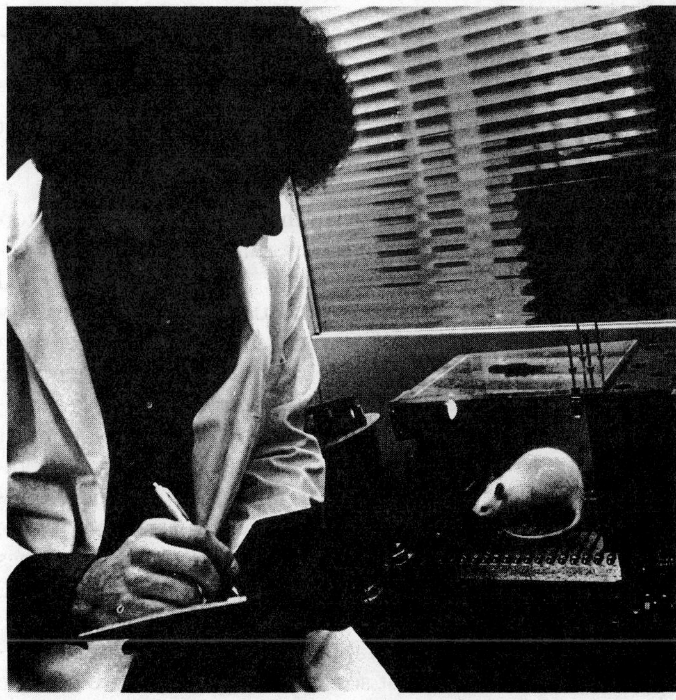

By using a Skinner box, researchers can study the impact of various types of reinforcement on bar-pressing behavior of rats. (*Sybil Shelton/Monkmeyer Press Photo Service*)

Table 5-3 Variations in Partial Reinforcement

Reinforcement Schedule	*Reward Method*	*Example*
Fixed-ratio	Reward given after a *specific* number of responses	A child receives a gold star for every 10 math problems done correctly. Work on the 9 unrewarded problems is maintained by a fixed-ratio schedule.
Variable-ratio	Reward given *on the average* after some number of responses	A person playing a slot machine wins *on the average* after every 10 plays—sometimes after 5 plays, other times after 15, and so on. Continuous play on nonreinforced trials is maintained by a variable-ratio schedule.
Fixed-interval	Reward given after a *specific* amount of time has passed and responding has continued.	A worker is paid once a week for working an entire week without receiving pay each day. Working on days other than payday is maintained by a fixed-interval schedule.
Variable-interval	Reward given after a variable period of time but *on the average* occurs after some identifiable interval.	A salesperson's rewards come irregularly in the form of commissions. If sales occur intermittently, rewards occur intermittently. Selling between commissions is maintained by a variable-interval schedule.

responses vary according to different reinforcement schedules. Specifically, extinction of responses doesn't occur as readily when they are reinforced intermittently rather than continuously. Partial reinforcement approximates the real world better because it is rare in reality for *every* response to be followed by a reinforcer. Behavioral stability seems to depend on partial reinforcement. A stapler is a good example of a machine that usually provides us with continuous reinforcement. In using a stapler, we usually extinguish after one or at most, two, nonreinforcement trials. If no staple comes out, we will stop to check whether another response is needed, such as reloading the stapler. However, if we have a stapler that sometimes sticks and we become accustomed to receiving a staple anywhere from every one to ten presses, when the stapler is empty (that is, extinction has begun), we may go on pressing a large number of times before we check for reloading. We continue to press the stapler long into extinction because of the partial reinforcement effect. Partial reinforcement can be given in various ways and according to a variety of schedules. As seen in Table 5-3, many real-life behaviors can be seen as maintained by partial reinforcement schedules.

Not only are types of reinforcement schedules important, but the concept of reinforcement or reward, per se, has been the object of considerable study in operant psychology. A reinforcer may be defined as any event that, when presented after a given behavior, tends to increase the probability of occurrence of that behavior. E. L. Thorndike (1913) proposed the *law of effect*, one of the earliest and most influential conceptualizations of reinforcement:

Most vending machines provide 100 percent reinforcement. People's coin-insertion behavior extinguishes rapidly if not reinforced. (*©1985 Peter Norem/Charles A. Scaravilli*)

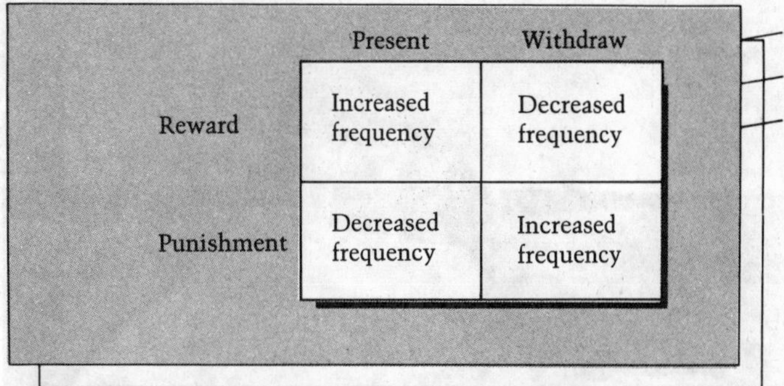

	Present	Withdraw
Reward	Increased frequency	Decreased frequency
Punishment	Decreased frequency	Increased frequency

Figure 5-8 Differential effects upon frequency of behavior of presenting or withholding reinforcers. Positive rewards include such things as money, privileges, or verbal praise. Punishments might include having to rewrite a term paper or pay a fine.

> By a satisfying state of affairs is meant one which an animal does nothing to avoid, often doing such things as to attain and preserve it. By a discomforting or annoying state of affairs is meant one which the animal commonly avoids and abandons. (p. 245)

Besides being thought of as a satisfying event, a reward can also be seen as a *drive-reducing event*. The drives which are reduced may be biological or psychological, and the experience of their reduction will be associated with an increase in the frequency of behavior. For example, a hungry child is reinforced by food because food reduces the hunger drive. A description of how the frequency of behaviors can be varied using the law of effect and drive reduction theory is seen in Figure 5-8. Note that both positive as well as negative experiences can be manipulated to either increase or decrease behavioral frequency. These phenomena will be especially important when we discuss the behavioral approaches to treatment of abnormal behavior.

Classical and Operant Conditioning and Abnormal Behavior

The concepts of conditioning, generalization, and discrimination are especially important in understanding abnormal behavior. A clear application of these concepts to the development of abnormal fears came from the noted behaviorist, John Watson. In 1929, Watson and Rayner performed an experiment in classically conditioning fear in an 11-month-old infant named Albert. In the procedure, the UCS was a noise from a hammer striking a steel bar behind the child's head when he wasn't expecting it. The UCR was the infant's startle reaction to the loud noise (screaming, trembling, and shrieking). The CS was a white rat that was shown immediately before the presentation of the loud noise. After a few trials, Albert responded to the

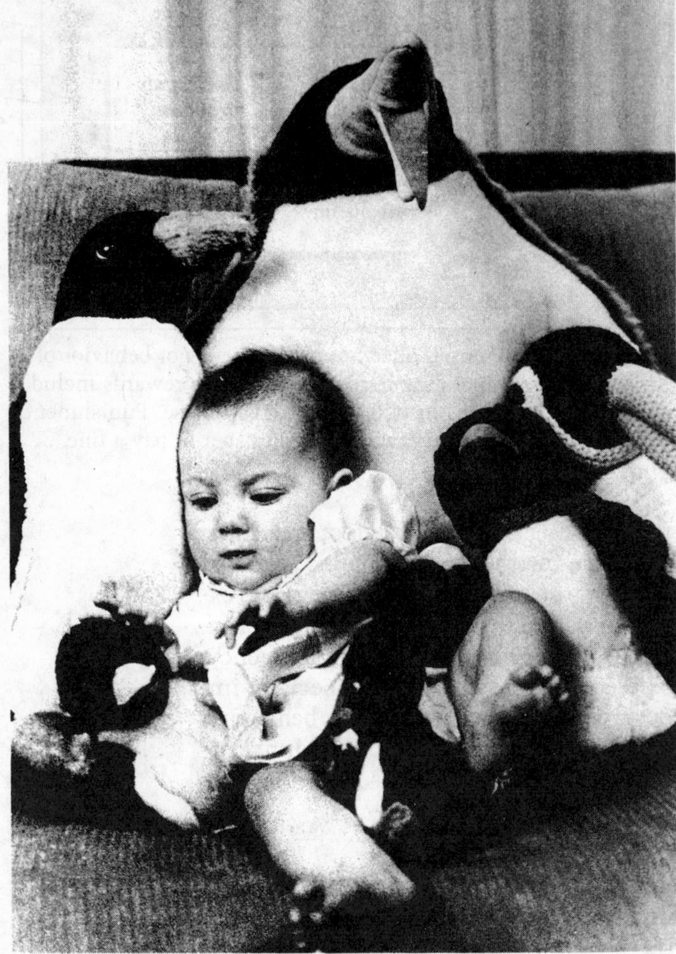

According to Watson and Rayner's work with Albert, if a loud noise were sounded near this baby, the baby might learn to fear stuffed animals. (*Mimi Forsyth/Monkmeyer Press Photo Service*)

furry rat alone in the same fearful way that he originally responded to the loud noise. The white rat was now a CS for the fear response and Albert's startle reaction was a CR. Later theorists have termed this type of classically conditioned fear a *conditioned emotional response.* Albert's bout with classical conditioning was not over at this point, however, for stimulus generalization from the original CS occurred and he manifested fear of a number of other white, furry things such as stuffed animals, his grandfather's white beard, and even Santa Claus. In this experiment, Watson and Rayner demonstrated that a phobialike irrational fear could be created by means of classical conditioning.

Operant conditioning theory also can explain abnormal behavior patterns. For example, simple positive reinforcement of any behavior usually will result in its increase. Parents can reward children (purposefully or unknowingly) for withdrawal from others and can shape them to be "loners." By responding to children only when they break something or violate some rules, parents may unwittingly be reinforcing aggressive behavior. By listening and attending only to sadness, weeping, and self-pity, parents may increase the frequency of depressive behavior. In these ways, operant rules may be seen to be at work in the development of both normal and abnormal personality patterns.

While operant conditioning alone can be useful in explaining acquisition of certain abnormal behaviors, there is evidence that a combination of classical and operant theories may provide an even fuller perspective on the learning of abnormal patterns. This *dual process theory* was used to explain the production of abnormal behavior in animals by Solomon and Wynne (1954). These experimenters trained dogs to jump across a barrier between two sides of a box in order to escape from a strong shock. After the dogs learned how to escape from the shock, they were kept in a limited area of the box and given a number of "unavoidable" shocks (UCS) that were paired with a buzzer (CS). When escape once again was made possible, the buzzer was sounded to determine whether the dog would jump the hurdle to escape from it. Over 80 percent of the dogs did so, manifesting what could be described by someone unaware of their previous training as "irrational fear" of a buzzing noise. Solomon and Wynne's procedure is called *avoidance learning* and works so well that the actual aversive situation (the shock in this case) is rarely, if ever, faced again. In fact, even after Solomon and Wynne removed the shock grids from the experimental box and tried to "show" their dogs that the threat was gone, most of their animals continued jumping at the sound of the buzzer and never extinguished their conditioned emotional response.

Dual process development and maintenance of a fear response also can be helpful in understanding simple phobias in humans. Consider the person who has an irrational fear of tall buildings. Imagine that the fear originated when as a child she became separated from her mother on the top floor of a 30-story skyscraper. The fear (the UCR) she felt at being lost (the UCS) may have become associated with the tall building via classical conditioning. Later, when approaching other tall buildings (now CSs), the CR of anxiety occurs. Because anxiety is aversive, the person attempts to reduce it by turning and walking away from the building, thereby dissipating the anxiety. However, the reduction of the anxiety is a reinforcer, and operant theory dictates that this reinforcer will increase the strength of the response it follows (i.e., turning and walking away from the building). Continuing avoidance of tall buildings in this way will prevent the person ever from determining that buildings are not actually harmful. Like the jumping of Solomon and Wynne's dogs, the phobic avoidance of tall buildings will be maintained by operant and classical conditioning and may never extinguish without carefully controlled relearning.

Behavioral Approaches to Treatment

The carefully controlled relearning often necessary to alter abnormal behavior within the learning theory perspective is generally termed *behavior modification* or *behavior therapy.* In behavior modification, basic laboratory-derived and tested rules of behavior are applied to the alteration of abnormal patterns of responding. Some behavioral approaches are designed to increase the frequency of desired behaviors (e.g., helping a person who is fearful of planes to fly) and some are designed to decrease the frequency of undesirable behaviors (e.g., overeating or excessive drinking).

Increasing the Frequency of Behaviors

Frequency-increasing behavior therapies may be directed at people who either don't know how to emit desired behaviors or who can't emit them because of fear. Depending on which of these conditions is present, therapists may choose different approaches.

Systematic desensitization (Wolpe, 1958) is a behavioral approach designed to increase the frequency of behaviors by reducing the fear associated with their emission. In developing the technique, Wolpe realized that certain pairs of behaviors or feelings were *reciprocally inhibitory*; that is, if one member of the pair were present, its reciprocal could not be. Some examples of reciprocally inhibitory pairs are relaxation-tension and sexual arousal-tension. The reciprocal response found most helpful in inhibiting anxiety was muscle relaxation (Jacobson, 1938). Wolpe reasoned that if he could replace tension in response to a particular stimulus with relaxation, he could prevent the occurrence of anxiety and "cure" phobias. A glance at Figure 5-9 may help to explain: Note that the maladaptive stimulus-response pair is weakened and replaced with a new, more adaptive pairing. The specific way in which the old stimulus-response (S-R) pair is weakened and replaced is called systematic desensitization. In this procedure, a hierarchy of increasingly fearful situations is carefully reassociated with relaxation so that once frightening stimuli are no longer avoided and approach behaviors are increased in frequency. Systematic desensitization has

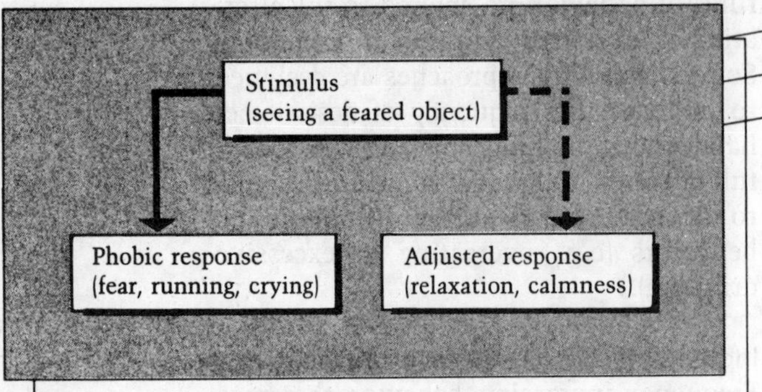

Figure 5-9 The mechanism through which systematic desensitization operates to replace a maladaptive S-R pair with a more adaptive response.

been used with fears such as the fear of flying in a traveling salesperson or fear of blood in a medical student.

Like systematic desensitization, *implosive therapy* also is directed at increasing response frequency through fear reduction (Stampfl & Levis, 1967). The major difference in the methods is in where on the anxiety hierarchy treatment should begin. Wolpe believes that a slow buildup of resistance to anxiety is best, so he begins with the least feared stimuli. Stampfl, however, believes that once people experience the *worst* of their fears and are still all right, their fears will be reduced. Thus Stampfl forces his clients to face their fears, to think the unthinkable; he starts at the very top of the fear hierarchy:

> Therapist: Imagine that you are in a room—the room is dark—you are alone. Suddenly you begin to hear a faint scratching sound at the base of the closed door. You look and see several small shadows in the light coming in under the door. Then you can see some forms coming in under the door; there are hundreds of small forms—you can see tiny legs and wings and antennae. You

Fear of crowds can prevent people from participating in many pleasurable activities. (*Michael Weisbrot and Family*)

> know at once what they are—large brown and black cockroaches with spiny wings and legs—coming at you. You can't see them in the dark, but you know they are there and they are coming closer—closer. Suddenly you feel something on your toe—a faint wisp of feeling—they've found you. You're frozen with fear—you can't move. They're on you! Hundreds of them crawling up your legs! You try to brush them off, but they stick to your hands! . . .

Implosion describes the use of *imaginary* trips to the peak of anxiety, but a complementary response-frequency-increasing behavioral method, *flooding*, involves the actual facing or handling of feared objects or situations (Ullmann & Krasner, 1975). In flooding, people might be asked to touch cockroaches and even to allow them to walk on their hands. In both approaches, the basic notion is that a majority of phobic anxiety is built up in a person's mind and facing feared objects can put things into a more realistic perspective.

Systematic desensitization and implosion may be preferred when people fear some external object or situation, but not when the frequency of desired behaviors is reduced due to personal timidity or interpersonal hesitancy. In these cases, *assertion training* may be used. In assertion training, people who, for fear of "stepping on others' toes," may have difficulty in insisting upon their legitimate rights can be taught to express themselves with less fear. Nonassertive persons probably would not be able to protest appropriately if someone broke into a theater line ahead of them. Instead, they might ruminate about what they *should* have said with the result that they might not enjoy the rest of their evening.

In assertion training, clients are presented with a series of situations in which they must practice defending their own rights. An originator of the method, Salter (1949) encouraged people to use more *facial talk* (communicating feelings with facial expressions as well as words) and *feeling talk* (e.g., I like this place. I'm glad we . . . came). Appropriate assertiveness was increased by clients when they disagreed more frequently with others' personal ideas and feelings and when they agreed more often with statements of personal praise.

Decreasing the Frequency of Behaviors

Abnormality does not always involve "too little" of a particular behavior; very often a particular response occurs too frequently. Examples of this class of responses might include alcohol consumption, drug use, sexual deviations, theft, hallucinations, anxiety, muscle tension, and headaches. Excessive frequency of behaviors may be due to a lack of means of controlling them, lack of desire to control them, or lack of awareness that a behavioral frequency problem exists.

One widely used behavioral method of reducing behavioral frequency is *aversive therapy* in which noxious or painful stimuli such as electric shock or nausea-producing drugs are associated with the emission of undesirable responses. For example, Barker and Miller (1973) reported the successful treatment of a man who had been "addicted" to slot machines for 12 years. During treatment, the client was wired to a 70-V shock source and was asked to play the machine as usual. While playing, he received shock for putting tokens into the machine, for picking up his winnings, and for other behavior associated with the gambling pattern. After 6 hours, he "chose" to stop gambling and was permitted to remain at the machine for another 6 hours with the absence of shock being associated with "no gambling." He reported that his desire to gamble had ceased and he said that he did not gamble for at least 18 months after treatment. Similar successes have been reported in treating alcohol consumption by the use of emetic drugs that cause nausea upon the ingestion of alcohol (Selzer, 1980).

In aversive therapy the usually positive associations found in drinking or gambling are reversed. (*©1985 Peter Norem*)

Although effective in some situations, aversive therapies using shock and drugs are difficult to administer, often require much unwieldy equipment, and may have ethical problems. A more easily administered approach and equally as effective in reducing behavioral frequency is *covert sensitization* (Cautela, 1967). In the basic procedure, imaginary scenes are composed by the therapist in which clients are led to associate their undesirable behaviors with nausea, vomiting, fear, embarrassment, shame, and a host of other aversive stimuli. Since the associations are in the imagination, they aren't dependent on the presence of wires or chemicals and generalization to a wider variety of real-life settings is possible. Likewise, scenes can be "tailor-made" to fit specific people's behavioral patterns. An example of a covert sensitization scene dealing with alcohol use may help to demonstrate this technique:

> Close your eyes and imagine that you are walking down the street. It's a sunny day and you're feeling very good. You pass in front of your favorite bar; you stop and decide to go in and get a drink. Just as you open the door to the bar you get a queezy feeling in your stomach. Sort of like you ate some food that disagreed with you. You say to yourself, "Maybe a drink will settle my stomach." You ask the bartender for a scotch and water. Just as you do this you sort of burp up some food. Little chunks of sour food are in the back of your throat. You swallow the chunks down, but that sour smell and taste are still there; the queasy feeling is stronger now. You get your drink and raise it to your lips. Just as it touches your lips (therapist makes a gagging sound) you vomit. You vomit all over your hands and into your drink. You see the pieces of food and mucous mixed in with the scotch in your glass. You can smell the odor of the vomit mixed with the aroma of the scotch. . . .

Another behavioral therapy method of reducing behavioral frequency, *negative practice,* is based upon the laboratory-established phenomenon called *satiation.* Simply conceptualized, satiation refers to the repetition of a particular behavior until the individual tires of emitting it. In negative practice, rather than being discouraged, undesirable behaviors are temporarily encouraged. The procedure may be exemplified by the work of Ayllon and Michael (1959) who treated a hospitalized woman with the undesirable habit of hoarding as many as 30 soiled towels in her room. These behavior therapists decided to give her all the towels she wanted. At first, she eagerly took towel after towel to her room. Then as the number of towels grew to 600 or more, she began to stop taking new ones. She soon seemed to tire of so many towels and the clutter they produced and *asked* that they be removed. She had been allowed to emit the undesirable response as often as she liked, soon became satiated, and the behavior reduced in frequency.

The Cognitive Perspective

Whereas the behaviorists view people's behavior primarily as a passive process controlled by external stimuli and reinforcements, those adopting a *cognitive* interpretation of the psychosocial paradigm emphasize people's abilities not only to respond to but to actively organize their experiences. A basic notion of the cognitive theorists is that prior to responding to them, internal and external situations are "filtered" through cognitive structures composed of thoughts, beliefs, attitudes, and expectations. These cognitive structures may differ from person to person in terms of flexibility and adaptability.

Bandura's Cognitive Approach to Behavior

Among the leaders of the cognitive school of thought is Bandura, whose work is widely associated with the development of social learning theory and *cognitive behaviorism* (Loftus & Wortman, 1981; Bandura, 1977). Bandura's major contributions have centered around his belief that actual reinforcement and punishment in specific real-life situations are not necessary for learning to take place. He has shown that rather than through direct experience, the majority of human learning is through observation, or more formally, *modeling*. In one study, Bandura and his colleagues (1961) showed that children could learn to exhibit aggressive behavior toward an inflatable clown doll simply by watching a film of another child hitting the doll without being stopped or punished. In addition to aggressiveness, Bandura believes that through observation, people learn expectations, attitudes, and social perceptions and that these "cognitive skills" are constantly being stored for future use in appropriate situations. Bandura (1977) proposed that reinforcement is not necessary for the learning of cognitive skills, but is only required if the skills are to be exhibited, such as when a situation calls for their use. Thus, although on the basis of countless

After watching another child being aggressive in a movie, this child used that same aggressiveness in his play. (*Mimi Forsyth/Monkmeyer Press Photo Service*)

Western movies each of us probably knows how to find water in a cactus when lost in the desert, most of us did not learn this through direct experience, and will never be reinforced for the knowledge, nor will we exhibit it.

In addition to their focus on active involvement in the acquisition of behavior, cognitive theorists also emphasize *expectancies* and *subjective values* in the determination of behavior (Mischel, 1976; Rotter, 1966, 1975). An expectancy may be described as a belief that if one acts or responds in a certain way, a specific outcome will result. For instance, if students believe that if they study hard enough they will be able to pass a major exam, their expectancy will probably lead them to study.

While expectancies generally predict the probability of a specific outcome in a particular situation, subjective values determine the importance to an individual of that particular outcome. To a student who values academic achievement very highly and wants an A, receiving a B can be very upsetting. On the other hand, to another student who doesn't value academic progress as highly, a B might be very acceptable.

To cognitive theorists, concepts such as expectancies and reinforcement values represent individuals' contributions to their own behavioral patterns. Expectancies seem to play an important role in the determination of *what* people do. Subjective values of outcomes seem to be involved in *how we feel* about events happening to us. Both, therefore, are clearly related to normal and abnormal patterns of behavior.

Cognitive Theory and the Treatment of Abnormal Behavior

In general, the cognitive or social learning view directs professionals to attend to the roles of social experience, modeling, beliefs, and attitudes in the development, maintenance, and alteration of behavior. Psychopathology is typically seen as being based in some way on faulty social learning, maladaptive or distorted attitudes and beliefs, or exposure to inappropriate models. Given this perspective, several cognitively based therapeutic approaches have emerged, among them rational emotive therapy, modeling, and cognitive behavior modification.

Rational emotive therapy (Ellis, 1973) focuses on irrational beliefs as the core of behavior disorders. Ellis's assumption is that emotional disturbances stem not from *what* people experience, but from *how* people perceive what happens to them. He proposes that when a highly emotional response *C* follows a significant activity or event *A*, *A* does not actively cause *C*. Rather, *B*, the individual's perception-belief about *A*, causes *C*. Thus, *A* may be a dirty carpet in the living room and *C* may be crying. Dirty carpets don't cause crying, but the irrational belief *B* that one must be a perfect housekeeper or face unbearable shame and embarrassment *can* cause crying in response to a dirty carpet.

Since irrational beliefs are seen as being at the core of emotional problems, the goal of the rational emotive therapist is to rid the client of such beliefs so that the client is free to have a logical existence filled with appropriate emotion (Corey, 1977). Ellis seeks out the particular type of irrational thinking in clients (See Table 5-4 for some examples) and then encourages them to alter their distorted cognitive structures.

Whereas Ellis's focus is on irrational beliefs per se, other cognitive therapists focus more on the *source* of such beliefs, the *models* upon whom people tend to base many of their ideas about the world. Just as modeling or observational learning can produce maladaptive behavior patterns, it can also be used to correct such patterns. This method is certainly not new, for its

Table 5-4 Ellis's Listing of 11 Basic Irrational Thoughts

1. It is essential that one be loved by virtually everyone in his community.
2. One must be perfectly competent, adequate, and achieving to consider oneself worthwhile.
3. Some people are bad, wicked or villainous and therefore should be blamed and punished.
4. It is a terrible catastrophe when things are not as one wants them to be.
5. Unhappiness is caused by outside circumstances and the individual has no control over it.
6. Dangerous or fearsome things are causes for great concern and their possibility must be continually dwelt upon.
7. It is easier to avoid certain difficulties and self-responsibilities than to face them.
8. One should be dependent on others and must have someone stronger on whom to rely.
9. Past experiences and events are the determiners of present behavior and cannot be eradicated.
10. One should be quite upset over other people's problems.
11. There is always a right and perfect solution to every problem, and it must be found or the result will be catastrophic.

Source: From A. Ellis, *Reason and Emotion in Psychotherapy.* Copyright 1962 by Lyle Stuart, Inc. Reprinted by permission.

use was recorded by Mary C. Jones as early as 1929. Jones treated a child with an irrational fear of animals. To help overcome the child's fear, Jones had the child observe other children happily playing with the feared objects.

Bandura and his colleagues (1968) treated snake phobias by allowing clients to observe a responsible looking, fearless model who calmly approached and handled some snakes. Working at their own pace after watching the model, almost all of Bandura's subjects eventually were able actually to hold a snake and to pet it. In another vein, Gordon et al. (1974) used modeling to help a young girl overcome an intense fear of the dentist. Using side-by-side chairs, these researchers allowed the patient to watch her older sister being treated by a kindly dentist. Over a period of several days, the girl changed from being very frightened and refusing to approach "her" chair, to being calm and interested enough to have a routine dental exam.

While modeling focuses on reexposure to new and more adaptive sources of behavior, *cognitive behavior modification* as developed by Meichenbaum (1977) and Beck (1976) is directed at reducing maladjustment by a more internal reorganization of beliefs and attitudes. In cognitive behavior modification, therapists attempt not only to resolve past difficulties produced by maladaptive beliefs but to "innoculate" people against future problems as well. For example, Meichenbaum has helped people with test anxiety (fear of taking exams) by training them to say aloud or silently to themselves such things as "I have studied this material completely, so I know the answers to the questions I will be asked. I know how to relax and so I don't have to be overwhelmed by anxiety." These self-instructions are believed by Meichenbaum (1977) to interfere with the person's own self-defeating and anxiety-causing self-instructions, thereby changing his or her emotional reactions to tests.

In a slightly different approach, Beck (1976) uses prescribed activity schedules, special cognitive tasks, and a variety of "emotional homework" to help people gain more rational views of their lives and the self-defeating attitudes that he believes they allow to harm them. In one particularly interesting case Beck described the cognitive treatment of a college professor:

> The patient had been preparing to give his first lecture to a large class. He became increasingly anxious as he began to think that he would perform ineptly. As his anxiety increased his thoughts dwelt on the possibility that he might not be able to prepare the lecture and, furthermore, that he would have a mental block

> and would be unable to speak to the class. From this point he conjured up a series of catastrophic consequences: he would lose his job; he would be unable to make a living; he would end up on skid row—a social outcast and a disgrace to his family.
>
> By unravelling the thought content that was generating his anxiety, the patient was able to gain more objectivity about his immediate problem. Alternative courses of action—such as telling the chairman of his department of his difficulty—were considered. Also, the probability that he could manage at other types of work, even if he were unsuccessful as a teacher, was discussed. As the patient attached less credence to his fears, his anxiety dissipated; he was able to prepare the lecture and to teach his class successfully. (Beck, 1976, pp. 148–149)

Concluding Comments

It is apparent that a lot of energy has been spent over the years trying to develop *the* best psychological theory of human behavior deriving from the psychosocial paradigm. However, there is reason to believe that this may have been a misdirected enterprise on at least two counts. First of all, it seems that those people who would be the "consumers" of such a theory are not looking for one. Garfield and Katz (1976), in fact, reported that only 10 percent of a large sample of clinical psychologists expressed a preference for *any* one psychological theory over another; most (over 55 percent) described themselves as *eclectic,* that is, as using a number of different approaches as warranted by the specifics of cases with which they were working. Further, there are some psychologists who believe that such an eclectic approach may be better than the specific derivatives we discussed in this chapter and in Chapters 4 and 6. For example, in endorsing a position termed *prescriptive eclecticism,* Dimond et al. (1978) suggest that disturbed people should be assessed, understood, and treated on at least *five* different levels. These are the behavioral, the humanistic-existential, the intrapsychic, the biophysical, and the social-environmental. Thus rather than trying to establish a priori which theory should be used, it may be that *all* of them should be routinely applied to a total view of a particular behavior pattern. We believe that such an eclectic approach probably is the most clearly reflective of the multiple-interactive etiology of psychopathology and may represent the most effective approach to the explanation and treatment of psychopathology in its many forms. To this point we have discussed the first four of Dimond et al.'s suggested levels of behavioral analysis. In the next chapter we will turn to the fifth level, the view of human behavior guided by the third major current scientific perspective on psychopathology, the systems paradigm.

Summary Chart

The application of the psychosocial paradigm has been diverse. We began our overview of its diversity with the psychoanalytic perspective:

Unconscious, preconscious, and conscious minds
Id, ego, superego
Defense mechanisms
Psychosexual development: Oral, anal, phallic, latency and genital stages
Thanatos, libido, primary process thought, secondary process thought
Pleasure principle, reality principle
Psychoanalysis: Free association, resistance, transference
Neoanalysts: Erikson, Sullivan

The next major interpretation of the psychosocial paradigm was the humanistic/existential view:

Rogers and Maslow: Self-actualization, hierarchy of needs, client centered
Perls and Yalom: Choice and awareness, confrontations with existence

We then turned to the behavioral position:

Classical conditioning: CS, UCS, CR, UCR, acquisition, extinction, spontaneous recovery, stimulus generalization, continuous reinforcement
Operant conditioning: Reinforcement (continuous and intermittent), schedules of reinforcement, conditioned emotional responses, dual process theory
Behavior modification methods: Desensitization, flooding, assertion training, aversive therapy, covert sensitization, negative practice

The final view deriving from the psychosocial paradigm was the cognitive perspective:

Thoughts, beliefs, and attitudes
Bandura: Cognitive behaviorism, observational learning, vicarious reinforcement, modeling
Cognitive therapies: Rational emotive therapy, cognitive behavior modification

CHAPTER 6

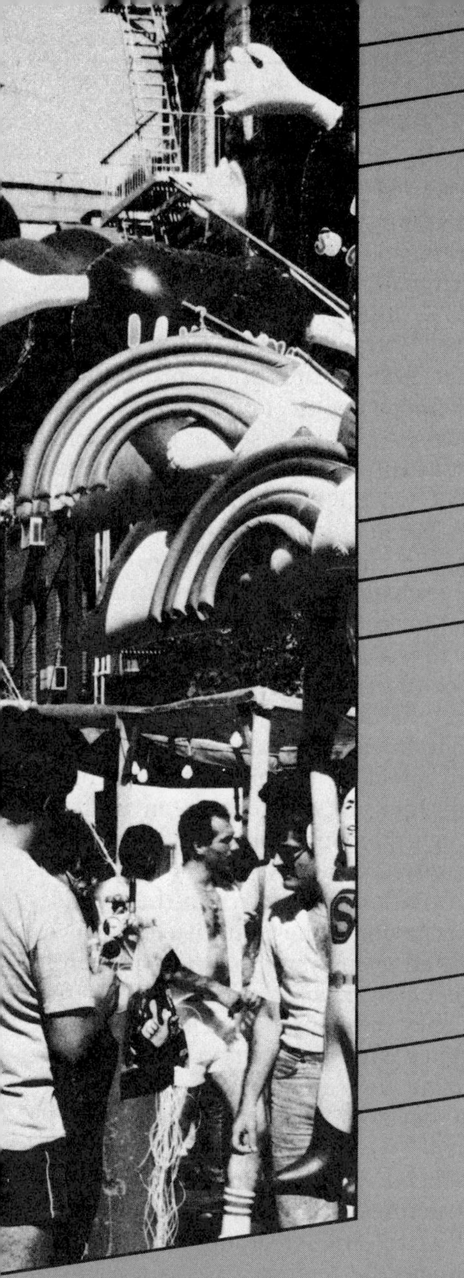

The Systems Paradigm

While professionals adopting the biological and psychosocial paradigms have sought clues to solving the puzzles of psychopathology in such things as brain biochemistry and genetic material or in faulty personality development or learning, those guided by the *systems paradigm* have sought to understand behavior at the level of group, family, societal, and/or cultural systems. To those sharing the systems perspective, people are not to be studied in isolation. Rather, their behavior is seen as a result of living within a number of structures or systems which they at once affect and are affected by. Systems thinking suggests that a clearer understanding of the interactions between people and the systems they are part of can lead to greater insights into the causes of abnormality and the ways to deal with it.

Explanations for Abnormal Behavior

As we noted in the history of the shared beliefs guiding abnormal psychology, the view that people interact with the systems of which they are part is not a new one. However, it is only within the last quarter century that the systems perspective has been more formally recognized and written about.

General Systems Theory

Whereas the systems *paradigm* is a global view of the world, general systems *theory* is a specific theoretical view deriving from it (von Bertalanffy 1967, 1975, 1981). It is a basic assumption of general systems theory that rather than being relatively passive products of biological, psychosocial, and sociological factors, people are "active organismic systems capable of self-regulation, goal-seeking, and growth and learning and are internally active as well as externally responsive." (Marmor, 1983, p. 833). In this perspective (von Bertalanffy, 1981; Davidson, 1983; Miller & Miller, 1985), people are seen as *open systems* as opposed to *closed systems.* Closed systems, such as TV sets or automobiles, don't usually change significantly from day to day. On the other hand, because they have *permeable boundaries,* open systems can change in reaction to information exchanged with the internal or external environment. An example of an open system is a committee working on a task; the committee may generate ideas from among its members (develop internal information) as well as seek information from outsiders (obtain external information). Information passing in and out through the permeable boundaries of the committee typically results in continuous variation and growth in the attitudes and behavior of the committee. However, while an open system such as a committee is changeable, it also has an inherent tendency to maintain itself and an ability to increase in complexity over time. Thus, over the course of its task, a committee may develop subcommittees and new tasks.

General systems theory may be applied to structures as large as entire cultures as well as to smaller groups and families. With specific reference to its use in understanding personality and psychopathology in individuals, Marmor (1983) suggests that:

> Personality develops out of the interactions of the human biological substrate with the matter, energy, and information coming from outside the biological system, that is, from the physical environment, the nuclear family, the school system, peer groups, the commu-

An extended family is an example of a large, open system that allows information to pass among its members through permeable boundaries. (*Michael Weisbrot and Family*)

> nity, the nation, and the culture at large. By the same token, the origins of psychopathology are not sought within the individual alone, but rather in his total system of relationships, including his physiology, his nuclear family, and even the patterns of his culture. (p. 833)

The general systems perspective also leads to unique research and treatment approaches in abnormal psychology. For example, given that people are both systems in themselves as well as parts of other systems like families, they should be studied in their systemic context. Thus, for example, to obtain an accurate picture of their behavior, children should be studied in the context of their homes, schools, families, or neighborhoods. Reflecting this view, Marmor (1983) notes that some symptoms of abnormality may have to be reconsidered in light of the general systems theory approach:

> A child with a reading disability in our culture would not be regarded as having a problem in a society in which the written or printed word did not exist, just as color blindness would not be a defect in a society in which the ability to distinguish red from green had no functional importance. (p. 834)

As a perspective deriving from the more global systems paradigm, general systems theory introduces and emphasizes the concept of people as open systems with permeable boundaries. However, the theory does not describe the mechanisms by which information passing through these permeable boundaries may contribute to the development of abnormal behavior. For proposals regarding such mechanisms, we need to look at other systems paradigm–based approaches. It is to discussions of two of these approaches that we shall now turn.

Societal Reaction Theory

One view of the mechanisms by which systems like communities and societies can adversely affect their members is *so-*

cietal reaction theory. Also known as labeling theory, societal reaction theory was developed in the early 1960s primarily by sociologist Thomas Scheff (1966, 1975; see also Ullmann & Krasner, 1969, 1975; and Miles, 1981). A basic notion of the perspective is that psychopathology may best be understood as a special form of *social deviance.* Scheff identifies two types of deviant behavior. In *primary deviance* people are labeled as deviant because they break some societal rule. Examples of primary deviance are stealing or assaulting someone. Primary deviance may have a cultural, social, psychological, or biological basis, but it is not the deviant behavior per se that makes an individual a recognized problem to the self or societal systems. Rather, it is the societal system's *reaction* to acts of primary deviance that is most crucial in the development of a stabilized pattern of abnormal behavior.

The social reaction of labeling a person as deviant results in a state of *secondary deviance* in which the person's social identity is changed. For example, the primary deviant may be described as "a person who has stolen something," whereas the secondary deviant is called a "thief." With regard to society's role in producing deviance in some of its members, Becker (1963) has stated: "Social groups create deviance by making rules whose infractions constitute deviance and by applying these rules to particular people and labeling them as outsiders" (p. 9). Simply breaking society's rules does not constitute secondary deviance, however, for to be so classified a person must break a rule *and* be reacted to as a deviant for his actions.

According to Scheff and the societal reaction theorists, the label of deviant, once applied, is very difficult to remove. As demonstrated in the case history below, once begun, it is difficult to reverse the labeling process. If not reversed, the process can eventually lead to the stable secondarily deviant behavior patterns known as mental disorders.

A seven year old boy was brought to a psychologist with his parents' major complaint being that he showed little interest in school. He was constantly being teased and upset by his peers. His teacher complained that he would daydream in class, fail to complete homework, and often pick fights with other children. After extensive evaluation, the psychologist determined that informal testing by an inexperienced kindergarten teacher had resulted in the child's being labeled as having a learning disability. Consequently, teachers working with the child were more likely to see him as having some difficulties that in reality he really did not have. Although they provided him well-meaningly with special help, they also produced in him a belief that he had special problems. The children in his class came to see him similarly and teased him about being a "dummy." Soon he saw himself as different, the children saw him as different, and his teachers and parents saw him as different. As a result, the child was upset each day before and during school and his work suffered immensely. His major problem seemed to be that he had become what he originally was erroneously labeled as being.

Scheff (1966) states that in the development of mental disorders, the rules broken during the primary deviance phase are quite special. They are rarely, if ever, openly stated or formally written down. Rather, they are rules *left over* after all the usual categories of societal regulations are exhausted. It is when people frequently break these *residual rules,* under inappropriate circumstances that they commit acts of primary deviance that can ultimately lead to the secondarily deviant label of "mentally ill."

Scheff argues that *stabilization* of residual deviance into a pattern of abnormal behavior is the result of societal reaction to continuous or inappropriate residual rule violation. Thus, if by some stroke of bad luck or poor judgment, people are observed in an act of significant residual rule violation, they may be pulled into a social labeling process beyond their control. This labeling process may begin with the simple violation of residual rules and end with the application of the label, "mental patient."

According to Scheff, the number of residual rules is quite large. A good way to generate a list of some residual rules would be to consider those social guidelines that we take so much for granted that we only notice them when they are violated. Some examples are "an adult must be involved in some task when in public"; "one should not stand too close to another person when conversing"; or "one does not laugh aloud in church during a funeral service."

Outside observers may not always be necessary for the labeling of behavior as deviant (Ullman & Krasner, 1969; 1975).

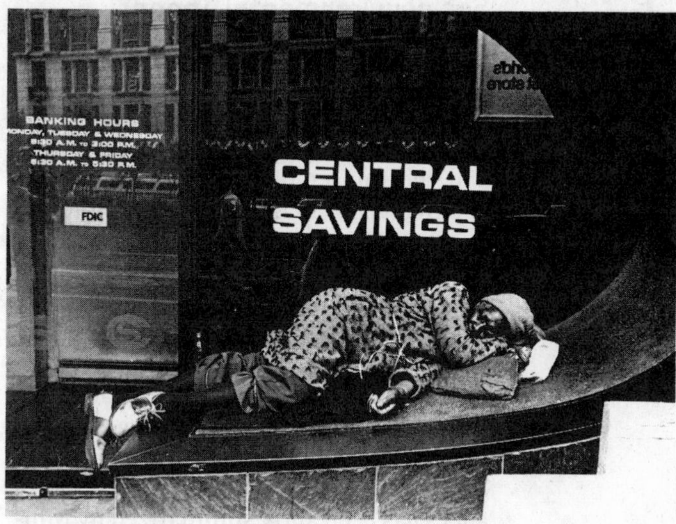

Once labeled a deviant, a person will have a difficult time achieving normal status again. (*Gloria Karlson*)

To some extent we observe ourselves, and if we perceive ourselves as violating residual rules, we may *self-label* and cause ourselves to suffer many of the same detrimental effects of secondary deviance as someone labeled by a powerful person like a teacher or psychiatrist. An example of the power of self-labeling is shown in the following case history:

> During early adolescence a young man and a close male friend sporadically engaged in mutual masturbation. Neither thought anything of it at the time, and such behavior often was accompanied by their poring over pornographic magazines depicting nude females. During the patient's third year of high school his basketball coach discussed the "horrors" of homosexuality during a team meeting. Trying to instill a masculine image in his players, he described behaviors such as mutual masturbation as "sick" and "disgusting," and told his players that if they were approached regarding such behavior they should take violent action against their accoster. Although he laughed and joked along with everyone else about the discussion, the young man began to feel anxious and guilty on his way home. By the time he arrived home he had convinced himself that he was indeed a deviant of the type spoken about by his coach. He began to label himself as sick and emotionally disturbed. From that point on he discontinued dating girls and became somewhat of a loner. He feared that his friends would discover (via his looks or actions) that he was disturbed sexually. Although this young man had lived comfortably with his mutual masturbatory behavior for many years, it was not until he had labeled himself as disturbed that his psychological problems began.

Socioenvironmental Theory

Rather than focusing on an individual's interactions with society's labeling process, *socioenvironmental theorists* emphasize the frequency of changes in people's lives and the impact of these on adjustment (Dohrenwend, 1975; Kohn, 1972; Meyers et al., 1971, 1974, 1975; Miles, 1981). A basic notion is that the greater the number of internally or externally generated changes with which people must cope, the greater their chances of developing behavior disorders. The view that changes in internal (personal) and external (social) systems in which people live can cause emotional stress and behavioral disturbances has been aptly summarized by Murphy et al. (1984):

> It is well known that numerous social and psychiatric theorists have suggested that the prevalence of mental illness is rising due to noxious factors that characterize the way of life in modern society.
>
> The impersonality and anonymity of increasing urbanism may destroy resources for achieving a sense of inner worth and of being valuable to others. Increased residential mobility may damage opportunity for human bonding and participation in supportive social groups. The rapidity of social changes in the spheres of family life and work may tax the ability to adjust and maintain personality integration and ego strength. The mass media may personalize the threats of nuclear destruction and the continuing lack of control over major diseases like cancer. The quickened pace of life associated with high speed technologies may intensify the pressures that erode mental health. In fact, most aspects of contemporary life have been viewed as creating difficulties

Table 6-1 The Social Readjustment Rating Scale*

Rank	*Life Event*	*Value*	*Rank*	*Life Event*	*Value*
1	Death of spouse	100	23	Son or daughter leaving home	29
2	Divorce	73	24	Trouble with in-laws	29
3	Marital separation	65	25	Outstanding personal achievement	28
4	Jail term	63	26	Wife beginning or stopping work	26
5	Death of close family member	63	27	Beginning or ending school	26
6	Personal injury or illness	53	28	Change in living conditions	25
7	Marriage	50	29	Revision of personal habits	24
8	Fired at work	47	30	Trouble with boss	23
9	Marital reconciliation	45	31	Change in work hours or conditions	20
10	Retirement	45	32	Change in residence	20
11	Change in health of family member	44	33	Change in schools	20
12	Pregnancy	40	34	Change in recreation	19
13	Sex difficulties	39	35	Change in church activities	19
14	Gain of new family member	39	36	Change in social activities	18
15	Business readjustment	39	37	Loan for lesser purchase (car, TV, etc.)	17
16	Change in financial state	38	38	Change in sleeping habits	16
17	Death of close friend	37	39	Change in number of family get-togethers	15
18	Change to different line of work	36			
19	Change in number of arguments with spouse	35	40	Change in eating habits	15
			41	Vacation	13
20	Loan for major purchase (home, etc.)	31	42	Christmas	12
21	Foreclosure of mortgage or loan	30	43	Minor violations of the law	11
22	Change in responsibilities at work	29			

Source: From Holmes & Rahe, 1967, p. 216.

*All life stresses are not equal. Holmes and Rahe (1967) developed a rank order of life events and the degree of stress associated with each. The idea is that each person can cope with only a limited number of Life Change Units (LCUs); upon passing this limit, added life stresses, especially negative ones, may result in psychological disorders.

> for people; and each new generation has been seen as facing larger trouble than the previous, with the consequence of a growing burden of mental illness. (p. 990)

Socioenvironmentalists such as Myers et al. (1971, 1974, 1975) believe that significant life changes are the mechanisms which are involved in the production of abnormality. These researchers have found that the greater the number of significant life events (see Table 6-1) experienced by people in a given period of time, the greater the likelihood that they will develop psychological problems. From this perspective *any change* in life pattern—but especially negative ones—may produce stress that challenges one's ability to cope. Thus, negative changes in school, work, or family systems all can contribute to increasing stress in an individual. Although the life-events–stress relationship has been supported in a number of studies by Meyers et al., there are some people who experience many significant life changes during a year and yet manage to remain relatively well-adjusted. Likewise, there are some people who have few negative changes in their lives but still develop behavioral disorders.

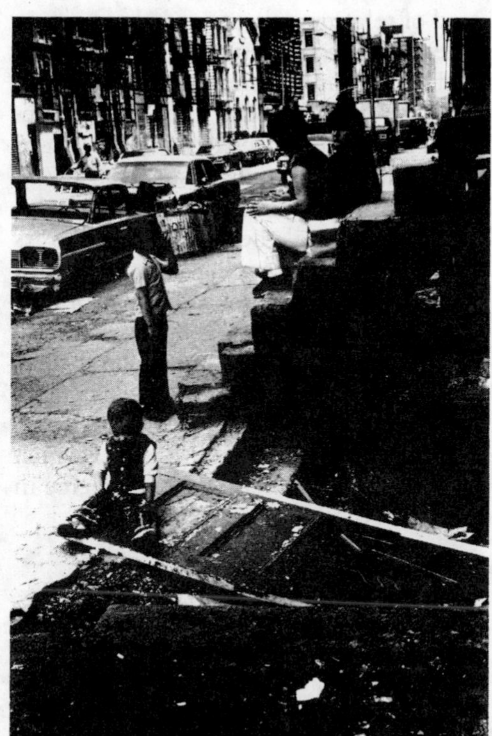

A major life stress is poverty. (©*Rhoda Galyn*)

The Treatment of Psychopathology

Professionals following the systems paradigm believe that individual disturbances result from or reflect disturbances in social groupings. Thus, rather than directing therapeutic efforts toward an individ-

Socioenvironmentalists believe that some abnormal behavior arises from the stresses and strains of modern urban society. (© *Eric Kroll 1979/Taurus Photos*)

ual per se, interventions are aimed at the systems of various types of which people are members. These systems include artificially organized structures as in the case of *group therapy* or naturally organized systems as in the cases of *family therapy* and *community intervention approaches.* The therapies deriving from the systems paradigm have in common the premise that effective systems have effective members and that problems developed within systems can be corrected via alteration of those systems.

Group Therapy

Quite accidentally, the therapeutic effects of a group upon its members were first observed by Joseph Pratt (1906) in his efforts to help outpatients who were adjusting to their disease after discharge from a tuberculosis sanitorium. Pratt noted that the adjustment of his patients was improved dramatically as a result of their meeting as a group to discuss their experiences. It was apparent to him that the "whole could be more than the sum of its parts"; that is, people in groups adjusted far better than any one of them could have done individually. Here was a clear demonstration of the manner in which joining a system such as a group could help people in need (Yalom, 1970).

While all group therapy involves the treatment of individual problems within a group context, there are a number of specific group techniques, each deriving from a different theoretical use of the systems paradigm. Some specific group approaches will be described at various other places in the text. Here, we will limit our discussion to some of the characteristics common to group treatment as a general therapeutic mode.

Most therapy groups are artificially organized systems which are composed of a varying number of members (somewhere between 7 and 12) and one or more leaders. Typically, members are interviewed by the leaders before they join a group and are usually assigned to groups on the basis of their problem, the type of people already in the group, and the specific desires of the leaders as to group composition. Some therapists, for example, prefer *homogeneous groups* composed of people with similar characteristics such as age, marital status, sex, or problem type. Other leaders may choose *heterogeneous groups,* whose composition may be decided on a first-come, first-served basis or on the basis of some desired "mixture" sought by the therapists for either practical or theoretical reasons. Groups usually meet for anywhere from 1 to 1½ hours (except for special groups called *marathons* which may meet continuously for a day or longer) and begin and end promptly. Members usually sit in a circle. As a rule, groups meet regularly, at the same time and place, and may continue meeting for a predetermined limited time or for an unlimited period lasting as long as several years. Instead of relating only to one other person, a therapist, people in group therapy must react to a number of people. The therapeutic use of this social interaction is believed to be the definitive mechanism of therapeutic change (Nichols & Zax, 1977).

Group therapy is not simply "watered-down" individual therapy but, due to its systems basis and emphasis, represents a unique approach to the treatment of psychopathology. Yalom (1970) describes the basic procedures and fundamental characteristics of groups and provides insights into *why* group therapy seems to work. Yalom describes 10 *curative factors* which are present to a lesser or greater degree in different types of group therapy:

> *Imparting of information.* Groups provide didactic instructions about adjustment and disturbance; some groups offer advice, suggestions, and guidance.
>
> *Instillation of hope.* Being in a group with others who are showing progress helps

instill and maintain hope for one's own chances of recovery.

Universality. Group members may learn that they aren't the only ones with problems and that their own problems may not be unique. Great relief can be obtained from this realization.

Altruism. In the course of group therapy, members typically help one another through support, reassurance, and the like. Helping others can make members feel valuable and enable them to accept help more easily themselves.

Corrective recapitulation of the primary family group. Groups are like families, with leaders being like parents and members being similar to siblings. Experiencing a healthy "family" can help correct early damage done by maladjusted family life.

Development of socializing techniques. Social learning occurs in groups, in which members learn new ways of relating to other people and can practice these new social skills in a warm, accepting atmosphere before trying them out in the "real" world.

Imitation of adaptive behavior. Group therapists can serve as models of better adjustment and often provide members with temporary new behaviors while they develop patterns comfortable to them.

Interpersonal learning. One of the two most important curative factors, interpersonal learning, describes the acquisition of corrective emotional experience in groups. Members exist in a social microcosm where their problems may be magnified, assessed, and corrected among understanding and accepting others.

Group cohesiveness. The other most important curative factor, group cohesiveness, is the therapy analogue of a relationship or intimacy. Members of a cohesive group often value their group above themselves: they may weep when one member is sad and rejoice if one of them achieves some progress. The sense of belonging seems to be of crucial therapeutic importance.

Catharsis. Group members can experience relief after releasing long-pent-up feelings of sadness, anger, joy, and so on. Ventilating feelings among those to whom one is close can be curative.

Family Therapy

Pioneering theorists in family therapy, such as Ackerman (1963), J. Bell (1975), Bowen (1971), Haley (1976), and Satir (1964) were similar to their group therapy counterparts in their shared belief that individual symptoms can be understood and treated within a systems context. However, their specific view was that the most important "group" on which to focus is the family. Generally, the philosophy of family theorists is that ineffective or disturbed family systems produced emotionally troubled individuals. The goal of family therapy, therefore, was primarily to restructure the family group and its communication patterns so that stress on its members would be reduced and normal functioning would once again be possible for all the family members. Two representative approaches to dealing with family systems are *structural family analysis* and *strategic family therapy.*

Structural Family Analysis

In structural family analysis (Minuchin, 1974; Minuchin & Fishman, 1981) the therapeutic focus is on the organization and structure of family interaction and communication. A family is seen as a system organized around the *support, regulation, nurturance, and socialization* of its members. If the family is structured in such a way that these functions cannot be fulfilled, one or more of the family members (called *identified patients*) may manifest "symptoms" or signs of the breakdown of the system. The treatment for these symptoms may not be therapy for the individual or identified patient but help for the system of which he or she is a part. For example, while the reason for

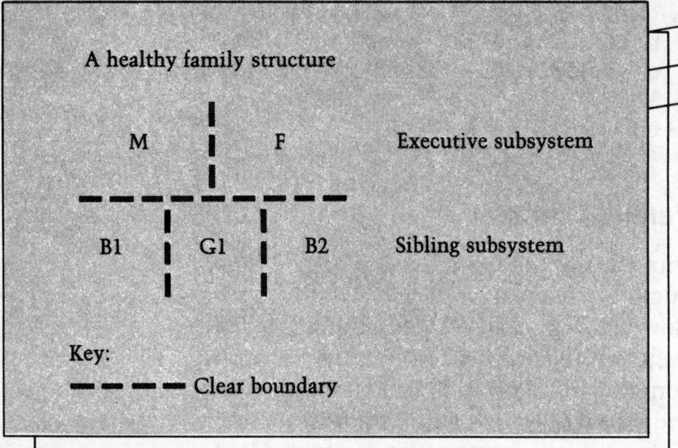

Figure 6-1 Structural Family Analysis. (*Adapted from Families and Family Therapy, by S. Minuchin. Copyright ©1974 by Harvard University Press. Used by permission of the President and Fellows of Harvard College.*)

a family's seeking professional help may be that their 10-year-old throws tantrums, the structural family therapists might look for problems in specific relationships among family members (e.g., the marital relationship between the parents) as a cause for the tantrum behavior in the child.

Table 6-2 Critical Events in the "Life" of a Family

Each of these events requires alterations in basic family function and structure.
Birth of first child
Speech in first child
First child goes to school
First child becomes a teenager
First child leaves the home
First child marries
Wife's menopause
Husband's climacteric
Birth of first grandchild
Death of one of the spouses

Source: After Satir (1964).

To better understand families, Minuchin has developed methods for analyzing the underlying structures of families and the patterns of communication that characterize their interactions. According to Minuchin, families are made up of individuals who must first of all be separated by *clear boundaries.* That is, each person needs to be independent of other family members, yet be able to communicate freely with them. In contrast, if such independence isn't felt, as when two children are treated and perceived by parents as being totally alike, a *diffuse* boundary may exist. When no communication is possible between two family members, as in the case where parents are not talking to each other, a *rigid* boundary exists. Both diffuse and rigid boundaries are considered undesirable elements in a family structure.

In addition to the boundaries between individuals, Minuchin also describes *family subsystems* as important sources of behavior. Most important are the *executive subsystem* and the *sibling subsystem* (see Figure 6-1). In the effective family, the executive subsystem is composed of the parents; in many disturbed families, one or more of the children may be elevated to the executive system and act like a "parent" because the real parents either cannot or will not fulfill their responsibilities. To Minuchin, such a situation is problematic because children cannot really handle such adult roles. Instead, children need to participate in the family as members of the sibling system which is usually subordinate to the executive subsystem.

When boundaries and subsystems are clear and open, the family system usually functions well. However, as with any open system, the structure can and should change over time. Among the major sources for this change are normal growth as manifested in the 10 common family developmental crises outlined by Satir (1964) and presented in Table 6-2. If these normally occurring changes result in adjustment of the family system, all goes well. However, if at some point, due to an inability to flexibly alter the system's structure, clear boundaries and proper subsystem membership are replaced by diffuse or rigid boundaries and improper subsystems, "symptoms" may appear somewhere in the family group.

For Minuchin, family therapy involves an active restructuring of family systems through meetings with spouses alone, with children alone, and with many other combinations of family members. Using warmth, cajoling, and active involvement, Minuchin directs the family toward a more adaptive family structure. Some family therapy experts (Nichols, 1984) suggest that Minuchin's approach is among the most effective methods of family treatment yet developed. An example of a structural family therapy interaction may help to familiarize you with the method.

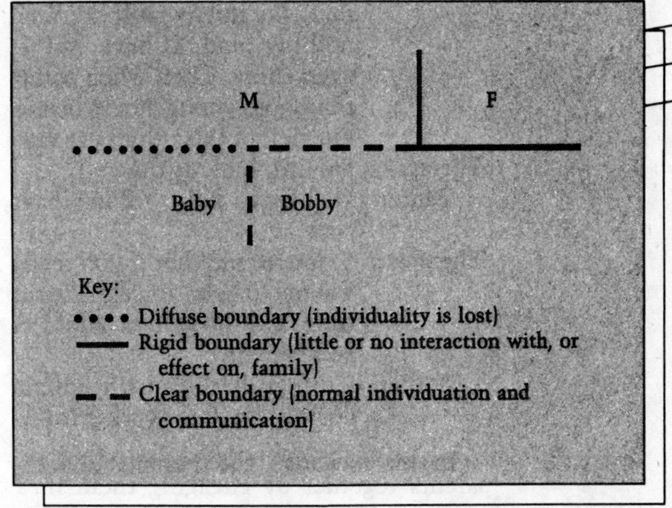

Figure 6-2 The structure of the disturbed family described in the text. (*Adapted from Families and Family Therapy, by S. Minuchin. Copyright ©1974 by Harvard University Press. Used by permission of the President and Fellows of Harvard College.*)

Therapist: Ok, what's going on this week?

Mother: All right—are you ready? This week Bobby did just terribly in school. He won't do his work, his teacher calls us up. Jim (father) won't do a thing about it.

Father: You know I'd like to. How can I? I've got to work, you know. You have more time than I do.

Mother: But I've got the baby to take care of. I can't just leave him. He hasn't been easy this week. The colic has been bad.

Therapist: You're both pretty angry about this. How do you feel about all of this, Bobby?

Bobby: I don't like all the noise.

Mother: We wouldn't fight if you did better in school. Why don't you do your work, for heaven's sakes.

Therapist: So Bobby makes you fight? It's his doing?

Father: I could help him with his homework, but I don't have time.

In this situation, the parents are fighting and making Bobby the focus of *their* battle. The family members are separated by maladaptive boundaries, as depicted in Figure 6-2.

Therapist: You know, I think this is a problem between Mom and Dad. Bobby, you go out and play in the waiting room. (The baby is not at this session.) OK, now, Mom and Dad, what's going on between the two of you?

Here the therapist forces the parents to face their own conflicts by isolating them from the sibling subsystem.

Mother: Well, he leaves me and when he gets home and there's trouble with Bobby, he screams at me. Like its my fault! He does nothing and I have to do everything. Then when something goes wrong, I'm to blame. I'm sick of this! (Starts to cry.)

Therapist: So, Jim, look at this!

Father: I'd like to help. I don't have time.

Therapist: Seems to me that if you really wanted to help, you'd make the time. I think you're afraid to be a parent.

Mother: I think that's a little unfair, doctor. He does work hard.

In this exchange, the therapist gets the parents together by engaging them in a conflict with him. By manipulating interpersonal communication and by following some clinical hunches, the therapist helps the family move toward a more effective and flexible structure. Having a clear structural goal in mind seems to help the structural family therapists to see where they are going and to know when they have gotten there. This quality makes Minuchin's approach especially attractive to clinicians and researchers alike.

Strategic Family Therapy

Minuchin's structural family approach is but one of several which conceptualize families as systems. A second such perspective is *strategic family therapy* (Haley, 1973). As described by Nichols (1984), "Strategic therapists take a systemic view of problem maintenance and a strategic (pragmatic) orientation to change. The analysis (of problems) is based on general systems theory, but the interventions are strictly pragmatic" (p. 426).

As in the structural family approach, the strategic therapy perspective conceptualizes disturbed behavior as reflecting dysfunctions in the family system and is best modified by changing the system (Weakland et al., 1974). However, it is here that the similarities end. For the strategists, there is no ideal family structure to move toward; for them families do not necessarily need to be rebuilt. In fact, they seem to believe that often only minor changes in a family may be sufficient to change even the severe abnormal behavior of one of its members.

An important concept to the strategic family therapist is the effect of *circular* patterns of behavior that are regularly repeated and involve three or more persons in the family (Selvini-Pallazoli et al., 1978; Haley, 1976). Circular patterns of behavior must be differentiated from *linear* patterns. In a linear view of behavior, a specific event is seen as preceding and causing a particular behavior and occurs independently of the behavior. For example, a misbehaving child may "cause" a parent to respond with anger. In contrast, circular thinking proposes that the misbehavior and anger in our example are related in an interlocking fashion. Thus, the misbehaving child causes its mother to be angry and irritable which causes the child to continue misbehaving, which maintains the mother's anger, etc. To strategic therapists, this sort of circularity occurs in triads in disturbed families. Haley (1976) provides an example:

> An example of a circular sequence of behavior—
>
> 1. Father becomes unhappy and withdraws
> 2. Child misbehaves
> 3. Mother doesn't deal effectively with the child
> 4. Father gets involved with mother and child
> 5. Child behaves
> 6. Mother becomes more effective; expects more from father and child
> 7. Father becomes unhappy and withdraws
>
> (Cited by Nichols, 1984, p. 433)

Directives and instructions play a major role in strategic family therapists' efforts to alter maladaptive sequences. Once a problem sequence like the one described above is identified and a goal for its change established, the therapist begins to design pragmatic strategies for blocking the symptomatic behavior. However, pragmatic does not necessarily mean commonsensical, for strategic therapists believe that commonsense approaches are rarely successful. Further, they also believe that insight and awareness are not always useful in bringing about behavior change. In fact, strategic family therapists often present their directives and instructions in the form of *paradoxes*, that is, statements which seem nonsensical and not-goal directed, but which can "shake up" a maladaptive sequence sufficiently to allow it to change for the better.

Rohrabaugh et al. (1977) describe three forms of paradoxes used by strategic therapists to bring about changes in maladaptive circular behavioral sequences. In *prescribing* strategies, therapists advise clients to continue or even increase the frequency of their troubling behaviors. For example, a family which has a rebellious adolescent might be told to encourage his rebelliousness or the family of an insomniac individual might be told to try to keep the person awake even when he or she wants to go to sleep. A different approach is used in *restraining* strategies where clients might be advised to go very slowly (too slowly) into the process of change. For example, a client might be "warned" that trying to change too quickly could be quite dangerous and that he or she might want to reconsider the decision to seek help. Finally, Rohrabaugh et al. describe *positioning* strategies in which therapists exaggerate the family's view of things. Thus, if a family member says things are "discouraging" at work, the therapist might suggest that they are probably worse than that and encourage the person to resign immediately. Regardless of their specific form, each type of strategy is assumed to motivate change by causing family systems to break out of their maladaptive sequences; sometimes change takes place via the family joining together in disagreement with the therapists, other times through a good laugh associated with the things that they find themselves doing as they try to follow the paradoxical directives.

An example may be helpful in showing how paradoxical strategies can help alter maladaptive system patterns. Watzlawick et al. (1974) describe an effective paradoxical intervention with a young couple who were bothered by their parents' treating them like helpless children:

> Watzlawick, Weakland, and Fisch (1974) describe a young couple who were bothered by their parents' tendency to treat them like children by doing everything for them. Despite the husband's adequate salary, the parents continued to send money and to lavish gifts on them, refused to let them pay even part of a restaurant check, and so on. Watzlawick and his colleagues helped the couple solve their difficulty with their doting parents by having them use reverse psychology. Instead of trying to act more competent, the couple was told to act helpless and dependent, so much so, that the parents got disgusted and finally backed off. This approach was clever and successful; but the therapists seem to assume beforehand that having the couple explain to their parents that they wanted more independence wouldn't work, and so they went directly to a paradoxical maneuver. (From Nichols, 1984, p. 447)

Other Family Approaches

In addition to structural family analysis and strategic family therapy, there are a number of other family therapies currently in use. Similarly based on the systems paradigm, each of these other approaches focuses on the family as the basic unit of treatment, but they differ in their specific methods. For example, in *multiple family therapy* (MFT) (Laqueur, 1972), several complete families are seen at one time and help one another work out their problems. In *social network therapy* (Speck & Attneave, 1972) the entire network of people surrounding a troubled family becomes involved. Typically including distant relatives, friends, and neighbors, such a social network may number over 40 people in a therapy session! While the methods do vary, all the family approaches are similar in their derivation from a paradigm which emphasizes the importance of the systems in which we function.

Community Psychology

Efforts to treat families as primary sources of psychopathology are clearly effective, but just as individuals are embedded in family systems so are they members of larger interlocking systems called communities and societies. *Community psychologists* believe that therapeutic interventions at these larger system levels can have even greater impact on the degree and frequency of individual problems. As defined by Zax and Specter (1974):

> Community psychology is regarded as an approach to human behavior problems that emphasizes contributions made to their development by environmental forces as well as the potential contributions to be made toward their alleviation by use of these forces. (p. 3)

Just as it is necessary for family therapists to have a basic knowledge of family structure and characteristics in order to deal with family systems, it is also necessary for community psychologists who focus on society as a system to be aware of its structure and characteristics. But families are relatively small systems which typically can be studied and worked with within the confines of a home, school, or professional office. Conversely, a system as large as a community or society cannot be analyzed or "treated" in the same way. In light of this, rather than describe and work toward some "ideal" system, community psychologists have redefined their task. In their view, their challenge is twofold. First, they must discover the nature of the "real" social system and, second, they must develop ways to work within the confines of that system. The task of determining the nature of the real system and the way in which its characteristics relate to the occurrence of abnormal behavior is called *epidemiology.* The effort to bring about changes in the mental health of people by intervening at the level of community and societal systems is called *community intervention.*

Epidemiology

Epidemiological research reveals the frequency of various diseases in specific subgroupings of a population and can lead to efforts to isolate the possible factors associated with the occurrence of those diseases. For example, epidemiological surveys first determined the relationship between smoking and lung cancer; this finding spurred researchers to identify the carcinogenic properties of tobacco use. In like manner, it is believed that epidemiological data can lead to clearer understanding of mental disorders.

In their efforts to establish how disorders are distributed, epidemiologists use a variety of concepts. *Demographic variables* (such as people's age, sex, and race) are examined to determine their relationship to the *incidence* and *prevalence* rates of disorders. The *incidence rate* reflects the number of new cases of a disorder within a given period of time (usually a year) per a given number of people in a population (usually 1000). Thus, a hypothetical incidence rate for phobias for the year 1980 might be stated as 3 per 1000 (3/1000). The *prevalence rate* reflects the *total* number of cases of a type of disorder in existence. Prevalence rates can be presented in a number of different ways. *Point prevalence,* for example, refers to the number of cases in existence at a particular point in time such as on a given day. *Period prevalence* refers to the number of cases that were in existence over some longer period of time like 1 month, 6 months, or 1 year. *Life prevalence* represents the number of people per 1000 who have had the disorder during their lifetimes. For example, the life prevalence for the common cold is very high, whereas the life prevalence for schizophrenia is much lower.

Data for prevalence estimates come from a number of different places. One source is those people who seek help for their mental problems. Prevalence rates based on these data are typically lower than rates based upon some truer indicator of *all* cases in a population. Called *true prevalence rates,* these latter estimates provide a more accurate picture of the number of people with a disorder.

The rates of mental disorders in large social systems like cities and countries have been the focus of a number of studies throughout the history of abnormal behavior (Regier et al., 1984). The most recent and ambitious epidemiological effort to date is the National Institute of Mental Health (NIMH) Epidemiological Catchment Area Survey (Regier et al., 1984). In this study, over 20,000 people in five different locations in the United States were interviewed and assessed for the presence of 1 or more of 15 DSM-III diagnosable disorders ranging from caffeine addiction to various forms of psychosis. The results of the NIMH study probably represent our best estimates of the prevalence of mental disorders in the United States and, as such, provide a view of the social system–abnormal behavior relationship.

Though lifetime prevalence rates for each of the 15 selected DSM-III disorders were reported by Robins et al. (1984), we will only describe their findings for overall mental disorders here. The rates for the specific patterns will be noted in the chapters in which we discuss them.

Depending on the site studied, between 25 and 38 percent of people interviewed in the NIMH study had experienced at least one diagnosable mental disturbance *in their lifetimes.* However, prevalence of

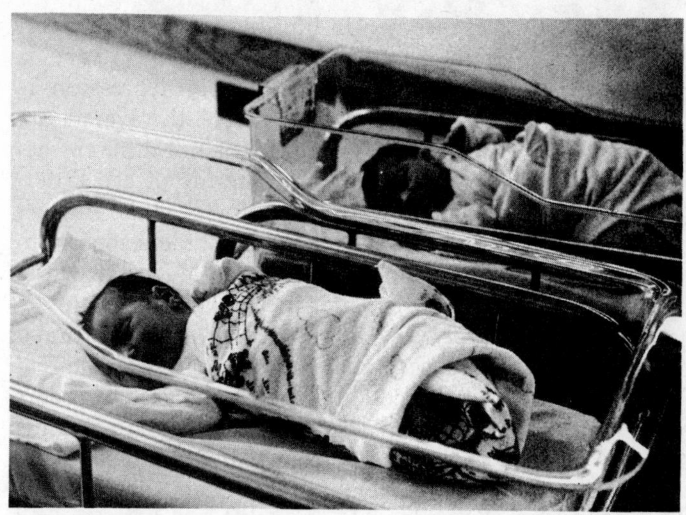

If current NIMH lifetime prevalence rates for mental illness hold, then these babies have about one chance in three of having a mental disturbance that can be diagnosed. (*Gloria Karlson*)

general mental disturbances was somewhat lower when examined within the 6-month period prior to the NIMH interviews (Meyers et al., 1984). In their analysis of 6-month prevalence rates Meyers et al. reported frequencies ranging from 14.8 to 22.5 percent of the population. These figures are not significantly different from the 16 to 25 percent rates reported in an earlier study (Dohrenwend et al., 1980).

Overall prevalence rates reflect the frequency of mental disorders in the general population, but they do not identify groups within a societal system which seem to be associated with inordinately higher or lower frequencies of abnormality. To identify such groups, prevalence rates are analyzed according to such demographic characteristics as sex, age, race, education, place of living, social class, religion, marital status, and country of origin. These data have also been reported by Robins et al. (1984) and Dohrenwend et al. (1980).

Robins et al. (1984) have reported that while there are differences between men and women in lifetime prevalence of certain disorders (e.g., drug dependence is more common in males, depression is more common in women), the overall rate of mental disturbance is not different between the sexes. In terms of age differences, it has been found that the highest rate for most DSM-III disorders appears to be in the 25- to 44-year-old range while the lowest lifetime prevalence is in the over 65-year-old age group. Additional analyses indicated that there were no real differences in lifetime rates of disorders between blacks and whites. Finally, Robins et al. reported that college graduates had fewer psychiatric disorders during their lives than those with less education and that people living in rural areas suffered from fewer disturbances than people living in cities.

While not yet reported for the 1984 NIMH data, there has typically been an important relationship between social class and mental symptoms. In a recent report, Dohrenwend et al. (1980) have stated:

> The lowest social stratum is almost always reported to have a higher rate of disorder than the highest class. . . . Across all studies (21 were examined) psychopathology in general was found to be at least two and one half times more prevalent in the lowest class than in the highest class. (p. 56)

Other demographic variables also help to provide a sense of the nature of the societal system–mental disorder relationship. Among these are religion, national origin, and marital status. Concerning theological beliefs, data compiled by Srole et al. (1975) suggest that there are, in reality, few differences among the three major religious groups in the United States with regard to overall rates of disturbance.

In contrast to religion, nationality appears more clearly related to differences in frequency of mental disorders. Generally, it appears that the overall rates for European countries are somewhat lower than those for the United States. For example, Schwab and Schwab (1978) have estimated that the point prevalence rate for all mental disorders in Europe is about 12 percent as compared with the rate of 25 percent for the United States reported by Dohrenwend et al. (1980).

In addition to data on religion and nationality, demographic information has also been collected on marital status. Data provided by Dohrenwend et al. (1980) indicate that divorced and separated persons seem to be at greatest risk for mental disturbance. Further, Gove and Howell (1974) have shown that not only do divorced and separated people experience more disturbances, but their symptoms are also more severe than those experienced by married people.

Although there are clearly many people in need of psychological help throughout society, not everyone who needs help gets it. Data regarding the rate of utilization of mental health services indicate that while up to 25 percent of the population may require help within a 6-month interval, only a little over 6 percent of the population obtains mental health services within that same time period (Dohrenwend et al., 1980; Shapiro et al., 1984). Although these figures might suggest that many people who need help are not getting it, it must be noted that people with more severe symptoms tend to get help at higher rates than those with milder problems. For example, over 40 percent of persons diagnosed as schizophrenic receive professional help (Dohrenwend et al., 1980). However, even with this in mind, it is still apparent that the number of people needing help far outweighs our capabilities to provide help via traditional individual, family, or group therapeutic approaches. To deal with problems of such magnitude requires interventions of similar magnitude, interventions designed to alter the nature of systems as large as communities or societies. Such interventions are possible within the framework of community psychology and psychiatry.

Community Intervention

The epidemiological identification of groups "at risk" for specific kinds of problems is only the first step in the application of the systems paradigm to the amelioration of mental disorders at the societal level. A second step is the development of a framework to guide professionals in their therapeutic interventions. One framework that has been especially useful is the community intervention approach proposed by Caplan (1974).

Caplan believes that people progress through specific stages from birth to death, and that at each stage they need certain "supplies" which help them through that stage and into the next. The three kinds of "supplies" are *physical* (such as food, shelter, and exercise), *psychosocial* (cognitive and emotional satisfactions received through interactions with others), and *sociocultural* (fulfilling the expectations of others concerning one's social roles and activities). The real or threatened loss of any of the three types of supplies can trigger a *crisis.* Caplan believes that crises are a normal part of development and help in the growth process. A crisis is a state in which a problem has arisen that resists being resolved by usual means; the old ways of dealing with the problem simply don't work anymore. Therefore, people in a crisis are forced to find new ways of behaving in order to solve their difficulties. A crisis has the potential to lead to growth or disability. Should people successfully resolve their crises, they may end up stronger psychologically. However, failure to handle crises adequately may leave people less confident and psychologically more vulnerable.

Caplan separates the more predictable *developmental crises* from unpredictable *accidental crises.* In the former, the crisis typically involves passage from one stage to the next and the changes in "supply"

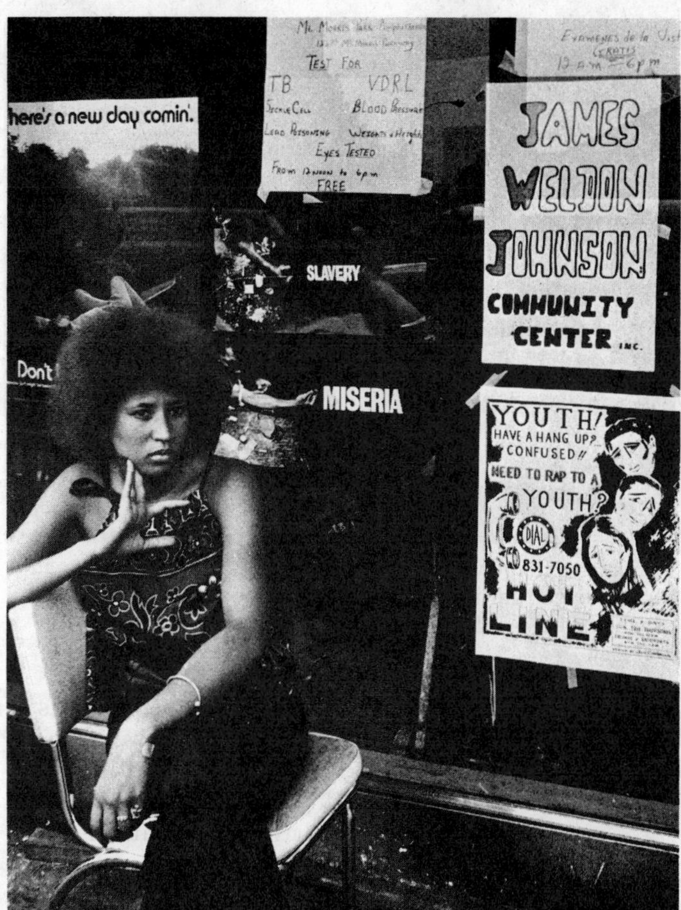

Community Mental Health Centers provide help to those in need close to where they live. (*Marion Bernstein*)

needs and availability which naturally occur. An example would be the "crisis" surrounding a student's leaving home to begin college. By contrast, accidental crises can be destructive psychologically and usually involve sudden and unexpected losses of "supplies," such as the death of a parent or spouse. Although they differ in intensity, Caplan views both types of crises as opportunities for growth.

Caplan proposes two ways to prevent crisis-based disordered behavior: *social action* and *interpersonal action.* Social action refers to improving the environment in which people live and interact so

In Caplan's framework of community intervention, crises can provide opportunities for psychological growth as well as psychological problems. (*Strickler/Monkmeyer Press Photo Service*)

that there are soon adequate amounts of all three kinds of supplies available. To ensure supplies are there, community mental health professionals must be involved in legislative and political activities. These activities are required to help guarantee the availability of physical supplies (for example, creating work opportunities that allow families to stay together), psychosocial supplies (perhaps reducing the isolation of certain "at risk" groups like the aged), and sociocultural supplies (such as providing ties to the community or society at large).

Interpersonal action usually refers to face-to-face interaction between a mental health professional and an individual or group. Since professionals can see only a few members of a community, they should choose to spend their time with individuals who are most likely to have impact upon large segments of a community. By selecting those who are in positions to supply the needs of other members of a community (such as prison wardens, political leaders, informal social leaders, or others in positions of respect or authority), the mental health worker can have maximum impact.

Be their major methods social or interpersonal, community psychologists agree that the best ways to reduce the frequency of mental disorders in large social systems is to *prevent* them in the first place. Caplan sees community intervention primarily in terms of three types of prevention—primary, secondary, and tertiary.

Primary prevention involves efforts to change social structures so that fewer people develop behavioral disorders. Such programs may be exemplified by the development of communities that have been carefully planned to avoid many of the "unhealthy" components of many freely developed population centers. One attempt at developing a new community based on this use of the systems paradigm is the city of Columbia, Maryland.

The opportunity to build the planned community of Columbia, Maryland, arose in the early 1960s. The city was to contain 100,000 people, and it presented an extraordinary opportunity for city planning. Panels of experts from many fields were convened. A health and welfare committee was given the responsibility for planning the community so that its physical structure might be maximally beneficial to the health of the townspeople. This task proved to be immensely complex. Struggles among members of the committee often centered about political and ethical considerations, but there was agreement on certain issues. For example, it was agreed that comprehensive physical and mental health facilities should be close at hand. It was also decided that it would be very difficult for members of Columbia to have a sense of community with 100,000 people, so smaller social units of around 10,000 to 15,000 were planned for. It was within these smaller social units that planning for neighborhoods and shopping centers took place. The planners also decided on having a downtown area with high-rise structures and to mix socioeconomic groups within social units. One major goal of the social scientists was to reduce sources of stress within the small social units. Therefore, some care was given to welfare planning and to several types of prevention programs, such as parent education, adult education, and access to counseling. Further, the planners sought to make recreational, occupational, and vocational opportunities widely available for all age groups. It was hoped and believed that such careful planning would produce a social milieu which would reduce the stress felt by people living in cities and contribute to lower rates of mental disorder.

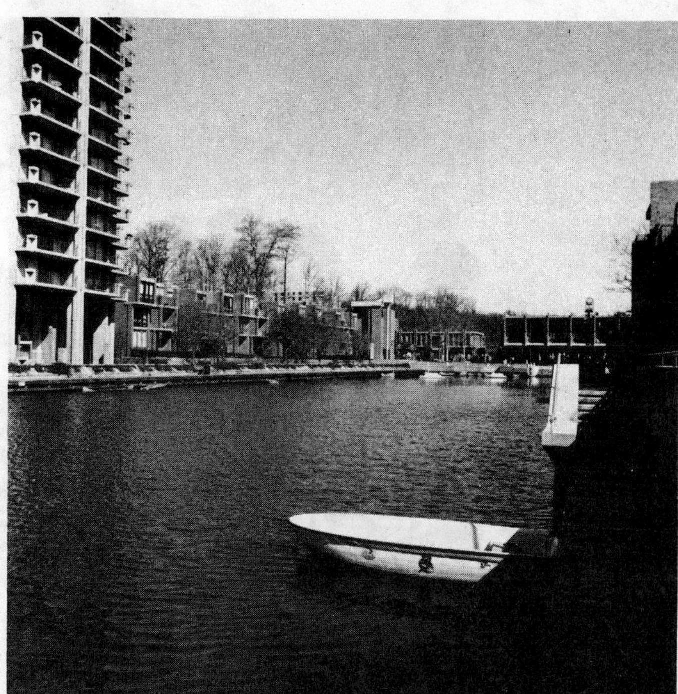

One application of the primary prevention of abnormal behavior is through the use of psychological principles in planned communities. (*Russell A. Thompson/Taurus Photos*)

Whereas primary prevention programs focus on avoiding the development of disorders in a general population, *secondary prevention* programs usually require that a "population at risk" (a group with a higher than average chance of developing a mental disorder) be identified and that attempts be made to reduce the incidence or prevalence of disordered behavior within that population.

An example of secondary prevention was the Residential Youth Center (RYC) program reported by Goldenberg (1971). The purpose of RYC was to create a residential setting in which personal growth of inner-city adolescents and their families (the populations at risk) could take place. The program differed in a number of ways from the more traditional juvenile home programs (tertiary prevention): It was based in the neighborhood where the youngsters lived, nonprofessionals living in the area usually were used as staff members, and goals and decisions affecting the program were arrived at cooperatively by staff and residents. The organization of RYC was unusual in that its structure was horizontal with all members, staff and client alike, sharing jobs ranging from administration to cooking. Staff members were chosen primarily on the basis of their knowledge of inner-city life, their experience in working with adolescents, and their willingness to voice dissatisfaction when necessary. Those chosen as staff members came from a wide variety of occupational backgrounds, ranging from mechanics to professional singers.

The 20 youngsters chosen for the RYC program were selected from a group of adolescents who had been "given up on" by other agencies. They all had made poor progress in school and had police records. During the day, the boys were expected to work outside of the center; RYC staff took this opportunity to meet with the boys' families. In addition to working with the boys personally, staff members worked directly on the environment surrounding the youngsters by setting up special days and programs for families and for the entire community. Boys and their families

One successful way to help hospitalized mental patients learn responsibility and practice social interaction is through milieu treatment. (*Marion Bernstein*)

had free access to the RYC building at any time of the night or day. The staff worked tirelessly to provide environmental support for all instances of new and positive behavior. The efforts of the RYC secondary prevention program seemed to be worthwhile. In an evaluation of the effects of the program, Goldenberg reported that, in comparison with a control group, RYC boys showed better records of employment, had less feeling of alienation, and had fewer run-ins with the law.

Unfortunately, it is often the case that efforts at primary or secondary prevention are not available or successful, and mental disorders do occur. Once this happens, the community psychologist must use *tertiary prevention* (also called rehabilitation or traditional treatment). All forms of intervention designed to shorten the time of disturbance are included under the rubric of tertiary prevention. However, within the systems paradigm, the societally sanctioned level of tertiary prevention would be *hospitalization* or removal from the community of an individual whose behavior is deemed to be disturbed (or disturbing). Hospitalization reflects the end-point of what Ullmann and Krasner (1975) termed the social process of mental illness.

Once in the mental hospital setting, a person may be exposed to a number of varying therapeutic environments ranging from locked wards to open patient-run communities. One example of such an open community is that developed by Maxwell Jones (1953, 1968) and described by Kraft (1976). Based upon the systems paradigm view that the social milieu can be a primary instrument of change, the *therapeutic community* represents a carefully structured and controlled attempt to establish a corrective environment. "All of the social and interpersonal processes in the hospital are considered important

The past decade has seen growing interest in defining and defending the rights of mental patients. (*Mimi Forsyth/Monkmeyer Press Photo Service*)

and relevant to the overall treatment of members of the community. No elements of hospital life are seen as outside of treatment and all transactions are important and potentially therapeutic" (Kraft, 1976, p. 163).

Evaluation of therapeutic community programs in mental hospitals has generally been favorable. As a result of Jones' original success, a number of similar programs developed in England and in the United States in the early 1960s (Sanders, 1967) and through the 1970s (Kraft, 1976).

Even though therapeutic communities and other hospitalization programs have been shown to be effective methods of tertiary prevention, some people are concerned about these applications of the systems paradigm. Beginning in the early 1960s, for example, the ability of psychiatric hospitals to provide active cure-oriented treatment above and beyond custodial care was called into question. Spurred by anti-institutionalization people such as Goffman (1961) and Szasz (1970, 1976, 1982), a number of researchers studied the effects of long-term hospitalization and found that people who stay in hospitals for a long time sometimes become "worse" than those institutionalized for short periods (Goldstein & Halperin, 1977; Ritzler, 1977; Romney & Leblanc, 1975).

The findings that some people did not seem to benefit from extended hospitalization in turn raised concerns about *the rights of mental patients to adequate treatment.* At the forefront of this movement was a hospitalized mental patient by the name of Kenneth Donaldson (Donaldson, 1976). A modern-day Clifford Beers, Donaldson had been hospitalized for over 10 years and despite continuous efforts, he could not obtain his own release. In 1960, he read about a lawyer-physician named Morton Birnbaum who had pub-

BOX 6-1

HOW DOES SOCIETY FEEL ABOUT MENTAL HOSPITALS AND THEIR PATIENTS?

In a series of studies by Phillips reported by Miles (1981), groups of New Englanders were asked five questions regarding their preferred degree of association with psychotic, neurotic, and normal people. As seen in part A of the table below, there was a clear lack of desire to allow current mental patients too close. Part B shows the subjects' preferences for ex-mental patients. Note that the percentage of people who would allow a marriage to, or rent a room to, a "normal" ex-mental patient is very low as compared with the percentages for a "normal" who has not been a patient before. One conclusion is that the respondents did not really believe that hospitalization or psychiatric treatment can "cure" mental illness; another conclusion is that they believe that mental illness cannot be cured at all. Probably both of these factors are involved, but a striking aspect of Phillips' data is that the mental hospital experience seems to make people *less* rather than more acceptable to society.

Table A Percentage of Subjects Willing to Associate with Mental Patients, Ex-mental Patients, and Normals

Level of Association	*Paranoid Schizophrenic, %*	*Phobic-compulsive, %*	*Normal, %*
Part A. Responses with Regard to Current Patients and Normal People			
Allow child to marry	1.7	60.0	98.3
Rent a room in house	3.3	88.3	100
Work with	11.7	98.3	100
Have in club	43.3	100	100
Have as neighbor	70.0	100	100
Part B. Responses with Regard to Ex–mental Patients			
Allow child to marry	0.0	1.7	16.7
Rent a room in house	1.7	16.7	40.0
Work with	8.3	73.3	86.7
Have in club	11.7	88.3	95.0
Have as neighbor	43.3	93.3	96.7

Source: After Phillips, cited by Miles, 1981.

lished his beliefs that mental hospitals were more like "mental prisons" and that rather than being simply "imprisoned" permanently with little hope of release, all patients had rights to treatment for their problems. Further, Birnbaum believed that if patients were not receiving such treatment, they had a right to be discharged at their request. Donaldson engaged Birnbaum as an attorney and, based on his claim that he was being denied his right to receive treatment, he was released from his hospital in 1971. In 1975, the Supreme Court supported Donaldson's (and hence other patients') rights to adequate treatment (Golaan & Fremouw, 1976). The Supreme Court's decision, in combination with decisions on a number of cases to follow (Stickney, 1976), has led to several requirements for involuntary hospitalization (commitment) and patients' rights to treatment: (1) People are not to be committed to hospitals unless they are deemed "dangerous to themselves or others"; and (2) if people are committed to a hospital, they may not be held indefinitely unless they are receiving adequate treatment. While these guidelines seem straightforward, they are still subject to varying interpretation. Because of this, Szasz (1982) has proposed that people prepare "psychiatric wills" stating their attitudes about psychiatry and hospitalization should they ever suffer severe disturbance and require treatment. Such wills would need to meet legal standards but would represent an exercise of the individual's legal rights to accept or refuse various types of help.

While the Donaldson case appears to be a victory for the rights of mental patients, it has also created some difficulties for some professionals charged with caring for disturbed people. As a result of the legal requirement to provide "adequate treatment" and the understaffing of many large institutions, many hospitals have been forced to discharge numerous disturbed long-term patients into the community at large. Because of their difficulties in adjusting to the stresses of community life, many of these expatients drifted throughout the lower echelons of society, sleeping in streets or on park benches or residing in decrepit hotels or rooming houses (Cohen & Sokolovsky, 1979; Lamb, 1979, 1980).

Obviously, the solution to the problems caused by the right-to-treatment decisions does not lie in releasing people because we cannot treat them, but rather in finding ways to treat them more effectively within the hospital setting. (Further, as Box 6-1 suggests, the community may not really be ready to accept ex-hospital patients back into its midst so easily.) Unfortunately, there remains a conflict between the legal requirement for rights to treatment and the abilities of many mental hospitals to provide such care. The innocent victims of this conflict are the mental patients whom both sides are trying to help.

Concluding Comments

The epidemiological data have shown that mental disorders are indeed a widespread social problem. If the current estimates of up to 38 percent of the population having some sort of diagnosable disorder during their lifetimes are accurate, we are including about 60 million people in the United States! However, Dohrenwend et al. (1980) and Shapiro et al. (1984) have concluded that only about 6 or 7 percent of people in need of mental health services may be receiving treatment. To be sure, the more severely disturbed people are more likely to have been identified and helped, but there remain large numbers of less disturbed but still needy people who could benefit from some form of mental health care. It is for the consideration of this large number of people that the community approaches based upon the systems paradigm seem particularly well-suited. Intervention at the community or societal level can have an impact on significant segments of the populace. In reflecting upon this, Hobbs (1964) termed community psychiatry "mental health's third revolution," for in it he saw a potential for effects on the understanding and relief of mental disorders which would be equivalent to the advances brought about by Pinel's unchaining the insane in 1793 and Freud's development of psychoanalysis. In the years since Hobbs' hope for a "third revolution," the Vietnam War, social unrest, and economic turmoil all have served to slow the progress of positive social change. Although Hobbs' contention would have us elevate the systems paradigm to a level of predominance, we must conclude that, at least for the time being, this global view must still be considered as being simply one of *three* major perspectives in modern abnormal psychology.

Having concluded our examination of each of the major paradigms in abnormal psychology, we will turn now to the consideration of the specific forms of mental disturbance. As we describe each form, we will make an effort to view it from the perspective of the three major paradigms. While all three perspectives will not be equally effective in dealing with various patterns of psychopathology, in our overview of the range of abnormality each global view will play an important and productive role.

Summary Chart

In Chapter 6 we examined the systems paradigm and its impact upon the science of abnormal psychology. We looked first at some of the major theories which have derived from the systems view:

General systems theory: People as open systems, how systems affect their members, and vice versa

Societal reaction theory: Labeling theory, primary and secondary deviance, residual rule violation

The socioenvironmental formulation: Life events and mental disorder, life change units and stress

We then examined some of the therapeutic approaches stemming from the systems paradigm:

Group therapy: Curative factors, varieties of types

Family therapy: Structural family analysis, strategic family therapy

Community psychology

Epidemiology: NIMH catchment area survey

Community intervention: Primary, secondary, and tertiary prevention

Rights of patients to receive treatment

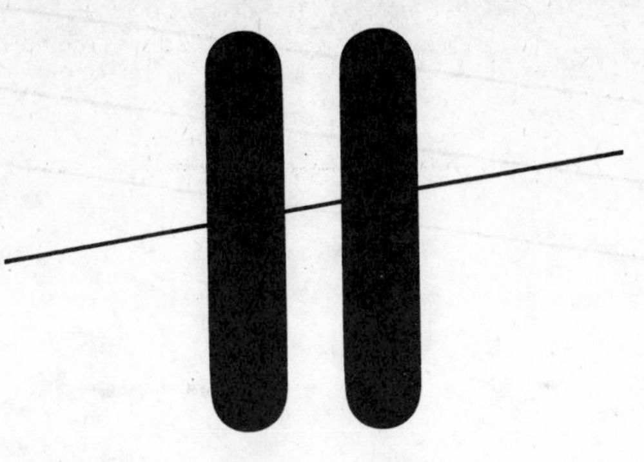

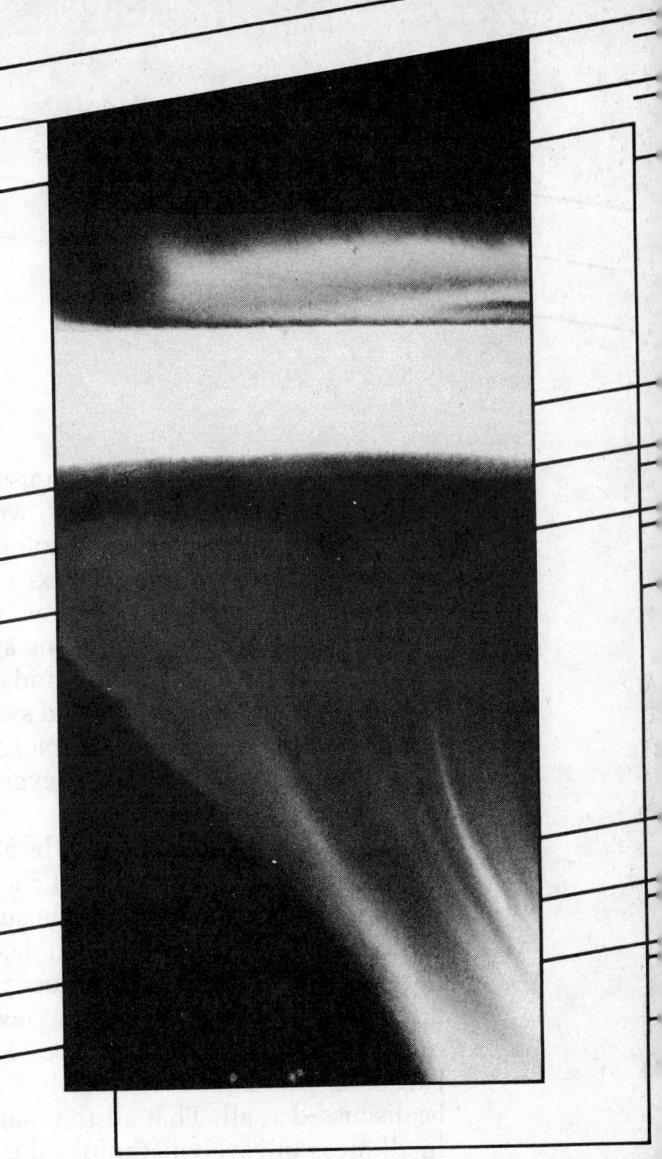

Patterns of Psychopathology

Having described the three major shared beliefs which guide the current course of abnormal psychology, we turn now to an examination of the specific patterns of psychopathology to which these paradigms have been applied. At this point in our text we begin a series of chapters in which we will consider the varieties of psychopathology classified in DSM-III. Each chapter will include descriptions and examples of the class of disorders under review as well as explanations and treatments deriving from (where applicable) the biological, psychosocial, and systems paradigms. We will try to demonstrate the manner in which these paradigms may have guided both researchers and clinicians and will attempt to evaluate their relative contributions.

While it would be ideal for us to be able to discuss all patterns of psychopathology from the perspective of each of the three major paradigms, the nature of modern abnormal psychology is such that all paradigms have not been equally applicable or fruitful in dealing with every form of disturbance. In light of this, in different chapters the order of presentation and the depth of discussion of the paradigmatic views will vary to reflect their differential importance for a particular type of abnormal behavior. In some chapters, a particular paradigm may have had such minimal impact that it will not be discussed at all. That all the major paradigms have not been used effectively in all areas of psychopathology does not necessarily indicate a failure on the parts of researchers and clinicians as much as it may reflect a potential failure of the paradigms themselves (Marmor, 1983). More will be said of this view when we discuss some emerging alternative paradigms in Chapter 19.

We will begin our discussion of the specific patterns of psychopathology with the schizophrenias, a set of very severe (*psychotic*) disturbances. The schizophrenias are not only the major and most devastating form of mental disturbance [lifetime prevalence over 3 percent of the U.S. population (Regier et al., 1984)], they are also disorders to which all three major paradigms have been applied. In this sense, they afford us an opportunity to examine most fully the way in which abnormal psychology as a paradigmatic science can be utilized in an effort to understand and alter disordered behavior.

CHAPTER 7

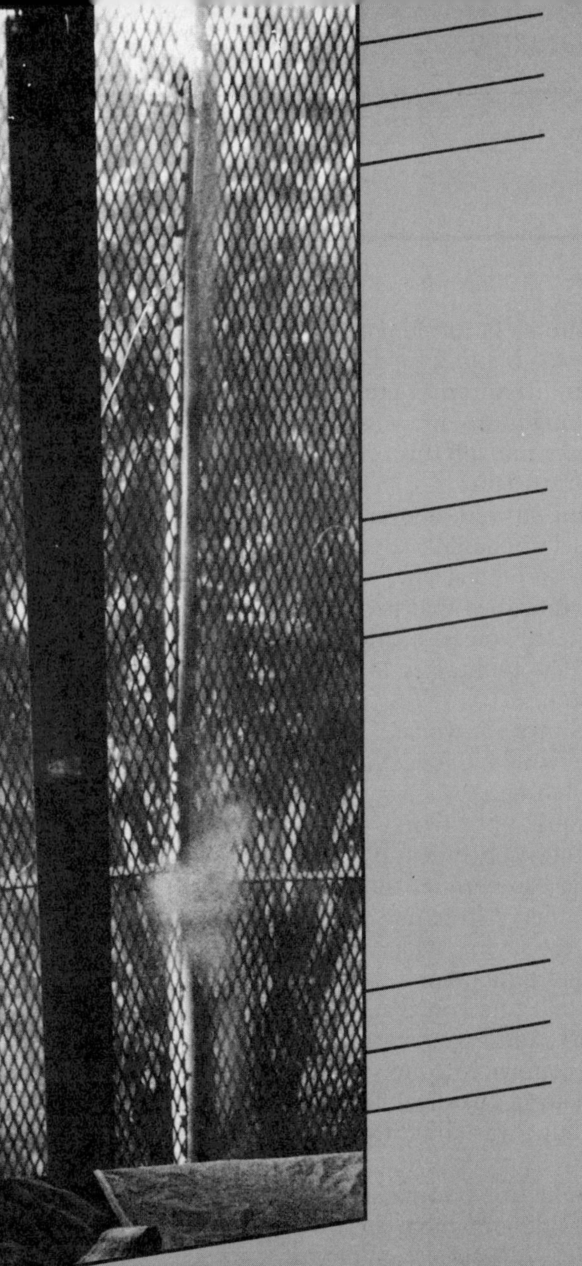

Description and Classification of Schizophrenia

Personal Experience: Schizophrenia

When my first episode of schizophrenia occurred, I was 21, a senior in college in Atlanta, Georgia. I was making good grades, assistant vice president of my chapter in my sorority, president of the Spanish club, and very popular. Everything in my life was just perfect. I had a boyfriend whom I liked a lot, a parttime job tutoring Spanish, and was about to run for the Ms. Senior pageant.

All of a sudden things weren't going so well. I began to lose control of my life and, most of all, myself. I couldn't concentrate on my schoolwork, I couldn't sleep, and when I did sleep, I had dreams about dying. I was afraid to go to class, imagined that people were talking about me, and on top of that I heard voices. I called my mother in Pittsburgh and asked for her advice. She told me to move off campus into an apartment with my sister.

After I moved in with my sister, things got worse. I was afraid to go outside and when I looked out of the window, it seemed that everyone outside was yelling "kill her, kill her." My sister forced me to go to school. I would go out of the house until I knew she had gone to work; then I would return home. Things continued to get worse. I imagined that I had a foul body odor and I sometimes took up to six showers a day. I recall going to the grocery store one day, and I imagined that the people in the store were saying "Get saved, Jesus is the answer." Things worsened—I couldn't remember a thing. I had a notebook full of reminders telling me what to do on that particular day. I couldn't remember my schoolwork, and I would study from 6:00 p.m. until 4:00 a.m., but never had the courage to go to class on the following day. I tried to tell my sister about it, but she didn't understand. She suggested that I see a psychiatrist, but I was afraid to go out of the house to see him.

One day I decided that I couldn't take this trauma anymore, so I took an overdose of 35 Darvon pills. At the same moment, a voice inside me said, "What did you do that for? Now you won't go to heaven." At that instant I realized that I really didn't want to die, I wanted to live, and I was afraid. I got on the phone and called the psychiatrist whom my sister had recommended. I told him that I had taken an overdose of Darvon and that I was afraid. He told me to take a taxi to the hospital. When I arrived at the hospital, I began vomiting, but I didn't pass out. Somehow I just couldn't accept the fact that I was really going to see a psychiatrist. I thought that psychiatrists were only for crazy people, and I definitely didn't think I was crazy yet. As a result, I did not admit myself right away. As a matter of fact I left the hospital and ended up meeting my sister on the way home. She told me to turn right back around, because I was definitely going to be admitted. We then called my mother, and she said she would fly down on the following day.

I stayed in that particular hospital for 1 week. It wasn't too bad. First I was interviewed, then given medication (Trilafon). There I met a number of people whose problems ranged from depression to having illusions of grandeur. It was quite interesting. I had a nice doctor, but he didn't tell me that I had schizophrenia—only that I had an "identity crisis." I was then transferred to a hospital in Pittsburgh. I did not care for my doctor. He told me that I was imagining things and constantly changed my medication. For instance, if I had a stomach ache, he would say I imagined it. At this stage of my recovery I was no longer imagining things, but I was afraid. I feared large crowds of people and therefore avoided going shopping, dancing, or riding buses (anywhere large crowds existed). It took me from September until March to recover. By the way, this particular doctor diagnosed my case as an "anxiety-depression reaction." In the meantime my family was very supportive of me.

In April, I decided that I was well and didn't need medication anymore (not knowing that I had schizophrenia and that it was incurable), and I also stopped going to the doctor's office. I got a job, from which I was terminated after a week. I became hypertensive and nervous without realizing it. My friends and family said I was behaving strangely, but I took no notice. I went out dancing practically every night to make up for the time lost while being afraid. I felt as if I were on top of the world—as if I were free.

The summer passed quickly. I had decided to return to Atlanta in the fall and complete my senior year. After all, I only had 1 measly year toward my Bachelor of Arts degree in Spanish, and I wanted to complete my education at the college where my education began. My parents, however, suggested that I finish in Pittsburgh, in case anything else might occur. I didn't listen, and somehow thought they were plotting against me. Next, I found myself in Atlanta and sick once again. I was taken to another psychiatric hospital. This time things were twice as bad as the first. I no longer heard voices, but the things I saw and dreamed about were far more traumatic. I recall at one point thinking I was Jesus Christ and that I was placed on this earth to bear everyone's sins.

My stay in that particular hospital was absolutely terrible. Each time I saw things I was placed in seclusion. They constantly used me as a guinea pig to discover which medicine would best suit my needs. However, I met many people (patients), some of whom became very close friends. I remained in the hospital 1 month and 2 days and was finally prescribed Loxitane, which I am presently taking.

After I was released, I returned to Pittsburgh and became an outpatient at Western Psychiatric Institute and Clinic. My doctor is very good and I respect her a lot. She's really a great person. It took me 6 months to recover. Again I was afraid of crowds of people, and I avoided them whenever I could.

Now I have been taking Loxitane for almost 2 years with considerable results. All of the symptoms seem to have vanished. I have my own apartment, I am back in college in Pittsburgh, president of my chapter of my sorority, and, above all, more confident and happier than I have ever been in my life. I reflect back on the pains of the past and consider them a learning experience. I foresee the future as a bright challenge. My doctor once asked me what do I think taking medicine means and I replied, "not being sick." Today I take medicine daily, just as a person with high blood pressure or a diabetic does. It doesn't bother me. Today I am really free!

The woman in this example is suffering from a form of schizophrenia, the most common form of *psychotic* (severe) mental disturbance. Schizophrenia is characterized by an extremely broad set of symptoms ranging from disturbances in thought to difficulties in behavior, affect, perception,and verbalization. It is estimated that upwards of 500,000 people in the United States may be treated for schizophrenia in any one year and that at any one time there may be as many as 2 million patients with this diagnosis in the country (Kolb & Brodie, 1982; Kaplan & Sadock, 1981a; 1985). It has been further estimated that as many as 3 out of every 100 people may experience some schizophrenic disturbance at some time during their lifetimes (Regier et al., 1984). Another way to put the extent of the problem is that "There are as many schizophrenics in America as there are people in Oregon, Mississippi, and Kansas, or in Wyoming, Vermont, Delaware, and Hawaii combined" (President's Commission on Mental Health, 1978). Schizophrenia costs the United States economy billions of dollars per year, but while the monetary cost is extremely high, it cannot be compared with the degree of human suffering it produces.

Chapters 7 and 8 will focus on schizophrenia as a clinical phenomenon and as a major research area. In Chapter 7 we focus on the history, classification, and symptoms of the disorder. In Chapter 8, current research on the possible causes and treatments for schizophrenia are examined.

A Short History of Schizophrenia

It is probably safe to say that schizophrenia is as old as humankind, but it was not until the eighteenth century that a systematic, scientific attempt to identify, understand, and treat the disorder was undertaken. One of the earliest written descriptions of the schizophrenia *syndrome** was provided by Connoly in 1849:

> Young persons not infrequently fall into a state somewhat resembling melancholia, without any discoverable cause of sorrow, and certainly without any specific grief; they become indolent or pursue their usual occupations or recreations mechanically and without interest; the intellect, the affections, the passions all seem inactive or deadened and the patients become utterly apathetic. (p. 56)

Shortly after Connoly's statement regarding the syndrome, the Belgian psychiatrist Morel applied the term *dementia praecox* to describe the case of a young teenage boy who appeared with the symptoms described by Connoly (1849). *De-*

* A syndrome may be defined as a cluster of symptoms which tend to occur together. Syndromes form the basis for diagnostic classification.

mentia is a term applied to the progressive loss of mental abilities associated with physical and/or mental disease. Following Morel's identification of "early dementia" (the literal translation of *dementia praecox*), some more specific forms of the disorder were identified and named. A most important figure in this effort was certainly Kahlbaum who described a hyperexcited form of the disturbance which he termed *hebephrenia* and a condition characterized by immobility and withdrawal for which he coined the term *catatonia*.

However, it was left for Kraepelin (1918), another pioneer psychiatric diagnostician, to integrate the variety of observations and syndromes previously described by others. In 1896, Kraepelin described a single disease entity, *dementia praecox*, that was expressed in various forms such as hebephrenia and catatonia. Kraepelin was an early adherent of the biological paradigm in that he believed very strongly that the disorder he described was based upon some genetic "injury" which led to progressive weakening of the emotions, the intellect, and the will.

Kraepelin's contributions helped prepare the way for Bleuler's more modern terminology for and conceptions of schizophrenia. In 1917, Bleuler (1930) proposed that Kraepelin had underplayed the importance of environment and the family in his thinking. Bleuler believed that the disease was not one of dementia, or a weakened mental capacity, but rather one of "disharmony" of the mental apparatus in which a number of confusing and often contradictory states of mind existed simultaneously. Based upon this idea of a "split" in the mental functions (a psychosocial paradigmatic view), Bleuler proposed as a name for the syndrome a word derived from the Greek *schizo* for "split" and *phrenum* for "mind": the new term—*schizophrenia*. Besides introducing a new terminology, Bleuler also designated a set of primary symptoms that could be used in diagnosing the syndrome. Known as the "four As," they included problems with *association, affect, ambivalence, and autism* and referred to difficulties in thinking, feeling, decision making, fantasy, and withdrawal. Seemingly favoring psychosocial or systems bases for schizophrenia, Bleuler also proposed extensive psychotherapy and environmental change as primary forms of treatment.

Fundamental Characteristics of the Schizophrenias

In addition to a set of broad-ranging *general* difficulties in functioning, people diagnosed as schizophrenic will manifest *specific* dysfunctions of at least one of the following types: behavioral, perceptual, affective, cognitive, and verbal. We will discuss each of these specific fundamental dysfunctions, but we will begin with a look at the more general qualities of schizophrenia.

General Dysfunctions

Almost all schizophrenic persons (Lehmann, 1980), show five general characteristics. *Symbolism*, the first, is the pronounced use of indirectly related patterns in speech, thought, and behavior. Colors may take on new important meanings. In one patient the color purple meant happiness and yellow meant sadness. In another, the days of the week held special symbolic meaning regarding relationships. Wednesday, because it was the middle of the week, related to the failure of those who chose the middle of the road in their relationships. Therefore he would never date on Wednesdays. Symbolic meanings are very individualistic and attempting to unravel them can be very difficult.

Schizophrenic people also show increased *sensitivity* to sensory and emotional stimulation as in the following personal experience.

Personal Experience: Sensitivity to Stimuli

Occasionally during subsequent periods of disturbance there was some distortion of vision and some degree of hallucination. On several occasions my eyes became markedly oversensitive to light. Ordinary colors appeared to be much too bright, and sunlight seemed dazzling in intensity. When this happened, ordinary reading was impossible, and print seemed excessively black. (Torrey, 1983, p. 9)

This excessive responsiveness appears to be present in some patients from as early as birth. To complicate matters, the schizophrenic person also can be hypersensitive to *internal* as well as to external stimulation, making intrusive thoughts and experiences harder to disregard when necessary.

A third general characteristic of schizophrenia is *social withdrawal.* With few exceptions, the schizophrenic person remains isolated and alienated from others and usually cannot establish close interpersonal relationships. Although the reasons for this kind of social difficulty may vary, the following personal experience reflects how difficult it is for schizophrenics to relate appropriately to others.

Personal Experience: Relating to Others

During the visit I tried to establish contact with her, to feel that she was actually there, alive and sensitive. But it was futile. Though I certainly recognized her, she became part of the unreal world. I knew her name and everything about her, yet she appeared strange, unreal, like a statue. I saw her eyes, her nose, her lips moving, heard her voice and understood what she said perfectly, yet I was in the presence of a stranger. To restore contact between us I made desperate efforts to break through the invisible dividing wall but the harder I tried, the less successful I was, and the uneasiness grew apace. (Torrey, 1983, p. 17)

It is not uncommon for schizophrenics to sit near one another for hours without ever acknowledging each other's presence. Not surprisingly, in nonhospital settings, many schizophrenic people may be extreme loners or recluses.

In addition to their problems relating to others, schizophrenic people also may have trouble dealing with themselves. They may manifest a *loss of ego boundaries* and seem unable to know where *they* end, and *others* begin. Thus, schizophrenics may believe that others can read their minds or understand their bizarre speech. Conversely, some schizophrenics may feel they can read others' thoughts. In extreme cases of loss of ego boundaries, people may see themselves as being merged or fused with inanimate objects such as rocks or TV sets. In the following personal experience the patient felt fused with the entire universe. His answer was in response to the question, "Everything disappeared and disintegrated around you? All your senses?"

Rather than referring to any particular

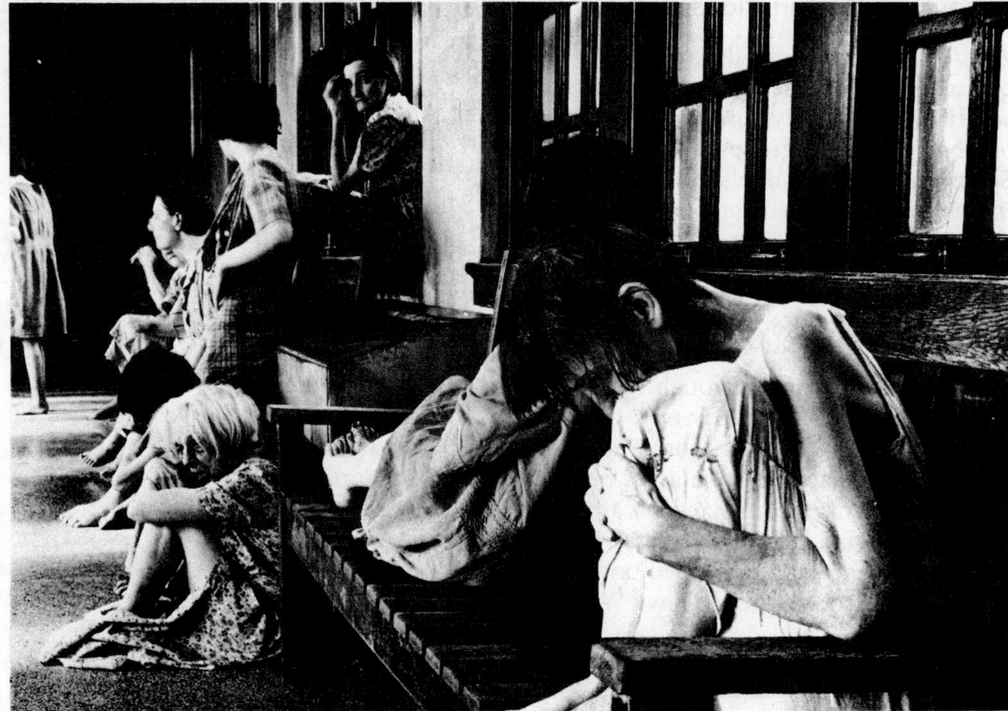

Those diagnosed as schizophrenics seem to be in their own world. They pay little attention to those around them. (© *Jerry Cooke 1975/Photo Researchers, Inc.*)

Personal Experience: Loss of Ego Boundaries

Everything except for my voice. This happened to me while I was in bed resting. And it was like a dream but it was just an escape into my subconscious—into the universe which is my subconscious. It's a microscopic cell and there's nothing else around but that. It couldn't happen for real—it could only happen that way to show me that I was the universe. It didn't happen automatically. Things didn't have to disintegrate but there it went. That was everything, everything had to do with that you know, to preserve me.

concrete behavior, the fifth general characteristic of schizophrenia, *variability*, refers to the overall unpredictability and inconsistency of schizophrenic behavior. In contrast to normal people, whose behavior is ordinarily only moderately variable and basically predictable, schizophrenic people can make us uneasy because we don't know what they will do next. For example, a schizophrenic person may be completely incoherent in the morning and quite rational and communicative that same afternoon. This unpredictable fluctuation in behavior can be quite demanding on family members and mental health professionals.

Behavioral Dysfunctions

Whereas the general dysfunctions are common to most schizophrenic people, additional *specific* dysfunctions also may be observed in subgroups of individuals. Schizophrenic individuals may be *over- or underactive*, and their activity may be bizarre and unpredictable as well. While behavioral dysfunctions may vary from person to person, we can delineate at least four different kinds. Grotesque grimacing and unusual movement of the arms or legs are examples of *psychotic mannerisms.* Some schizophrenic people may stare downward or upward while exhibiting a wry smile.

Personal Experience: Observing a Schizophrenic Individual

I watched Walter through the one-way observation window. He was a big adolescent, nearly 6 ft. in height and over 200 lb. He was attempting to do his classroom assignment. As he sat at his desk his face changed shape. He grimaced, he stretched and contorted his mouth. Then his face relaxed for a moment and he looked down. When he looked up his face was screwed into another bizarre expression. The facial grimacing continued until I left 30 minutes later. Attempts by classmates or teacher to have Walter stop these facial grimaces were unsuccessful.

Although these mannerisms typically mean little to an observer, they often seem to be very meaningful to the schizophrenic person. Further, because of their ego-boundary problems, some schizophrenics may believe that others understand what their idiosyncratic movements mean.

Besides strange mannerisms, schizophrenic people may evidence *echopraxia,* or the mimicking of other's behavior. Patients rarely seem to realize the negative impact of their mimicking behavior on those around them. Requests to stop the echopractic behavior are usually ignored.

In *stereotyped behavior,* rather than repeating others actions, schizophrenic people repeat their own self-initiated behaviors, such as continuously pacing back and forth for hours. One of the authors observed a patient who, for a year and a half, rubbed her index finger up and down on her forehead once every minute. Her stereotyped behavior resisted repeated attempts at alteration, in spite of the behavior's apparent lack of purpose and creation of a painful sore.

While the dysfunctions described thus far affect speech or movement, the last behavioral signs are the typical *slovenly appearance* and *poor social manners* of the schizophrenic individual.

Personal Experience: Observing Slovenly Appearance in a Schizophrenic Individual

Gary is liked by staff and peers alike, but he looks like he's dressed in a windstorm. Overweight and suffering from eye problems, Gary already appears a bit weird and different to others. However, in addition his pants seem too big and always are falling down around his hips. Buttons on his shirt are almost always buttoned wrong, and his shirt is half in and half out of his pants. There is always a good chance that Gary's underwear is showing. Everything seems at once too big and too small on him. Nothing seems to fit. He may burp in the middle of talking to you or scratch himself. Intervention from others seemed to have little impact on his dress or social behavior.

In some mental hospitals, one can still observe patients who have not washed or bathed in days and who show few, if any, of the social graces. Social skills are rarely used by schizophrenic individuals; for example, they may not say "hello" or return a smile. Although not as frequent as they once were, public masturbation and other sexual activity have also been observed among long-term hospitalized schizophrenic patients.

Perceptual Dysfunctions

In addition to deviations in behavior patterns, schizophrenics also may manifest perceptual dysfunctions. Distortions in, or absence of, accurate perceptions of the real world have been described by Lehmann (1980):

> [The schizophrenic] frequently sees objects and people change their dimension, their outline and their brightness . . . before his eyes. . . . Time may become devoid of any structure or meaning and the experience of passing of time may expand or contract. . . . [Perceptual] disturbances include hypersensitivity to light, changes in perceptions of other people's faces, misperception of movement, hypersensitivity to sound or smell or taste. (p. 983)

Hallucinations are the most common perceptual dysfunction seen among schizophrenics. Hallucinations may be defined as sensory experiences for which there are no external stimuli. In fact, for many professionals the presence of hallucinations is a primary indicator of schizophrenic disorder (Kolb & Brodie, 1982; Kaplan & Sadock, 1981a; 1985). Further, the presence of hallucinations suggests a poor prognosis for recovery in schizophrenia (Moller et al., 1982; Prentkey et al., 1980).

Most frequently, hallucinations are *auditory*. People hear voices (their own, God's, their family's) talking, screaming, whispering, or singing. If they are experiencing the loss of ego boundaries described earlier, it is frequently impossible for hallucinators to know whether the voices come from inside them or from such often claimed sources as radiators, TV sets, computer terminals, or air vents. This is reflected in the following personal experience.

Everyday objects can make some unexpectedly frightening changes as schizophrenics experience hallucinations. (*Michael Weisbrot and Family*)

Personal Experience: Loss of Ego Boundaries and Auditory Hallucinations

The voices . . . were mostly heard in my head, though I often heard them in the air, or in different parts of the room. Every voice was different, and each beautiful, and generally, speaking or singing in a different tone and measure and resembling those of relations or friends. There appeared to be many in my head, I should say upward of fourteen. I divide them, as they styled themselves, or one another, into voices of contrition and voices of joy and honour. (Torrey, 1983, p. 30)

Not as frequent as auditory hallucinations are *visual* hallucinations.

Personal Experience: Visual Hallucinations

I was sitting listening to another person and suddenly the other person became smaller and smaller and then larger and then . . . smaller again. (Torrey, 1983, p. 29)

Some schizophrenic people claim to see things of a frightening or symbolic nature, usually in conjunction with an auditory hallucination. Thus, the person who *hears* God's voice may also *see* God in the room.

Although they are far less frequent than the auditory and visual misperceptions, hallucinations of smell, taste, and touch also can occur as in the following description by a patient.

Personal Experience: Olfactory Hallucinations

On many occasions when I was stressed, smells would become quite important to me. I would smell sweet smells that triggered memories of childhood when I was happier. I would also smell acrid smells that reminded me of burning flesh and these would make me sad and I could cry. I can't control the smells and there's nothing I can do to stop the smells and the memories and feelings they bring.

Beyond these disturbances in "normal" sensation, Lehmann (1980) also describes *cenesthetic hallucinations*, or sensations felt in bodily locations not neurologically "wired" for experiencing such feelings. People may feel a burning sensation in the brain or a cutting sensation in a bone.

Cognitive Dysfunctions

While hallucinations refer to sensations with no basis in reality, *cognitive dysfunctions* are ideas and thoughts without adequate basis. There are two primary types of cognitive disturbances, *delusions* and *dysfunctions of thinking*.

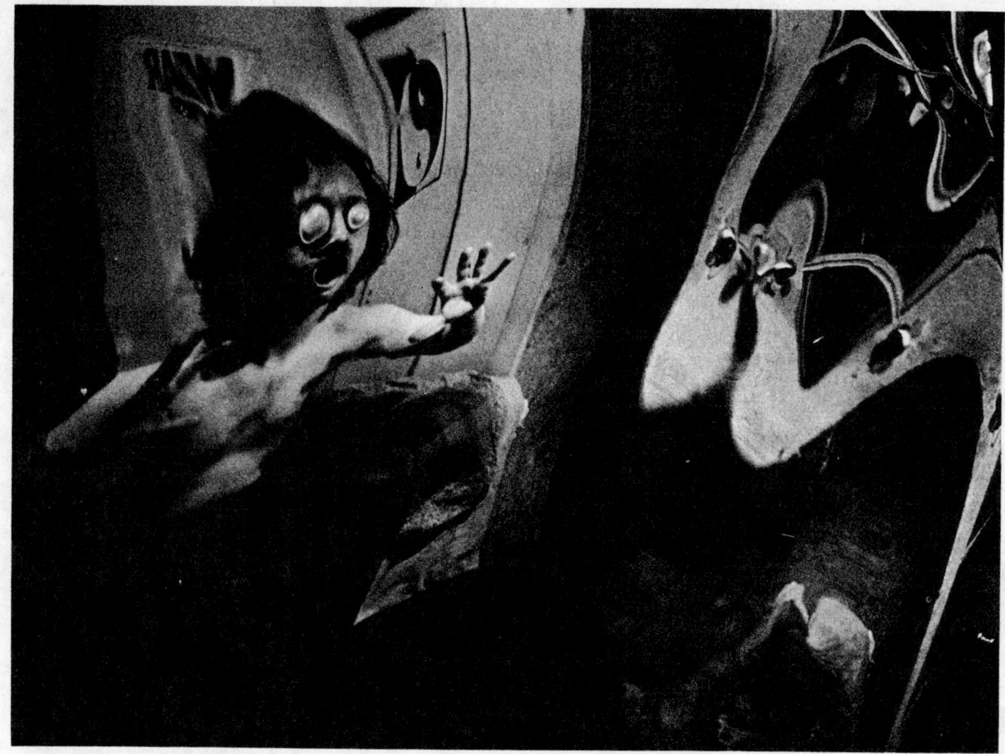

The world is a frightening place to those who are having difficulty holding onto reality.
(*Michael Weisbrot and Family*)

A common feature in many cases of schizophrenia, delusions are incorrect beliefs that are very resistive to correction by discussion or logical argument. The content of delusions can vary widely as seen in Table 7-1. It is important to keep in mind that "delusional" thought exists on a continuum anchored on one end by normal suspiciousness or skepticism, and on the other by severe irrational ideas.

Table 7-1 Some Common Patterns of Delusional Thought

Delusion of influence	A belief that others are influencing one by means of wires, TV, and so on, making one do things against one's will.
Delusion of grandeur	The belief that one is in actuality some great world or historical figure, such as Napoleon, Queen Victoria, or the President of the United States.
Delusion of persecution	The belief that one is being persecuted, hunted, or interfered with by certain individuals or organized groups.
Delusion of reference	The belief that others are talking about one, that one is being included in TV shows or plays or referred to in news articles, and so on.
Delusion of bodily change	A belief that one's body is changing in some unusual way—for example, that the blood is turning to snakes or the flesh to concrete.
Delusion of nihilism	A belief that nothing really exists, that all things are simply shadows; also common is the idea that one has really been dead for many years and is observing the world from afar.

Thus, most of us probably develop some fairly firm ideas or beliefs that are not soundly based in fact. For example, some college students are firmly convinced that as a group professors are "out to get them." Likewise, some college professors may be just as convinced that many college students will do anything to avoid work. It is likely that neither the students nor the professors are completely correct—each is probably "deluded" to some degree. People with pathological or paranoid delusions, however, are usually quite alone in their misperceptions of the world. There is usually little or no basis in fact for the schizophrenic person's delusional ideas, and their unrealistic quality is apparent to most people as is shown in the following personal experience.

Personal Experience: Delusions

I know why people have trouble with one another . . . why relationships don't work. See at one time there were no men and women . . . just people. There was no sex . . . people just stayed with one another and were happy. Then we sinned and we were punished and separated . . . men and women . . . and now we want to get together and be one but God still wants to punish us for our sins. That's why there's divorces and why husbands kill wives and mothers beat children. We all just want to be one.

Dysfunctions of thinking differ from delusional thought processes in that they emphasize the *manner* in which schizophrenics mentally process information rather than the *content* of such information. One example of thought disturbance is the use of special rules of logic called *paralogic* by Arieti (1966). An illustration of paralogical thinking is the following: "The Virgin Mary was a virgin. I am a virgin: therefore, I am the Virgin Mary" (p. 37). Matte-Blanco (1959) described what is called the *pathological symmetry* of schizophrenic logic: "John is Peter's father,

Table 7-2 Some Examples of Cognitive Dysfunction in Schizophrenia

Mystical-magical thinking Confusion between fantasy and reality. "I think that I am invincible, therefore I am going to jump off this building and not be hurt."

Concretization Abstraction is not possible so figurative thoughts and actions become literal. If asked to tell the meaning of a proverb like "A stitch in time saves nine," a schizophrenic might say, "I should sew nine buttons on my coat."

Overinclusion Inability to exclude irrelevant stimuli and cues. Reading this table, a schizophrenic might be unable to "tune out" the color of the room, the feel of the chair under him, or the sound of his own breathing.

Inability to hold a set Schizophrenic people cannot use a "Ready!" signal to improve performance on tasks like reaction time. So "Ready, Set!, Go!" may result in the same speed of response as just plain, "Go!"

Sudden blocking of stream of thought Often the schizophrenic person's thought will suddenly stop in midsentence. After a few seconds or minutes of seeming confusion, he or she may begin an entirely new topic.

Source: After Lehmann, 1980.

therefore Peter is John's father" (p. 254). (See Table 7-2 for some other instances of schizophrenic thinking dysfunctions.)

Chapman (1981) has reviewed the literature on other aspects of schizophrenic thought and concluded that these patients may have significant *problems in attentional processes* (Cromwell et al., 1979). Other evidence of the schizophrenic's being easily distracted from normal thinking processes also comes from the work of Oltmanns and Neale (1978), who demonstrated the adverse effects of auditory distracting stimulation on digit memory test performance. A possible reason for this distractability is found in the following personal experience.

Personal Experience: Distractability

My trouble is that I've got too many thoughts. You might think about something, let's say that ashtray, and just think, oh! yes, that's for putting my cigarette in, but I would think of it and then I would think of a dozen different things connected with it at the same time.

My concentration is very poor. . . . If I am talking to someone they only need to cross their legs or scratch their heads and I am distracted and forget what I was saying. (Torrey, 1983, p. 10)

Chapman (1981) also pointed out that schizophrenic people have problems with memory. For example, Koh (1978) has found that schizophrenic people in remission (not actively psychotic) cannot recall information as well as normal people. However, they can recognize previously seen stimuli just as well as normals. Thus, if shown a list of words, a schizophrenic person might have difficulty in reproducing the list from memory, but would do as well as a normal person in indicating whether or not words on a new list were among those on the old list. It was proposed by Koh that this recall deficit in schizophrenia is probably due to the lack of organizing structures such as mnemonic devices in their thought processes.

Flat affect is a significant characteristic of many schizophrenics. (*Michael Weisbrot and Family*)

Affective Dysfunctions

Although primarily a disorder of thought and perception, schizophrenia also can include *alterations in affective or emotional responsiveness* (Lehmann, 1980; Kolb & Brodie, 1982). Most notable among these affective alterations is reduced emo-

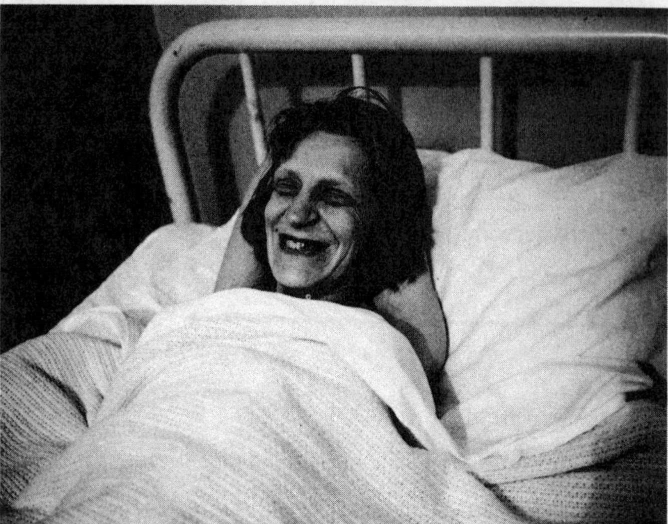

Inappropriate and uncontrolled elation may accompany severe psychological disorders. (*Mary Ellen Mark/Archive Pictures, Inc.*)

tional responsiveness or *blunting*. Many schizophrenic people exhibit "flat" affect; that is, they tend not to respond to situations with normal levels of feeling. Venables and Wing (1962) suggested that schizophrenic people may be so involved in responding to internally generated stimuli that they can't respond to anything else. In contrast, Mednick (1958) proposed that their reduced reactivity may be explained by the idea that schizophrenic persons actively "protect" themselves from stimuli with which they cannot cope by "turning themselves off."

Perhaps even more common than emotional blunting are the *inappropriate emotional responses* shown by some schizophrenic individuals. For example, a schizophrenic person may smile or laugh while talking about a very sad or frightening event. Generally, the more pronounced the inappropriateness of emotion, the more severe the schizophrenia. Indeed, the return of appropriate affect and reduction of emotional blunting often herald the patient's beginning recovery.

Verbal Dysfunctions

Sometimes related to occurrences of affective dysfunctions, the verbal deficits typical of schizophrenia are frequently the first to be observed by family and friends and are among the most disconcerting. Verbal dysfunctions can take a variety of forms, each representing some degree of deviation from normal conversation.

In one pattern called *mutism* the schizophrenic person might not utter a sound for anywhere from a few hours to several days. Typically encouragement or prodding have little to do with the return of speech, but even upon its return, the speech pattern may still be abnormal.

In *echolalia* rather than saying nothing as in mutism, schizophrenic people answer questions in such a way as to repeat most of the words of the question. Or perhaps even more disconcerting, they may repeat every statement they hear.

Incoherent speech differs from echolalia in that rather than simply repeating other's words, schizophrenic persons may speak as if they were saying something very definite, but in actuality they make little sense. Often they become quite animated in their presentation and may become angry if they do not receive a reply. The following example demonstrates incoherent speech:

Therapist: Why are you here?
Patient: I cannot fail to let him see that I am barren and wasted. The Prime Minister is raving and yelled at me but I feel cold.
Therapist: But why are you here?
Patient: You don't hear me or need to hear me. I cannot see the trees any longer for they are barren and wasted. The leaves are dead and my mother. Witches are Halloween Eve. The sky is Black and shoe polish. Hail to the walfordstefkin.

The final word in the above example, *walfordstefkin*, exemplifies a fourth form of verbal dysfunction in schizophrenic people, the creation of *neologisms*. Literally "new words," neologisms probably are constructed by schizophrenic persons because no word in normal language can express the idea they are trying to convey. For example, upon investigation, the word *walfordstefkin* was found to mean that the patient's brother Walter's car (a Ford) was being kept by his wife Stephanie's relatives. However, most neologisms aren't possible to decipher and remain understandable only in the private domain of the schizophrenic's disturbed thoughts.

Verbigeration refers to the senseless repeating of the same word or phrase for hours or even days. Thankfully, verbigeration is rare. It is the verbal equivalent of the stereotypic repetition of certain behavior which also characterizes the psychosis of schizophrenia.

Some Precautions Regarding the Diagnosis of Schizophrenia

Even with attempts to clearly delineate characteristics such as those we have just reviewed, the diagnosis of schizophrenia often remains a most frustrating task. As noted by Fenton et al. (1981), the diagnosis of schizophrenia is quite different from other medical diagnostic efforts. While in most medical diagnosis agreement is not only possible but is the rule and diagnoses are capable of being corroborated by subsequent examinations and laboratory tests, in psychiatric diagnosis of schizophrenia and other disorders, decisions can be affected by at least *nine* nonillness-related factors *other than the disorder itself*. Thus, as depicted in Figure 7-1, numerous interfering variables are present and can result in major errors in diagnostic classification. Even the most skillful and well-meaning diagnostician

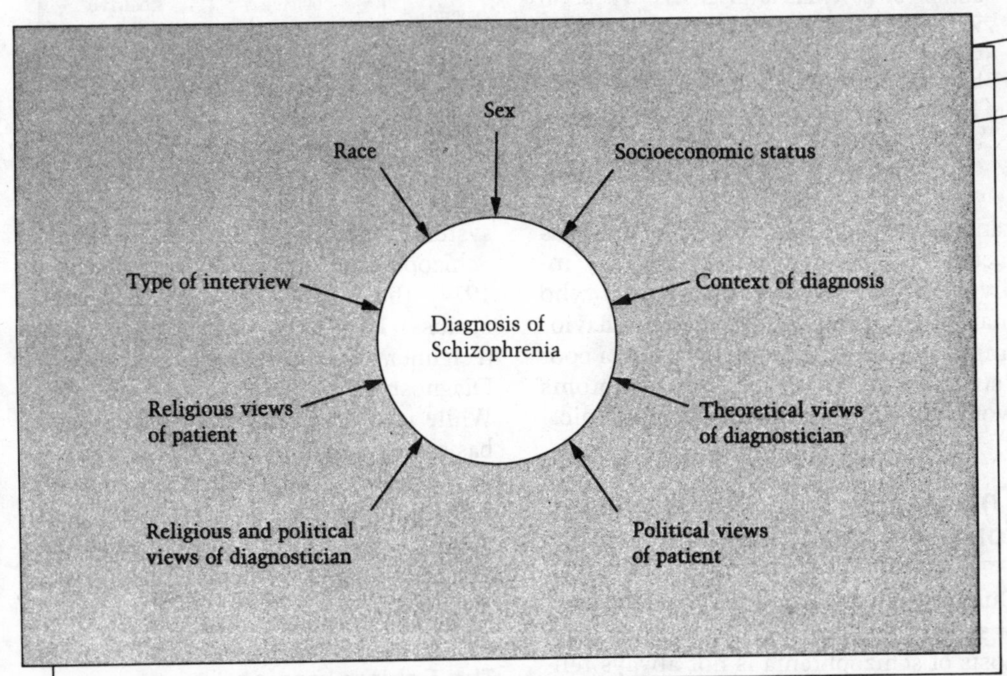

Figure 7-1 Factors other than the disorder itself that may contribute to the diagnosis of schizophrenia.

BOX 7-1

THE USE OF THEORY OF SIGNAL DETECTION IN EVALUATING DIAGNOSTIC SYSTEMS

A communication theory approach called *Theory of Signal Detection* (TSD) is used in the evaluation of psychiatric diagnostic approaches. Briefly, TSD deals with the probabilities of people detecting stimuli (such as sounds and the like) when exposed to them. A glance at the diagram below will help clarify the process. Note that there are four different probabilities represented in the diagram. *False positives* occur when a stimulus sound is not presented but people say they heard one. *False negatives* occur when people say they did not hear the stimulus sound, but one was in fact presented. *True positives* occur when people state that they have heard a stimulus and one was actually presented. Finally, *true negatives* occur when a stimulus is actually not present and people report hearing nothing.

TSD may be usefully applied to the evaluation of psychiatric diagnosis. To begin with, a good classification system should be one in which the rate of true positives is high but the rate of false positives is low. That is, the system should identify actual schizophrenics as schizophrenic, but it should not label nonschizophrenics as being schizophrenic. Further, an effective classification system should have a low rate of false negatives and a high rate of true negatives. This is to say, it would identify very few actual schizophrenics as being nonschizophrenic and a major proportion of nonschizophrenics as being nonschizophrenic.

TSD can be a fine way of judging the efficacy of the diagnostic systems for schizophrenia to be discussed in the text. It represents another example of the way in which the *science* of psychology is intertwined with its clinical aspects.

	Signal present	Signal absent
Subject perceives signal	True positive	False positive
Subject does not perceive signal	False negative	True negative

can sometimes be affected by extraneous factors. For example, a very wealthy individual from a well-known family who manifests bizarre thoughts and behavior might be seen as "eccentric" while a poor "street person" with the same symptoms would probably be called schizophrenic.

The DSM-III Classifications for the Schizophrenias

Due in some measure to the wide variety of symptoms associated with it, the diagnosis of schizophrenia is not always reliably accomplished (see Box 7-1). In fact there are at least five different systems for diagnosing this disorder: the first rank system (Schneider, 1959), the New Haven Schizophrenia Index (Astrachan et al., 1974), the flexible system (Carpenter & Strauss, 1974), the longitudinal system (Feighner et al., 1972) and the Research Diagnostic Criteria (Spitzer et al., 1978). While it is really too early to tell on the basis of copious published research, investigations of some preliminary forms of DSM-III (Spitzer et al., 1979, 1980; Regier et al., 1984) suggest that the approach yields very high levels of diagnostician agreement.

The Schizophrenias

Rather than describing schizophrenia as a single disorder, DSM-III recognizes that "schizophrenia is most likely a group of disorders of differing etiologies" (p. 181) which have been gathered under the rubric of, simply, schizophrenia. Included in this group are several patterns which represent clear cases of schizophrenia and others that *appear* to be very much *like* schizophrenia, but which may actually be forms of other severe disturbances. Later in this chapter we will describe these latter schizophrenia-like patterns. However, we will begin our discussion of the DSM-III categories with a look at the diagnostic signs for and categories of the true schizophrenic disorders.

General Characteristics and Signs of Schizophrenic Disorder

The primary characteristics of schizophrenic disorders are summarized in DSM-III as follows:

> . . . the presence of certain psychotic features during the active phase of the illness, characteristic symptoms involving multiple psychological processes, deterioration from a previous level of functioning, onset before the age of 45, and a duration of at least six months. (p. 181)

According to DSM-III, the course of schizophrenic disorder follows a specific pattern. In the beginning, or *prodromal phase*, patients may show social withdrawal, odd behaviors, deterioration in personal hygiene, inappropriate emotional reactions, unusual ideas and problems in communication. The length and severity of this prodromal phase is important to diagnosticians, for when there is a short prodromal phase associated with some specific environmental precipitating stress (*reactive schizophrenia*) the prognosis for recovery is quite good. On the other hand, with a protracted prodromal phase associated with progressive nonstress-related deterioration (*process schizophrenia*), the prognosis becomes poorer.

At times because of some identifiable psychosocial stressor and at times for no observable reason, the prodromal phase of schizophrenia moves into the *active phase.* In the active phase, schizophrenic individuals manifest many of the general and specific dysfunctions described earlier in this chapter. The active phase may last a few days to many months, but eventually it is replaced by a *residual phase* in which the person returns to a pattern of behavior very similar to that shown in the prodromal phase. Rarely do people with schizophrenic disorder return completely to their *premorbid state,* i.e., the condition of functioning prior to the onset of the prodromal phase. While a minimum of 6-months duration of these three phases is required for diagnosis of schizophrenic disorder, Huber et al. (1980) have reported on the basis of a long-term follow-up study of schizophrenic patients that the average total duration of the illness was 22.4 years.

DSM-III Subtypes of the Schizophrenic Disorders

DSM-III identifies five basic subtypes of the "true" schizophrenias. Each subtype shares the basic pattern of schizophrenia but differs from the others in certain salient features. For example, in *schizophrenic disorder, disorganized (hebephrenic) type,* the salient features are frequent incoherent speech, changeable and bizarre delusions and hallucinations, inappropriate or silly affect, facial grimacing, odd mannerisms, and extreme social impairment. The following personal experience of an actively excited schizophrenic shows a lack of clear response to our initial question and a special type of thinking distortion called *clang.* In clang, the person speaks in rhymes; new thoughts and topics arise as a result of a rhyming relationship with the previous thought. Thus, *knees* (niece) leading to *nephew* is an example of a clang association made on the basis of sound rather than content.

BOX 7-2

PETT SCANS: THE DSM-IV DIAGNOSTIC SYSTEM?

The future of diagnosis in schizophrenia and other severe psychological disorders may lie in the application of some new, very sophisticated computer-based analyses of specific brain functions. One of these promising techniques which may form the basis for DSM-IV is *Positron Emission Transaxial Tomography*, or the PETT scan (McKean, 1982; Reivich et al., 1981). In a PETT scan, a mildly radioactive sugarlike substance called 18F-fluorodeoxyglucose is injected into the bloodstream and makes its way to the brain where its metabolism is measured via a special method designed to represent differing rates of metabolism in different colors on a screen. Persons with diagnosed mental disorders of various kinds manifest differing patterns of colors than normals. PETT scans have been made of large numbers of mental patients with varying diagnoses. Some of the researchers making these scans [e.g., Farkas and Wolf and their associates (1984) at Brookhaven National Laboratories] claim to have established a different pattern for different disorders (schizophrenia, mania, depression, and paranoia). While still in the experimental stage, it is quite possible that in the future PETT scans will be an integral if not definitive component of psychiatric diagnosis and classification.

Personal Experience: An Excited-type Schizophrenic Person Speaks in Clang

Interviewer: How does it feel to have your problems?
Patient: Who can tell me the name of my song? I don't know, but it won't be long. It won't be short, tall, none at all. My head hurts, my knees hurt—my nephew, his uncle, my aunt. My God, I'm happy . . . not a care in the world. My hair's been curled. The flag's unfurled. This is my country, land that I love (singing), this is my country, land that I love.
Interviewer: But how do you feel?
Patient: Happy! Don't you hear me? (Mumbles some incomprehensible things.) Why do you talk to me? Rowf! Rowf! (Barks like a dog.)

While the excited type of schizophrenia is differentiated from the others by primary disturbances in speech and affect, *catatonic type* is characterized by salient features reflecting severe psychomotor difficulties. Further, differences in the specifics of these motor disturbances characterize two basic patterns of catatonic-type schizophrenia— *stuporous catatonia* and *agitated catatonia.* Stuporous catatonia is marked by *mutism, automatic obedience, and waxy flexibility.* Automatic obedience refers to the person's tendency to follow all instructions, even the most absurd (e.g., "Pat your head and stand on one foot"). In waxy flexibility there is compliance of a more passive sort in that the person can be placed in a wide variety of awkward postures and may even remain in that position until moved out of it.

Case: Catatonic Schizophrenia

Mr. A is a 29-year-old white male graduate student who had never before been diagnosed or treated for schizphrenia. Three months before admission to the Western Psychiatric Institute and Clinic (WPIC), he first experienced auditory hallucinations of a frightening nature consisting of voices commenting on his behavior. During this time he neglected his personal hygiene and isolated himself in his apartment. On the day of admission he was found kneeling on the ground outdoors staring at the sidewalk and was brought to WPIC by the police. He was alert and oriented and responded to questions with vague one- or two-word answers, mainly stating that he had been "under stress."

On examination the following morning he was found seated on his bed nearly immobile with his arms held stiffly at his sides. He was staring into space but would occasionally move his eyes to follow objects. Although he was slightly tremulous, no true tremors or other abnormal movements were noted. Because he was not cooperative at this time, a full neurological examination could not be performed. The cranial nerves that could be tested were noted to be intact. He appeared to perceive pain and would open his mouth on deep pressure but would not respond when lightly touched with a sharp object. Motor strength could not be directly tested, but the patient was able to stand with minimal weakness when assisted. Waxy flexibility was present (the patient's arms could be placed in awkward positions, which he would maintain for more than 2 minutes). . . .

The next day. . . . A neurological examination showed no abnormal findings. He later complained that he had been experiencing frightening auditory hallucinations during the time of the catatonic episode the previous day, and stated that he heard voices which made him "afraid to move. . . . "

Five days after admission he received antipsychotic medication for the first time . . . the dose resulting in a marked diminution in the auditory hallucinations. Shortly after discharge, however, the patient stopped taking his medication and began hallucinating again . . . and was lost to follow-up. (Lohr, 1985, pp. 172–173)

Agitated catatonia is characterized by *motor excitement* in which the patient manifests wild, uncontrollable behavior which is unceasing and often very destructive. Prior to the advent of the major tranquilizing drugs, agitated catatonia also was known as *fatal catatonia* (Stauder, 1934), because the unceasing activity characteristic of this disorder could lead to a state of total exhaustion and death.

Rather than motor disturbance, the salient features demarcating *schizophrenic disorder, paranoid type*, are delusions and hallucinations. While a number of different types of delusions are possible, the primary indicators for paranoid-type disorder are *persecutory and grandiose delusions.*

Case: Paranoid Schizophrenia

The patient—a 33-year-old, white unemployed husband and father of six living children—dates the onset of his distress to . . . (when) His maternal grandmother had broken her leg, and his mother had died of cancer. After the birth of a sixth child, his wife had her gallbladder as well as her remaining ovarian tube removed. After he had signed the form giving consent for his wife's sterilization procedure, he became quite upset at the prospect of having no more children as he felt this had destroyed him. He thought that because he had signed the sterilization consent form, he too had been sterilized. Since the operation, he felt his wife had less vaginal lubrication which made it difficult for them to have intercourse. He felt the doctors had put a tube in his wife's vagina and the tube, in turn, had been introduced into his penis, which made him impotent. Eventually, he began to smell odors, the nature of which was impossible for him to describe. But the smells would be persuasive and would in fact drive him toward or away from that which he was to do, almost as if there was an invisible wall of smell he could not penetrate. At times, the messages from the smell would be simiar to the impressions he would get from his boss to hurry up at work. Some of the smells were unpleasant; some were vaginal smells. Smells had powers over him.

In some way the town banker was involved with the smells, and he told the banker to "quit it" because he had heard voices telling him that the banker had drugs in the bank. Later he heard voices—including the voice of the man who had sold him his house—telling him to "Change your sewer system," which he proceeded to do. He had peculiar tactile sensations. He felt houseflies in an envelope, and the vibrations told him not to throw it away. Upon picking up the mail, he could tell through smell and touch whether or not to open it. He was aware of other smells on his children's school papers. He heard voices saying, "We don't care," and he thought this meant that he should kill himself. He almost did this with his shotgun but stopped after he thought about leaving his wife and children alone. There was evidence of thought broadcasting, thought insertion, and somatic hallucinations, including the feeling of a hammer hitting him on his tailbone, rump, scrotum, and penis. He said he had trouble maintaining an erection. He said there were wires in his nose and head with repetitive banging, almost like a heartbeat. (Romano, 1979, pp. 2–3)

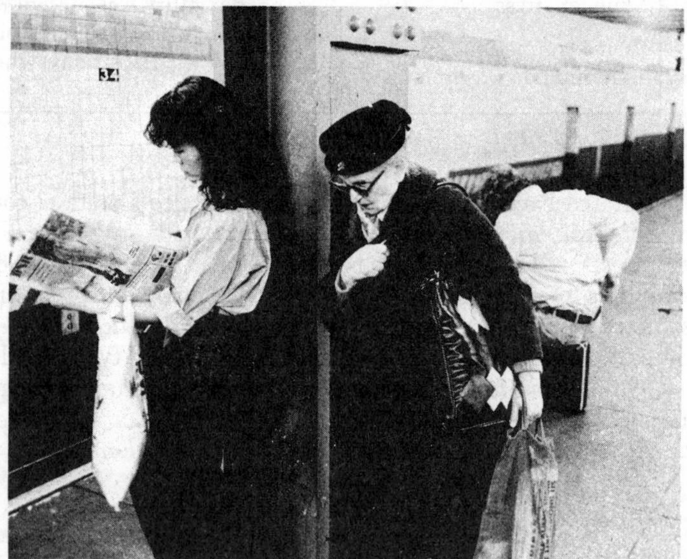

Paranoid-type schizophrenia is characterized by extreme suspiciousness of others. (*Michael Weisbrot and Family*)

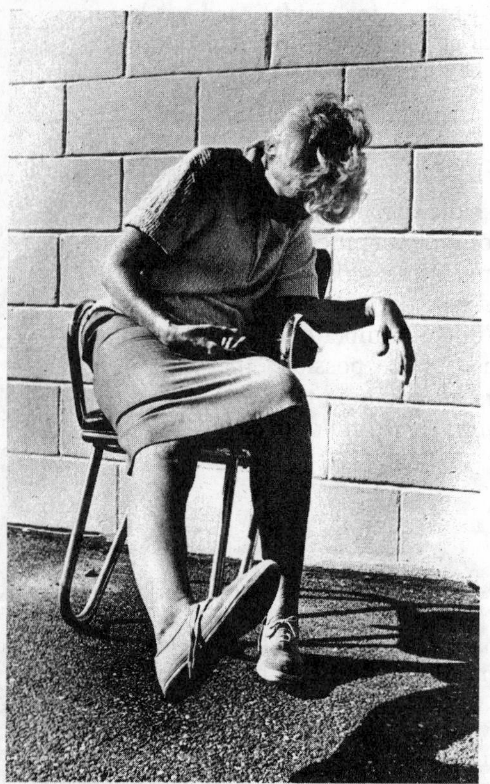

Catatonic-type schizophrenia is characterized by "waxy flexibility" or the ability to be placed in and maintain awkward positions. (*Elinor S. Beckwith/Taurus Photos*)

BOX 7-3

IS PARANOID SCHIZOPHRENIA, PARANOIA OR SCHIZOPHRENIA?

There is some confusion regarding how to classify paranoid-type schizophrenia. Part of this confusion arises because of similar symptoms shared by this type of schizophrenia and the patterns in DSM-III called the *paranoid disorders.* Characterized primarily by the presence of delusions of persecution and jealousy and the absence of hallucinations, the paranoid disorders may take three forms. In *acute paranoid disorder,* delusional symptoms last less than 6 months and are most commonly seen in people whose environments have dramatically changed, e.g., refugees, combat soldiers, flood or fire victims. Common distorted beliefs may involve invoking powers like communism or space visitors as explanations for the calamities. The condition known as *paranoia* differs from the acute pattern in that the symptoms last for more than 6 months and develop into an almost unshakable network of unbased beliefs. A final pattern is *shared paranoia* (also known as *folie à deux*) in which due to their dependence upon one another and their isolation from the rest of the world, two or more people develop a shared delusional system which may become very stable over time.

But is paranoid-type schizophrenia more like these paranoid conditions than like the other schizophrenias? In answering, we must consider several points. First among these is the unusual-for-schizophrenia clarity of thought and maintenance of personal hygiene often seen in the paranoid schizophrenic person. Further, the age of onset for paranoid schizophrenia is more similar to the middle to late adult age range of the paranoid disorders than to the younger adult onset more common for the schizophrenic disorders. These considerations, combined with the tendency for paranoid schizophrenics to behave differently from other types in studies of schizophrenic process, lead one to wonder whether it might be better simply to classify paranoid-type schizophrenia as a fourth paranoid disorder. Perhaps DSM-IV may reflect this opinion as well.

Paranoid type schizophrenia differs from the other types in several important ways. Typically, these people show minimal impairment in functioning and few affective symptoms and manifest the disorder later in life as compared with the other subtypes. Further, in research observations paranoid schizophrenics tend to behave differently from groups composed of the other types. These differences suggest to some researchers and clinicians that paranoid type may not be a "true" schizophrenia and may belong to a different group of conditions, the *paranoid disorders* (see Box 7-3). There is so much confusion surrounding the paranoid diagnoses that the DSM-III notes that it is not possible to describe clear differences between paranoid type schizophrenia and the other paranoid disturbances.

If a person manifests the major signs of schizophrenia but none of the specific patterns demarcating the excited, catatonic, or paranoid types, then he or she would probably be diagnosed as *undifferentiated type.* Usually diagnosed by exception (i.e., if none of the other symptom patterns is present, then it is undifferentiated), the primary symptoms of hallucinations, delusions, and bizarre behavior are usually present as is evidenced in the following case description.

Case: Undifferentiated Schizophrenia

A 28-year-old man appeared in a hospital emergency room complaining that he was confused, fearful, and depressed. He said he had been hearing voices and "seeing colors." His history showed that he had become very involved in a splinter religious group and that most of his time was spent in "church" activities. He claimed to be "the ambassador of Christ" and felt he had a special mission. On a visit to the World's Fair he upset his family by making bizarre "religious" gestures, standing and staring at people, and laughing and crying for no apparent reason. He was picked up by police in a major department store where he was shoplifting clothing in a very obvious manner. He claimed that he was not stealing because "everything belongs to God." At the time of his admission to the hospital, he claimed to hear the voice of God and to see the face of the Devil. (Adapted from Spitzer et al., 1983)

The four subtypes discussed thus far represent diagnostic patterns observed during the active phases of schizophrenia. A final category, *residual type,* is reserved for those people who have passed through the active phase of the disorder and are in a postdromal state characterized by social withdrawal, moderately eccentric behavior, loosening of associations, and illogical thought. The major change from the active phase would appear to be the absence of hallucinations and delusions.

A case may be helpful in illustrating the nature of residual-type schizophrenia.

Case: Residual-type Schizophrenia

There was a "bag lady" who frequented the T_________T college cafeteria. Each day she appeared at 7:00 a.m. and set up at "her table." She would spread out several paper bags in a specific place, put her purse on a particular chair, and set out her newspaper. She then would begin what was to be one "day-long" meal in which she would first get some tea, then go back and get some toast, and so on throughout the day. Students would come and go for breakfast, lunch, and dinner and she would always be there. She rarely spoke to anyone and seemed very uncomfortable if people even sat at the table next to hers. Her dress was rather shabby and she wore thick cotton stockings in summer and winter. She made grimacing movements with her face when she ate and was frightening to some, but she was simply a poor soul who could not function in any other way.

Other "Schizophrenias"

The disorders described thus far may be seen as clear forms of schizophrenia in that they fulfill the diagnostic requirements of symptoms *and* duration set forth in DSM-III. However, there are two forms of severe schizophrenic-*like* psychoses which, although fulfilling the symptomatic requirements, do not satisfy the duration guidelines. Diagnostically, it is on the basis of this duration variability that *brief reactive psychosis* and *schizophreniform disorder* are discriminated from schizophrenic disorders.

Brief Reactive Psychosis

Characterized by sudden onset and a duration lasting from a few hours to a maximum of 2 weeks, brief reactive psychosis may include bizarre ideas, mutism, inappropriate affect, silliness, and *transient* hallucination and delusions. Most often, the disorder is precipitated by some severe psychosocial stressor such as the death of a loved one, severe accident and injury, or combat experience. The rapid onset, however, also is typically followed by a rapid remission and recovery to the premorbid level of functioning. In common parlance, the brief reactive psychoses are probably best known as "nervous breakdowns" such as that described below.

Case: Brief Reactive Psychosis

A 35-year-old woman was admitted to the psychiatric ward of a county hospital by her family. Following the death of her oldest child in an auto accident 3 weeks earlier she had begun to show signs of extreme agitation and perceptual distortion. Her family became concerned when she began spending several hours a day in the child's room talking with the child whom she insisted was in there with her on "a special visit from God." On the day prior to her hospitalization, her husband discovered her lacing the family supper with chemicals. When she claimed that her son (the lost child) told her to do this so that the family could "be together again," the husband called their family physician who recommended hospitalization. Following a stay of 8 weeks as an inpatient she was released in a much improved state.

Schizophreniform Disorders

If the symptoms of schizophrenia last longer than 2 weeks but less than 6 months, the diagnosis of *schizophreniform disorder* would most likely be applied. Similar to the brief reactive psychosis in that it also is often referred to as a nervous breakdown, this short-lived psychosis differs from the schizophrenias not only in duration but in the fact that essential recovery to premorbid adjustment again is more likely. Further, there does not appear to be as clear a genetic link for the schizophreniform psychoses as with the schizophrenias. The following case history exemplifies schizophreniform disorder.

Case: Schizophreniform Disorder

A 43-year-old woman who worked with her husband in a mail order business suffered a psychotic disturbance which led to hospitalization. While working under great pressure to complete their Christmas catalog, she began to have vague fears that her husband was going to hurt her. After experiencing what she called "an evil presence" in her home, she ran away to stay with a friend. While there, she tried to type a letter to her husband, but began to believe that each of her typestrokes was "canceling out" another person on earth and that she soon would be the only one left. She began "seeing" meaning in the glances of people on the street and heard a voice saying to her, "G. is nuts." When admitted to the hospital she spoke incoherently, appeared very frightened, and cried frequently. The presence of bizarre delusions, delusions of reference, and auditory hallucinations of more than 2 months duration led to the diagnosis of schizophreniform disorder. (Adapted from Spitzer et al., 1981, pp. 227–228)

Schizoaffective Psychosis

Sometimes the diagnosis of schizophrenia is complicated by the presence of manic and/or depressive symptoms in conjunction with the basic signs of "true" schizophrenia. In DSM-III it is assumed that as long as the presence of affective (emotional) components are secondary, schizophrenia still may be diagnosed. However, there are instances in which affective symptoms are so strong that a diagnostician cannot decide whether the pattern is one of schizophrenia with strong affective aspects or affective psychosis (such as depression or mania) with significant schizophrenic involvement. It is for these cases that the DSM-III category of *schizoaffective disorder* is reserved (Meltzer, 1984; Tsuang & Simpson, 1984).

Case: Schizoaffective Disorder

Hospitalized for treatment of severe depression, a 44-year-old woman reported that 1 year earlier she had become psychotic after breaking up with her lover. Symptoms of this acute psychosis included being afraid someone was trying to kill her, hearing voices of people plotting her death, thought broadcast, and thought withdrawal. She locked herself inside her apartment, stayed up all night listening to the voices and could not eat. After approximately 2 months of treatment, she recovered from this psychotic pattern but a *severe* depression remained and continued for the next 9 months. During this time she did little except sit in her apartment and stare blankly about her. Since she manifested clear signs of schizophreniform disorder (the schizophrenic symptoms lasted less than 6 months) as well as major depression, the best diagnosis was considered to be *schizoaffective disorder*. (Adapted from Spitzer et al., 1981, pp. 235–237)

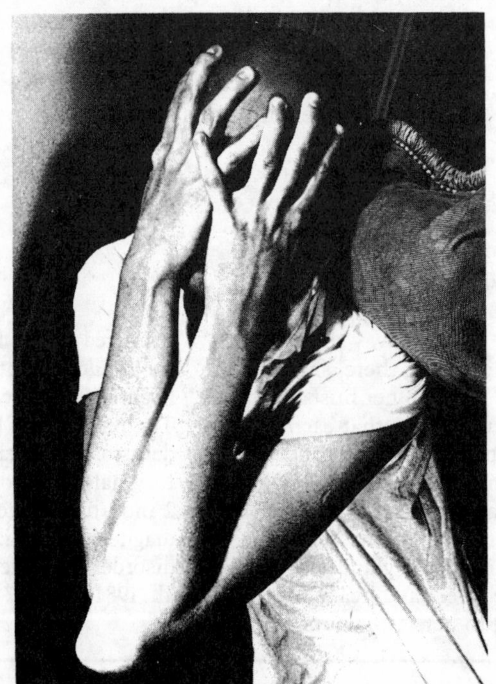

Brief reactive psychosis, which is characterized by a sudden onset of symptoms, is what lay people most often refer to as a "nervous breakdown." (© *1981 Susan Rosenberg/Photo Researchers, Inc.*)

Concluding Comments

In this chapter we began the exploration of the puzzling pattern of psychopathology called schizophrenia. Testimony to the complexity of this disturbance may be found in several of the major topics we covered. We saw that simply arriving at an acceptable name for the pattern encompassed decades of controversy. Further, the symptoms associated with schizophrenia are not only very broad-ranging but sometimes contradictory and mutually exclusive (e.g., verbigeration and mutism; stupor and hyperactivity). However, we also saw the personal misery and fear described by those diagnosed as schizophrenic. To schizophrenic individuals the world is a frightening, unpredictable, and foreboding place.

From this groundwork of reliable classification and rich personal experience we next move to a consideration of the considerable research that has been done to discover the how and why of schizophrenia. It is through the shared methods of research that it may be possible to begin to unravel many of the answers to the mysteries that enfold schizophrenic disorders. Research has yielded many promising possibilities that will be described in Chapter 8.

Summary Chart

Due to its severity and worldwide frequency, schizophrenia has drawn immense amounts of theoretical and empirical interest in the science of abnormal psychology. Reflecting this, we have set aside two chapters to deal with this psychosis. In Chapter Seven, we focused on general symptoms of the disorder and classification of its various forms.

We began with a short history of schizophrenia and then described some of its fundamental characteristics:

General dysfunctions: Withdrawal, loss of ego boundaries

Behavioral dysfunctions: Mannerisms, stereotyped behavior, slovenly appearance

Perceptual dysfunctions: Hallucinations

Cognitive dysfunctions: Delusions, thought difficulties, attentional deficits

Affective dysfunctions: Blunting, inappropriate affect

Verbal dysfunctions: Mutism, echolalia, neologisms

We continued with an examination of the DSM-III classifications for the schizophrenias and exemplified each of the following:

Phases of the disorder: Prodromal, active, residual

Subtypes: Excited, catatonic, paranoid undifferentiated, residual

Special forms of schizophrenia: Brief reactive psychosis, schizophreniform disorder, schizoaffective psychosis

CHAPTER 8

Research, Theory, and Treatment of Schizophrenia

The intensive efforts to identify and classify accurately the disorder called schizophrenia have been matched by equally massive attempts to explain and cure the disorder. As a result, several explanations and treatments for schizophrenia have evolved from the biological, psychosocial, and systems paradigms. The paradigmatically based research, theories, and therapies for schizophrenia are the main focus of this chapter. However, prior to describing these, a note of caution is necessary, for historically the findings of schizophrenia researchers have sometimes been misinterpreted. The major misinterpretation has stemmed from the confusion of *correlates* of the disorder with its *causes*. To reduce the chance of similar misinterpretation of the findings to be presented here, we believe it advisable to digress briefly.

The Question of Causation versus Correlation

Before delving into the specific research on the causes of and treatments for schizophrenia, it is necessary to clarify the difference between *correlates* of the disorder and its *causes*. Much of the work to be reviewed next might mistakenly be seen as identifying causes of schizophrenia. However, in order to identify a cause of schizophrenia or any other disorder, researchers need to perform studies paralleling those used to identify the causes of *physical* diseases. For example, take the diagnosis of tonsillitis. To establish that tonsillitis is *caused* by a bacterial infection, at least three kinds of information are necessary. First, the suspected bacteria must be found in people manifesting tonsillitis. Second, exposure of healthy individuals to the suspected bacteria must result in a greater incidence of the disease than is observed in a group not so exposed. Finally, the destruction of the suspected bacteria (i.e., removal of the suspected cause) should result in a reduction or disappearance of tonsillitis symptoms.

To determine "causes" for schizophrenia, similar sorts of data must be gathered. A first step would be to determine which characteristics, be they biological, psychosocial, or systems-based, seem to be associated with the presence of schizophrenia. Next, a group of people must be identified as possessing these characteristics or they must be exposed to certain identifiable *schizophrenogenic* (schizophrenia-producing) agents or experiences. The people exposed to these conditions should then develop schizophrenia. Finally, when people can alter or avoid exposure to suspected causative agents, schizophrenic symptoms should abate or not appear.

Because it is not possible to perform studies that actually try to produce schizophrenia in normal people, alternative methods of investigation must be used. One such alternative method is to use a *cross-sectional* methodology in which groups of diagnosed schizophrenics are compared with groups of nonschizophrenics. Differences between these groups are then sought as possible clues to causation. Cross-sectional studies, however, can be misinterpreted. For example, in 1932, J. Freud and Dingemanse published an article in which they reported finding a significantly greater amount of a specific biochemical in the blood of a group of schizophrenics as compared with a group of nonschizophrenics. They gave the substance the name *catatonine* and concluded that it was a cause of schizophrenia. The optimism generated by their discovery was dampened, however, when

Correlation vs. causation? Subway stations are most crowded just before a train arrives. Will getting a group of people to fill up a station make the train come sooner? (© *1985 Peter Norem*)

1 year later they reported that their mystery substance actually was simple *nicotine* (Dingemanse & Freud, 1933). Indeed, what these researchers had shown was that hospitalized schizophrenics smoked more cigarettes than the people with whom they were compared.

The Freud and Dingemanse studies illustrate a major concern for researchers in schizophrenia. When are differences between schizophrenics and normals a function of some directly causative factor and when are they merely *correlative*? Just as the excessive smoking of the schizophrenics (a common correlate of schizophrenia) resulted in higher nicotine levels, it may be the case that many of the more recent potential "breakthroughs" to be described later also may simply be correlates of schizophrenia. Thus, reduced blood levels of the biochemical monoamine oxidase may be a *correlate* of schizophrenia, not a *cause*; or extreme levels of family stress may be a correlate of schizophrenia and have little causative impact (see Figure 8-1).

The Biological Paradigm and Explanations for Schizophrenia

Adopting the global view of the biological paradigm results in researchers and clinicians seeking to explain abnormal behavior at the physical level. This perspective has been exceedingly productive in the study of the schizophrenias. The view has led to a variety of explanations including the genetic, psychophysiological, biochemical, neuromuscular, and viral approaches.

The Genetic Approach

The genetic approach leads scientists to consider the *heritability* of disorders like schizophrenia (see Chapter 4). The main thrust of the research, therefore, is to identify family patterns, concordance rates among identical (MZ) twins and fraternal (DZ) twins, and concordance rates among children of schizophrenics who were raised by adoptive families.

In many treatment settings and schools, children who are hyperactive are placed on sugar-free diets. In many cases, this action is taken due to an interpretation of research findings which show that difficulties with sugar metabolism have been observed in overly active children. In this interpretation, sugar intake is assumed to be related in a *causative* manner to hyperactivity:

Sugar metabolism problems ⟶ hyperactivity
(cause)

However, the coexistence of sugar metabolism problems and hyperactivity may be *correlative* rather than causative. This is to say that these phenomena may coexist because both of them are caused by some third factor. For example, if this third factor is a genetic predisposition:

Genetic predisposition ⟶ elevated activity levels
(cause)

and ↕ (correlation)

Genetic predisposition ⟶ difficulty in sugar metabolism
(cause)

In this case, activity level and sugar metabolism may be statistically correlated, but one does not *cause* the other. If only a correlative relationship exists between activity and sugar metabolism, assuming causation and implementing sugar-free diets would represent an error in scientific interpretation. Similarly, in the interpretation of the scientific data collected in an effort to identify the etiology of psychopathology, care must also be taken not to confuse causation and correlation.

Figure 8-1 Causation versus correlation: a potential source of error in scientific conclusions

Family Patterns

The example in Chapter 4 of the Kallikak family demonstrated that mental and behavioral as well as physical disorders tend to concentrate in close relatives. However, the genetic transmission of mental and behavioral characteristics is typically not so simple as the Mendelian determination of eye color; rather the genetic process is extremely complex and, for the most part, beyond our scope. However, based on a review of many years of research on the genetics of schizophrenia (Kessler, 1980a; Lukoff et al., 1984; Slater & Cowie, 1971), we can draw certain conclusions regarding the role of inheritance in the development of schizophrenia. Table 8-1 presents the estimates of risk for schizophrenia as a function of degree of family relatedness. The biological paradigm suggests that if a genetic component is present for a disorder, the risk rates should be greater the closer the blood relationship. Such a relation appears to be true for schizophrenia, leading us to suggest that there is *some* biologically transmitted family-centered genetic component in the development of the disorder. Unfortunately, the precise nature of this involvement remains unclear.

Table 8-1 Risk for Schizophrenia among Relatives of Schizophrenics

Relationship	*Risk*
Parents	4.3
Siblings (neither parent schizophrenic)	7.5
Siblings (one parent schizophrenic)	13.2
All siblings	8.0
Children	11.0
Children (both parents schizophrenic)	36.0 (or higher)
Half-siblings	3.2
Aunts and uncles	1.8
Grandchildren	2.7

Note: Risk equals the probability that a particular type of relative of an identified schizophrenic also will be identified as a schizophrenic.
Source: Based on data derived from Rosenthal (1971) and Slater and Cowie (1971).

The Twin Method

While the estimate of risk research focuses on all relatives of a given schizophrenic, the *twin method* hones in on the difference in concordance rates for monozygotic versus dizygotic twins (see Chapter 4). While early investigators showed MZ concordance rates to be as high as 86 percent (Kallmann, 1938), more recent studies have shown this figure to be somewhat lower though still significantly higher than the DZ rates. In Table 8-2, several twin studies of concordance in schizophrenia are summarized. Note that in each instance, the MZ rate is higher than the DZ rate, which is consistent with the idea that the greater the shared genetic endowment, the greater the chances of developing schizophrenia. Note also that, as compared with the nontwin sibling rate of 8.0 percent in Table 8-1, the DZ twins have still higher concordance rates of around 16 percent. Given that the DZ twins are not any more genetically similar than full siblings born at different times, one may conclude that the shared *environment* of the DZ twins also may have contributed in some way to their higher concordance rate (i.e., the systems paradigm receives some support here as well).

Table 8-2 Concordance Rates in Twin Studies of Schizophrenia

Studies	*MZ Rate, %*	*DZ Rate, %*
Kringlen (Norway, 1967)	45	15
Tienari (Finland, 1971)	35	13
Fischer, Harvald, and Hauge (Denmark, 1969)	56	26
Gottesman and Shields (U.K., 1972)	58	12

Source: Adapted from Kessler, 1980.

Adoption Studies

The specific contributions of heredity and environment in the development of schizophrenia are sometimes confused in the twin studies. One way of unraveling the interaction of these two effects was proposed in the mid-1960s by Heston (1966). Because of the turmoil often inherent in families with schizophrenic members, a significant number of children born into such families are adopted by normal families. Heston used this happenstance to develop the *adoption methodology* for the study of heritability of schizophrenia. The basic advantage of the method is that adoption allows researchers to observe whether a child who is genetically at risk for schizophrenia will or will not be likely to develop the disorder when reared in a nonschizophrenic family environment. If genetics are a primary cause, then rates for schizophrenia in children born of schizophrenic parents should be higher *regardless* of where they are raised. On the other hand, if environment is more of a key factor, children of schizophrenics raised in normal homes should have rates for schizophrenia that are not different from those of children born of *nonschizophrenic* parents.

In a series of studies, Rosenthal and Kety and their colleagues have demonstrated the usefulness of the adoption methodology (Rosenthal, 1977; Rosenthal & Kety, 1968;

Studying adopted children helps researchers to separate the effects of heredity and environment on behavior. (*Irene Bayer/ Monkmeyer Press Photo Service*)

Fieve et al., 1975). For instance, Rosenthal et al. (1971) studied 76 children born to schizophrenic parents (termed the *schizophrenic index cases*) and 67 children born to normal parents. All the children shared the fact that they had been adopted at birth and reared in foster homes which were schizophrenia-free. Results indicated that 30 percent of the schizophrenic index cases received a diagnosis of *schizophrenia spectrum disorder*,* as compared with only 17.8 percent of the nonschizophrenic index cases. As shown in Table 8-1, the 30 percent risk figure for the schizophrenic index cases is not really different from the 35 percent figure for children raised by their biological parents. Such small differences suggest that schizophrenia may be likely to develop *regardless* of the rearing environment.

Some notes of caution are necessary here. First, even though the adoption study data may suggest a genetic basis for schizophrenia, there remain up to 70 percent of index children whose parents were schizophrenic and who *did not* develop schizophrenia in foster homes. As Kessler (1980a) has noted, "...although in many cases a genetic predisposition to schizophrenia may be a necessary condition, it is by no means a sufficient condition to produce the disorder. Both genes and environment play a substantial role in the etiology of schizophrenia" (p. 21). In addition, Lidz (1976, 1977) and Lidz and Blatt (1983) have questioned the validity of what Lidz terms the "presumption" of a genetic basis for schizophrenia. Lidz's position is that genetic researchers have failed to consider sufficiently the effects of family environment in the etiology of schizophrenia. Lidz and Blatt (1983) state that the role of genetic factors in the etiology of schizophrenia is "far from definite or proven" (p. 426).

Reflecting the controversies in the schizophrenia research literature, environmental theorist and researcher B. Dohrenwend (1975, 1976) feels that we must recognize a standoff between the genetic and environmental explanations. In a similar vein, Gottesman and Shields (1976) have argued that the resolution of the genetic findings and sociological factors leads to a "sophisticated detente known as diathesis stress theory" (p. 371). These interactionists (using more than one major paradigm in an interactive manner) suggest that the *liability* to develop schizophrenia may be inherited, but not schizophrenia itself. Further, they believe the development of schizophrenia may be dependent upon the occurrence of severe life stresses in those people *diathetic* for (predisposed to or vulnerable to) schizophrenia (Zubin & Spring, 1977). Anticipating a modern interactionist view, the diathesis-stress model of Meehl (1962) can explain much of what is known about the occurrence of schizophrenia among relatives. According to Meehl's theory, an inherited predisposition, *schizotaxia*, must interact with a *schizophrenogenic environment* to produce schizophrenia.

Most recently, the interactional view has been restated by Nuechterlein and Dawson (1984a) in their vulnerability-stress model for schizophrenia. These researchers propose that:

> ... certain characteristics of individuals may serve as vulnerability factors and that environmental stressors may precipitate psychotic periods in vulnerable individuals. Certain information processing deficits, automatic reactivity (problems), and social competence and coping limitations are viewed as potential vulnerability factors. Stressors in the form of discrete life events as well as the prevailing level of social environmental stress are seen as factors that interact with preexisting vulnerability characteristics to produce vicious circles, which lead, in turn, to psychotic episodes. (1984a, p. 300)

*Schizophrenia spectrum disorders include a variety of disturbances ranging from schizoid personality to schizophrenia per se. The concept was developed to include in concordance rate estimates the occurrence of other possibly inherited disorders related to schizophrenia in relatives of schizophrenics.

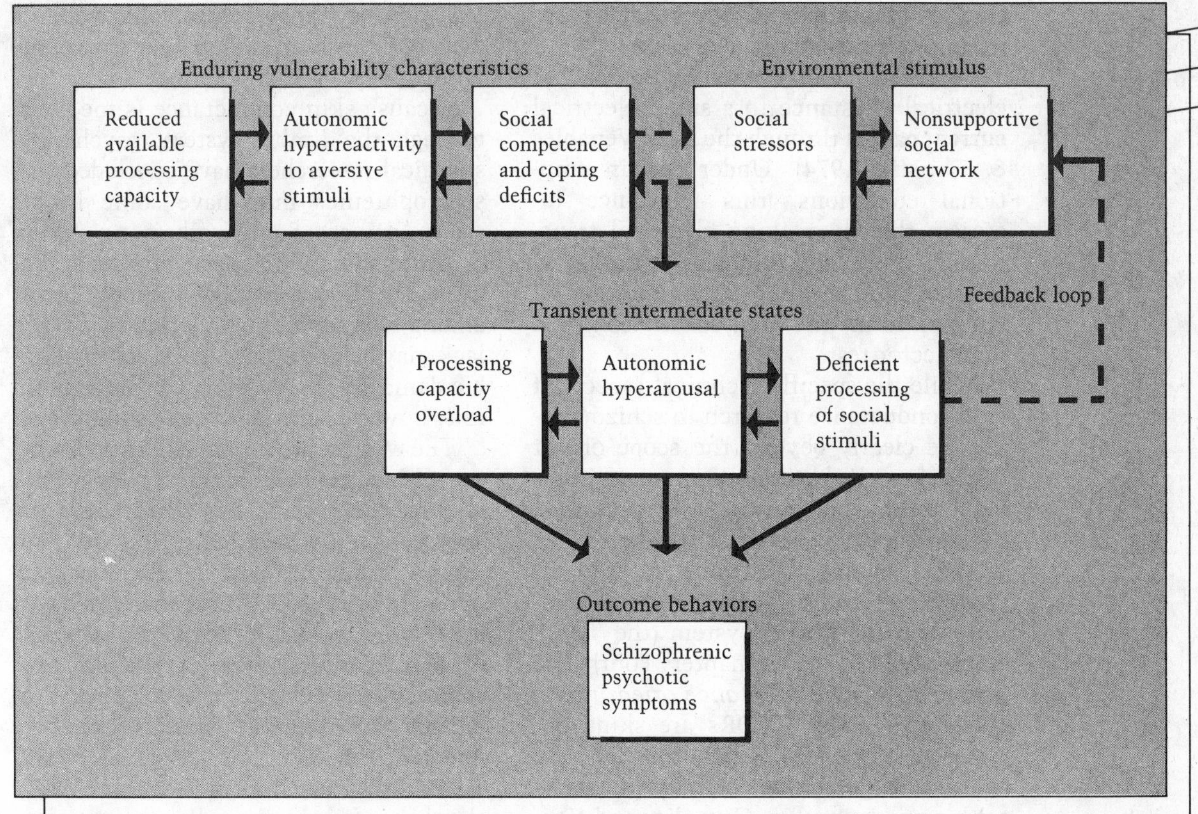

Figure 8-2 A tentative, interactive vulnerability/stress model for the development of schizophrenic psychotic episodes.

Nuechterlein and Dawson, demonstrating their perspective graphically, have offered the chart presented in Figure 8-2. As can be seen, the final outcome of schizophrenia may be produced via the interaction of many personal and environmental factors. As such, the disorder is considered to be based on neither biological nor environmental factors exclusively, but it reflects both genetic as well as experiential contributions.

The Psychophysiological Approach

Besides possible genetic differences between schizophrenics and normals, researchers also have identified a number of ways these groups differ *psychophysiologically*. Psychophysiology, according to Spohn and Patterson (1980), "involves methods of recording and processing bioelectric signals from the surface of the skin. Such bioelectric signals typically reflect the activity of the central nervous system (CNS) and the peripheral nervous system (PNS)" (p. 581). Through psychophysiological methods it has been possible to identify differences between normals and schizophrenics in electrical properties of the skin, in cardiovascular activity, in eye movement patterns, and in brain waves (*electroencephalograms* or EEGs) (Dawson & Nuechterlein, 1984). Here again, however, the difference between causation and correlation must be kept in mind. Many of the psychophysiological abnormalities found in schizophrenic people seem more correlative than causative. However, *clear* correlates of a disorder can have significant value because their presence or absence may become reliable bases for difficult diagnostic decisions.

Skin conductance refers to the level of electrical resistance to a small electrical current passed through the skin (Venables & Christie, 1974). Under certain emotional conditions, this resistance increases thereby making electrical transmission more difficult. The variation in skin conductance (SC) in varying states of emotion forms the basis for the common lie detector test.

While the specific technical aspects of skin conductance research in schizophrenia are clearly beyond the scope of our discussion, the basic findings are of interest. For example, working with monkeys, Bagshaw and her associates (Bagshaw et al., 1965; Bagshaw & Kimble, 1972) demonstrated a link between abnormal conditions in the limbic system (the "emotional brain"; see Chapter Four) and abnormal *skin conductance orienting responses* (SCORs). SCORs are skin conductance responses which are observed when an organism is initially presented with a new stimulus. Gruzelier and Venables (1975) extended Bagshaw's work to human beings. They found that over 50 percent of schizophrenics showed *no* SCORs (i.e., they did not respond to new stimuli), while the remainder of their sample showed SCORs which did not *habituate* (disappear with repeated presentations and increasing familiarity with the stimulus). Thus, while the specific SCOR patterns differed within the group of schizophrenics, *all* the schizophrenics manifested some sort of SCOR disturbance.

More recent work involving psychophysiological dysfunctions in schizophrenia has been reported by Dawson and Nuechterlein (1984). These researchers identified two abnormalities in schizophrenics: (1) abnormally high sympathetic arousal and (2) an abnormal absence of SCORs. They conclude that these factors as well as other psychophysiological indicators may someday be used in a diagnostic fashion to help identify people vulnerable to schizophrenia.

Because skin conductance is mediated through the limbic system, psychophysiological researchers have concluded that schizophrenics may have some limbic system damage. Some workers (e.g., Spohn & Patterson, 1980) have proposed that given the higher rate of difficult births among schizophrenics, perinatal oxygen lack may be among the causes of this limbic damage. The viability of this hypothesis, however, has not been established.

The work of psychophysiologists studying schizophrenia holds great promise not only for the possible identification of the sources of schizophrenia, but for improved diagnosis as well. For example, since abnormal SCORs are found in a vast majority of schizophrenics, the presence of these abnormal electrical patterns may someday serve as a reliable diagnostic indicator. Longitudinal studies currently underway in Denmark (Mednick et al., 1978) and Great Britain (Venables, 1977) should contribute to a fuller evaluation of the potential of the psychophysiological approach.

The Biochemical Approach

Whereas psychophysiological research focuses on a more general level of analysis, the biochemical approach leads investigators to stress the *micro* aspects of neural function and their possible relationship to the etiology of schizophrenia. Owing much of its current viability to the work of Kety, Rosenthal, and their colleagues, the biochemical perspective suggests that observed abnormal behavior is based on defects in one or more neurochemical systems (see Donaldson et al., 1983). As is true of most other researchers gathered under a nominal umbrella, scientists examining biochemical aspects of schizophrenia are quite varied in their specific focus. The variations in focus we will describe are those examining dopamine, monoamine oxidase, endorphins, and endogenous hallucinogens in the development of schizophrenia.

The Dopamine Hypothesis

In the *dopamine hypothesis* schizophrenia is seen to result from abnormalities in the availability of the neurotransmitter dopamine in various parts of the central nervous system (Bunney, 1978; Carlsson, 1977, 1978). These abnormalities may be in the form of excess dopamine found at the dendritic receptor sites or in the synapses (Carlsson, 1977) or in hypersensitivity of dopamine receptors. This hypersensitivity seems to occur for as yet unknown reasons and can produce above-normal reactivity in the nervous system even with a relatively constant amount of actual dopamine present (Langer et al., 1981).

In examining the dopamine hypothesis, researchers (e.g., Walinder et al., 1976) have found that reduction of dopamine can lead to significant decreases in psychotic symptoms. Similarly, Bird et al. (1979), in a postmortem study of diagnosed schizophrenics, reported abnormally high levels of dopamine in certain areas of the limbic system. Despite different methodologies, the convergence of research suggests that dopamine is involved in schizophrenia, but whether this involvement is causative or correlative is as yet unclear.

The Monoamine Oxidase Hypothesis

In addition to examining the role of specific neurotransmitters like dopamine, researchers also have focused on mechanisms involved in the production and/or metabolism of these neurotransmitters (see Box 8-1). One chemical involved in the breakdown of dopamine, for example, is the neural enzyme, monoamine oxidase, or MAO. MAO has been the focus of biochemical research in psychopathology because low levels of this enzyme can result in elevated levels of transmitters like dopamine. As reviewed by Wyatt et al. (1979), researchers focusing on MAO have found a relationship between schizophrenic symptoms and *low levels of MAO* in the blood platelets of diagnosed schizophrenic patients. In turn, low platelet MAO levels appear to correspond to the occurrence of auditory hallucinations and delusions (Schildkraut et al., 1976) and to elevated psychosis scores on the MMPI (Haier et al., 1979). Further, MAO abnormalities appear to run in families and have been shown to be discriminators among disturbed and undisturbed family mem-

BOX 8-1

BREAD AND MILK: STAPLES OF LIFE OR CONTRIBUTORS TO SCHIZOPHRENIA?

Clearly, every possibility must be explored in the effort to identify biochemical bases for schizophrenia. One intriguing idea which has not as yet enjoyed widespread examination proposes that schizophrenia may be caused by the abnormal entrance into the brain's cerebrospinal fluid of *gluten*, a chemical found in cereal grains and in milk products (Rudin, 1979). For example, damage to the *choroid plexus* (the source of spinal fluid in the brain ventricles) has been found in several autopsies of schizophrenics. Such damage may result in malfunction of the brain's normal barriers to potentially interfering chemicals like gluten. Upon passing the brain's barrier, it has been suggested that the gluten may disturb the normal functioning of neurotransmitters like dopamine. Support for this idea comes from results of studies showing that gluten-free diets for 3 weeks ameliorated the symptoms of schizophrenia (Dohan & Grosberger, 1973; see also Singh & Kay, 1976).

bers (Baron et al., 1984). On the other hand, low platelet MAO also has been reported among people with alcoholism (Sullivan et al., 1978) and with affective disorders (Orsulak et al., 1978). This leaves us with the possibility that rather than being associated in some *specific* way with schizophrenia, low platelet MAO may be associated in a more *general* way with psychopathology.

The Study of Endorphins

Research on the roles of dopamine and MAO in schizophrenia has been underway for quite some time compared with the more recent work on the *endorphins* (Snyder, 1978). Endorphins are biochemicals (see Chapter 4) which are known to reduce pain and produce euphoria. Preliminary research results suggest a relationship between endorphins and schizophrenia. For example, several investigators have reported significant reduction in psychotic symptoms with the administration of endorphins (Kline et al., 1977; Verhoeven et al., 1979). However, at least one other study has found that schizophrenic people have abnormally *high* levels of endorphins in their cerebrospinal fluid (Lindstrom et al., 1978). Given the growing interest in the endorphins and their early promise as correlates of schizophrenia, research will help to clarify their role in the disorder.

According to the transmethylation hypothesis, schizophrenic perceptions may be a result of internally produced hallucinogens. (*Michael Weisbrot and Family*)

The Study of Endogenous Hallucinogens

While little is understood about the mechanism by which endorphins may cause schizophrenic symptoms, more is known about how hallucinogenic drugs like LSD-25 produce psychosis-like effects. LSD-25 and similar compounds such as psilocybin and mescaline are produced outside the body and must be ingested. However, it appears that hallucinogenic chemicals also can be produced inside the body. One biological paradigm–based theory of schizophrenia stemming from this idea of *endogenous* (produced within the body) *hallucinogens* is called the *transmethylation hypothesis*.

The transmethylation hypothesis assumes that schizophrenia is a result of internally produced compounds similar to LSD, mescaline, and psilocybin (Rosengarten & Friedhoff, 1976; Bowers, 1980). First proposed by Osmond and Smythies (1952), the hypothesis is based upon the observation that a small change in the chemical structure of norepinephrine or dopamine could result in a compound quite similar in structure and effect to mescaline (see Figure 8-3). It was hypothesized that a genetically caused aberration in the metabolic system might cause norepinephrine to break down and create schizophrenia-producing hallucinogens. Data supporting the transmethylation hypothesis have continued to be gathered over the years. For example, Baldessarini et al. (1979) reported that endogenous hallucinogens appear to block normal neurotransmitter function, thus possibly producing perceptual distortion. Further support for

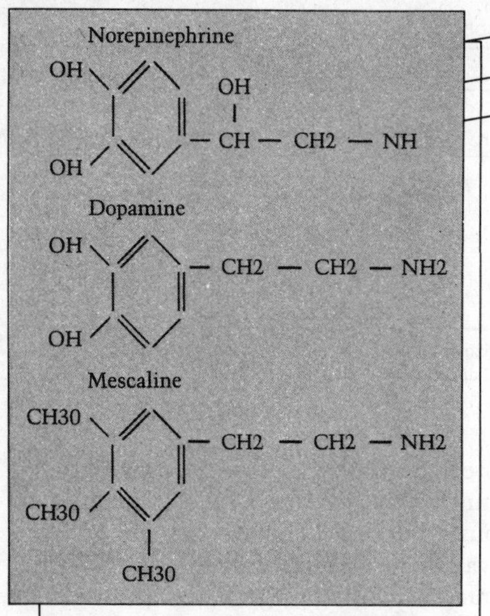

Figure 8-3 Similarities between normal biochemicals and hallucinogens.

the role of endogenous hallucinogens in the development of schizophrenia comes from studies in which researchers have found small quantities of bodily produced hallucinogens in the cerebrospinal fluid of schizophrenic patients (Smythies, 1976; Christian et al., 1975). Also Gillin et al. (1976) have proposed that the hallucinogen, dimethyltryptamine (DMT), may be involuntarily produced within the nervous system of schizophrenics. Finally, Murray et al. (1979) not only found DMT in the urine of schizophrenic patients, but noted that it decreased when patients began to show clinical improvement.

Certainly, the possibility that internally generated hallucinogens cause schizophrenia is intriguing. However, there is some difficulty with the endogenous hallucinogen hypothesis. First, it is not known whether the hallucinogens are causative in themselves or just play a part in the process of producing hallucinations or other forms of perceptual distortion. Second, actual schizophrenia can be different from the *schizophrenic-like* experiences described by people who use hallucinogens. One major difference is that normal people using hallucinogens typically *are aware* that they are in fact experiencing hallucinations and delusions; i.e., they do not seem to lose touch with the differences between reality and fantasy. On the other hand, schizophrenic people usually cannot make this distinction—their hallucinated perceptions seem real; their delusional ideas seem to represent truth. The endogenous hallucinogen hypothesis may be only an explanation for the emergence of schizophrenic-*like* behavior but not for schizophrenia itself.

The Neuromuscular Dysfunction Approach

The majority of biochemical research discussed thus far is based on the idea that a disturbance of thoughts and feelings like schizophrenia should have observable causes or consequences in the chemistry of the *central* nervous system. However, there is a body of literature which focuses on chemical aspects of *peripheral* neuromuscular dysfunctions among schizophrenics. For example, using the presence of creatine phosphokinase (CPK) as an indicator of skeletal muscle deterioration, Meltzer (1976a) has found disease-related elevations of CPK in a variety of psychiatric patients, including schizophrenics (see Table 8-3).

In addition to chemical signs, Meltzer has used the presence of abnormal muscle tissue as an indicator of nerve disease in schizophrenics. As seen in Table 8-4, the percentage of schizophrenic patients with abnormal musculature is very high as compared with normal people. Further, close relatives of schizophrenics manifest higher than normal levels of abnormal muscle tissue.

Meltzer's work suggests that something may be physically wrong with the

Table 8-3 Percentage of Patients with Creatine Phosphokinase (CPK) Elevations

		Time of CPK Elevation			
Diagnosis	*N*	*Admission*	*Later*	*Any Time*	*Never*
Nonpsychotic	19	0	5.3	5.3	94.7
All psychotic	187	47.1	60.4	75.9	24.1
Acute schizophrenic	123	50.4	61.0	78.9	21.1
Chronic schizophrenic	40	42.5	65.0	70.0	30.0
Bipolar—manic phase	12	33.3	58.3	75.0	25.0
Psychotic—depression	12	41.7	41.7	66.7	33.3

Source: From H. Meltzer, "Neuromuscular Dysfunction in Schizophrenics," *Schizophrenia Bulletin,* 1976, *2,* 106–135. National Institute of Mental Health, U.S. Department of Health, Education, and Welfare.

schizophrenic person. However, while neurological disease may be present, the mechanism by which such physical-neurological disease is translated into schizophrenic behavior remains largely unknown.

The Viral Hypothesis

While Meltzer's work has focused on one sort of physically based problem in schizophrenia, some other researchers guided by the biological paradigm have hypothesized another type of disease process—a *long-acting virus* (Torrey & Peterson, 1976; Torrey et al., 1978). Generally, *the viral hypothesis* for schizophrenia states that certain "slow viruses" (active over long periods of time as opposed to the more familiar 24-hour flu-like viruses) may interact with genetic predispositions to produce schizophrenia. Initial viral infection may occur prior to birth and cause abnormality in the same way that a German measles (rubella) virus infection during pregnancy can cause later difficulties in the form of mental retardation. Acquisition of the virus prior to birth could help account for the higher concordance rates for schizophrenia among monozygotic twins than dizygotic twins, inasmuch as MZ twins share the same placenta and would be more likely to be simultaneously affected.

Some evidence in support of the viral hypothesis has accumulated. Penn et al. (1972) have isolated a viral infection in a case of fatal catatonia, a disorder characterized by schizophrenic behavior, high fever, and cerebral hemorrhage. Further, Torrey and Peterson (1976) reported data from over 4000 schizophrenic patients that indicated a significantly higher incidence of abnormal finger, foot, and palm prints compared with normal people. More recently, others have reported finding a virus-like agent in the cerebrospinal fluid of schizophrenic patients (Crowe et al., 1979; Tyrell et al., 1979).

A final line of evidence for viral involvement is the finding that births of schizophrenics do not seem to be randomly distributed throughout the calendar year as would be expected of a purely genetic disease. Rather, in the Northern Hemisphere, more schizophrenic people

Table 8-4 Percentage of Psychotic Patients and Relations Showing Abnormal Muscle Biopsies

Group	*N*	*Abnormal, %*
Controls	34	14.7
Nonpsychotics	19	5.3
All psychotics	166	69.3
Acute schizophrenics	108	69.9
Chronic schizophrenics	36	38.3
First-degree relatives	26	50.0

Source: From H. Meltzer, "Neuromuscular Dysfunction in Schizophrenics, *Schizophrenia Bulletin,* 1976, *2,* 106–135. National Institute of Mental Health, U.S. Department of Health, Education, and Welfare.

are born in January through April than at any other time of the year (Dalen, 1974; Hare et al., 1974). Torrey and Peterson (1976) point out that many viruses, such as rubella and measles, show peaks of occurrence at these same times. Such peaks are consistent with the hypothesis that infants are infected during their mother's last trimester of pregnancy or shortly after their birth and only manifest symptoms many years later.

The viral hypothesis provides a real possibility for the identification of a causative agent. Unlike the other biochemical factors we have discussed, it is not likely that a slow virus would be a correlate of schizophrenia. Further, unlike an excess of dopamine which clearly affects neural transmission, a virus itself cannot clearly be so influential in the actual process of symptom development. Thus, it is possible that a virus could be the *cause* of the other biochemical abnormalities. Further, a viral hypothesis also can explain family and twin concordance rates in schizophrenia. For example, the schizophrenia-causing virus may be passed among family members in much the same way that other viral infections are transmitted.

The Psychosocial Paradigm and Explanations for Schizophrenia

While the biological paradigm leads to a focus on physical aspects of schizophrenia, the psychosocial paradigm generates approaches which reflect the belief that this disorder is caused by or expressed in behavioral, cognitive, perceptual, experiential, or interpersonal dysfunctions (Harrow et al., 1983; Lukoff et al., 1984; Nuechterlein & Dawson, 1984b). The major psychosocial conceptualizations include the psychoanalytic, the arousal-motivational, the learning-oriented, and the sociopsychological positions.

Schizophrenia as Regression

Psychoanalytic theorists view schizophrenia as a return to a much earlier level of functioning. According to Freud, at the earliest stage of personality development the *id* is not yet differentiated from the *ego.* Thus, infants are unable to discriminate between self and nonself because only primary process thought exists. Schizophrenia is seen as a loss of contact with reality and a regression to the oral stage of psychosexual development. The regression occurs because of either an uncontrollable increase in id demands or an unbearable degree of guilt or moral anxiety produced by the *superego.* Regardless of the specific internal or environmental precipitator of regression, schizophrenic symptoms are thought to be caused by a sequence of events that follows the initial break with reality. In the first phase of this progressive sequence, *regressive symptoms* occur that reflect a return to the infantile level. These regressive symptoms include feelings of depersonalization, sense of loss, delusions of grandiosity and self-importance, passivity, vegetative existence, and primary process thought (Lehmann, 1980). When regression is complete and contact with reality has been surrendered, the schizophrenic person attempts to regain reality through *restitutional symptoms*: To replace the lack of perceptions grounded in reality, hallucinations may develop; to replace reality-based beliefs, delusions emerge; to reestablish verbal communication, bizarre and incoherent speech occurs. Thus, when the person is seen for diagnosis, he or she shows primarily restitutional symptoms which reflect intrapsychic conflicts that have led to regression in the face of unbearable stress.

Arieti (1955), like Freud, also proposed a regression hypothesis. Based upon the neurological rule of thumb that higher brain centers tend to control lower, more primitive centers, Arieti believed that, in

In the psychoanalytic view, regression is a primary aspect of schizophrenia. (© *1985 James Fitzgerald*)

the face of extreme stress, a *teleological* or purposive regression occurs. People then experience a "functional paralysis" of higher brain centers, forcing them to readjust their level of behavior downward to a lower level where stress is reduced to a degree with which they can cope. According to Arieti's view, schizophrenics regress further and further back in their search for lower stress levels until they reach a point at which higher mental functions, such as logical thought and speech, break down and the typical symptoms of psychosis are clearly observable.

Schizophrenia as an Arousal and Motivation Dysfunction

Whereas the regression theorists tend to focus on complex intrapsychic conflicts, a significant number of other psychosocial explanations of schizophrenia focus on just one or two specific causative dysfunctions. For example, there are data implicating specific difficulties in arousal and motivation among schizophrenics. Motivation theorists generally perceive schizophrenia as an inability to receive, process, or respond to internal and external stimulation (Nuechterlein & Dawson, 1984a).

One arousal theorist, Mednick (1958), believes that prodromal schizophrenia is characterized by excess arousal in the form of massive anxiety. Because of stimulus generalization (Chapter Five), a great number of ordinarily ignored stimuli become associated with this massive anxiety. Therefore more and more environmental and internal stimuli have the power to make the person anxious and fearful. A vicious circle may then develop in which more and more stimuli are associated with anxiety. Soon the person is so aroused that he or she responds with anxiety to nearly every event or experience. According to Mednick, when this point is reached, the person may be seen as suffering from acute schizophrenia.

To cope with the intense anxiety of acute schizophrenia, the person tries to find ways to *reduce* the aversive feelings. One way to do this is to stop responding to the real world and to attend to small numbers of tangential, irrelevant events and stimuli. The physiological result of this attentional shift is a dramatic reduction in arousal to a lower-than-normal level; the person's behavior is now consistent with that of an underaroused and nonresponsive chronic schizophrenic. Research evidence for poor arousal levels among schizophrenics may be exemplified by the work of Zahn (1975; Zahn et al., 1978) who found that schizophrenics are not aroused in the same way as normal people by important environmental stimuli.

Another explanation for schizophrenia deriving from the psychosocial paradigm, *attentional-interference theory,* focuses not on arousal and motivation per se but on problems associated with thinking and meaningful attention and perception. A pioneer researcher in interference theory, Shakow (1962) believed that schizophrenic people have difficulty in attending to and focusing on relevant aspects of a situation and cannot "not attend" to peripherally important aspects. The net result of this attentional problem is that unimportant stimuli interfere with the ability to process and deal with important stimuli. This interference effect is illustrated in Figure 8-4 in which you may get some idea of how normal filtering and schizophrenic nonfiltering of stimuli may be experienced. McGhee and Chapman (1961) believed that schizophrenic symptoms are the result of the patient's basic inability to select, process, and control the stimuli impinging on internal and external sensors. Further clarification of interference theory also came from Payne (1962) who stated that the major problem for schizophrenic people is their inability to *exclude* unimportant stimuli—in that they respond to everything, their responses are often inappropriate and bizarre. The schizophrenic person's difficulty in focusing and thinking clearly has also been studied by Harrow et al. (1984) in their examination of *intermingling* in thoughts and speech patterns. Intermingling "involves the blending of personal material from one's experiences into one's thinking and communication leading to bizarre and inappropriate speech" (p. 354). Harrow et al. note that intermingling occurs frequently among schizophrenic persons and represents a clear cognitive indicator of the psychosis.

In addition to cognitive interference, other evidence indicates that attentional deficits may also be reflected in the schizophrenic's inability to attend visually to moving stimuli (Holtzman et al., 1973) and in his or her difficulty in screening out distracting auditory stimuli (Oltmanns & Neale, 1978; Oltmanns et al., 1978). An interesting complement to these findings is that 44 percent of close relatives of schizophrenics also seem to have the same trouble in attending to and tracking visual stimuli (Holtzman et al., 1974).

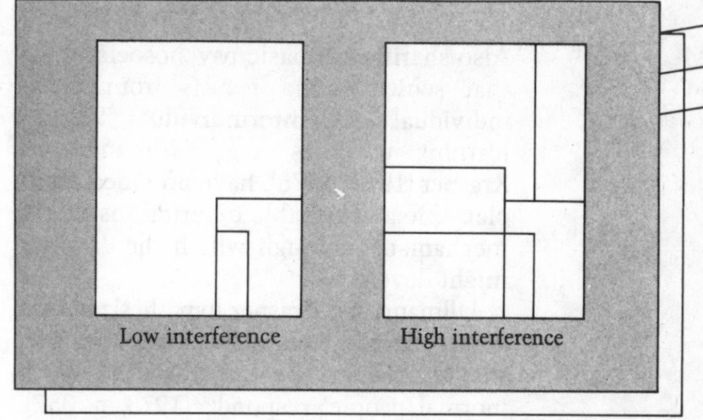

Figure 8-4 The effects of interference on perception. Find an "F" in each of these diagrams.

An inability to filter out internal and external stimuli has been associated with schizophrenia. (© *Rhoda Galyn*)

Schizophrenia as Learned Behavior

Also sharing the basic psychosocial view that schizophrenia results from intraindividual and interindividual factors, learning theorists, e.g., Ullmann and Krasner (1969; 1975), have provided some plausible and testable descriptions of the mechanisms through which the disorder might develop.

Ullmann and Krasner hypothesized that schizophrenia results from the "*extinction* of attention to social stimuli to which 'normal people' respond" (1975, p. 357). Put another way, schizophrenics have not been reinforced by others for attending to appropriate social cues; they may even have been actively punished for doing so. In a self-protective manner, the attentional response is extinguished and the person begins to respond to asocial, culturally unacceptable stimuli. For example, instead of attending to what his wife is saying and speaking with her, a schizophrenic man may communicate with a TV set. As inappropriate responding continues, he may be considered deviant by those around him. Ullmann and Krasner (1975) suggest that this societal reaction then can change the primary deviance (see Chapter Six) of the person into more permanent secondary deviance, thereby firmly establishing the nonattender as schizophrenic.

The Systems Paradigm and Explanations for Schizophrenia

As compared with a focus on individual psychodynamics and learning, in the systems perspective, schizophrenia is perceived as being either caused by, or exacerbated by, aspects of the social systems in which people live. The systems theorists emphasize the deleterious effects of sociocultural and environmental life stresses and the adversity of certain family patterns.

Social Stress and Schizophrenia

As stated by Dohrenwend (1975) and Dohrenwend and Dohrenwend (1974) and as reviewed by Lukoff et al. (1984), the social stress perspective assumes that environmental stresses can produce failure to cope, which may in turn lead to schizophrenic symptomatology. One line of evidence for this view is that many otherwise well-adjusted people exposed to the extreme stresses of war have been known to develop psychotic symptoms. Clearly, severe stress can produce behavioral deterioration, but stresses as severe as war are not everyday events. Normal life events also must be shown to produce stress if the *social stress hypothesis* is to be supported. Using the scale of life events devised by Holmes and Rahe (1967) (see Table 6-7), several researchers have found relationships between severe psychological disorders and the occurrence of divorce, death of a spouse, loss of a job, and the like (Dohrenwend, 1973; Markush & Favero, 1974). Further, Gersten et al. (1974) have reported similar relationships between stress and symptom development among children as well as adults.

Family Aspects of Schizophrenia

Also deriving their theoretical impetus from the systems paradigm, some researchers examine the family lives of schizophrenics in the belief that it is in the more global interactions among family members of these patients that we will find some of the sources of this disorder (Liem, 1980; Lukoff et al., 1984). These investigators have identified a number of family characteristics that seem to correlate with (and perhaps cause) the development of schizophrenia.

Family Power Patterns

Among the first family characteristics to be associated with schizophrenia were the family power patterns of *marital schism* and *marital skew.* In marital schism, parents remain together yet bicker and argue constantly, thereby producing a highly volatile, tense home environment. By contrast, in marital skew, overt happiness and harmony frequently mask deep parental dissension and hatred. In such a home, it is not unusual to find that one of the parents is deeply emotionally disturbed and the other family members sacrifice their growth and happiness to help cover up the disturbed member's dysfunction. A child being reared in a maritally skewed home often lacks a sense of self-importance and a feeling of security, core characteristics of schizophrenia. In a study of 256 families, half of which had produced at least one schizophrenic child, Friedman and Friedman (1972) reported that parents of patients manifested more psychopathology and thought disturbances than parents of normal children. Further, Wynne and Singer (cited by Keith et al., 1976) also have found a significant relationship between parental psychopathology and level of schizophrenic symptomatology among offspring.

Family Communication Patterns

In addition to power patterns within families being potentially influential in the development of schizophrenia, several important deviant *communication patterns* among family members also have been proposed and researched. Building on the early work of Bateson et al. (1956) who emphasized the importance of communication in the development of psychopathology, Wynne and Singer (1963; Singer & Wynne, 1965) identified two forms of schizophrenogenic communication. In the *amorphous style,* communications are very vague, loose, and indefinite. For example, "You can go or not, it's OK, I'm not sure what you ought to do." A second pattern, the *fragmented style,* is marked by disruption and lack of closure. A typical statement of this type might be, "I told you to stop or I'll. . . . Oh, go ahead and do it, but . . . wait . . . I'll tell you what I think later" (the speaker in this instance never really tells).

After the initial work of Wynne and Singer, data from other studies have supported the position that deviant family communication can be associated with schizophrenia (Doane, 1978; Reiss, 1976). In reviewing these studies, Liem (1980) has concluded that "of all aspects of family life, disordered communication is the most likely to be associated with the development of schizophrenia" (p. 91).

Paradigmatically Based Treatments for Schizophrenia

Given the large amount of research and theory regarding schizophrenia deriving from the existing major paradigms, it should come as little surprise that many therapeutic efforts also have emerged from the biological, psychosocial, and systems views. Most of the general treatments described in Chapters 4 to 6 have been used in working with schizophrenic people and will not be rediscussed here. Instead, several paradigmatically derived therapies especially useful in schizophrenia will be highlighted.

The Biological Paradigm in the Treatment of Schizophrenia

The most widely used and often most successful of the treatments for schizophrenia deriving from the biological paradigm is *drug therapy* (Donaldson, et al., 1983). Cole et al. (1966; 1964) were among the early researchers to demonstrate the effectiveness of this approach and it continues to serve as a mainstay of psychiatric care. As can be seen in Table 8-5, even when administered independently of any other form of therapy, antischizophrenic drugs reduce schizophrenic symptoms. The specific impact on the schizophrenic pattern of the antischizo-

Table 8-5 Effects of Treatment of Schizophrenic Patients with Antipsychotic Drugs versus Placebos

	Treatment Mode, %	
	Antipsychotic Drugs	*Placebo*
Effect on symptoms		
Worse or no change	8	60
Minimally or much improved	92	40

Source: After Cole et al. (1966) and Davis et al. (1980).

phrenic drugs has been described by Davis et al. (1980):

> Antipsychotic drugs seem to have a normalizing effect. They improve typical schizophrenic symptoms such as hallucinations and delusions, as well as other types of abnormal behaviors. The antipsychotic drugs are not uniformly sedating. Under their influence, retarded schizophrenics "speed up" and excited schizophrenics seem to "slow down." (pp. 70–71)

The chemicals used in the treatment of schizophrenia have traditionally belonged to the groups known as the major tranquilizers (see Chapter 4). Included in this set of medications are the phenothiazines, thioxanthenes, and butyrophenones. However, in recent years, it has been determined that drugs once believed to be effective in other severe disorders such as mania and depression also hold promise in the treatment of schizophrenia. Donaldson et al. (1983), for example, have reviewed research which indicates that certain schizophrenic symptoms can be relieved by the use of the antimanic drug,

While moderate conflict is common in many families, severely distorted communication is often seen in the families of schizophrenic people. (© *Shirley Zeiberg/Taurus Photos*)

BOX 8-2

ARE DRUG THERAPIES REALLY BEST FOR SCHIZOPHRENIA?

In most settings drug treatment is typically used in combination with the psychological therapies. However, do these combined therapeutic efforts make for significantly better treatment than one or the other alone? Is one clearly better? One important study addressing these questions was performed by May et al. (1976) (see table below). These researchers examined four groups of schizophrenic subjects who received varying treatment procedures, and they reported that patients receiving psychotherapy alone showed no more improvement than a no-treatment control group and were, in fact, even *worse* off when it came to relapse rates. Further, drugs alone and drugs plus psychotherapy did not differ in their effects, suggesting that the psychological treatments added little to the drug therapy. While *discouraging* from the perspective of those guided by a psychosocial paradigm, the results reported by May et al. are surely *encouraging* from the perspective of the biological paradigm.

Effects on Outcome and Readmission in Schizophrenics as a Function of Mode of Therapy

	Treatment Groups			
	No Drugs, No Therapy	*No Drugs, Therapy*	*Drugs, No Therapy*	*Drugs, Therapy*
Percent released from hospital	59%	64%	95%	96%
Days back in hospital during 3 years after first admission	350	390	220	225

Source: After May et al., 1976.

lithium, as well as by several antidepressant medications.

In addition to their use in the reduction of schizophrenic symptoms, drugs also are widely used in maintaining adjustment once the active phase of the disorder has been resolved. Given the possibility of frequent relapse in schizophrenia, this aspect of drug treatment is vital to consider. In a summary review of almost 30 studies assessing the percent of relapse of patients on placebo versus those on antipsychotic medication, Davis et al. (1980) reported an average percent relapse on placebo of 58 percent as compared with only an average of 19 percent relapse rate for drug treatment. Apparently, not only can antipsychotic drugs resolve the symptoms of schizophrenia, they also can play a major role in preventing their recurrence.

Along with the positive aspects of drug treatment, however, there are also a number of undesirable side effects. *Short-term side effects* can include shakiness, dryness of the mouth, allergic reactions, and slowing of motor function. Most of these side effects are relatively mild and can be controlled through careful variation of dosage and/or administration of additional medications specifically geared toward counteracting them. On the other hand, *long-term side effects* can be more severe, disabling, and even irreversible. Among these long-term effects are *skin discoloration, visual impairment* and, most severe of all, *tardive dyskinesia.* Symptoms of tardive dyskinesia may last for years *after* all antipsychotic medication has ceased and include uncontrolled facial grimacing and tongue movements, jerky or convulsive-like movement of the arms, slowed movement of the upper extremities, and contraction of the neck and back. These symptoms typically appear shortly after the cessation or reduction of antipsychotic medication which has been taken for a lengthy period of time. The pattern of tardive dyskinesia is so serious that any long-term use of antipsychotic drugs *must* be accompanied by a serious consideration of the drug's benefits weighed against the chance of this severe side effect. Prognosis for recovery from tardive dyskinesia is generally poor and to date there is no reliable way of identifying those patients in whom it is most likely to occur.

Treatments Deriving from the Psychosocial Paradigm

While therapies deriving from the biological paradigm are aimed at altering the physical state of schizophrenic people, treatments derived from the psychosocial paradigm may be seen as modifying their psychological state. Specific methods may be exemplified by the individual therapies deriving from the psychoanalytic and behavioral applications of the psychosocial paradigm (Mosher & Keith, 1980; May, 1984; Klerman, 1984).

Individual psychotherapy for schizophrenia has been the subject of a fair amount of research and theory (Bendetti, 1980; Beck et al., 1981; May, 1984; Klerman, 1984; Gunderson et al., 1984; Stanton et al., 1984). In many of these studies, individual psychotherapy has been found to be an effective treatment method. However, it must be remembered that approaching a *psychotic* person in one-to-one "talk" therapy can be quite different from the typical conversational interaction characteristic of the treatment in milder disorders (as described in Chapter 4; see also Chapter 10). Thus, special techniques have been developed that seem to lend themselves better to the individual treatment of schizophrenia.

A technique devised by Rosen (1953), *direct analysis* is a type of psychotherapy in which schizophrenic people are strongly encouraged to accept that they are severely disturbed and that the therapist is a parent-like, omnipotent provider of all their needs. Scheflen (1961) describes Rosen as using "with resourcefulness and persistence a dramatic barrage of powerful maneuvers to persuade the patient to relinquish his psychotic behavior, promising and rewarding, threatening and punishing, coercing . . . using group pressure, ridiculing and shaming, . . . imitating and caricaturing . . . and using shocking interpretation."

Rosen's theoretical base is psychoanalytic, and he seems to believe that much of schizophrenia lies in faulty mother-child relationships. His goal in direct analysis is to replace the faulty parent of the schizophrenic person with himself as the benevolent, yet authoritarian, parent who will guide the person to better adjustment. As seen in the sample of a Rosen-type interview below, some of his focus is on psychosexual difficulties:

Patient: I don't know what you want.
Therapist: I want you to love me.
Patient: Huh?
Therapist: That's right, I want you to love me. I want you to come right up to me and kiss me on the mouth!
Patient: I don't wanna do that.
Therapist: What's the matter? Does it scare you to think about loving a man—about kissing a man?
Patient: Yeah.
Therapist: Does that make you a homo-

sexual? Or me a homosexual? I love some other men and so do you.

Patient: No I don't.

Therapist: How about your father? You loved your father, didn't you?

Patient: Uh-h.

Therapist: Answer me! I can't understand you when you say "Uh-h."

Patient: Yes, I guess I loved my father.

While techniques like Rosen's are based on psychoanalytic theory, *behavior modification* with schizophrenics is derived from laboratory-tested techniques of altering behavior through the systematic application of basic principles of learning. In a classic example of applying behavior modification in the treatment of schizophrenia, Isaacs et al. (1960) used chewing gum as a reinforcer to establish verbal communication in a mute, withdrawn patient. Each time the patient made an approximation to speech, he was rewarded with a piece of gum. After a period of time, the patient had to *ask* for gum prior to receiving it. Using operant conditioning (Chapter 5), the response of speech was reinstituted and generalized to numerous people throughout the hospital. Prior to this therapeutic intervention, this schizophrenic person had not uttered a word for 19 years.

In another application of learning theory, Ayllon and Azrin (1968) developed the now widely used program called the *token economy*. The token economy is a small economic structure within a treatment setting. Behaviors of importance, such as attending therapy groups, cleaning rooms, and the like, are "paid for" by staff with tokens such as stamps, poker chips, or stars. With earned tokens, patients are able to "buy" things they like (reinforcers). Common individual reinforcers on a psychiatric ward can include such things as TV time, sleep time, candy bars, and extra recreation time. In a review of the token economy and other behavioral techniques used in the individual treatment of schizophrenia, Liberman (1972) stated:

> The token economy . . . has been shown to be effective in increasing the adaptive repertoire of institutionalized schizophrenics. Behavioral interventions are effective, even when phenothiazine medication is withdrawn from chronic psychotics. (p. 47)

Treatments Deriving from the Systems Paradigm

While treatments deriving from the psychosocial paradigm focus primarily on individual care, therapies deriving from the systems paradigm stress group, family, and societal routes to the reduction of schizophrenic symptoms.

Group Therapy

Special group approaches to the treatment of schizophrenia include *recreational therapy, art therapy, music therapy,* and more traditional *talk-oriented group therapy.* Whereas all these methods are widely used, the majority of research has been focused on traditional group approaches, but with equivocal results. For example, Pattison et al. (1967) reported little improvement in schizophrenic symptomatology as a result of psychoanalytic group treatment. However, Vitalo (1971) demonstrated a significant reduction of symptoms in a sample of schizophrenics in group therapy. Unfortunately, these changes in clinical pattern did not appear to be translated into permanent personality changes. Although about two-thirds of the studies of the efficacy of groups showed little positive effect (Mosher & Keith, 1980), group therapy seems to many clinicians to be an important and effective part of the treatment of schizophrenia.

Family Therapy

In addition to group treatment, the repertoire of therapists working from the systems perspective also includes *family therapy.* This approach owes much of its popularity to the work with schizophrenics of Fromm-Reichmann (1948). Fromm-Reichmann proposed that a major environmental determinant of schizophrenia was a *schizophrenogenic mother,* a woman who produced in her children intense, often insoluble conflicts which, when combined with an inherent tendency toward schizophrenia, resulted in the development of the disorder.

Fromm-Reichmann's method of overcoming the effects of the schizophrenogenic mother often was literally to move into the patient's life and take over. However, more recent forms of family therapy for schizophrenia deal with the *family context* in other ways. Among these are the structural family analysis of Minuchin and the other family approaches described in our more general discussion of family treatment in Chapter 6.

In contrast to the research on group therapy, the findings regarding the effects on schizophrenia of family therapy are clearer—and positive. Ro-Trock et al. (1977), for example, have reported that family treatment is clearly related to reduction in rehospitalization rate for schizophrenics (see Table 8-6). These positive results have been corroborated by Goldstein et al. (1978). Further, Falloon and Liberman (1983) have noted that "Family interventions . . . may contribute significantly to the clinical and social outcomes achieved by optimal pharmacotherapy" (p. 545). These authors also add that the use of family and social interventions actually can enhance the effectiveness of drug treatments. That is, antischizophrenic medication appears to work better in people who are also receiving some form of psychosocial or family treatment.

Table 8-6 The Effects of Family Therapy on Rehospitalization Rate among Schizophrenics.

	Outcome of Treatment, %	
	Not Readmitted	***Readmitted***
Family therapy (n = 14)	100	0
Individual therapy (n = 14)	57	43

Source: Based on Ro-Trock et al., 1977.

Societal Intervention and Prevention

While group and family treatment for schizophrenia is applied after the disorder has appeared, the systems-paradigm-based approach of *prevention* is an attempt to avoid the disturbances altogether. In prevention of schizophrenia, initial efforts are directed at identifying, before the onset of the prodromal or active phases, those people who are *at risk* for the disease. This being accomplished, energies are then directed at trying to avert the disorder or soften its impact in some way. A third aspect of the preventive effort involves research in which at risk children are identified and their environments carefully studied in an attempt to isolate those factors which seem to be related to increases or decreases in the incidence of schizophrenia.

The basis for the preventive approach in schizophrenia has been traced by some (Lewine et al., 1981) to the work of Mednick and McNeil (1968) who proposed that rather than continue the often frustrating and sometimes fruitless efforts to identify the etiology of schizophrenia by studying persons already suffering from schizophrenia, researchers should turn to the study of the offspring of schizophrenic parents (i.e., persons at "high risk" for schizophrenia who have not as yet developed the disorder). In this way, it was believed that clearer precipitators of schizophrenia could be isolated while preventive efforts could be simultaneously developed and applied.

While efforts to identify populations at risk are numerous and could be presented through verbal description, we have chosen to introduce you to this "treatment" effort in a slightly different way. We have asked a psychologist who has obtained a major federal research grant for the study of children at risk for schizophrenia to provide a brief narrative of her work (Goodman, 1982).

Personal Experience: A Prevention Project Director Describes Her Research Experience (Sherryl Goodman, Emory University)

Project PACT (Parents and Children Together) is a research-demonstration project which implements and evaluates the effectiveness of three models of primary prevention with children of severely disturbed mothers. Children of schizophrenic and of depressed mothers are considered to be at risk of developing a variety of psychological problems regardless of whether one ascribes to a genetic, psychogenic, sociogenic, or early neglect model for the development of psychopathology.

The preventive intervention model was derived from existing reports on theoretical models, research, and prior attempts at intervention. That review of the literature lead to the following guidelines for designing a prevention program:

1. A major goal is to reduce or prevent the disruptive experiences to which the children are subjected, that is, fewer separations and more consistent child rearing. The implication is that the most effective intervention program would be one which identifies and begins to work with children within the youngest age range and as quickly as possible after the mother's problems begin to develop. Another possible implication is that in some cases helping the family to arrange for alternative parenting may be needed.
2. Rather than aiming to compensate for deficits in the parenting or home environment, more of a health or competence perspective needs to be taken. That is, children and parents can be trained on specific skills or strategies to cope with their situation, e.g., social problem solving, reality testing.
3. For problems that derive from a poor home environment and lack of resources, interventions aimed at linking families with available resources (material and social) are appropriate.
4. For problems that derive from faulty parent-child relationships, interaction-based interventions are called for. The focus of these interventions could include the mother's attitude toward her child, her expectations and ability to perceive the child, and her ability to manage the child's daily behavior.
5. Clearly, the intervention requires an evaluation component so that the most effective strategies can be identified and replicated in this or other communities.

While it appears from the above narrative that high risk for schizophrenia research is a most valuable and exciting field, it also has its problems. Most crucial among these is difficulty with diagnosis; that is, the parents of the children at risk must be accurately diagnosed as schizophrenic if their offspring are to be included in the study sample. In "at risk" studies, diagnostic errors have been traced to such factors as sex bias, country in which the diagnosis takes place, and system of diagnosis used (Lewine et al., 1981). In spite of its drawbacks, the preventive effort which focuses on at risk populations is special in that, as mentioned, it combines research and treatment in its systems-paradigm-based effort to overcome schizophrenia.

Concluding Comments

In this chapter some of the major paradigmatic foci in the search for a better understanding of schizophrenia have been examined. Through our considerations of the biological, psychosocial, and systems perspectives, it seems apparent that the puzzle called schizophrenia is not going to be solved with the correct placement of any one piece but with a combination of many. The so-called "silver bullet" belief that some day *the* one cause for this set of disorders will be found must fade in the face of growing research-based knowledge of schizophrenia. Perhaps, an ultimate explanation of schizophrenia will be similar to that based on an integrated paradigm proposed by Cools (1975). Cools hypothesized that life experiences such as family problems, life stresses, genetic and psychological factors all combine to bring about biochemical alterations which then produce the symptoms of schizophrenia. For thinkers like Cools, schizophrenic symptoms may represent a *final common pathway* produced by one or several of the biological, psychosocial, and systems factors which have in the past been examined as possible unilateral causes of this devastating disorder. Alternatively, our future understanding of disorders like schizophrenia may be enhanced by ideas such as those of Petho (1984) who proposed that we view psychopathology as if it were the constriction found at the middle of an hourglass. Below the constriction one can imagine a broad range of etiological factors such as genetics and stress. Above the constriction, one may hope for a reemergence of useful, adaptive behaviors which appear as a person recovers. Although speculative, perhaps these views or others like them may represent the kinds of alternative sets of shared beliefs which can guide future efforts to solve the mystery of schizophrenia.

Summary Chart

Having discussed the methods of classifying schizophrenia, we turned in Chapter 8 to a focus on theories and treatments for this widespread psychosis. We opened the chapter with a word of caution regarding the differences between causation and correlation and then moved to an overview of paradigmatically based explanations.

Views from the biological paradigm were:

The genetic approach: Heritability, twin studies, adoption studies, diathesis-stress models

The psychophysiological approach: EEGs, skin conductance, orienting responses

The biochemical approach: Dopamine, MAO, endorphins, endogenous hallucinogens

The neuromuscular dysfunction approach: CPK, family patterns of CPK

The viral hypothesis: Slow-acting viruses, a possible causative agent

Theories deriving from the psychosocial paradigm were:

Schizophrenia as regression: The psychoanalysts, Freud

Schizophrenia as an arousal dysfunction: Overinclusion, intermingling, overarousal, underarousal

Schizophrenia as learned behavior: Extinction of appropriate behaviors, learned maladaptive patterns

The systems paradigm also has yielded perspectives on schizophrenia:

Social stress and schizophrenia: Stressful life events

Family patterns and schizophrenia: Power patterns, family schisms, skewed families, maladaptive communication patterns

We closed Chapter 8 with a broad overview of some paradigmatically based treatments for schizophrenia:

The biological paradigm: Antipsychotic drugs, benefits and concerns

The psychosocial paradigm: Individual therapy, direct analysis, behavior modification, token economies

The systems paradigm: Group therapy, family therapy, prevention projects

CHAPTER 9

The Affective Disorders

Personal Experience: Depression and Mania

The dawn soon hid itself in the brilliancy of a perfect June day. Never had I seen a brighter—to look at; never a darker—to live through,—or a better to die upon. Its very perfection and the songs of the robins, which at that season were plentiful in the neighborhood, served but to increase my despair and make me the more willing to die. As the day wore on my anguish became more intense, but I managed to mislead those around me by uttering a word now and then, and feigning to read a newspaper, which to me, however, appeared an unintelligible confusion of type. My brain was in a ferment. It felt as if pricked by a million needles at white heat. My whole body felt as though it would be torn apart by the terrific strain under which I labored. (Beers, 1910, pp. 17–18, describing his depressive despair shortly before and during a suicide attempt)

What could be more delightful, thought I, than the furnishing and financing of ideas of a magnitude such as would stagger humanity. My condition was one of ecstatic suspense . . . The city of my birth was to be made a garden spot . . . Churches were to give way to cathedrals; the city itself was to become a paradise of mansions. . . . Art galleries, libraries, museums and theaters of a dream-like splendor were to rise wherever and whenever I should will. Why absurd? Was it not I who would defray the cost? The famous buildings of the Old World were to be reproduced, if, indeed, the originals could not be purchased, brought to this country, and re-erected. (Beers, 1931, p. 192, describing a period of mania)

We have all experienced milder forms of the feelings described by Clifford Beers. However, for the most part our normal "lows" and "highs" usually are realistic reactions to the stimulation of everyday life. Beers' feelings of depression, on the other hand, were so severe as to be considered psychotic and precipitated a suicide attempt; his feelings of elation led him to lose contact with reality and to develop such outlandish views of his own power and importance that he required hospitalization in an asylum. When the normal range of human emotions reaches extremes such as those described by Beers, a diagnosis of *affective disorder* may be applied.

The affective disorders are similar to the schizophrenias we described in Chapters Seven and Eight in that they are extremely severe and typically warrant hospitalization. However, they differ from the schizophrenias in several ways. One difference is that the affective disorders are associated primarily with disturbances of emotion rather than thought. Furthermore, whereas it is often quite difficult to identify a precipitating event for schizophrenic episodes, such a precipitator can usually be found in the affective psychoses. Finally, while the course of schizophrenia is difficult to predict and the prognosis for recovery often very poor, people with affective disorders usually recover from a particular episode within a few months to a year.

Although both extreme depressive and manic mood states are possible, depressive disorders are much more frequent. Boyd and Weissman (1981) estimated that at any point in time, up to 20 percent of the general U.S. population may be experiencing severe depression. Similarly, Regier et al. (1984) have noted that the lifetime prevalence for these disorders is higher than that of schizophrenia. Perhaps due to its frequency, it seems also that a greater amount of scientific and therapeutic energy in the science of abnormal psychology has been directed at the symptom of depression (Akiskal & Webb, 1983; Coyne & Gotlib, 1983). In this chapter on affective disorders we will reflect this differential emphasis by focusing more heavily on depression as well. Prior to examining the affective disorders from the perspectives of the biological, psychosocial, and systems paradigms, we will describe the major patterns of these disturbances of mood.

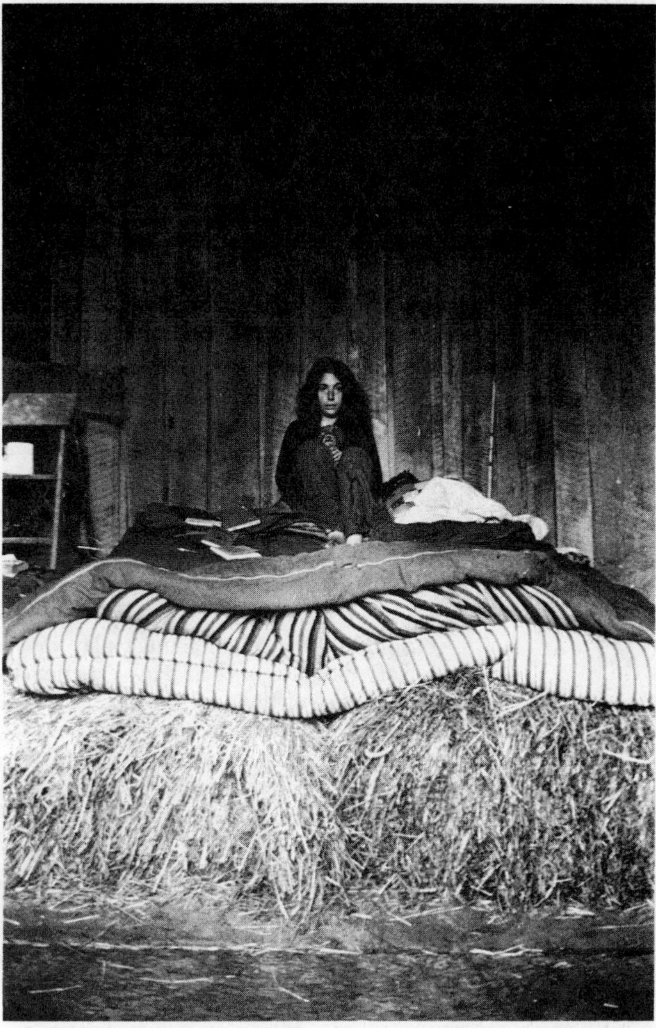

Depressed people often feel like being alone, but withdrawing from others can also maintain a sense of sadness. (*Michael Weisbrot and Family*)

The Affective Disorders

In DSM-III, the affective psychoses may take the form of either *major depression* (which also may be termed *unipolar affective disorder*) or *bipolar affective disorder* which can involve episodes of major depression intermixed with episodes of manic (or highly energized) behavior.

Major Depression

Major depression is characterized by *dysphoria* or the loss of interest in or enjoyment of usual activities and events. In the depressive state, there may be "appetite disturbances, weight change, sleep disturbance, psychomotor agitation or retardation, decreased energy, feelings of worthlessness or guilt, difficulty concentrating or thinking, and thoughts of death or suicide or suicide attempts" (American Psychiatric Association, p. 210; Nelson & Charney, 1981). To be diagnosed as having a severe depressive episode, people must show a number of these symptoms for at least 2 weeks. Depression is much more frequently diagnosed in women than in men (see Box 9-1).

Severely depressed people may describe themselves as sad, hopeless individuals who care little about anything or anyone.

BOX 9-1

WHY IS DEPRESSION MORE COMMON IN FEMALES?

Up to six times more women than men receive the diagnosis of depression. Antidepressant drugs are prescribed for women eight times more frequently than for men (Penfold, 1981). Why? Are women, as a sex, more prone to depression? Is depression sex-linked? Is it a disorder genetically programmed in women? In an attempt to answer some of these questions, Penfold (1981) has noted that depression in women is typically seen by professionals and lay people alike as a dysfunction of the person herself; this being the case, it is seen as incumbent upon *her* to change in order to return to normal. Penfold proposes that many depressions in women, however, may in fact be *externally* produced and then maintained at such a high frequency because of the role which females must play in our society, because of their daily experiences, and because of their upbringing.

In her examination of the psychoanalytic perspective on depression, Penfold notes that the Freudian account of the development of depression is very similar to that presented for the development of the female personality. Also, she disagrees strongly with the idea that there is a physiological link between menopause and certain forms of depression or that depression in new mothers is solely due to the extreme hormonal fluctuations they experience during pregnancy.

In sum, Penfold takes exception to the assumption that there is a relationship between the physiology of women and their propensity for depression. She notes that some writers seem to mistakenly believe that depression is a dysfunction in women which *causes* many of their problems in living. Penfold proposes that the inverse is true, that depression is the *effect* and is caused by women's roles in society and by the lack of proper concern for their special needs in such areas as childbirth and mothering.

In support of Penfold's view, some nonpsychiatric writers have described the daily lives of many women as paths to resentment, misery, frustration, boredom, and fatigue. Feminist Betty Friedan called these reactions "the problem with no name." Sheila Rowbotham, in her book, *Woman's Consciousness, Man's World,* has termed the problem "the neurosis of nothingness." And in a chilling self-description, Adrienne Rich (*Of Woman Born*) wrote, "I weep and weep, and the sense of powerlessness spreads like a cancer through my being" (cited by Penfold, 1981, p. 29)

They may withdraw from friendships and once-enjoyable activities may seem like drudgery. Because their eating habits sometimes change radically, they may gain or lose significant amounts of weight. Sleep patterns may also be affected so that people may either sleep too much (*hypersomnia*) or not enough (*insomnia*). The following case description reflects many of the prime characteristics of major depression (Cameron, 1947).

Case: Major Depression

On admission to the hospital, the patient sat slumped in a chair, frowning deeply, staring at the floor, his face looking sad and drawn. When questioned he answered without looking up, slowly and in a monotone. Sometimes there was such a long pause between question and reply that the patient seemed not to have heard. Every now and then he shifted his position a little, sighed heavily and shook his head from side to side. His first verbal response was, "It's no use. I'm through. All I can think is I won't be any good again." In response to further inquiries he made the following comments, relapsing into silence after each short statement until again asked a question. "I feel like I'm dead inside . . . like a piece of wood . . . I don't have any feeling about anything; its not like living anymore . . . I'm past hope. . .there's nothing to tell. I've lied to everybody. My family is ashamed of me. I've messed up my life. I'm no good to anybody. . . . My memory is gone. I forget everything. I can't look people in the eye anymore. I've done everything wrong. You're wasting your time on me." (Cameron, 1947, p. 508).

Motorically, depressed people may either increase or decrease their rates of behavior. When showing an increased rate, as in *psychomotor agitation,* they may have difficulty remaining still, may pace, wring their hands, pull at their hair, skin, or clothing, and may shout loudly and unpredictably. In contrast, in *psychomotor retardation* depressed people talk and move very slowly and seemingly labor over their every action and thought.

Whether they are agitated or retarded motorically, most depressed individuals also tend to feel inadequate, guilty, and worthless. In fact, the presence of these kinds of feelings in agitated individuals is one way of discriminating them from people involved in manic patterns of behavior who typically express greater than normal happiness. Depression also can cause difficulty in concentrating, forgetfulness, and unrealistic worrying about illness and death. As in the case of Clifford Beers, these feelings can often lead to suicide attempts. (More will be said about the relationship between depression and suicide later in this chapter.)

Although immobilizing and life-threatening, depressive symptoms tend to be relatively short-lived. In many cases, with or without specific treatment, major depression may lift over a period of a few months. However, on the negative side, more than half of the people who experience one episode of major depression will experience a relapse at least one more time in their lives.

Bipolar Affective Disorder

When episodes of major depression occur in some alternating or intermixed fashion with episodes of *mania,* the diagnosis of *bipolar disorder* is made. The term "bipolar" reflects the fact that in this form of affective psychosis, both extremes of mood disturbance may be observed at dif-

During manic episodes, people feel very energized, euphoric, and grandiose. (*Michael Weisbrot and Family*)

ferent times. In this sense, the major depression pattern we have just described is seen as a *unipolar* disorder in that only one form of mood alteration is observed. However, while such unipolar depression is relatively common, unipolar mania is rarely, if ever, observed. One result of this rarity of unipolar mania (i.e., a manic episode without a depressive episode at some other time in a person's life) is that the very experience of a manic episode is often a sufficient basis for the diagnosis of bipolar disorder. Since the depressive episode of bipolar disorder is essentially the same as the major depression, we will not describe its symptoms again. Rather we will outline the characteristics of the *manic episode.*

In contrast to the low energy and lack of interest shown in severe depression, manic episodes are characterized by "hyperactivity, pressure of speech, flight of ideas, inflated self-esteem, decreased need for sleep, distractibility and excessive involvement in activities that have a potential for painful consequences" (American Psychiatric Association, p. 206). During his manic state, for example, Clifford Beers seemed tireless in his effort to rebuild his home city into a showplace. Like Beers, most manic people are euphoric and seem to be "on top of the world." However, their euphoria seems tenuous, for, if crossed, they can quickly become quite angry. They seem unable to control their internal pressures to do things, and their flow of energy seems boundless. While in a manic episode, people may be quite impulsive and do things like call friends in the middle of the night and describe "wonderful plans," spend money illogically, or drive recklessly. The hyperactivity characteristic of the manic state may also result in loud, rapid, and difficult-to-interpret talking such as in the following example of psychotic speech (Cameron, 1947):

Case: Psychotic Speech During a Manic Episode

"You go out and stand pat—pat, you hear! Who was Pat? What does he wear when he's in Ireland? This hair won't stay out of my eyes (brushes it aside and touches pillow). See this pillow (raising it behind head)? Now is it even, even or odd? Even or odd, by God; I take it even, by God. By God we live, by God we die, and that's my allegiance to these United States. See my little eagle (bedsheet wrapped around feet and stretched taut)? These are my wings. No, I have wings of a girl." Patient sings *Prisoner's Song,* making flying movements with her arms to accompany the lines, "Over these prison walls I would fly." Then sings, "One little Indian, two little Indians," and suddenly shouts, "Heap big Indian chief! I'm not afraid. I got a heart right there, I've got a key to my heart. I don't want instant death. No, not one little teensy, eensy, weensy, not one little teensy, eensy, wittsy, wonsy bit. Right is right, wrong is wrong, two rights don't make a wrong. So they are, all over the world. God made the world, but this isn't Adam speaking, it's me. Mr. Adam, you can't just walk out of here. It's O.K. by me, I've said my say. Out you go! Take me if you want to or leave me. Shoot if you want to. I have just one heart, a right heart. I'm so tired. So shoot, shoot, but only once. Point the gun at the right breast. I'll know him wherever I see him, dead or alive. Shoo-oot, 'Oh, Columbia the gem of the ocean' (sung). Shoot, I'm ready, 1-2-3, shoo-oot! (hand over heart, eyes closed). My husband, my heart aches, oh, it aches, I'm tired, I'm tired, I'm tired." (Cameron, 1947, p. 205)

This example helps to demonstrate several classical characteristics of manic speech. *Clang association* or connections of ideas on the basis of sound rather than meaning is seen in the sequence: "Now it is even, even or *odd.* Even or odd, by God . . By God we live. . . . " *Flight of ideas* is demonstrated by the rapid shifts from one topic to another as in, "The hair won't stay out of my eyes. See this pillow?" Finally, *distractibility* is shown by the patient's inability to remain on any topic for more than just a brief moment.

As shown in the selection from Beer's memoirs at the start of this chapter, manic episodes may also be marked by inflated self-esteem, a sense of grandiose self-importance, and a belief in one's ability to accomplish just about anything. The following personal experience demonstrates some of these expansive manic qualities:

Personal Experience: Manic Expansiveness

I just remember feeling wonderful—on top of the world. God I felt good—inside me it was like a glass of pop with too many bubbles—they just came busting out and I laughed and sang. Everybody else had a good time. I know they did—we were all laughing until our sides hurt, and tears came running down our faces. Wow—what a time. Yes, I remember everyone else stopping, but I didn't—I couldn't—it was as if I was out of control. I was having a great time—but it was a little scary, too.

Manic episodes intermixed with depressive episodes comprise the symptom pattern called *bipolar affective disorder.* In some people these episodes may alternate in a regular manner with interspersed periods of normal mood lasting for months or even years. In others, several manic episodes may occur sequentially followed by the appearance of depressive episodes later in life. In most cases, each episode is limited in time and the person recovers and returns to a symptom-free life. However, during the manic or depressive episodes themselves a psychotic disturbance is clearly present. (DSM-III also describes some nonpsychotic forms of the affective disorders which seem to mirror the more severe forms but are much less intense. See Box 9-2.)

Developmental Patterns of Depression

While DSM-III represents the "official" diagnostic classification system and encompasses the major patterns of affective disturbance, it describes the disorders of mood as they occur primarily in adults. However, it is apparent that many symptoms of psychopathology seem to be age- or role-related. This is to say that depression in a young person is not necessarily the same symptomatically or etiologically as depression in adulthood or old age. In light of these developmental differences, several special patterns of depression have emerged as foci of much clinical and research attention. These include *depression in childhood, postpartum depression, and involutional melancholia.*

Depression in Childhood and Adolescence

Kraepelin (1896), a trailblazer in the classification of mental disorder, observed that the prime time for onset of the first attack of a bipolar disorder was in the age period of 15 to 20 years. He noted that it was rare to find such cases in children younger than 13. However, according to Winokur and his colleagues (1969) and more recently to Toolan (1981), Call and Bland (1979), and Akiskal and Webb (1983) cases of affective psychosis in children and adolescents are increasingly common.

BOX 9-2

MILDER FORMS OF AFFECTIVE DISTURBANCE

In addition to the major affective psychoses described in the text, DSM-III also includes two other forms of mood disturbances, *cyclothymia* and *dysthymia.* These patterns were originally grouped with the neuroses in DSM-II, but due to the similarity of their symptoms and those of the affective psychoses, they have been reclassified. The milder affective patterns are not of psychotic proportion, less frequently require hospitalization, and usually have no clear point of onset. Both tend to occur more frequently in females, to "run" in families, and to appear relatively early in life (before age 30).

Cyclothymic disorder is characterized by chronic (as defined by at least 2 year's duration), recurrent mood disturbances involving repetitive periods of *moderate* depression alternating with a mild form of mania called *hypomania.* Like its more severe counterpart, the bipolar affective disorder, the depressive and manic symptoms in cyclothymic disorder may be clearly separated by periods of normal mood, and may occur in either alternating or intermixed irregular fashion. In the table below are some common manic and depressive symptom "pairings" seen in the cyclothymic pattern.

Dysthymic disorders are characterized by all the symptoms of major depression, only to a more moderate degree. Much more common than psychotic depression, dysthymia is often passed off as a case of "the blues" and occurs most frequently in females. With or without treatment, the dysthymic pattern will usually subside in a few days or weeks, but as is true of psychotic depression, it tends to recur.

Contrasting Symptomatology of Moderate Depression and Hypomania in Cyclothymic Disorder

Hypomanic Period	*Depressive Period*
More energy than usual	Less energy than usual
Reduced need for sleep	Hypersomnia; insomnia
Inflated self-esteem	Feelings of worthlessness
Increased sexuality	Decreased sexuality
Restlessness	Slowing down
Increased talking	Decreased talking
Optimism	Pessimism
Laughing, joking	Crying, humorlessness

Source: Adapted from DSM-III, American Psychiatric Association, p. 220.

Case: Bipolar Disorder in a 12-year-old

Mary W., 12 years old, was seen in the clinic in a state of hyperactivity, exhilaration, and extreme talkativeness. Menstruation at that time had not yet begun. She had had her first attack of affective disorder at the age of 10 years, which was 15 to 24 months before she was seen in the clinic for the first time at age 12. At 10 years she would not go out of the house and was afraid that people were watching her. She had feelings of derealization and expressed the feeling that she did not belong to the world. There was little in the way of spontaneous talk. This depression (which started at the age of 10 years) continued for 7 months, after which she became excited, talked excessively, sat in peculiar positions, and had flighty thoughts. She then went into a period of 4 months in which phases of depression and excitement alternated every 2 weeks. This, in turn, was followed by a depression that lasted for 3 months. A normal mental state intervened for a month, and her illness recurred. It was then that she was seen in the clinic (age 12 years), showing alternating periods of depression and excitement. Her illness remitted in 9 weeks, and she was well for 2 years, during which time the first menstruation occurred. At 14 years of age she again entered the clinic in a state of excitement that had developed after a period of depression; this time she was exhilarated, distractible, boisterously overactive, and continuously talking. In a period of 3 months she improved and was home until the age of 19 years, when she again became excited and had to be admitted to a state hospital. This excitement disappeared in a few weeks, and she regained her normal health. Eight years later another attack requiring hospital admission occurred. This particular case appears to be one in which affective disorder, showing both mania and depression, started considerably before puberty (17 months to 4 years prior to menstruation). There is an adequate follow-up to indicate that the patient's illness was indeed a rather typical manic depressive psychosis (From C. Winokur, P. Clayton, and T. Reich, *Manic-Depressive Illness*, pp. 23–24. Copyright 1969 by C. V. Mosby Company. Reprinted by permisson of the authors.)

Toolan (1981) suggested that one possible reason for believing that depression did not occur in younger children was the assumption that mood disturbances in youngsters would take the same form as they do in adults. However, if we assume that *normal* emotional reactions of 5-year-olds and 50-year-olds differ significantly, then we can assume that *abnormal* reactions may differ as well. This *pathoplastic effect of age* * leads us to accept the possibility that a "depressed" child might act differently from a "depressed" adult. Toolan (1981) notes further that it may not be until age 20 that depression in young people takes on adult form.

While childhood affective disorders were seen infrequently because we used adult symptoms to diagnose children, some researchers believe that the rarity of affective disorders in adolescents may be due to other factors. For example, Bowden and Sarabia (1980) concluded that affective disorders tended to be *underdiagnosed* among teenagers. Whereas researchers find *actual* prevalence of schizophrenia and affective disorders in teenagers equal to that of adults, the diagnosis of schizophrenia is used up to nine times more frequently for adolescents. Bowden and Sarabia believe that this overuse of the schizophrenia diagnosis may be due to hesitancy in applying the affective diagnosis because of a continuing belief that while schizophrenia occurs in young people, affective disorders do not.

*The pathoplastic effect of age refers to the fact that the same disorder will be manifested in different ways in different age groups. For example, symptom pathoplasty is exemplified in a disease like chicken pox which, in infants, is typically a mild disease, but which, in adults, can be quite serious and painful.

Mild depression may be experienced as an extended period of pensiveness or malaise. (*Michael Weisbrot and Family*)

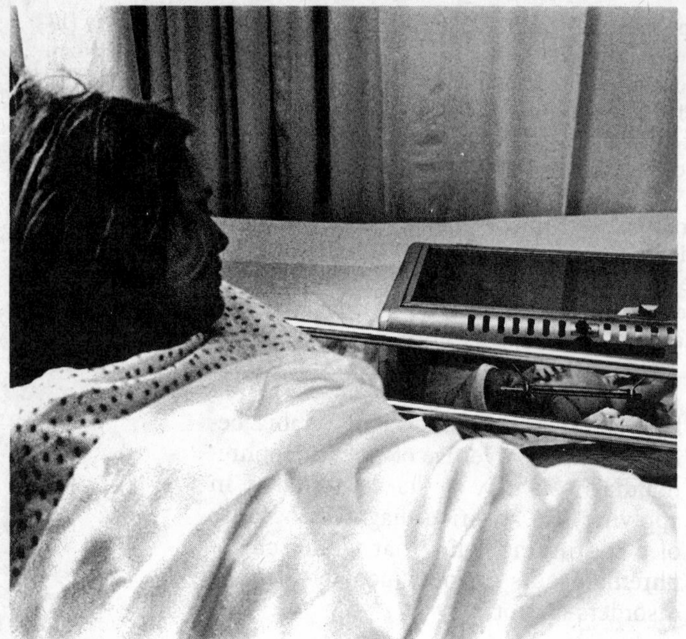

In some new mothers the joy and excitement of childbirth are replaced by postpartum depression. (© *Eric Kroll 1984/Taurus Photos*)

Postpartum Depression

In addition to there being special forms of depression associated with childhood, there are also specific patterns which occur in conjunction with new motherhood. Called *postpartum depression,* a moderate to severe affective disturbance can follow the birth of a child. During this period of time when many mothers experience a mild case of the "blues," some may have problems severe enough to require psychiatric intervention. Penfold (1981) notes that greater attention paid to what she terms the "fourth trimester of pregnancy" could have significant impact on reducing postpartum reactions. O'Hara et al. (1982) would likely agree since they found that many postpartum depressions could be prevented given greater sensitivity to the special stresses experienced by expectant and new mothers. The personal experience of one young mother may help to demonstrate the impact of postpartum depression.

Personal Experience: Postpartum Depression

I think the "blues" started right there in the hospital. I felt unable to relax at all. Now that I was a mother I had many important duties. I didn't feel sure I could live up to these responsibilities and at night in the hospital bed I didn't sleep, but outlined my daily schedule in my mind. I knew that when the baby and I got home I would have to be busy keeping the place in such a condition to be a "wholesome environment" for a child. I decided that I would have to force myself to stick to this schedule.

After we were home for awhile I began to feel like a shell. I did the same thing every day. While the baby was awake I was his servant and when he was asleep I cleaned and checked on his breathing. Nothing could upset my routine. If I knew a friend might call I took the phone off the hook or simply didn't answer its ring. I couldn't see anyone or go anyplace because it would upset my routine and I would be an unfit mother.

Although it's called postpartum "blues" I remember feeling incapable of being blue. I just felt profoundly "empty." There was no feeling for anything. I was quite sure that I didn't and couldn't love my husband or child.

The very worst day was when our baby was baptized. It was a bright spring day. I remember that a shaft of sun shone in from the porch that morning and I somehow saw it as a symbol that there was light and life somewhere but "I" would never be part of it.

After about six months I began to have bad stomach aches and diarrhea. Everytime I went out (which was not often and only to the grocery store or on some short errand) I would develop severe stomach pains and have to come home. Soon I began to think that I'd probably die.

By this time my husband, who had been very patient and kind, insisted that I see a doctor. The doctor found nothing wrong with me and spent quite a while talking with me—gently prodding. At last I cried, sobbed in fact, and told him that I felt nothing, loved nothing, and was nothing.

After this visit to the doctor I realized that I had a "real problem." Somehow just knowing this helped. Maybe I wasn't just empty, maybe I was unwell. Very, very slowly I started to feel better. I think I could have gotten better faster with professional help. Now that the "baby" is six, I am better than I ever was but I do regret that I never let myself enjoy his babyhood.

Involutional Melancholia

Major differences between involutional melancholia and the other types of affective psychosis lie in the age of onset of depression and the lack of significant history of depressive episodes (Akiskal & Webb, 1983). Occurring three times more frequently in females than in males, *involutional melancholia* typically affects females between the ages of 50 and 60 and males between the ages of 60 and 70. In women, the onset of the disorder usually follows menopause by a maximum of seven or eight years.

Generally, as involutional melancholia develops, people begin to experience periods of insomnia and feelings of inner tension. They may become easily fatigued, both mentally and physically, and show a reduced need for food or sexual activity. Fears for personal health and complaints of a continuous headache are frequent. Gradually, the person with involutional melancholia may develop a sense of despondency accompanied by constant weeping and loss of interest in favorite activities. As involutional melancholia deepens, insomnia worsens,

Some older people suffer from involutional melancholia, which is characterized by feelings of helplessness and depression. (© *1983 Larry Racioppo*)

weight loss increases, and numerous bodily ills may be imagined. The person typically presents a picture of extreme sadness mixed with agitation, often in the form of hand-wringing, pacing, repeated pleas for help, and self-deprecating statements. In severe cases, the person may experience delusions of guilt and bodily changes. For example, those suffering from involutional melancholia may believe that their insides have turned to concrete or that future bowel movements will be impossible. The following personal experience of involutional melancholia demonstrates many of the characteristics we have described.

Personal Experience: Involutional Melancholia

I don't know what went wrong with me. I had always been strong and stable, but now I feel so terrible and frightened. I can't sit still, and I'm always so tense and irritable. I cry at the drop of a hat. My children try to get me to do things, but they only succeed in making me mad. Even my grandchildren irritate me—can you imagine that? Nobody can stand me anymore. I nag and cry and nag and cry and can't be satisfied. I feel like nobody can help me and I really don't deserve to be helped.

Paradigmatically Based Explanations for the Affective Disorders

There are a number of explanations proposed for how the disorders of mood originate. For some scientists, the patterns are seen as inherited or biologically based in some other way. Others explain depression and mania on the basis of psychosocial factors like learning or cognitive processing problems. Finally, many researchers believe that life stresses are the major contributor to the development of affective symptomatology.

Biological Paradigm-based Explanations for the Affective Disorders

Explanations for affective disorders deriving from the biological paradigm focus on *physical* factors such as neurochemistry and heredity and their possible relation to depression and mania.

The Neurotransmitter Substances

Much of the biological paradigm–based research on the affective disorders has focused on neurotransmitter substances and their roles in emotional behavior (Anisman & Zacharko, 1982). Among the first group of substances to be implicated in the affective psychoses were the *catecholamines,* one of which is *norepinephrine* (Van Praag, 1980). Wherever it is found in the nervous system, an appropriate amount of norepinephrine seems to allow for smooth and normal synaptic transmission. However, the presence of too much norepinephrine at synapses can cause nerves to fire inappropriately and too frequently; conversely, too little of the substance can result in a slowing of the nervous system in which neurons may not be able to respond to normal impulses from adjoining cells. In view of these norepinephrine effects, Schildkraut (1970) proposed the *catecholamine hypothesis* which states that depression is related to a deficiency in brain norepinephrine and mania is related to an excess of this neurotransmitter.

Research has supported the catecholamine hypothesis (see Teuting et al. 1981; Anisman & Zacharko, 1982). For example, different groups of antidepressant drugs, though working in different ways, affect the amount of norepinephrine available at brain synapses. One group of drugs, the *monoamine oxidase inhibitors,* elevates the concentration of norepinephrine by slowing the action of the enzyme that metabolizes it. Another group of drugs, the *tricyclics,* increase amounts of norepinephrine by inhibiting the reuptake of the neurotransmitter into the synaptic vesicles after neuron firing (thereby leaving more norepinephrine in the synaptic space to ease transmission). In further support of the catecholamine hypothesis is the finding that the drug, *lithium carbonate,* now used in the treatment of manic episodes, produces a marked *decrease* in norepinephrine available at certain brain synapses. It is thought that this reduction in available norepinephrine in turn decreases the hyperresponsivity of the nervous system and slows neurotransmission to a normal level (Teuting et al., 1981).

Other evidence for the catecholamine hypothesis has come from research with selected groups of mental patients. Kety (1975) reported lower than normal levels of norepinephrine in the urine of depressed people and higher than normal levels in manic patients. In a study of treatment effects, Maas et al. (1972) have shown that the reduced levels of catecholamines in depressed individuals seems to return to normal when they are successfully treated by antidepressant medication (see also Teuting et al., 1981).

In addition to the catecholamines, another group of neurotransmitters, the *indoleamines,* also seem to play a part in the patterns of affective psychosis (Anisman & Zacharko, 1982). One indoleamine, *serotonin,* has been shown to be deficient in depressed (Shaw et al. 1967; Goodwin et al., 1978) *and* manic people (Coppen, 1972; Van Praag et al., 1973; Van Praag, 1981). Since serotonin is depleted in both forms of affective psychosis—not depleted in depression and excessive in mania as in the case of norepinephrine—indoleamine involvement may be somewhat more difficult to explain. One effort to explain this depletion pattern in both types of affective disorders and to integrate this phenomenon with the variation in norepinephrine is the *permissive amine hypothesis* described by Kety (1975) and Prange et al. (1974).

The permissive amine hypothesis has evolved because the regular and predictable variations in the affective disorders of both the catecholamines and the indoleamines suggest that neither of the neurotransmitter hypotheses alone can explain fully the biochemical basis for manic and depressive behaviors. In the permissive amine explanation, it was proposed that the biological predisposition to affective psychosis is expressed through an inherent serotonin deficiency. According to Kety (1975), serotonin is believed to regulate the reactivity of synapses by exerting a stabilizing influence upon variations in available catecholamines. If serotonin level is lower than normal, catecholamines are "permitted" to vary without sufficient control and can reach pathogenically high or low levels (see Figure 9-1). Kety has stated that "a deficiency of serotonin at central synapses, is an important generic or constitutional requirement for affective disorder, permitting what might otherwise be normal and adaptive changes in norepinephrine activity and the resultant mood states, to exceed the homeostatic bounds and progress in an undampened fashion to depression or excessive elation" (p. 184). Thus, from the permissive amine view, variations in mood in the affective psychoses may be attributable specifically to norepinephrine variation, but the predisposition to overreaction in the form of these norepinephrine variations is a result of a genet-

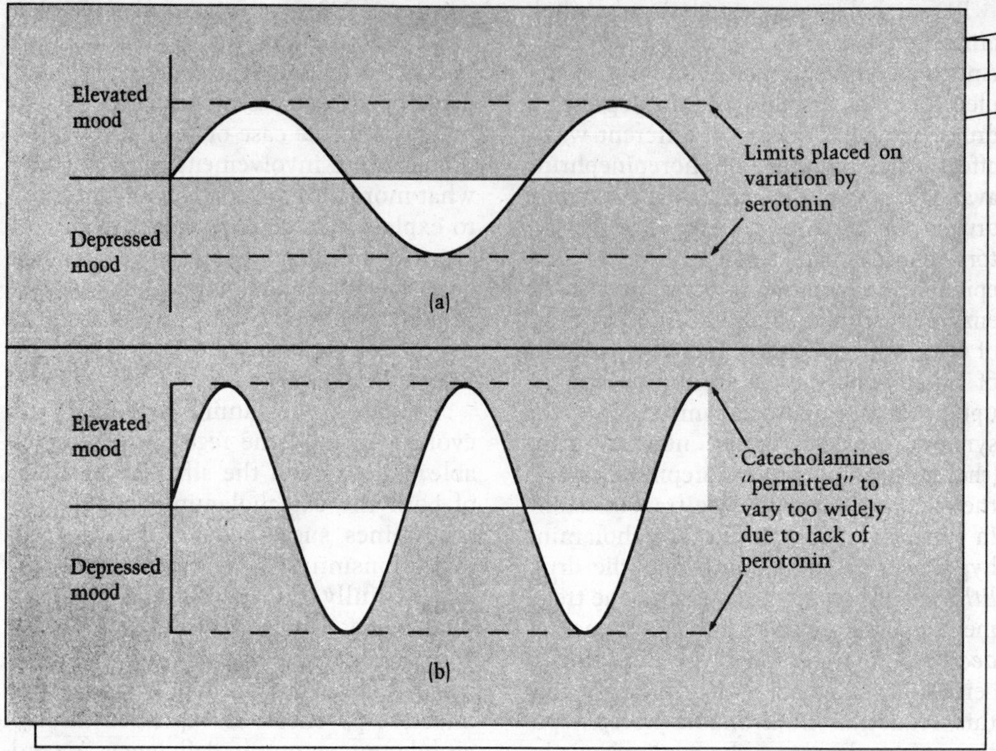

Figure 9-1 A schematic representation of the permissive amine hypothesis: (a) variations in catecholamines with normal amounts of serotonin (result—normal highs and lows); variations in catecholamines with below normal amounts of serotonin (result—abnormally high or manic moods, abnormally low or psychotically depressed moods).

ically caused lack of adequate amounts of serotonin.

While the neurochemical hypotheses are fairly well researched and seem promising, they require a cautionary note. Just as it was difficult to separate correlation and causation in the study of the biochemistry of schizophrenia, it is also difficult to determine if variations in neurotransmitter levels are a cause or an effect of affective psychosis. There are some researchers who believe that the biochemical differences observed in people with affective disorders may be a result of severe and unusual life stresses and, as such, are basically symptoms in themselves (Anisman & Zacharko, 1982). This should not, however, diminish the importance of this biological paradigm-based perspective.

Heredity

In addition to the focus on neurobiochemical function, the belief in the biological paradigm also has directed researchers to study the degree to which genetic factors may be involved in the development of the affective disorders. Genetic researchers have studied families, twins, and adoptees in their efforts to identify hereditary components of mood disturbances. Tsuang (1978b), Johnson and Leeman (1978), and Akiskal and Webb (1983) have reported that relatives of people with affective disturbances had a higher than normal rate of affective disorders. Studies comparing concordance rates between monozygotic and dizygotic twins seem to lend further support to a genetic component in affective patterns. Gershon et al.

BOX 9-3

THE ANTIDEPRESSANT EFFECTS OF LIGHT: A NEW APPLICATION OF THE BIOLOGICAL PARADIGM

So-called "seasonal" depressions occurring during the winter months were described by Kraeplin in the early part of this century (1921). People with this disorder are described as follows:

> During the winter, individuals feel depressed, slow down, and generally oversleep, overeat, and crave carbohydrates. In spring and summer they are elated, active and energetic and generally function well. (Rosenthal et al., 1985, p. 163)

In an interesting application of the biological paradigm, N. Rosenthal et al. (1985) reasoned that the crucial variable in winter was the reduction in the amount and intensity of daylight. Given lack of light as a "cause" for seasonal depression, it followed that administration of light would be a logical treatment for it. Specifically, seasonally depressed patients were exposed to light in such a way as to simulate the long daylight hours of summer. At the time the "light therapy" began, 22 of 24 patients in the study were suffering from major depressive episodes and 2 were diagnosed as dysthymic. The exposure to light resulted in improvement in patient moods within 2 days. So long as the light therapy continued, patients felt well. However, if allowed to return to the normal winter light schedule, most patients relapsed into depression within 72 hours. Further, reinstituting light therapy could not lift this relapsed depression in many instances. The authors noted that their treatment did not work with ordinary household lighting; rather bright lights several times as intense were needed to achieve therapeutic effects.

In concluding their report, Rosenthal et al. noted:

> We believe that patients with marked and predictable behavioral responses to the seasons provide clinical investigators with a unique opportunity for studying the interaction between vulnerable individuals and their physical environment. Light may prove to be an important element in the treatment of such patients and is a valuable key to understanding their condition. Behavioral and psychological effects of light may be important both in clinical practice and in public health planning. (p. 169)

While tested only with a relatively small group of patients thus far, light treatment reflects an application of the biological paradigm which may eventually be used more widely. For example, lighting in mental hospitals may be altered or traditional drug treatments for depression may be replaced. As with any new interpretation of a major paradigm, ensuing research will determine whether the therapeutic use of light is a temporary part of the scientific process or a permanent addition to the body of knowledge in abnormal psychology.

Source: Rosenthal et al. (1985).

(1977) and Gershon (1978) found a concordance rate for affective disorders among MZ twins to be as high as 71 percent as compared with a rate for DZ twins of no higher than 13 percent. Such a MZ-DZ difference is consistent with there being a genetic component in the transmission of the mood disorders.

Though their results are generally taken as supportive of a genetic hypothesis, studies using twins are often criticized because they usually do not control adequately for environmental influences. Studying children born to people with affective disorders but adopted and raised by "normal" parents helps to overcome this problem. Cadoret (1978) and Mendlewicz and Rainer (1977) found that adoptees who had biological parents diagnosed as having affective disturbances had a higher prevalence of depression than adoptees whose biological parents were normal.

While data from family, twin, and adoptee studies suggest the existence of a genetic component in affective disorders, the mechanism by which this component is transmitted or expressed is less clearly understood. Some researchers have proposed and found evidence for mood disturbances being linked to the female or X chromosome. Evidence for this supposition comes from studies which show that certain other, better understood and established X chromosome linked characteristics such as color blindness also tend to occur more frequently in people with forms of affective disturbance (Gershon & Bunney, 1976). Since it is known that certain X chromosome linked characteristics are transmitted in genetic clusters, if an individual inherits one identifiable characteristic, then other, less easily identified characteristics are likely to be present as well. The X, or female, chromosome linkage for affective disorders also has been suggested as an explanation for the greater incidence of these problems among females (Gershon & Bunney, 1976).

Feelings and actions associated with the normal grief process are often similar to those seen in depression. This observation is an important part of the psychoanalytic explanation for the disorder. (*Michael Weisbrot and Family*)

The Psychosocial Paradigm-based Explanations

Whereas the biological explanations for affective psychosis focus on the physical level of analysis, the psychosocial paradigm leads theorists to search for causes at intrapersonal and interpersonal levels of human functioning. The psychosocial explanations for affective disorders began with the work of the psychoanalysts and eventually broadened to include the views of the ego analysts, neoanalysts (interpersonal theorists), and the learning theorists.

The Psychoanalysts

One of the first psychosocial conceptualizations of manic-depressive disorder was provided in 1911 by the psychoanalyst, Karl Abraham (Robertson, 1979a,b). Abraham believed that people prone to develop affective disorders were egocentric and so ambivalent about love and hate for themselves and others that they couldn't express one feeling in the absence of the other. Their inability to express love which was not blurred by hate led to feelings of inner emptiness. These feelings of emptiness are thought to originate from a fixation at the oral stage of psychosexual development caused by an ambivalent attitude toward the mother. Such people grow up being unable to relate adequately to *love objects* (parent, spouse, and lover) who frustrate their attempts to obtain gratification from them. Failing to relate successfully to love objects, they are forced to regress to the oral level where they can relate to themselves with the same love-hate ambivalence that they felt toward others. The result is that at times they overly hate themselves (depression) and at other times they overly love themselves (mania).

Freud also wrote about the origins of depression from the psychoanalytic perspective. In *Mourning and Melancholia* (originally published in 1917), he noted the similarity between grieving behavior and depression. Just as bereaved people mourn the loss of important others, Freud believed that depressed individuals mourned the loss of their own egos. Freud reasoned that since the ego was involved to the extent of identifying with the love object, itself, the loss of that love object (e.g., the loss of a parent) is felt by the ego as depression. Freud also proposed that depression could result from anger that derived from the love-hate feelings held toward the love object. People who cannot express the aggression associated with the hate component of their feelings may turn these feelings inward, against themselves, and experience despair which may be so severe as to lead to suicide (the ultimate form of aggression turned inward). In support of Freud's view, Kendall (1973) found that in societies where expression of aggression is either encouraged or more freely permitted, there seems to be a lower incidence of depression.

Other psychoanalytic thinkers see *loss of self-esteem* as the most crucial event in the development of depression. Jacobson (1953) states:

> Manic-depressives manifest a particular kind of infantile narcissistic dependency on their love object. What they require is a constant supply of love and moral support from a highly valued love object, which need not be a person, but may be represented by a powerful symbol, a religious, political, or scientific cause, or an organization. . . . As long as their "belief" in this object lasts, they will be able to work with enthusiasm and efficiency (p. 67).

According to Jacobson, depressed people overly value their love objects and undervalue themselves. Thus, when there is a loss of their love object, all that they have left is the depression associated with the low self-esteem of their undervalued ego.

According to theorists like Jacobson, the basic mechanism in depression seems to be the ego's realization that, on its own, it is helpless to realize its aspirations (Bibring, 1953). Depressed people tend to set unrealistic goals for themselves, and their self-esteem is attached to the achievement of these goals. When goals are not achieved and self-esteem drops, the ego begins to feel that greater helplessness is imminent. In psychologically stable individuals, this threat of helplessness typically leads to activities directed at increasing self-esteem. Among these activities might be the lowering of goals or the use of defense mechanisms to mildly distort the perception of the world. However, instead of being spurred to constructive activities, in the face of imminent helplessness, depressed individuals may become passive, immobile, and resigned to failure. Using a similar analysis, Bibring (1953) suggests that manic excitement may be a result of a distorted belief that unrealistic goals actually are being met even though in reality they are far from being achieved.

The Cognitive Theorists

While psychoanalytic thinkers find the source of affective disorders in the malfunctioning of the intrapsychic processes, the *cognitive theorists* focus on difficulties in people's thinking processes. According to Coyne and Gotlib (1983), who reviewed the cognitive approaches to depression, symptoms may result from problems in one or several of five major areas—expectations and evaluations of performance, perception of environmental information, recall of information, cognitive biases, and attributional processes. These authors note that there are two major theories which attempt to explain affective disorders within the context of these five areas. These are Beck's model of depression and Seligman's learned-helplessness explanation.

Beck takes the position that affective disorders can reflect *cognitive errors* caused by the use of faulty *schemas* (Beck, 1967,

1976). Cognitive errors are erroneous conclusions reached about the nature of a particular situation. Schemas are organized clusters of attitudes, beliefs, and assumptions about events in the internal and external world that mediate between what people perceive and their responses to their perceptions. Beck believes that psychological disorders develop when biased sets of schemas adversely affect a person's ability to see the world accurately and to behave adaptively. Affective disorders usually involve problems in important schemas about the *self*, the *outer world*, and the *future*. For example, a depressed person faced with a term paper might filter perceptions through all of his or her distorted depressive schemas. The resultant conclusions might be "I can't write a good term paper. I'm not good at writing" (distorted self-schema); "I'll never do it with all the other things I have to do. There's no use trying" (distorted outer world schema); "I'm going to fail—I just know it" (distorted future schema). As a result of these three distorted schemas, depressed individuals theoretically find their worlds filled with unreachable goals, unscalable obstacles, and hopelessness.

From the perspective of Beck's model, as compared with depressed individuals, manic people use a different set of distorted schemas. They tend to see themselves, their outer worlds, and their futures in an unrealistically *positive* light. Thus, they would tend to feel much happier and optimistic about the very same events which the depressed person might find very upsetting. For cognitive theorists, then, the difference between the manic and the depressive person lies not in their mental processes but in the patterns of their distorted schemas.

While Beck's view of depression derived primarily from work with people, Seligman and his coworkers (Seligman, 1975; Maser & Seligman, 1977; Abramson et al., 1978; Abramson et al., 1980) have presented a cognitive theory of affective disorder based initially on their work with laboratory animals. It is their view that depression in humans is caused by extensive experience of being exposed to situations beyond one's control and the sense of *learned helplessness* caused by this experience:

> When a person finds that he is helpless, he asks *why* he is helpless. The causal attributions he makes determine the generality and chronicity of his helplessness deficits as well as his later self-esteem. (Abramson et al., 1978, p. 50)

The sequence in the development of symptoms is as follows:

> *Objective* noncontingency—*Perception* of present and past noncontingency—*Attribution* for present or past noncontingency—*Expectation* of future noncontingency—*Symptoms* of helplessness. (Abramson et al., 1978, p. 52)

In other words, Abramson et al. (1978) propose that depression develops in a way similar to the following: First people notice that they have no control over some things happening to them; they then realize that this is a continuous pattern now and in the past; they then attribute their inability to control things to either themselves or to powerful others or both; a belief that they never will be able to control their experiences then emerges; this belief is accompanied by depression and loss of self-esteem.

Seligman and his colleagues began their study of learned helplessness with an investigation of dogs attempting to learn how to avoid a strong electrical shock. To train "helplessness," they restrained their animals and then submitted them to an unavoidable shock. Later, these same dogs were placed on one side of a divided box and were again given a strong, painful shock. Now, however, because they were not being restrained in any way, they could escape the shock merely by jumping over a low barrier to the other side of the box. A control group of dogs which did not receive the "helplessness" pretraining soon learned how to escape the shock in this manner. However, when the dogs who had been restrained and exposed to unavoidable shock and learned to be "helpless" were introduced to the barrier jumping situation, they behaved quite differently. Even though the painful shock lasted up to 1 minute, these dogs did not jump to avoid it; they simply stopped moving, lay down in a corner of the box, and whined.

Once induced, the state of learned helplessness usually has tremendous staying power, as Seligman discovered during his attempts to "cure" his affected dogs. He and his colleagues removed the barrier in the jumping box, tempted the animals to jump with food, and even *dragged* the animals from the shock side of the box to the safe side. With few exceptions, Seligman's efforts were unsuccessful; most of the dogs simply sat and took the shock. In some cases, however, after being dragged repeatedly across the barrier, a dog would overcome the helplessness. Seligman speculated that in a manner similar to his dogs, due to unfortunate and uncontrollable life experiences, some people may learn to perceive themselves as being unable to control what happens to them. As a result of such an attitude, they may react to pain and disappointment by becoming passive, withdrawn, and depressed.

The Operant Theorists

While the cognitive theorists are drawn to internal factors like schemas, operant theorists emphasize concepts like external stimuli and reinforcement in their views on the development of affective disorders. One operant theorist (Ferster, 1965), for example, described how an elderly woman developed a depression when her sister died. In operant terms, she became depressed because the main source of reinforcement for a large proportion of her behaviors was gone, and she no longer received a positive response for appropriate normal behavior. This lack of reinforcement resulted in her feelings of sadness and helplessness. In like fashion, operant theorists believe that we can explain the sudden depressions that often result from significant changes in our families, friendships, or environments.

Operant theorists Lewinsohn and Atwood (1969) have a slightly different view from that of Ferster. Rather than depression occurring because of a *loss* of reinforcement, these researchers believe that people become depressed because, due to their poorly developed social skills and often aversive personal characteristics, they *receive* little love, attention, and sympathy from those around them (McLean, 1976). Their resulting "low positive reinforcement schedules" lead them to feel guilty, self-deprecatory, and fatigued. Summarizing this operant perspective, McLean (1976) suggests that depression is brought about by an interaction between an individual's personal characteristics and societal reaction to those characteristics.

The Systems Paradigm-based Explanations for Affective Disorders

Although the psychosocial paradigmatic explanations for affective disorders focus attention on individual perception and cognitive functioning, it is clear that much of what they emphasize happening *within* individuals is in some way related to what is happening *to* them in the systems in which they live. The systems theories for affective disorders focus on these things that happen *to* people and try to relate the occurrence of such stressful life events to the development of affective disorder.

One application of a systems paradigmatic approach to the explanation of affective disorders has been provided by Billings and Moos (1982). These authors view depression as stemming from an interaction of environmental events and in-

Environmental stressors . . . develop from personal and environmental factors and include specific events (divorce, death of spouse, job loss), chronic life strains associated with major social roles (a stressful job, marital discord), and medical conditions and illnesses (arthritis, cancer).

Personal resources include dispositional characteristics such as self-concept, sense of environmental mastery and attributional styles, as well as social skills and problem solving abilities. *Environmental resources* refer to informational material and emotional support provided by intimates, other family members, and non-kin social network members. It is in the context of these environmental and personal resources that individuals *appraise* particular stressors: that is, perceive and interpret specific events. Along with the appraisal process, individuals use *coping responses* that are intended to minimize the adverse effects of stress. The outcome of this process influences the individual's level of *functioning* and adaptation.

Figure 9-2 The interaction of environmental and personal factors in depression. (*From Billings & Moos, 1982, pp. 214–215.*)

dividual abilities to cope with them. Billings and Moos conceptualization is depicted in Figure 9-2.

From Billings and Moos' perspective as well as in the view of others believing that affective disorders stem from stressful life events (Lloyd, 1980a, b), the things that happen to people within the context of the systems of which they are a part can be a major source of their difficulties. The systems may be as small as a family or as large as a company, neighborhood, or city; when stressful events are so great that people cannot cope with them, psychological symptoms result.

An Integrated Paradigm Explanation for the Affective Disorders

While theories deriving from the biological, psychosocial, and systems paradigms can explain some aspects of the affective disturbances, no one approach seems complete enough to account for the variety of observed patterns. For example, some depressions are clearly caused by life stresses such as the death of a loved one, but there are other depressive episodes for which there seems to be no identifiable psychosocial or environmental cause. In an attempt to overcome these and other problems brought about by the limitations of the single-factor paradigms, researchers such as Akiskal and McKinney (1973, 1975) and Anisman and Zacharko (1982) have proposed *integrative models of affective disorders.*

In Akiskal and McKinney's integrative model (see also Akiskal & Webb, 1983), depression is defined as the outcome of an interaction among three levels of function: *the experiential, the biochemical, and the behavioral.* As seen in Figure 9-3, severe affective symptoms are seen as a *biological final common pathway* reflecting a variety of interacting experiences and events. As Figure 9-4 shows, the initial cause of an affective disturbance may be biological and/or psychosocial. For instance, psychosocial stress in the form of adult object loss, physical disease, learned helplessness, and the like can begin the process of depression. Also, however, these same symptoms can begin as a result of a genetic predisposition to develop the disorder. Even with their different sources, Akiskal and McKinney note that once depressive reactions have begun, they are biologically mediated in the same way. Hence, deficits in norepinephrine and abnormal levels of serotonin are likely to be present whether a particular depression is physiologically, psychosocially, environmentally, or genetically based.

In another interactive view of affective disturbance, Anisman and Zacharko have

Experiential
Nonrelatedness
Anhedonia
Hopelessness
Loss of control
Chemical
Alternation in functional level of catechotamines and indoleamines
Electrolyte disturbance
Behavioral
Disturbances in sleep or appetite
Psychomotor dysfunction (slowing or agitation)

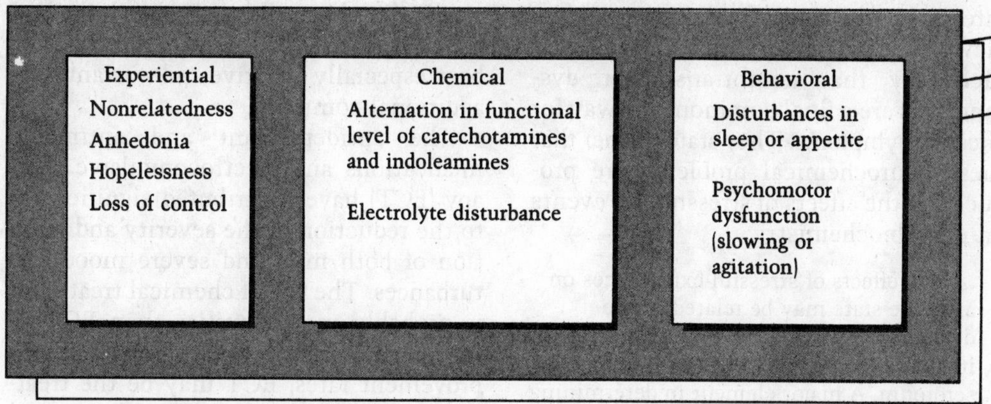

Figure 9-3 Definition of depression as a multilevel interaction. (*From "Overview of Recent Research in Depression," by H. Akiskal and W. McKinney, Archives of General Psychiatry, 1975, 32, 285–305. Copyright 1975 by the American Medical Association. Reprinted by permission.*)

Physiological stressors
Reserpine
Hypothyroidism
Viral infection
Genetic predisposition
Leaky presynaptic membrane
Decrease in postsynaptic receptor sensitivity
Psychosocial stressors
Adult object loss
Chronic frustration
Developmental predisposition
Early object loss
Learned helplessness
Alterations in functional level of biogenic amines
Production of faulty neurotransmitters
Intraneuronal sodium accumulation
Diencephalic final common pathway
Melancholia

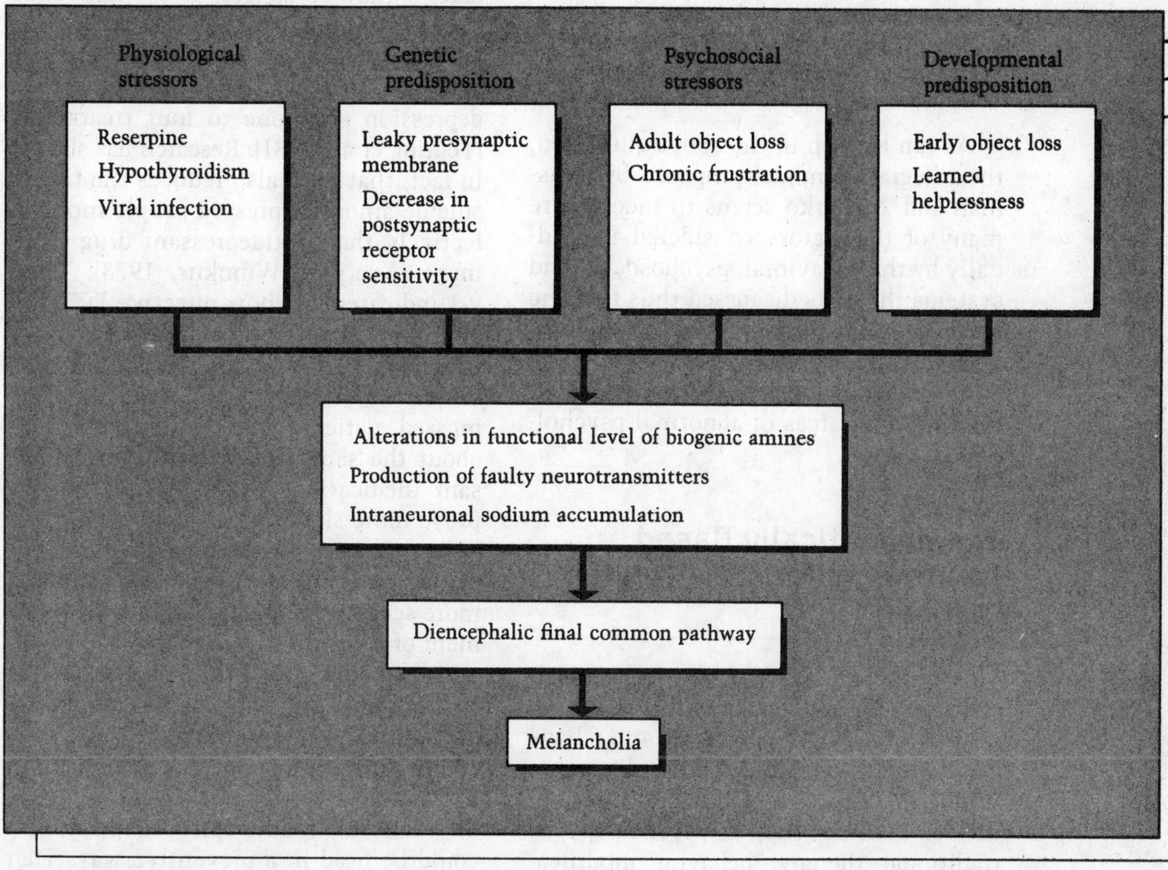

Figure 9-4 Depression as a final biological pathway. (*From "Overview of Recent Research in Depression," by H. Akiskal and W. McKinney, Archives of General Psychiatry, 1975, 32, 285–305. Copyright 1975 by the American Medical Association. Reprinted by permission.*)

integrated the biological and systems views. They agree with Akiskal and McKinney that neurotransmitter dysfunctions are a final common pathway for affective symptoms. They state further that these neurochemical problems are produced by the effects of stressful life events on neurobiochemistry:

> . . . the effects of stressful experiences on affective state may be related to the depletion of several neurotransmitters, including norepinephrine, dopamine, and serotonin. A major element in determining neurochemical changes is the organism's ability to cope. . . . When behavioral coping is possible, neurochemical systems are not overly taxed (and) behavioral pathology will not ensue. However, when there can be no behavioral control over the stressful stimuli, or when the life experience is perceived as uncontrollable, increased emphasis is placed on coping through . . . neurochemical mechanisms. (Anisman & Zacharko, 1982, p. 89)

As can be seen in the above quotation, the integrative model proposed by Anisman and Zacharko seems to incorporate many of the factors considered individually by the behavioral, psychosocial, and systems theorists discussed thus far. The need for and seeming efficacy of such integrated paradigmatic views may be seen as a foreshadowing of such integrative efforts in other areas of abnormal psychology as well.

Paradigmatically Based Treatments for the Affective Disorders

Most of the basic biological, psychosocial, and systems-based treatment methods described more fully in Chapters 4 to 6 have been applied to the affective disorders. While the psychosocially and systems-derived methods such as psychoanalysis, traditional therapy, behavior modification, group and family therapy, and hospitalization have all been helpful, the biologically based treatments seem to have been especially effective and warrant brief additional comment.

The antidepressant and antimanic medications and electroconvulsive therapy (ECT) have contributed significantly to the reduction of the severity and duration of both mild and severe mood disturbances. The use of chemical treatment is probably more familiar than ECT to most people. However, in terms of improvement rates, ECT may be the treatment of choice for depression for several reasons (as outlined in Chapter 4). One reason is that antidepressant medication can require up to 10 days to take effect and in instances where depression is so severe as to increase the likelihood of suicide, it may be dangerous to wait for so long for symptom relief. A second reason is that ECT seems to be relatively safe and can reduce major symptoms of depression after one to four treatments (Teuting et al., 1981). Research has shown, in fact, that ECT also reduces the rate of suicide among depressed people more effectively than antidepressant drug treatment (Avery & Winokur, 1973). Table 9-1 indicates just how effective ECT can be compared with other approaches to the treatment of depression. Note that even with *no* treatment (the placebo group) depressed patients eventually recover at about the same rate as with antidepressant medication, although they do improve more slowly.

As has been the case throughout our discussion of the affective disorders, much more seems to be known about the treatment of depression than mania. However, with the advent of lithium carbonate as an antimanic drug, the success rate for reducing manic symptoms increased appreciably. Initially it appeared that lithium was indeed a "miracle" drug, for not only did it shorten manic episodes, but it also could be used in a preventive way. That is, people who were prone to repeated manic episodes could take a daily dose of lithium and avoid future recurrences of mania. However, continued research on the extended use of lithium has been associated with kidney failure in some patients (Vestergaard, 1980). Also, Carroll (1979) has found that not everyone with manic symptoms responds well to lithium treatment. Although, as with any medication, there may be limits to lithium's usefulness as a treatment, it presently stands as an effective application of the biological paradigm.

Table 9-1 Comparative Effectiveness of Different Types of Treatment for Severe Depression

	Degree of Improvement, %	
Treatment Method	***Marked***	***Marked or Moderate***
ECT	76	92
Antidepressant drugs	49	76
Placebo	46	69

Source: Based on Crow & Johnstone, 1979.

Suicide

Any examination of depression must include a discussion of its most devastating "symptom," *suicide.* Likewise, any treatment for depression must reduce the risk of self-destruction so often associated with it. Since by its severity, frequency, and impact, suicide is in so many ways more than just "one of the symptoms" of severe depression, it in itself has been the focus of much research and theory deriving from the biological, psychosocial, and systems paradigms.

Nearly 30,000 people in the United States take their own lives each year (Miles, 1977). Victims may be rich or poor, city dwellers or country dwellers, young or old. They may vary in a great number of ways, but each shares the experience of deep despondency and suicide with such personalities as Marilyn Monroe, Nero, Amy Vanderbilt, Vincent van Gogh, Virginia Woolf, Hannibal, Cleopatra, Ernest Hemingway, Brutus, Marc Antony, and Sylvia Plath. All of these well-known people seem to have shared a feeling of unbearable anguish that pushed them to the dramatic act of taking their own lives. Why do people kill themselves? While people have pondered this question for centuries, only recently has there been a concerted scientific effort to provide an answer. *Suicidology,* the study of suicide, has grown significantly over the past two decades and has contributed much to our understanding of self-destructive behavior.

In the United States, suicide ranks third as a cause of death in people 15 to 34 years of age, and ninth in people over 55 (Holinger, 1980; Vital Statistics of the United States, 1981). More men than women commit suicide, although over three times as many women as men *attempt* suicide. The higher rate of completed suicides among males is usually attributed to their more frequently choosing highly lethal means of attempting suicide such as guns. Women seem to complete suicidal acts less often because their preferred methods tend to be less immediate and more reversible ones such as drugs or poison.

As well as differing by sex, the suicide rate also seems to vary with age. Beginning in adolescence there is steady increase in the suicide rate which reaches a peak in the 45 and over age group. However, Seiden and Freitas (1980) report a change in this trend with rising rates for younger people during the 1970s. Seiden reported that there seems to be a rise in suicide attempts in the 15- to 24-year-old age group. Although the frequency of attempts has risen in younger people, however, the chance of completing suicide tends still to be higher in older individuals.

Given its rate and impact, great effort has been expended in trying to find ways of assessing suicide potential and preventing people assessed as suicidal from taking their own lives. There are many beliefs about how one can know when someone is suicidal; some of these beliefs are supported by scientific data and others may be considered "myths" (Shneidman & Farberow, 1961). In Figure 9-5, we have provided a list of some of the realities and myths surrounding suicide. Among the myths we can find attitudes which can cost a life; among the realities we can find *clues* which can help in suicide prevention. Shneidman and Farberow (1961) have attempted to apply their study of the myths and realities of suicide by developing the basic clues that can help determine whether a person is seriously planning self-destruction.

1. *Myth:* People who talk about suicide don't commit suicide.
   Reality: Eight out of ten persons who completed suicides made previous attempts, and retrospective studies of suicidal persons show most gave ample warning through verbal and other behavioral signals.
2. *Myth:* Suicide happens without warning.
   Reality: Most suicidal people give ample warning of what they are contemplating.
3. *Myth:* Suicidal people are fully intent on dying.
   Reality: Most attempters of suicide are ambivalent about dying, and, as just mentioned, most will let others know about their plans in various ways.
4. *Myth:* Once a person is suicidal, he or she is suicidal forever.
   Reality: Research has shown that the critical period within which suicidal behavior will probably occur is brief.
5. *Myth:* Improvement after a suicidal crisis means that the suicidal risk is over.
   Reality: Most suicides occur three months after a previous attempt when the people have the energy to carry out their objective of killing themselves.
6. *Myth:* Suicide occurs more often among the rich, or conversely, it occurs almost exclusively among the poor.
   Reality: Suicide occurs in all strata of society.
7. *Myth:* Suicidal tendencies are inherited or run in the family.
   Reality: There is no support for the assumption that suicidal behavior is genetically determined.
8. *Myth:* All suicidal persons are mentally ill, and suicide is always the act of a psychotic person.
   Reality: Data show that there is no necessary connection between mental illness and suicidal behavior.

Figure 9-5 *Suicide: myths and realities. (From Shneidman & Farberow, 1961.)*

Paradigmatically Based Explanations for Suicide

Historically, the basic paradigms used to explain suicide have been either psychosocial or systems-based. However, recent attempts to apply the biological paradigm to self-destructive behavior also seem to hold promise.

The Psychosocial Paradigm: Psychoanalytic Theories

A major psychosocial explanation for suicide comes from the psychoanalytic school of thought. Freud postulated that people have an innate need to be aggressive and that this aggressive drive may be expressed in fights, arguments, and wars. Like hunger and thirst, aggression is a drive that needs satisfaction in the form of reduction. However, while hunger and thirst contribute to the maintenance of life, Freud postulated that aggression was part of the death instinct, *Thanatos*. He stated:

> A more fruitful idea was that a portion of the death instinct is diverted toward the external world and comes to light as an instinct of aggressiveness. In this way the instinct itself could be pressed into the service of Eros, in that the organism was destroying some other things, whether animate or inanimate, instead of destroying its own self (Freud, quoted in Litman, 1967, p. 324.)

To Freud, restriction of the aggressive drive by either the environment or by psychic structures such as the superego could result in self-destructive behavior. He therefore believed that suicide was in large part the result of repressed hostility which could find no acceptable external outlet.

Freud pointed out that aggression can take either an outward or inward route. A later analytic thinker, Menninger (1938), added that the inward turn of aggression also can take a variety of forms, but that only one of them might be considered clear suicide. As support for his view that other methods of self-destruction also can occur, Menninger cited the self-destructive behavior of drug addicts and alcoholics (which he termed *chronic suicide*), the need for self-mutilating surgery expressed by some neurotic individuals *(focal suicide)*, and the psychophysiological patterns of frustrated rage as expressed through ulcers or high blood pressure *(organic suicide)*. According to Menninger, the self-destructive component of these disorders is often obvious to outside observers, but rarely are they included as examples of aggression turned inward.

In addition to utilizing the concepts of repressed hostility and aggression turned inward as explanations for suicide, psychoanalytic theory also suggests that self-destruction possibly occurs when a person who is *both hated and loved* is *introjected* or psychologically incorporated into a person. If this introjected other should do something, such as reject the person, which leads to the removal of the love component of the attachment, then the person is left with only introjected hate. This hate then becomes dominant, is transformed into strong self-hate, and can lead to suicide. The following example may make this psychoanalytic view clearer: A man identifies with and introjects the qualities of his father whom he both loves and hates. Later, he finds that his father has run away with another woman, leaving him and his mother alone. At this point, the love component of his attachment to his father is neutralized and all the man has left is introjected hate, which he may try to get rid of by attempting suicide.

The Psychosocial Paradigm: Social Learning Theory

Unlike psychoanalytic theory, which seems to focus less on the effects of the environment in the development of suicidal behavior, social learning theory assumes that suicidal behavior is highly dependent upon learning from others. A person may learn that indulging in potentially self-destructive acts (such as car racing or skydiving) frequently attracts attention and caretaking from other people. This learning process can direct a person toward suicidal behavior especially if his or her family members or close friends have exhibited such behavior in attempts to solve problems. To the social learning theorist, this kind of observational learning can help explain why there seems to be a greater likelihood of suicidal behavior in individuals who have known someone who has committed suicide. From such a perspective, a person faced with seemingly insurmountable problems may indulge in suicidal behavior based on the expectation that this behavior will have some previously observed effect upon others. Many suicidal people seem to believe that they will be able to obtain satisfaction of their anger against others through knowing that these others will be sad, guilty, or otherwise affected.

Menninger has suggested that drug abusers are expressing a self-destructive attitude that could be termed "chronic suicide." John Belushi may have been such an individual. (© *1980 Steve Kagan/Photo Researchers, Inc.*)

The Systems Paradigm: Societal Integration Theory

Moving even further than the learning theorists toward a focus on environmental factors in suicide, Durkheim (1951) created a systems paradigm model to explain the incidence and prevalence of suicidal behavior. Durkheim believed strongly that there was a connection between suicide rates and social conditions. Specifically, he proposed that suicide frequency was inversely related to the integration and organization of society. When society is loosely organized and the individual isolated, the suicide rate should be higher. Durkheim classified three basic kinds of suicide, differing primarily according to the victim's relationship to society: egoistic, altruistric, and anomic.

In Durkheim's first class of suicide, *egoistic*, victims are individualistic and thus not a part of society. Either they have rejected society, or society has rejected them; but in any case, they are not really a part of the general cultural group.

For some World War II kamikaze pilots, altruistic suicide was both an honorable and a joyous death. (*U.S. Naval Institute*)

Altruistic suicide is directly opposite to egoistic suicide and occurs when individuals are too closely bound to society and feel required for the common good to perform some act of sacrifice. If they were not to perform the act of sacrifice, the societal pressures could cause them to experience unbearable shame. Altruistic suicide may be exemplified by the behavior of kamikaze pilots in World War II, who used their airplanes as bombs in attempts to destroy enemy ships.

Anomic suicide differs from egoistic and altruistic suicide in that it occurs when people's usual relationship to society is shattered and they find themselves alienated from a group of which they used to be a part. When Hitler took power in Germany, many educated people suddenly found themselves outside society. Their choice was often either to flee or to experience *anomie* (not feeling part of established society). Similarly, many poor people are subject to anomie, especially if they perceive that they were once in a better situation and thus are aware of a difference between their present situation and their goals. However, from this perspective, if disadvantaged people can prize what they have and are satisfied, they may not be considered anomic and may not be more prone to suicide.

The Biological Paradigm

Neither the psychosocial nor the systems explanations of suicidal behavior address the possibility of biochemical etiology in suicidal behavior. However, Snyder (1975) reviews the biological work most closely related to suicide and concludes that "many biological factors may be construed as 'relevant' to the study of suicide" (p. 126). The major focus on biological factors generally involves the neurotransmitters, such as norepinephrine, and their impact on functioning. Citing the catecholamine hypothesis of depression, Snyder concluded, "If there is

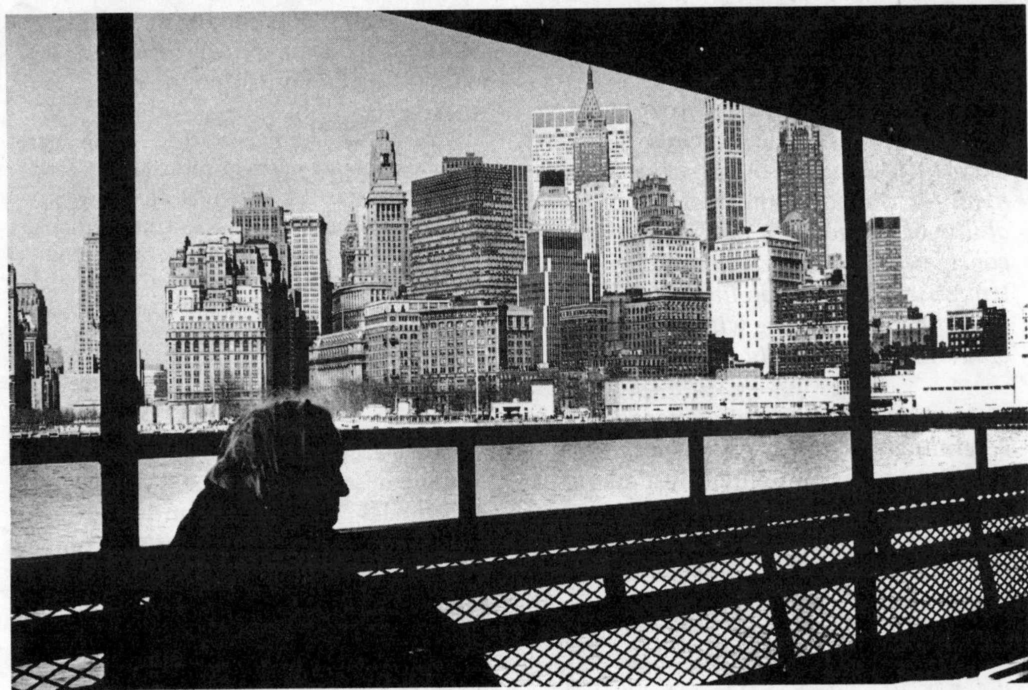

Even in the most populous of cities, people can be lonely and find little to live for. (*Louise E. Jefferson/Monkmeyer Press Photo Service*)

a unique biological substratum of that state of mind that eventuates in a person taking his own life, our present knowledge of brain function might elect a possible alteration in catecholamine dispositions as the major candidate" (p. 127). The major assumption in this explanation is that catecholamine dysfunction may be the cause of depression, which in turn is the cause of suicidal behaviors. Snyder points out that the majority of biological research on depression has been accomplished with animals and that we shouldn't conclude that human depressive states are caused by or are identical with lowered brain catecholamine levels. However, recent evidence adds further support to the biological perspective. Greenberg (1982) reviewed the work of Stanley and Gordon at the National Institute of Mental Health who have identified a biochemical correlate of suicide (low serotonin) and of Kety who, in a study of adoptees in Denmark, has proposed that suicide runs in families. Further, a new drug, zimeladine, is being tested which may hold promise for the prevention of suicide.

Paradigmatically Based Treatments for Suicide

Unlike other forms of psychopathology, suicide is not a disorder which can be treated after it has appeared. As such, "treatment" of suicide must be defined within the context of *prevention.* While the biological paradigm has led to the use of antidepressant medication in the reduction of suicidal feelings, most efforts at suicide prevention have derived primarily from the psychosocial and systems perspectives.

The Psychosocial Paradigm: Assessment and Reduction of Suicide Potential

From a psychosocial perspective, effective prevention of suicide depends on three factors. These are the *accurate assessment of suicide potential, the availability of methods for dealing with those considered to have elevated suicide potential, and the availability of people who are trained in working with those considered to be dangerously suicidal.*

Assessment of Suicide Potential The determination of the seriousness of suicide potential is quite literally a matter of life and death. According to experts (Shneidman, 1969, 1971, 1975), a person's potential for suicide consists of three components: *lethality, perturbation, and inimicality.*

The first component of suicide potential, lethality, refers to the probability that the person will commit suicide. How "lethal" a person is at any given time may be seen as a combination of past and present experiences and circumstances. Table 9-2 presents some factors often used in assessing lethality.

Perturbation refers to how distressed, disturbed, or agitated a person is judged to be. The greater the degree of perturbation, the more likely a suicide attempt will occur. Although lethality and perturbation are interrelated, they are also seen as independent components of suicide potential and are typically assessed separately. As Shneidman points out:

> One can be highly perturbed—in an acute schizophrenic episode, for example—and not necessarily be suicidal; the converse is, in a curious sense, also true. Although, admittedly, no one in his normal mind commits suicide, it is perfectly possible—indeed it happens much too often—that a person need not be in a discernable state of high perturbation in order to kill himself. (1975, p. 1778)

Thus, according to Shneidman, one can be quite upset (perturbed) and yet not really be suicidal; more importantly, however, one can appear to be relatively unperturbed and yet be lethal enough to attempt self-destruction. It may be this very lack of perturbation that often keeps people close to a possible suicide victim from actively intervening.

The third component of suicide potential, inimicality, refers to a person's general life-style. It is here that general and pervasive patterns of self-defeating or high-risk behavior (such as auto racing, sky diving, or snake handling) may be looked for. These patterns, if continued, might significantly shorten a person's life. Alcoholics, smokers, drug abusers, and those who refuse to follow prescribed medical regimes, for example, might be considered high in inimicality.

Table 9-2 Factors Associated with Increased Suicide Potential

Symptoms—feelings of depression or hopelessness, sleeplessness, alcohol or drug abuse
Age and sex—male, over the age of 50
Stress—recent loss of loved one, loss of job, onset of physical illness
Type of onset of stress—sudden onset
Suicide plan—presence of a feasible suicide plan and the means to carry it out
Prior suicide attempts—history of one or more attempts or history of many threats
Support system—absence of friends or family who are willing to help
Physical status—failing health or presence of chronic illness
Family contacts—communication with family members has deteriorated or ceased
Reactions of others—loved ones all rejecting, punitive, or unsupportive

Source: Based on suicide prevention materials from several suicide prevention centers.

Besides the accurate assessment of a person's suicide potential, prevention must take into account three additional features of the suicidal state: *its brief duration, the ambivalence of the suicidal person with regard to death, and the dyadic nature of suicide* (Shneidman, 1975).

The period of high lethality for suicide typically lasts only a brief time. A person will not stand on a window ledge for 2 months deciding whether or not to jump, nor will anyone stand for a week in a room with a gun pointed at his or her head. Since the lethal period is so brief, it is usually during that short time that major means of prevention must be applied.

Prevention also can be based upon the fact that many of those who attempt suicide are ambivalent as to whether they wish to live or die. It is often the case that at the same time that the person is planning to die, he or she may also be fantasizing about being rescued from the brink of death. Also, the attempted suicide may frequently represent a "cry for help" in which the person cannot ask for aid in any other way. It is for reasons similar to these that prevention efforts must always be directed at the portion of the person that wants to live.

A final feature of suicide which can aid in its proper "treatment" is that it is often a dyadic event. Thus, although the psychological conflict may seem to be waged within the victim's mind, other people such as a parent, loved one, child, spouse, or colleague may also be involved. A person's death is not an isolated event; it leaves lasting marks on those who survive. As Toynbee (1968) concluded, "The two-sidedness of death is a fundamental feature of death . . . the sting of death is less sharp for the person who dies than it is for the bereaved survivor" (p. 23). Unlike other forms of death among family members, suicide seems to have a way of stigmatizing survivors, who often must deal with their own guilt from within and accusations from without. For this reason Shneidman concludes strongly:

> On these grounds alone the psychiatrist is advised to minimize or totally disregard those well intentioned but shrill writers in the field who naively speak of a person's right to commit suicide . . . as though the suicidal person were a chronic, univalently self-destructive hermit. (1975, p. 1780)

Reducing Suicide Potential Once psychosocially-based assessment procedures have been effective in identifying people whose suicidal potential is very strong and who have a high probability of succeeding in efforts at self-destruction, the psychosocial paradigm also guides efforts to prevent the suicidal act. Shneidman (1975) suggests a number of hints for dealing with people assessed as being suicide risks:

1. Continuously monitor the patient's lethality.
2. Actively take the "side of life" by helping the patient deal with his problems in a realistic manner.
3. Mobilize community resources such as churches and organizations on the "life" side of the patient.
4. Obtain consultation from peers to help in deciding on the right course of action for the person.
5. Hospitalize the person only after careful consideration, because hospitalization tends to complicate treatment and should be brief if it is deemed necessary.
6. Use all the benefits the therapist can gain from "transference." Here the therapist-patient relationship can be a very positive force.
7. Involve the significant others in the life of the suicide attempter.
8. Bend the rules of confidentiality between the therapist and patient if necessary. Suicide plans cannot always be treated as secrets.
9. Therapists should limit themselves to seeing only a few lethal patients at any one time. The tension generated in treating such patients takes great

energy. When a therapist loses a patient through suicide, studies show that he or she reacts much like anyone else with feelings of guilt, anger, inadequacy, grief, and self-blame (Litman, 1965).

The Systems Paradigm: Suicide Prevention Centers

Along with traditional mental health professionals dealing with suicide from the psychosocial paradigmatic perspective, a more recent approach specific to suicide prevention is the *crisis center* movement deriving from the systems paradigm. Historically, the Salvation Army was among the first socially minded organizations to found centers to help both suicide attempters and their families deal more effectively with the conflicts surrounding suicide. Begun at the turn of the century, these Salvation Army centers flourished for a time in North America and Europe and then, inexplicably, they disappeared (Shneidman & Farberow, 1961). It was not again until the 1960s with the rise of community psychology that centers to deal with suicide crises once again became widespread.

Based on the fact that not all crises occur between the hours of 9:00 a.m. and 5:00 p.m., modern crisis centers typically offer 24-hour services. Usually the telephone is the main means of communication between staff and suicidal individuals. The majority of telephone staff are lay people who are specifically trained by professionals.

Most crisis centers operate on the basis of *crisis intervention theory* as introduced by Lindemann (1944) and expanded by Caplan (1964). According to crisis theory, not only are people in most danger when in a state of crisis, they are also most malleable and vulnerable to helping efforts. However, the state of crisis is usually brief, so that whatever intervention is attempted, it must be done rapidly. The importance of rapid intervention is shown in the following personal experience of one of the authors:

Personal Experience: Suicide Prevention

As a graduate student, one of us worked at a suicide prevention center in a rural area. Most of the work at the center was done by volunteers from the nearby large city. These volunteers participated in long hours of workshops, honing their telephone skills, before beginning to work at the center. Most of their work wasn't very dramatic. Phone calls came in at a fairly constant rate, but most involved routine requests for information about other mental health facilities. Although valuable, answering phones and giving information isn't the world's most exciting work. However, not all calls are routine.

Late one evening, just after a routine call, a man phoned and told the counselor who answered that he was going to kill himself. The counselor, a woman in her forties, used all of her considerable counseling skills to try to talk this man out of suicide. She was able to collect enough information from him to know that, by all indices, the caller was highly lethal and probably would try to kill himself. No matter what verbal ploys she tried, the man appeared to be moving inevitably toward killing himself with a .45 caliber pistol he had next to his phone.

The call went on for nearly 2 hours and police and hospital facilities were alerted and ready to move as needed. At the end of this tense 2 hours, the caller wished the phone counselor good luck and good-bye, and declared that he was now going to shoot himself. All held their breath, waiting for the shot to be fired. At this point, the phone counselor broke down and started to cry. Sobbing, she told the caller that he couldn't kill himself, that she cared too much about what happened to him for him to commit suicide. With tears rolling down her cheeks, this reserved middle-aged woman was begging a man whom she had never met not to kill himself. In response to this unorthodox and unplanned approach, the man also began crying. With both people sobbing, the caller's resolve to kill himself melted, and he told the counselor where he was.

The man who called the crisis center is alive today because of the availability of the phone and the people who cared enough about others to be willing to answer it. Although these sorts of spectacular occurrences don't occur frequently, they happen enough to warrant keeping crisis centers and help-lines open. There may be no other work in the field of mental health quite so valuable as that focused on saving another person's life.

Although the theory underlying the development of crisis centers seems sound, there is only limited empirical support for their effectiveness (Litman, 1965; Weiner, 1969). However, it is known that such centers are used a great deal, as shown by the thousands of contacts made each year. The telephone is apparently a less threatening means of communication than face-to-face interaction and it may be an easier first step for many troubled people. Thus, although conclusive support for this systems paradigm based method is lacking, given our limited mental health resources, the crisis center must be considered to be among the mainstays of suicide prevention.

The Systems Paradigm: Help for the Survivors

Despite preventive efforts such as those exemplified by crisis centers, many people do succeed in taking their own lives. However, the involvement of mental health professionals must not stop even if preventive methods have failed. The emotional effects of suicide frequently extend far beyond the individual victim. Those who survive a suicide victim are often left with many problems and emotions which also require professional intervention. Shneidman (1973), for example, believes that the survivors of suicides constitute a significant mental health problem. To help these thousands of people who are adversely affected by others' suicides every year, Shneidman has proposed a process called *postvention.* Based upon the community and family perspective growing out of the systems paradigm, the goal of the postvention process is to lessen the aftereffects of suicide and to facilitate the recovery of surviving family and friends. Survivors of a suicide can experience a potpourri of emotion such as grief, guilt, and shame, many of which can render them increasingly vulnerable to both physical and mental illness (Wallace, 1973).

Although there are traditional religious

and cultural procedures such as sitting "shiva" or holding "wakes" that seem to approximate postvention, the concept emphasizes that grieving is a long-term process that takes months and years, not just days, to be completed. On the basis of his clinical experience with the grieving process, Shneidman suggests that postvention work should begin immediately after a suicide, because many survivors wish most to talk to a helping person at that time. Shneidman further suggests that a survivor needs rational discussion rather than a focus on feelings toward the suicide victim. Lastly, Shneidman believes that the medical state of the survivors should be constantly monitored, for they seem to be more vulnerable to a variety of physical disorders such as heart attacks or high blood pressure. In its focus on the suicide victim as part of a larger network in need of help, postvention represents an application of the systems paradigm in the understanding and treatment of disordered behavior.

Concluding Comments

In many ways, the affective disorders are enigmatic. On the one hand, they are more likely than the other psychoses to go away with—or, at times, without—treatment. On the other hand, however, they are also more likely to recur throughout the lifetime of an afflicted person. At the beginning of the 1980s, affective disorders were considered the most prevalent of the major mental illnesses and the leading cause of U.S. hospital admissions for mental illness (Teuting et al., 1981). Worldwide, up to 150 million people suffer from some form of affective disturbance, with at least 15 percent of those experiencing its depressive form attempting suicide. There can be little doubt that the problem is of immense magnitude. From the view of abnormal psychology as a science, the affective disorders may reflect important developments. While all three major paradigms have been fruitfully applied to these disturbances of emotion, it seems safe to say that no one approach has established clear preeminence. While the psychosocial theories are many and varied, the psychosocial treatments are not the most effective. Further, although life stresses clearly are involved in some episodes of depression and mania, there seem to be some environment-independent instances as well. Finally, although there appears to be copious research in support of a biochemical component in affective disorder, the disturbance is still not definitively curable or preventable through biological means. From the perspective of its scientific development, therefore, it seems that the current paradigms in abnormal psychology may have begun to reach their limits in the search for causes and cures for the disturbances of mood. Reflecting this state of affairs is the emergence of "new" paradigms in the form of integrated perspectives such as those of Akiskal and McKinney and Anisman and Zacharko. As these views are applied and tested and as they begin to replace the existing unifactorial perspectives, we may be able to observe the scientific process Kuhn termed a "Gestalt switch" at work. Out of the tension produced by the limits of existing paradigms, new paradigms emerge.

Summary Chart

In Chapter 9 we considered the disorders associated with emotion, the affective disturbances. We began by looking at the symptoms and varieties of these patterns:

Major depression: Dysphoria, sleep problems, motor symptoms, appetite problems

Bipolar disorder: Depressive pattern interspersed with manic episodes, manic episodes marked by distractibility, excitement, flight of ideas, expansiveness

Dysthymia: A milder form of severe depression

Cyclothymia: A milder form of bipolar disorder

A developmental view of depression provided a different perspective on affective symptoms:

Depression in childhood
Depression in adolescence
Postpartum depression
Involutional melancholia

Our attention then turned to the paradigmatically based explanations for affective patterns:

The biological paradigm: Neurotransmitter difficulties, heredity, use of drug treatments and electroshock therapy

The psychosocial paradigm: Psychoanalytic approaches, cognitive approaches, operant approaches

The systems paradigm: Life events and affective disorders

An integrated paradigm: Final common pathway, multiple etiologies

We then discussed a number of treatment approaches for affective disorders before examining in more detail the most catastrophic symptom of depression, suicide.

Clues to suicide, myths about suicide
Explanations

Psychosocial paradigm: Psychoanalysis, social learning theory

Systems paradigm: Societal integration theory, anomie

Biological paradigm: Genetic basis, biochemical basis

Treatments: Hotlines, prevention centers, help for survivors

CHAPTER 10

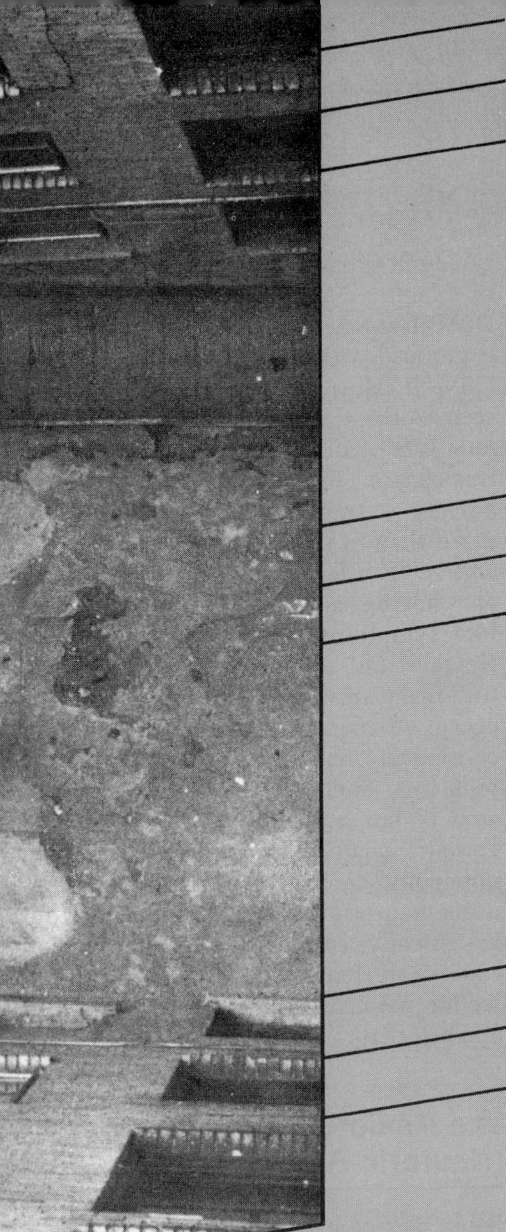

THE ANXIETY DISORDERS (NEUROTIC ANXIETY)
Anxiety States
Phobic Disorders
Obessive-Compulsive Disorders
Stress-related Adjustment Disorders
THE SOMATOFORM DISORDERS (CONVERSION NEUROSIS)
Somatization Disorder
Psychogenic Pain
Hypochondriasis
Conversion Disorders
DISSOCIATIVE DISORDERS (NEUROTIC DISSOCIATION)
PARADIGMATICALLY BASED EXPLANATIONS
The Psychosocial Paradigm: Psychoanalytic Theory
The Psychosocial Paradigm: Learning Theory
The Biological Paradigm: The Genetic Basis
The Systems Paradigm
PARADIGMATICALLY BASED INTERVENTION APPROACHES
The Psychosocial Paradigm: Individual Psychotherapy
The Psychosocial Paradigm: Behavior Modification
The Biological Paradigm: Biofeedback
The Biological Paradigm: Drug Therapy
Systems Paradigm: Family Therapy
CONCLUDING COMMENTS
SUMMARY CHART

The Anxiety, Somatoform, and Dissociative Disorders

Less severe and less pervasively incapacitating than the schizophrenias and affective psychoses, anxiety, somatoform, and dissociative disorders hamper individuals in milder, more circumscribed ways. In DSM-I and DSM-II, these moderate disturbances were defined as being *neuroses*; a group of disorders with varying symptoms, which could be organized around the central components of anxiety and/or reactions to anxiety. The developers of DSM-III have seen fit to alter this grouping and to class the neuroses with other patterns mostly on the basis of symptom similarity. For example, as noted in Chapter Nine, dysthymia, which in DSM-II was termed neurotic depression, is grouped with the affective disorders in DSM-III. However, anxiety may still be seen as the thread that relates the three new sets of disorders to be described in this chapter. In the *anxiety disorders* the anxiety is more easily seen and recognized than in the *somatoform* and *dissociative disorders* where it may be thought of as having been converted into physical-like symptoms or memory difficulties. However, all three types tend to substitute maladaptive (self-defeating) and self-deceptive maneuvers and strategies for conscious, reality-based responses to problems. Such strategies help to avoid anxiety but at the cost of continual or episodic signs of fatigue, tension, and unhappiness. Because of their symptoms, neurotic people may be kept from realistically coming to grips with the causes of their anxiety, and their behavior patterns may become stabilized and self-perpetuating.

The experience of intense anxiety is especially frightening and disquieting. (© *Suzanne Szasz, 1981/Photo Researchers, Inc.*)

The Anxiety Disorders (Neurotic Anxiety)

Being blessed or cursed, as the case may be, with the ability to remember and to anticipate physical or emotional danger, people can experience anxiety, a form of fear based not upon the present alone, but on actual or fantasied experiences of the past and future as well. Overtly anxious people feel physically tense and look emotionally pained. The manner in which people handle their excessive fear determines the specific type of anxiety disorder. In the *anxiety states* people experience the unbridled impact of anxiety without relief. In contrast, in *phobic disorders,* the anxiety can be controlled if individuals can avoid the feared object or situation. In the *obsessive-compulsive disorders,* anxiety can be avoided by carrying out specified sequences of thoughts or actions. Finally, in the *stress-related adjustment disorders,* we return to easily observable anxiety that takes a variety of forms.

Anxiety States

Some 5 percent of the population is estimated to experience some form of diagnosable anxiety with women outnumbering men at a 2 to 1 rate (Nemiah, 1980). In one form of anxiety state, the *panic attack*, the fear is so intense that some people are driven to attempt suicide. About 1.5 percent of the population will experience a panic attack some time during their life (Robins et al., 1984). Some writers have tried to put the experience of "raw" anxiety into words. Though the following personal experience is somewhat dated, the writer's description of fear is not. He was an English professor whose intense fear of locomotives would precipitate his panic attacks.

Personal Experience: Panic Attack

I light a cigar in the doorway . . . just as a train is passing over beyond the meadows . . . my eye sees the horrible phantom in the map once more. I suffer the intensest seizure of terror sensations. . .I say nothing. . .try to "walk it off". . .within a hundred feet I throw the cigar away, saying it seems to make me feel worse (a truth uttered by the subconsciousness, with a different purport from that intended, while the throwing away was an attempt to get rid of the unknown factor of torment). I recover a little. I feel a sinking loneliness, an uneasy, a weird isolation. The locomotive-phase of road-house and cigar of less than an hour before has already lapsed from consciousness. I take off my hat; I mop my head; I fan my face.

Sinking . . . isolation . . . diffused premonitions of horror. I am alone, alone, in the universe. My subconscious knows what the torture is; and makes my voice shriek, as I rush back and forth on the bluffs: "My God, won't that go; my God, won't that train go away!" I smash a wooden box to pieces, board by board, against my knee to occupy myself against panic. I watch the train . . . it seems so slow . . . so slow . . . if it will only get across the flats . . . out of hearing. (W. Leonard, 1927, *The Locomotive God*, New York: Century Co.)

In contrast to those in a *panic state*, in *generalized anxiety disorders* people usually do not experience a rapid onset of fear. However, they do live in a constant state of tension that testifies to the failure of their attempts to handle anxiety.

An account of a woman who developed a generalized anxiety state is presented next. The narrative shows how she began with panic attacks but soon came to experience a generalized anxiety disorder.

Case: Generalized Anxiety Disorder

A 32-year-old woman reported that for the past 6 months she had been experiencing episodes of severe anxiety. These episodes would start without identifiable precipitants, build up "like a wave" to a level of panic over 15–20 minutes and gradually subside by the end of an hour. When having these attacks, the patient experienced the following: "My chest tightens, my ears clog, my palms sweat, I have a sense of dread and it feels like I'm losing control." These episodes occurred in a variety of situations where rapid exit was difficult, such as: supermarket lines, buses, crowded stores, restaurants, and elevators. In each case the patient would immediately cease what she was doing and flee the situation, even if it meant, for example, abandoning a basket full of groceries for which she was waiting to pay. Furthermore, she had begun to limit her activities because she feared having a panic attack. Thus, she avoided restaurants and department stores, took taxis instead of buses, and shopped at times when there were no lines in the supermarkets. The patient noted that she had currently been upset and worried by her elderly father's declining health over the past year. She had also suffered a miscarriage 8 months before her anxiety symptoms began. Finally, she had experienced several weeks of "unrelenting criticism" by her supervisor at the magazine where she worked as an editor. This occurred in the period immediately prior to the onset of her panic attacks. (Liebowitz & Klein, 1979, p. 436)

Phobic Disorders

Whereas people with anxiety states typically cannot identify a source for their tension, *phobic* individuals can, but the source is usually recognized as harmless. It is estimated that between 13 and 14 percent of the population will experience a diagnosable phobia (Robins et al., 1984). However, if the feared object or situation is not avoided, phobic individuals will become intensely anxious as depicted in the next personal experience.

Personal Experience: Phobic Fear of Moths

Terror is the only thing that comes close to describing how I feel when I think of moths. Their willowy, see-through wings always seem filthy. I remember being stuck in a car with a huge moth and my date, not knowing how terrified I was of moths, thought I was kidding when I told him I was afraid. It was terrible! I can feel it right now, feeling trapped and the moth with its ugly body flitting around so quickly. I couldn't anticipate where it would go next. Finally, that creature hit me in the arm and I screamed—it felt dirty and sleazy and then it hit me in the face and I began to scream uncontrollably. I had the terrible feeling it was going to fly into my mouth, while I was screaming, but I couldn't stop. By this time, my date believed my terror and stopped the car. I jumped out and ran screaming down the street. Finally, I stopped by a tree, sat down and began to cry. It took me 15 minutes to calm down and to feel foolish.

Although up to 14 percent of the general population is estimated to have phobias, only 1 percent of these disorders are serious enough to be called "disabling." Phobias usually become disabling when the source of the fear is present in the

Table 10-1 Some Common Forms of Object Phobias

Name	Object(s) Feared	Name	Object(s) Feared
Acrophobia	High places	Hematophobia	Blood
Agoraphobia	Open places	Monophobia	Being alone
Ailurophobia	Cats	Mysophobia	Contamination
Algophobia	Pain	Nyctophobia	Darkness
Anthropophobia	Men	Ocholophobia	Crowds
Aquaphobia	Water	Pathophobia	Disease
Astraphobia	Storms, thunder, and lightning	Pyrophobia	Fire
Claustrophobia	Closed places	Syphilophobia	Syphilis
Cynophobia	Dogs	Thanatophobia	Death
		Xenophobia	Strangers
		Zoophobia	Animals or a single animal

immediate environment and interferes with people's ability to perform valued tasks. For example, having a fear of closed places (claustrophobia) may be disabling to a coal miner or an elevator operator but probably not to someone who works in open places.

DSM-III describes three types of phobias, classified as *simple or object phobias, situational phobias, and social phobias.* Though they are the most common, object phobias are also the least disruptive. Frequent examples are fears of dogs or bugs (see Table 10-1, for a list of common-object phobias). By contrast the *situational phobias* can be far more disturbing. *Agoraphobia*, a fear of open places, can spread to any number of situations like theaters, public transportation, elevators, and open places. To reduce the likelihood of setting off an anxiety reaction, agoraphobic people may limit their outside activities even to the point of never leaving home. Probably because of its negative impact on everyday life, agoraphobia makes up more than one-half of all cases of phobia brought to the attention of clinicians.

The most infrequent of the phobias, *social phobias* reflect an inordinate concern about appearing stupid while talking, writing, eating, or urinating in the presence of others. The following case presentation describes three women who had fears of writing or signing their names in public.

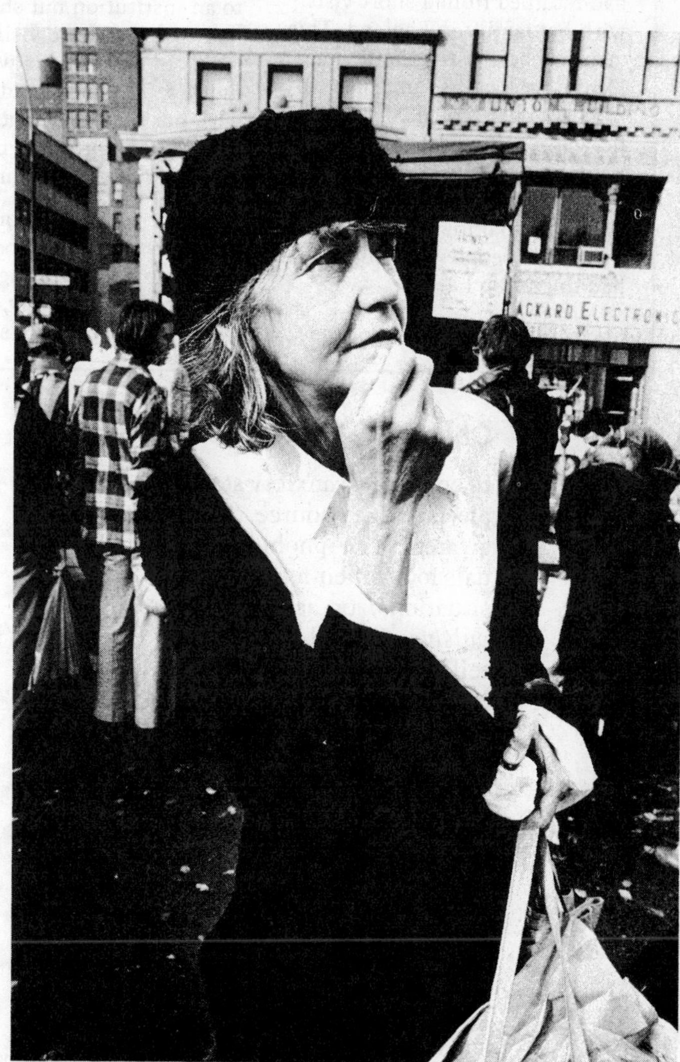

Crowds can be terrifying for someone suffering from agoraphobia. (*Jean-Marie Simon/Taurus Photos*)

Case: Social Phobia

Subject A, age 37, had experienced her first phobic reaction at the age of 16 when waiting in line in a bank. In the preceding year her father had died, an event that she reported to have been "overwhelming" for her.

The onset of phobia in subject B, age 49, had occurred 16 years earlier, after she and her husband had returned from a short visit with her family in England. This visit had been a traumatic one. Her father had died unexpectedly soon after her arrival. She resumed her job as a secretary immediately upon returning to the U.S., but became aware of the fact that her hand was shaking while writing in front of people. Eventually, she had to give up her job.

Subject C, age 41, first noticed the problem in high school. Her first phobic experience had occurred when she was requested to sign her name in an autograph book. Although no traumatic event was associated with the onset of the phobia for this subject, she felt that the problem was somehow related to her family situation. Her older sister was mentally ill and committed to an institution but she visited home often. These visits always involved bitter fights with the mother. The subject identified with her sick sister and felt anger toward her mother for committing her sister to the institution.

All three subjects reported that these first incidents soon developed into a debilitating phobia and persisted this way, unabated, with the exception of subject A who experienced short remissions during each of her two pregnancies. None of the subjects could purchase items with a check or credit card, rarely went to a bank, and did not vote. The three subjects avoided any recreational or social activity which involved writing in public. Subject A was working part time as a clerk/typist but was experiencing much difficulty with the job because of her problem. The other two subjects wished to work outside their homes but their fear prevented them from even applying for a job. All three women were married and had arranged for their husbands to take care of those situations and tasks they avoided. (Biran et al., 1981, p. 525).

Obsessive-Compulsive Disorders

In contrast to anxiety states in which people push the source of their fear out of awareness or phobias in which individuals focus their fears on harmless objects, situations, or activities, *obsessive-compulsives* control their anxiety through intellectualization and rituals. Up to 50 percent of obsessive-compulsive people are unmarried and most are members of the middle and upper classes. Though they make up only 2.5 percent of the general population, they probably are overrepresented in mental health agencies because they tend to seek professional help at relatively early ages (Robins, et al., 1984).

Although termed obsessive-compulsive disorder, the typical pattern is characterized by *either* obsessive thinking or compulsive actions, although mixtures of these symptoms also may be found.

Obsessive Reactions

Beginning in adolescence or early adulthood, obsessive individuals report experiencing persistent and unshakable thoughts and unwanted and unpleasant sexual or hostile impulses (Salzman & Thaler, 1981). Although their impulses rarely, if ever, are acted upon, these people live with the recurrent fear that their dreaded feelings may break through as in the following personal experience.

Personal Experience: Obsessive Reaction

I can tell you how it is when I'm being obsessive. It's a tiring experience. I've always been an organizer . . . so that from the time I get up in the morning until I go to sleep at night I'm thinking about what's going to happen. I worry, but I can take it and it's not too bad . . . but it's when those terrible thoughts come into my head that I become afraid. The thoughts are all different, and they're sickening and terrible. Like when I was outside with my child, I thought of what would happen if my metal rake slipped and flew over and hit my child in the head. I don't know why I would think of this. It made me feel like a crazy person, and then I'm worried sick the rest of the day that I'm going to think that thought again. Here's another example of what I mean. While eating dinner the thought suddenly came to me . . . how would it look if I drove my fork through the eye of my husband . . . I mean my husband's eye. I can see the fork puncture the eye and the liquid squirts out . . . and then I break out in a cold sweat and have to leave the table. I'm a kind person . . . I go to church . . . It makes me feel crazy and different. Even telling you makes me feel weird about myself.

Compulsive Reactions

In the obsessive pattern, "forbidden" impulses are usually not acted out, but are "headed off" by ritualistic thinking. In *compulsions*, on the other hand, people feel a need to carry out certain, often admittedly senseless, often "magical" actions or sequences of actions in their efforts to avoid experiencing anxiety. Among the numerous forms of compulsive reactions, many seem to be related to guilt about sex, as is shown in the following personal experience of an adolescent girl responding to beginning menses.

Personal Experience: Compulsive Reactions

I remember how embarrassed I was when I found that my panties were soiled. I was at school. My mother really never prepared me for this happening and I get mad at her even now. Anyway . . . ever since then I've had to go through the same washing order or I get so uptight that I cry. Although it means I have to get up 2 hours earlier than I used to, I get up so that I can have enough time to complete the washing. I start with my toes, washing each individually, and then I have to go over every inch of my body twice. For every major part of me I have to use a new washcloth. It takes from 10 to 12 washcloths to complete the washing. The morning washing only makes me feel okay until the afternoon. I couldn't wait until I could get home and wash. It got so bad that I used to carry washcloths and soap to school so that I could slip into the lavatory and wash. I lived in fear that one of my friends would see me, but I just had to do it. My parents don't understand . . . and I guess I don't either . . . but I have to wash . . . I just have to or I feel so dirty and slimy and junky. I hate that feeling.

In addition to single sets of compulsive behaviors such as washing, anxiety may also be reduced by specific ordering procedures as in *serial compulsions.* It is characteristic of most compulsive rituals to take up more and more of a person's time and energy. The following case history reveals some of the frustration people can feel when they are compelled to do "senseless" things in order to limit the pain of anxiety.

Case: Compulsive Reactions

A young unmarried woman developed an irresistable need to think of a different person with each separate act she performed in a given series, until she finally reached a point at which gainful employment and marriage were both out of her reach. This magical practice began originally as a technique of distraction from sex preoccupations, which had induced severe anxiety reactions in the patient as she walked each morning to work. She established a rule that each step on or off the curb at a corner must be accompanied by the thought of some adult she knew, the adult must be a different one for each step on or off the curb, and she must have one clearly ready in her imagining ahead of time. If she thought of the same person twice on the same street something terrible might happen. The provisions of her ritual made a frequent change of street convenient and this obliged her to start to work earlier and to shun company, both because talking interfered with preparation for the curb crises, and because her changes of course were hard to justify to someone else.

Because her anxiety over possible lapses continued, the patient's magical practice spread to other situations. As she put on or took off each article of clothing she had to think of a different person, and the same rule eventually applied to eating, to washing and drying dishes, dusting and tidying the house, inserting typewriter paper and carbons at work, opening and sealing envelopes or filing letters. She had to give up her job, finally when the ritual crept into her typing in spite of everything she did to prevent it. She could not help daydreaming as she typed and sooner or later forbidden thoughts would start up her protective device. This first cut her speed down and later destroyed her accuracy also. Of her complicated ritual, she said, "For a long time I couldn't break it, and now it just seems easier to go on." (Cameron, 1947, p. 296)

Compulsive magical behavior may be related in some ways to superstition. There is a great deal of similarity between compulsive persons who must arrange their clothes in a certain order before going to sleep at night and the athletes who must wear the same "lucky" socks or shirt when competing. Although athletic and theatrical performers may admit their superstitious behavior is senseless, they also admit that interruption of the "lucky" activity can cause them to become anxious. For example, a famous baseball player had to touch second base running onto the playing field and first or third base running off; an Olympic gold medal winner in the men's 800 meters had to wear a golf hat held in place with bobbie pins while racing; and a famous actress had to wear the same bra whenever beginning a new movie. However, in contrast to superstitious individuals, compulsive people seem never to be quite sure that their rituals will succeed in controlling their anxiety. As a result of this insecurity, they often add new elements to their compulsions in the mistaken belief that they can somehow "cover all possibilities." With time, as in the unfortunate case of the secretary described above, such additions can compound the compulsions into an almost unbearable burden.

There is some similarity between superstitions and compulsive behavior. However, superstitious behavior does not spread like compulsive actions do. (*Mimi Forsyth/Monkmeyer Press Photo Service*)

Stress-related Adjustment Disorders

In contrast to people who are diagnosed as having generalized anxiety states, phobias, or obsessive-compulsive disorders, those with stress-related adjustment problems such as *posttraumatic stress disorders* have symptoms usually caused by severe external stressors (Andreasen, 1980). DSM-III defines *posttraumatic stress disorder* as follows: "The essential feature is the development of characteristic symptoms after the experiencing of a psychologically traumatic event or events outside the range of human experience usually considered to be normal. The characteristic symptoms involve reexperiencing the traumatic event, numbing of responsiveness to, or involvement with, the external world, and a variety of other autonomic, dysphoric, or cognitive symptoms." New to DSM-III, this disorder involves a single syndrome that reflects people's reactions to experiencing a variety of severely stressful situations like war

Disasters cause difficulties that can be expressed in posttraumatic stress disorders. Here a lone soldier guards against looters after an earthquake. (© *Bruce Roberts 1980/Photo Researchers, Inc.*)

time combat, prisoner of war camps, accidents in planes, cars, or ships, and civilian disasters like fires, earthquakes, and floods.

Chamberlin (1980) has reviewed the research on the impact of extreme environmental disasters on the psychological functioning of survivors. She suggests that between 10 and 50 percent of the survivors will show diagnosable stress syndrome disorders immediately following the traumatic event. There is less information on the long-term effects, but generally the more severe the stress the more likely it is that survivors will show psychiatric symptoms. Hocking (1970), for example, found 100 percent of the concentration camp survivors and prisoners of war to have psychiatric symptoms years after their experience.

The most recent military experiences in Vietnam have left a number of psychiatric casualities as is shown in the following case.

Case: Posttraumatic Stress Disorder in a Vietnam Veteran

I treated A. B., a 35-year-old veteran, for several months on a weekly basis following his hospitalization for attempted suicide by drowning. Throughout the time we worked together his attitude was cynical and derisive. A. B.'s mood was intermittently depressed. He went into a rage whenever he perceived other people to be unreliable or unworthy of trust. As a result of his fierce antagonism, A. B.'s business had failed and he increasingly became socially isolated. He used the few marital meetings we had to actively convince his wife that she was foolish to have any faith in others. At the same time he discouraged and rebuffed her efforts to engage him in any form of meaningful companionship. A. B. remarked more than once that a dog was his only true friend. He continued to persist in the idea that it was others—the government and the war—that were the cause of all his difficulties.

This veteran's dream life vividly confirmed the cynical mood of his waking state. In one dream A. B. saw himself shoot a man with a hunting rifle. However, he was unable to shoot a duck flying overhead. The dream was understood as a sardonic expression of his attitude that a duck's life was worth more than a man's. A. B.'s profession had been taxidermy and his favorite sport was duck hunting. In a second dream he purchased a pair of shoes from an Oriental salesman, and discovered the two feet of his dead combat buddy in the shoebox. As he peered into the box in disbelief the salesman and other Orientals in the store tormented him with their ridicule and laughter. The manifest content of the dream highlights not only the theme of death and vengeance, but the pained disappointment and mortification he experienced as a consequence of trusting others. This dream alludes to the death of A. B.'s closest friend who was blown up by a land mine and only his feet could be recovered for burial. A. B. deduced that a peasant family nearby had prior knowledge of the mine. He gunned them down to avenge his friend's death. He denied having misgivings or feeling guilt, and persistently blamed the government for putting him in a position in which he had to behave in this manner.

A. B. derisively described himself prior to the war as having been naive and as having uncritically accepted the values of peers and persons in authority.

A. B. terminated therapy abruptly after wrongly accusing me of not having kept my promise to be available to see him for psychotherapy twice a week. I was unsuccessful in making him realize that by assuming that his desire for more sessions would make them a fact, he was actively setting himself up to be disillusioned once again in a relationship.

A special feature of this case was the veteran's active homicidal and suicidal wishes. The homicidal feelings were not necessarily directed towards any particular person, and not clearly differentiated from the suicidal feelings. His cynicism and rage were expressions of a profound disillusionment with those who represented authority and secondarily with himself. (Glover, 1984, p. 448)

Concentration camps and war create severe stress. Civilians have experienced the negative impact of severe stress through such disasters as floods and plane crashes. The following is a description of a plane crash that occurred recently in Atlanta and some of the negative effects it had on survivors.

On a spring day in 1977, a Piedmont Airline's plane took off from Birmingham, Alabama, on a flight that was supposed to take it within an hour to Atlanta, Georgia. As the plane reached a high altitude, it ran into a severe springtime thunderstorm. Hailstones and torrential rain battered the plane. In a short time the hailstones intensified to the point that they plugged up the jet engines. The plane lost power and began to fall. The pilot radioed ahead to Altanta's Hartsfield International Airport to say that he was going to try and make it to the field. When it became obvious that the plane would not be able to make Hartsfield, the pilot radioed other fields in the vicinity to see if he could find a landing site. However, time ran out and the pilot was forced to try and land the aircraft on a county highway. The plane crashed with only 10 of the 137 crew and passengers surviving.

One response to a disaster is psychic numbing or a constriction of emotional responsiveness. (*Michael Weisbrot and Family*)

Many of those who survived the Atlanta crash experienced the posttraumatic stress syndrome. In most cases, the symptoms of the syndrome began within 24 hours after the tragedy and followed a regular sequence. First was a disconcerting tendency for the survivors to "reexperience" the traumatic event. Most often this occurred through dreams or nightmares that usually left survivors in a state of terror. One of the survivors of the plane crash frequently felt as though she were back on the plane as it was falling. These feelings would occur suddenly and without warning. She could feel herself falling and would run screaming throughout her house until the reality of where she was would calm her again. Such *dissociative states* are frequently seen in stress disorders and can last anywhere from a few minutes to several hours, or in rare cases even days.

Besides reexperiencing the disaster, survivors also showed *psychic numbing* or a constriction of emotional responsiveness. Survivors of the plane crash felt detached from other people and complained of being unable to feel emotions of warmth or happiness. Their sexual activity almost completely stopped.

In many ways the last group of symptoms described above shows that life after a traumatic event is much more difficult than it was before. Survivors frequently experienced difficulties in long- and short-term memory even to the point that they forgot the phone numbers of relatives or the name of the family pet. In addition, they often became hyperalert, had trouble concentrating, and were easily startled by loud noises. Another common reaction was *survivor guilt*, or "Why should I have survived when so many others did not?" Some survivors spent much of their time examining their lives to find what could have "earned" them, and not their peers, "extra" life. Not surprisingly, after disasters many survivors devoted themselves to religious or moral causes.

In the case of the Atlanta plane crash, at least one of the survivors developed an intense fear of leaving the house (agoraphobia). Long after the crash, she could not leave the safe confines of her house without experiencing intense anxiety. Though behavioral methods were used to alleviate her "phobic" reactions to open spaces, the symptoms resisted change for months.

Like most survivors of disasters, those who survived the airplane crash also experienced an *acute stress reaction* that began and ended within 6 months. During this time, they became irritable, restless, fearful, depressed, and constricted. They felt rage toward the source of the trauma even though in most instances they realized it was inappropriate (Krupnick & Horowitz, 1981). It is not unusual for traumatic stress to interact with a person's personality style in determining the form and intensity of the posttraumatic stress syndrome. Therefore, clinicians are usually aware that while a single stress syndrome may occur, the flavor of the symptoms shown in that syndrome may be affected by the particular personality of the survivor.

Extending beyond its impact on individuals, a disaster can reach others beyond the survivors of the actual event. Three years after the Atlanta plane crash, the air traffic controller who was in charge of the communications between the plane and the ground was arrested and accused of killing his wife during an argument. During the trial, his lawyers argued that their client had changed significantly since the time of the Atlanta plane crash. He was described as being irritable, unable to sleep at night or concentrate on his job during the day. He eventually lost his job and soon after that his wife divorced him. His episodes of anger and irritation increased until they culminated in the argument with his estranged wife during which he shot and killed her. During the court proceedings, the controller testified, in tears, that he still had nightmares about the plane crash and felt intensely guilty that he couldn't do anything to help the plane land safely. Those who knew him were apalled at the way he looked during the court proceedings. Witnesses testified that he looked like he had aged 15 years since the plane crash. His hair had turned from dark brown to nearly completely white. The air traffic controller's 3 years of symptoms were consistent with a diagnosis of a *chronic posttraumatic stress disorder*, where symptoms must last for at least 6 months or begin 6 months after the traumatic event.

The Somatoform Disorders (Conversion Neurosis)

Unlike the anxiety disorders and stress disorders, where anxiety is clearly observable, in somatoform types of disorders, anxiety is less obvious because it appears to be expressed in physical symptoms. The DSM-III divides the *somatoform* disorders into two main groups. In the first group are patterns involving physical symptoms similar to those seen in actual physical diseases: *somatization disorder, psychogenic pain, and hypochondriasis.* Often the psychologically based symptoms in this group are so "real" that they are quite difficult to discriminate from physically based problems. The second group of somatoform patterns are the *con-*

version disorders in which the symptoms are more easily discernable from actual physical disorders. Overall these disorders affect about 0.25 percent of the population (Robins et al., 1984).

Somatization Disorder

DSM-III defines *somatization disorder* as "recurrent and multiple somatic complaints for which medical attention is sought: they are not apparently due to any physical illness, begin before early adulthood (prior to age 25), and have a chronic but fluctuating course." In somatization disorders people usually complain about headaches, fatigue, chest pains, genitourinary or abdominal symptoms, vomiting, and fainting.

More common in women than men, somatization disorders are characterized by dramatic, exhibitionistic, seductive, and manipulative behaviors. Because they are able to present their physical complaints so intensely and persuasively, these patients can convince physicians to complete unneccessary diagnostic and surgical procedures.

Psychogenic Pain

Internists, rather than mental health workers, are probably the most likely to have first contact with people carrying the diagnosis of somatization or psychogenic pain. *Psychogenic pains* usually involve the back and neck and are often precipitated by a significant change in relationships. Individuals in psychogenic pain, however, are unaware of the connection between their "pain" and the emotional stressors that may be involved with precipitating it. On the contrary, they are likely to argue that emotional difficulties have nothing to do with their pain. As a consequence of their attitude, they are very difficult to treat psychologically.

Hypochondriasis

Although complaints in psychogenic pain sound similar to those in *hypochondriasis*, it is usually more difficult to identify specific environmental causes in the latter. Hypochondrical people tend to misinterpret normal physical feelings and sensations as indicating severe physical

Many people who see physicians with somatic complaints actually may be suffering from a somatoform disorder. (*David S. Strickler/Monkmeyer Press Photo Service*)

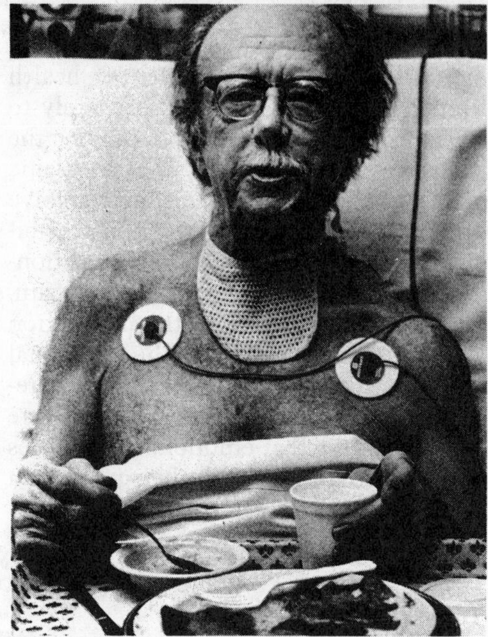

Some people fit snugly and happily in the role of a "sick" person. (© *1981 Richard Falco/Photo Researchers, Inc.*)

illness. Though any part of their body may be involved, the physiological complaints generally involve the stomach and heart. Attempts by physicians to reassure these patients of their good health often have little, if any, impact. True to the self-defeating quality of this disorder, hypochondriacal people build much of their lives around visiting physicians in spite of doctors' apparent inability to successfully treat their problems.

In part, because of their negativistic style, people diagnosed as hypochondriacal usually have a poor prognosis for recovery. In a study of 118 hospitalized people with a diagnosis of hypochondriasis, only one in five was discharged as improved as compared with two in five who were discharged as being worse (Kenyon, 1980). In fact, after 6 months only six of the patients discharged as being improved had remained symptom-free.

Hypochondriacal people may be characterized as fitting snugly into the role of a sick person. Their apparent sickness can elicit sympathy and attention from others, as well as provide an excuse for failure. The following letter exemplifies how a hypochondriacal person might attempt to gain attention.

> Dear Mother and Husband:
>
> I have suffered terrible today with drawing in my throat. My nerves are terrible. My head feels queer. But my stomach hasn't cramped quite so hard. I've been on the verge of a nervous chill all day, but I have been fighting it hard. It's night and bedtime, but, oh, how I hate to go to bed. Nobody knows or realizes how badly I feel because I fight to stay up and outdoors if possible.
>
> I haven't had my cot up for two days, they don't want me to use it.
>
> These long afternoons and nights are awful. There are plenty of patients well enough to visit with but I'm in too much pain. The nurses ignore any complaining. They just laugh or scold.
>
> Eating has been awful hard. They expect me to eat like a harvest hand. Every bite of solid food is agony to get down, for my throat aches so and feels so closed up. (Menninger, 1945)

Conversion Disorders

In contrast to the somatoform patterns in which some physical problem may be observed, the most salient feature of conversion disorder is a physical disability without an identifiable physical basis. However, although conversion disorder symptoms seem to be copies of certain physical disorders, they are typically easy to discriminate from actual physical disease syndromes and are quite often symbolically related to psychological conflicts. It is as though in conversion disorders people were able to "convert" their anxiety and psychological conflict into a physical disability. This conversion can work so well that they often lack much of the overt tension that is observed in other neurotic disorders. This relative lack of tension or anxiety in the face of an apparently debilitating physical ailment is called *la belle indifference,* or the *noble lack of concern.* The presence of la belle indifference may lead one, incorrectly, to suspect a person of *malingering* or consciously faking disease. However, the fact is that although people with conversion disorders may receive a great deal of *secondary gain* in the form of attention and sympathy from others for their apparent illness, they are usually not consciously aware of the connections among their physical disorder, their psychological conflicts, and the attention they receive. Conversions can take place in the sensory, motor, or autonomic systems.

In *sensory conversions* there is difficulty in receiving or processing sensory stimuli. For instance, some people have a patch of skin that is insensitive to pain. To proponents of the once-popular supernatural paradigm, such patches served as "proof" that an individual was a witch and thus a candidate for torture or death.

The presence of a *tactual anesthesia,* or the inability to sense touch, is a primary diagnostic sign of sensory conversion disorder. Usually the loss-of-feeling pattern is neurologically "impossible" and may be delimited by clothing areas rather than by neurophysiology (see Figure 10-1). In *glove anesthesia,* for example, people lose feeling in their hands up to their wrist; in *swimsuit anesthesia,* the buttocks and groin areas become numb.

At the opposite extreme from the loss of sensitivity or feeling of anesthesia is *hyperesthesia,* in which people are oversensitive to stimuli. In one case of hyperesthesia, a man could only wear light cotton clothing regardless of the temperature because any other clothing caused him intense discomfort. Although no physiological basis could be found for his extreme sensitivity to the touch of his clothing, his subjective experience of pain was no less real.

Rather than disturbances in their sensory functioning, people with *motor conversions* may experience such symptoms as uncontrollable muscular contractions, tremors, or even seizures without physical basis. However, these seizure symptoms are easily discriminable from those associated with actual physical disease in a number of ways. First, the conversion "convulsion" is not characterized by rhythmic movements, as are physically based seizures, but rather by chaotic thrashing about. Second, people with con-

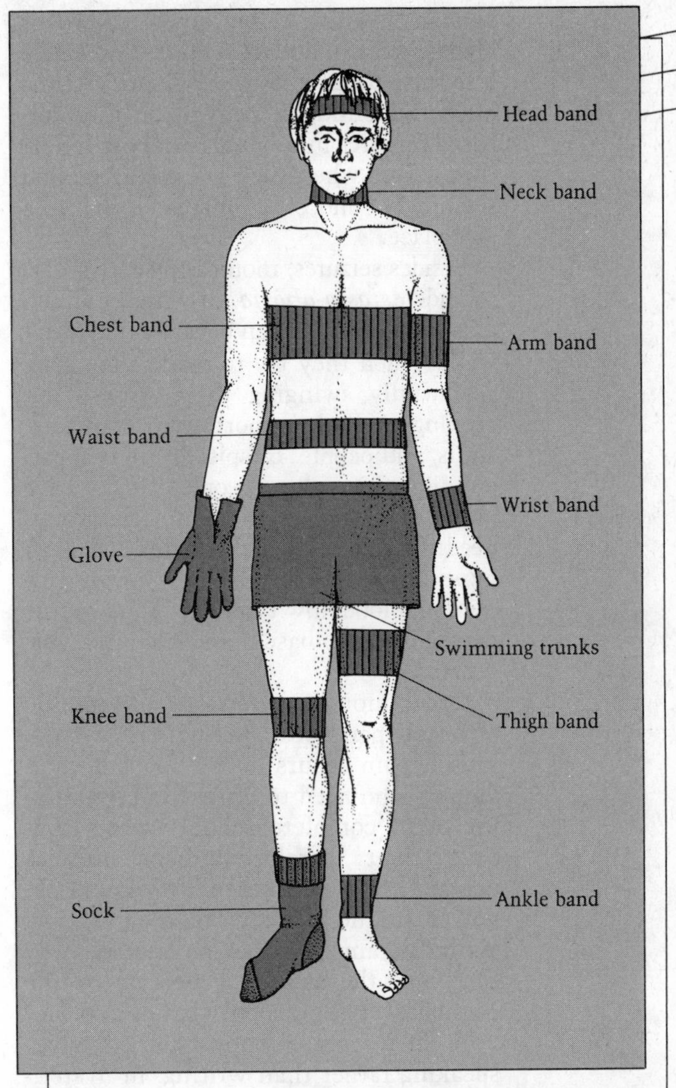

Figure 10-1 Common sites for sensory conversions. Loss of sensation in such circumscribed areas is usually physiologically impossible and is typically psychologically caused.

version disorders will rarely lose bowel or bladder control during seizures and won't bite their tongues as true seizure victims often do. Third, in conversion disorder-based seizures individuals rarely will hurt themselves when they fall to the ground seemingly "choosing" instead to fall in a safe place.

Besides seizures, motor conversions also include *astasia-abasia*, in which individuals may be bedridden because they can't walk. When they try to walk, they stagger, wildly swinging their arms about seeking to find support from furniture, walls, and people. In spite of their apparent difficulties, these people actually have physical control of those muscle groups needed for standing and walking and show none of the muscle atrophy or impairment of blood flow typically found in true neurologically based muscle-tone disorders.

Other motor conversions can mimic physical paralyses. In *writers cramp,* muscle pain occurs in the hands of individuals who need to write to make a living or to complete school work. Typically, their "paralyzed" hand muscles operate quite well when they aren't involved in the stressful task of writing. Writer's cramp may be one effective way to escape the anxiety generated by the possibility of losing a job or failing a course.

A final motor conversion involves speaking rather than writing. In *hysterical aphonia,* people cannot speak above a whisper. As in other conversion disorders, people manifesting aphonia often can be manipulated into behaving normally, as shown in the following incident:

> A forty-five-year-old married woman felt badly treated and neglected by her husband. This had been particularly aggravated following the departure of their two grown children from the home. After one in a series of angry scenes with her husband, she suddenly developed aphonia. Following examination, the physician spoke to another person present. In a whispered tone, but loud enough to insure the patient's overhearing, he said, "That old gal is an awful fake. There is nothing wrong with her. Of course she could talk if she really wanted to." The angry response of the patient was an indignant vocal denial. This proved the doctor "right", and he announced her cured. (Laughlin, 1956, p. 263)

The sensory and motor conversions we have been describing primarily involve the peripheral nervous system. On the other hand, the *autonomic conversions* affect the digestive, eliminative, and reproductive systems. Among the most complex of the autonomic conversions is *pseudocyesis,* or phantom pregnancy. In pseudocyesis, women not only may stop menses and suffer "morning sickness" but also may have enlarged breasts and abdomen. It is as though these women desire children so much that they, in essence, take on the appearance of being pregnant. The following personal experience took place 6 months into a phantom pregnancy. It is a conversation between one of the authors and a 16-year-old girl who had just been told she wasn't pregnant.

Case: Pseudocyesis

Interviewer: How do you explain the fact that you had all the signs of pregnancy and now find that you're not?

Woman: (Calmly) I guess God willed it to be so. Probably there was something wrong with the baby.

Interviewer: Then you still believe you were pregnant?

Woman: Sure . . . didn't you see my belly . . . I had a baby.

Interviewer: But the doctors said they could find no proof of a baby.

Woman: Well, they're wrong. Don't worry, I'll get pregnant again.

Dissociative Disorders (Neurotic Dissociation)

While anxiety is actually experienced in the anxiety disorders and is "converted" into physical concerns or symptoms in the somatoform disorders, in the dissociative disorders anxiety-producing thoughts or aspects of personality are separated from awareness. This separation, or *dissociation*, results in reduction or avoidance of anxiety and may take any of several forms, such as *psychogenic amnesia, psychogenic fugue, multiple personality, and depersonalization disorder.*

The most common type of dissociative reaction is *psychogenic amnesia*, or total loss of memory associated with a traumatic event. According to DSM-III, there are several kinds of psychogenic amnesia. In *circumscribed amnesia*, people lose their memory for a specified period of time. This type of forgetting is reflected in the commonly reported absence of memory surrounding the funeral of a loved one. In *generalized amnesia* all memory is lost for past experiences, names, and places. Finally, in *continuous amnesia*, people forget each successive behavioral event as it occurs. For example, when one patient attempted to read a novel, she ended up reading only the first page over and over again. After an entire day's reading, the patient couldn't even remember the name of the book (Janet, 1925).

Under intense stress, psychogenic amnesia may be accompanied by a psychogenic fugue state in which people forget who they are. In some cases, they may run away and reappear thousands of miles from home with a new name and a new life. People in fugue states rarely question the fact that they can't remember their past and probably make up a fair number of the "amnesia victims" described in newspapers or characterized in detective stories, soap operas, and melodramas.

Unlike amnesia and fugue states, which most often affect only a part of a person's thinking, *multiple personality* affects the person's entire functioning. Multiple personality is a pattern in which an individual alternates between two or more personalities as in the literary work, *Dr. Jekyll and Mr. Hyde*. Dr. Jekyll's personality split into "good" and "evil" parts with the aid of a chemical potion. However, real-life cases of multiple personality don't necessarily split into good and evil parts and they don't need a chemical to achieve their sometimes dramatic and abrupt personality transformations. Generally, the new *secondary personalities* are less conservative, inhibited, and morally constricted than the original *primary personality*. Although each of the personalities typically has its own set of memories and behavior patterns, usually the secondary personality is aware of the primary personality but not vice versa. The primary personality generally has amnesia for the time that the other personalities are in control.

There seems to be no limit to the number of personalities that can develop. Women are more likely than men to show

In the various forms of dissociative disorders, people appear to be trying to run away or distance themselves from the source of their anxiety, never realizing that the source of their anxiety is within themselves. (*Paul Conklin/Monkmeyer Press Photo Service*)

this disorder, and in rare instances there are gender identity or sexual orientation difficulties within the secondary personalities. For example, two of one woman's 20 personalities were male even to the point of claiming they had male genitalia (Schreiber, 1974).

The following is a case of a 21-year-old white female who developed five personalities.

Case History: Dissociative Disorders—Multiple Personalities

"Kathy" is a 21-year-old white married female who, after having taken an overdose of sleeping pills in her home, was accidentally discovered by her husband and admitted to hospital. This overdose was attributed to her inability to cope with her responsibility as a wife and mother. The husband reported that several times he had found food burning in the oven, and on one occasion the patient was saved from a fire in the home, but was unable to recall how it had started. The patient also denied ever having had a sexual relationship with her husband, although she was the mother of three children.

Kathy had an extraordinary traumatic history. She was the only child of a middle-class family. Her mother had suffered two miscarriages before Kathy was born and was close to death during her birth. Early development was uneventful except for temper tantrums and nightmares. The nightmares began at about age three when the parents would entertain in their home and the child was left alone to cry for hours. She would eventually fall asleep only to wake up frightened and screaming.

At age four, she had her first traumatic experience. As long as the patient could remember, her parents had slept in different rooms. One night she found her father naked and in bed with her five-year-old neighbour. She said that she was stunned with fear and surprise and ran away to her room. Her father followed her and gently persuaded her to take off her clothes and to join him and the other girl in their sexual play. Later, alone in her room, she felt guilty and cried for several hours, denying to herself what had taken place, and only got relief when she attributed what had happened to someone else other than herself, whom she called "Pat". The second day when approached by her father and the girl, she insisted on being called "Pat", who continued to engage in oral sex with the father, for nearly five years.

At age nine, she experienced her second traumatic event, when she was discovered by her mother. The mother became angry with father, wept for some time and insisted on taking her daughter to bed with her every night. After a short time, the mother encouraged the daughter to have what she described as a "safer" sexual relationship with her. "Kathy" could not accept this, but the mother was insistent. Again, this was denied and the patient attributed the new relationship to a new person, "Vera", who continued the relation with the mother for another five years.

At age 14, she suffered her third traumatic experience. This was rape by an older man, who was her father's best friend. "Kathy" became very depressed and was frightened of telling her parents of the incident. She insisted on living in a separate room away from her mother, and called herself "Debby". At that time, she was described by the parents as being very miserable and refusing to talk. The parents then admitted her to a hospital, during which time she showed a mixture of depression, dissociation and trance-like symptoms, with irritability and much manipulative behaviour that caused confusion and frustration among the hospital staff (according to past hospital records).

Following discharge from hospital she was seen by a therapist to whom she became very attached. He showed marked curiosity about the different personalities and became fascinated with her case. He suggested hypnosis as a treatment for her condition. His hypnotherapy session focused on the rape incident, as he felt that "Debby" was the strongest of the personalities, but instead of concentrating on "Kathy," he encouraged "Debby" to dominate the therapy sessions and encouraged her to talk about "Pat" and "Vera", reinforcing their roles as dominant personalities. At the same time he prescribed antidepressant medication to "Kathy." His diagnosis was "depressive neurosis in a hysterical personality with dissociative episodes." The patient continued outpatient hypnotherapy for eighteen months during which time she experienced no change. She decided then to terminate treatment; and it was at this period the parents reported that she began calling herself "Kathy", "Pat", "Vera", and "Debby" at different times.

At age eighteen, she had her fourth traumatic experience. "Kathy" became very attached to a boyfriend in town. Her parents opposed the relationship and refused to allow her to meet with him. Her mother was constantly warning her that men could not be trusted, pointed to the example of her own marriage and how the father abused and neglected her. The patient became "confused and frustrated", as she was unable to trust either of her parents, and ran away from home to another town. She could not find a job and due to need for money, she became a prostitute, who called herself "Nancy". "Nancy" was rejected by "Debby" and was forced by her to take an overdose of sleeping pills, with the result that this patient was admitted to the hospital. On this occasion, she met her present husband, who had also been admitted following a drug overdose after his girlfriend had left him. The husband knew about his wife's multiple personalities through the patient's records. The patient continued hypnotherapy for two years, but felt no change, as her therapist repeated the same mistake as the first one. Since then she had continued to change therapists every few months for the last nine years.

Following her admission to hospital, she was put on unit restriction, suicidal precaution and close observation. The nursing staff observed her change of voice and behaviour. During her initial interview, she called herself three different names in a period of an hour; she denied being called "Kathy" and insisted on being called "Pat," then changed to "Vera," then to "Debby". In the second interview "Kathy" denied her "change" of names, but after a few minutes, she began to expose parts of her body, altered her tone of voice and called herself "Nancy", and the diagnosis of multiple personality was confirmed.

Physical examination showed no abnormality; repeated neurological examination, electroencephalogram and X-rays were negative. Psychiatric evaluation showed "Kathy" to be of average intelligence, her mood was appropriate and she was well oriented. She showed no formal thought disorder, concentration was good, speech was normal and there was no cognitive impairment. She was very articulate, and was able to talk freely about her difficulties at home. Her change of personality was quite noticeable; while carrying on a conversation, she would suddenly get a glazed look in her eyes, assume another tone of voice, and begin to speak on a different topic. She would identify herself as one of the other personalities, and during that time, I could easily order any one of the other personalities to appear and talk. After a few minutes, she would look at me and say something to the effect of not knowing what she had just said and would blame me for not continuing with the previous conversation. The original "Kathy" showed no knowledge of the other personalities, but the other four personalities shared a kind of relationship with each other, each with her particular hobbies and interests and all hated "Kathy." (Salama, 1980, p. 569)

Rather than manifesting one or more complete additional personalities, people who experience a *depersonalization disorder* lose the one personality they have. The world around these people seems somehow different and they no longer feel like "themselves." Depersonalization often occurs when people face new, stressful circumstances. Not only do they sometimes lose their capacity to "experience" emotions (even though they may be able to "express" them), people may even feel as though they are actually observing themselves from outside. As seen in the following personal experience, depersonalization can be extremely unnerving.

Personal Experience: Depersonalization

I had gone to Florida as a reward for finishing my first year of graduate school successfully. I had driven myself hard throughout the year, but now I was done and could finally relax. I had never been to

Florida. It was good to be away from the stress, but rather than relaxing me, being in Florida made me feel strange and ill at ease. The buildings were so different from what I was used to and the warm temperatures instead of being comforting added to the alien quality of the situation. My wife and I went out to dinner. We had been outside all day and I was ravenously hungry. I remember we had lobster with melted butter and I ate my portion quickly. About 15 minutes after I finished and we were having coffee, I began to feel very strange. At first things around me became strange. The people in the room seemed to be talking too loudly. I began to sweat. Next, I began to feel very weird. I can only say that I felt unreal and disconnected to the people and things around me. It was terrifying. I felt so apart from everything. I got up and went to the rest room but the weird feelings stayed with me. I felt so alone and completely unattached to anything. I told my wife that I was ill and she had to drive me back to the motel. The feelings disappeared in a few days but I would have done anything to escape them and still fear their return.

Paradigmatically Based Explanations

Historically beginning with the study of hysteria, the psychosocial perspective has been a rich source of explanation and treatment for what are now called the anxiety, somatoform, and dissociative disorders. Because of its historical and present-day usefulness, the theoretical explanations springing from the psychosocial paradigm will be described first.

The Psychosocial Paradigm: Psychoanalytic Theory

Freud (1936) basically viewed neuroses as the result of an interaction between anxiety and defense against anxiety. By anxiety, Freud generally meant a specific state of "unpleasure" that signaled danger. He described three different kinds of anxiety: *realistic*, *neurotic*, and *moral*. Though not differing in their experiential impact, each type of anxiety has different antecedents.

Realistic anxiety is adaptive since it helps alert people to actual dangers in their environment. It is an early-warning system that alerts people about potential harm in the world. Being afraid of cobras in India or of muggers in a city's dark alleys are examples of realistic anxiety.

To understand *neurotic anxiety*, it is necessary to refer back to the psychoanalytic concepts of the id, ego, and superego. Neurotic anxiety is believed to arise from the ego's realization that, if the unrealistic aggressive or sexual urges of the id show themselves, they may elicit punishment from outside sources. Neurotic anxiety then is the tension felt from the struggle between the ego and the id for the determination of an individual's behavior.

While neurotic anxiety arises out of ego-id conflicts, the source of *moral anxiety* is the superego. Through guilt or shame, the superego punishes even the thought of inappropriate behavior. Thus, moral anxiety originates in the tension that an important rule or code of behavior may be broken.

For example, assume a boy is thinking about stealing a toy car from a store. If he is anxious because he is afraid of getting caught by the watchful storekeeper, he probably is experiencing realistic anxiety. However, his anxiety would be regarded as neurotic if it occurred because his ego perceived the stealing as the expression of hate toward his father, who is symbolized by the storekeeper. Lastly, the boy is morally anxious if the source of his feelings is his having been taught that stealing is a sin against the rules of his religion.

In psychoanalytic theory, the primary functions of the ego are to maintain the individual's emotional stability and avoid severe anxiety by mediating among the id, superego, and reality. The ego defense mechanisms are sometimes used to help accomplish these tasks. When they are overused or rigidly applied, the defenses significantly contribute to the development of anxiety-related disorders.

From the psychoanalytic perspective, people use defenses to help deal with earlier childhood-parental conflicts. In anxiety states, for example, *repression* hides the source of upset from awareness. By this defensive process individuals use procedures that, though they reduce anxiety, also make it difficult to come to grips with the original source of their anxieties.

In the phobias, the defense of *displacement* allows for the refocusing of most feared id impulses to some object, situation, or social function, that though harmless usually has a symbolic connection to the original Oedipal conflict (Nemiah, 1981). Although phobias sometimes have their beginnings at earlier levels, obsessive-compulsive reactions more often are seen as resulting from a fixation at the earlier psychosexual anal stage. The fixation usually reflects an attempt to control aggressive feelings developed in reaction to harsh toilet-training experiences. If angry feelings lead to aggressive behavior, the child may be punished. Therefore cognitive or behavioral rituals are developed to dissipate the angry feelings before they become angry actions. Reflective of the anal period, many of the compulsive rituals involve cleanliness (Dowson, 1977). The greater the possibility that anger will be expressed, the more intense become the obsessive and compulsive rituals.

As in the development of anxiety disorders, psychoanalytic thinkers assume that somatoform and dissociative symptoms result from the mishandling of the Oedipal complex. These patients have become too dependent on the defenses of *repression and displacement* to soften their feelings of anxiety and inadequacy (Krohn, 1978). These two defenses originate during a fixation at the phallic stage of psychosexual development when heterosexual feelings directed at opposite-sexed parents are first awakened. These forbidden feelings are quickly repressed and remain dormant during the latency phase. According to Nilsson (1982), these repressed sexual feelings for the opposite-sexed parent are reawakened during young adulthood. In those who have not satisfactorily resolved the Oedipal crisis, reawakened sexual feelings produce intense feelings of anxiety. Anxiety can be reduced by being converted into physical symptoms as in the somatoform disorders, or by being compartmentalized as in the dissociative disturbances. Within the dissociative disorders, amnesia, fugue, and multiple personality could be viewed as the result of an increasingly intense application of the defenses of repression and displacement in an effort to wall off unacceptable sexual impulses.

The Psychosocial Paradigm: Learning Theory

Learning theorists such as Skinner (1938) and Ullmann and Krasner (1975) believe that they may be able to explain the occurrence of anxiety with simpler concepts than those used by psychoanalysts. The learning theory concepts of anxiety are tied very closely to the basic phenomena of motivation, learning, and reinforcement discussed in Chapter 5.

To learning theorists, physiologically based *primary drives* such as sex, thirst, and hunger are important motivators of basic, survival-oriented behavior. However, it is the learned, or *secondary drives*, that are often most important in determining behavior. Secondary drives such as those for money, prestige, and security are learned through association with primary drives like needs for food, water, sexual contact, and avoidance of pain.

Like the needs for food, water, and sexual contact, the pain-avoidance drive appears to be biologically programmed into all animals and is crucial to species survival. The anticipation of pain is equated with the feeling of anxiety. Thus, people may not only feel anxious before receiving an injection, an event associated with pain, but since anxiety itself is so unpleasant, they can learn to avoid the situation that causes it as well. Thus anxiety functions as a *secondary, or learned, avoidance drive* whose strength varies according to the intensity of the anticipated pain and the number of times the person has experienced the painful situation.

Watson and Rayner (1920) in their classic study of Little Albert (see Chapter 5) used the concept of a learned avoidance drive to explain the development of phobias. As you may remember, after placing Albert in a crib with a white rat, Watson loudly banged a steel bar behind the baby's ear. The noise so frightened Albert that he cried. After several repetitions, Albert showed signs of anxiety when presented with objects resembling the original white rat. These toy animals had become secondary, or learned, sources of anxiety by being associated with the aversive stimulus of painful sound.

Albert's anxiety spread beyond white rats and furry toy animals through the process of *generalization.* In generalization original associations with anxiety-producing stimuli (such as the loud noise for Albert) become increasingly complex. Anxiety can generalize in three major ways. First, people learn to fear objects associated in *time, place, and circumstance* with the originally feared stimulus. By association, once-neutral objects or circumstances can themselves become anxiety-evoking cues. Little Albert became anxious when placed again in the crib where the original conditioning occurred.

Besides generalizing across time, place, and circumstances, anxiety also can spread along the *stimulus similarity* dimension. That is, people learn to fear objects or situations that are experientially or descriptively similar to the originally feared event. In Albert's case, he showed signs of anxiety not only to the white rat, but also to his mother's furry hand warmer and a mask of Santa Claus. Albert's anxiety had generalized across a stimulus similarity dimension to a wide variety of furry stimuli.

Anxiety can also spread through people's ability to label, categorize, and abstract their behavior verbally and mentally. This *mediated generalization,* for instance, helps people learn that a stove, match, and fire are all associated with the word "hot" and if one shouldn't be touched, neither should the others. Without this sort of verbally mediated generalization, the education of a child regarding the dangers of the world would be more difficult. Along with the other forms of generalization, verbally mediated generalization can make it difficult to trace the original source of maladaptive anxiety.

Operant theorists believe that since anxiety is a secondary drive, it should respond to procedures that reduce the strength of such drives and its reduction should be a reinforcing event. According to the rules of reinforcement outlined in Chapter Five, behaviors followed by a reduction of an aversive stimulus usually are strengthened. Thus, since avoiding feared objects is usually followed by a reduction in anxiety, it reinforces the maintenance of behaviors. In a practical example, avoiding airports reduces anxiety and maintains the fear of flying because the feared object is not confronted.

Many learning theorists believe that the same processes of conditioning and generalization that produce phobias also produce anxiety states. The main difference is that while phobic individuals can avoid their feared objects or situations, thereby reducing anxiety, people with anxiety states feel anxious most of the time because they have been classically conditioned to a range of stimuli so wide that they inevitably encounter something that makes them anxious (Ost & Hugdahl, 1981).

In addition to phobias, conditioning principles also can be used to explain the development of obsessions and compulsions. From the operant learning perspective, people learn to use compulsions because these behaviors reduce feelings of anxiety. For instance, some compulsive people find that cleaning and organizing help reduce their anxieties and make them feel better. Logically then, if they become increasingly anxious, they may respond by increasing their compulsive cleaning behavior lest their anxiety intensify further.

Skinner (1938) provided some experimental evidence for the operant conditioning explanation for obsessive and compulsive reactions. In an animal analogue of human behavior, he found that pigeons tended to repeat behaviors which they were emitting when they were rewarded. If a pigeon were hopping when food was presented, it would begin hopping the next time it became hungry. This sort of *superstitious* behavior seems very similar to some of the unusual rituals and behaviors shown by compulsive individuals. In support of the suggestion that phobias and anxiety response patterns are learned through these operant procedures, Ost and Hugdahl (1981) surveyed 106 patients and found that 58 percent of them attributed their fears to conditioning experiences. Somewhat the same results were found by Wolpe (1981).

Some learning theorists believe that most maladaptive behavior is not directly learned through reinforcement and generalization but is acquired primarily through imitation. Those espousing this position consider *modeling* a better explanation for the acquisition of patterns of fear responding than operant and classical conditioning. According to modeling theory, people may become phobic via *vicarious conditioning*. In vicarious conditioning, people learn to be fearful of objects or situations by observing others become fearful. A child may watch his or her mother fake touching a stove, see her act as though she had burned her hand, and hear her say "hot." By observing their mothers in this way, children can vicariously learn to avoid the stove, without ever having to actually be burned themselves. While this is an instance of modeling adaptive behavior, abnormal patterns also can be learned in this way. If children observe a parent become very anxious before visiting a dentist, they may develop a dental phobia without ever having experienced any real pain in a dental office.

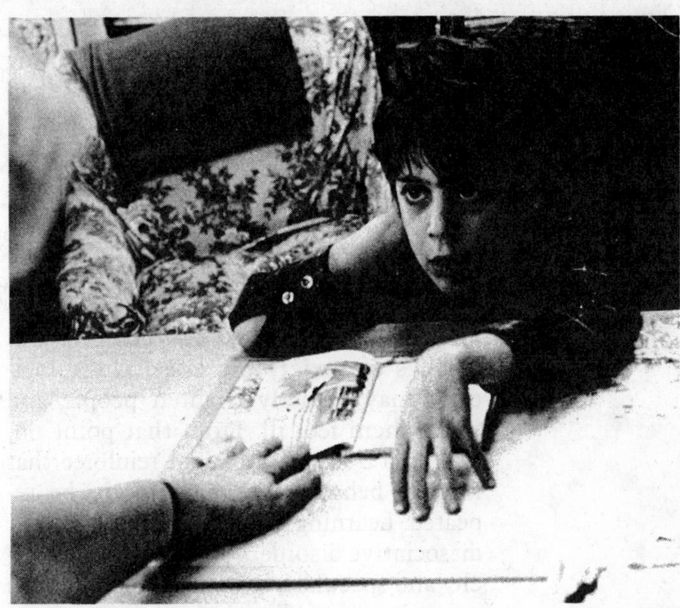

In vicarious learning, people can learn by observing the actions of others. (*Shirley Zeiberg/Taurus Photos*)

Learning theorists seem to have a somewhat more difficult time explaining somatoform and dissociative disorders than they do anxiety states, phobias, or obsessive-compulsive reactions. Ullman and Krasner (1975) believe that in somatoform disorders, people behave consistently with the way they think sick people do. When they show disease-like behavior, they receive attention from others that reinforces the activity. It is also possible that feelings of anxiety expressed physiologically may actually frighten people and make them feel ill. From that point on, attention from others might reinforce that kind of behavior and cause it to be repeated. Learning theory statements about dissociative disorders are even more sketchy and speculative. Usually they involve generalizations based on memory research. For instance, it may be that the same mechanisms underlying amnesia underlie the development of dissociative disorders. Hirst (1982) has formulated the concept that information that is usually processed automatically in normal people, for some unknown reason, requires conscious effort in people who have memory problems. Therefore the reason amnesics have memory difficulties is because they have to expend more energy and effort to take in and process information. Dissociative behavior may result from a similar process. More research is needed before amnesia or other memory difficulties can be assumed to be related to dissociative processes. At present there does not seem to be a cohesive learning theory explanation of dissociative disorders.

The Biological Paradigm: The Genetic Basis

Rather than internal psychic processes, learning, or modeling, those favoring the biological perspective have examined the possibility that anxiety, somatoform, and dissociative disorders are inherited. One genetic explanation offered by Eysenck is that the level of autonomic reactivity is inherited and plays a part in the development of these disorders.

The dimension of neuroticism is conceived in terms of individual differences in the reactivity and lability of the autonomic nervous system, and the autonomic lability itself is seen as an inherited characteristic of the organism. Eysenck and Rachman (1965) suggest that some people are innately predisposed to respond more strongly, more lastingly, and more quickly with their autonomic nervous system when presented with stressful stimuli (Gossop, 1981, p. 125).

Consistent with a genetic explanation, phobic individuals have been shown to have greater autonomic nervous system lability than normals (Lacey, 1967). Torgerson (1979) studied twins and found that there were more similar and more intense phobias in monozygotic twins as compared with dizygotic twins.

Those diagnosed as obsessive-compulsive show higher arousal levels than normals when working on problems that call for information-processing abilities (Ciesielski et al., 1981). Higher arousal states are consistent with a tendency to become more anxious under pressure. Thus higher arousal tendencies might predetermine the development of greater anxiety and the need for anxiety-reducing strategies. More support for the possibility that level of arousal is inherited was presented by McGuffin and Mawson (1980). They found two identical twin pairs who developed a similar obsessive-compulsive disorder even though separated from each other. The odds of finding even one pair of identical twins with obsessive-compulsive disorder is estimated to be 1 in 400,000, while the probability of finding *two* pairs who are concordant for obsessive-compulsive reactions is estimated to be well over 1 in 600 million. One of the two sets of twins is described in the following case.

BOX 10-1

THE BIOLOGICAL PARADIGM IN THE STUDY OF ANXIETY DISORDERS

Although historically the biological paradigm has not contributed greatly to the understanding of severe anxiety disorders, recent research suggests that this view may be beginning to emerge as an important source of theory, research, and treatment. Sheehan (1983) has proposed that there are actually *two* types of anxiety disorders. The first of these, *exogenous anxiety*, is caused primarily by stressful life events and other identifiable precipitators. Exogenous anxiety seems best explained through application of the psychosocial and/or systems perspectives. A second form of anxiety is *endogenous* and, according to Sheehan, represents an inherited vulnerability in which panic symptoms occur without warning and with no apparent precipitator. Sheehan believes that this form of sudden, unexplained panic should be called *anxiety disease* rather than anxiety disorder. He estimates that up to 5 percent of the U.S. population may suffer from the anxiety disease.

Some researchers have also adopted the view that some anxiety reactions are biologically based and have collected data in support of their beliefs. For example, Charney et al. (1985) studied people with panic disorders of undetermined origin. These people suffered unpredictable attacks characterized by rapid heartbeat, senses of impending doom, increased muscle tension, sweating, and so forth. Charney et al. found that when these people were administered doses of caffeine during calm periods, within minutes they began to experience anxiety, tremors, and other feelings described as "not different from the symptoms of their spontaneous panic attacks." Such strong effects of caffeine were not noted in a group of control subjects. Charney et al. concluded that there may be some physical abnormality in the biochemical system (most likely the neurotransmission system) of people with anxiety disease, such that they respond to certain dietary chemicals with a sense of panic while most people respond with a simple elevation in alertness.

Given a biological basis for certain anxiety disorders, it would follow that biological treatment such as dietary controls or use of certain drugs which alter neurotransmission would be more effective in anxiety disease than psychosocial or systems-based approaches such as psychoanalysis, behavior modification, or group therapy. According to Sheehan (1983) this may be the case. He reports that in many cases of anxiety disease and the phobic-like avoidance of situations often associated with it, simple drug therapy (Nardil) has helped people to feel better within a matter of a few weeks. Many of the people helped in this way had been treated with other approaches unsuccessfully. A note of caution is in order here. Sheehan's work suggests that *all* anxiety disorders are not psychologically or systems-based, but that *some* are biological in nature. It would be a mistake suddenly to assume that *all* anxiety disorders are probably biological and to cast aside the psychosocial and systems approaches which have worked in many cases in the past. The emergence of a biological view needs to be placed in its context as a step forward in the process of the science of abnormal psychology.

Case: Obsessive-Compulsive Reaction in Identical Twins

The "W" Twins

The proband, Jean, a housewife, developed her symptoms at 24 years of age a few months after her marriage when she acquired a fear of contamination by dirt with severe washing and cleansing rituals. At the time of her referral to this hospital three years later she was washing her hands between sixty and eighty times per day, spending twelve hours a day cleaning and disinfecting her house, and using up to 20 litres of liquid disinfectant a week. Her daughter, aged 2 and one half years, was not toilet trained and was restricted to one room of the house in order to avoid spread of contamination, and her husband had been obliged to give up sport for fear that his soiled sports clothes would introduce dirt to their home. Since she considered that sexual activity also involved risk of contamination it had ceased completely. On admission to hospital the skin of her hands was roughened, red, cracked and bleeding. She was moderately depressed. Jill, the co-twin, a social worker, developed her symptoms at the age of 22 when she and Jean were leading separate lives and had little contact with each other. Her traits of neatness and cleanliness became more pronounced and she developed particular rituals concerned with washing her bath and washing up the crockery and cutlery, which had to be started immediately after a meal was finished, any delay resulting in severe anxiety; the washing of the dishes and utensils had to proceed in a specific order and failure to comply with the routine, or an attempt by others to relieve her of her task, provoked great discomfort. She attempted to resist carrying out her rituals which she considered were silly and unnecessary but the time spent on them increased and interfered with her social life and home studies for a postgraduate qualification.

Their father, a retired clerk, was fastidiously neat and orderly in his habits but neither he nor other family members had received psychiatric treatment.

Jean was the first-born twin. Their early development and childhood were unremarkable, and at school both did well academically. They attended separate universities where Jill graduated in history and Jean obtained a first-class degree in physics, but declined an academic career in favour of nursing. Both the twins were normally outgoing and sociable and both had personality traits of orderliness, determination and conscientiousness. Neither of them had suffered any previous illness and they only learned of their similar obsessional problems after Jean began treatment with clomipramine and behaviour therapy, which effected considerable improvement, enabling her to return to work as a nurse. Jill received no formal treatment but her obsessional disorder underwent a spontaneous remission after more than a year. (McGuffin & Mawson, 1980, p. 285)

Other researchers have studied same-sex twin pairs. Slater and Shields (1982) found that monozygotic twins shared the same "neurotic" diagnosis in 29 percent of the pairs as compared with only 4 percent of the dizygotic pairs. In a somewhat different approach, Katsching and Shepherd (1978) looked at "neurotic" symptoms rather than people who were diagnosed as neurotic. They found significantly higher concordance rates for these kinds of symptoms in monozygotic as compared with dizygotic twins.

Carey (1982) found that the pooled risk for second-degree relatives was significantly less than that for first-degree relatives. These data are consistent with a simple genetic model since it is assumed that relatives share half as many genes with the proband as the first-degree relatives do.

Only a few adoption studies have been completed on those with neurotic diagnoses. Shields (1978) reported that there were more disturbed children among those adopted away from neurotic parents than from normal parents.

The relatively few studies concerning genetic components of neurosis usually involve small, nonrandom samples, in which neurosis is unreliably defined. These limitations have led to conflicting results. However, data of studies do seem to provide suggestive evidence of genetic factors in anxiety disorders, although there is little or no evidence for genetic factors in the somatoform and dissociative disorders.

The Systems Paradigm

There is little written that relates systems theory to the specific development of anxiety, somatoform, and dissociative disorders. From any of the major systems theories, it could be assumed that anxiety derives from skewed community or family systems. From the perspective of

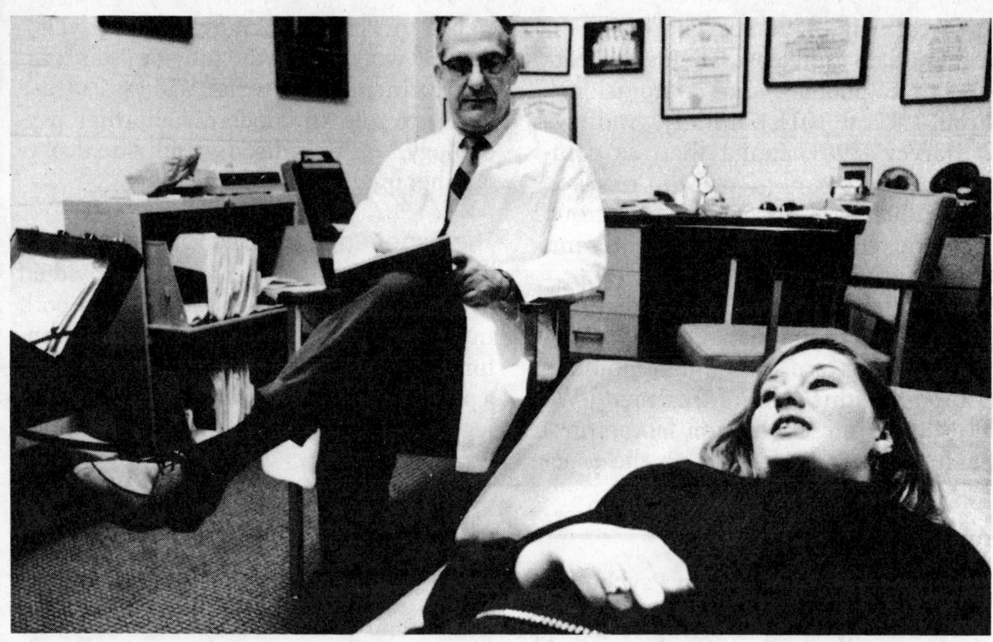

In most forms of psychotherapy, individuals face each other. However, in clinical psychoanalysis, the therapist usually sits behind the client. (© *Van Bucher, 1970/Photo Researchers, Inc.*)

Minuchin's structured family therapy approach, anxiety would develop from inappropriate boundaries between family members and abnormally constituted subsystems. In terms of prevention, theorists usually do not focus on the anxiety, somatoform, and dissociative disorders. While we are not certain about the reasons for the lack of present-day theorizing, historically, prevention theorists have dealt with the more severe rather than milder disorders. There is a need for systems theorists at either the family or community level to develop explanations for and complete research focused on the etiology and maintenance of anxiety, somatoform, and dissociative disorders.

Paradigmatically Based Intervention Approaches

Many of the traditional individual psychotherapies originating from the psychoanalytic, client-centered, and gestalt approaches described in Chapter Five were described in this chapter. More recently, behavior modification from the psychosocial perspective, biofeedback and drug treatment from the biological view, and family therapy from the systems paradigm have been effectively used to deal with the anxiety, somatoform, and dissociative disorders.

The Psychosocial Paradigm: Individual Psychotherapy

In individual psychotherapy one or more professionals apply a variety of psychosocially derived techniques of behavior change in an effort to help a single individual. Since many of the different forms of individual therapy originated in the treatments of anxiety, somatoform, and dissociative disorders, it is no surprise that they have most often been applied to them. Research has shown that individual therapy is among the most effective methods in the treatment of "nonpsychotic depressions, mild to moderate anxieties, fears and simple phobias and compulsions" (Parloff, 1982, p. 101). Similarly, Andrews and Harvey (1981) found that, as compared with a control group who received no individual care, 75 percent of a group of neurotic persons were significantly improved after individual treatment.

While there are literally hundreds of different forms of individual therapy (Harper, 1975), there are several common factors regarding this form of treatment. We will examine these common factors in a general fashion that focuses on the experience of psychotherapy, why psychotherapy works, and who provides this form of treatment. Due to its widespread use and key role in modern abnormal psychology, we will discuss individual psychotherapy in some detail.

The Experience of Psychotherapy

The personal experience of individual psychotherapy may be studied from both informal and formal perspectives. The informal perspective is represented here by a personal experience obtained from a college student in individual psychotherapy.

Personal Experience: Being in Psychotherapy

At the beginning of therapy I felt apprehensive and excited about starting. I was unsure of what the therapist would think of me and my chances for changing and becoming happier. The excitement increased and I felt very optimistic about being committed to changing. However, my enthusiasm diminished as I saw that change was hard and would be slow in coming. It seemed as if there was so much to tell my therapist about my past so that he would understand me and not make any snap decisions, but my present life problems were also demanding attention. I had to rely on his judgment, knowing his understanding of me would be incomplete. My confidence in what was going on in therapy would vary from week to week. At times, I felt the therapist was not particularly attentive or concerned and that he was marking time with me and just trying to earn some money. At other times, I felt exhilarated and very confident of myself and what we were doing together. The continuity from one session to the next was often absent, and then I would feel as if therapy were just a crisis-oriented maintenance exercise. Nevertheless, most of the time I felt I really needed his attention and suggestions for my current crisis. We are now making some gradual headway in developing my understanding of what forces motivate me that I'm not aware of. Then I will have a reasonable chance, I hope, of being able to change those things about myself that hold me back.

Although the informal perspective on the experience of psychotherapy can be informative, it is difficult to know whether a single experience reflects what goes on with others. Howard and Orlinsky (1972; Orlinsky & Howard, 1975) studied the experience of a number of people in psychotherapy. Using a standardized report form,

Table 10-2 Typical Therapeutic Experiences

Patient wants to:	"Get a better understanding of my feelings and behavior."
	"Get help in talking about what is really troubling me."
	"Work out a problem that I have."
	"Work together with my therapist on a person-to-person basis."
	"Get advice on how to deal with my life and with other people."
Patient talks about:	"Feelings and attitudes toward myself."
	"Social activities and relationships, friends and acquaintances."
	"Relationship with spouse, boyfriend, or girlfriend."
Patient feels:	"Anxious."
	"Tense."
Patient relates by:	Leading.
	Being interdependent.
	Being friendly.
	Being animated or feeling.
Therapist tries to:	"Increase my patient's insight and self-understanding."
	"Move my patient closer to experiencing her real feelings, what she really is."
	"Engage my patient in an honest person-to-person relationship, work together authentically."
Therapist feels:	"Interested."
	"Calm."
	"Involved."
	"Alert."
	"Confident."
	"Sympathetic."
Therapist relates by:	Reciprocating.
	Being interdependent.
	Being friendly.
	Being feeling.
Patient gets:	"A sense of having an honest person-to-person relationship with my therapist, of working together."
	"Help in being able to talk about what was troubling to me and really important."
	"Better insight and self-understanding."

Source: Reprinted by permission of the publisher from David E. Orlinsky and Kenneth I. Howard, *Varieties of Psychotherapeutic Experience* (New York: Teachers College Press, Copyright © 1975 by Teachers College, Columbia University), p. 73.

these investigators compiled data for 60 subjects in psychotherapy. In all, 890 therapy sessions with 17 different therapists were analyzed. The summary of these findings is presented in Table 10-2. The results suggest that many of the same feelings described in the personal experience just recounted are shared by others. Orlinsky and Howard (1975) note: "To the extent that these findings are representative gives an idea of what most likely happens in the ordinary therapy session as it occurs in everyday practice" (p. 72).

The Effectiveness of Psychotherapy

It is possible to identify common characteristics of psychotherapy sessions scientifically, but whether these characteristics are of any value in helping people is a separate question. This issue has been addressed in investigations called *therapy-outcome studies.* There has been much controversy surrounding the possibility that psychotherapy may do little more good than no treatment at all. Early fuel for the fire of this controversy was provided by the interpretation of outcome studies by British psychologist Eysenck (1952, 1965, 1978). In 1952, using records of the discharge rates of those in the New York State hospital system and those who were waiting to receive psychotherapy, Eysenck claimed that up to 72 percent of neurotic people improved without the benefit of psychotherapy. He concluded that these patients improved because of *spontaneous remission*, or just getting better on their own. Since the people who received no treatment seemed to improve at the same rate as those who were involved in psychotherapy, he asked whether there was a need for psychotherapy at all.

Needless to say, Eysenck evoked quite a response from the psychotherapeutic community. Numerous criticisms have been leveled at his conclusions. One major criticism has to do with his "no treatment" groups. Did these people really receive no treatment? It seems safe to say that these distressed people on a waiting list didn't stop seeking relief from their discomfort. Chances are they talked with friends, perhaps with other professionals such as ministers, teachers, and the like, or perhaps even with other therapists. Merely being placed on a waiting list doesn't mean that a person is necessarily going to stay and wait passively to improve. Some people do seem to improve spontaneously, but they are usually diagnosed as depressed (Kiesler, 1966, 1973).

Eysenck's interpretation has also been challenged because of his criteria for success. For example, is being discharged from a large state mental hospital equivalent to termination of a successful psychotherapeutic interaction? In some instances, state hospitals believe their obligation is met and patients have been successfully treated when they have been given drugs and "stabilized." Even the rate of spontaneous remission of 72 percent cited by Eysenck has been seriously questioned. Bergin (1971) has noted that, in long-term (up to 20 years) follow-up studies of untreated people, spontaneous remission occurs only about 30 percent of the time. The 30 percent figure is significantly lower than the improvement rate reported in a review of recent therapy-outcome studies (Bergin & Suinn, 1975).

More recently the debate has continued over the use of *meta-analysis* to evaluate the impact of psychotherapy. Smith and her colleagues (Smith & Glass, 1977; Smith et al., 1980) and Shapiro and Shapiro (1982) have completed a thorough application of meta-analysis to the psychotherapy area. In meta-analysis the results from many divergent studies of psychotherapy are transformed in such a way that they can be combined with one another to obtain the overall effect of psychotherapy. Reviewing over 400 studies it was concluded that the average psychotherapy client was better off than 75 percent of the untreated controls. While the studies have been criticized because of statistical analyses used, relative absence of data from both behavioral and psychoanalytic studies, and equating problems presented for psychotherapy (Eysenck, 1978; Rachman & Wilson, 1980), it appears that meta-analysis has given significant support to the assumption that psychotherapy is an effective intervention for a number of disorders.

How Psychotherapy Works

Whereas outcome studies are directed at determining *whether* psychotherapy works, *process studies* are directed at determining *how* it works. Process researchers attempt to isolate the factors in the psychotherapeutic experience that may be responsible for bringing about the positive changes documented in outcome studies. Some factors may be general enough to span most types of therapy; others may be specific to certain approaches. The following are some general factors that seem to cut across therapies.

The Placebo Effect and the Barnum Effect The first general factor proposed to account for the general effects of psychotherapeutic approaches comes from the fact that people tend to place faith in members of the healing professions (Parloff, 1984). This faith allows for what are called *placebo effects* in psychotherapy (A. Shapiro, 1971). Placebo effects occur when a person is led to expect benefit from a therapeutic procedure or chemical substance that actually is neutral in its effects. For example, for some patients, physicians may prescribe pills that are no more than candy. Nevertheless, in some patients these pills seem to have significant impact in eliminating discomfort or problems. In psychotherapy, the placebo effect may occur when "new" approaches are first used. If improvement is due to a placebo effect, then the positive effects usually will diminish as time passes and the placebo effect weakens.

Named for its similarity to the promotional ability of P. T. Barnum, in the Barnum effect the therapist actively "talks up" a mode of treatment to such a degree that the client's faith in the therapy magnifies the placebo effect. However, if faith in and acceptance of the therapy diminish, so can the effectiveness of the therapy.

Despite their possible beneficial characteristics, the placebo and Barnum effects can interfere with attempts to get a clear answer to the question of how psychotherapy works. Therapists could believe that their specific techniques are helpful when, in fact, it is not the techniques but the placebo or Barnum effect that produces change. Further, specific techniques may be helpful, but their actual potency may be distorted by variations in the placebo and Barnum effects (Prioleau et al., 1983).

Therapist Variables The personal characteristics of the therapist may have a significant impact on the therapeutic process. These characteristics can be viewed from both experiential and scientific perspectives.

Experientially, most therapists would agree that all therapists cannot work with all clients and that some therapists do especially well with certain types of clients. In the following statement from an experienced therapist, we can see some of the therapist characteristics important to the process of psychotherapy.

Personal Experience: Being a Therapist

Having been a therapist for about 11 years now, I find myself loving what I do more and more. I've learned many things over the years. For one thing, I know that I'm not cut out to see married couples—I just don't feel comfortable with them, and I'm not sure that I can really help them. On the other hand, I *know* I can do individual therapy as well as any of my colleagues. I feel right in a one-to-one situation—I feel good. I've been able to train myself to shut out everything but my client during the therapy session. Sometimes that's hard, especially when I'm worried about some personal problem myself. But, to be a good therapist, I've got to be able to concentrate every ounce of my energy on the relationship with my client. I find therapy to be a draining experience; when I've had a good session (and, to tell the truth, I do have bad ones now and then), I feel almost shot for the rest of the day. I can't really handle more than three intense hours like that in any one day—some therapists can; I can't.

I've been able to help many people during my career, and I feel good about having touched the lives of my clients in some positive way. And my clients have touched my life as well. Each relationship has changed my life in some way, most times for the better, a few times for the worse. Being a therapist is an intense experience, one that is hard to describe in words. I can say, however, that it is an emotional, deeply human endeavor with which I continue to be enthralled.

Informal observations of differences among therapists have been documented by a variety of formal, scientific efforts. Some research has focused on the effects on the progress of therapy sessions of daily variations in the therapist's mood (Gurman, 1972, 1973; Orlinsky & Howard, 1967, 1975). Other efforts have been directed primarily at identifying more long-standing personality characteristics of effective therapists and even attempts to "match" therapists with the kinds of clients they would be most likely to help (Carson & Heine, 1962). Parloff et al. (1983) conclude that therapy outcome was not directly related to the personality characteristics of the psychotherapists. However, others (e.g., Truax & Carkhuff, 1967) suggest that the therapist's personality may be helpful in setting the kind of conditions within which the clients would feel comfortable about disclosing their difficulties. It would seem safe to conclude that since personality characteristics are important in determining the quality of most relationships, they should also significantly impact on the therapy relationship as well (Ellis, 1982).

There are three major groups of therapists. According to a recent survey of clinical psychologists (Norcross & Prochaska, 1982), 30.9 percent were identified as eclectic, 30 percent as psychodynamically oriented, and 14.4 percent as behaviorally oriented.

Client Variables Client characteristics can also affect success in psychotherapy. Bordin (1974) concluded that differences among clients served by therapists were more responsible for differences in success rates than the specific therapies used.

Informally, a number of therapists believe that the so-called YAVIS person may be the best candidate for successful psychotherapy. The letters Y-A-V-I-S stand for young, anxious, verbal, intelligent, and successful. In other words, clients who aren't very disturbed and can focus on and deal with a clearly defined set of problems probably will do best in psychotherapy. In one review of research on the role of client factors in the therapy process, Bordin (1974) has noted that successful clients generally stay in therapy longer, are dissatisfied with their level of functioning, experience emotional pain, have hope that they can be relieved of emotional pain, and can allow themselves to become temporarily dependent on the therapeutic relationship. For example, Schramski (1984), found that clients who made, as well as maintained, therapy gains were from higher rather than lower social class, were younger rather than older, and were anxious rather than calm.

Who Does Psychotherapy?

Up to this point, we have attempted to show what it's like to be in psychotherapy and the factors related to effective psychotherapy experiences. With this basic background of information, it now seems appropriate to look at *who does* the psychotherapy.

Psychotherapists are specially trained in the application of the psychotherapies. Many people erroneously equate *psychotherapist* with *psychiatrist*. In truth, there are a number of professional groups trained in the practice of psychotherapy. Most of the treatment methods to be presented aren't the sole province of any one profession.

Psychiatrists Psychiatrists are physicians who specialize in treating the mentally disturbed. In addition to college and medical school, psychiatry requires 3 to 5 years of professional psychiatric residency. Because of their medical training, psychiatrists are the only mental health professionals permitted to prescribe drugs or administer shock therapy. *Psychoanalysts* most often are psychiatrists who take additional training in Freudian therapy techniques. Not all psychiatrists are psychoanalysts, but almost all psychoanalysts are psychiatrists.

Clinical and Counseling Psychologists Clinical and counseling psychology are applied subdisciplines of psychology. In contrast to psychiatrists who have medical degrees (M.D.s), clinical and counseling psychologists hold a doctoral level degree (Ph.D. or Psy.D.), which requires 4 to 6 years in graduate school and a year of additional training in a clinical internship. Clinical and counseling psychologists are the only mental health professionals specially trained in developing, administering, and interpreting psychological tests. Psychologists are trained in a wide variety of therapeutic approaches, from the psychoanalytic to the humanistic or the behavioral. Clinical and counseling psychologists who hold a research degree (the Ph.D.) are also trained in research methodology. Clinical psychologists more often work with the severely disturbed clients as compared with counseling psychologists who more often help less disturbed individuals. Both types of psychologists must have licenses or certification in most states in order to practice.

Psychiatric Social Workers Although clinical psychology is primarily a post-World War II phenomenon, psychiatric social work has been a profession since the early 1900s. Fully trained social workers hold M.S.W. (Master of Social Work) degrees and belong to and are approved by a national organization called ACSW (Academy of Certified Social Workers). Social workers can provide psychotherapy to individuals and groups. They often work in the homes or working environments of disturbed people.

Psychiatric Nurses In contrast to social workers, who traditionally work in the community, psychiatric nurses usually complete a postgraduate program in psychiatric nursing within a medical setting. Often in more direct contact with patients than any other professional, psychiatric nurses may administer medications (under a physician's guidance) and provide physical care as well as individual psychotherapy.

Pastoral Counselors In addition to psychiatrists, psychologists, social workers, and nurses, psychotherapy can also be provided by pastoral counselors—clergy who are specially trained in working with those who have behavioral and emotional disturbances. Pastoral counselors often serve internships in mental hospitals or other special mental health facilities.

The Psychosocial Paradigm: Behavior Modification

Whereas the traditional psychotherapist's goal is generally to search out the underlying conflicts that lead to the formation of symptoms, behavior modifiers typically focus on the symptoms themselves. From the behavioral perspective, since disordered behaviors are learned, learning principles should guide interventions as well. Three interventions called habituation, reciprocal inhibition, and in vivo desensitization have been used with special success in treating phobias (Wolpe, 1973).

In *habituation*, people with phobias are forced to experience their feared object, situation, or activity repeatedly until they become so used to it that they no longer respond to it with anxiety. In a somewhat less stressful approach called *reciprocal inhibition*, a weakened form of the phobia is paired with an antagonistic response like relaxation. For instance, applying a reciprocal inhibition procedure to treat a fear of flying in an airplane, the therapist helps a client to compose a graduated list of fears from the least to the most anxiety-producing fear involving flying. The first and least feared item might be: "You are notified that in a year you will have to fly to New York to present at a conference." The client is instructed to relax while imagining receiving the news of a trip to New York. If clients can think about less feared items on the list without feeling anxious, they then are allowed to move on to the next more feared ones. When the entire list can be thought about without anxiety, the client may then be asked to experience the feared situations in the real world. Called *in vivo desensitization*, it would mean that clients who fear flying in an airplane might have to go out and visit an airport or actually sit in an airplane.

Habituation, reciprocal inhibition, and in vivo desensitization have been applied successfully in a number of instances. Benjamin and Kincey (1981) have used specially trained nonprofessional therapists to successfully treat hospitalized agoraphobic patients by having them actually experience walking out of doors, traveling by bus, and shopping.

As with the traditional psychotherapies, of the other anxiety states, somatoform and dissociative disorders, phobias appear to be the most responsive to behavioral interventions (Emmelkamp & Kuypers, 1979; Goldfried & Davison, 1976; Munby & Johnston, 1980). After reviewing 39 studies concerned with the treatment of phobias, Linden (1981) concluded that in vivo exposure (i.e., in vivo desensitization) seems to be the behavioral treatment of choice. Others have noted that *applied relaxation*, in which people are taught to relax quickly in response to the beginning signs of anxiety (Jerremalm et al., 1980), and *self-hypnosis* (Spiegel et al., 1981) are also effective, especially with social phobias.

Behavioral methods also have been successfully applied to other disorders besides phobias. *Response prevention* has been used to reduce obsessive-compulsive behavior. In response prevention, people are placed in the type of environmental situation that produces the obsessive-compulsive behaviors, but they are prevented from expressing their disordered reactions. If someone, for example, has a hand-washing compulsion, placing him or her in a room without washing facilities prevents that disordered set of behaviors from occurring. During the time that the response is "prevented" in this way, the person can learn that his or her anxiety can be dealt with in newer, more adaptive ways.

The Biological Paradigm: Biofeedback

In biofeedback, people are directly taught to control the functioning of their autonomic nervous system, and through this control, to decrease their feelings of anxiety. Blanchard and Young (1974) present a case of a 50-year-old man who would be diagnosed as being in an "anxiety state." Although the anxiety left him tired and weak, he seemed most upset by his speeded-up heartbeat. To decrease his heart rate, the man was connected to biofeedback equipment that continuously monitored his beating heart. Whenever he relaxed enough to slow his heartbeat, the sound coming from the monitoring equipment changed from an unpleasant to a pleasant tone. As added reinforcement, he was given 1 cent for every 10 seconds his heartbeat fell below a certain rate. At the beginning of biofeedback training, the man had an average heart rate of 96 beats per minute; at the end of 19 sessions his average rate was 14 beats slower and remained so even after training and monetary rewards stopped. Moreover, the man reported feeling less anxious and stronger.

Recent work has shown that some biofeedback procedures are better at reducing anxiety than others. Frontalis EMG feedback appears to reduce anxiety significantly more effectively than such techniques as EEG alpha biofeedback.

More research may establish other differences between various biofeedback techniques and their impact on particular disorders.

The Biological Paradigm: Drug Therapy

The most widely used intervention for the anxiety, somatoform, and dissociative disorders based on the biological perspective is the tranquilizing drugs. The tranquilizing drugs can be effective in temporarily eliminating feelings of tension and anxiety. It appears that most tranquilizing drugs (like benzodiazepine) impact on panic attacks but *not* on the anticipatory anxiety that characterizes anxiety-related disorders (Davis et al., 1981). Some professionals suggest that clients need support to overcome the anticipatory anxiety that seems unaffected by the tranquilizing drugs. For example, in the case of agoraphobia, after taking a drug like phenelzine to neutralize a panic attack, clients can then be helped to confront the feared phobic situation or object.

Although tranquilizers such as meprobamate and valium can decrease the tension level in a dissociative disturbance, they generally have less of an impact on the disorder's other symptoms such as memory difficulties. As a result of their limited impact, most physicians who prescribe drug therapy would probably agree that drugs should be used only in conjunction with a therapeutic program that includes some form of psychotherapy or behavior modification. Without a therapeutic relationship, the danger of becoming psychologically dependent on, and in some cases physiologically addicted to, the tranquilizing drugs increases dramatically. As Nemiah (1975) advised: "Drugs should never be allowed to become a substitute for a relationship with a doctor" (p. 1263).

The Systems Paradigm: Family Therapy

The use of systems-based approaches to deal with anxiety, somatoform, and dissociative disorders is quite recent. Historically, individual approaches have been most often applied to these disorders. Psychotherapeutic and behavioral interventions traditionally are completed on a one-to-one basis. It also appears that family therapies have had some limited success with these disorders as well. From the perspective of Minuchin's structured family therapy, family members are helped to change rigid and diffuse boundaries to clear ones so that the identified clients may more easily communicate with their family members in a constructive fashion. Without such clear boundaries, subsystems can become distorted. For example, anxiety states may be caused when people are asked to perform roles in a family system that they are not qualified for. An adolescent who is pulled into behaving like a parent may become very anxious when he or she has to make parent-like decisions and actions. Family intervention here focuses on getting the parents to take responsibility for the parental subsystem and helping the adolescent relate to his or her own subsystem.

Family approaches have proven successful elsewhere. Dollinger (1983) reported the successful remediation of dissociative blackouts in a 15-year-old girl and Hafner et al. (1981) reported the successful treatment of two cases of obsessive-compulsive disorder through family therapy procedures. More research is needed to evaluate the worth of systems approaches to treating anxiety, somatoform, and dissociative disorders especially in comparison with the much more commonly used psychosocially based individual psychotherapy procedures.

Concluding Comments

While it was possible to find instances in which all of the three major paradigms were applied in the study of schizophrenia and the affective disorders, this was not the case in our presentation of the anxiety, somatoform, and dissociative disorders. As we have surveyed these patterns associated with anxiety and its avoidance, we have found that much theoretical and therapeutic work has been derived from the psychosocial paradigm. Unfortunately, the same thing cannot be said about the biological and systems paradigms. To be sure, the biological paradigm has led to the use of drug therapy that can, in some instances, control anxiety; however, the use of these biologically grounded treatments is not as clearly based upon an understanding of the physiology or neurochemistry of the disorders as it is in the cases of biologically based treatments for the schizophrenias or affective disorders. The systems paradigm also seems to have contributed relatively little to our understanding of the differential development of anxiety, somatoform, or dissociative disorders. One of the most promising applications of the systems view, family therapy, has only recently been used extensively to treat these disorders and more time is needed to evaluate its worth.

In light of the inability of two of the three major paradigms to generate either cogent theoretical or treatment approaches, it may be said that, for abnormal psychology as a science, the anxiety, somatoform, and dissociative disorders pose serious problems. The problems become even more serious in the case of somatoform and dissociative disorders. While almost all interventions, regardless of the perspective, showed some success with anxiety state disorders in general and phobias in particular, with the exception of psychoanalytic theories, explanations and specific treatments for somatoform and dissociative disorders are sparse. The difficulty of all three major paradigms to yield consistent progress could create the kind of tension that forces scientists to begin to look elsewhere than in the traditional paradigms for answers. The future of the study of these disorders seems ripe for the development of new paradigms that might suggest more appropriate explanations and interventions.

Summary Chart

In Chapter 10 we focused on a set of moderately severe disorders which have in common an involvement with anxiety. Among the most frequently occurring disorders, the anxiety, somatoform, and dissociative disturbances rarely require hospitalization.

The anxiety disorders: Anxiety states, phobic disorders, obsessive-compulsive disorders, stress-related adjustment disorders
The somatoform disorders: Similar to actual physical disease or not similar to actual disease, psychogenic pain, hypochondriasis, conversion disorders
Dissociative disorders: Amnesia and fugue, multiple personality, depersonalization

We then examined some paradigmatic explanations for the disorders:

Psychosocial paradigm: Psychoanalytic theory
Psychosocial paradigm: Learning theory
Biological paradigm: Genetic bases

In our discussion of treatments for the anxiety, somatoform, and dissociative disorders, we took the opportunity to examine psychotherapy in some detail. This reflects the fact that this form of treatment works especially well with this group of disturbances.

The effectiveness of psychotherapy
How psychotherapy works
Who does psychotherapy

We closed with an examination of the major paradigmatically based efforts to alter anxiety, somatoform, and dissociative disturbances:

The psychosocial paradigm: Individual psychotherapy
The psychosocial paradigm: Behavior modification
The biological paradigm: Biofeedback
The biological paradigm: Drug therapy
The systems paradigm: Family therapy

CHAPTER 11

Psychological Factors Affecting Physical Condition

Personal Experience: Heart Attack

I probably would not have been able to talk about my heart attack right after it happened, so it's better that it's been some time since it happened. I know that I will probably be very intellectual in my description, but let me assure you that I can still feel how it was to experience a heart attack. I'm not a young man, being 63 years of age, but then one never really thinks of oneself as being old. I was fairly active. I played golf about two or three times a week, cut the grass, and even jogged a little. My father had a bad heart, but I really had no inkling that I would have heart trouble. Then one night in October it began. Business had really been rough; competition with another firm was making work a living hell. Everybody was always trying to do something to someone else. So I had to think about the business night and day. Anyway, it was just after dinner and I wasn't feeling very well. But my stomach had been acting up lately anyway so I didn't make very much out of it. It felt like gas and I wondered if maybe I ate too fast. About an hour later it was still there but getting worse. I began to get flushed and to feel very uncomfortable. I couldn't sit, but it was getting to be painful to walk. I did not want to alarm my wife so I didn't make very much out of it. I managed to stand the pain until about one o'clock in the morning. That's when my arm began to hurt like I threw it out playing ball. When I found that I could not move it without severe pain, I called out to my wife and she got help from the hospital. By the time I got to the hospital, I knew it was serious and that I might not live through the night. I thank God I survived; it has made me appreciate life again.

The personal experience of a heart attack points out that unlike the somatoform disorders described in Chapter 10, *psychophysiological disorders* reflect actual physical damage that can be life-threatening. When such physical damage is more the result of psychological factors like stress than actual disease processes, the symptom patterns are classed as psychiatric conditions. Work on the psychophysiological disorders must, by necessity, include significant interactions between the biological and psychosocial paradigms. As a result, rather than specifying a number of different primary diagnostic patterns as was done in DSM-I and DSM-II, DSM-III identifies psychophysiological disorders in terms of combinations of Axis I and Axis III categories. In each psychophysiological disorder, the Axis I diagnosis is *psychological factors affecting physical conditions*, and the specific nature of the disorder is then indicated by the medical problem entered on Axis III. Thus the diagnosis for chronic heart disease not based on physical disorder would be:

Axis I: Psychological factors affecting physical condition

Axis III: Chronic heart disease

By combining Axes I and III, designers of the DSM-III have recognized that psychophysiological disorders are "real" medical problems that can be painful and life-threatening and contain a significant psychological component in their etiology.

Before describing the major psychophysiological disorders, additional differences between them and the somatoform disorders need to be clarified. As mentioned earlier, one important difference is that psychophysiological disorders do cause physical damage whereas somatoform patterns typically do not. In addition, symptoms in psychophysiological disorders usually involve internal organs like the lungs, viscera, or, as shown in the initial personal experience, the heart. Lastly, patients suffering from psychophysiological disorders typically are quite concerned and anxious about their symptoms, feelings that are missing in the "la belle indifference" shown by those with somatoform symptoms.

Some General Considerations Regarding the Etiological Bases of Psychophysiological Disorders

People diagnosed as having psychophysiological disorders make up a small proportion of admissions to state mental hospitals and of those visiting private psychiatric practitioners (less than 1 percent). Yet due to their often life-threatening consequences, these disorders demand a great deal of theoretical and research effort. While many specific theories have been offered for particular disorders, much of the general theoretical effort is devoted to investigating the reasons why different individuals "choose" different organ systems as sites for psychophysiological disturbance. It is not known exactly why some individuals suffer respiratory-system breakdowns (asthma), and others gastrointestinal-system breakdowns (ulcers). There are at least three major "guesses" made by researchers and clinicians as to why a particular psychophysiological disorder might be "chosen." One view is that the specific psychophysiological disorder occurs in the organ system that is physically the weakest. The weakness in a specific organ system may have a genetic or environmental cause. Thus, for example, if the respiratory system is a person's weakest organ system and the person experiences continued stress, this could lead to a breakdown of that system in the form of asthma.

A second explanation suggests that there are differences in inherited patterns of response to stress that may predispose people to develop specific system breakdowns. For example, some people respond to stress with elevated blood pressure, whereas others respond with increased acid production in the stomach. Lacey and Lacey (1958) have shown these differences in individual physiological reactivity to stress to be fairly stable over time. Some of the varieties of physiological responses to anxiety are shown in Table 11-1. These responses were obtained by asking psychology students to write down what physiological reactions they experienced as anxiety.

A third theory suggests that specific types of personality—and "not" weak organ systems or inherited response patterns—are the chief reasons for the development of certain psychophysiological disorders. For instance, people who have dependence-independence conflicts may be more prone to develop ulcers (Alexander, 1934). Consistent with this personality explanation, people tend to express different attitudes, depending on the type of psychophysiological disorder they have. Therefore an ulcer patient might more often "feel deprived," whereas the hypertensive person "feels threatened with

Table 11-1 Physiological Correlates of Anxiety in College Students

Physiological Response	*Percent of Students*
Increased heart rate	20
Digestive upset	17
Sweat, cold sweat	15
Sweaty palms	15
Increased breathing rate	11
Alertness, heightened senses	11
Muscular tension	10
Tire easily, weakness	9
Knots or butterflies in stomach	8
Pulse-rate increase	6
Whole body tense, tight	6
Hypertension	6
Weak legs, legs buckle	6
Light-headed, faint, dizzy	5
Shaky	5
Cry easily	5
Lose appetite	5
Nauseated	5
Hands and feet tap	5
Can't sit still	4
Sudden movement, twitches	4
Talk a lot, fast, loud	3
Headaches	2
Jittery laugh	2
Can't sleep	2
Mind blanks	2
Frequent urge to go to bathroom	2
Break out in blemishes	2
Flushed	2
"Cotton mouth," tough speaking	2
Clenched fists	2
Increased metabolism	2
Cold hands	2
Hot ears	1
Tension behind eyes	1
Burning inside	1
Teeth grind, sore jaws	1
Chilled	1
Loss of feeling	1
Hair on legs stands out	1
Skin rash	1
Bite nails	1
Smoke	1

harm." However, these relationships when found are usually correlative rather than causative and as such they help little in evaluating the worth of this theoretical approach.

Cardiovascular Disorders

The cardiovascular disorders involve diseases of the heart and blood vessels which are either produced or aggravated by psychological factors. The most destructive and prevalent of these disorders are coronary heart disease (CHD) and essential hypertension.

Coronary Heart Disease

Ranking first as a cause of death in adults, coronary heart disease may account for as many as half the yearly deaths in the United States. Many more men than women are victims of CHD, with a healthy male child in the United States having one chance in five of developing some form of CHD before he is 60 years old.

The most common form of coronary heart disease, *myocardial infarction*, is referred to as a heart attack. These attacks usually are caused by an obstruction of one of the heart arteries which can lead to the destruction of portions of the heart muscle. If the destroyed heart muscle was responsible for maintaining heart functioning, then the heart attack will probably be fatal. The experience of a myocardial infarction is uniquely frightening and can generate a great deal of anxiety as is shown in the following personal experience.

Personal Experience: Anxiety in Reaction to a Myocardial Infarction

Is there really nothing which can prevent me feeling my heart—that vital machine whose slightest deviation from the normal is enough to upset the entire body—suddenly give out, get painfully irregular, to be thrown for hours into an unimaginable state of crazy fear, while at the same time the lungs seem to be turned into cotton-wool which lets no air pass, and in a few moments a glacial cold, such as I have never experienced at any other time, penetrates the whole of my being and turns it into a block of ice? Shall I then always be liable to those states of collapse when, in indescribable agony, gasping and feeling death imminent. I find myself as incapable of resistence of defense as a plant whose stalk is suddenly cut. (Pastorelli, 1936, pp. 32–33)

A less serious, but still very painful, form of coronary heart disease is *angina pectoris* in which people experience intense pain in the chest, especially in the area behind the breast bone, and from the shoulder radiating down the left arm. These symptoms typically are caused by fatty deposits that block the arteries leading to the heart resulting in a decrease of oxygen to the organ itself. While the reduced blood flow creates pain, it is rarely fatal. Either emotional or physical exertion may trigger an attack of angina pectoris.

The lethality and prevalence of CHD has stimulated research from the perspective of all three major paradigms. For example, from the view of the psychosocial paradigm, attempts have been made to identify a *coronary personality*. One significant attempt was begun by Friedman and Rosenman (1959). They concluded that there was a major behavior pattern, called *type A personality*, that was associated with increased incidence of CHD. As compared with their opposites, called *type B personalities*, type A people seem to live as though they were continually under pressure. They have difficulty relaxing and behave as though they are under time demands to complete tasks. Type A individuals seem driven to win at everything they do; they are intensely competitive and losing a game or a business deal often can trigger an inappropriately extreme emotional reaction. Type A people also have difficulty tolerating waiting in lines or for traffic lights. They are in constant motion tapping their fingers, wiggling their legs, or moving from side to side. Their verbal interactions also may be abrupt. Type A individuals are almost always too much in a rush to stop and "smell the roses"; instead they seem to be more interested in accumulating objective indices of their achievements such as awards, money, or property.

Research evidence has lent some support to Friedman and Rosenman's thinking. For example, Suinn (1978) found that type A males in the 39- to 49-year-old age group had six times as many heart attacks as type B males. In an extensive study, Rosenman et al. (1975) followed more than

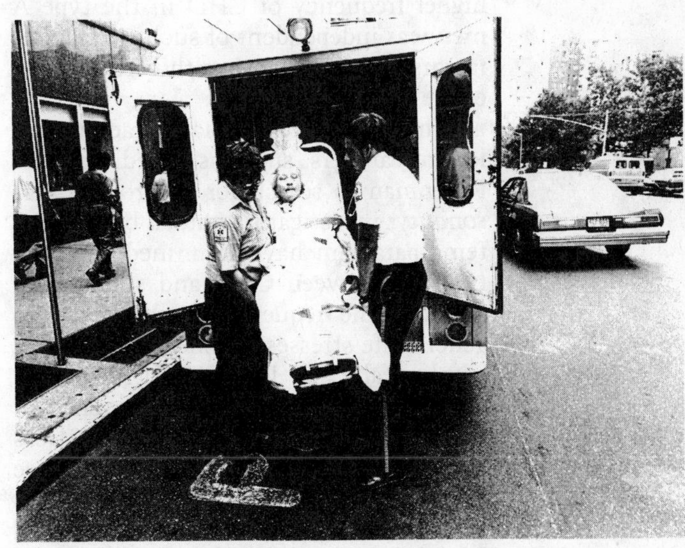

The experience of a heart attack is frightening and affects emotions of survivors for years. (*Michael Weisbrot and Family*)

Type A personalities, who are more prone to have heart disease, seem to be under continual time pressure. (*Michael Weisbrot and Family*)

3000, 39- to 59-year-old men over an 8-year period. Results showed that type A individuals were more than twice as prone to develop coronary heart disease as type B people. Further, in those men who already had evidence of coronary heart disease, type A men were five times as likely to have a second heart attack. Also the higher frequency of CHD in the type A men was independent of such extraneous factors as education, health care, and exercise levels.

While the psychosocial paradigm has led researchers such as Friedman and Rosenman to search for a *coronary personality*, investigators guided by the systems paradigm have examined the relationship between CHD and such social factors as the frequency of and reaction to general life stresses. In one study, for example, Rahe and Lind (1971) reported a relationship between the occurrence of heart attacks and higher rates of life stress as measured by life change units (see Chapter Six). However, their finding was not replicated by Byrne and White (1980) who found no real differences in average life stress between a group of CHD patients and a control group. However, Byrne and White did find that CHD patients interpreted their life events as being more emotionally stressful and reported themselves as significantly more depressed and helpless in response to what happened to them.

The psychosocial and systems perspectives have produced some important insights into the factors contributing to CHD. However, there is a growing belief that a paradigm that integrates biological, psychosocial, and systems perspectives is needed to reflect the true nature of coronary heart disease. In a theory deriving from such an integrated paradigm, Lipowski (1980a) has identified six major factors that appear to be related to the development of coronary heart disease.

1. Dietary factors: Diets that are habitually filled with high levels of saturated fats, cholesterol, and calories (a biological factor).
2. Blood chemistry: Elevated levels of various innate chemicals such as cholesterol (a biological factor).
3. Organ disease or dysfunction: Disorders like kidney disease or diabetes mellitus (a biological factor).
4. Living habits: A deadly trio of smoking, overeating, and physical inactivity (a psychosocial factor).
5. Environmental factors: Chronic dissatisfaction with life and work (a systems factor).
6. Familial factors: A family history of CHD and related disorders (a systems and biological factor).

Although Lipowski's six factors are known to be related to coronary heart disease, their identification has not yet drastically changed people's habits nor decreased the incidence of this disorder. There are many possible reasons for a lack of responsiveness to the factors isolated by Lipowski; people may deny the possibility that the disorder could happen to them, they may be lazy, or they may even have a need to be self-destructive. Regardless of these considerations, however, an integrated paradigm seems to have provided some insight into the causes of CHD.

Just as an integrated paradigm has led to improved understanding of coronary heart disease, it also has led to integrated treatment efforts. One such approach, derived from a combined biological-psychosocial-systems perspective, focuses on helping heart attack patients deal more effectively with their illness. Generally, patients will adopt one of four possible coping responses to their coronary heart disease. In the first response, patients may make a *realistic appraisal* of the damage and realistic attempts at rehabilitation, but in the second response patients may show *excessive dependence* accompanied by anxiety and depression. In other responses, patients may *deny* their illness and attempt to live as though they were never affected, or they may attempt to use the heart attack as a way to *manipulate* others for attention. Because they have a difficult time accepting the seriousness of their illness, many of those hospitalized for coronary heart disease exhibit significant signs of depression and anxiety. Of the more than 2 million annual heart attack victims, about 20 percent cannot return to a normal, productive life for "psychological" reasons (Lipowski, 1975, 1980a).

Support given to both victims and their families during hospitalization can have significant effects on the psychological aspects of coronary heart disease. Brief psychotherapy can shorten the hospital stay considerably by reducing the anxiety and depression surrounding the illness. Likewise, counseling with patients and their families can help make the transition to home a smoother one and lessen the chances for complications while convalescing.

In addition to methods of helping people cope with CHD, some other approaches have been developed to help *prevent* heart disease from beginning or, if present, from worsening. Jenni and Wollersheim (1979) examined 27 men and 15 women classified as type A personalities to evaluate the effectiveness of two types of stress management training. While the two treatments used different methods to reduce tension, one approach utilized muscle relaxation while the other focused on changing attitudes about living, both reduced self-reported anxiety levels effectively.

Essential Hypertension

Unlike the dramatic effects of heart attacks, *essential hypertension* (or chronic high blood pressure) works its destruction insidiously and often without the victim's awareness. It is estimated that of the 23 million people with hypertension, probably half are unaware they have it. Even moderately high blood pressure that

Realization that so many people are unaware of their hypertension has led to various ways to increase public awareness and to make assessment of blood pressure easier. (*Michael Weisbrot and Family*)

persists for an extended time can shorten life expectancy. Further, if people with high blood pressure also smoke or have high cholesterol levels, they increase their risk for a variety of heart and lung diseases that also shorten life expectancy. High blood pressure seems to be more frequent in populations undergoing rapid cultural change, migration, or socioeconomic mobility, and in urban as opposed to rural populations. Although prevalent in all ages and socioeconomic groups, hypertension is present in about twice as many blacks as whites with black males being affected most.

Physiologically, hypertension can result from either an acceleration of the heart rate or constriction of blood vessels; however, the mechanisms by which psychological factors make the heart beat faster or the blood vessels constrict are not clearly understood. The most thoroughly developed theories for hypertension seem to derive from the psychosocial paradigm.

Psychoanalysts believe that people with high blood pressure have few effective outlets for aggressive impulses. According to most psychoanalysts, hypertensive individuals, unlike anxiety state, somatoform, and dissociative patients described in Chapter Ten, may be unable to make efficient use of defenses and must rely on constant, conscious monitoring to control their aggressive impulses.

Some empirical support consistent with the psychoanalytic explanation of hypertension was obtained by Davies (1970), who studied 123 factory workers divided into high, middle, and low blood pressure groups. Davies found that subjects with the lowest blood pressure were more likely to use "neurotic" defenses like fantasy and repression during their childhood. The use of retrospective data spanning many years should lead to some caution in accepting these results. It is difficult enough to make the case that low blood pressure groups tend to use "neurotic" defenses now, let alone trying to conclude what they had done years earlier. However, the results of this study do give researchers a solid direction to turn to.

Also supportive of an analytic explanation is the continuing work of McClelland (1975, 1979), who tested the proposition that suppressed hostility, as measured by inhibited power motivation, played a significant role in the development of high blood pressure. He believed that the difference between people's need to control others (need for power) and their need to be with others (need for affiliation) reflected their tendency to be assertive or angry. McClelland suggested that inhibited power motivation would be related to the development of high blood pressure. In three samples of men varying in age and baseline level of blood pressure, it was found that the inhibited power motive syndrome was associated with significantly higher blood pressure.

In other research based on the psychosocial perspective, Hokanson and his colleagues studied the possibility that inhibition of aggressive impulses was related to hypertension. In a series of studies (Hokanson & Burgess; 1962 Hokanson et al., 1971), an experimental situation was set up in which two subjects were to cooperate in completing a task. In reality, one of the subjects was always a colleague of the experimenter whose function was to engage in behavior that frustrated the subject and hampered the completion of the task. This experimental procedure was successful in raising the subject's blood pressure. Afterwards, the subject was placed in one of a number of experimental situations that differed primarily in the available method of dissipating frustration and thus lowering blood pressure. Hokanson found that, if males could aggress against the source of the frustation (their work partner), their blood pressure usually decreased, but if they could not, it generally remained high. In an interesting sex difference, Hokanson reported that females' blood pressure decreased when they were able to "reward" the source (their work partner) of their frustration.

This apparent sex-related divergence in dealing with the source of frustation led Hokanson to look for some common denominator between the two sexes. He hypothesized that males and females who had lowered their blood pressure had exercised control over the source of their frustration, but had done so in the socially acceptable ways dictated by their sex roles. In an experiment to test this hypothesis, two groups of subjects performed a symbol-matching task in which they were shocked for wrong responses. One group of subjects had control over how many 1-minute rest periods they wanted to take. Their blood pressure was compared with that of a second group of subjects, who were given the same rest period and number of shocks, but had no control over when they could take their rest periods. Consistent with the hypothesis that control over the source of frustration is related to lowered blood pressure, Hokanson found that the group with no control over the occurrence of their rest periods showed higher blood pressure, regardless of sex.

Although Hokanson doesn't deal with long-term effects of frustration on high blood pressure, the results of his studies suggest that if people have to "sit on" their anger for long periods of time, their blood pressure may rise and stay high even after the cause of their frustration has been removed. The suggestion that suppressed anger can raise blood pressure even when the source of frustration is gone may explain why compared with white people, a large proportion of black males are hypertensive. Hokanson's conclusion regarding inhibited anger and high blood pressure are in agreement with the conclusions of black psychiatrists Grier and Cobbs, as reported in their book, *Black Rage* (1968). On the basis of clinical observations and a commitment to a systems paradigmatic explanation for hypertension, these psychiatrists concluded that blacks feel rage at being oppressed by white society. However, since black men's rage has few avenues of socially acceptable expression, it had to be suppressed to protect them from the possible retaliation of white society. Blacks living in unpleasant and unsatisfactory situations, experiencing feelings of rage they cannot express, should be especially vulnerable to developing hypertension. In support of this systems-derived hypothesis, research results suggest that it may be race and not membership in a lower social class that seems to be related to hypertension. For example, a study of people in the city of Detroit (Gentry et al., 1973) selected "high-stress" and "low-stress" areas of the city. White males and black males were compared within each area, thus controlling for social class. It was found that when environmental stress was low, white and black

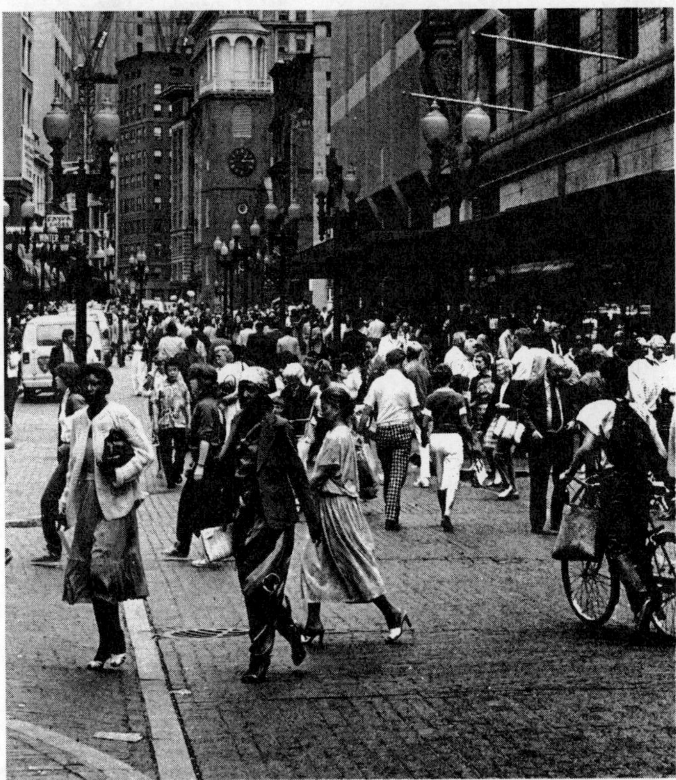

Todays high pressure society creates anger and stress that is assumed to be involved in the development of hypertension. (© *Richard Wood 1984/Taurus Photos*)

males did not differ in blood pressure; but in the high-stress areas, black males had significantly higher average blood pressure than white males. Only further work can resolve whether it is uniquely systems-derived or caused in some part by genetic predispositions for blacks to develop hypertension.

In addition to theories deriving from the psychosocial and systems views, some researchers guided by the biological paradigm have suggested that there may be genetic predispositions for the development of hypertension. Consistent with such reasoning, Hodapp et al. (1975) proposed that hypertensives inherently overreact to novel situations. They found that hypertensive patients showed increased blood pressure when working on a difficult cognitive task as well as when they were viewing some slides of pleasant landscapes. Normal control subjects showed increased blood pressure only when they were completing the stressful tasks. Consistent with this finding was work showing that air traffic controllers who showed inherently greater blood pressure reactivity to their work situation were more likely to develop hypertension later (Rose et al., 1978). From the biological perspective, inherent hypersensitivity and overreactivity may predispose certain people to develop high blood pressure when under stress.

Although the most well-developed and researched explanations of essential hypertension derive from the psychosocial and systems paradigms, treatment of the disorder is largely based on a biological perspective. However, while drug treatment is most common, it may be combined with early detection and psychosocially based counseling to produce an integrated intervention program.

One possible treatment application of the psychosocial perspective is the use of operant-conditioning techniques to help people obtain control over their blood pressure. In one study (Benson et al., 1971), seven patients who were hypertensive completed 22 training sessions in which they were attached to biofeedback machines that gave a certain tone when blood pressure was reduced. Subjects were told to try to make the machine produce the tone reflecting the lowered blood pressure. All but one subject showed a decrease in blood pressure after training.

Other therapists guided by the psychosocial view examined the effects of *anxiety managment training* and relaxation training in reducing levels of hypertension. Jorgensen et al. (1981) assigned male patients who had been diagnosed as having essential hypertension before the age of 55 to an anxiety management training program or a waiting-list control group. In the initial phase of anxiety managment training, subjects were taught deep muscle relaxation. Later in the training process the subjects received structured rehearsal in using relaxation skills to cope with feelings of stress. At the end of treatment, the subjects were instructed in how to use tension as a cue for applying their relaxation-based coping skills in real-life situations. Those subjects who had received anxiety-management training showed a decrease in base level blood pressure. Follow-up showed that not only was there satisfactory maintenance of reduced blood pressure level, but actual reductions in the already lowered blood pressure as well.

Gastrointestinal Disorders

Like the cardiovascular system, the gastrointestinal (GI) system is a common channel through which people express their emotions. It is thus also a primary site for possible psychophysiologial disorders. While any part of the GI system can be affected by psychological factors, two of the more prevalent and destructive disorders are ulcers of the stomach and inflammation of the colon (colitis).

Ulcers

Ulcers of the stomach and duodenum are among the best known psychophysiological disorders. While sometimes the topic of jokes about overworked and driven businessmen, the following personal experience of a vivacious, popular college student demonstrates that ulcers can attack anyone and are no laughing matter.

Personal Experience: Ulcers

What its like to have an ulcer—Stage I, finding out. I was 16 years old when I went to the doctor because of these terrific stomachaches I was getting. No matter what I ate, drank, or thought about resulted in a stomachache that not even Maalox could handle. I was just your basic nervous kid who let everything bother her. I was very sports-oriented and competition and tryouts and such didn't help matters any. And I always got all As and had to be the best—No.1! Needing to have both an upper and lower GI series of tests made me a nervous wreck. I had heard a lot about the tests and they were worse than I ever imagined. I cried and vomited through it all. The only other thing I remember is the doctors and nurses who, while they were performing the tests, kept whispering ". . . and she's only 16 years old. . . ."

I was put on a very bland diet which didn't last long because "heaven forbid" it made me gain weight! The medication was no fun either. I stuck with that for a year or so and have stayed with extra-strength Maalox ever since.

Stage II—Dealing with "it." "It" is a combination of problems with my stomach and my nervous system. "It" works in strange, invisible ways. I don't feel nervous, yet my foot shakes underneath the table. Some people just call me "hyper." I don't feel nervous, yet I have no patience with people who can't keep up with me or understand me. I don't feel nervous or upset, yet the slightest comment or action from someone can release a flood of tears. My emotions run high—I don't often yell or scream or stomp my feet . . . I wring my hands and usually cry. Or else food that goes in goes right through or comes right back up—that's all—simple as that.

I'm destined for a life of never slowing down or being able to take it easy—I don't have time for that—I've gotta move on—I drive a lot of people crazy—mostly my mother.

An ulcer gets in the way of having a normal day. Just when things get a little out of hand and things don't go your way—something inside gets triggered and doubles the uneasiness. You tend to get impatient and short with people even when you don't want to. You can't put things off to another day hoping you'll feel better—you could wait a long time.

An ulcer gets in the way of ever being an optimist. You can't! Something is bound to go wrong. You're nervous about big things, little things, and sometimes nothing at all and you don't know why. An ulcer can very easily make you into a complainer because the hurt is sometimes so constant that you lose sleep for days. You can't concentrate and you really can't explain to people what it feels like so they'll never know. It's frustrating! . . . and no one likes a complainer . . . that's more frustrating.

An ulcer gets in the way of ever eating like a "normal" person. If you splurge on too much of anything "good," you're reminded of it almost immediately that day and the next. A Friday night date to the movies, then pizza . . . Nope! A tall glass of OJ after a run or for breakfast . . . Nope! So you attempt to put up with it and OD on Maalox or something similar. I think it's almost impossible in this day and age to actually take care of yourself as you should having an ulcer without becoming a recluse within your social and working worlds!

An ulcer is an inflammation or opening in the lining of the stomach wall that has been produced by excess amounts of gastric secretions. Gastric secretions primarily are made up of *mucous*, which protects the stomach lining, *pepsin*, which breaks down proteins, and *hydrochloric acid*, which aids in digestion. In the development of an ulcer, gastric secretions (especially pepsin) may be produced in amounts well beyond what is needed to digest food adequately, and the excess secretion destroys stomach-lining tissue (Weiss, 1977).

Because they work under continual stress, air traffic controllers are prime candidates for a variety of psychophysiological disorders. (*Jacques Bourgeois/Taurus Photos*)

Recently, Cheren and Knapp (1980) suggested that gastric and duodenal ulcers may have different etiologies. Compared with gastric ulcers which tend to appear during the sixth decade, duodenal ulcers occur most frequently when the people are in their 40s and 50s. As well as appearing earlier, duodenal ulcers more frequently are found in lower social classes and in more women than men. Explanations for the development of ulcers have been derived primarily from the biological and psychosocial paradigms. Biological theories focus on innate physical differences in people, while psychosocial theories emphasize the effects of conflict and stress.

The predisposing biological condition for an ulcer is thought to be acquired genetically. For example, it has been found that compared with normal controls people with certain types of ulcers have larger, hypersecreting stomachs and produce more acids and pepsins (Cheren & Knapp, 1980; Weiner, 1977). It appears, then, that the biological conditions necessary for the creation of an ulcer may be present long before the ulcer actually forms. This partly explains why, when two people experience the same degree of stress, only one may develop an ulcer.

While there is a modicum of evidence for a genetic contribution to the development of ulcers, much more is known of the psychosocial factors involved. Evidence has been gathered from research with animals as well as people. Research with animals has shown that conflict situations can be related to increased acid production which in turn leads to generally higher frequency of stomach disturbances. Devised first by Sawrey (1961), a basic ulcer-producing procedure entailed placing rats in a situation where they were shocked every time they attempted to eat or drink. Present-day refinements of this procedure can cause an ulcer in certain kinds of rats in as little as 6 hours (Wald et al., 1973). Supporting what is known about ulcers in humans, autopsies of rats subjected to ulcer-producing procedures show that their ulcers seem to be caused by a higher percentage of pepsin in the gastric secretions.

The cause of oversecretion of pepsin in higher animals such as primates and people is still largely unknown, but one hypothesis is that only specific kinds of stress may produce destructive kinds of acid production. An animal experiment often cited in support of the specific stress view was completed by Brady (1958). Brady had two monkeys sit next to each other in restraining chairs. Both monkeys received electric shock, but only one, called the *executive monkey*, could prevent the shock from occurring to both monkeys by pressing a lever. The other monkey also had a lever, but it had no effect on whether the shock occurred. Both monkeys received the same number of shocks. After 23 days of such experience, the executive monkey died. An autopsy revealed that he had developed a severe ulcer. A subsequent autopsy of his partner monkey showed him to be ulcer-free. The results of Brady's experiment were quoted in the popular press, for it was easy for the layperson to see the similarity between the stress placed on the so called executive monkey and the stress experienced by the human business executive. Seligman (1975), however, criticized Brady's results on methodological grounds. He pointed out that, in Brady's procedure, the more active monkey was likely to become the executive monkey; and the monkey that was more active might also be more prone to develop ulcers. Further, in contrast to Brady's findings, Seligman has found that, in higher animals, those subjects who do not have control of aversive stimuli are more likely to develop ulcers.

Other psychosocial paradigm-generated work done with human subjects also suggests that specific types of emotions may be related to ulcer production. Observations pertinent to human ulcer production have been gathered fortuitously from people who have suffered accidents. Wolf and Wolff (1947) had a "ringside seat" to observe what was going on in one man's stomach. At the age of 9, the man had drunk some scalding hot soup that burned out the end of his esophagus. Some time later, physicians attempted to insert a tube into his stomach so he could be fed, but the operation had to be stopped because the patient was in danger of dying. The incomplete operation left the man with a large hole through which part of his stomach protruded. Amazingly, the patient adjusted fairly well to such inconvenience. He reportedly first chewed his food for taste and then deposited it into a funnel that carried the food down a rubber tube into his stomach. The patient worked at a hospital and, in return for his medical care, he allowed doctors to observe his stomach activity. From observations of the man's stomach, Wolf and Wolff learned that the type of stomach secretions varied depending on the kinds of emotions the man was experiencing. When he was angry, there was an oversecretion of gastric fluids; when he was sad or otherwise emotionally aroused, lesser amounts of fluid were produced. The association between anger and ulcers is similar to that

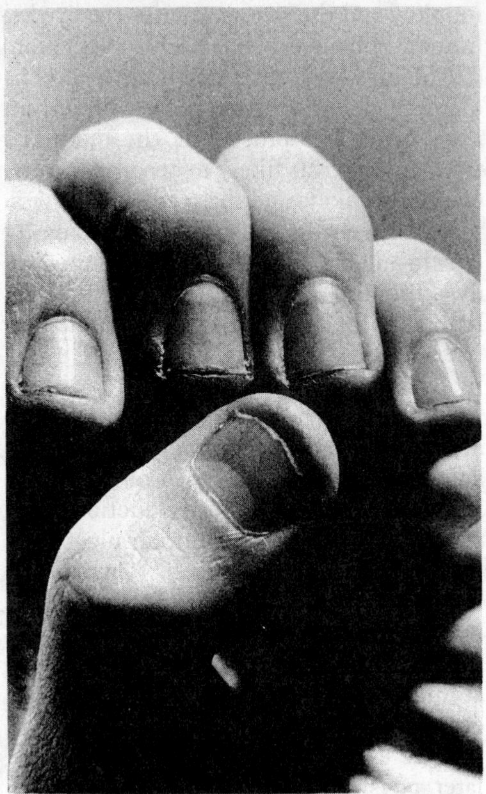
Suppressed anger and its resultant tension can be shown in several ways. (*Van Bucher/ Photo Researchers, Inc.*)

found between anger and other psychophysiological disorders.

The psychosocial paradigm in the form of psychoanalytic theory suggests that separation from parents might create the kinds of stress that translate into peptic ulcers. To investigate this possibility, Ackerman et al. (1981) used information from hospital records, tape-recorded admission interviews, and follow-up questionnaires to assess whether adolescents who were separated from their parents were more prone to develop peptic ulcers. In support of this relationship more adolescent-aged peptic ulcer patients were found to have experienced separation from parents in the year prior to admission compared with appendicitis patients.

Like the explanations offered for their development, treatment for ulcers reflects psychosocial and biological perspectives. In one study (Brown & Richards, 1980) patients with duodenal ulcers were taught to manage anxiety and to express negative emotions appropriately. Eleven of the 22 male patients who had confirmed x-ray diagnosis of duodenal ulcers completed this training in eight 75-minute sessions over a 2-week period. The other 11 patients received an attention placebo treatment. Those patients who had received training consumed less antacid, reported fewer days of symptomatic pain, and experienced less severe symptoms over the entire follow-up period. In fact, after 3½ years, the treatment group did show a significantly lower rate of ulcers.

Although psychotherapy may be effective in helping people handle stress more adequately, it probably doesn't directly change underlying inherited physiological predispositions; that is, on a genetic basis, people who tend to hypersecrete stomach acids probably will be most vulnerable to developing ulcers when stressed. In light of this, people who develop ulcers should be made aware of the possibility that proneness to ulcers doesn't necessarily reflect a psychosocial defect or weakness; it may simply be the result of chronic gastric hyperactivity over which they have no control.

Colitis

Less well known and studied than stomach ulcers, *colitis* can be just as painful and potentially as damaging a gastrointestinal disorder. There are two kinds of colitis, mucous colitis and ulcerative colitis. In *mucous colitis*, the mucous lining of the colon is dissolved and the patient may experience pain whenever eating or eliminating. To avoid such discomfort, people with mucous colitis typically eat less and, as a result, may become tired, listless, run-down, and irritable. In *ulcerative colitis*, an ulcer forms in the mucous membrane of the colon, causing bleeding. It is a disorder that occurs most frequently between the ages of 30 and 50 and is more common among Jews, whites, urban dwellers, and members of the higher socioeconomic levels.

The psychosocial paradigm is most often applied to the study of colitis. Engel (1975) describes colitis patients as neat and orderly, with an almost "uncanny perception of hostility or rejecting attitudes on the part of others" (p. 1645). In addition, he sees colitis patients as frequently having a dependent relationship with one key person, most often a parent, and few, if any, other satisfying or deep relationships.

From the psychoanalytic perspective, the mother is extremely important in determining whether a person will develop colitis. In some cases of colitis, patients have a close, almost symbiotic relationship to their mother's feelings and needs. Typically, in the patient's family the father may be unable to stand up to his wife and cannot protect his child from her. In the person who already has either a genetic or prenatal potential to develop some form of inflammatory bowel disease, these family-generated stresses may produce colitis (McKegney et al., 1970).

Treatment methods for colitis derive primarily from the psychosocial and biological paradigms and include psychoanalytic psychotherapy and drugs. Drug treatment, however, is primarily directed at reducing symptoms and not at remediating the underlying cause. In psychoanalytic therapy on the other hand, the therapist seeks to become the "key" person in the colitis patient's life and through this relationship to help the patient learn new, more effective ways of relating to people, thereby changing the course of the colitis.

In a thorough study of the effects of psychotherapy on ulcerative colitis patients, Karush and his colleagues conducted a 30 year follow-up of people who had received various combinations of treatment involving psychotherapy and medical and surgical procedures (Karush et al., 1977). They found that patients who had received psychotherapy were more improved than others.

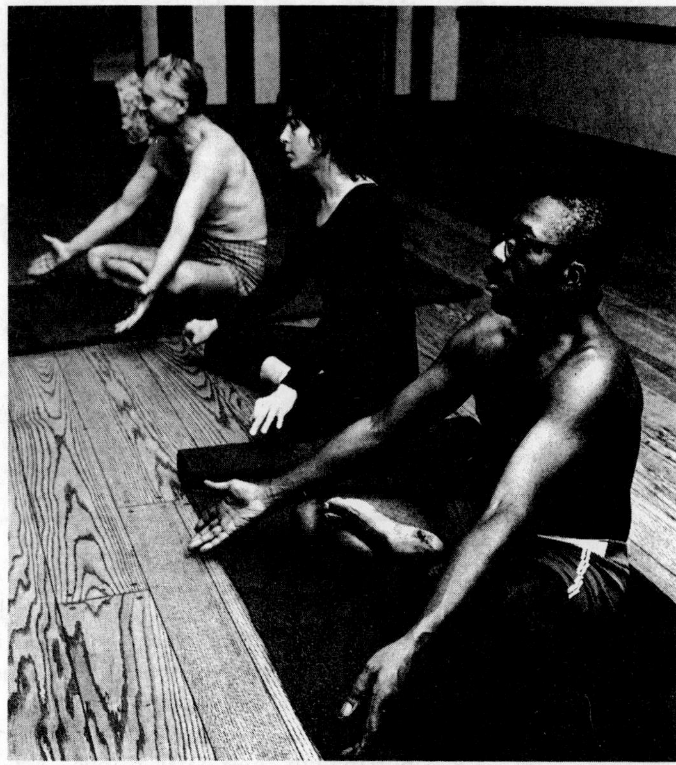

Learning to relax is one way to offset the debilitating effects of stress. (*Nancy Hays/Monkmeyer Press Photo Service*)

If psychosocial methods and drugs don't calm the colon, then surgery may be indicated. Surgical treatment of colitis usually involves an *ileostomy* (making an opening in the ileum which is the lowest part of the small intestine leading to the large intestine) or a *colectomy* (removal of all or part of the colon or large intestine leading to the rectum). Surgery is suggested only if there is intractable diarrhea or the threat of further disease such as cancer.

Respiratory Disorders

Although they are not as lethal as cardiovascular disorders nor as common as digestive disorders, psychophysiological respiratory disorders affect a significant number of people. Respiratory disorders may take the form of hyperventilation, dyspnea, and asthma. *Hyperventilation*, or overbreathing, is most clearly a consequence of anxiety. Individuals who overbreathe may begin to feel light-headed, dizzy, and tingly in their hands and feet. Often, these frightening behavioral sensations tend to make people even more anxious. Shortness of breath, or *dyspnea*, most often is also of psychogenic origin, but it occurs in cardiac and pulmonary conditions as well.

In *asthma*, the airways of the throat and lungs constrict. The airways may be narrowed by increased sensitivity to substances ingested or inhaled, by bacterial infection, or by stress. Asthma attacks usually are characterized by *wheezing* and *rales* (whistling sounds made when air is expired) and can be very frightening events as shown in the following personal experience.

Personal Experience: Asthma

I had asthma as a child. I no longer have asthma attacks, but I can remember quite vividly what they were like. One attack I remember especially clearly because it took place just before my seventh birthday party. My mother was getting everything in readiness for the party. My friends from school were going to come over at 4 o'clock, and I was putting out their party things . . . you know, the plates and favors and decorations. About quarter to 4—I remember the time because I was asking my mother the time at 5-minute intervals—I suddenly began to have a hard time catching my breath. The more I tried to take a deep breath the less I was able to succeed. I stopped and sat down and tried to take a breath and found that I could not; no matter how hard I tried to get that breath that I needed to feel like I was getting enough air, I could not. I began to gasp. My mother was in the kitchen and so did not know my plight. I felt really frightened at that point . . . all alone, unable to get any air. My gasps became louder and more labored, and that's when my mother heard me and came rushing into the room. By that time I was on the floor and if my mother's expression was any indication of how I looked, I must have looked bad. By the time the emergency police van arrived I was nearly blue and making the most horrible noises. I remember them and so does my mother to this day. The feeling of being able to breathe again after the oxygen was given to me was absolutely wonderful. I was so tired, though, that I slept on the way to the hospital. It's funny, even telling you this, you know makes my palms sweat and makes me feel very uncomfortable.

The asthma experience as observed by outsiders can also be very stressful. In the experience that follows, the mother of the person whose personal experience was just presented gives her impressions of the same event.

Personal Experience: Observing an Asthma Attack

I can remember that seventh birthday very clearly. My son had trouble with asthma up until he was about 10 or 11 but he never had a worse attack than that one on his birthday. I remember hearing those horrible wheezing and whistling sounds even though I was at the opposite end of the house getting things ready for the party. I thought he was dying. I dropped an entire tray of dishes and rushed as fast as I could to his bedroom. He was on the floor, thrashing about like he was having a seizure. His face was turning blue and his eyes were bulging out as he fought for breath. I can still remember how he sounded . . . it was terrible. I felt so helpless. I tried to comfort him but I'm sure my voice carried my fears rather than calmness to my son. I called the emergency number, but I can't remember to this day whether I left him or took him with me to make the call. The time between the call and help arriving seemed like hours even though I was told it was only 6 minutes. I was so afraid I was going to lose my son. I'll never forget how he sounded and looked.

Asthma occurs three times more frequently in male than female children, but this difference decreases in adults past the age of 45 (Weiner, 1980). Rees (1980) reported that nearly half of the cases of asthma began before puberty with 38 percent occurring before the age of 5.

There are at least two main forms of the disease—the *extrinsic* (caused by external factors like allergies or bacteria) and the *intrinsic* (caused by internal psychological factors). Rees (1980) estimates that about 40 percent of all cases are caused by extrinsic, allergic factors. While extrinsic asthma tends to develop before the age of 40, intrinsic asthma more often occurs in those people over the age of 40 who have no hereditary or allergic components in their etiological history.

In large measure, because it consists of frightening symptoms and strikes at all ages, asthma has generated a great deal of theoretical interest. Research has been generated by each of the three major paradigms and by an integration of their perspectives.

Working from the psychosocial paradigm, psychodynamic theorists postulate that asthma may be caused by an uncon-

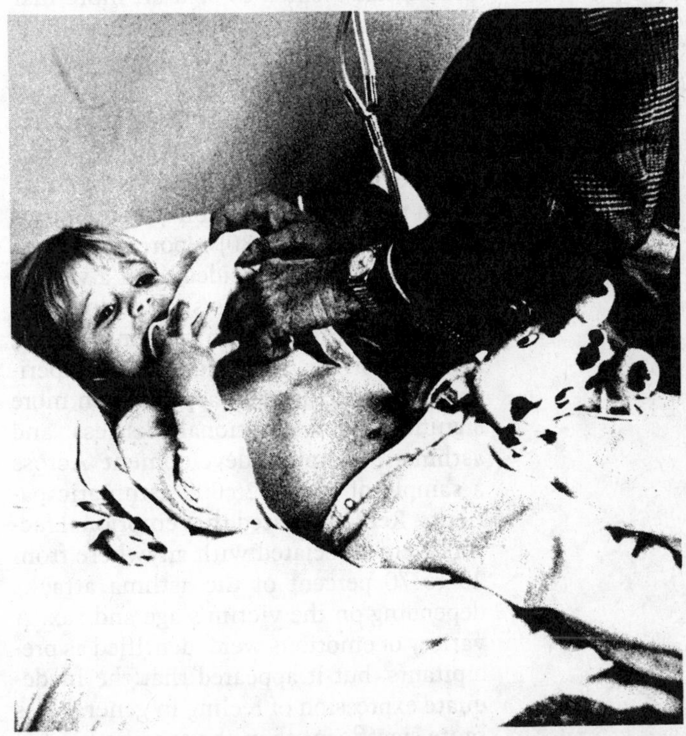

In asthma attacks the airways of the throat and lungs constrict. Medical intervention may be necessary to restore breathing. (© *Ed Lettau 1976/Photo Researchers, Inc.*)

scious fear of loss of the mother. For example, based on the findings of a study of 27 asthmatic patients undergoing psychoanalytic treatment, it was concluded that the central emotional component of asthma was the repressed cry for the lost mother (Alexander, 1952). Other analytic researchers believed that the major emotions prior to an asthma attack may be anger or anxiety caused by the loss of the "mothering one" (Knapp et al., 1970). Rees (1980) found a higher incidence of anxiety states compared with controls in both children and adult samples. However, in another investigation, Graham et al. (1967) studied the personality structure of a large population of 9- to 11-year-old children. Although psychiatric difficulties were more frequent in asthmatics than in physically normal children, these symptoms were no more frequent than in children who were normal but suffered from some other "physical" disorder. In essence, asthmatics seemed to be a bit more maladjusted and nervous than those who weren't asthmatic, but they possessed no unique set of "asthmatic" personality characteristics (Rees, 1980; Tamarin, 1963; Van der Valk, 1960).

Other psychological variables appear to play a role in the initiation of some forms of asthma. Rees (1980) reported that the onset of asthma coincided with a variety of psychosocial stresses such as loss of a significant other person, accidents to self, school worries, and frightening experiences. The relationship appears even more significant for emotional distress and asthmatic symptom development. Across a sample of nearly 25,000 asthmatic patients, Rees estimated that emotional factors were associated with anywhere from 20 to 70 percent of the asthma attacks depending on the victim's age and sex. A variety of emotions were identified as precipitants, but it appeared that the inadequate expression of feeling in general was more significant than the specific kind of emotion not expressed.

The systems perspective has led researchers to focus less on individual personality traits than on family patterns in asthmatic people. Thus, parental overprotection, overt rejection, and perfectionism have been associated with asthmatic patients (Cheren & Knapp, 1980). It could be that having a "sick" child would elicit these parental behaviors, but after reviewing data on 25,000 asthma patients, Rees (1980) concluded that parental attitudes could not be explained as a reaction to a child with asthma in most cases. Lipscomb and Parker (1979) found that parents of asthmatic children were perceived as being more overprotective of these "sick children" than they were of their siblings. Notably, Lipscomb and Parker implied that it was overprotectiveness in the father and not the mother that was associated with asthmatic symptoms.

Instead of focusing on personality traits or family factors, researchers guided by the biological paradigm look for causes of asthma in such areas as central nervous system functioning. For instance, some biological explanations have linked asthma to abnormal brain wave patterns as measured by electroencephalograms (EEGs). Although some investigators believe the abnormal EEG readings mean that asthma may be related to a specific nervous system defect, most investigators don't yet know how. However, most agree that the nerve center controlling respiratory activity may become hyperexcited for some unknown reason, triggering asthmatic behavior. Asthma attacks could be prevented if these hyperactive nerve centers could be quieted. The fact that drugs calming these nerve centers also reduce the number and intensity of asthma attacks is taken as support for the involvement of the nervous system (Weiner, 1980).

While each of the three major paradigms has been applied to asthma, none has been totally satisfactory. Thus, as could be expected, integrated approaches have been tried. In one integrated approach, it is assumed that both psychosocial and biological theories are accurate and that asthma may be produced in more than one way. Among the earliest of the integrative theorists, Rees (1964) proposed three major causes of asthma: an "allergic" cause (a biological sensitivity to substances such as dust), an "infective" cause (infectious diseases), and a "psychosocial" cause (emotional instigators like anxiety, anger, or tension). Each of these three causes is believed to be responsible for a significant proportion of asthmatic disorders. In a similar vein, another integrative theorist, Teirmea (1979) after studying 100 adult asthmatics, concluded that the biological, psychosocial, and systems etiological factors interacted in a complex fashion to produce asthmatic symptoms.

Also reflecting successful integration of paradigms, treatments for asthmatic behavior generally have derived from the psychosocial and biological perspectives. Working from the perspective of a combined psychosocial-biological paradigm, Phillip et al. (1971) investigated the differential effects of hypnotism and relaxation training on ease of breathing in asthmatics. These researchers assumed that asthmatic people could be separated into groups based on the different triggering mechanisms for their asthmatic attacks. They reasoned that psychosocial treatment in the form of hypnotism would be more effective in changing respiratory behavior of those subjects who had a psychosocial cause for their asthma attacks than for those subjects who had an infective cause. As they hypothesized, asthmatics who didn't respond to skin-testing for an allergic basis for their symptoms were more responsive to suggestion and behavioral relaxation procedures than others. In addition, Phillip et al. found that, regardless of the triggering source, most asthmatics were helped by relaxation training in terms of gains in respiratory efficiency. By helping to break up the vicious circle of perceived shortness of breath, tension, feelings of loss of control, and fear, and back to shortness of breath, relaxation training may help asthmatics gain some control over the occurrence, or at least the severity, of attacks (Kotses et al., 1976).

All researchers are not so impressed with relaxation training, however. Erskine-Millis and Schonell (1981) reviewed a number of studies and concluded that muscular relaxation therapy alone appears to have little effect on asthmatic people. It did appear though, based on their review, that certain mental relaxation techniques such as transcendental meditation, systematic desensitization, and biofeedback-assisted relaxation produced a variety of positive changes such as increased ease of respiration and feelings of well-being. King (1980), however, sounds a clear note of caution regarding the effects of behavioral interventions. He suggested that the "efficacy of such intervention strategies for asthmatic children is in doubt . . . and that intervenors should seek to develop mulifaceted treatment programs built around the individual case" (p. 169).

Headache

While not all people will experience the distress of ulcers or suffer through an asthma or heart attack, almost everyone has experienced headaches caused by psychosocial factors. An important examination, a baby crying, or a boring neighbor are only a few of the many potential causes of headaches. Most headaches may be classified as *muscle-contraction headaches* and are caused by sustained tension in the skeletal muscles of the scalp, shoulders, neck, and face. The muscle-contraction headache may be part of the price of living in a high-powered society, but it has been the subject of limited research. Far more research and theoretical interest has been directed toward a less fre-

While nearly all of us have experienced a headache, the symptoms of a migraine are much more severe and long lasting. (*Mimi Forsyth/Monkmeyer Press Photo Service*)

quent, but a far more serious, painful, and disabling kind of headache, the *migraine*.

More correctly called a vascular headache of the migraine type, the migraine typically has the following symptom pattern:

1. Recurrent throbbing pain, usually on one side of the head at onset
2. Nausea, vomiting, and irritability at the height of the headache attack
3. Temporary visual disorders preceding the headache
4. A history of migraine headaches in the immediate family
5. Dizziness, sweating, and other vasomotor disorders
6. Positive response to administration of the drug ergotamine tartrate if given early in attack
7. Variable duration, but usually 2 to 8 hours.

The following personal experience demonstrates how much more serious a migraine headache is compared with the more common muscle-contraction headaches.

Personal Experience: Migraine Headaches

I'm describing how it used to be when I had an incapacitating migraine (while I still get headaches, they're no longer severe enough to be incapacitating). The pain was confined to my right temple and would radiate outward from there. Any movement of my head or exposure to light or noise would amplify the pain. Consequently, I was forced to lie down in a dark and quiet room for hours at a time—often 6 to 8 hours—unable to sleep. Occasionally, I would drift into sleep but awaken with the headache still there. I am fortunate in that I do not suffer concomitant nausea and vomiting, a frequent complaint.

The forced inactivity in a dark, silent place tended to produce feelings of frustration, depression, and occasionally intense self-pity. These feelings were especially likely when the attacks clustered within a short period of time, which often they did. When the headache at last disappeared, I felt absolutely flat—great fatigue and no emotion. I would sleep a dreamless sleep—sort of a "sleep of the dead."

The National Migraine Foundation (1980) estimates that there are nearly 12 million individuals who suffer from the kind of headache described in the personal experience above. When one adds to this number the more than 42 million others who suffer from other types of headaches, the extensiveness of this symptom complex becomes clear. In fact, Delozier and Gagnon (1975) estimate that over 1 year's time, headaches accounted for 12,314,000 visits to physicians' offices. Seventy percent of these visits were made by women and 80 percent by whites as opposed to other racial groups. Migraines typically begin about age 20 but the symptoms have been reported in children as young as 7 years old (Vahlquist, 1955). Generally, people experience from one to four migraine attacks per month with each attack lasting anywhere from 4 to 24 hours. A variety of precipitating factors for migraine headaches have been identified. For instance, emotions, visual glare (such as found in a flickering light or television), foods, and oral contraceptives have been implicated as precipitants.

Efforts to explain migraine headaches have been guided by the biological and psychosocial perspectives as well as by at least one attempt at a paradigm integrating the two. Biological explanations for migraine headaches are most often focused on vascular activity. The vascular explanation of migraine headaches states that pain-sensitive extracranial arteries dilate and cause intense discomfort. However, there is other work suggesting that it is the constriction of these same arteries, especially the carotid artery, that causes the pain of the migraine. In any case, the flow of blood through the cranial arteries seems to be implicated as the major cause of the pain experienced by the migraine sufferer. These vessels constrict or dilate in response to the release of biochemical substances such as serotonin and histamine. The mechanisms by which these chemical substances are released is not entirely clear, but researchers espousing a psychosocial paradigm have proposed some answers.

There has been substantial documentation of the role of psychosocial factors in the etiology of migraine headaches. Kolb (1963b) described a typical migraine-headache victim as a tense, driving, obsessional perfectionist with an inflexible personality maintaining a store of bottled-up resentments that can neither be expressed nor resolved. Consistent with the description, when asked to report the circumstances preceding their migraine attacks, many victims state that they were in an emotionally stressful situation and felt tremendous amounts of rage. Harrison's (1974) review of studies of migraine headaches also concluded that unexpressed anger was involved in the disorder. In an attempt to find empirical support for a psychosocial explanation of migraine headaches, Henryk-Gutt and Rees (1973) compared office workers who had migraine headaches with those who did not. They found that migraine sufferers "subjectively" experienced more symptoms of emotional distress than controls, but they didn't differ in the degree of real-life stresses that were objectively assessed.

Although there is little argument with the conclusion that psychological stresses can be a significant precipitant of migraine attacks, there is some reason to believe that migraine subjects may be predisposed by constitutional, and not environmental, factors. In his synthesis of the biological and psychosocial paradigmatic perspectives, Wolff (cited in Dalessio, 1972) postulates that individuals who have a genetic predisposition or vulnerability toward migraine headaches are more likely to respond to stress with headaches than people not as inherently predisposed.

Integrated approaches such as that of Wolff have led to therapeutic views that migraine headaches are due to an interaction of a learned overreaction to stress with an inherited hypersensitivity of the cranial nerves and arteries. In light of this interaction, treatment of migraine headaches typically focuses on both the biological and the psychosocial components of the etiological pattern. Some of the more successful, but primarily symptomatic, biological treatments for migraines are tranquilizers, antidepressant drugs, histamine desensitization, surgery, and special diets. However, the most effective biological treatment for migraine headaches has been the administration of ergotamine tartrate and its derivatives (trade name, Cafergot or Migral). Administration of ergotamine tartrate early in the migraine-headache attack usually restores the dilated vessels to their original state and reduces the severity of the headache. Some attempts have been made to find drugs that would prevent headaches, but few have been found that seem to be worth the danger, the side-effects, or the risk of addiction (see Cutler et al., 1976; Medina & Diamond, 1977).

Of all the biological approaches, variants of biofeedback procedures also seem to hold much promise. Holroyd et al. (1980) compared EMG biofeedback training with psychotherapy or a symptom monitoring control group. Only the biofeedback procedure effectively reduced headache symptoms. The efficacy of biofeedback procedures was further established by Andrasi and Holroyd (1980), Cram (1980), and Anderson et al. (1981) who used a variety of techniques to lessen the pain brought about by migraine headaches. These results reinforce the conclusions of Adams et al. (1980) that "a biofeedback approach directed at modifying the peripheral pain mechanism in migraine appears to be a promising treatment technique for this disorder" (p. 217).

From the psychosocial perspective, behavior modification has been advocated by some as a treatment for headaches (Philips & Hunter, 1981). Behavioral techniques are based on the assumption that, if a person could relax in response to the cues that a migraine headache was developing, this might lessen the response of the endocrine and autonomic neurons. Using a population of 17 migraine-headache sufferers, Mitchell and Mitchell (1973) found that pitting relaxation against the tension of migraine-headache cues was successful in reducing the number and duration of migraine episodes. In fact, after reviewing a large number of studies, Adams et al. (1980) concluded that "hypnotic intervention, relaxation training, various behavior therapy techniques, and thermal and blood volume pulse biofeedback appear to significantly alter migraine activity" (p. 221).

Concluding Comments

Some investigators have attempted to meet the challenge presented by psychophysiological disorders by developing integrative paradigms. However, these new perspectives have had relatively little impact. At present, psychophysiological disorders account for nearly one-third of all work days lost to "illness." Despite being the focus of study for over a century, rather than decreasing, psychophysiological disorders have increased especially among women and children (Alexander, 1975). Recent research has revealed that, besides the traditional disorders discussed in this chapter, an entire new variety of diseases may be added to the classification of "psychological disorders affecting physical conditions." Called *auto-immune disorders*, they refer to diseases that result from a breakdown of the natural immune systems of the body that protect it from the invasion of dangerous disease entities. Without the protection of this system, infectious diseases could fatally attack people. Recent discovery of and publicity surrounding *auto-immune deficiency syndrome* (AIDS) has focused even more attention on a group of disorders that includes rheumatoid arthritis, psoriasis, and pernicious anemia. Psychological stress appears to play an important role in the development of these diseases (Hall, 1983). Perhaps the 1980s will see an intensified study of the possibility that these, as well as other seemingly physiologically caused diseases, may have significant psychological components. If so, the need for more complex paradigms to guide researchers and clinicians will become all the more intense.

Summary Chart

Among the physical conditions affected by psychological factors are patterns of actual physical disease either produced by or exacerbated by emotional and behavioral conditions. We first examined the theories concerning why a particular physical system falls prey to such disorders:

Weak organ theory

Inherited predisposition to stress

Personality type may be associated with symptom type

We then examined a number of forms which the so called psychophysiological disorders may take:

Heart disease: Type A/type B personality, coronary personality, biological, psychosocial, and systems factors

Essential hypertension: Chronic high blood pressure, a neurotic defense, suppressed aggression

Gastrointestinal disorders: Ulcers (genetic basis, stress-related), colitis (psychosocial factors, seems to respond well to treatment)

Respiratory disorders: Hyperventilation, dyspnea, asthma (related to family patterns, related to CNS functioning, helped by relaxation training and medication)

Headaches: Muscle contraction, migraines (stress-related, helped by relaxation and medication)

CHAPTER 12

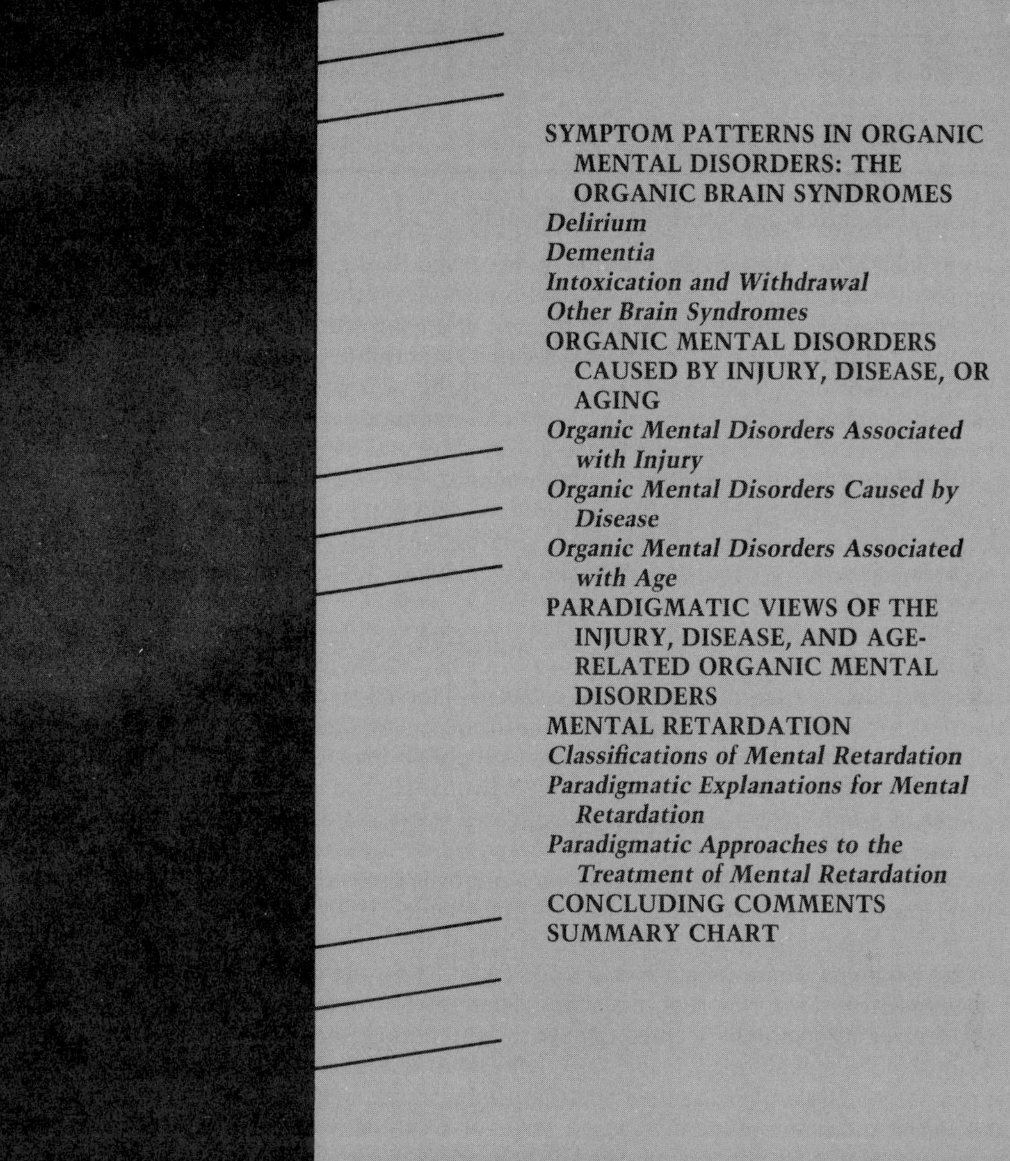

The Injury, Disease, and Age-related Organic Mental Disorders and Mental Retardation

Personal Experience: Organic Mental Disorder

Uncle Dave was keenly intelligent. He loved to engage in mental games, debated any issue, and concerned himself with the intellectual development of us children. He was the son of a fruit peddler who, through hard work and much ability, became the head of a flourishing law firm. Not only was Uncle Dave smart, but he was precise and exacting with a rigid sense of appropriate and inappropriate behavior. He and Aunt Gracie appeared to have a very solid and happy marriage with clearly defined roles that they both enjoyed and fostered: Aunt Gracie, the charming hostess, busy volunteer, and doting mother—Uncle Dave, the benevolent despot who lovingly issued orders in accordance with his prudish reality and gave advice, both solicited and unsolicited.

Five years ago, I visited him after not having seen him for over 6 years. He still looked healthy and dapper, but his whole manner had changed. Rather than discussing and debating, Uncle Dave repeated stories three and four times that, at least to me, seemed pointless and irrelevant. Most startling was his endless supply of dirty jokes that he accompanied with a slap-on-the-back attitude. He had started on a course of progressive senility that had affected every male in his family for the past three generations.

I visited Uncle Dave again just a few months ago. While he still looked well, he did so only because of Aunt Gracie. He had begun to put on his clothes backwards and, 2 weeks before, had left the house in his pajamas. He no longer had any idea who I was, nor was he sure of the identity of my mother, his sister. There was no semblance of real conversation and he seemed to have forgotten most social responses. Aunt Gracie kept saying, "Dave, say 'thank you' to Linda for the present," or "Dave, Linda asked about our new grandson." There were no longer moments of lucidity, just a sense of a hollow being who really did not exist any longer. Maybe the saddest of all was watching this once purposeful, dynamic man wandering aimlessly as he would lose his way to the bathroom in the house he had lived in for 35 years.

"Uncle Dave" is the victim of an *organic mental disorder* which has affected the functioning of his brain and nervous system. DSM-III describes three main groups of disorders in which brain malformation, disruption, or damage are a primary cause of observed symptoms. These groups are the *age-*, *disease-*, or *injury-based organic mental disorders, the substance-induced organic mental disorders, and mental retardation.* In this chapter, we will discuss the organic brain disorders associated with injury, disease, and aging as well as the forms of mental retardation. We have grouped these together because we believe they represent patterns of behavioral disturbance which, in large measure, are biologically based, as well as beyond the control of their victims. In Chapter Thirteen, we shall describe a second group of organic brain disorders, those associated with the use and/or abuse of drugs. In the drug-induced organic mental disorders, people may actually desire to produce specific brain syndromes and are in many ways victims of their own behavior patterns more than they are victims of injury, disease, aging, or mental retardation.

Symptom Patterns in Organic Mental Disorders: The Organic Brain Syndromes

While organic mental disorder may be caused by diseases, injuries, or substances, it is characterized clinically by the presence of symptom patterns called *brain syndromes.* It must be emphasized that these brain syndromes *are not* considered to be disorders per se, but like difficulty in swallowing, fever, and chills in the case of tonsillitis, they are only the symptoms of underlying disruption of brain function. When these symptom patterns are combined with a specific causative factor, be it a disease or the use of a drug, the combination of the two comprise the organic mental disorder (Parsons & Hart, 1984). Thus, in the case of Uncle Dave, memory loss, intellectual deterioration, and personality change were symptoms comprising a brain syndrome called "dementia." However, only when these symptoms were combined with their cause, "progressive degenerative nerve disease," did Uncle Dave's difficulty become a diagnosable organic mental disorder.

The organic brain syndromes are symptom patterns reflecting temporary or permanent disruption of brain function regardless of cause. They can be either *acute* (reversible with rapid onset) or *chronic* (mostly irreversible and with slower, more insidious onset), but in either case they may be characterized by both physical and mental disturbances. Generally, brain syndromes are marked by difficulties in orientation, memory, perception, judgment, intellect, and emotion. Thus, people may not always know where or who they are and may not be able to remember recent activities and experiences. They may have difficulty in reproducing on paper visually presented stimuli (see Figure 2-5), or may be unable to plan future behavior or make sound decisions. Finally, they may be incapable of retrieving and using facts and information and may show inappropriate emotional reactions. Rarely are all these general characteristics of brain syndromes present in any single case; more typically, the actual pattern of deficit varies as a function of the specific type of brain syndrome in question. DSM-III describes the major brain syndromes of delirium, dementia, intoxication, and withdrawal, as well as a group of less frequently occurring patterns involving amnesia, hallucinations, delusions, and affective and personality changes.

Delirium

The basic feature of delirium is a "clouded state of consciousness . . . manifested by difficulty in sustaining attention . . . sensory misperceptions and a disordered stream of thought" (American Psychiatric Association, p. 104). The symptoms may vary in severity, but in all cases they begin quickly and last a relatively short time. Formally called *acute brain syndrome,* in delirium people may have difficulty attending to conversations or, when speaking, may shift from topic to topic. Frequently, they also misinterpret sensations; for example, the backfiring of a car may be mistaken for a rifle shot. People with delirium can experience symptoms ranging from simple drowsiness to stuporous or comatose states and from simple hyperactivity to severe agitation and insomnia. While delirium can occur at any age (especially if it is substance-induced), the syndrome occurs most frequently in association with physical diseases in children and in adults over age 60 (Strub & Black, 1981).

Dementia

While delirium is usually short-lived and primarily affects consciousness, *dementia* includes more permanent deterioration of intellectual abilities, especially in the realm of memory (See Table 12-1). Memory difficulties may range from forgetting of things that one is about to do to an inability to remember names of close relatives, birthdays, or even one's own name or occupation. People with dementia may show impaired judgment and poor impulse control and if the dementia continues will become increasingly "different" and "not like themselves." For example, they may show an increasing frequency of poor social and business decisions.

The rate of onset and duration of symptoms of dementia will vary with its cause. If caused by accidental brain damage, then the loss of intellectual abilities is rapid but does not progressively worsen. On the other hand, in cases of degenerative nerve diseases (as in the example of Uncle Dave), the pattern may develop more slowly but progressively intensify. Finally, when dementia is caused by brain tumors or chemical poisoning, its symptoms may be reversible if appropriate medical treatment is applied (Joynt & Shoulson, 1985). As people become aware of losing their intellectual abilities and of their difficulties in compensating for these losses, they often become frustrated and depressed. This reaction may be seen in the following:

Personal Experience: Reaction to Brain Damage

Look at me . . . I'm sweating like a pig! Four f—— pieces and I can't even put them together. The harder I try, the worse I do. You'd think I was doing the world's toughest puzzle. I try to be cool and not let it bother me, but my grandson could put this together . . . you and I both know that. I can't tell you how frustrating it is to see something you could do easily before . . . you know . . . but something you can't do now. I feel like some kind of ass . . . some kind of stupid ass. But I know in my head how to do things . . . Somehow when I start to put things together it just won't work. I wonder if I'll be this way the rest of my life . . . as long as that might be at the rate I'm going.

Intoxication and Withdrawal

While delirium and dementia can be caused by injury and disease as well as by chemical substances, the symptom pattern of *intoxication* occurs only in reaction to drug use. Probably the most common example of intoxication syndrome is drunkenness. Intoxication involves disturbance in perception, attention, thinking, judgment, and emotions that are clearly caused by the recent use of a chemical substance like alcohol or other drugs. The course and severity of intoxication depends on the amount of drug used, how it was administered, the person's

Table 12-1 Clinical Differentiation of Delirium and Dementia

	Delirium	*Dementia*
Onset	Acute	Usually insidious; if acute, preceded by coma or delirium
Duration	Usually less than 1 month	At least 1 month, usually much longer
Orientation	Faulty, at least for a time; tendency to mistake unfamiliar for familiar place, person	May be correct in mild cases
Thinking	Disorganized	Impoverished
Memory	Recent impaired	Both recent and remote impaired
Attention	Invariably disturbed	May be intact
Awareness	Always reduced, tends to fluctuate during daytime and be worse at night	Usually intact
Alertness	Increased or decreased	Normal or decreased
Perception	Misperceptions often present	Misperceptions often absent
Sleep-wakeful cycle	Always disrupted	Usually normal for age

Source: After Z. J. Lipowski, *Delirium: Acute Brain Failure in Man.* Springfield, Ill.: Charles C Thomas, 1979.

physiological tolerance for the substance, the individual's personality, and the circumstances in which the drug is used.

Extended use of a number of chemical substances such as alcohol, heroin, and barbiturates often leads to *tolerance,* or the need for increasing amounts of a drug in order to achieve the desired effect. When people try to stop using a drug for which they have built up a tolerance, they can experience a brain syndrome called *withdrawal.* The exact pattern and severity of withdrawal varies with the type of substance involved but generally can include nausea, vomiting, sleep disturbances, disturbances in temperature regulation, and breathing difficulties that typically last no more than 1 week. Much more will be said about the specific pattern of intoxication in Chapter Thirteen.

Other Brain Syndromes

Although delirium, dementia, intoxication, and withdrawal represent the most frequently seen symptom patterns, DSM-III describes several other brain syndromes. *Amnestic syndrome* (also known as Korsakoff's syndrome), for example, is characterized by two types of memory disturbances. In *retrograde amnesia,* memories established prior to the onset of the organic disorder are lost; in *anterograde amnesia,* there is a reduced ability to remember newly occurring events (Lipowski, 1980b).

Rather than memory problems, hallucinations are the major symptom of *organic hallucinosis.* Although typically a reaction to the use of, or withdrawal from, substances such as alcohol, cocaine, or hallucinogens like LSD, hallucinosis has also been observed in cases of syphilis, migraine headaches, and brain tumors.

In *organic delusional syndrome,* the primary isolated symptom is the presence of irrational beliefs during states of wakefulness (that is, not during periods of delirium). As in the case of hallucinosis, in delusional syndrome, symptoms may last beyond the immediate effects of the causative agent (drug or head injury) and could become permanent. Besides perception and cognition disturbances, mood alteration also can characterize a brain syndrome. When this occurs, it is called *organic affective syndrome.* In this pattern, the brain dysfunction may result in extreme depression or elation. A last symptom pattern is characterized by more global changes than the specific ones discussed thus far. In *organic personality syndrome,* disturbances are observed in overall personality style, general behavior patterns, impulse control, and activity and interest levels. In some cases, the brain syndrome may alter people's usual behavioral repertoire so that they behave very differently from the way they did previously.

Case: Organic Personality Syndrome

I can remember what John was like before the accident. He was a "Marine" from head to toe. After he got out of the service, he maintained his level of fitness, ran every day, lifted weights, spoke with a strong deep tone and feared no one or no thing. Then the accident happened—he was working on a construction job and a beam fell from the second floor. It hit John on the left side of his head and dug a hole in his skull the size of a child's fist. At first I was afraid that he might die, but after I saw what he was like after he began to recover, I actually felt sorry sometimes that he didn't. He was a frightened, whimpering man who jumped at the slightest noise. He would do no exercise, ate all day, and let his body go to pot. He couldn't read anymore, couldn't do the simplest arithmetic problems, would forget what I said to him in just a few seconds. He was a stranger to me. His face looked the same, but his eyes were different. It was almost as if God had taken his very being out of his body and replaced it with someone else.

The Organic Mental Disorders Caused by Injury, Disease, or Aging

The brain syndromes we have just described are reflections of temporary or permanent interruption of normal brain functioning. As such, according to DSM-III, they do not represent actual diagnostic categories or disorders per se. In order to be labeled as part of a diagnosable *disorder,* a particular brain syndrome must be coupled with a specific cause such as brain damage, brain disease, invasion of a toxic substance, or aging. In Table 12-2, we list some of the many etiologies of the common brain syndromes of delirium and dementia. In the discussion to follow, we will highlight a selection of these.

Organic Mental Disorders Associated with Injury

As a result of falls, blows to the head, automobile accidents, or other sources of trauma, the brain may be damaged. If trauma is mild as in the case of *concussion,* people may experience the temporary brain syndrome of delirium. When damage is more extensive so that brain tissue is destroyed, other brain syndromes like dementia may occur.

The specific form and content of symptoms observed in the injury-based brain disorders depend on an interaction between the area of the brain which is affected and the premorbid personality of the individual. Table 12-3 provides a description of the kinds of symptoms typically associated with damage to particular

Table 12-2 Some Causes of Delirium and Dementia

Delirium: Alcohol, inhalation of gasoline, glue, or solvents; lack of oxygen; endocrine disorders; systemic infections; intercranial infections; head injuries; epilepsy; migraine headaches; tumors; exposure to extremes of temperature; food allergy

Dementia: Degenerative diseases like Alzheimer's and Pick's diseases; senility; multiple heart attacks; metabolic disorders; head trauma; epilepsy; meningitis; encephalitis; heat stroke; electric injury; multiple sclerosis

Source: Adapted from Lipowski (1980b) and Parsons & Hart (1984).

parts of the brain. For instance, damage to the frontal lobe is associated with deficits in thinking, whereas destruction of certain parts of the temporal lobe are related to memory problems. When there is significant tissue destruction, the symptoms described in Table 12-3 are permanent. However, in some cases, nondamaged parts of the brain can take over responsibility for lost function through a process called *equivalence of function.* Unfortunately, the "recovered" function is rarely of the same quality and effectiveness as it was originally.

In addition to trauma, toxic levels of chemicals also can cause brain injury severe enough to produce a diagnosable mental disorder. Such chemicals may enter the body through the ingestion of normal foodstuffs, as in the case of fruit sprayed with harmful compounds, or through the eating of nonfood materials such as lead-containing paint chips by children. In either case, a buildup of chemicals may occur which can either temporarily or permanently damage the brain and produce brain syndromes such as delirium, dementia, hallucinosis, or personality alteration. Among the more common damaging chemicals involved in organic disorders are lead, industrial solvents, household cleaners, gasoline vapors, and manganese and mercury vapors. Kaplan and Sadock (1981a) describe the symptoms of the temporary pattern called "manganese madness":

> Symptoms include headache, irritability, joint pains, and somnolence. An eventual picture appears of emotional lability, pathological laughter, nightmares, hallucinations, and compulsive and impulsive acts. Gait is impaired and speech may be monotonous and rigid. There may be tremors of the extremities and a strange, mask-like look on the face. The psychological effects tend to clear three or four months after exposure. (p. 411)

Symptoms similar to those produced by manganese also are produced by prolonged exposure to mercury vapors. Kaplan and Sadock even conjecture that since mercury was an integral part of the production process for felt hats in the 1800s, the behavior of the Mad Hatter in *Alice in Wonderland* may have been a result of "mercury madness."

Auto accidents are among the most common causes of brain syndromes. (© *Eric Kroll 1979/Taurus Photos*)

Table 12-3 Correlation of Deficits and Behavior with Area of Brain Damage

Site of Brain Lesion	*Deficits*	*Behavioral Correlates*
Frontal lobe	Inferior quality of thinking, abstraction, and synthesis; failure to inhibit ongoing activity	Perseveration, concreteness, preference for old behavioral patterns, impulsiveness, tactlessness, indifference, incapacity for decision, aggressive behavior, increased libido, euphoria, lack of productive thinking, demanding attitude, childish behavior, lack of foresight and insight, loss of moral, ethical, and social standards
Temporal lobe		
Bilateral	Retrograde and anterograde amnesia, dementia	Korsakoff's psychosis, dementia
Left	Poor verbal recall, intellectual loss	Memory problems, difficulty with verbal material, atypical schizophreniform psychoses, personality changes
Right	Visual-ideational sequencing problems, difficulty with auditory perception	Difficulty in identifying incongruities in pictures, difficulty in arranging pictures, inability to appreciate musical tone, loudness, timbre, etc.
Brainstem and diencephalon	Alternation of drive states, alteration of mood, diminished alertness	Apathy, sluggishness, depression, hypomania, lability of affect, increased thirst, bulemia, anorexia, changed libido, stupor, coma, sleep alterations
Parietal lobe	Spatial disorientation, body agnosia	Disorientation, ignoring portions or an entire half of the body
Left hemisphere	Ideational and ideomotor apraxia	Inability to express thoughts, blocking, difficulty in initiating action
Right hemisphere	Visual-constructional spatial apraxia	Difficulty in copying designs, difficulty with jigsaw puzzles, spatial disorientation, increased incidence of behavioral changes
	Symptoms showing no correlation with site or degree of injury (therefore, more likely to be psychological in origin)	Headache, giddiness, irritability, sensitivity to sensory stimuli, anxiety, fatigue, difficulty in concentration

Source: From Peterson (1980).

Organic Mental Disorder Caused by Disease

Besides injuries due to trauma and chemical toxins, a number of brain syndromes are caused by contracted or hereditary diseases, tumors, and nutritional deficiencies. Sometimes the diseases have clearly identifiable causes, as in encephalitis and meningitis, or advanced syphilis, but at other times their origins are less clearly definable, as in epilepsy.

Encephalitis and Meningitis

In encephalitis and meningitis, brain function is disrupted due to infection. In the case of encephalitis, there is an inflammation of the brain itself, whereas in meningitis, the outside layers or meninges surrounding the brain are affected. In either case, people will be confused, disoriented, and unable to remember recent events or to perceive accurately what is going on around them. With proper diagnosis and treatment, the symptoms of encephalitis and meningitis can be typically reversed.

Syphilis

In contrast to the possible reversibility of symptoms in brain infections, those of *general paresis*, one of the results of advanced syphilis, are more permanent. General paresis occurs in about 10 percent of cases of untreated syphilis. In fact, as we mentioned in Chapter 3, the discovery of the biological basis of general paresis gave early credence to the biological theories of mental disorders. The initial venereal infection, called primary syphilis, can be treated effectively with antibiotics. If untreated, however, the symptoms of primary syphilis usually disappear, and the individual may believe mistakenly that the problem has remitted. However, the absence of symptoms may signal the beginning of the incubation period, or secondary phase, of the disease that can last anywhere from 5 to 30 years. About 2 out of 10 of those with secondary-stage syphilis will have their nervous systems invaded by the syphilis-producing organism *Treponema pallidum*. Subsequent inflammation and degeneration of the central nervous system result in the outward signs associated with general paresis.

Personality disturbances are among the initial behavioral signs of this tertiary phase of syphilis. People may become more irritable and inconsiderate of others, sexually promiscuous, moody, depressed, and apathetic. In time, psychotic symptoms such as delusions, hallucinations, and bizarre behavior may appear, as well as deficits in motor skills, memory, and judgment. Death will occur about 4 years after the onset of the tertiary symptoms. Most of such deaths are unnecessary and preventable if the possible signs and symptoms of venereal disease appearing a few days or weeks after sexual contact are treated.

Epilepsy

Unlike the etiology of general paresis which has been clearly identified through the application of the shared methods of science (see Chapter 3), epilepsy is an organic mental disorder for which there is often no known cause. Epilepsy victims experience unpredictable seizures where they lose consciousness. While some seizures may be produced by directly identifiable tumors, inflammation, or trauma in the brain, about 75 percent of epileptic disorders are termed *ideopathic*, that is, are of unknown (but assumedly, biological) origin. The following personal experience may convey what is like to have an epileptic seizure.

Personal Experience: Epilepsy

But on October 31, just as I was going to eat my lunch, having done a whole morning's washing, I was shown abruptly that there was no truth yet in believing myself better.

The food was on the table, the oil stove lit. I picked up the coffee percolator to fill it. Just as I reached the sink and was standing in the doorway, I found I could not move, could not remember what I wanted to do. It seemed a long time that I stood there (actually perhaps a few seconds) saying to myself, "This is nothing. It will be all right in a moment and I shall remember *all the rest*." Then I felt my head beginning to jerk backwards and my face to grimace. Then the percolator fell from my hand into the sink. But still some dogged part of me kept saying, "All this is really controllable." I was still conscious and felt violent gestures and spasms were shooting all over me, even till I felt my knees give and I fell down on the concrete floor. As I went, it shot through me, the astonishment: "As bad as this, then?"

The next thing I remember was the B____s' kitchen and Betty B____, God bless her, giving me tea and talking to me in the tone mothers use to little children coming out of nightmares. Rosie was by me, sitting at my feet. I asked the time. They said it was two o'clock. Half an hour had *gone.* I had not the slightest recollection of picking myself up or walking 100 yards up the road or going into their kitchen. Nor, for an hour or two, of what had happened before I fell. (From M. Evans, *A Ray of Darkness,* London: B. Calder, 1978)

The epilepsies may be categorized on the basis of the type of seizure manifested (Heilman & Valenstein, 1985). To some extent the specific type of seizure manifested depends upon heredity factors (Parsons & Hart, 1984), but the exact nature of the inherited defect transmitted is not yet known.

Grand mal seizures are what most lay people think of when they consider an epileptic disorder. The initial sign in these seizures may be an aura, or a sense of impending seizure, felt a few seconds prior to onset. Auras can be very individualistic and may consist of events varying from numbness, tingling, a sense of distress in the stomach, hallucinated light flashes, voices, odors, or motor symptoms such as twitching or stiffness.

As the seizure begins, air is suddenly expelled from the lungs, producing a crying-out sound. The individual loses consciousness and falls to the ground. The first phase of the seizure is called the *tonic* phase; as the person falls, his or her entire voluntary musculature goes into a continuous contraction lasting from 10 to 20 seconds. Breathing may stop momentarily, bladder and bowel control may be lost, and in males erection and ejaculation may occur.

Following the tonic phase, the *clonic* phase begins. This phase is characterized by intermittent periods of relaxation and contraction, resulting in jerking movements. During this time the individual can seriously damage the tongue by biting it. After the clonic phase, the person may sleep for a few hours and awaken confused and suffering a loss of memory for the events immediately preceding the sei-

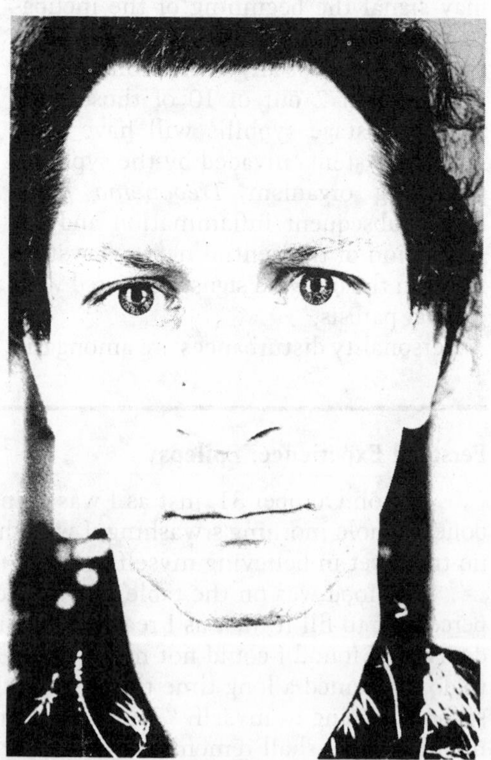

A dazed look may be the only outward sign of a petit mal seizure. (*Michael Weisbrot and Family*)

zure. In rare instances, instead of reviving, some people may experience a continuous sequence of seizures. Called *status epilepticus,* this condition is a medical emergency, it will cause death if it is not treated. However, in most cases of grand mal seizures, the affected people will complete the seizure pattern in a few minutes, fall into a deep sleep, and recover unharmed. Usually all that outsiders can do is to turn the victim on their side so that the tongue is not swallowed and make them as comfortable as possible.

Less well known, and less frequently found, are *petit mal seizures.* A petit mal seizure may be seen as an incomplete grand mal seizure. Typically, there is a brief loss of consciousness and awareness lasting for anywhere from 5 to 30 seconds. There is no aura. The person doesn't fall down, and in some instances, individuals aren't even aware that they have experienced a seizure. To an outside observer, those experiencing a petit mal seizure may merely look like they have a blank expression. Some individuals can have up to 100 petit mal seizures a day.

Whereas grand mal and petit mal seizures may involve more general brain dysfunctions, *focal seizures* are related to specific parts of the brain (usually indicated by abnormal EEG activity). One type of focal involvement is a *Jacksonian seizure,* which begins with a tingling or numbing sensation around the corner of the mouth or in a thumb that usually spreads to adjoining parts of the body until half the body is involved.

Like Jacksonian seizures, *psychomotor seizures* are associated with abnormal EEG readings from specific parts of the brain. Psychomotor epilepsy produces changes in perception, self-awareness, thought patterns, and mood. When affected by psychomotor seizures, people may behave irrationally, even to the point of committing aggressive acts for which the person is amnesic. There has been some conjecture that Jack Ruby, the murderer of Lee Harvey Oswald, the accused assassinator of President John Kennedy, was suffering from psychomotor epilepsy.

As in epilepsy, alteration of consciousness is the prime symptom in the brain syndromes of *narcolepsy* and *cataplexy.* In narcolepsy, the person may fall asleep involuntarily in the middle of an activity, and may sleep anywhere from a few seconds to half an hour or more. The primary symptom of cataplexy is a sudden loss of muscle control and power that leads the victim to fall limply to the ground. Laughing sometimes may produce cataplectic attacks in those susceptible to them. The causes of narcolepsy and cataplexy are unclear at this time.

Other Disease-related Organic Mental Disorders

Less frequent than the infectious, general-paretic, and epileptic chronic brain syndromes are a number of disorders with a wide variety of causes (Heilman & Valenstein, 1985). *Pellagra,* caused primarily by a niacin deficiency, includes a reddening of the skin, as well as psychological symptoms of paranoid delusions and hallucinations. If treated rapidly, pellagra-induced psychosis usually is reversible. However, if not quickly treated, permanent damage may result, in the form of chronic brain syndrome and dementia.

Like niacin deficiency, *cranial neoplasms* (tumors) also may produce chronic psychological and emotional symptoms. Early signs of a potential brain tumor are impairment of consciousness, headache, loss of energy, and an exaggeration of existing personality disturbances.

People who were anxious before the development of brain tumors may become even more anxious. Specific symptoms will vary depending on the type and placement of the tumorous growth. Generally, the more localized the neoplasm, the more likely it is that specific symptoms will result.

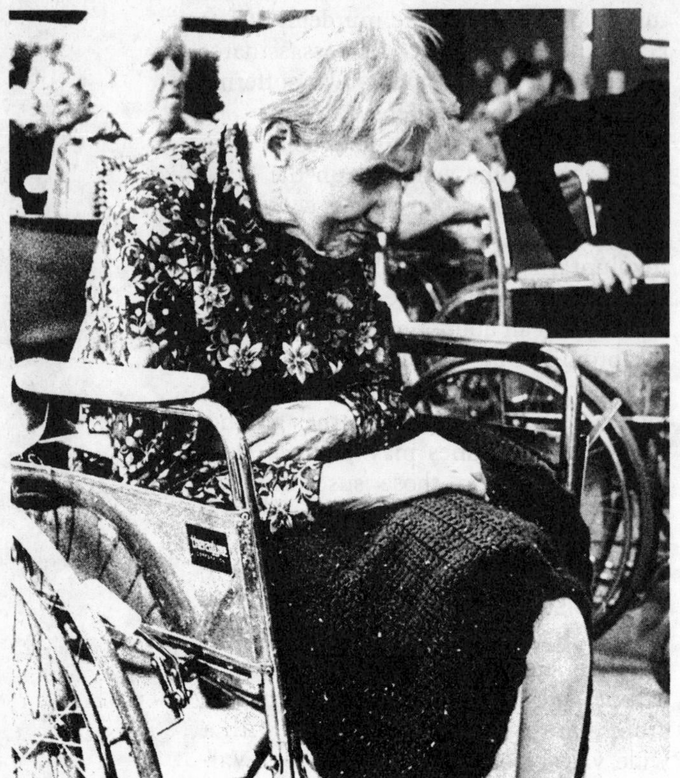

Victims of Parkinson's disease steadily lose control of their motor abilities and may have to be confined to a wheelchair. (*Martin M. Rotker/Taurus Photos*)

Nutritional deficiencies and neoplasms are two known causes of chronic brain syndromes. However, there are organically based disorders for which there are as yet no known causes. For example, *paralysis agitans* (Parkinson's disease) is characterized by muscular rigidity, difficulty in movement, and slow, rhythmic tremors of the hands and feet. Many people with this disorder become morose and irritable in response to their increased dependency and loss of behavioral freedom.

Known to be inherited, but through some as yet unknown mechanism, and of unknown specific cause, *Huntington's chorea* usually manifests itself between the ages of 30 and 45. At first, the person may show mild irritability; later, suspiciousness, paranoid ideas, hallucinations, and dementia inevitably occur. The person may exhibit *choreiform movements* that are clumsy, jerky, and irregular. As the disease progresses, the muscles needed for speech, eating, and motion also may weaken. In Huntington's chorea, depression can become severe, and potential for suicide is high. Huntington's chorea usually results in death about 15 years after the first symptoms appear. There is no known cure.

Organic Mental Disorders Associated with Age

Brain syndromes, injury, or diseases can occur at any age. However, there are a number of disorders which seem to be more clearly related to the aging process. The *senile degenerative nerve diseases* occur in persons over the age of 65 and are marked by memory loss, slowing of thought, and personality changes. Organic mental disorders of advancing age are so frequent that they account for 75 percent of all first admissions to mental hospitals among people age 65 to 74 years. Among people over 75 years of age, 90 percent of first admissions are for senile organic mental disorders (Strub & Black, 1981). But advanced age is not the only time of life when age-related neurological deterioration may occur. It can also be produced in people as young as 40 by *presenile* occurrences of dementias such as Alzheimer's disease and Pick's disease (Heilman & Valenstein, 1985). Since it occurs about 50 times more frequently than other forms of presenile dementia, we will discuss Alzheimer's disease most thoroughly.

The onset of Alzheimer's disease may be sudden or gradual. Emotional changes, loss of interest in work and home activities, and increased irritability can be among the early signs. Typically, people feel as if "something is wrong," but they cannot determine the source of their difficulties.

The joy and involvement of the retirement years are denied to victims of Alzheimer's disease. (*Michael Weisbrot and Family*)

Depression, anxiety, and increasingly bizarre speech and behavior are also part of the symptomatic picture. People may complain of memory problems and be unable to learn new facts. Even routine tasks can become burdensome or impossible. As seen in the example in Box 12-1, great stress is often on the family as well as the Alzheimer's victim.

As Alzheimer's disease progresses, language may begin to fail and mood swings may become more severe and unpredictable. People may wander about aimlessly, get lost easily, and involve themselves endlessly in such things as folding and unfolding clothes or picking lint from their clothing (Strub & Black, 1981). As time goes on, names for things are forgotten, familiar objects are unrecognizable, and previously learned "automatic" skills become disrupted. Strub and Black, for example, describe one patient's problems with a simple block of sugar:

> We watched one woman carefully unwrap a lump of sugar for her coffee only to be baffled about what to do thereafter. She had the sugar in one hand, wrapper in the other, and after painful deliberation, she put the paper in the coffee and threw away the sugar (p. 126).

In the final stages of Alzheimer's disease, patients become almost totally uncommunicative. They manifest uncontrollable laughing, aimless wandering, and little social interaction. Eventually, they become bedridden and physically weakened. Death is usually the result of pneumonia or some other infection and is the inexorable endpoint of Alzheimer's disease. From the start of the process to its end requires an average of 7 years, although some patients live as long as 20 years after the onset of symptoms (Heilman & Valenstein, 1985).

Although similar in many ways to Alzheimer's disease, Pick's disease tends to

THE EFFECT OF ALZHEIMER'S DISEASE

BOX 12-1

Days in the Life

Ruth Conroy is grateful for all the traveling she and her husband, Bill, did together—hiking and camping all over New England, sailing their boat from Massachusetts to Long Island, skiing in Austria, touring Pakistan and Russia. "I'm glad we did those things without waiting to retire," the 56-year-old Brighton, Mass., woman says "You never know what life is going to hit you with."

Bill, a handsome 57-year-old Harvard graduate, was diagnosed as having Alzheimer's three years ago at Massachusetts General Hospital. He stays home now while Ruth holds down a part-time job in Boston. Before she leaves each morning, she neatly lays out plates and silver on the kitchen counter and leaves his breakfast in the refrigerator. She also puts handwritten notes around the house—"Get name and phone number," "Turn gas off," "Don't go out—back at 2:30." Occasionally, Bill takes walks by himself, but, for the most part he stays home and aimlessly passes the time. When his wife asks if he listened to music or watched television while she was away, his reply is usually something like "Can't do anything now. Dropped everything."

After Ruth comes home, they occasionally take walks around the reservoir near their condominium or watch football practice at Harvard. But she finds it increasingly difficult to think of things for them to do together. "Dinner gets to be earlier and earlier," she says. And recently, communication between the two has become difficult because Bill often speaks in cryptic, fractured sentences, "I don't want to burn myself," he said one day recently. "I found myself; I was gone. I have to go back again. Everything bang! Right out of me." Ruth wonders if he was referring to his disease. When she asks him if he's talking abut Alzheimer's, he replies: "It's the same thing. I can't figure." He sometimes can't remember the names of his stepchildren, or even his wife, but he may try to cover such lapses. When groping for a name, he'll stall by saying, "Wait a minute, I want to hear what they are saying." Sometimes he asks Ruth when they are going home, even though they are sitting in their own living room.

Ruth has begun to show the stress. Once, she rushed to the emergency room, complaining of severe chest pains, afraid she was having a heart attack. But she was told the symptoms were simply the result of being on edge. Now and then, she blows up. "Last night, he brought me a can of beer, and I reminded him I like it in a glass," she says. "He must have gone back and forth to the kitchen four times and returned with the same can of beer. I yelled at him, then I felt terrible."

But most of the time, a bond of deep affection helps both of them cope. "He tries so hard to please me," says Ruth. "He is so grateful." Occasionally, Bill will take her hand and, looking into her face, he will say simply, "I would be dead by now." As much as possible, Ruth strives to make their present life together resemble what it was before Bill's illness. "I am taking every good thing that I can now because I know it's not going to last," she says. "But I don't dwell on what's ahead."

Source: From Newsweek, Dec. 3, 1984.

occur in somewhat younger people. While Alzheimer's patients typically first experience changes in their *thinking* abilities, in Pick's disease the *personality* seems to be affected most in the early stages of the disorder. Further, while patients with Alzheimer's disease are usually aware that something is wrong and that they are changing, Pick's patients can seem quite flippant and unconcerned about their deteriorating condition. The two forms of dementia become more similar as they progress; in their later stages, they may be indistinguishable.

A FUTURE APPLICATION OF THE BIOLOGICAL PARADIGM

BOX 12-2

Mouse Brain Transplant Is Successful

San Francisco—A piece of brain has been successfully transplanted from one mouse into another, where it not only survived but correctly connected itself and functioned near normally, a scientist reports.

"This is what I call my science-fiction experiment—except that it works," said Dr. Dorothy Krieger, chief of endocrinology at Mount Sinai Medical Center in New York City.

Although the partial brain transplant succeeded in seven out of eight tries with mice, Krieger said, "I will make no speculation as to any possible relation of this (procedure) to humans. I wouldn't touch that with a 10-foot pole. This is only the first experiment. . ."

She said the transplants use a specially bred strain of mice that produces both normal animals and some mutants that completely lack a crucial substance called luteinizing hormone releasing hormone. The hormone, produced in the brain, controls production of yet another set of hormones, the gonadotropins that affect development of sex organs.

The adult transplant recipients were genetically male, although without the sex hormones they were virtually asexual, with minute testes and no sperm production.

The donor brain tissue came from unborn fetuses that were normal, although from the same strain that produces the mutation.

"We looked three months after the brain transplant and the pituitary gland (a hormone controller at the base of the brain) was making gonadotropin, the testes had gotten bigger and they were making sperm," Krieger said.

In the transplants, she said, the part of the brain that normally makes luteinizing hormone—a piece smaller than the head of a match—is taken from the donor brain and dropped into a natural cavity of the thimble-sized brain of the adult mouse.

"Then," she said, "we just leave it alone."

The brain cells grow in the cavity, which is near their normal location, and begin to send out nerve fibers that hook up with the rest of the brain.

"Somehow," Krieger said, "the nerves know just where to grow . . . and they make the right connections."

The fibers establish a pathway, just as in a normal mouse, into the bottom of a brain structure called the hypothalamus, she said. How they manage that remains a question, although she noted that a variety of cell-to-cell communication systems exist and said the mice are genetically programmed to be males even if the switch isn't turned until adulthood.

The transplants seem to become permanently functioning parts of their new brain, Krieger said.

Although sex hormones are greatly increased after the transplants, they remain lower than normal.

Source: The Denver Post, June 18, 1982.

Paradigmatic Views of the Injury-, Disease-, and Age-related Organic Mental Disorders

Given the clear physical basis for the organic mental disorders we have discussed thus far, it should come as no surprise that the biological paradigm seems to have been most effective in the understanding of these patterns of abnormal behavior. However, while the causes of most of these disorders are biological, treatments deriving from the biological paradigm are most effective in cases of reversible symptoms such as those caused by nutritional deficiencies, ingestion of toxins, and the like. Unfortunately, no biological treatment has as yet been discovered which can reverse the progress of senile and presenile dementias or replace damaged brain tissue (although such replacement may be a reality in the future as seen in Box 12-2).

Brain tissue implants such as those described in Box 12-2 represent an application of the biological paradigm in an effort to restore behaviors lost due to brain damage. Although the method remains experimental and has not been used with humans, scientists and neurosurgeons are already considering its potential application in people. For example, it may be possible to replace brain tissue lost through injury or disease with new tissue which, after reconnecting with neighboring structures, may replace lost functions. Similarly, the ravages of Alzheimer's disease may be reversible once the mechanisms of the brain implant process are understood and applied in such a way as to make brain tissue regenerate. Someday, hopefully, the idea of a *brain graft* may not be so inconceivable as it seems now (Labbe et al., 1983). In the nineteenth century, few people would have believed that the heart transplants of today would ever be possible.

Although biologically based, the specific form taken by a particular brain syndrome is significantly affected by psychosocial and systems factors. For example, the particular behaviors on which Alzheimer's patients may perseverate are often based upon their learning history. Further, the personality distortions observed in organic personality syndrome may be based upon the individual's predisorder personality. Similarly, the kinds of hallucinations experienced by different people also may vary according to their unique life experiences. At a systems level, the manner in which people are affected by and deal with their organic mental disorders often can be positively or negatively influenced by the responses of their families or social groups. Elderly persons in accepting, supportive, and stimulating environments often manifest slower deterioration as compared with those in more isolated circumstances (Ernst & Badash, 1977). In addition, the commitment of family members to help in the daily functioning of a person such as Bill Conroy, the Alzheimer's patient described in Box 12-1, can help make that person's remaining years as happy as possible despite the continuing progress of the disease. Indeed, even though the organic mental disorders are clearly biologically based, each of the three major paradigms seems to have made productive contributions to our understanding and treatment of them.

Mental Retardation

Prior to the onset of their symptoms, persons with organic mental disorders based upon injury, disease, or aging are typically normal, fully functioning individuals. It is primarily due to the disruption of their normal brain function that they begin to manifest intellectual and behavioral deficits. On the other hand, there are some people who, because of physical, psychosocial, and/or systems factors never achieve a level of fully normal intellectual or behavioral functioning. These individuals are termed *mentally retarded.* Because a significant portion of those who are mentally retarded have clear biological causation and the rest have varying degrees of biological involvement, it is included here. However, it should be noted that psychosocial and systems factors play important roles in almost all cases of mental retardation.

Classifications of Mental Retardation

Mental retardation is defined by the American Association on Mental Deficiency (AAMD) as "significantly subaverage general intellectual functioning existing concurrently with deficits in adaptive behavior and manifested before the age of 18" (Grossman, 1973; 1983). It is generally agreed that approximately 3 percent of the U.S. population, or about 7.5 million people, may be considered retarded (Drew et al., 1984), although some estimates place the incidence of retardation as high as 9 percent (Baird & Sadovnick, 1985). The mentally retarded are often shunned, placed in separate schools, ridiculed, and even feared by the general public. However, mental retardation, like the brain syndromes discussed earlier in this chapter, is best seen as a symptom that may result from a variety of biological, psychosocial, or systems-based difficulties (Robinson & Robinson, 1976; Rodgon, 1984). Regardless of its etiology, the symptom pattern termed mental retardation always involves reduced intellectual performance and hampered abilities to adapt to many of the requirements of everyday life.

The classification of mental retardation is fraught with problems of social stigma. Early scientific categories included such descriptive labels as "idiot," "imbecile," "moron," and the like. With time, these labels were used in denigrating fashion and were dropped from official usage. The current definitions of mental retardation stem from two main sources, the manual of the American Association on Mental Deficiency and the DSM-III. The most basic definition is the one provided by the AAMD which we noted above (Grossman, 1983). The AAMD carefully defines each of the key terms in this definition:

> *Mental Retardation* . . . denotes a level of behavior performance without reference to etiology. Thus, it does not distinguish between retardation associated with psychosocial or polygenic influences and retardation associated with biological deficits. Mental retardation is descriptive of current behavior and does not imply prognosis [chances for recovery]. Prognosis is related more to factors such as associated conditions, motivation, treatment, and training opportunities than to the mental retardation itself.
>
> *Intellectual functioning* may be assessed by one or more of the standardized tests developed for that purpose;
>
> *Significantly subaverage* refers to performance which is [significantly] below the average of the tests. On the two most frequently used tests of intelligence, Stanford-Binet and Wechsler, this represents I.Q.'s of 67 and 69 respectively.
>
> The upper age limit of the *developmental period* is placed at *18 years.*
>
> *Adaptive behavior* is defined as the effectiveness or degree with which the individual meets the standards of personal independence and social responsibility expected of his or her age and cultural group. Since these expectations vary for different age groups, *deficits in adaptive behavior* will vary at different ages.
>
> During infancy and early childhood, sensory-motor, communication, self-help, and socialization skills ordinarily develop in a sequential pattern reflective of the maturation process. Delays in the acquisition of these skills represent potential deficiencies in adaptive behavior and become criteria for mental retardation.
>
> The skills required for adaptation during childhood and early adolescence involve more of the learning process. . . . Attention should not only focus on the basic academic skills and their use, but also on skills essential to cope with the environment, including concepts of time, money, self-directed behaviors, social responsiveness, and interactive skills.
>
> In the adult years, vocational performance and social responsibilities assume prime importance assessed in terms of the degree to which the individual is able to maintain himself independently in the community and in gainful employment as well as by his ability to meet and conform to standards set by the community. . . . Only those individuals who demonstrated deficits in both measured intelligence *and* adaptive behavior are to be classified as mentally retarded.

> Within the framework of the definition . . . an individual may meet the criteria . . . at one time in his life and not at some other time. A person may change status as a result of changes or alterations in his intellectual functioning, changes in his adaptive behaviors, changes in the expectations of society, or for other known or unknown reasons. (Grossman, 1973, pp. 11–14)

The AAMD definition of retardation is presented in such a way that it is possible to ascertain the degree of retardation by using a combination of assessment devices. The first of these are standardized tests of intellectual abilities, such as the Wechsler Scales we described in Chapter Two. The second method involves the use of nonintellectual measures such as the Adaptive Behavior Scales that reflect the degree of socially appropriate behavior for individuals (Nihira et al., 1974). By administering tests of intellectual and social abilities, one can determine the specific classifications of mental retardation.

Based upon AAMD definitions, DSM-III demarcates four categories of mental retardation. Although supposedly based upon intellectual ability *and* adaptive behavior, severity of retardation is typically keyed to IQ scores. As summarized in Table 12-4, however, the intellectual realm is far from the only area of functioning affected by the various patterns of retardation.

Mild Mental Retardation

One of the general criteria for a diagnosis of retardation is an IQ score of less than 70. People diagnosed as *mildly* retarded have IQs ranging from 50 to 70 and, according to DSM-III, about 80 percent of retarded people score somewhere in this

Table 12-4 Characteristics of Mentally Retarded Children

Area of Functioning	*Mild*	*Moderate*	*Severe and Profound*
Self-help skills	Feeds and dresses self and cares for own toilet needs.	Has difficulties and requires training but can learn adequate self-help skills.	No skills to partial, but some can care for personal needs on a limited basis.
Speech and communication	Receptive and expressive language are adequate. Understands communication.	Receptive and expressive language are adequate. Has speech problems.	Receptive language is limited to good. Expressive language is limited to poor.
Academics	Optimal learning environment—third to sixth grade.	Very few academic skills. First or second grade.	No academic skills.
Social skills	Has friends, can learn to adjust adequately.	Capable of friends but has difficulties in many social situations.	Not capable of having "real" friends. No social interaction.
Vocational adjustment	Can hold a job. Competitive to semicompetitive. Primarily unskilled work.	Sheltered work environment. Usually needs constant supervision.	No employment for the most part. May be in an activity center. Usually needs constant care.
Adult living	Usually marries, has children. Needs help during stress.	Usually does not marry or have children. Dependent.	Always dependent on others. No marriage or children.

Source: Chart from William R. Van Osdol and Don G. Shane, *An Introduction to Exceptional Children* Dubuque, Iowa: William C. Brown, 1977, p. 68.

range. Only about 1 percent of mildly retarded people ever require institutional care. The remainder usually are able to complete schooling in special classes and, as adults, frequently fill unskilled jobs. Measurable brain damage or other forms of neurological difficulties are infrequently found among mildly retarded persons.

Moderate Mental Retardation

Moderately retarded people have IQs in the range of 35 to 49 on the Wechsler Scales. About 12 percent of all retarded individuals are classified as *moderate.* Unlike the mildly retarded, the majority of the moderately retarded show significant evidence of brain damage or other neurological disorder. Some moderately retarded individuals may be institutionalized, but most of them are capable of living within the protective environments of their families and homes. Moderately retarded people may be capable of learning simple skills and can often earn money through jobs in sheltered workshops.

Severe Mental Retardation

With IQs ranging from 20 to 34, *severely* retarded people represent less than 7 percent of retarded individuals. The majority of these persons are permanently institutionalized and require constant care. They usually have difficulty learning even the simplest tasks. Severe retardation usually is associated with some genetic disorder or with severe brain damage due to accident or birth difficulty.

Profound Mental Retardation

The *profoundly* retarded, who represent less than 1 percent of retarded people, have IQs of less than 20. Almost always hospitalized, profoundly retarded people have difficulty attending to basic physical needs and usually require significant amounts of nursing care. Such a level of retardation is usually a result of severe disorders where gross deformities of the brain, head, and body are often observed. Partially because of the intensity of their general physical problems, a large proportion of profoundly retarded people die at very early ages.

Although the four categories we have described are associated with intelligence test scores, it must be remembered that adaptive functioning also plays a significant part in reaching a diagnosis of mental retardation. According to this system, a person with an IQ score of 60 who scores very high on an adaptive behavior scale might *not* be considered mentally retarded. Similarly, an individual with an IQ over 70 who cannot take care of his or her basic needs may be considered to be mildly retarded.

Case: A Nonretarded Person with a Low IQ

Maria, a forty-four year old Mexican mother of five, scored 65 on an intelligence test. . . . Maria completed the ninth grade and subsequently worked as a fruit packer. She reports no serious illness, operations, or accidents, regularly attends the Roman Catholic church, and leads an active informal social life visiting friends, family and neighbors. . . . She enjoys watching Spanish-language television broadcasts and listens to the daily news. . . . Although Maria scored low on the intelligence test measure, there is nothing about her style of life nor the characteristics of her children (all of whom appear to be successful) that would indicate inadequacy in parental or other social roles. (Mercer, 1979, pp. 194–195)

Before closing our discussion of classification of mental retardation, we believe it important to mention the growing belief that a two-category system may be preferable to the traditional four-category approach. As stated in Zigler et al. (1984), the two-category view is based on the fact that about 30 percent of all retardates are clearly biologically based, whereas about 70 percent are clearly psychosocially determined. Further, the vast majority of biologically based retardation fall into the moderate, severe, or profound category, whereas most levels of psychosocial retardation are mild. Zigler et al., therefore, have proposed the following two categories: *retardation associated with organic defect* and *retardation not associated with organic defect.* Zigler et al. propose that such a discrimination would be easier to make and would help guide therapeutic efforts more effectively than the four-group system.

Paradigmatic Explanations for Mental Retardation

Explanations for the symptom patterns of mental retardation derive from each of the major paradigms. In general, the biological paradigm serves as the best guide for understanding the moderate, severe, and profound levels of retardation, while the psychosocial and systems views tend to fare better with the mild form.

The Biological Paradigm: Genetic Factors in Mental Retardation

The symptom of mental retardation has been found to be associated with a number of genetic syndromes (Abuclo, 1983). In each of these syndromes, intellectual or physical abilities and often physical appearance are adversely affected by some genetic difficulty. In some instances, the genetic difficulty is the result of extra chromosomes or mutant chromosomes; in other cases, dominant or recessive genes produce a disorder that is accompanied by retardation. A specific, detailed account of types of genetic syndromes associated with retardation is beyond the scope of this book. We will limit our discussion to two genetic syndromes whose role in producing retardation is reasonably clear: Down's syndrome and phenylketonuria.

Down's Syndrome Also known as *mongolism,* because of the oriental facial features of its victims, Down's syndrome is probably the single most common chromosomal cause of moderate to severe mental retardation (Robinson & Robinson, 1976; Drew et al., 1984). The disorder occurs once in about 660 births, with the risk dramatically increasing with the age of the mother. Down's syndrome is caused by a genetic defect at one of the chromosomes. With modern amniocentesis techniques, in which samples of the fluid surrounding the fetus can be taken and analyzed, it is often possible to determine whether Down's syndrome is present in an unborn fetus by the seventeenth week of pregnancy. However, such tests usually are performed only when there is reason to believe the disorder may be present.

The signs of mental retardation in a child with Down's syndrome can be present from about age 1. As the child grows, developmental milestones are typically reached later and later than by peers. Most Down's syndrome children have IQs in the range of 40 to 54 (moderately retarded) and are capable of living at home. There is some evidence (Belmont, 1971) that Down's syndrome children tend to show fewer signs of severe psychological disturbance than other types of retarded people. In fact, such children have been characterized as "lovable little creatures full of affection and tenderness" (Benda, 1946, p. 61).

The child with Down's syndrome manifests not only the intellectual and adaptive disabilities of the mentally retarded person, but also a well-documented set of particular physical features, such as floppy muscles, a small and flat nose, eyes that slant upwards, a short neck, small hands with short fingers, and sparse body hair. Most of these features don't affect the child's health directly, but they can be used as diagnostic criteria. However, physical defects such as the reduced size of the brain and the high incidence (40 percent) of heart malfunctions do represent serious threats to physical well-being. About 20 to 30 percent of Down's syndrome babies do not survive their first 2 years; those who do are usually characterized by incomplete sexual development and infertility.

There are indeed many things that combine to make Down's syndrome victims different. Note, though, that Down's syndrome is *not* a type of mental retardation; rather, mental retardation is one of the symptoms of the disorder.

Phenylketonuria (PKU) In contrast to Down's syndrome which is caused by an extra chromosome, phenylketonuria (PKU) is caused by a genetic error in which the enzyme responsible for the metabolism of the biochemical *phenylalanine* is not present at birth. The result of this genetic error is that phenylalanine can build to dangerous levels, producing severe brain damage and consequently mental retardation. Incidence of PKU has been found to range from 1 in every 6800 births to 1 in every 14,000 births (Murdock, 1975). The average IQ of children with untreated PKU is about 50, placing the majority of them in the moderately to severely retarded range.

PKU was first described in 1934 by Folling (Robinson & Robinson, 1976), a veterinarian who developed an interest in a strange disorder present in a newborn child of a relative. The child's mother complained to several physicians that there was a strange odor emanating from the child's urine; dissatisfied with the physicians' claims that there was nothing to worry about, Folling went on to study the problem and to discover the PKU defect.

Caused by a genetic defect, individuals with Down's syndrome have a characteristic set of Oriental-like facial features. (© *Bruce Roberts 1979/Photo Researchers, Inc.*)

Generally, the PKU child appears normal for the first few weeks of life, but usually motor problems appear around 6 months of age. The child may not be able to sit at age 1, and may not walk by 4 years of age. About one-third of PKU children never learn to walk or to control defecation or urination, and about two-thirds never learn to talk. Unlike the usually friendly Down's syndrome children, typical PKU children may be wild, uncontrollable, and generally unpleasant to be around. Psychologically, they may be fearful, restless, and so hyperactive that they require restraint and institutionalization.

Fortunately, the effects of PKU are preventable if the disorder is identified in the newborn infant. A simple urine or blood test for PKU given at birth is now a requirement in most hospitals. When PKU is identified, the infant can be placed immediately on a special phenylalanine-free diet. If done in time, this early dietary restriction usually prevents severe retardation. Berman and Ford (1970) report that successfully treated PKU children tend to perform within the average range of intelligence. The Collaborative Study of Children Treated for PKU (1975) reports that, in 95 percent of cases, neurological examinations are normal at ages 2 to 4, and that IQs are within the average range. Thus, simple control of diet can result in the avoidance of some of these devastating behavioral and intellectual deficits.

The Biological Paradigm: Physical and Environmental Hazards and Mental Retardation

In addition to genetic causes, mental retardation can also be produced by neurological damage brought about by other means. One way to categorize these physical and environmental factors is according to the developmental periods in which they may occur (Lott, 1983). We will consider hazards to normal development at the prenatal, natal, and postnatal periods of early life.

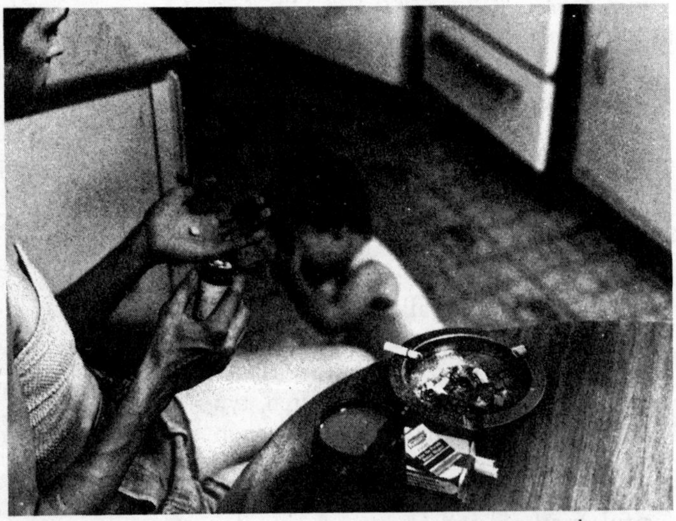

Principle causes for mental retardation sometimes can be traced to ill advised maternal behavior during the prenatal period. (© *1985 Peter Norem*)

Prenatal Hazards The unborn child is vulnerable to several types of hazards that may result in the symptom of mental retardation. One such hazard is *maternal undernutrition during pregnancy.* In a study of animals, Winick and Rosso (1972) found that malnutrition in pregnant rats results in a reduction of as much as 15 percent in the number of brain cells in their offspring. The same authors also have noted that malnutrition in humans resulted in significantly lower birth weights in infants. These lower birth weights may reflect lower brain weight and reduced intellectual ability as well.

Maternal malnutrition may be controllable, but the presence of *acute maternal infection* is more difficult to avoid. About 5 percent of pregnancies may be accompanied by some viral infection (Hellman & Pritchard, 1971). These are most dangerous during the first 3 months of pregnancy. Although most viruses and bacteria are prevented from reaching the fetus by the placental barrier between mother and child, certain damaging agents can get through. Among these viruses are those causing measles, chicken pox, smallpox, polio, and rubella (German measles). Rubella is an acute infection that has been most frequently implicated in the production of birth defects and mental retardation. Of mothers who contract rubella, up to half of their fetuses also become infected while in the womb. The rubella-infected child can show growth deficiency, heart disorders, deafness, blood diseases, *and* mental retardation. Chess et al. (1971) reported moderate mental retardation in 25 percent of rubella-infected children and mild retardation in another 25 percent. As in the case of PKU, knowledge of the cause of rubella-induced retardation and disease has led to effective efforts to prevent its occurrence. Vaccination against rubella for women of childbearing age has drastically reduced the incidence of rubella in pregnant women.

A prenatal hazard also may be present when there is a *chronic maternal infection.* Among the kinds of chronic infections that have been implicated in this group of hazards are herpes infection (type II) and syphilis. Both of these can result in mentally retarded offspring. However, deleterious effects from both disorders can be avoided with adequate medical care, identification, and treatment prior to the eighteenth week of pregnancy.

Besides maternal malnutrition and infections, mental retardation can be caused prenatally by the mother taking *unsafe drugs and medications.* Shepard (1974) noted that at least 20 drugs can produce defects in the human fetus. In the 1950s, a supposedly harmless tranquilizer given to mothers called thalidomide produced eyeless, limbless, hopelessly retarded children in 1 out of 5 women using it. Such occurrences are grim reminders of the potential harmful effects of unsafe drug use during pregnancy. Alcohol also is included among the damaging drugs pregnant women may not use safely. Researchers have shown that physical as well as mental deficiencies tend to be more common among infants born to female alcoholics (K. Jones et al., 1974). Milkovich and Vandenberg (1974) have reported similar results among pregnant women who use some of the minor tranquilizers, such as chlordiazepine and meprobamate (Librium and Miltown).

The unborn child may encounter a variety of other hazards, such as radiation poisoning, Rh incompatibilities, and increased age and stress in the mother. Although these hazards may not always lead to a retarded child, each is capable of changing a normal, healthy fetus into a damaged one.

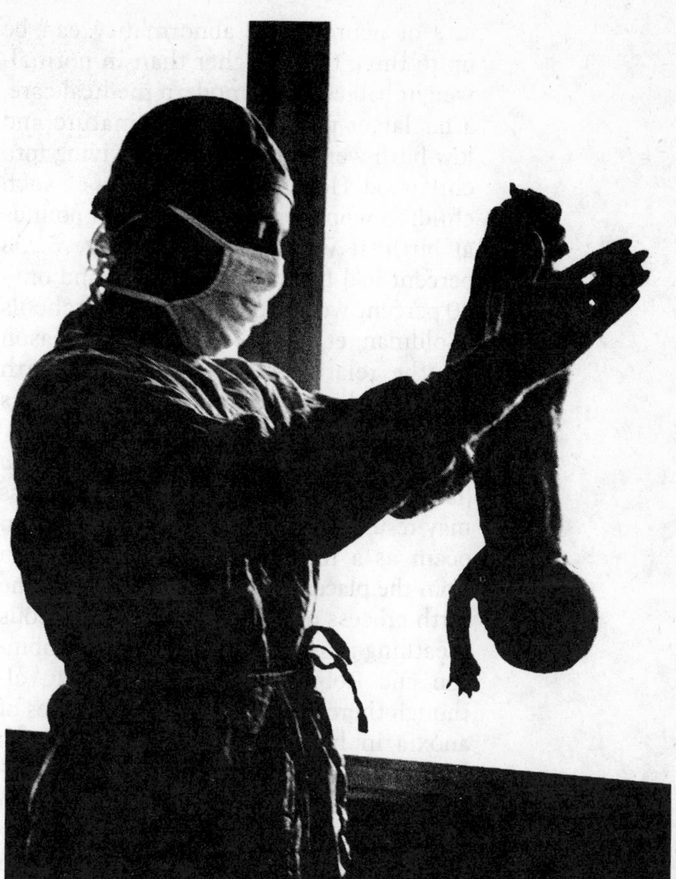

Mild retardation can sometimes be caused by difficulties encountered during the birth process. (*Merrim/Monkmeyer Press Photo Service*)

Natal Hazards Natal hazards are those present during the birth process itself. Generally, these are responsible for mild retardation. The main natal hazards fall into three categories: prematurity, birth anoxia, and kernicterus.

Premature birth usually results in an infant whose birth weight is far below normal (under 5.5 lb). Low birth weight is known to be related to a variety of possible physical and mental difficulties. For example, Niswander and Gordon (1972) reported that the death rate for low-birth-weight infants is 25 times higher than for normal-weight infants. In addition, among those who survive low birth weight, the rate of neurological abnormality can be up to three times higher than in normal-weight babies. With modern medical care, a far larger proportion of premature and low-birth-weight infants are surviving into childhood. However, in a study of 55 such children who weighed less than 3 pounds at birth, it was found that at age 5, 58 percent had IQs of less than 80, and only 30 percent were attending regular schools (Goldman, et al., 1974). The exact reason for the relationship between low birth weight and its concomitant disabilities is not clear.

In addition to low birth weight, *anoxia* (lack of oxygen) during the birth process may result in mild retardation. Anoxia can occur as a result of an early separation from the placental blood supply during the birth process or from lack of spontaneous breathing immediately after birth. Robinson and Robinson (1976) note that, although there are few controlled studies of anoxia in humans, studies in monkeys have demonstrated that anoxia can be associated with permanent brain damage. In a study of human children with a history of breathing difficulties at birth, Graham et al. (1963) reported that these children exhibited more neurological abnormalities and intellectual disabilities than normal controls.

Kernicterus, a disorder resulting from inability of the liver to function adequately in the newborn, can also cause retardation. When levels of a biochemical called bilirubin reach too high a level in the child's body, it can produce the yellowness of the skin characteristic of liver dysfunction, severe destruction of brain cells, muscular disorders, and seizures—in addition to retardation. Careful medical treatment of such infants with blood transfusions and special lights to metabolize bilirubin now have reduced the damaging effects of kernicterus.

Postnatal Hazards Even with uneventful prenatal and natal periods of development, physical hazards can occur shortly *after* birth in several ways. Accidental head injuries account for a large number of the postnatal hazards; the degree of ensuing retardation and disability in these instances usually depends upon the extent of actual damage to the brain. Generally, the more damage, the more severe the retardation.

In addition to head injuries, postnatal brain damage can occur as a result of infections involving the brain. *Encephalitis,* in which the brain itself is inflamed, and *meningitis,* in which the wrappings around the brain and spinal cord are infected, both may be implicated in the development of mental subnormality. Because of its viral nature, encephalitis often cannot be treated with antibiotics, and the chances of permanent brain damage in severe cases may be as high as 1 in 3. Common meningitis, however, is bacterial and can usually be treated with modern medications. Early diagnosis and treatment reduce the possibility that mental retardation will result.

Cranial neoplasms, or brain tumors, can also cause impaired intellectual functioning, seizures, loss of vision, a staggering gait, and headaches. With early identification and treatment, the negative effects of the tumor can be reduced.

The Psychosocial and Systems Paradigms: Retardation Due to Sociocultural Disadvantage

Although striking in their severity, the forms of retardation produced by clearly observable physical abnormalities represent only about one-third of all retardations (Zigler et al., 1984). The majority of retarded individuals are diagnosed as mildly retarded and little or no biological basis can be found for their problems. In these cases, research has shown that the primary sources of intellectual or adaptive deficits are psychosocial or systems-based (Grossman, 1983; Drew et al., 1984; Switzky & Haywood, 1984).

The relationship between adverse social and economic conditions and lowered intellectual abilities is clear. Vogt (1973) reported that in children from families earning less than $3000 per year, illiteracy rates were as much as three times the national average. Inability to read in and of itself does not indicate retardation, but it does make it difficult for a person to function adaptively in society. Further, Cassell (1973) reported that the incidence of mental retardation was consistently higher in poor urban areas.

Among the possible factors implicated in the relationship between social disadvantage and mental retardation is the poor physical health of lower socioeconomic groups. Bauer (1972) notes that most of the physical or environmental hazards to development and the chances of contracting infectious diseases after birth occur more frequently among the poor. The health of children and pregnant women who are poor generally is at greater risk than that of people at higher socioeconomic levels. Without proper prenatal care, many avoidable hazards are not avoidable and can do great harm to lower-class people.

Along with poor health, an inadequate home environment often is found in poorer segments of our society. Houses may be infested by disease-carrying rodents, and they may be overcrowded or unsafe and lack proper heating. These factors make it more likely that a child will suffer brain damage from disease or accident.

In addition, disadvantaged people may have attitudes that contribute to lower intellectual functioning in children. For example, adults may value a passive and conforming child who may fail to experience stimulating learning situations. Likewise, many disadvantaged children have little preschool exposure to the kinds of things they will be doing when they get into formal classrooms. These children may not be able to adjust well to school, may fall behind, and may deteriorate in-

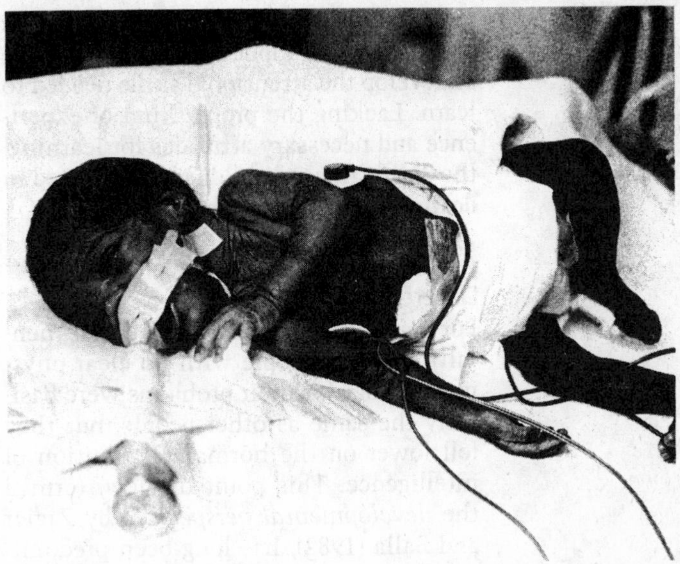

The greater physical problems faced by premature infants become even more difficult to overcome when social and economic deprivations are also experienced. (© *Phiz Mezey/ Taurus Photos*)

Environmental factors are often implicated as the primary cause in instances of retardation. (*H.U.D.*)

tellectually. Also, such children may be overloaded with input and may not be able to develop the attentional skills needed to learn. Lacking the proper kind of experience and necessary attitudes for learning, the disadvantaged child is handicapped in dealing with formal schooling.

A Different View: The Developmental-Difference Controversy

For many years it was assumed that mentally retarded people with no clear physical etiology for their problems were basically the same as other people, but they fell lower on the normal distribution of intelligence. This point of view, termed the *developmental perspective* by Zigler and Balla (1982), has long been predominant. However, in recent years a second perspective representing a combination of the biological and the psychosocial paradigms, has emerged. Termed the *difference perspective* by Zigler and Balla (1982), this view holds that mildly retarded people have basically different capacities for thinking and conceptualizing. That is, they seem to have some biologically based slowing of intellectual processing and their brains seem to work less efficiently than persons with normal intelligence. At this point, there exists much controversy surrounding the developmental versus difference perspectives on mental retardation. Depending upon which view is adopted, perceptions of mentally retarded people and efforts to help them will vary considerably.

Paradigmatic Approaches to the Treatment of Mental Retardation

Reflecting its multiple causality, treatments for mental retardation have also derived from various paradigmatic perspectives. In retardation due to brain damage or hereditary defects, treatment goals may be limited to optimal adaptation to an unchangeable disability. However, in retardation due to psychosocial disadvantage, some "catching up" may be possible through application of the psychosocial and systems paradigms.

The Psychosocial Paradigm: Psychotherapy

Although the major problem with many retarded people is irreversible physical damage and its concomitants, there usually are additional emotional maladjustment problems as well. With the greater stress placed upon the retarded person by simple daily problems of living, it is no wonder that a large number of retarded people also manifest some kind of psychological symptoms. Often these symptoms take the form of acting-out behavior in which the person becomes violent, abusive, or irritable; other times, depression and anxiety may add to the basic intellectual difficulty. When the psychological components of the symptom pattern of the retarded person become so strong as to hinder efforts at education and adaptation, psychotherapy often becomes a major part of treatment (Nuffield, 1983). Generally, the therapeutic approaches are of four types: individual psychotherapy, group psychotherapy, behavior modification, and observational learning. All four can be useful regardless of the "causes" of the retardation.

Individual Psychotherapy Individual therapy with a retarded individual typically involves a professional trained in the areas of mental retardation and psychopathology engaging in a one-to-one relationship with the disturbed individual. Individual therapy with the retarded may be of either the nonverbal or the verbal type, depending upon the client's age and degree of retardation.

Nonverbal individual-therapy techniques represent a variety of approaches to the treatment of the retarded person. *Play therapy* has been adapted to the special problems of the retarded by Leland and Smith (1965, 1972). In their approach, differing combinations of structured or unstructured play materials and structured or unstructured therapeutic techniques are used in an effort to match the therapy to the level of the individual. With severely retarded and disturbed children, unstructured materials (water, finger paint) may be used in a free, unstructured therapy atmosphere. With mild retardates, structured materials (puzzles, coloring books) may be used in a more highly structured atmosphere. A child may be seated at a desk and required to relate more formally to the therapist. In addition to play therapy, other nonverbal techniques useful with adults include art therapy, occupational therapy, and music therapy.

Verbal psychotherapy can be used only with those who are capable of communicating in words. The majority of retarded people in this category will be mildly retarded adults. As is true of individual psychotherapy in general, treatment of emotionally disturbed retarded people may include support, advice, insight, relaxation, or a number of other particular goals. The relationship between therapist and client is often the key factor in successful treatment and recovery.

Group Therapy There is ample evidence that a group-therapy approach has certain advantages over the individual approach. Group therapy is often a more economical mode of treatment, given the shortages of professionals qualified in therapy for the retarded. Further, the group atmosphere allows for safe practice in relating to peers, which may be problematic in individual therapy. Finally, group therapy affords members with models for better adjustment and re-creates a sense of safety and "family feeling" that can be extremely helpful to the frightened or depressed retarded person, regardless of age (Robinson & Robinson, 1976).

Behavior Modification Behavior modification has shown itself to be an effective form of intervention with retardates as well (Drew et al., 1984). Behavior modification involves the application of basic laboratory-derived principles of punishment and reinforcement to the alteration of behavior. To the behavior modifier, the behaviors present in the retarded child or adult can be altered by applying suitable reinforcement.

Behavioral approaches used with retarded people have included operant conditioning, in which reinforcers are given whenever desirable behaviors are performed; aversive conditioning, in which punishments are administered whenever undesirable behaviors are performed; and token economies, in which points or tokens earned for "good" behavior may be traded for candy, gum, movies, or the like. Many professionals believe that behavioral methods have been the most effective form of treatment for the problems of the mentally retarded (Gardner, 1970).

Observational Learning Observational-learning approaches depend upon the presentation of people who model correct behavior after whom retarded people may pattern themselves. Researchers have shown that imitation learning (Bandura, 1969; see also Chapter 5) makes it possible to teach severely and moderately retarded children such basic skills as using the telephone (Stephan et al., 1973) and communicating simple ideas to peers (Talkington et al., 1973). Imitation learning seems to be a highly valuable asset to a therapist working with retarded children. With attractive models, almost all retarded children can learn via imitation.

The Systems Paradigm: Special Education for Retarded People

Although limited in ability, some mentally retarded people are taught how to take care of many of their daily needs. Without such education, the majority of retarded individuals would probably sink lower and lower into intellectual and social deficit. Nevertheless, there is some controversy regarding the necessity of special training for retarded pupils. Some people believe retarded children should be educated separately from normal children, but others feel such separation may be unnecessary and even harmful because it prevents their access to effective normal models.

Special Education Programs From the perspective of those who believe in specialized education for retarded people, the scheme of classification proposed by the AAMD falls short. For special education, retarded people are usually classified into two groups, the *educable mentally retarded* (EMR) and the *trainable mentally retarded* (TMR).

EMR people generally fall into the IQ range of 55 to 70. They may be expected to reach a level of anywhere between third and sixth grade by the time they finish school. Social adjustment and ability to take care of themselves are the primary objectives of their schooling. Special classes for EMR children generally are small and emphasize social competence and occupational skills rather than academic achievement. There are special EMR classes and programs for people of different ages (Robinson & Robinson, 1976):

Infant stimulation class: For children from birth to 3 years of age, infant stimulation involves parents and teachers providing maximum healthy stimulation in the developing child.

Preschool class: For children 3 to 6 years old with mental ages from 2 to 4 years, preschool classes introduce group experiences and continue healthy stimulation.

Elementary primary class: For EMR children 6 to 10 years of age with mental ages from 3 to 6 years, primary classes are generally preacademic. Experience such as those of a regular kindergarten are provided in hopes of building self-confidence, early language development, and security in the school situation.

Elementary intermediate class: For EMR children 9 to 13 years of age with mental ages of 6 to 9 years, intermediate classes designed for children who cannot remain in regular classrooms due to inability to sit quietly and to exhibit other social skills necessary for regular schooling. Focus in class is on academic tools of reading, writing, and mathematics, as well as on practical everyday skills.

Secondary school classes: For EMR children at junior and senior high school levels, secondary school classes emphasize vocational training and domestic skills. Students are taught to apply basic tools to everyday problems such as use of money, reading of newspapers, application for jobs, and the like.

Postschool programs: For persons who have completed formal schooling, postschool programs provide a place where continued vocational and educational guidance is available. Examples of such programs are sheltered workshops and rehabilitation agencies such as the Salvation Army and Goodwill Industries.

With few exceptions, TMR children are more severely retarded than EMR children and present a different set of educational problems. TMR children have IQs in the range of 25 to 55 and may not be expected to achieve any more than the slightest mastery of academic skills. Primary goals for TMR children usually involve their being able to care for themselves and to sustain themselves in simple occupational endeavors. Regular schooling is generally impossible for TMR children, and very few of them can function in the most liberally organized EMR classes. Contributing to the TMRs' difficulties in school is the frequency of physical problems in this more severely retarded group. Children who have seizures, who lack control over elimination, and who show other characteristics often associated with more severe retardation aren't readily accepted by regular schools.

Burton (1974) has stated that the term *education* may be a misnomer for the services needed by TMR children. The goal of the TMR class is to develop basic skills that normal and EMR children usually learn as they grow. TMR children must learn such "simple" tasks as washing themselves, eating properly, speaking, following simple directions, and the like. Instead of books, they must learn to read important signs: signs indicating "Danger" or "Stop" may be much more important to read than simple stories. Efforts to educate the TMR child can be frustrating. In some cases, there is evidence that special programs for TMR children are able to teach little more than the child could learn at home (Dunn, 1973). However, the sense of accomplishment that accompanies seeing a severely retarded child do something as basic as brush his teeth alone for the first time is hard to measure scientifically.

It may sound as if we're saying that special classes for TMR children do as much for teachers and parents as they do for the children themselves. In fact, Kirk (1972) has noted that relieving parents of some responsibility and helping them to see their children's disabilities more realistically are indeed two results of special classes. Kirk notes that the effects on children of TMR classes are hard to assess: "Invariably, the children improved from year to year, but whether this improvement stemmed from the program or from maturation was hard to know" (p. 234).

Normalization of Education of Retarded Children As we noted earlier, not all of the professionals involved in the care of mentally retarded children agree that EMR children need special education. Although it is obvious that TMR children need special attention, there is concern that special education for mildly retarded children may only make these children look and feel more different than they are. The proponents of *normalization*, or *mainstreaming*, believe that mildly retarded children should be integrated into regular classrooms and not placed in special classes (Gottlieb et al., 1983). The idea of mainstreaming retarded children gained impetus in the late 1960s. The beginning of the movement can be traced to the change of position effected by Lloyd Dunn, a long-time advocate of self-contained special classes for the educable retarded child. Dunn (1968) said the following:

> I have loyally supported and promoted special classes for the educably retarded for most of the last 20 years, but with growing disaffection. In my view, much of our past and present practices are morally and educationally wrong. We have been living at the mercy of general educators who have referred their problem children to us. . . . And we have been generally ill-prepared and ineffective in educating these children. Let us stop being pressured into continuing and expanding a special education program that we know to be undesirable for many of the children we are dedicated to serve. (p. 5)

Dunn's statement gave life to a movement away from special placement and toward integration of EMR children into regular classrooms for the majority of the school day. To be sure, all special education has not ceased. Rather, modern education for the EMR child involves a combination of special and regular classes. Special classes may be better while a child is learning to adjust to school, with regular classes tried a few hours a day in certain subjects, such as art or physical education. However, the goal of mainstreaming is to fit the EMR child as much as possible back into his normal peer group.

Several assumptions about the efficiency of mainstreaming may provide further support for its wider implementation (Robinson & Robinson, 1976). One assumption is that the "special classroom is an isolating experience" (p. 383). In general, children from special classes within regular public schools are avoided by the other pupils and often feel lonely, unwanted, and negatively valued. In the mainstream approach, EMR children tend to play with their normal classmates and feel more a part of the entire school group. Another assumption behind mainstreaming is that EMR children are "better able to achieve socially and academically if they are exposed to models whose achievement in both areas is more expert than their own" (p. 383). This assumption is supported by the fact that retarded children placed in regular classrooms may be less disturbed than those forced to remain in special programs. It's also true that a "regular classroom bears a greater resemblance to the real world" (p. 393). By being exposed to the realities of existence among other children, the mainstreamed student will be better able to adjust to life outside the protection of the special program. A final assumption behind mainstreaming is that "exposure to mentally handicapped children helps other children to understand and accept them" (p. 384). From the perspective of labeling theory and general societal reactions to those who are different, this seems a sound argument for normalization. If the prejudice against retarded children can be reduced by education alongside normal children, the threats to the emotional adjustment of the retarded child might be dramatically reduced.

The concept of mainstreaming is so recent that there is little conclusive research bearing upon its efficiency. Mesibov (1976) has noted that the data evaluating mainstreaming generally have been mixed. First of all, the hopes that normal children's attitudes toward retarded children will be improved by normalization haven't been fully realized. Further, MacMillan et al. (1976) have noted that, regardless of specific components of a mainstreaming program, teachers' attitudes toward retarded children in their regular classes may be the major deter-

The great majority of retarded individuals live and work outside of permanent residential institutions. (*Irene B. Bayer/Monkmeyer Press Photo Service*)

minant of the success of normalization programs. MacMillan et al. urge that the *principle* of mainstreaming be separated from its *implementation.* Although early research has shown that the implementation of mainstreaming may be ineffective, the principle may still be sound.

The Systems Paradigm: Residential Placement

Residential placement of retarded people is different from education and psychotherapy in that it typically involves total control of the retarded person's life. Once known as *institutionalization*, residential placement involves removing retarded people from their homes and placing them in a setting where they may live either permanently or for some extended period of time. Although many moderately retarded individuals live in residential facilities, the majority of those who are institutionalized fall in the severely and profoundly retarded categories. In 1982, the number of retarded people in residential centers in the United States was about 250,000 (Hauber et al., 1984). Since about 7 to 9 million people in the United States may be considered mentally retarded, the number in permanent residential status is relatively small. This testifies to efforts to maintain retarded people in the community as part of the mainstream.

The decision to place a child in a residential facility is a stressful and emotional one for most parents. Yet there comes a time in the life of some families with a retarded child when this decision must be faced.

Personal Experience: The Father of a Severely Retarded Child

We had Ronnie put in an institution a year ago . . . and my wife still cries whenever she sees his picture. We visit him a couple of times a year, but that doesn't seem to help 'cause it just brings back all the sadness that we feel because he's not with us and because he had to be born retarded. It's really not fair for something like that to happen to a kid or to the rest of the family. Maybe there's something we could have done to prevent it . . . I don't know . . . the doctors don't know exactly what caused it. His brain didn't get enough oxygen when he was born. If it had, he would be living with us today. We just couldn't help him at home. He wasn't learning anything, and we were all pretty upset most of the time. We must have taken him to 10 different specialists and tested him, but nothing helps. Maybe he's happier there, but it hurts no matter where he is. It would have been easier for him and us if he hadn't lived. . . . At least then the grief would have gone away.

The decision to place a child in a residential facility is complex. An extensive study by Saenger (1960) of factors related to the decision to institutionalize a retarded child suggests several basic conclusions. First, the more severely retarded a child, the more likely it is that residential placement will be chosen. Nearly 9 out of 10 of Saenger's sample of profoundly retarded people were hospitalized as opposed to 1 out of 10 of the moderately to mildly retarded group. Saenger also noted that the presence of behavior problems *outside the home* was significantly related to institutionalization. A child who caused little or no trouble for parents was less likely to be placed in a hospital. Another reason for institutionalization is that the retarded person causes unbearable stress and trouble at home. Finally, the fact that outpatient care is not readily available to many lower socioeconomic groups may leave institutionalization as the only recourse for the family of a poor retarded person. Many families probably would prefer to keep a retarded person at home, but when their choice is limited to no treatment or residential treatment, they frequently are forced to decide in favor of the latter.

Residential treatment can take any of several forms. There are the traditional state or private hospitals, as well as a variety of residential programs that can provide positive experiences. One example of an alternative to the state hospital is the *group home,* a sort of boarding house in which a limited number (perhaps 40) of retarded people live under the same roof with a staff of professionals. In this protected environment, home members can carry on simple vocational tasks, produce saleable items in sheltered workshops, take part in group therapy, and live as nearly normal a life as possible. The group home can avoid many of the detrimental aspects of the large institution and maintain many of the characteristics of a real "home" for the retarded person.

Concluding Comments

In few other forms of psychopathology is it possible to see so clearly the relationship between brain function and abnormal behavior as in the organic mental disorders and mental retardation. Throughout this chapter, we have described patterns in which identifiable brain damage has been found to be the cause of cognitive, emotional, and behavioral changes and deficits in people. However, we have also seen that even in these clearly biologically based disorders, the psychosocial and systems paradigms have been able to make significant contributions. The lesson to be learned here can be an important one, for it suggests that even when a clear basis for a disorder is identified, scientists and practitioners should not assume that amelioration of that disorder can only derive from the paradigm which best explains it. For example, if it is assumed that the course and symptoms of Alzheimer's disease are purely biological, then the helpful effects of psychosocial and systems interventions might never be realized. Many older persons might be simply left alone and in fact harmed by the erroneous assumption that since their problems are biologically based, nonbiological intervention will be of little use. Similarly, if retarded individuals are believed to be biologically limited, efforts to improve their level of adaptive functioning might not be undertaken. We believe that to use the paradigmatic perspective to its fullest, means to try to apply each major paradigm in all cases of behavioral disturbance. The paradigm which best explains a disorder may not always be the only paradigm which can be applied in efforts to treat it.

Summary Chart

In Chapter 12 we discussed two forms of disorders in which brain functions or dysfunctions are related to psychopathology. We began by describing the variety of brain syndromes or symptom patterns associated with organic mental disorders;

The brain syndromes:

Delirium: Acute, temporary, clouding of consciousness

Dementia: More permanent, progressive, loss of intellectual abilities

Intoxication and withdrawal: Most commonly associated with chemical use

Other brain syndromes: Amnestic syndrome,

organic hallucinosis, organic delusional syndrome, organic personality syndrome

We then examined the organic mental disorders associated with injury, disease, and aging.

Disorders associated with injury: Trauma, toxic materials

Disorders associated with disease: Encephalitis, meningitis, syphilis, epilepsy, nutritional disorders, neoplasms, Huntington's chorea

Disorders associated with aging: Senile dementia, presenile dementias, Alzheimer's disease, Pick's disease

After discussing briefly the applications of the biological, psychosocial, and systems paradigms to the treatment of the organic mental disorders, we turned our attention to a second group of disorders in which brain dysfunction is often involved, mental retardation. We discussed first the classification of mental retardation:

Classification is based on intelligence *and* adaptive behavior.

Mild mental retardation: 50 to 70 IQ, typically nonneurological

Moderate mental retardation: 35 to 49 IQ, frequent brain damage

Severe mental retardation: 20 to 34 IQ, most in institutions, often genetic

Profound mental retardation: Less than 20 IQ, cannot attend to even basic needs

Following are paradigmatic explanations for mental retardation:

The biological paradigm: Genetic factors as in Down's syndrome and PKU

The biological paradigm: Physical and environmental hazards, prenatally, natally, and postnatally

The psychosocial and systems paradigms: Retardation due to sociocultural disadvantage deriving from economic, health, and educational conditions

Several treatment approaches have been derived from the various paradigms as well.

The psychosocial paradigm: Psychotherapy (individual, group, and behavioral)

The systems paradigm: Special education programs for educable and trainable mentally retarded people; mainstreaming of mentally retarded people

The systems paradigm: Residential placement

CHAPTER 13

Organic Mental Disorders Associated with Substance Abuse

Certainly few people would purposely injure their brains or attempt to contract degenerative nerve diseases in order to experience the effects of disrupted brain function in the form of a brain syndrome. However, many people in our society use chemicals purposely to produce such disruptions and attain certain "desirable" symptom patterns. Due to the voluntary nature of many forms of drug usage, those who induce brain syndromes chemically are considered by many to be responsible for their own problems and often are not seen or treated as disordered. Further, the use of certain chemicals, such as alcohol, caffeine, and nicotine, is so widespread among "mainstream" society that it is sometimes hard for people to see the habitual use of these chemicals as a mental or behavioral problem. Nevertheless, in terms of the number of people adversely affected both directly and indirectly by the abuse of chemicals, the organic mental disorders associated with drug use represent a major problem for the science of abnormal psychology, a problem in which each of the three major paradigms has been extensively applied.

Patterns of Organic Mental Disorders Associated with Substance Abuse

According to DSM-III, the occurrence of brain syndromes caused by the use of drugs are classified as *substance-induced organic mental disorders.* Thus, the symptom pattern of intoxication which follows ingestion of large amounts of alcohol would be termed an *alcohol organic mental disorder,* or the withdrawal syndrome associated with cessation of heavy use of barbiturates would be termed a *barbiturate organic mental disorder.*

Substance-induced organic mental disorder is diagnosed in *each instance* in which one or several brain syndromes are caused by the use of a drug. However, repeated, voluntary, and habitual production of individual substance-induced organic mental disorders represents yet another category of DSM-III diagnoses, *the substance-use disorders.* Previously termed "drug abuse" and "drug addiction," there are two types of substance-use disorders in DSM-III—*substance abuse* and *substance dependence* (Bennett et al., 1983).

Substance abuse (or pathological drug use) is defined on the basis of three criteria. The first criterion requires constant (daily) drug use leading to intoxication that cannot be stopped even when physical symptoms associated with the drug are worsened. Thus, an alcoholic may continue drinking even in the face of extreme illness associated with liver disease. The second criterion for substance abuse is met when people's use of a substance has resulted in problems with family, friends, employers, or the law. The third and final criterion involves pathological substance use for more than 1 month.

Reflecting a much more severe drug problem than substance abuse, in *substance dependence* the pathological use of drugs leads to a physiological need for the substance. Physiological dependence may be shown by increased tolerance for the drug and the occurrence of a withdrawal syndrome when the drug usage is stopped. Depending upon the specific substance to which people are "addicted" (dependent), withdrawal symptoms can range from mild tension and irritability, as in the case of caffeine, to life-threatening disruption of body functions, as may be seen in the abuse of alcohol and heroin (Pattison & Kaufman, 1982). See Figure 13-1 for a chart describing the kinds of symptoms associated with the abuse of varying chemicals.

Organic Mental Disorder Associated with Alcohol

Although DSM-III categorizes alcohol abuse as one pattern among many involving the ingestion of chemicals to achieve desired brain syndromes, due to its impact and frequency (see Figure 13-2), it deserves, and will be given, somewhat more of an emphasis (Johnston et al., 1982). Estimates of the prevalence of alcoholism in the United States suggest that as many as 1 in 20 Americans is addicted to this substance. Given that the drinking problems of each of these 11 or 12 million people affect an average of three other people (spouse, children, etc.), it is estimated that up to 45 million people live with an alcohol-induced problem (Pattison & Kaufman, 1982). There is no other physical or mental disorder with such an impact. Alcohol can adversely affect people in all walks of life and at every socioeconomic level. The chemical is the most freely available of abused drugs and, although sometimes seen as different in some way from other addictive compounds, it is widely abused and associated with the largest number of self-induced organic brain syndromes (see Figure 13-3).

Alcohol use is associated with a variety of organic brain syndromes including intoxication, amnestic disorder, dementia, delirium, withdrawal, and hallucinosis (Robins, 1982; Seixas, 1981; Nathan & Hay, 1984). The popularity of alcohol usage in our society is reflected in the nearly 120 million people who are estimated to have experienced an alcohol-based brain syndrome (Seixas, 1981).

Alcohol can produce both abuse and dependence. Alcohol abuse is characterized by a need for daily use or regular *binge* drinking, inability to cut down, occasional loss of memory ("blackouts") for periods of hours or days, and drinking of nonbeverage sources of alcohol such as vanilla extract, Sterno, hair tonic, or aftershave lotion. In alcohol dependence, peo-

Alcohol is not always associated with a good time. (*Michael Weisbrot and Family*)

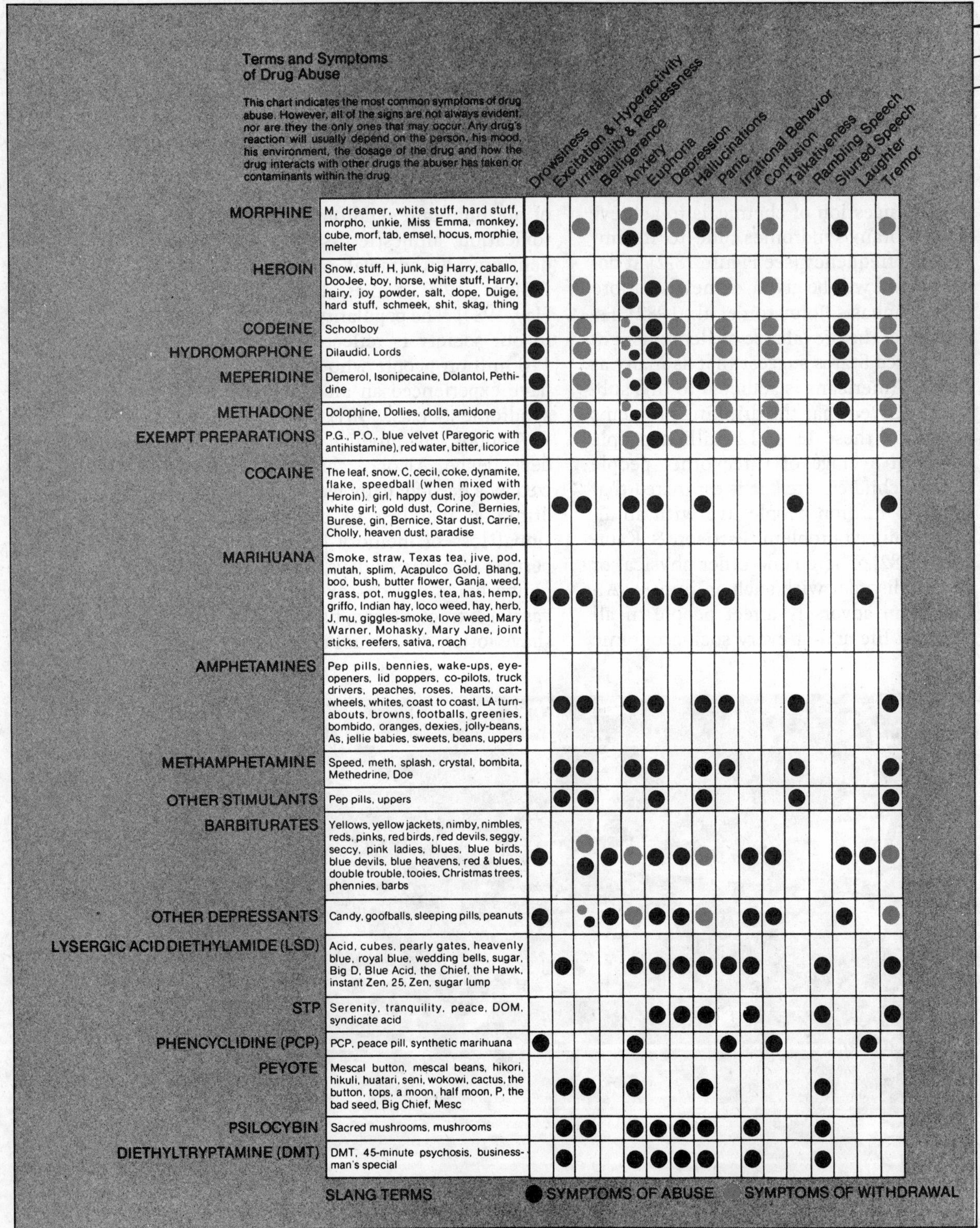

Terms and Symptoms of Drug Abuse

This chart indicates the most common symptoms of drug abuse. However, all of the signs are not always evident, nor are they the only ones that may occur. Any drug's reaction will usually depend on the person, his mood, his environment, the dosage of the drug and how the drug interacts with other drugs the abuser has taken or contaminants within the drug.

	Slang Terms	Drowsiness	Excitation & Hyperactivity	Irritability & Restlessness	Belligerence	Anxiety	Euphoria	Depression	Hallucinations	Panic	Irrational Behavior	Confusion	Talkativeness	Rambling Speech	Slurred Speech	Laughter	Tremor
MORPHINE	M, dreamer, white stuff, hard stuff, morpho, unkie, Miss Emma, monkey, cube, morf, tab, emsel, hocus, morphie, melter	A		W		W/A	A	W	A	W		W			A		W
HEROIN	Snow, stuff, H, junk, big Harry, caballo, DooJee, boy, horse, white stuff, Harry, hairy, joy powder, salt, dope, Duige, hard stuff, schmeek, shit, skag, thing	A		W		W/A	A	W		W		W			A		W
CODEINE	Schoolboy	A		W		W/A	A	W		W		W			A		W
HYDROMORPHONE	Dilaudid, Lords	A		W		W/A	A	W		W		W			A		W
MEPERIDINE	Demerol, Isonipecaine, Dolantol, Pethidine	A		W		W/A	A	W	A	W		W			A		W
METHADONE	Dolophine, Dollies, dolls, amidone	A		W		W/A	A	W		W		W			A		W
EXEMPT PREPARATIONS	P.G., P.O., blue velvet (Paregoric with antihistamine), red water, bitter, licorice	A		W		W	A	W		W		W					W
COCAINE	The leaf, snow, C, cecil, coke, dynamite, flake, speedball (when mixed with Heroin), girl, happy dust, joy powder, white girl; gold dust, Corine, Bernies, Burese, gin, Bernice, Star dust, Carrie, Cholly, heaven dust, paradise		A	A		A	A		A				A				A
MARIHUANA	Smoke, straw, Texas tea, jive, pod, mutah, splim, Acapulco Gold, Bhang, boo, bush, butter flower, Ganja, weed, grass, pot, muggles, tea, has, hemp, griffo, Indian hay, loco weed, hay, herb, J, mu, giggles-smoke, love weed, Mary Warner, Mohasky, Mary Jane, joint sticks, reefers, sativa, roach	A	A	A		A	A	A	A	A			A			A	
AMPHETAMINES	Pep pills, bennies, wake-ups, eye-openers, lid poppers, co-pilots, truck drivers, peaches, roses, hearts, cartwheels, whites, coast to coast, LA turnabouts, browns, footballs, greenies, bombido, oranges, dexies, jolly-beans, As, jellie babies, sweets, beans, uppers		A	A		A	A		A	A			A				A
METHAMPHETAMINE	Speed, meth, splash, crystal, bombita, Methedrine, Doe		A	A		A	A		A	A			A				A
OTHER STIMULANTS	Pep pills, uppers		A	A			A		A				A				A
BARBITURATES	Yellows, yellow jackets, nimby, nimbles, reds, pinks, red birds, red devils, seggy, seccy, pink ladies, blues, blue birds, blue devils, blue heavens, red & blues, double trouble, tooies, Christmas trees, phennies, barbs	A		W/A	A	W	A	A	W		A	A			A	A	W
OTHER DEPRESSANTS	Candy, goofballs, sleeping pills, peanuts	A		W/A	A	W	A	A	W		A	A			A		W
LYSERGIC ACID DIETHYLAMIDE (LSD)	Acid, cubes, pearly gates, heavenly blue, royal blue, wedding bells, sugar, Big D, Blue Acid, the Chief, the Hawk, instant Zen, 25, Zen, sugar lump		A			A	A	A	A	A	A			A			A
STP	Serenity, tranquility, peace, DOM, syndicate acid						A	A	A		A			A			A
PHENCYCLIDINE (PCP)	PCP, peace pill, synthetic marihuana	A				A				A		A				A	
PEYOTE	Mescal button, mescal beans, hikori, hikuli, huatari, seni, wokowi, cactus, the button, tops, a moon, half moon, P, the bad seed, Big Chief, Mesc		A	A		A			A					A			
PSILOCYBIN	Sacred mushrooms, mushrooms		A	A		A	A	A	A		A			A			
DIETHYLTRYPTAMINE (DMT)	DMT, 45-minute psychosis, businessman's special		A			A	A	A	A		A			A			

SLANG TERMS ● SYMPTOMS OF ABUSE ● SYMPTOMS OF WITHDRAWAL

(A = symptom of abuse, black dot; W = symptom of withdrawal, grey dot)

Figure 13-1 Terms and Symptoms of Drug Abuse. (*United States Department of Justice, Drug Enforcement Administration.*)

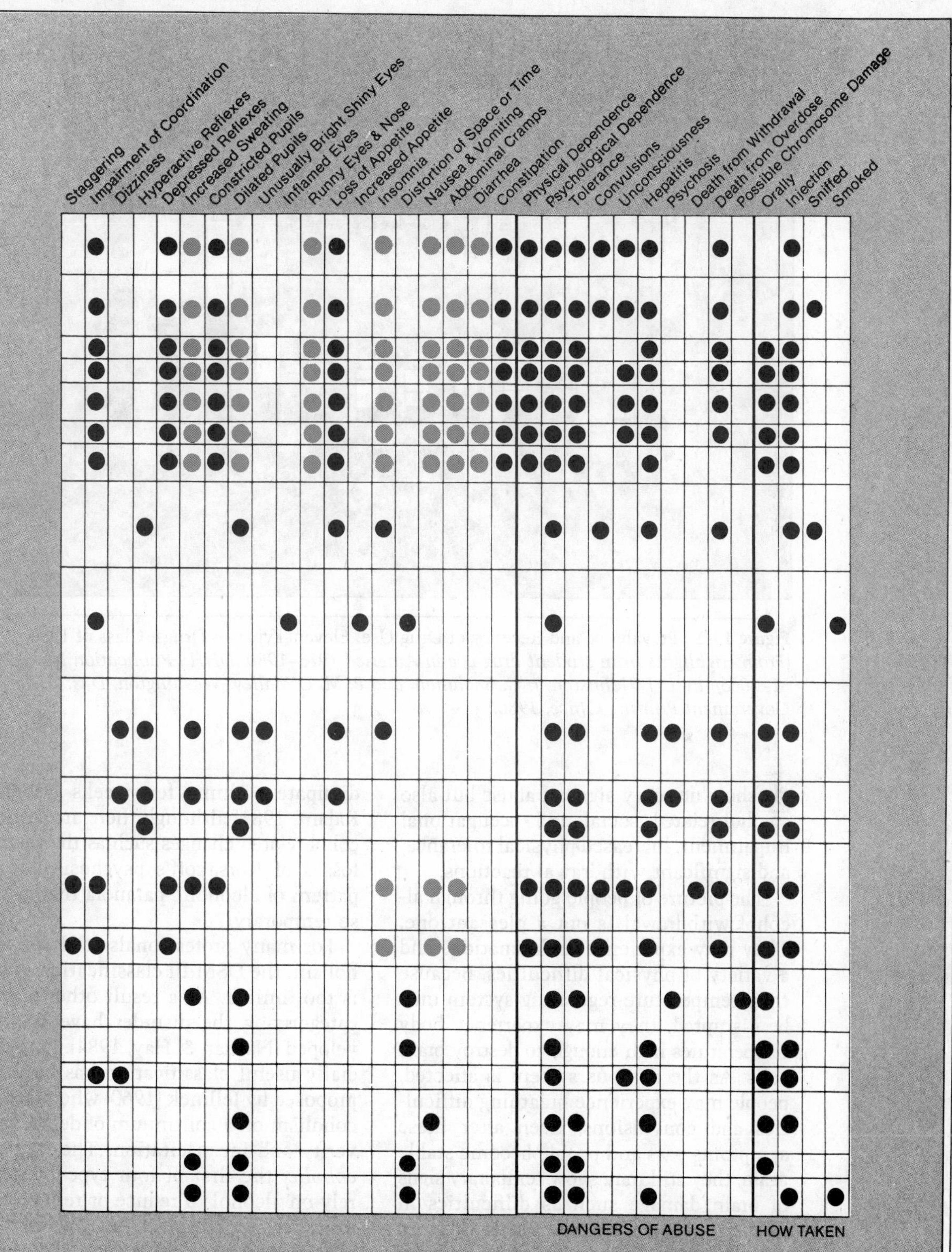
Staggering
Impairment of Coordination
Dizziness
Hyperactive Reflexes
Depressed Reflexes
Increased Sweating
Constricted Pupils
Dilated Pupils
Unusually Bright Shiny Eyes
Inflamed Eyes
Runny Eyes & Nose
Loss of Appetite
Increased Appetite
Insomnia
Distortion of Space or Time
Nausea & Vomiting
Abdominal Cramps
Diarrhea
Constipation
Physical Dependence
Psychological Dependence
Tolerance
Convulsions
Unconsciousness
Hepatitis
Psychosis
Death from Withdrawal
Death from Overdose
Possible Chromosome Damage
Orally
Injection
Sniffed
Smoked
DANGERS OF ABUSE
HOW TAKEN

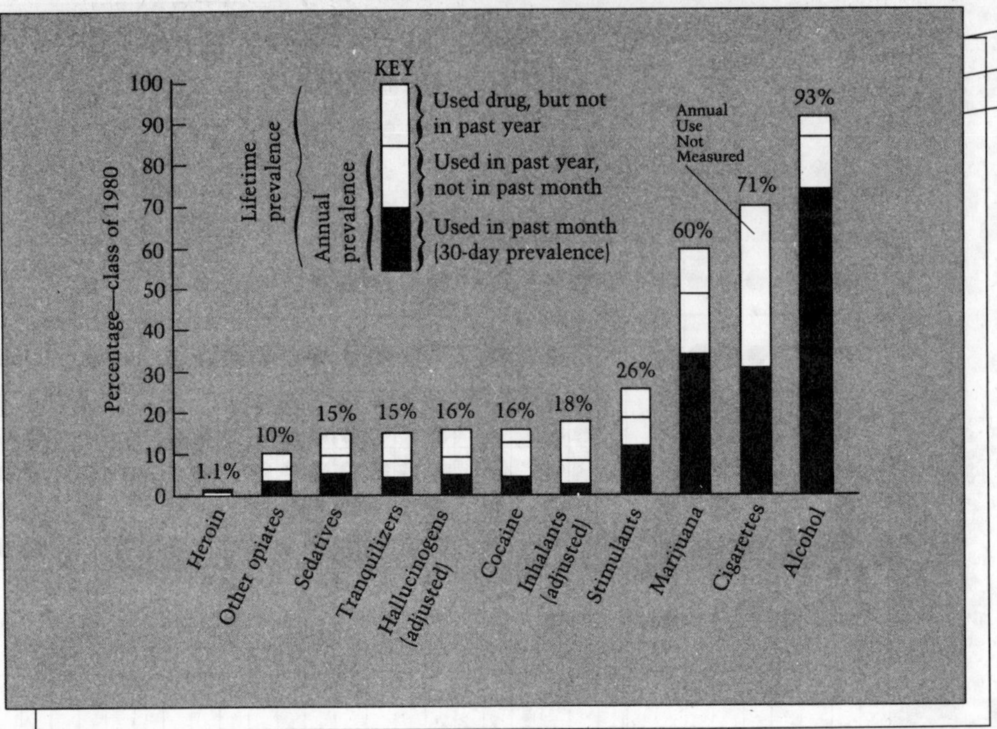

Figure 13-2 Prevalence and Recency of Drug Use. Eleven Types of Drugs, Class of 1980. [*From Highlights from student drug use in America 1975–1980* (*DHHS Publication No. ADM 81–1066), by L. D. Johnston, J. G. Bachman, and P. M. O'Malley. Washington, D.C.: U.S. Government Printing Office, 1980.*]

ple show not only signs of abuse but also alcohol-related social and occupational impairment, increased physical tolerance, and significant withdrawal reactions.

The picture of people going through alcohol withdrawal is not a pleasant one. They may experience hallucinations and a variety of physical difficulties. Because their temperature-regulating system may be disrupted, they may experience body temperatures high enough to destroy brain cells. As the nervous system is affected, people may experience breathing difficulties and convulsions. Even after these symptoms pass and people become stable again, they still may show temporary signs of brain damage such as difficulties in writing or dialing a phone. Fortunately, in most cases these neurological disabilities dissipate within a few weeks (Sellers & Kalant, 1981) although there are some alcohol-related changes such as the memory losses of Korsakoff's psychosis and the pattern of alcoholic paranoia that are not so temporary.

For many professionals studying alcoholism, the DSM-III classification system is too limited. As a result other ways of categorizing the disorder have been developed (Nathan & Hay, 1984). One especially useful classification has been that proposed by Jellinek (1960) who placed alcoholism on a continuum of degree of severity and incapacitation. The *alpha alcoholic,* the first of four types, tends to rely on alcohol to reduce or relieve emotional or physical pain, but does not usually lose control over the use of the drug.

The National Institute of Alcohol Abuse and Alcoholism (NIAAA) has published (1972) a lengthy report on the occurrence of drinking problems. We will mention some of the more stable of their findings so that you may see how alcohol-related problems manifest themselves.

Consumption rates: Americans consume, on the average, 2.61 gallons of alcohol per year. The Pacific states and New England lead with averages of around 3 gallons per year; the south-central states (Alabama, Mississippi, Louisiana, and Arkansas) trail with a rate of 1.63 gallons.

Sex: Men drink more than women and are much more likely to become alcoholics. Heavy drinking is most likely to occur in both men and women between the ages of 45 and 49.

Occupation: Most professionals and businessmen (83 percent of them) drink, but they are less likely to become heavy drinkers than people lower on the occupational ladder. Generally, the lower the occupational level, the more likely alcoholism is to develop out of heavy drinking.

National origin: Americans whose fathers were born in Ireland, Italy, or Great Britain report the highest percentage of drinkers among them (around 90 percent). Of these three nationalities, the Irish claim the highest percentage of *heavy* drinkers (33 percent).

Socioeconomic level: Among both men and women, the lowest socioeconomic group had a *smaller* percentage of drinkers than the highest group. The percentage of *heavy* drinkers, however, did not differ according to socioeconomic status.

National drinking patterns: France and Italy are by far the leaders in world alcohol consumption (6.53 and 4.01 gallons per year per person, respectively). The United States is in the middle of the pack (2.61), with Finland (1.03), Iceland (0.96), and Israel (0.82) claiming the lowest alcohol intake. Occurrence of alcohol-related problems seems to parallel these consumption rates fairly closely.

Figure 13-3 Alcoholics—Who Are They?

Interpersonal relationships may deteriorate when the person finds that the use of alcohol is frequently more important than relating to others. In the second type, the *beta alcoholic,* physical problems caused by the use of alcohol occur in addition to interpersonal difficulties. These physical diseases may include cirrhosis of the liver and ulcers, but physical or psychological *dependence* is not present. The *gamma alcoholic* is one step worse than the beta. There is physiological dependence such that cessation of drinking produces a withdrawal syndrome. Gamma drinkers have usually lost control of their alcohol use and may exhibit significant signs of physical, psychological, and social deterioration.

The last and most severe form Jellinek described is the *delta alcoholic.* Here the drinker *cannot* abstain from drinking for any period of time and usually does not experience the brief periods of sobriety of the gamma drinker. In the delta alcoholic, cessation of drinking usually leads to severe withdrawal symptoms. The delta alcoholic is psychologically and physically dependent upon alcohol and experiences the most severe social deterioration. It is not uncommon for family, friends, and job to be sacrificed or lost as drinking becomes the all-consuming behavior pattern of the individual.

While there have been other efforts to develop special classifications for alcoholism (see Pattison & Kaufman, 1982; Morey et al., 1984), Jellinek's seems to be an excellent aid in thinking about the stages of alcoholism. The process of deterioration described by Jellinek, however, is only part of the picture, for there seem also to be specific stages in the recovery of an alcoholic person. As proposed by Glatt (1974), this overall process of addiction and recovery is depicted in Figure 13-4. As can be seen, alcoholism invades all aspects of human function, and it is often necessary for a person to "bottom out" completely before being ready to turn to professional help.

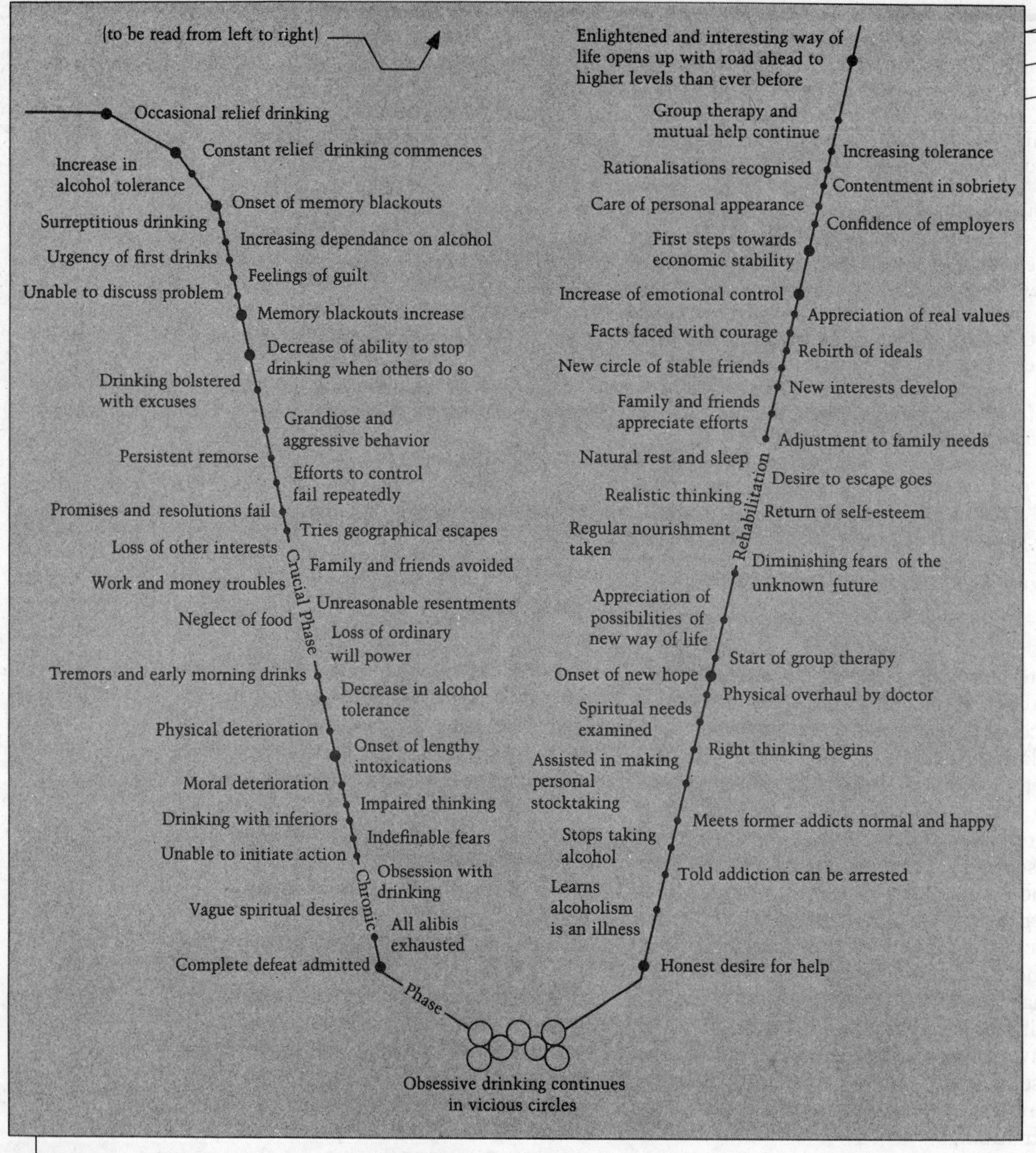

Figure 13-4 A Chart of Alcoholic Addiction and Recovery. (*From A Guide to Addiction and Its Treatment, by M. Glatt. Copyright 1974 by MTP Press, Ltd. Published in the U.S.A. by John Wiley & Sons, Inc. Reprinted by permission.*)

Organic Mental Disorder Associated with Barbiturates, Sedatives, and Other Hypnotic Drugs

Although alcohol is often used for its sleep producing effects, the most common chemicals used to produce drowsiness and sleep are the barbiturates (e.g., secobarbital and phenobarbital), common sedatives, the minor tranquilizers (e.g., Valium and Librium), and the mild hypnotics (e.g., chloral hydrate and Quaalude). All these chemicals in great enough doses can produce the brain syndromes of intoxication, withdrawal, delirium, and amnestic disorder (Sadava, 1984).

As with alcohol, both substance abuse and substance dependence occur with the sedative-hypnotics group. Withdrawal from these chemicals can be even more severe and dangerous than from alcohol and may result in severe anxiety, nightmares, tremors, nausea, vomiting, seizures, and delirium.

Personal Experience: Organic Mental Disorder with Use of Valium

In her book, *I'm Dancing as Fast as I Can,* Barbara Gordon has described her experience of substance dependence on Valium. She stated that she began taking the drug after a back injury. Over a period of 10 years, her dosage increased from 4 to 30 milligrams a day. She "took pills before she went to a department store, rode a bus, or walked in the streets." The drug became as much a part of her daily ritual as "putting on lipstick." A very successful producer of television documentaries, Ms. Gordon knew she had a problem when she "couldn't get out of the house without taking them. I was taking them before an anxiety attack, to try to ward it off, or to minimize the terror. And it didn't always work, either." (Gordon, 1980)

Organic Mental Disorders Associated with the Opioids

The opioid substances, which include heroin and morphine, may be taken either orally, intravenously, intranasally (sniffed), or subcutaneously (injected under the skin) (American Psychiatric Association, DSM-III, 1980; Deneau & Mule, 1981; Sutker & Archer, 1984). Opium is derived from the milklike sap of the opium poppy and has been used medicinally for at least 5000 years as a pain reliever. Although morphine is used medically, it and the other opioids are frequently misused, causing intoxication and withdrawal. Opium intoxication is characterized by symptoms such as euphoria, apathy, inactivity, drowsiness, slurred speech, and impairment in attention and memory. Withdrawal from opioids can produce tears, a runny nose, high fever, raised blood pressure, and insomnia. Long-term abuse of, or dependence on, the opioids has also been associated with progressive physical deterioration as shown in the following excerpt from a 1962 Supreme Court Decision in the case of *Robinson vs. California*:

> To be a confirmed drug addict is to be one of the walking dead. . . . The teeth have rotted out, the appetite is lost, and the stomach and intestines don't function properly. The gall bladder becomes inflamed; eyes and skin turn a bilious yellow; in some cases membranes of the nose turn a flaming red; the partition

"Cold turkey" withdrawal from heroin is accompanied by nightmares, sweating, and choking. (*Michael Weisbrot and Family*)

separating the nostrils is eaten away—breathing is difficult. Oxygen in the blood decreases; bronchitis and tuberculosis develop. Good traits of character disappear and bad ones emerge. Sex organs become affected. Veins collapse and livid purplish scars remain. Boils and abscesses plague the skin; gnawing pain racks the body. Nerves snap; vicious twitching develops. Imaginary and fantastic fears blight the mind and sometimes complete insanity results. Often times, too, death comes much too early in life. . . . Such is the torment of being a drug addict; such is the plague of being one of the dead.

Organic Mental Disorders Associated with Cocaine

Like opium, cocaine has long been used medicinally, primarily as an anesthetic. It is derived from the leaf of the shrub, *Erythroxylon coca,* and can be chewed, brewed, injected, sniffed, snorted, or smoked in the form of a paste which is mixed with tobacco or marijuana (Van Dyke, 1981). Due to the chemical characteristics of cocaine, the body does not build up a tolerance for it; thus, there is no physiological withdrawal syndrome and hence no DSM-III diagnosis of substance dependence. In fact, the only cocaine-produced brain syndrome is intoxication and the only cocaine-associated substance use disorder is *cocaine abuse* (Sadava, 1984).

Personal Experience: Cocaine Use

I got a mental craving for more and more, buying additional "coke" from other addicts and occasionally exchanging "H" for extra "C." I could use all my supply of "C" [5 g] within four hours and I had none left in the afternoon. . . . I kept shooting it up. . . . Many people gave themselves overdoses of "C." . . . I once nearly killed myself through such an overdose: I felt a terrible explosion in my head and my heart beat violently. On that occasion the "C" crystals were damp so I didn't know how much I was using . . . the effects were much stronger than usual. Ordinarily after mainlining "C" the "flash" came within seconds: my heart started beating fast, there was a nervous excitement which usually scared me. . . . The first time when I took "C" I got the "flash," although I only took very little, perhaps ⅓ g, but later on I needed more to get the "flash." I liked the stimulation but every time I took "C" I had a fear of overdosing myself.

Source: From M. Glatt, *A Guide to Addiction and its Treatment.* Copyright 1974 by MTP Press, Ltd. Published in the U.S.A. by John Wiley & Sons, Inc. Reprinted by permission.

The absence of tolerance and withdrawal may at first make cocaine seem like a "safe" drug. However, even though it is among the most widely used "recreational" drugs, recent evidence suggests that cocaine may be more dangerous than it may seem. Van Dyke (1981), for example, has reported that oral, nasal, and intravenous administration of cocaine can produce an increased sense of well-being, increased activity level, feelings of grandiosity, increased blood pressure, nausea, anorexia, or vomiting. However, he warns that the cocaine smokers or "pastaleros" are placing themselves in particular danger the more they continue the drug's use. Smoking of cocaine paste can produce, in addition to the desired "high," undesired personality changes, depression, hallucinations, and paranoid psychosis requiring hospitalization (Jeri et al., 1978).

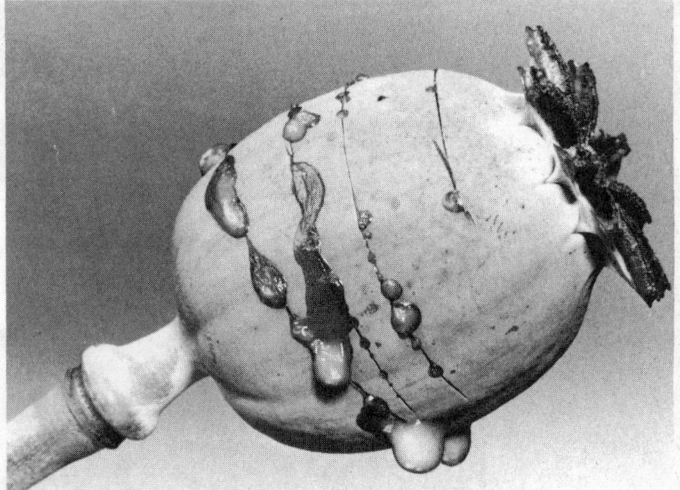

When slit, the opium poppy oozes raw opium. (*Charles Marden Fitch/Taurus Photos*)

Organic Mental Disorders Associated with Amphetamines

While cocaine is considered by many to be "the" drug of the 1980s, many experts feel that the drug of the 1950s and 1960s was amphetamine (Morgan, 1981). More commonly known as "speed," the amphetamines can produce a number of organic brain syndromes including intoxication, delirium, delusional disorder, and withdrawal. Also, however, a unique reaction called *amphetamine delusional disorder* rapidly develops in some people after taking amphetamines. It is marked by paranoid ideas of persecution, distortion of body image, and misperception of other people's faces. At times, people may hallucinate insects or worms crawling under their skin. The reaction usually lasts for about 1 week, but can continue for as long as a year.

Both abuse and dependence can occur with habitual amphetamine use. Withdrawal from amphetamines is characterized by severely depressed mood and fatigue, disturbed sleep patterns (either sleeping too much or too little), and increased dreaming. Although the more severe symptoms of amphetamine withdrawal usually last for only a few days, people can remain irritable and depressed for months.

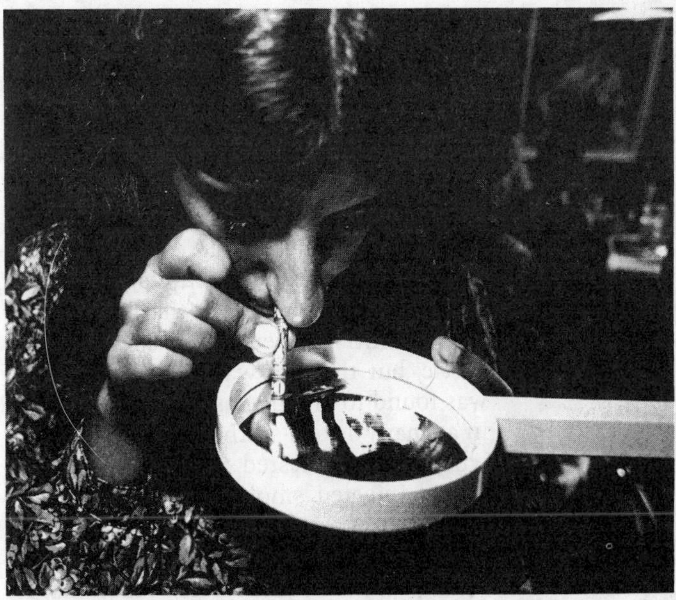

While use of heroin is often a solitary undertaking, use of cocaine is increasingly common at many social gatherings. (*Michael Weisbrot and Family*)

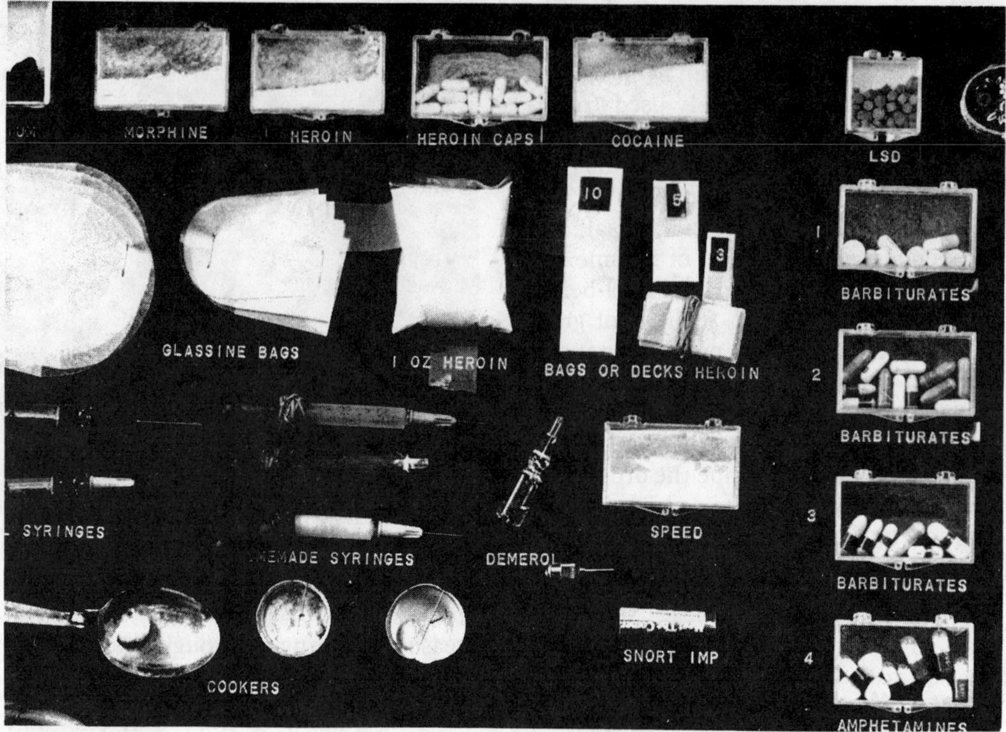

The variety of types or forms of abused drugs is remarkable. (*Mimi Forsyth/Monkmeyer Press Photo Service*)

Organic Mental Disorders Associated with Phencyclidine

Commonly known as "PCP" or "Angel Dust," phencyclidine produces euphoria, grandiosity, sensation of slowed time, diminished responsiveness to pain, agitation, anxiety, and synesthesias ("seeing" sounds or "hearing" pictures) (Luisada, 1981). First discovered in the late 1950s, it was initially developed as an anesthetic, but this use was stopped when it was found to produce psychotic reactions in as many as one-sixth of the patients on whom it was tested. PCP may be ingested, injected, smoked, or inhaled. In its early use as a recreational drug, it was usually ingested, but because this method often produced such adverse reactions, it rapidly fell from favor. However, according to Luisada (1981), PCP is now sometimes "disguised" by combining it with marijuana. The combination may be called "Wacky Weed," "Super Grass," or "Killer Weed."

With the switch to smoking as the primary mode of administration, PCP is now being more widely used. In DSM-III, it is associated with the brain syndromes of intoxication and delirium. Since, as with cocaine, physiological tolerance and withdrawal do not occur with PCP, the diagnosis of substance dependence is not appropriate. However, *PCP abuse* describes habitual and maladaptive or pathological use of the chemical. A most serious warning needs to be added here. Although research shows that dosage of PCP administered nasally, intravenously, or through smoking is somewhat controllable, ingesting PCP is not. Since ingested PCP takes up to 1 hour to produce its effects, users sometimes will take an additional dose for fear that the first "isn't working." Such increased dosage can be fatal with PCP doses as low as 5 to 10 milligrams (Luisada, 1981).

Organic Mental Disorders Associated with the Hallucinogens and Marijuana

While PCP is often classed as an hallucinogen (Ungerleider & DeAngelis, 1981; Sadava, 1984), in DSM-III it is placed in a separate diagnostic category from the more "traditional" hallucinogens like *lysergic acid* (LSD), *mescaline, psilocybin, and cannabis (marijuana).* All these drugs are capable of producing the brain syndromes of hallucinosis and delusional disorder, but only cannabis causes intoxication syndrome. Hallucinogenic hallucinosis is marked by distortions of auditory and visual perception, depersonalization, and synesthesias while awake. The symptom picture can be compounded further by many people's fearful reactions to the perceptual distortions and by the sense of loss of control often produced by the hallucinogens.

The sixties saw the rise of the flower children, who helped popularize the use of marijuana and other consciousness-affecting drugs. (*Anthony A. Scaravilli*)

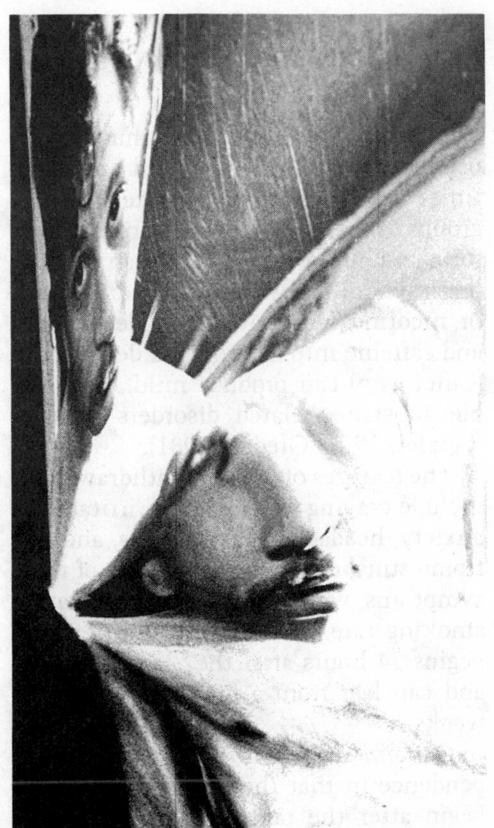

The perceptual distortions produced by LSD can be quite frightening to some people. (*Michael Weisbrot and Family*)

Also known as the *psychedelics* and the *psychotomimetics,* hallucinogenic drugs like mescaline, psilocybin, and peyote have been used in the religious and mystical rites of certain Indian tribes and historically among ancient peoples like the Aztecs. LSD was discovered in 1943 when it was accidentally compounded by Dr. Albert Hoffman, a Swiss chemist (Cashman, 1966). Hoffman accidentally ingested some of the chemical and reported the following experience:

Personal Experience: LSD

I can remember the following were the most outstanding symptoms: vertigo, visual disturbances, the faces around me seemed grotesque, colored masks; marked motoric unrest, alternating with paralysis; an intermittent feeling in the head, limbs, and entire body, as if they were all filled with lead; dry, constricted sensation in the throat; feeling of choking; shouting half-insanely or babbling incoherently; I sometimes felt as if I were out of my body. (Cashman, 1966, p. 31)

Unlike LSD, marijuana has been in use for thousands of years as a muscle relaxant, analgesic, and anticonvulsant. Most recently it has been used in the amelioration of some of the discomfort associated with chemotherapy for cancer patients and in the treatment of glaucoma (Grinspoon & Bakalar, 1981). Marijuana is the most widely used hallucinogen and the only one that can produce the physical tolerance necessary for the diagnosis of substance dependence.

Although more a part of everyday life than many other drugs, cigarettes and coffee are also addictive. (© *Bob Krueger/Rapho Photo Researchers, Inc.*)

Organic Mental Disorders Associated with Tobacco and Caffeine

While the drugs discussed thus far are usually obtained illegally and are sometimes associated with "counter-culture" groups, the legal and traditional "cigarette and cup of coffee" also can produce brain syndromes when overused. Tobacco or nicotine withdrawal and dependence and caffeine intoxication and dependence (caffeinism) can produce mild, diagnosable substance-related disorders (Jaffe & Kanzler, 1981; Greden, 1981).

The features of tobacco withdrawal can include craving for cigarettes, irritability, anxiety, headaches, restlessness, and gastrointestinal distress. The severity of these symptoms varies with the precessation smoking rate, but typically the reaction begins 24 hours after the "last cigarette" and can last from a few days to several weeks.

Caffeinism differs from nicotine dependence in that the primary symptoms begin after the taking of the substance rather than after its cessation. Generally, after two to four cups of coffee (or four or more cups of tea) mild symptoms occur

BOX 13-1

SUBSTANCE ABUSE IN THE "FUTURE"

Although the recreational and medicinal use of drugs has been a constant for thousands of years, the specific drugs used and their mode of use has varied. The psychedelics of the early 1960s were replaced by the amphetamine use of the later 1960s. In the 1970s, sedative-hypnotics seemed most popular and the 1980s seem to have begun with cocaine as the glamour substance. It is clear that there will continue to be changes in drug use patterns as time goes on and at least one writer (Cohen, 1981) has attempted to predict the future of substance abuse.

Cohen predicts that the "nasal trip" (i.e., sniffing, inhaling, or snorting) will increase in popularity because of "the rapid entry into the bloodstream, no need for syringes, and the bypass of the liver and its detoxifying enzymes" (1981, p. 844). Cohen also believes that rather than simply for recreational purposes, drugs will be used increasingly in religious experiences as well as for relief of general daily distress. The search for pleasure, Cohen contends, will continue: "Some people believe that what this country needs is a safe, 5-cent euphoriant." (p. 845)

like nervousness, excitement, insomnia, and stomach distress. After four or more cups of coffee, some people's muscles may begin to twitch, their speech may ramble, their ears may ring, and their heart rate may increase. Although researchers who study caffeinism (Greden, 1981) contend that dependence and withdrawal can occur with this substance, DSM-III does not yet include a substance use disorder associated with caffeine.

Organic Mental Disorders and Volatile Substances

Like caffeine dependence, the abuse of volatile substances or inhalants also is not yet included in DSM-III. More often observed in lower socioeconomic groups, the inhalation of substances in order to achieve a "high" is relatively widespread with about 12 to 15 percent of U.S. high school students having admitted to such behavior (Johnston et al., 1982). Besides the glue inhaled or "sniffed" as early as the 1950s and 1960s, people now may also inhale gasoline, paint thinner, deodorant sprays, PAM cooking spray, lighter fluid, nail polish remover, shoe polish, hair spray, and liquid paper thinner (Sharp & Korman, 1981).

All inhalants present a common danger. Because they are quite toxic chemically and because the dosage is difficult to control, brain damage and death may result from their use. The danger represented by the inhalation of volatile substances is compounded by the fact that it seems to be more common among more disturbed people. Alapin (1973) reported that one-third of his sample of "sniffers" were diagnosed as schizophrenic. Similarly, Comstock (1978) found that nearly 100 percent of a group of inhalers he studied had some diagnosable psychiatric disorder. In spite of the fact that some researchers feel that nasal administration will be the primary method of drug use in the future (See Box 13-1), it probably is responsible for producing more long-term physical and mental damage than any other method.

Paradigmatic Perspectives on Substance-induced Organic Mental Disorders and Substance-use Disorders

Because drug abuse and dependence are such widespread problems in our society, they have come under the scrutiny of researchers using a number of paradigms. Lettieri et al. (1980), for example, have presented a "selection" of 36 contemporary theories of drug use. Paradigmatically, these 36 theories can be placed into several major groupings—the basic biological, psychosocial, and systems views, and some integrations of these three approaches.

Regardless of their paradigmatic roots, each group of theories attempts to explain four crucial aspects of substance abuse—its *initiation, continuation, transition from use to abuse,* and its *cessation* (Lettieri et al., 1980). No one paradigmatically generated group of theories seems to handle all these aspects well, but each appears to increase our level of understanding of the overall problem of drug use. In keeping with the relationship between theory and treatment, we shall describe therapeutic efforts in conjunction with the explanations from which they are derived.

The Biological Paradigm and Substance-use Disorders

Scientists guided by the biological paradigm look for physical explanations and cures for drug use. Since the early 1960s, research evidence has been gathered based upon two adaptations of the biological paradigm. One group of researchers believes that there is a genetic basis for drug abuse and dependence. A second focuses more specifically on the possibility that recently discovered opiate receptors and endorphins and enkephalins in the brain are related to drug dependence.

According to scientists searching for a genetic basis for alcohol and drug addiction (Schuckit, 1980; Murray & Stabeneau, 1982; Goodwin, 1985), people may be born with certain levels of "genetically influenced biological predisposition toward alcohol and drug abuse" (Schuckit, 1980). Some genes may predispose a person "toward" alcoholism via an unusually strong anxiety-reducing effect in response to the drug or an extremely high level of pleasure associated with its ingestion. On the other hand, there may be genes which may help protect a person "against" alcoholism by being responsible for causing aversive reactions like nausea at low levels of alcohol ingestion. According to the genetic interpretation of the biological paradigm, inherited predispositions interact with specific life events either to increase or decrease the likelihood of a substance-abuse disorder developing. For instance, Robins et al. (1975), studying soldiers in Vietnam, reported that although the stressful war environment and the easy availability of heroin yielded a large number of addicts in the war zone, only a small percentage of the soldiers seemed "genetically compatible" with the drug to a sufficient degree to continue its use upon returning home. Overall, the genetic view suggests that whether people become substance abusers seems to depend upon the genetic predispositions interacting with positive and negative environmental factors (Schuckit, 1980).

Especially with regard to alcoholism, research supports the view that there are inherited predispositions for drug addiction. Kalj (1960) reported a monozygotic twin concordance rate for alcoholism of 60 percent as compared with a dizygotic rate of only 30 percent. Further, adoption studies have demonstrated increased risks for alcoholism among biological offspring of alcoholic parents reared by nonalcoholic parents (Schuckit et al., 1972). In addition, children of nonalcoholic parents raised by alcoholic parents do not seem to be more prone to alcoholism than if they were raised by nonalcoholics (Goodwin, 1979). Finally, Goodwin (1985) has reported that the genetic basis for alcoholism is such that 20 to 25 percent of the sons of alcoholics will become alcoholic as well. In a similar vein, Murray and Stabeneau (1982) note that concordance for alcoholism among MZ twins is as high as

70 percent, whereas concordance for DZ twins is only 28 to 33 percent. Such data clearly support the existence of a genetic component in alcoholism.

Data from studies with animals corroborate the findings with human subjects. Nichols and Hsiao (1967) were able to breed rats for high- and low-morphine preferences, and Schuckit (1980) reports that it has been possible to produce strains of animals with higher or lower preferences for drinking alcohol.

Given a genetic component in the etiology of substance abuse disorders, therapeutic efforts are most likely to be of a preventive nature. Thus, such efforts would focus on first identifying populations at high risk and then on genetic counseling to help reduce the chance of passing on genetic predispositions. Special groups like Alateen and AlaTot, run by Alcoholics Anonymous for the children of its members, may be seen as examples of therapeutic efforts based upon this perspective.

The genetic interpretation of the biological paradigm has led to important findings with regard to the etiology of substance abuse. However, recent research suggests that an even more microscopic understanding of the biological mechanisms of addiction may be possible. In specific, it has been proposed that the opiate receptors and the endorphins and enkephalins which are associated with them may eventually be found to play a role in the addiction process (Simon, 1980, 1981). For example, Su et al. (1978; cited by Simon, 1980) have found that administration of beta endorphin to morphine addicts results in "dramatic improvement" as shown by less severe withdrawal symptoms. After receiving a dose of the beta endorphin, Su et al.'s subjects reported feeling dizzy, sleepy, and warm for about 20 minutes. Following this initial reaction, the addicts experienced continuing reduction in withdrawal symptom severity for several days. Su et al. concluded that since beta endorphin reduced withdrawal symptoms in much the same way as the administration of more morphine, this neurochemical might play some role in the brain's processes of tolerance and dependence. Su et al.'s research is strengthened by their inclusion of a control group which received a "placebo" rather than the beta endorphin. In that there was little suppression of withdrawal symptoms in this group, the effectiveness of the beta endorphin is even more clearly demonstrated.

In another study, Gold et al. (1978) reported "elimination" of withdrawal symptoms in "all" members of a group of long-term heroin addicts to whom they administered *clonidine,* a neurochemical similar to beta endorphin. Prior to their involvement in the clonidine study, many of Gold et al.'s subjects had been maintained heroin-free via the administration of a drug called methadone, which, until the promising research on the endorphins may have been the best example of treatment for substance abuse deriving from the biological paradigm. Methadone treatment capitalizes on the opiate property of *cross-tolerance.* That is, the withdrawal symptoms of any one of the opiates may be delayed or abated by administration of any of the others. This phenomenon was applied therapeutically by Dole and Nyswander in the development of *methadone-maintenance therapy* (1965; 1980).

In the mid-1950s, Vincent Dole began a study of the metabolism of heroin. He later met and did collaborative research with Marie Nyswander, a specialist in addiction to heroin. Their research led to the discovery of a technique for detoxifying (withdrawing) heroin addicts through the administration in its place of a synthetic opioid, methadone (Dole & Nyswander, 1980; Lowinson, 1981). The success of methadone maintenance has been noteworthy. Through 1980 (Dole & Nyswander, 1980; Callahan, 1980) the dropout rate from the Dole-Nyswander pro-

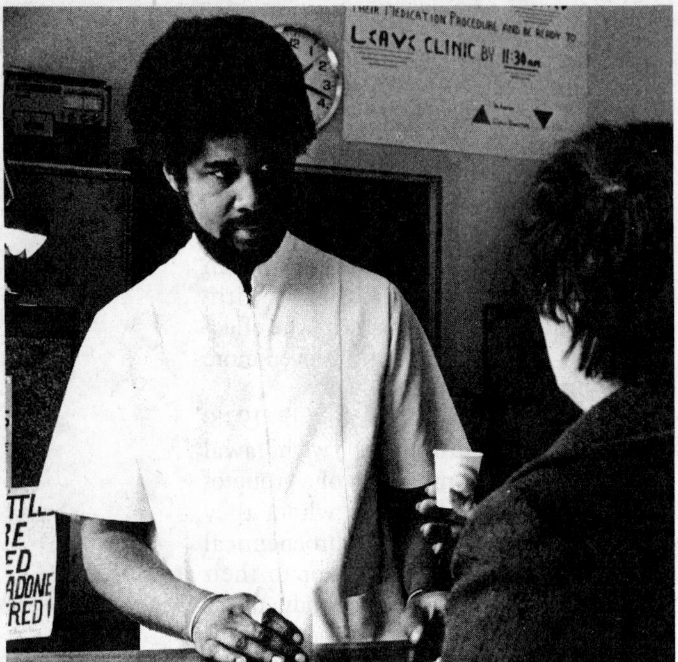

Under careful supervision, methadone can be an effective replacement for heroin. (© *Robert Goldstein 1982/Photo Researchers, Inc.*)

gram was less than 20 percent. Further, since they no longer need to obtain expensive and illegal heroin, the crime rate among methadone patients is reduced. However, there also have been some negative aspects of methadone maintenance therapy programs. Among these are the illegal acquisition and sale on the streets of methadone doses and the focus on methadone treatment centers and their patients as sites for illegal drug dealing to patients who have not totally switched their addiction over to methadone (Callahan, 1980).

The therapeutic effects of methadone seem so similar to the withdrawal symptom suppression effects of the endorphins and enkephalins that one might speculate that the use of methadone may have been a foreshadowing of current and future biological understanding of the causes, correlates, and treatments of substance abuse. In this light, Simon (1980) reports the discovery of a specific receptor site in the brain for the tranquilizer, benzodiazepine (Valium). At this point in the development of our knowledge, however, we must be cautious, yet optimistic, regarding the coming contributions of the biological paradigm to our understanding of substance abuse and dependence.

The Psychosocial Paradigm and Substance-use Disorders

As was the case with the biological paradigm, there are also several ways in which the psychosocial paradigm has been applied in the study of substance-use disorders. The major interpretations are the *psychodynamic* and the *behavioral/learning* perspectives. The general view of the psychodynamic approach is that, like all behaviors, substance abuse may be seen as a meaningful reflection of mental processes which are part of total functioning (Wurmser, 1981; Forrest, 1984). On the other hand, learning theorists (e.g., Frederick, 1982; Marlatt & Donovan, 1982) generally view drug abuse as behavior which is emitted in order to reduce anxiety or other unpleasant feelings and in turn is reinforced by the reduction of such feelings.

Wurmser (1981) describes the psychodynamics of substance abuse in terms of *triple layering.* Proposing that drugs themselves are early "attempts at self-help which fail" (p. 65), substance abuse is seen as a first, or "superficial layer" which may initially appear as "the" disease. However, at a second layer, drug use is seen as a "mere symptom, functioning as artificial positive feelings which replace a vague, diffuse, but pervasive mood of anxiousness, tension, uneasiness and unhappiness" (p. 66). Wurmser goes on to suggest that the specific drug chosen may be correlated with the kinds of adverse feelings from which an individual is trying to escape:

> Narcotics and hypnotics are arrayed against rage, shame, jealousy, and the often panicky anxiety attacks derived from these partly repressed affects. Stimulants (including cocaine) are deployed against feelings of depression, weakness, inner emptiness and helplessness. Psychedelics tend to be chosen to ward off boredom, disillusionment, apathy, a sense of meaninglessness, painful isolation and detachment. Intense guilt, self-punishment, loneliness and longing are said to yield to alcohol. (p. 66)

From the psychoanalytic perspective, Wurmser suggests that beyond the symptom level lies a third and final level, of "unconscious conflicts," that the drug user attempts to escape. It is at this third level of understanding that childhood traumas, fixations, and unresolved stages of psychosexual development can come forth from their resting places in the unconscious and create problems later in a person's life. Wurmser goes on to propose that faulty psychosexual development in substance abusers may ultimately be traced to family patterns characterized by parental violence, intense exposure to sexual activity, overresponsiveness to aggression, secretiveness, inconsistency, and unreliability.

As might be expected, given the triple layering psychodynamic view of the development of substance-abuse behavior, treatment is directed at identifying unconscious conflicts of the third layer through "modified" psychoanalysis (Wurmser, 1981). In such treatment, efforts are made to seek out Oedipal and pre-Oedipal difficulties and to understand the need for the overuse of the ego defense of *denial*. Denial is an important component in understanding drug abuse because it is used by people to deny their pharmacological attempts to "rid themselves of undesirable inner and outer realities."

While basic to psychoanalysts, the triple-layering concept is not accepted by learning theorists who believe that the "symptom is the disease." They believe that layers of unconscious conflicts are not necessary components in the development, maintenance, and treatment of drug dependence and abuse. Not surprisingly, the behavioral view leads to a much different explanation of drug abuse. Anxiety, depression, or other forms of unpleasant emotion are seen to result from intense stimulus situations which people feel powerless to change. To escape these adverse feelings, people may learn directly or through observation of others that use of certain chemicals can reduce their unpleasant experiences. Drug ingestion results in the reduction of unpleasant feelings and this reduction of unpleasant feelings is a reinforcer. By this process, over a period of time, drugs become strong reinforcers not only because they are a source of pleasure but also because they reduce aversive feelings (Frederick, 1982).

Given the behavioral view that drug abuse is learned and maintained by reinforcement, it follows that treatment for substance-abuse disorders would involve learning of alternative responses to reduce tension and/or changing the perception of drugs from that of a reinforcer to that of an aversive stimulus. To provide alternative modes of responding to tension or depression, behavior modifiers have used interventions like systematic desensitization and relaxation (see Chapter 5). To decrease the positive associations to drug use, per se, some behaviorists may use aversive conditioning in which drugs are systematically reassociated with electric shock or nausea (Cheek & Miller, 1981). Other behaviorists prefer not to use real shock and drugs to make people ill. In *covert sensitization* the imagination is used to associate drug use with unpleasant feelings and events (Cautela, 1967). An example of a covert sensitization procedure used to change the perception of alcohol from positive to negative is provided in Box 13-2.

BOX 13-2

A COVERT SENSITIZATION SCENE

I want you to close your eyes and imagine the scene I'm about to describe. See yourself clearly doing all the things I suggest. You are walking down the street. It is a sunny day and you're feeling particularly good. Suddenly, you pass in front of your favorite bar. You stop for a moment and decide to go in and get a drink. You walk toward the door of the bar and just as you open it, you get a queasy feeling in your stomach. Sort of like you ate some food that disagreed with you. You say to yourself, "Maybe a drink will settle my stomach." You walk up to the bar and ask the bartender for a scotch and water. [This part is tailored specifically to the patient's own habits and preferences.] Just as you do this you kinda burp up some food. Little chunks of sour food are in the back of your throat. You swallow the chunks down but that sour smell and taste are still in your mouth; the queasy feeling is even stronger now. The bartender brings you the drink and you grasp the glass and take it to your lips. Just as it touches your lips—[therapist makes a vomiting sound] you vomit. You vomit all over your hands and into the drink. You look down into the glass and see the pieces of food and mucous floating around in the scotch and water. You can smell vomit mixed with the smell of the scotch. You vomit again. This time you spurt some vomit onto the bartender. He's looking at you in horror and disgust. You can smell the vomit and see it floating in your drink. You take the drink and throw it away. Suddenly you are outside again. You are clean and fresh-smelling. The sun feels warm on your back and the air is clear and stimulating.

The Systems Paradigm and Substance-use Disorders

Rather than believing that the cause and cure for substance-use disorders are to be found intrapsychically or behaviorally, theorists guided by the systems paradigm look for answers in social or familial structures and their effects on people (Alksne, 1981; Roman, 1982). With specific reference to substance-abuse disorders, the systems perspective assumes that the initiation, continuation, exacerbation, and cessation of drug use are determined through the interaction of people and the systems of which they are part.

One major systems approach, *structural-functionalism* (Alksne, 1981), is based on the idea that "the social system is built upon commonly shared values, norms, role expectations, and interactions that permit humans to relate in a mutually acceptable framework" (Alksne, 1981, p. 81). If everyone follows the rules of the game, the social system works. However, inherent in complex societies is the possibility for the development of a sense of detachment from shared norms and values which Durkheim (1952) called *anomie.* Those people who feel detached are more prone to develop *deviance,* such as drug abuse. Another sociologist, Merton (1949) believed that feelings of detachment increase when a society emphasizes goals which many people cannot achieve due to their minority status and economic difficulties. While all people experiencing detachment must adapt in some way in order to survive, Merton proposed that for the drug user the primary means of adaptation to detachment is "retreatism" in which people use chemical methods both to reduce the unpleasant sense of anomie and to demonstrate their rejection of its source, the goals and values of society (Lukoff, 1980).

While seemingly able to explain findings such as greater rates of drug abuse in minorities and lower socioeconomic groups, Merton's theory has garnered only limited research support (Lukoff & Brook, 1974; Waldorf & Daily, 1975). A major problem appears to be arriving at a satisfactory definition of society's "shared values and norms." Since the United States is composed of so many varied social groupings and subcultures, the identification of *one* set of values is a very difficult task. Without such a universally accepted set of values, the structural-functional perspective cannot be easily applied.

Despite its drawbacks, however, the structural-functional application of the systems paradigm continues to influence the study of drug usage and the development of treatment approaches. Most of these therapeutic efforts assume that to reduce deviant behavior, it is necessary (1) to make social goals more reachable by increasing opportunities and (2) to defend against anomie by encouraging and maintaining contact between people at risk for detachment and social institutions such as schools, churches, and local governments. Some examples of such structural-functional theory-based approaches are *Model Cities, Head Start, and Equal Economic Opportunities* programs.

To the structural-functionalists, substance abuse and other forms of deviance represent reactions "against" shared values and norms of society at large. However, to those systems theorists espousing a *socialization process* perspective, deviance such as drug abuse derives from an "acceptance" of and internalization of a specific subculture's set of values and norms. Thus, through what Sutherland (1939) originally termed "differential association," people can be socialized into patterns of drug abuse and dependence. The subgroups (subsystems) which serve as sources of deviant socialization can include people's families and peer groups. From the socialization perspective, exposure to parents who use excessive alcohol in dealing with problems can predispose children to alcoholism. Similarly, pressure from peer groups can lead some youngsters to see drug use as one of the "valued-shared goals" worth striving for (Lukoff, 1980).

In some ways, the socialization perspective could be viewed as a more sophisticated way of saying that people should not "hang around with bad company." The perspective guides clinicians toward the idea that if immersion in a faulty socialization system can produce drug-abuse behavior, then immersion in a corrective social milieu can alter deviant behavior. This application of the systems perspective underlies many of the general community psychology approaches (Chapter 6) as well as specific substance-abuse programs like Alcoholics Anonymous.

Alcoholics Anonymous (AA), probably the best-known systems-based therapeutic approach to alcoholism (Rosenberg, 1982), was started in 1938 by a physician who had conquered his own problem with alcohol. AA is based upon a Christian religious philosophy, but it has been used interdenominationally with great success. AA's approach to treating alcoholism is broken down into 12 steps (see Table 13-1), which alcoholics complete according to a loosely defined time schedule. Typically, alcoholics begin the resocialization process by publicly admitting in group meetings that they are alcoholics and cannot control their drinking. With support from other alcoholics, some of whom have recovered, new members come to value sobriety and to learn effective ways of controlling their drinking patterns.

In addition to the use of groups such as Alcoholics Anonymous and more recently Narcotics Anonymous to treat substance-abuse disorders, the systems perspective has also lead to a focus on family systems (Nichols, 1984). For example, Minuchin's structural family therapy was used in the treatment of drug addicts and their families by Stanton and

Table 13-1 The 12 Steps of Alcoholics Anonymous

1. We admitted we were powerless over alcohol . . . that our lives had become unmanageable.
2. [We] came to believe that a power greater than ourselves could return us to sanity.
3. [We] made a decision to turn our will and our lives over to the care of God *as we understood Him.*
4. [We] made a searching and fearless moral inventory of ourselves.
5. [We] admitted to God, to ourselves and to another human being the exact nature of our wrongs.
6. [We] were entirely ready to have God remove all these defects of character.
7. [We] humbly asked Him to remove our shortcomings.
8. [We] made a list of all the persons we had harmed, and became willing to make amends to them all.
9. [We] made direct amends to such people wherever possible, except where to do so would injure them or others.
10. [We] continued to take personal inventory and when we were wrong promptly admitted it.
11. [We] sought through prayer and meditation to improve our conscious contact with God *as we understood Him,* praying only for knowledge of His will for us and the power to carry that out.
12. Having had a spiritual awakening as the result of these other steps, we tried to carry this message to alcoholics, and to practice these principles in all our affairs.

Todd (1979). After restructuring the family systems, these researchers observed positive change in most of their patients. Further, this change was still evident upon one-year follow-up. In addition to structural approaches, many other forms of family therapy have also been applied successfully in the treatment of substance-use disorders (Nichols, 1984).

An Integrated Theoretical Paradigm and Substance-use Disorders

Responding to the occurrence of anomalies for which the unifactorial application of the three major existing paradigms have few definitive answers, some investigators have turned toward an integration of the biological, psychosocial, and systems paradigms. Such an integrated paradigm emphasizes the interacting effects of all three perspectives on human behavior. While there have been several efforts to effect a paradigmatic integration for drug disorders (see Bejerot, 1980; Jonas & Jonas, 1980), one proposal which may serve as an example is that of Van Dijk (1971, 1980).

Van Dijk contends that dependence or addiction should not be looked at as an entity, but as the final stage of a process beginning with *initial contact* with a drug, passing through *experimentation* with it, continuing with *ever-increasing intensity* of use, and ending with the *"terminal"* or *"disease" phase* of the disorder. The factors that begin, sustain, and culminate the process of drug abuse are biological (pharmacological or genetic), psychosocial (intra- and interpersonal), and systems-based (cultural, social, or familial).

Pharmacological factors have to do with variations in the "addictiveness" of drugs.

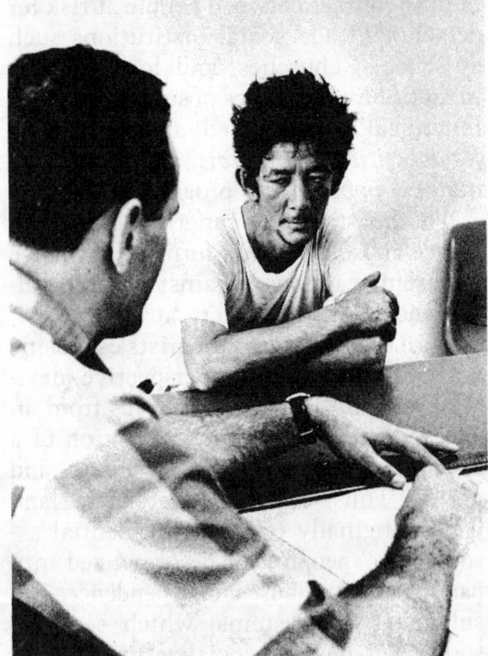

Many heavy drug users enter treatment programs only after they have done significant physical and psychological damage to themselves. (© *Bob Combs/Rapho Photo Researchers, Inc.*)

For instance, heroin is strongly and rapidly addictive, whereas aspirin is not. Personal factors of the user also play a contributing role. For genetic or psychological reasons, people differ in their predisposition toward substance abuse. Van Dijk notes that people at high risk for addiction tend to experience greater than normal levels of discomfort, tension, and displeasure in their lives and they typically find it impossible to allay these feelings without chemicals. Finally, the social meaning of drugs contributes to its use; such meanings can be quite complex:

> The ritualization of the use of drugs, and the social norms, habits and sanctions governing it . . . the significance of a drug as a symbol of sturdy, competitive, aggressive masculinity . . . the drugs as a symbol and signifier of differences between groups, classes and generations . . . the symbol of a progressive, nonauthoritarian attitude. (Van Dijk, 1980, p. 168)

Biological, psychosocial, and systems factors contribute in very basic ways to the early phases of the addiction process (i.e., contact wth the drug and increased intensity of its use), but Van Dijk contends that their involvement reaches higher levels of complexity in the individual who continues using drugs excessively. He proposes that these levels of complexity may be conceptualized as involving four "vicious circles" which, once entered into, become self-propagating and stable unless interrupted through treatment efforts. As depicted in Figure 13-5, the vicious circles are *pharmacological, cerebral, psychic, and social.*

In the *pharmacological circle,* excessive use of a drug results in changes in body chemistry and metabolism in the form of tolerance. Due to their physiological dependence on it, when people stop taking the drug they experience powerful withdrawal symptoms which can be stopped by reinitiation of drug use.

The circularity at the *cerebral* level in Figure 13-5 is due to drug-produced decreases in people's ability to control their own behavior (e.g., I want to stop, but I can't). This decrease in ability for self-control translates into a drop in ego-strength which in turn aggravates the entire coping system. With a weaker ego, multiple once-regulated motives (sex, aggression, and the like) break into consciousness further weakening the person's defenses against drug use.

Simultaneous with the ego-weakening in the cerebral circle, in the *psychic circle,* the awareness of drug dependence and its social, familial, and occupational implications results in feelings of guilt and shame, decreases in self-esteem, and rising concern about the future. According to Van Dijk, these negative feelings are "most easily and effectively gotten rid of with more drugs."

The final vicious circle in the addiction process is *social.* Drug use has social consequences in which the addicts become detached from many important support groups like family, friends, and fellow workers. Quarrels, conflicts, and other forms of interpersonal turmoil can lead people to withdraw from others. Feelings of detachment, isolation, and withdrawal can be so aversive that they produce extreme loneliness and anomie, which, again, can lead to a stronger need for more drugs.

Not only does Van Dijk's integrated view of substance abuse and dependence have implications for understanding the development and maintenance of patterns of addiction, such a paradigm also suggests a number of therapeutic approaches. Van Dijk suggests that therapeutic efforts can be aimed at breaking into any one of the vicious circles and that this, in turn, can have an impact on other circles as well. Thus, if the social circle were interrupted, it is likely that the psychic circle would be altered as well.

The pattern of treatment in many modern drug treatment facilities may be seen

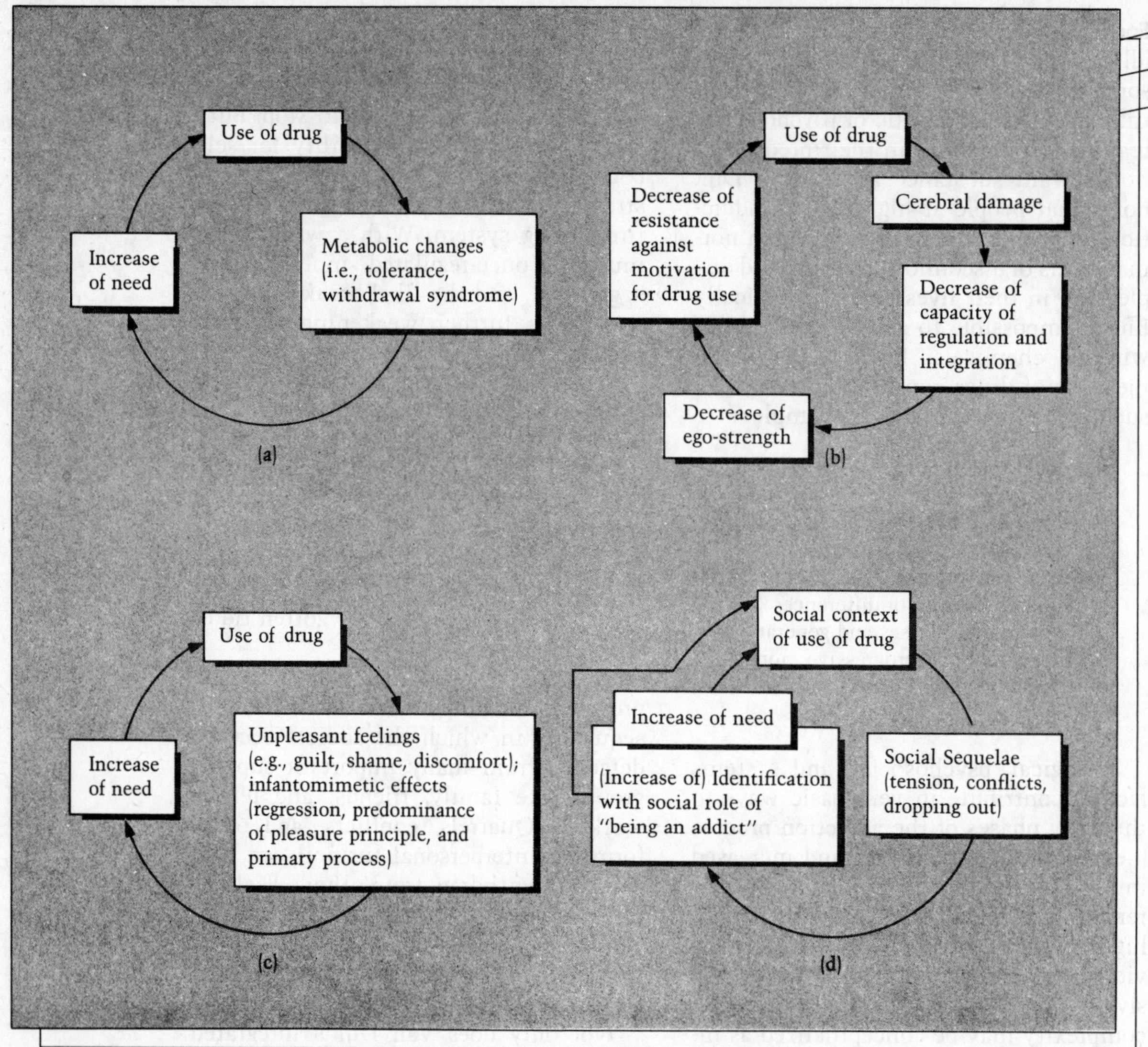

Figure 13-5 Vicious Circles in Drug Dependence: (a) Pharmacological Vicious Circle; (b) Cerebral Vicious Circle; (c) Psychic Vicious Circle; (d) Social Vicious Circle. (*From Van Dijk, 1980, pp. 170–172.*)

as a reflection of the integrated approach. In one such center patients are first medically withdrawn from drugs, thereby interrupting the pharmacological circle via medical management. They then begin a 30-day period in which they are exposed to individual and group psychotherapy and intense education regarding drugs; these efforts are designed to produce increased ego strength, to improve general coping skills, and to interrupt the cerebral and psychic circles. Following the first 30 days, treatment continues on a less intense basis and is characterized by efforts to interrupt the social circle by reintegrating patients into their families, social groups, and work settings. The eventual result of the integrated biological-psychosocial-systems treatment program is control over the addiction, recognition of sobriety by oneself and others, and an ensuing rise in self-worth and self-esteem.

Concluding Comments

Although we discussed the injury-, disease-, and age-related organic mental disorders separately from the drug-induced organic mental disorders, it must be noted that the authors of DSM-III have chosen to include them in the same grouping, *organic mental disorders*. The two groups of disturbances are clearly similar in that the feelings experienced and the behaviors observed in both are produced by disruption of the normal functioning of the brain and nervous system. They are not similar in that while people with head trauma and progressive brain disease would do anything to reverse their symptoms, in the case of drug dependence and abuse, this neurological disruption is voluntary and sought after. In this voluntary aspect of substance-induced disorders lies a major difference between the two groups of brain disorders and therein lies much of the pathology of substance abuse.

While the basis for the injury-, disease-, and age-related organic mental disorders is primarily biological, the etiology of the substance-abuse organic mental disorders is not so easily discernible. In fact, in the study of the substance-abuse disorders we have seen the application not only of the three major unifactorial paradigms, but of integrated or multifactorial paradigms as well. The integrated views are especially important from the perspective of abnormal psychology as a science, for their existence may reflect beginning efforts to resolve the "tension" arising from the difficulties encountered by unifactorial attempts to explain satisfactorily the existence of substance-abuse disorders. While each unifactorial paradigm has certainly led to plausible explanations and reasonable treatment approaches, the disturbing fact remains that disordered drug use continues to be a major problem in our society. Thus, although widespread efforts have been made within the existing paradigms, drug disorders may be seen as an anomaly for the science of abnormal psychology. From a Kuhnian perspective, this state of affairs is expected and energizes the scientific process. Through such stimulation, our understanding of drug disorders as well as several other patterns of psychopathology can only be enhanced.

Summary Chart

When brain syndromes are produced voluntarily and habitually through voluntary administration of chemical substances, a substance-use disorder exists. Among the chemical substances which produce brain syndromes and may be abused are:

Alcohol	Barbiturates and sedatives
Opioids	Cocaine
Amphetamines	PCP
Hallucinogens	Marijuana
Tobacco	Caffeine
Inhalants	

Habitual abuse of or dependence upon chemicals is a significant form of psychopathology and has been studied from all three major paradigmatic perspectives.

The biological paradigm: Genetic explanations, inherited predisposition to addiction, role of endorphins in addiction

The psychosocial paradigm: Psychoanalytic theory (layering), behavioral theory (reinforcing nature of drugs)

The systems paradigm: Anomie and deviance generate drug problems, subsections of society foster drug usage

We closed Chapter 13 with an examination of a view which integrated all three major paradigms:

Van Dijk's theory

Vicious circles: Pharmacological, cerebral, psychic, social

CHAPTER 14

Sexual Dysfunctions and Disorders

James was a quiet unassuming young man. He worked as an assistant to the general manager at a clothing business. Although shy, he was able to carry on normal conversations and interactions with his office peers. He rarely dated and spent most of his time at home watching television. Two or three times a week he walks over to the nearby college and sneaks around the women's dormitory, hides in the bushes so that he can catch glimpses of the women dressing and undressing. From his hiding place he also enjoyed watching the male students say good night to the coeds.

Although he was a very successful lawyer, Jerry had difficulty performing sexually with his wife unless he was dressed in women's clothing. His wife explained that Jerry was a satisfactory partner and his cross-sex dressing was only confined to love-making situations.

Judy and Sara were in the university library looking for a reference book describing the different kinds of textiles produced in Asia. Their search took them to one of the less populated parts of the library. As they turned the corner there was a man who was completely nude except for the fact he was wearing brown knee high socks and wing tip shoes. They screamed and ran for help. When they returned with the security guard he was gone.

Warren is a single, 21-year-old sailor on furlough. He picked up a young woman hitchhiker and drove to a roadside rest area. Although she resisted his advances, he believed that "she really wanted it but didn't want me to think she was easy." He overpowered her, forced her to submit to intercourse, and afterward asked her for a date later that same evening. Warren had committed four similar offenses in the space of a week but had no previous criminal or psychiatric history. (Groth & Birnbaum, 1980, pp. 22–23).

What is appropriate sexual behavior has concerned societies for thousands of years. Defining abnormal sexual behavior is complicated by the fact that it is still viewed with awe, mystery, and embarrassment by significant numbers of people. That is probably why, among other things, in this supposed age of enlightenment, sex education is actively opposed by significant numbers of parents and millions of people have contracted venereal diseases.

In the DSM-III and other traditional attempts to classify sexual behavior, it has typically been assumed that heterosexual intercourse is the single most important and normal way of satisfying sexual drives. When people have difficulties in completing sexual intercourse, they may be diagnosed as having a *sexual dysfunction*. However, when people do not attempt to meet their sexual needs through heterosexual intercourse, but rather use other methods, they are seen as having *paraphilias*. Both will be described in this chapter.

Sexual Dysfunctions

Sexual dysfunctions refer to a range of difficulties that reflect an impairment or inability to obtain sexual gratification. Usually, these difficulties arise for psychosocial or systems reasons and make completion of intercourse with orgasm a virtual impossibility. Although primarily psychosocially based, in a small number of cases sexual dysfunctions can be caused by drugs (Mitchell & Popkin, 1982) or vascular disorders (Wagner & Metz, 1980). Regardless of their source, sexual dysfunctions almost always affect others and can put great strains on relationships (Roffe & Britt, 1981). Until recently, these difficulties often were dealt with in private or not at all, with considerable strain on all those involved. Not until the work of Masters and Johnson (1970) did people with sexual dysfunctions become less stigmatized and have easier access to help.

Orgasmic Dysfunctions in Males

Personal Experience: Male Erectile Dysfunction

I had made love to my wife with no difficulty for well over a year. I never thought about "getting hard"; it just came naturally. That was until it didn't. I remember that it was a Sunday night. I was working hard on papers that I had to have ready for a big conference the next morning. The work was hard and I was really looking forward to going to bed and being with my wife. I needed to get enough sleep so I wouldn't be tired for the presentation and I thought making love would relax me so I could sleep. However, my wife decided that it was time to sew something or another and fix something else so by the time she came to bed it was late and I had been waiting for what seemed like forever. She was responsive to my foreplay but I noticed for the first time that I was not getting hard. The thought crossed my mind that my wife could be all excited and then I might not be able to enter her. That would really be embarrassing. And that's exactly what happened. No matter how much I tried and my wife helped I couldn't get hard. I felt like a failure. My wife, thank goodness, was very understanding. But, I wondered about my masculinity and it made me doubt my ability to do my job.

Previously known as impotence, *male erectile dysfunction* involves the male's inability to achieve or maintain an erection sufficiently firm to complete intercourse. In *primary dysfunction*, a male has rarely, if ever, experienced an erection during intercourse; in *secondary dysfunction*, he was previously able to achieve an erection but presently cannot. Although there are a number of possible physiological causes for an inability to achieve an erection (such as diabetes mellitus, cardiorespiratory disorders, certain drugs and alcohol) the majority of causes are psychosocial or systems based. Age also is not usually a factor. Nearly 80 percent of men maintain the physiological capacity to consummate the sexual act at age 70, and most maintain the capability to enjoy sex into the nineties (Kaplan, 1975).

Love and sex are very much a part of normal living. (*Rhoda Galyn*)

Psychosocial and systems causes of *erectile insufficiency* may include repressive upbringing, cultural pressure to perform up to some masculine image, or failures in early attempts at intercourse. Because an episodic inability to maintain an erection is a normal occurrence for most men, Masters and Johnson (1970) defined true dysfunction as a "failure in 25% of attempts at intercourse."

Ejaculatory Disturbances

Even if erection is normal, *ejaculatory disturbances* can occur. In *premature ejaculation*, a male cannot control his ejaculation for a sufficient length of time during intercourse to satisfy his partner in at least 50 percent of their coital connections (Masters & Johnson, 1970). LoPiccolo (1978) suggests that males should be able to experience at least 4 minutes of genital stimulation without ejaculation. It may be that some males with ejaculatory difficulties first tried to perform intercourse in tense situations where quickness of response was called for. The great majority of the reasons for premature ejaculation are psychosocially based and usually involve anxiety about "performing" the sex act.

The opposite of premature ejaculation, *retarded ejaculation*, occurs less frequently and refers to an inability to ejaculate during intercourse. Masters and Johnson reported that of the 17 cases of retarded ejaculation they treated the following causes were found: religious orthodoxy, male fear of pregnancy, lack of interest in or physical attraction to their partners, adverse maternal influences, and homosexuality. Kaplan (1975) reported basically similar etiologies in the cases she treated, adding the fear of being caught or interrrupted in the process of intercourse. Jacobs (1980) concluded that the males he treated were "extremely compulsive . . . with a failure to develop basic trust reflected in an obvious or concealed paranoid stance toward life" (p. 179). This tendency is reflected in the following case history.

Case: Ejaculatory Disturbance

The 32-year-old computer operator had been unable to ejaculate with oral or manual stimulation, or coitus for the eight years of his marriage and courtship. He had only learned when he was 24 that he was adopted at the age of six months. His diabetic mother died of complications of the pregnancy, and his biological father refused to take care of the baby, blaming the child for his wife's death. He then traced his biological brother with whom he developed a close relationship. This brother, raised by the father, provided him with more information regarding his biological parents. Both adoptive parents already in their forties when they adopted him, were described as emotionally remote and highly intelligent people who demanded perfection from him. He recalled having frequently had the impression that these were not his real parents. They told him later that, after weighing the pros and cons, they had decided to totally withhold his adoption from him, "to prevent damage". His only sexual experience with a woman prior to his relationship with his wife was limited to two consecutive failures to obtain an erection with a girlfriend who angrily called him "psychotic". It made him very wary of further contacts with women. Shortly after finding out he was adopted, he married a girl two years his junior, who was warm, conscientious, and with low neuroticism, notwithstanding her unusual family background. She was raised by her mother's sister who adopted her because the mother, who lived with the sister was too depressed to raise her. She was told about this at the age of four. No unresolved feelings were noticeable in her about her adoption.

The husband blamed his sexual problem on the girlfriend who rejected him: "After that, I never had an ejaculation except with masturbation." He was obsessive-compulsive, and complained of feeling exhausted. On closer questioning he revealed a paranoid stance toward people. Basically, he did not trust anyone. He felt he had been given a raw deal, and retrospectively explained his unhappy childhood and lack of occupational success mainly as the result of his adoption. All his misfortunes were attributed to his bad genes. He referred to himself as a mongrel dog. (Jacobs, 1980, pp. 179–180)

In addition to its psychosocial causes, certain neurological disorders also can cause retarded ejaculation, and certain antidepressant medications can prevent ejaculation even though an erection and sensation of climax are experienced. These possibilities must be evaluated before psychosocially based treatment is initiated.

Orgasmic Dysfunctions in Females

Once called "frigidity," female orgasmic dysfunction refers to the inability of a woman to experience orgasm. Freud believed the clitoral orgasm was an "immature orgasm," and that it took a mature woman to experience a vaginal orgasm. Thus for many years orgasmic dysfunction was erroneously defined as a woman's inability to experience a "vaginal" orgasm. We now know from the work of Masters and Johnson that the clitoris is the major source of the orgasmic experience for women and that there is no basis for the belief in the superiority of the vaginal orgasm.

As in males, Masters and Johnson (1970) identified primary and secondary female orgasmic dysfunctions. In *primary dysfunction*, women have never experienced an orgasm either through intercourse or by masturbation. *Secondary dysfunctions* are those in which orgasmic difficulties have appeared in women once capable of normal orgasm. Data gathered 30 years ago indicated that nearly one-third of the women surveyed never experienced orgasm before marriage (Kinsey et al., 1953). More recent data reported by Edwards (1983) revealed that less than one-fifth of the college women surveyed had never experienced orgasm. Apparently, women now are more likely to experience orgasm before they marry.

Other Dysfunctions in Females

Orgasm is not always the focus of sexual dysfunctions in women. Some women complain that they are unable to respond to sexual foreplay; nor can they produce the necessary lubrication of the vulva and vaginal tissues for comfortable intercourse. Called *arousal insufficiency*, it parallels the male's inability to achieve an erection because it can render intercourse impossible. Intercourse also can be prevented by *vaginismus*, in which there are involuntary spasms of the muscles controlling the entrance to the vagina. The following case history describes a woman who experienced vaginismus.

Case: Vaginismus

The case was a 26-year-old white female who was referred to her local mental health center by her gynecologist after a second separation from her husband. The couple had been married for six years and the marriage had not been consummated through sexual intercourse. Only partial penetration for a few brief seconds had been achieved once during the six years. After this painful incident the wife would not allow further attempts by the husband to penetrate.

The couple engaged exclusively in oral sex. The husband, an

understanding and rather submissive partner, finally initiated a six month separation. At that point the couple decided to reconciliate and sought professional counseling . . . with no apparent success.

The couple again separated, and after two weeks the woman was depressed, frustrated and guilt-ridden. She had lost fifteen pounds since the last separation, cried nightly and was extremely distraught and angry over her husband's involvement with another woman.

The initial session was used to collect information concerning the phobia and any incidences that might be connected to the fear. The wife reported that she was raised in a very conservative, rural family and her mother had never discussed sex. She had never masturbated nor experienced intercourse before marriage and, until therapy was initiated, had never masturbated with finger insertion. She had experienced a very painful and anxiety provoking pelvic exam as a part of her premarital examination. She had submitted to periodic pelvic exams after marriage, but with great ambivalence, pain, and fear. However, she could not allow herself to permit intercourse due to the cyclical pattern of her phobia; anticipatory anxiety—tightening of vaginal muscles—attempted penetration—reinforced phobia.

Two months after therapy was terminated, the patient reported she had finally realized her goal of achieving intercourse. The experience was complete with orgasm, and no pain or psychic trauma was evidenced. Four months after termination she called to report that she and her husband were back together. (Frutiger, 1981)

Paradigmatic Perspectives on Sexual Dysfunctions

Graber (1981) has noted that both the biological and psychosocial paradigms have been useful in explaining sexual dysfunctions. Generally the biological perspective focuses on the presence of certain neurological diseases or disorders of the genitourinary system that make intercourse painful. Dysfunctions can also be caused by certain tranquilizers and antidepressants whose side effects include suppression of the ability to ejaculate in males (Hatch, 1981).

People also can become very anxious if they do not meet their self-imposed, inordinately high standards of performance. This is trouble because anxiety is reciprocal to sexual arousal: If one is present, the other can't be. Thus if a man becomes anxious about his performance, he may not be able to achieve an erection; if he can't achieve an erection, he is sure not to live up to his standards; if he doesn't live up to his standards, he becomes even more anxious. This anxiety-dysfunction association often results in a vicious circle in which concerns about inadequacy seem to make performance all the more difficult.

From a systems perspective, sexual dysfunctions may be conceptualized as interpersonal events. Their occurrence is inseparable from the relationship in which they are embedded. Roffe and Britt (1981), for example, suggest that changes in power, hostility, independence, and intimacy can create stress in a relationship that can be experienced as sexual dysfunctions.

Of all the psychosocially based paradigmatic perspectives offered for sexual dysfunctions, there is most empirical support for a learning theory. Masters and Johnson (1970) have reported that many of their patients simply had not learned appropriate sexual behaviors. Graber (1981) compares learning sexual behavior with learning to ride a bike. Both are psychomotor acts that require attention and awareness to bodily functioning and a feedback mechanism to process the information. Once learned, the psychomotor skill becomes automatic and the learning process fades from awareness.

Paradigmatically Based Treatment for Sexual Dysfunctions

Until Masters and Johnson's (1970) program of treatment, most of the help available for those with sexual dysfunctions was derived from the psychosocial paradigm's psychoanalytic perspective. In this approach, the therapist used intensive analysis to discover and to work through the sources of the sexual "symptoms." Masters and Johnson also began with the psychosocial paradigm, but developed what is essentially a systems approach to sexual dysfunctions. Using this approach they were able to produce "cure" rates double or triple those of analytic therapists and in 2 or 3 weeks, not 2 or 3 years.

In developing their treatment program, Masters and Johnson used data gathered from their original research on the physiological correlates of intercourse and sexual pleasure. In essence, their treatment is based on their psychosocial belief that the causes for sexual disorders are to be found in the interaction between the partners. Masters and Johnson reasoned that past pressures changed a spontaneous sexual interaction into one in which either one or both partners adopted a spectator role and made it into a command performance. To correct this negative situation, Masters and Johnson begin the treatment process by having the couple come to stay near the treatment center. The couple is interviewed, both separately and together, by professionals of both the same and the opposite sex. To eliminate the possibility of biological causes for the sexual problems, each partner must complete a physical examination. Only about 1 percent of the patients were terminated from treatment for these problems (Kolodny, 1981). After the interviews and examinations, the couples meet with the therapists who give them their evaluation of the problem and explain the proposed treatment. In most cases the couple is instructed to undress in front of each other when they return to their room. While undressed, they are supposed to touch each other to find what is pleasurable to one another. However, they are instructed *not* to have intercourse. Psychotherapy counseling sessions focusing on major relationship problems are usually run concurrently with the exploring activity. Although therapists may discuss sexual techniques in these sessions, they make no demands for any increased level of sexual performance.

Masters and Johnson's program appears to be extremely successful in eliminating the disorders of vaginismus (100 percent success), premature ejaculation (98 percent success) and primary erectile disturbances (70 percent success). When followed up after a year, their clients showed an impressive 80 percent success rate for sexual dysfunctions in both women and men.

Since Masters and Johnsons' early work, the field of "sex therapy" has continued to grow. Clinicians using techniques closely paralleling Masters and Johnson's basic approach have reported progress in two-thirds of the patients (Crown & D'Ardenne, 1982). However, at least one researcher, Graber (1981), believes that movement toward a separate and unique approach to treating sexual dysfunctions is an error that has led some clinicians to apply sexual techniques uncritically. Rather, Graber believes that sexual dysfunctions should be treated with traditional psychotherapy techniques. Reviewers of behavioral approaches to treating sexual dysfunctions tend to support Graber's conclusions. They conclude that behavior therapists failed to properly assess the impact of treatment on partners and to use comparable criteria across studies (Cooper, 1981; Kilman, 1978; Marks, 1981).

Sex therapists in general and Masters and Johnson in specific, have been further criticized for reporting few treatment details, misreporting data, and for not being more helpful to other practitioners (Kaplan, 1979; Szasz, 1980; *Time Magazine*, 1983; Zilbergeld & Evans, 1981). Kolodny (1981), who is associate director of the Masters and Johnsons' institute, has responded to these criticisms. He points out that few couples are denied therapy at the institute even though they present a variety of serious disorders. Kolodny noted that details of treatment are presented in workshops under the guidance of qualified therapists. Finally, his plea to other workers who deal with sexual dysfunction is a good guide for research in this area. "Taking pot shots at one another cannot make up for a lack of research data and research cannot be magically conjured up—it requires long, hard hours, careful attention to detail, and a willingness to report the difficult problems as well as the comfortable solutions" (p. 316).

There are many ways in which paraphilias are fostered and maintained in our society. (*Mark Mellett/Taurus Photos*)

Paraphilias

Unlike the sexual dysfunctions, in which there are difficulties in the "normal" mode of sexual gratification, *paraphilias* represent methods of sexual gratification that are contrary to the established rules and mores of society. Generally these deviant behaviors are assumed to be modes of sexual release that are used when normal modes of release aren't available (Edwards, 1983). In most instances of true paraphilias, people cannot establish intimate, love-related relationships with others. They are forced, therefore, into the pursuit of alternative nonintimate and impersonal channels of sexual expression. The paraphilias are grouped into those characterized by abnormal "choice" of sexual object and those reflected by abnormal "method" of sexual gratification. Paraphilias also vary along a dimension of potential harmfulness to self and others. Within abnormal choice and abnormal method groupings, therefore, paraphilias should be expected to vary considerably in potential dangerousness.

Disordered Choice of Sexual Object

The disorders of sexual object are characterized by an attachment of sexual feelings to "abnormal" sexual articles. In that "normal" sexual objects are typically considered by society to be members of the opposite sex, sexual *gratification* with any other "object" would usually be considered abnormal. We have emphasized the word gratification because the use of many otherwise "abnormal" sex objects as part of foreplay is generally acceptable. It is when the objects rather than sexual intercourse become the primary source of sexual fulfillment that a paraphilia may be said to exist.

Fetishism

The center of sexual interest in fetishism is some inanimate object. Most often the object is an article of women's underwear, which typically is used by the male as a stimulus while masturbating. Stealing the articles seems to add to their stimulating value. The objects stolen may include bras, shoes, or even more unusual items. In one case, a man cut hair off unsuspecting young girls. He collected over 100 different samples before he was arrested. Another fetishist collected cardboard tubing found inside of such items as paper towels or waxed paper. Fetishes for exhaust pipes, baby carriages, and even baby food jars have been described. Some fetishists can be very devious in their attempts to obtain the objects they want for sexual excitement. One man posed as an agent from the Environmental Protection Agency who supposedly was checking the breathing capacity of women to see if it had been affected by radiation from an atomic power plant. As part of this "breathing test" he convinced a number of unsuspecting women to remove their bras so he could check their breathing.

Transvestism

Transvestites obtain sexual gratification and pleasure by wearing rather than stealing the clothing of the opposite sex. They obtain "primary" sexual excitement by the "feel" of such clothing. Most transvestites are male, heterosexual in sexual orientation, married, and they maintain their masculine identity in their families except for the fact that they frequently dress in cross-sex clothing for sexual excitement (Stoller, 1977). Cross-sex dressing more often occurs in the privacy of the transvestite's home.

Personal Experience: Transvestism

Its hard for me to talk about this. I know its not right. If my friends knew I had to dress in outfits they'd have nothing to do with me. It's one of the reasons I came in for therapy. The fear that I would be found out was beginning to make me tense. (Question: Was there an event that made you come in for help now?) Yes. My son woke up one night last week and came into our bedroom to ask for a drink of water. I was just putting on the first nylon stocking. What would have happened if he had come in five minutes later? How would I explain? (Question: How long have you been excited by wearing women's clothing?) When I was younger and living at home, I can remember my mother thinking I had nice curly hair. She liked to comb it for me and fix it in different ways. She sewed for all of us and for children at church and she sometimes asked me to put dresses on while she fixed them. Sometimes she would put the dresses on me and comb my hair and then step back and say that I would really make a cute little girl. I can remember her standing with her hands on her hips looking down at me with the nicest smile on her face and then she'd give me a hug, a long good hug. I can remember how she smelled; she smelled good. I didn't want to wear dresses but I didn't want to hurt her feelings. Really sounds Oedipal doesn't it doctor? I think I understand how it started but that doesn't help me to stop it.

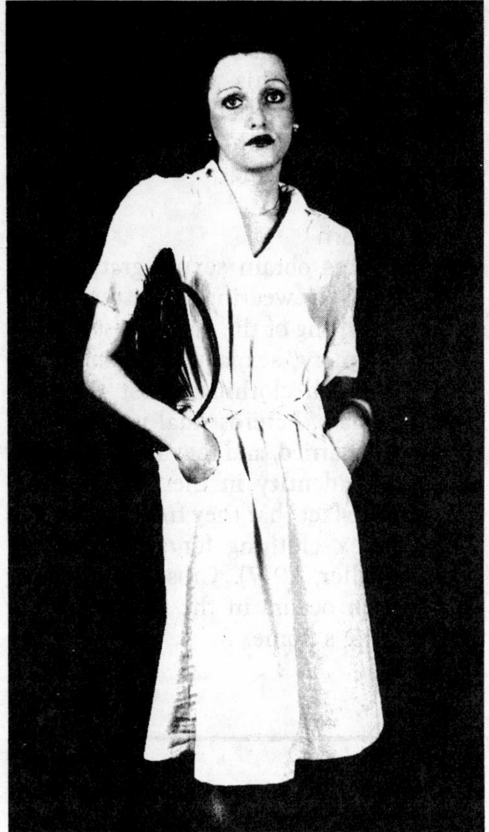

While some transvestites are clearly identifiable, others may be more difficult to notice. (left photo: © *1976 Eric Kroll/Taurus Photos* right photo: *Rhoda Galyn*)

It is a tribute to human adaptability that so many wives learn to live with their husband's strange dressing habits. However, it is dismaying that there is relatively little information on how the wives of transvestites deal with their husband's behavior. We also do not know how long transvestites continue their cross-dressing behavior. Although both behaviorists and psychoanalysts have reported some successes (Person & Ovesey, 1978), most attempts to change transvestism have been disappointing (Wise & Meyer, 1980).

Transsexualism

More formally called *gender dysphoria syndrome* in DSM-III, transsexualism is characterized by people feeling as though they are trapped in the body of the wrong sex (Levine & Lothstein, 1981). Unable to accept their own physical sex, they may dress in the clothing of the opposite sex, although, unlike transvestites, it is not for sexual excitement or gratification. The opposite-sex clothing simply feels more appropriate to the way in which they think about themselves. In *primary gender dysphoria*, people have always felt as though they should have been members of the opposite sex. Their histories are characterized by gender and sex-role confusion; males are likely to have been described as "sissies," and girls as "tom boys." In physical appearance and by most other criteria of hormonal and sexual attributes, transsexuals are quite normal; the differences lie primarily in the manner in which they think about themselves.

Personal Experience: Transsexualism

I've always been a woman! I know its hard for you to buy that, but it's true. I hate my penis. How would you like to be a woman and have a penis? It's like it was stuck on as an afterthought. As a child I always liked to play with the girls. It was easier to talk with them and be with them. Boys were always dirty and foulmouthed. They weren't any fun to be with. (Question: When did you decide to apply for sexual reassignment surgery?) I've thought about that since I read about somebody having done it. I was about 10 years old at the time. Adolescence was hell. Everybody expected me to grow out of my "troubles" and get on with being a sex-crazed male adolescent. I didn't. I am now 26 years old. I am bright. I am sane. I am reasonable. You know that, you've given me all the tests. I cannot live any more as a woman trapped in a man's body. The surgery will give me a chance for happiness. The thought of spending the rest of my life this way is depressing, almost intolerable, now that I realize I have a chance to change things.

Though a relatively rare disorder that occurs more frequently in males (1 per 100,000 people) than females (1 per 700,000 people) (Levine & Lothstein, 1981), treatments for transsexualism have attracted a great amount of attention. One of the primary ways of treating gender dysphoria is by *sex-reassignment surgery* (SRS), a method derived from a biological perspective on the disorder. Since the early 1950s when the case of Christine Jorgensen received so much publicity, hundreds of people have completed SRS. The surgery techniques, especially for males, have "reached an impressive degree of perfection" (Levine & Lothstein, 1981, p. 104). In males, surgeons can create female genitalia after removing the penis and testicles. Surgery with women is more difficult, however, because of the problems in building a functional penis.

Recently there has been a concerted effort to evaluate the effectiveness of SRS. Walinder and Thurne (1975) found that a combination of hormonal therapy, cross-gender living, and surgery resulted in favorable outcomes in 80 percent of the cases. However, Meyers and Reter (1979) and Pauly (1981) concluded from studies of 283 male-to-female and 83 female-to-male transsexuals that "sex reassignment surgery confers no objective advantage in terms of social rehabilitation as compared with a group of individuals who sought sex reassignment but remained unoperated on at follow-up" (Pauly, 1981, p. 45).

Even those who perform SRS conclude that it should only be used as a last resort (Lothstein, 1982). All types of psychotherapy approaches ought to be used to help people come to some resolution of their difficulties before SRS is decided on (e.g., Keller et al., 1981). Most SRS patients require at least 2 years of psychotherapy before surgery.

Incest

With the consideration of incest, we move to those disorders that involve other people as victims. *Incest*, or sexual activity among blood relatives, has been nearly always universally condemned (although intermarriage among royalty has been, at times, condoned). Estimates of the rate of incestuous behavior are very difficult to obtain because so many cases go unreported. While Summit and Kryso (1978) estimate that there are some 36,000 cases of father-daughter incest in the United States, these figures must be taken cautiously because only a limited percentage of cases are ever found. Although mother-son incest also occurs, it is much rarer than father-daughter involvement.

Generally the incestuous father has been described as immature, passive, timid, low in self-esteem, and fearful of mature women (Schultz, 1979). In some instances, however, the father will present himself in a mature yet hostile manner. In those instances where the father is angry and unable to control his impulses, there is a strong chance that the daughter can be abused physically as well as sexually. Such cases may be less likely to be reported because the daughter and perhaps her mother fear for the child's safety. Generally, hostile incestuous behavior takes place in families that can be described as chaotic and unsettled. This is reflected in the following case reported by Wells (1981).

Case: Incest

A 35-year-old married mother from a rural area wanted "to get a mental exam so I can get my daughter back." She began by telling how her oldest child had run away from home and how she, the patient, wanted to get her back—as did her husband. She seemed angry with the daughter and indicated that this child had always been "different," with temper tantrums as a toddler and more independence than the other children in the family. About a year prior to running away, she began to "act up" in school. The mother attributed this to bad companions and a bad teacher. There were apparently some accusations by other students that the daughter was stealing from them; her classwork deteriorated, and she was sent to live with her maternal grandparents. While there, she was arrested for shoplifting and returned home. She began to rather openly steal purses from the classmates and to put them in her mother's closet at home. The girl's father confronted her with these thefts and she turned her back on him, refusing to discuss them. He then lost his temper, shook her, and beat her severely. He went out to do his farm chores after administering this beating and the daughter ran away from home. She was located after 3 days and was placed in foster care at her request.

According to the girl, her father had been beating her frequently with belts and farm implements (including a baling hook) and he and an uncle had been sexually abusing her for many years. She refused to recount this history of abuse to the court. She indicated that her uncle had begun genital fondling when she was 7 and had commenced intercourse with her when she was 11. She said that her father had occasionally participated in these activities and had threatened to kill her if she told anyone. She indicated that her uncle and perhaps her father were currently engaged in genital fondling of all her sisters and overt intercourse with two of them.

In telling me this story of her daughter, the patient had a very flat affect and insisted that the girl had not been "really abused." She admitted that she had "walked into a baling hook her father was holding" on one occasion, and acknowledged that the child had lost a tooth or two during beatings. She acknowledged that while her husband had sexually abused the daughter and did beat her frequently, the sexual abuse had stopped and he had never "really hurt her." As for the uncle, the patient was aware of his incestuous behavior. The patient was "surprised but not angry" when she learned that this was true and said that she and her husband told the uncle to stop the sexual abuse. In discussing this man, the patient said, "You can't really blame him; after all he is not married". She went on to describe what she saw as an idyllic family life, with her 8 children doing chores and happily participating in farm life. She said that her marriage was "perfect" except for occasional disagreement about the daughter. Although she denied any anger toward her, she answered questions about the number of children she had by saying, "Eight; well, nine if you count her." The daughter was an unwanted child with whom the patient became pregnant immediately after high school. She married her husband, who was the girl's father, about six months into the pregnancy. (Wells, 1982, p. 198)

There is considerable conjecture as to what causes incest. Guided by the biological paradigm, Bixler (1981) suggests that incest results from natural selection; that it is a natural outgrowth of biological needs. On the other hand, workers using the systems perspective have gathered data which suggest that incest occurs where there is alcoholism, overcrowding, and increased physical proximity that prohibits extrafamilial contacts (Sadock, 1980).

Unfortunately, there is very little treatment available for people who need help for incestuous behavior (Rist, 1979). Most practitioners are ill-prepared to deal with the complex problems presented by families with incestuous members. Simari and Baskin (1980) believe that the best way to deal with incest is through early diagnosis and clarification of feelings of the people involved. Like other clinicians, they believe strongly that the whole family needs to take part if real progress is going to be made.

Pedophilia

Many incestuous adults could also be categorized as pedophiliacs, people who can only attain sexual gratification through sexual contact with children. As a group, pedophiles have been mentally defective, alcoholic, and inadequate (Meyer, 1980). They may subject young children to sodomy, fellatio, or coitus. Legally, pedophiles are described as people whose sexual contact is with children no older than 13, and who are at least 10 years older than their victims. Most pedophiles are men and most children molested are girls (at a ratio of 2 to 1). It is difficult to gauge the true number of sexual assaults by pedophiles because children may not always tell what has happened and even if they do, should a relative be involved families may wish to keep such experiences secret.

While most pedophiles do not do much more than interact with children in a brief sexual way, a significant proportion of them also may abuse the children they victimize. These *aggressive pedophiles* usually are strangers to the children, in their thirties, and drink to excess. Because of their poor impulse control, they may abuse children severely or even murder them to keep them quiet (Meyer, 1980). Aggressive pedophiles are among the most dangerous of all sex offenders.

Disordered Choice of Method of Gratification

Rather than using disordered *objects* for sexual satisfaction, in the paraphilias to follow people employ disordered *methods* of gratification. Those who must resort to deviant methods of gratification often have difficulty forming satisfactory, intimate love-related relationships. As a result they may choose to look at others from a distance as in voyeurism or they may attain sexual contact by force as in rape.

Exhibitionism

In exhibitionism, males expose their genitalia to women or children who usually are strangers to them. The more he can surprise and upset others, the more sexually excited he becomes. One exhibitionist hid in women's bath stalls, and when they were washing their hands he would step out and expose himself. While exhibitionists account for nearly one-third of the arrests for sex crimes, they make up only about 10 percent of those imprisoned for such offenses (Rooth, 1974). Seemingly, then, exhibitionism is seen by the law and society as a relatively "harmless" class of paraphilia (Gebhard et al., 1965; Meyer, 1980). We say relatively, for about 1 out of every 10 exhibitionists is involved in more violent forms of sexual offenses such as pedophilia and rape. Although two-thirds are married, exhibitionists appear to have difficulty in adjusting heterosexually and tend frequently to use masturbation and prostitutes for sexual satisfaction. There is no completely satisfactory explanation for exhibitionism, although from the psychosocial and systems perspectives, Blair and Lanyon (1981) report that many exhibitionists were loners as children and had families characterized as cold and uncommunicative.

Reviews of treatments for exhibitionism suggest that the psychosocial paradigm-based method of covert sensitization (see Chapter 5) has been most successful. However, Blair and Lanyon (1981) urge that individualized treatment procedures include behavioral as well as interpersonal and social factors to deal with the variety of symptoms presented by exhibitionists.

Personal Experience: Exhibitionism

The feeling just comes over me. It's not anything I'm proud of but what can I say. If I could control it I wouldn't be in prison now. (Question: What happened to get you in prison?) I showed myself. I did it before and I did it again. You've met my wife. She's a bitch! She's always nagging, getting on me to do this and do that; even in front of people. Makes me feel like shit. Sorry . . . But last Tuesday she got on my case at the grocery store. Right in front of the cashier she tells me that I'm stupid. That night about 10 o'clock, I left the house and went down to the college. I know the girls usually leave the library and walk back to the dorm. There's always a straggler or two. Those are the ones I wait for. I get excited waiting. Finally, I couldn't wait any more and I called to this girl. "Hey," I say, "Did you lose your purse?" As soon as she looks at me I give her a good view. By that time my penis is big as can be. She really gives it a look and screams and starts running. I started to masturbate there . . . I couldn't wait. That's how they caught me. They think I would have done something to hurt somebody I guess. That's why I'm here. Hell, I've done my thing a lot of times and I've never hurt anyone. In fact, I think the girls liked it.

Voyeurism

Whereas the exhibitionist wants others to see him, the voyeur prefers to hide himself. He obtains sexual gratification by observing others (without their awareness) in various stages of undress or lovemaking. Generally shy and immature, the voyeur is usually not interested in making any additional contact with the people he watches. Instead, he is more likely to masturbate either during or after his observations. The possibility of his being caught while voyeuring seems to add to the sexual excitement of the act.

Voyeurs combined with exhibitionists make up more than half of all arrests for sexual misbehavior. Like the exhibitionist, voyeurs rarely are involved in significant aggressive or dangerous actions.

Personal Experience: Voyeurism

I'm really upset about what I've done . . . I feel like a freak or something. I was brought up in a religious family, and I shudder to think what my pastor would say if he knew about me. But I think that my strict upbringing had much to do with what I wound up doing

. . . looking into dorm windows. I'm sort of frightened by them. Look at me . . . I'm not very good looking . . . very few girls would really want to go out with me. But I'm a male too, and I have a sex drive. I used to be able to satisfy myself by looking at Playboy pictures and all and then masturbating, but those girls weren't real . . . they're not alive. When I came to school, I learned from certain places it was easy to see into the girls' bathrooms in the dorm on the ridge . . . especially on hot spring nights when they open the windows. So, I got . . . binoculars, . . . and would tell my roommate I'd be studying late at the library. Then I'd go up and watch the girls take showers and fantasize that they were having sex with me. I'd masturbate while I watched and after I reached a climax, I'd go home . . . and I'd feel real bad . . . kind of dirty and sick, but in two or three days, I'd be right back doing it again.

Masochism and Sadism

While exhibitionists and voyeurs rarely touch or harm their victims, that is not the case for sadists and masochists. Generally the *sadist* experiences sexual excitement when harming another person, while the *masochist* becomes sexually excited by being harmed. Sadism is named for the Marquis de Sade, an eighteenth century nobleman who was known for his vivid literary descriptions of brutal, cruel treatment of women. Masochism is named for the pain-loving character type developed by Leopold von Sacher-Masoch, a nineteenth century Austrian author. While there are pure sadists and masochists, generally people can and often do play both roles (Meyer, 1980).

Although some aggressive behavior is present in most normal sexual interactions, it usually is more a result of the sexual passion than the cause of it. However, in the case of the sadist and the masochist, hurting or being hurt is *the* source of sexual excitement. Sadomasochistic individuals may use unusual methods to inflict or receive pain.

Personal Experience: Sadism

I've only agreed to talk to you about this because I'm concerned that you are writing about sadism in an abnormal psychology book. I want it known that sadism is "not" abnormal, but is the expression of a deeper sense of feeling for another person that is not possible with routine sexual patterns. I am not an uneducated person and I've not come to these conclusions out of lack of knowledge or experience. To me sadism is the icing on the cake, the cherry on top of the sundae . . . it adds a special something to sex. The inflicting of pain upon another person is the inflicting of your existence upon them; when you kiss another person she need not remember that kiss nor the feelings associated with your presence, but when you cut a person with a razor ever so lightly and you share the drops of blood which result, the relationship is sealed and never to be forgotten.

Unfortunately, some sadists go beyond simple infliction of pain and graduate to murder as the ultimate in sexual excitement. Some of the most bizarre mass murderers have been sadists who have punished and mutilated their victims for sexual gratification before killing them. "Lust" murders can be heterosexually or homosexually motivated. In rare instances, sadists may even have intercourse with their victims at the time of death (*necrophilia*).

Rape

Like sadism and masochism, rape is also characterized by aggression and infliction of pain. Sadock (1980) stated, "Rape is an act of violence and humiliation that happens to be expressed through sexual means" (p. 571).

Personal Experience: Rapist

(How were you feeling at the time of the incident?) I was very depressed at the time. Empty, lonely, out-of-it feeling. I was trying like a bastard to get someone to stop me. No one listened. I wanted to kill the woman; I didn't intend to rape her. In the struggle her clothes were ripped, so I got charged with attempted rape. They showed her dress in court; it was a mess. (Groth & Birnbaum, 1980, p. 19)

Sadism derives its name from the cruel sexuality described in the writings of the Marquis de Sade. (© *Mary Evans Picture Library/Photo Researchers, Inc.*)

According to statistics from the Uniform Crime Reports, there were 78,918 cases of forcible rape reported in the United States during 1983, but it is estimated that this figure represents only about 10 to 25 percent of the actual occurrences. Conservatively then, there may be between 200,000 to 450,000 rapes each year (Rabkin, 1977). Probably fear of their assailant and embarrassment over the incident play an important role in the fact that only 52 percent of the known forcible rapes were solved by arrest (Uniform Crime Report, 1983).

Sadock (1980) reports that 61 percent of rapists are under 25. The rapist will generally threaten a woman with physical force. Based on police data typical rapists are single, 19 years old, with a police record, from the lower socioeconomic classes, strongly heterosexual, and low in impulse control. FBI Uniform Crime Reports (1983) show that rape usually is not a one-time crime; rapists tend to repeat their rape behavior. Rapists seem to be more labile and responsive to violence than men in general (Quinsey et al., 1984).

Almost any woman may be the target of a rapist. Victims have ranged from 15 months to 82 years of age, but most frequent are females between the ages of 10 and 29. More often than not, rapes occur in the victim's own neighborhood and, in nearly half of the cases, the attacker is an acquaintance. Some rapists believe that all women secretly wish to be raped and that the more they resist, the more women want to be violated further.

Only recently, guided by the systems paradigm, have professionals begun to study the victim *and* her family and friends and their reactions to the rape experience. As they try to deal with being raped, victims move through five distinct phases; initial, denial, symptom formation, anger, and resolution (Forman, 1980). In the *initial* phase the victim usually is in a state of shock. After the shock wears off there may be a tendency to *deny* that the attack really happened. However, frequently the denial does not work and the victim may experience a variety of reactions including fear, headaches, irritability, and withdrawal. As she becomes more aware of the origins of her symptoms, she may become very *angry* at her rapist in specific or at all men in general. Through realistic assessment of the incident and her feelings about it, the woman can move to the final stage in which there is a positive *resolution* of the event.

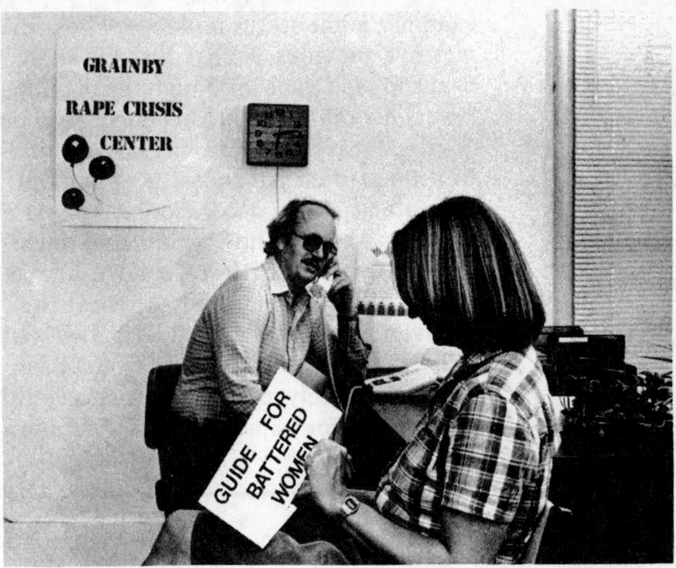

Rape crisis centers represent an application of the systems paradigm. (*Mimi Forsyth/Monkmeyer Press Photo Service*)

Researchers have found that, as compared with women who have not been raped, rape victims have lower self-esteem (Burgess & Holmstrom, 1979), greater feelings of fear (Kilpatrick et al., 1979), and lowered sexual activity levels and sexual satisfaction (Feldman-Summers et al., 1979). In other research, Norris and Feldman-Summers (1981) asked 189 adult rape victims to complete a questionnaire concerning their rape and their response to it and found that rape victims had a more positive recovery when they had male and female associates who were understanding and supportive.

Victims are not the only people who are hurt by the rapist; if she is married, the victim's husband also is significantly affected. Studies have shown that the spouse's initial reaction to the rape may often take the form of anger toward the victim (Burgess & Holmstrom, 1980) and/or anger toward the rapist and a desire for revenge (Holmstrom & Burgess, 1979). One group of researchers looked at the long-term effects of rape on married couples (Miller et al., 1982) and found that serious relationship difficulties can continue for years after the incident. Therefore they strongly suggest that spouses be included in postrape therapy sessions.

Deriving from the findings of research based on the systems paradigm, *rape-crisis centers* have developed to help women adjust to the trauma of being raped. Center activities include working with victims and their families, and putting political pressure on the legal system to deal more fairly and equitably with raped women (Underwood & Fiedler, 1983). For example, some states no longer allow the victim's previous sexual history as evidence in rape trials (although the previous sexual history with the defendant may be admissable if the victim has known him). In spite of such advances, it is still very difficult to obtain a conviction against a rapist and even if he is convicted, incarceration may do little to change his behavior. Since rapists tend to repeat their behavior, chances are good that they will rape again after being released from prison.

Unfortunately, there are few successful treatments for rapists. Some European professionals have even gone so far as to suggest the extreme biologically based treatment of castration (Heim & Hursch, 1979). Such radical interventions need to be discussed and evaluated, at length, before being used.

Therapeutic efforts are not only directed at rapists or their victims. One less radical, but effective intervention has developed out of the systems paradigm method of helping rape victims through improving communication and support from their families as is seen in the following personal experience.

Personal Experience: The Husband of a Rape Victim

It's been nearly 6 months and I still have trouble talking about it. I've never felt more anger. I'd kill the guy if I could. I remember how my wife looked that night. She had smudges on her face like when we clean up the garage together. At first glance she looked cute and then I could see the terror in her eyes. She had been hurt. Oh, God! I can't stand somebody in my family feeling pain or being hurt and here some scum had hurt the woman who is dearest and closest to me. I remember not knowing what to do to make her feel better. I held her but she didn't cry. I wish she would have, it would have made things easier for me. Following this set of feelings, I began to be angry with her. I asked her what she was doing that she could be attacked. I know she never is careful enough when she goes downtown. She's too friendly and naive. I've told her over and over again to be careful. Of course, she wasn't to blame. It was that. . . . It was so hard for me to get over my own feelings of anger and wish to kill that bastard so that I could help my wife deal with her own feelings of outrage. The anger is still there but counseling has helped me and her sort our feelings out so that we can build our relationship up rather than have that rapist tear it down. I think we're going to be stronger for having gone through this together.

Paradigmatic Perspectives on the Paraphilias

Considering the variety of paraphilias it may not be surprising that no single paradigm has produced a satisfactory comprehensive explanation. Generally, behavioral explanations are based upon the assumptions that biological/sexual needs serve as motivators and that the reduction of the biological sex drive is a reinforcing event (orgasm is pleasurable) and can strengthen any behavior that precedes such reduction. In people who have learned how to relate on a mature heterosexual level, sexual fulfillment reinforces that level. In people who cannot relate in biologically adaptable or socially acceptable ways, other sexual behaviors must serve as the primary tension reducer.

Reasoning from the psychosocial paradigm, Walker (1982) has suggested that paraphilias may develop from a basic reinforcement process. That is, behaviors that are reinforced will tend to repeat themselves. Therefore stimuli present when people become sexually excited might become capable of producing sexual arousal when presented again. In a study supporting this explanation, Rachman (1966) paired pictures of nude women with pictures of boots. Using increased blood flow to the penis as his dependent measure, he found that boots became capable of eliciting sexual arousal. People also are capable of fantasizing objects or situations while sexually aroused, and through this pairing, these fantasies may become capable of producing a sexual response.

Although theoretically sound and garnering some research support, there still is not conclusive empirical evidence for this explanation of aberrant sexual behavior. It should be possible to gather information from case histories and interviews to see if the antecedents for paraphilic behavior are present more in diagnosed cases than in the general population. As of yet such confirmatory evidence is lacking.

As will be described further when we discuss treatment, behavioral explanations assume two major aspects of misdirected sexuality must be changed. First, the positively valued abnormal sex object or behavior must be made aversive or negative. Second, the difficulties encountered when trying to satisfy biological drives through normal sexual intercourse need to be resolved.

Like the learning theory explanation of paraphilias, psychoanalytic theory is comprehensive but lacking in empirical support (Fenichel, 1945). Basically, paraphilias are assumed to develop from a mishandling of the Oedipal complex. Males fear that their sexual feelings toward their mother will be found out and they will be punished by their father for their indiscretion. One of the most feared repraisals is castration. Males may develop castration anxiety whenever they experience sexual feelings in other situations besides with their parents. This fear might motivate males to develop other ways of gratifying their sexual needs as described in the paraphilias. While we present some evidence for this explanation in our discussion of homosexuality, conclusive empirical evidence for the other paraphilias is not available.

At this point we present a recent general explanation derived from an integration of the psychosocial and systems paradigms. It assumes that the various paraphilias represent modes of sexual gratification which are alternatives to heterosexual intercourse. These alternative modes are abnormal in the sense that they are considered culturally unacceptable (Edwards, 1983).

According to Edwards (1983; Storr, 1964), sexual deviations may be seen as simple exaggerations of normal male sexual tendencies. For instance, normal males "exhibit" their masculinity in body-building, athletics, sports cars, and the like; deviant males may "exhibit" their masculinity by exposing their genitals or being voyeurs. Similarly, while many normal males are easily aroused by the sight or touch of female undergarments, the fetishistic male achieves gratification "only" through such objects.

Persons with sexual deviations often have deep-seated feelings that they are less than adequately masculine or feminine. Although almost everyone has been distressed by such feelings of "sexual inferiority" at one time or another, they seem to have a particularly powerful influence on behavior for the person with a sexual deviation. A male who sees himself as being inferior is likely to have problems relating normally to women and may settle on modes of sexual release which augment, or at least do not threaten, his fragile sense of masculinity. In a fetishist, an object such as a bra can take on the power of the female who wore it and substitute for her. The fetishist is guaranteed success in his interaction with the substitute and thereby increases his sense of masculinity. In pedophilia, the male is typically afraid of mature females and therefore chooses a child as an object. The child's powerlessness emphasizes the deviant's strength and masculinity and assuages his inferiority feelings.

According to theorists such as Edwards and Storr, sexual deviations may be understood as exaggerated normal patterns that may be used to satisfy needs for a sense of masculinity without the requirements of intimate personal relationships. In our society the pressures on males to conform to a highly idealized model of strength, competence, and virility can be enormous. Thus feelings of sexual inferiority are probably more strongly felt by males. This may be one reason why the sexual devations are much more common in men than women. However, these and other assumptions need to be verified by research evidence.

Paradigmatically Based Treatment for Paraphilias

While most people with psychological problems seek help because their symptoms make them uncomfortable and unhappy, that is not necessarily the case in the sexual disorders; these people may not seek treatment until they are forced to do so by actual or threatened legal action. Needless to say, "forced therapy" is difficult in unmotivated and uncooperative clients. Although traditional forms of individual psychotherapy have had inconsistent success in treating such clients, a further application of the psychosocial paradigm in the form of behavioral treatments has been more useful. The clients' apparent lack of motivation does not seem to bother some behavior therapists: "All that is necessary for change to occur is that the client agree to take part in the conditioning procedures; his degree of motivation during the procedures is not crucial" (Cautela, 1968).

Covert sensitization (Cautela, 1968, 1970a) is a good example of a therapy that focuses on making the positively valued deviant sex object or behavior aversive. It helps the client to produce aversions to his abnormal sex objects. In covert sensitization, sex objects that initially are positively valued are associated not with pleasure but with discomfort. For instance, in treating a sadist an image of inflicting pain on another may be paired with images of becoming nauseated. Soon, through classical conditioning, the image of pain infliction makes the person sick. In this way, the frequency of the deviant behavior may be reduced. Mahoney (1974) has concluded that covert sensitization is consistently effective with sexual paraphilias.

To control sexual fanatasizing, a "thought-stopping" technique may be used by itself or in combination with covert sensitization. In this procedure, the therapist asks the patient to close his eyes and talk about his sexual thoughts. At some point during this process the therapist will shout "stop!" After a period of time, the client will be instructed to say "stop" himself each time the unwanted thoughts begin to emerge. Parenteau and Lamontagne (1981) have applied thought stopping successfully to a number of paraphilias.

Once the deviant pattern of sexual behavior is halted through techniques like covert sensitization or thought stopping, it is necessary to help males come to a more realistic appraisal of their masculinity by focusing on the development of more adaptive social-interpersonal sexual skills (Edwards, 1983). Successful development of these skills would allow males to satisfy their sexual needs through normal channels. Both unstructured and structured procedures can be used. In *unstructured procedures*, clients usually are allowed to develop new skills in their own way and at their own pace. The therapist follows the lead of the client and rarely if ever gives advice. In contrast, *structured procedures* have the client follow various assignments made by the therapist. Here, a client might be assigned the task to make a date with a woman. To help develop the needed skills to complete the task, the client might role play asking a woman for a date. In this way, social skills that were absent may be learned, and the necessity for deviant modes of sexual behavior may disappear in the face of more mature modes of expression. The combination of new modes of expression and acquired aversion to deviant behavior can provide an effective treatment program for sexual paraphilias.

From a biological perspective, hormonal therapy has been a recent addition to attempted treatment. In this approach, antiandrogens are given to sex offenders to diminish sensitivity to circulating androgens. This reduces erotic arousal and desire. Money and his associates have been major investigators using this approach (Money et al., 1975). Usually, the dosage of medication is combined with psychological counseling for a period of 6 months to 2 years. Walker (1977) reports that patients report a sense of relief that their sexual compulsion no longer governs what they do. Money et al. (1976) found that sex-offending paraphiliacs (like exhibitionists and pedophiliacs) who remained for the completion of therapy reported a reduction of erotic imagery and fewer sex-offending incidents than those who dropped out of treatment. However, it should be remembered that hormonal treatment does not change the direction of the sexual urges, just the intensity.

While the approaches based on single paradigms like the psychosocial perspective have had some success in treating paraphilias, some scientists believe that combining one or more paradigms might be more useful (Berlin & Meinecke, 1981). For example, Crawford (1979) proposes that it is simplistic to view sexual deviance as only a problem of deviant arousal. Based on a review of research evidence, he has concluded that (1) sex offenders have difficulties in other areas of their life; (2) it is inconsistent to accept that normal sexual behavior is complex but deviant sexual behavior is simple; (3) more emphasis ought to be placed on increasing the sexually disordered person's nondeviant arousal and interests; and (4) it is unrealistic to consider paraphilias in isolation from other problems. In essence, Crawford calls for comprehensive treatment programs based on systems as well as psychosocial perspectives.

Homosexuality

Homosexuality differs from the sexual paraphilias in several important ways. First, many homosexuals are capable of mature, intimate, interpersonal, and sexual relationships. Second, their choice of object and mode of sexual satisfaction is primarily based, not upon distorted sexual abilities within their physically determined sex, but on the fact that emotionally and psychologically they experience themselves as oriented differently. Thus, many homosexual people are more comfortable being sexually intimate and loving with a member of the same rather than the opposite sex.

Characteristics of Homosexual Behavior

Homosexuality was included in the DSM-I under sociopathic personality disturbances; in DSM-II, it was included in a section on personality disorders. In 1974, six years before DSM-III was instituted, the

In addition to homosexuals, there are also other groups of people who support gay rights. (© *Rhoda Galyn*)

American Psychiatric Association voted to stop considering homosexuality in and of itself a mental disorder. In place of the previous classification this organization substituted a category called *sexual-orientation disturbance.* This category was intended for individuals whose sexual interests are directed primarily toward people of the same sex and who also are in some way uncomfortable with their sexual orientation. The spirit of this change in perspective was carried over to DSM-III. However, the term *sexual orientation disturbance* has been omitted and replaced by the classification *ego dystonic homosexuality* under the larger category of psychosexual disorders. According to DSM-III, unless homosexual individuals experience persistent distress regarding their own sexual orientation and have a strong need and desire to change their behavior, homosexuality is not a diagnosable disorder (Smith, 1980).

The history of attempts to classify homosexuality reflects its controversial nature. Data from survey studies suggest that there are not two distinct groups of people, heterosexuals and homosexuals, but rather a continuum of people who engage in sexual behaviors ranging from primarily homosexual through bisexual to primarily heterosexual (Kinsey et al., 1948; Masters & Johnson, 1970). In Kinsey et al.'s work, a 7-point scale reflected this continuum with people who were primarily homosexual placed at one end and people who were primarily heterosexual at the other. In rating homosexual and heterosexual behavior, Kinsey et al. used sexual arousal level and not manifest behavior as the most significant diagnostic sign. Based on Kinsey's data, 4 percent of adult men were classed as exclusively homosexual throughout their lives, with another 13 percent predominantly homosexual after age 16. Nearly one-third of all males interviewed had had an interaction with another male that led to an orgasm. Women's rates of homosexual experience were about one-half of those reported for men. Quite clearly Kinsey's data suggest that there are not exclusive heterosexual and homosexual groups, but rather groups of people who share more or less a homosexual or heterosexual orientation. Supporting the flexibility of sexual orientation, Schafter (reported in Green, 1980) found that 40 percent of the female homosexuals surveyed had had heterosexual intercourse during the previous year.

Although both male and female ego-dystonic homosexuality occurs, the sexes do differ in their patterns of interpersonal behaviors. Saghir and Robins (1973), for example, found that compared with female homosexuals, male homosexuals usually began masturbating earlier and masturbated more frequently, engaged in homosexual experiences earlier, had a higher number of homosexual contacts, were more promiscuous, and engaged in more oral-genital sex. Both males and females reported that they were erotically aroused by people of the same sex before adolescence and usually alternated between active and passive roles in lovemaking (Storms, 1981). In all, women tended to engage in fewer and longer homosexual relationships than males, who

BOX 14-1

HOMOSEXUALITY AND EMOTIONAL DISTURBANCE

Freud described homosexuality as occurring in "people who exhibit no other serious deviation from the normal . . . whose efficiency is unimpaired, and who are indeed distinguished by specially high intellectual development and ethical culture" (1953). However, other psychoanalysts differ with Freud. Bieber et al. (1962) view homosexuality as the result of disordered sexual development and as an impediment to a happy life.

Some biologists see homosexuality as inconsistent with the basic role of procreation. They point out that if everyone were homosexual, it would mean the end of the human race (Beach, 1948). From such a biological perspective the homosexual is perceived as abnormal and "out of synch" with the human species.

Those who believe there is no necessary link between homosexuality and emotional difficulties reason that researchers such as Bieber use data gathered from homosexuals who have gone to see psychiatrists to generalize about all homosexuals. If data obtained from heterosexuals who are in therapy were used to generalize about all heterosexuals, they too might be described as unhappy and maladjusted. In fact, Weinberg and Williams (1974) found homosexuals to show no greater incidence of psychological disturbance than heterosexuals, a finding replicated by Hart (1978). Likewise, Meredith and Riester (1980) caution that differences found between homosexuals and heterosexuals do not necessarily mean deficits. Rather, homosexuals may be showing stress arising from their status in society not from any innate deficit. This view is expressed in the theory of secondary deviance, derived from the systems perspective.

While there is little support for there being any greater rate of emotional disturbance among homosexuals, neither is there any indication of a lower rate. Some spokespeople for homosexual groups tend to give the impression that homosexuals may be better adjusted than heterosexuals and that the only basis for their emotional difficulties, should they experience them, may be found in their status in society. Most likely, this is not the case. There probably are proportionally as many murderers, schizophrenics, and other unhappy people among homosexuals as there are among heterosexuals. Being homosexual is not a safeguard against developing disordered behavior.

had more "one-night stands." These one-night stands often were engaged in compulsively. Some males participated in as many as 10 homosexual contacts in a single night at a variety of places such as public washrooms, public baths, autos, and public parks. The increased danger seemed to heighten sexual excitement. Saghir and Robins' basic findings have been replicated by other researchers (Hoffman, 1977; Lehne, 1978; Monteflores & Schultz, 1978; Peplau, et al., 1978).

It is estimated that over half of those men who participated in the impersonal sex of the public-bathroom circuit (called "tearooms") were married and lived with their wives and children in generally middle-class homes (Humphreys, 1970). As a group these men tended to be politically conservative and religious. Nearly half saw themselves as heterosexual and viewed the public-restroom meetings as a quick way of satisfying their sexual needs. Although married, many of these men seemed to have unsatisfactory sexual relationships with their wives. Women homosexuals less often engaged in impersonal homosexual interactions.

Paradigmatic Perspectives on Homosexuality

All three major paradigms have been involved in attempting to explain homosexuality. The explanations can be grouped into biological, psychosocial, and system views, and more recent attempts to combine them.

The Biological Paradigm

Researchers following the biological perspective suggest that homosexuality is caused by defective genes or some nervous or hormonal system defect. However, attempts to find support for such theories have been discouraging. Although, Kallmann (1952) found a concordance rate of 100 percent for homosexuality in a sample of monozygotic twins and a significantly lower rate for dizygotic twins, his findings have not been confirmed by others (Kolb, 1963a; Money & Ehrhardt, 1972). If there is a genetic cause for homosexuality, most theorists now believe that it would be in the form of a predisposition for individuals to become homosexual if they encounter a particular kind of environment.

While the genetic explanation for homosexuality has not received much support, other theorists sharing the biological view have proposed hormonal differences between homosexuals and heterosexuals. They suggest that homosexual men have lower levels of testosterone (the male sex hormone) and homosexual women lower levels of estrogen (the female sex hormone). Some evidence of testosterone deficits in male homosexuals has been found (Kolodny et al., 1971; Loraine et al., 1970). More recent work has implicated other hormonal substances called luteinizing hormones in the case of female homosexuals (Doerr et al., 1976; Meyer-Bahlburg, 1979). Other research suggests that homosexuality in both sexes may be due to abnormalities in fetal exposure to hormones that affect sexual development (MacCulloch & Waddington, 1981).

The role of hormones in causing and/or maintaining sexual orientation behavior may hold some answers to the question of how homosexuality arises, but not all theorists are convinced. Ross et al. (1978), for example, concluded that "an individual's hormonal condition plays no part in the determination of sexual activity or sexual preference in any of its forms, including homosexuality" (p. 315). If believed, such evaluations will lead researchers to use paradigms other than the biological in their search for causes of homosexuality.

The Psychosocial Paradigm

Rather than seeking answers in genetic and hormonal data, researchers guided by the psychosocial perspective look for evidence that homosexuality comes about primarily through psychological experiences. Freud, in his "Three Essays on the Theory of Sexuality" (1930/1953), suggested that all people were bisexual (attracted to both sexes) at the point in their normal development when they loved both of their parents. Homosexuality is seen as the result of an arrest of normal development at this bisexual (homoerotic) stage, or as a regression back to that stage. Freud further believed that people maintain vestiges of this homoerotic stage as they develop. Remnants of bisexual urges may be felt by some as *homosexual panic,* a sense of severe anxiety in response to normally occurring sexual thoughts about members of the same sex.

Freud implicated the mishandling of the Oedipal stage and the failure of the male child to form a satisfactory relationship with his father as a major cause for the retardation of normal sexual development. Freud believed the presence of a detached, cold, and even hostile father, together with a close, binding, seductive mother sets the stage for the development of a homosexual orientation. However, the presence of a truly loving and caring father probably could prevent the development of a homosexual orientation, regardless of what the mother was like. In the case of homosexual development, a boy must deal with his incestuous feelings toward his mother. From his attempts to handle these incestuous feelings, he may develop a fear of sexual contact with the opposite sex (*heterophobia*). This fear develops because the boy may observe that women have "lost their penises" and that the very same thing might happen to him if his father learned of his feeling toward women in general, and his mother in particular. Freud suggested that sex with a woman can awaken male fears of castration and may lead one to adopt a homosexual orientation.

Support for the Freudian explanation was gathered by Bieber and his colleagues (1962). Seventy-seven psychoanalysts provided access to the case histories of 106 male homosexuals seen in psychoanalysis. On the basis of these case histories and information gathered through interviews of the patients by their analysts, Bieber concluded that the most significant factor in the genesis of homosexuality was the particular parental constellation of cold father–seductive mother as hypothesized by Freud. As was also suggested by Freud, homosexual patients reportedly showed castration fears and an apparent aversion to female genitalia.

Generally, the data gathered by Bieber's group and others (Evans, 1969) hold only for males. Freud offers little about the development of homosexuality in women. Perhaps we can assume that, parallel to the explanation for males, there may be an inadequate identification with the mother and a fear of sexual relationships with males as a result of a poorly resolved Electra complex.

The criticisms of Bieber's work concern its narrowness and use of patients to generalize to all homosexuals (Bell & Weinberg, 1978). Further, since most of the data were based on ratings and those doing the rating knew the basic hypotheses, there was also a chance of their judgments being biased and inflating the relationships found. Further studies done with raters blind to the purpose of the study could provide a truer evaluation of Freud's hypotheses. Likewise, based on Freud's reasoning, there should be a higher rate of homosexuality in ghetto-type living situations, where there may be a higher proportion of absent fathers. Data do not support this assumption opening up the possibility that other environmental or genetic factors may need to be considered.

The assumption of frozen psychosexual development at a homoerotic stage is one of several theories deriving from the psychosocial paradigm. Another, based on learning theory, proposes that the "reinforcement" of inappropriate sex-role behavior is the most important contributor to the development of a person's homosexual orientation. In our culture, there is usually pressure on youngsters to adopt same-sex relationships for an extended length of time in their development (Werner, 1979). Boys interact with boys and girls interact with girls in such activities as sports, scouting, and social interactions. It often takes youngsters some time and great courage to overcome the embarrassment of peer pressure in order to make cross-sex contacts and establish relationships.

The Systems Paradigm

As mentioned earlier, some researchers (e.g., Meredith & Riester, 1980) feel that psychosocial approaches such as those espoused by Bieber do not fully reflect the problems of homosexuality. These scientists as well as others guided by the systems perspective believe that the status of homosexuals in society also contributes significantly to their classification as abnormal.

Society's role in the perception of homosexuality might best be conceptualized in terms of primary and secondary deviance as outlined in Chapter 6. Primary deviance, or the violation of societal rules involving sexual activity with same-sex partners, is not uncommon in our society. Kinsey reported that 37 percent of males have some sort of homosexual experience to orgasm after the onset of adolescence and that in males remaining unmarried past age 35 the percentage engaging in orgasmic homosexual behavior rises to 50 percent (Kinsey et al., 1948; see also Storms, 1981).

Primary deviant homosexual behavior seems quite frequent among males. However, those espousing a systems perspective believe that true homosexuality can only occur if these acts of primary deviance are *reacted to* by society in the form of labeling of the primary deviants as "abnormal." According to labeling theory, if society calls primary deviants "homosexual" and alienates, avoids, or punishes them, these individuals begin to move toward a condition of *secondary deviance*. Rather than being simply a person who experiences orgasm through activity with members of the same sex (primary deviant), the secondary deviant is a homosexual.

Once the label of homosexual is applied, not only does society treat the person as "different," but after a time the individual may also begin to see himself or herself as an outcast. Feeling unaccepted by the majority of society, the secondary deviant may gravitate to groups and places which feel more comfortable. In this way, he or she may be pressured to join a homosexual subculture and become more fully involved in and committed to a different life style. Labeling theory can help explain why from among the estimated 30 to 40 percent of adolescents who report experiencing same-sex orgasmic activity only a small percentage become fully active adult homosexuals.

An Integrated Paradigm

Although the application of a systems paradigm seems to explain some of the special characteristics of homosexual development and life style, any explanation for homosexuality needs to combine the biological, psychosocial, and systems perspectives. Each view in and of itself fails to account for significant factors in the development of a homosexual orientation. Money and Ehrhardt (1972) suggested that homosexual orientation came about through an interaction between a genetic predisposition and particular kinds of environmental situations. Noting that there is no one source for homosexuality any more than there is for heterosexuality or bisexuality, Money and Ehrhardt state:

> The most likely explanation of the origins of homosexuality, bisexuality, and heterosexuality of gender identity is that certain sexual dispositions are laid down in the brain before birth which may facilitate the establishment of either of the three conditions but are too strongly bivalent to be exclusive and invariant determinants of either homo- or heterosexuality, or of their shared bisexual state. The primary origins of the three conditions lie in the developmental period of a child's life after birth, particularly during the years of late infancy and early childhood, when gender identity differentiation is being established. (p. 253)

While they contend that biological and psychosocial factors seem quite important in the establishment of sexual orientation, Money and Ehrhardt also note that the expression of homosexual behavior has strong systems concomitants. As evidence, they describe research conducted in prison systems in which men who are actively heterosexual "on the outside" often become actively homosexual during their incarceration. Once released to the

According to the integrated view, the environment in which sex roles develop is as important as the genetic determinants of sexuality. (*Jean-Marie Simon/Taurus Photos*)

community system, they typically return once again to their original heterosexual preference. Thus in addition to genetic predispositions and developmental experience, systems in which people find themselves also contribute to the development of homosexual behavior patterns.

Though speculative, this integrated paradigm is quite similar to those also being used to explain mental disorders like the schizophrenias, affective disorders, and drug addictions. As seems to be the case for these other disorders, an integrated paradigm holds promise for improved understanding of ego-dystonic homosexual orientation.

Paradigmatically Based Treatments for Ego-dystonic Homosexuality

Of the many forms of intervention used in treating the ego-dystonic homosexual, most derive from the psychosocial paradigm. Traditional individual psychotherapy has been successful, especially with highly motivated clients under 35 years of age who have experienced some heterosexual satisfaction at some time in their lives and whose homosexual orientation is recently acquired (Green, 1980). Bieber et al. (1962) found that about one-third of 100 homosexually oriented males had acquired and maintained a heterosexual orientation for 5 years following psychoanalysis.

There are many complex issues of values and ethics involved when heterosexual therapists deal with homosexual clients (Riddle & Sang, 1978). Some clinicians suggest that special training may be needed to sensitize therapists to issues of their own sexuality and their personal reactions to homosexuals (Davison, 1978; Murray, 1981). Coleman (1978) has concluded that rather than try to help egodystonic homosexuals to change their orientations, therapists should assist homosexuals to recognize, accept, and value their sexual identity and to help them adjust to this identity in a predominantly heterosexual society.

In addition to traditional *talk* therapies, learning theory-based *aversion* training also has been used to change homosexual behavior. In this approach, the pleasurable association between sexual gratification and a same-sex partner is changed to a negative one. In some instances, therapists may administer a nausea-producing drug or deliver mild shocks to the wrist while the client is shown erotic slides of same-sex people. Through such classical conditioning, the once arousing same-sex stimulus becomes aversive. In some instances, the client can stop the shock by choosing to view an erotic slide of an opposite sexed individual. MacCulloch and Feldman (in Green, 1980) report that over half of the homosexual men experienced increased arousal to heterosexual stimuli as a result of aversive training.

Rather than actual painful shock as the source of aversion, covert sensitization (Cautela, 1968) also can be used. Clients are asked to imagine unpleasant mental images such as vomiting or suffocating. They then are asked to imagine being involved in a homosexual act and, at the moment of full sexual arousal, are instructed to imagine the noxious images they had previously developed. The unpleasant images are only stopped when the thought of homosexual interactions cease as well. At this point, clients are instructed to reward themselves with pleasant images such as walking on a beach or sitting by a brook in a forest.

To many people, the use of aversive conditioning raises serious ethical questions. Many clinicians do not favor the use of such techniques at all, while others only use them as a last resort in treatment. Reservations are especially cogent when it comes to changing homosexual behavior. Halleck (1976) suggests that therapists should help the homosexual client consider all alternatives, including remaining homosexual. Only in making clear all the possible options can therapists help their clients to make the best possible decisions concerning their sexuality and style of living.

Concluding Comments

As a biological function with psychosocial and systems consequences, sexual behavior seems to demand a paradigm that combines all these elements. However, as in the case of most of the patterns of psychopathology included in this text, researchers and clinicians have traditionally ascribed to one or the other of the three major paradigms. For example, the psychosocial and biological paradigms have been frequently applied in explaining the sources of sexual disorders. However, the treatment of sexual disorders has not been as successful as one might expect given the amount of research done on them. It could be that sexual disorders represent anomalies with which our current single-factor paradigms cannot adequately deal. The fact that so many sexually disturbed people are remanded to prisons for "rehabilitation" rather than to more appropriate "treatment" agencies suggests that society, too, is not confident in the ability of psychology and psychiatry to understand and alter patterns of sexual psychopathology. There seems to be a need for integrated paradigms to tease out relative contributions of different perspectives in the development and maintenance of sexual behavior.

Summary Chart

In our discussion of sexual disorders, we first examined patterns called sexual dysfunctions. These disturbances are usually treatable and occur with some frequency.

Orgasmic dysfunction in males: Ejaculatory disturbances
Orgasmic dysfunction in females: Orgasmic problems, vaginismus
Explained biologically and psychologically
Treated by modern sex therapy: Master's and Johnson's methods

Unlike the dysfunctions which occur in the "normal" course of sexual behavior, the paraphilias represent abnormal patterns of sexual object or method of sexual gratification.

Abnormal Choice of Object
Fetishism
Transvestism
Transsexualism
Incest
Pedophilia

Abnormal Choice of Method
Exhibitionism
Voyeurism
Sado-masochism
Rape

Efforts to explain and treat paraphilias derive from both the psychosocial and biological perspectives.

The psychosocial perspective: Exaggeration of normal patterns, covert sensitization, thought stopping
The biological perspective: Biochemical or neurological problems

We closed Chapter 14 with a discussion of ego-dystonic homosexuality.

The biological view: Genetic evidence, twin studies, hormonal factors
The psychosocial view: Psychoanalytic explanation dealing with Oedipal stage problems, difficulties in psychosexual development
The systems view: Theories of secondary deviance
An integrated perspective: Biological predisposition interacting with psychological and environmental factors

CHAPTER 15

Personality Disorders

Most of the sexual disturbances discussed in Chapter 14 are usually brought to the attention of professionals and treatment may be sought for them. Conversely, the majority of the personality disorders we will discuss in this chapter are often simply "lived with" or "passed through" without professional aid. Although most of these patterns are mild, they are accorded diagnostic status in DSM-III. In the case of the personality disorders, however, diagnosis is made along Axis II rather than Axis I indicating that the personality patterns are not considered to be true "mental disturbances." Typically, people with personality disorders have had long-term characteristic patterns of interacting with others. These patterns are integral parts of their personalities and may cause them or others degrees of difficulty ranging from very mild to very serious.

General Characteristics of the Personality Disorders

Vaillant and Perry (1980; 1985) conclude that "no group of emotional disorders is more often encountered in psychiatric practice than the personality disorders" (p. 474). However, they also point out that there probably is no other group who is more likely to refuse psychiatric help. Instead of cooperating, these people often will point out the shortcomings of those who are attempting to help and instigate unpleasant and frustrating interactions.

Why people with personality disorders create such interpersonal problems for mental health workers reflects the basic core of their disturbances. Although the symptoms may differ considerably from one person to another, "people with personality disorders respond with an inflexible and eventually maladaptive response to stress" that shows itself primarily in a wide variety of important social contexts (DSM-III, 1979). These maladaptive patterns are ingrained, inflexible, and recognizable by adolescence. As a result of their personality patterns, these people have considerable trouble interacting with others in work or intimate situations. Their inability to use strong emotion in a flexible and adaptive way drives others away. Because they have difficulty seeing themselves as others see them, people with personality disorders may misread interpersonal cues to fit their own narrow way of perceiving their world, as is seen in the case that follows.

Case: Personality Disorder

S., a 30-year-old single, government lawyer, was referred to me for analysis because of chronic anxiety and interpersonal difficulties. Intelligent, competent, and very ambitious, S. was constantly at odds with his supervisor over the handling of cases assigned to him. Suspicious and intrusive, he always seemed to be provoking arguments. S. had a habit of walking into bars and baiting bigger and stronger men. When they would threaten to hit him, he would menace them with legal action for assault and battery. Although his supervisor never objected, S. felt uneasy about extending his lunch hours in order to come to see me. One day he had a particularly stormy encounter with his supervisor over the handling of a case just before leaving for an hour. On the way to my office, he developed the conviction that the F.B.I. was following him to see how he was using government time. After discussing the incident with me, S. realized that his suspicion was probably related to the argument with the supervisor and it quickly vanished. (Lion, 1981, pp. 173–174)

As well as being difficult to deal with interpersonally, individuals with personality disorders present considerable problems in diagnosis. Although they were placed on a separate axis (Axis II) in the multiaxial DSM-III framework, Frances (1980) points out that personality disorders "as a group still attain the lowest reliability of any major category in the classification" (p. 1050). Partially, this lack of reliability results from the fact that personality disorders may be simply extremes of normally appearing personality traits. The continuous nature of personality dimensions makes diagnosing people into groups more difficult to do, especially with the failure of DSM-III to operationalize such terms as "inflexible" or "maladaptive." The reliance on clinical judgment regarding these terms can lead to inconsistency and lowered reliability in diagnosis.

Another source of lowered reliability results from the impact of what are called "trait" and "state" factors. A trait refers to a person's long-term personality characteristics, while a state factor reflects a personality characteristic that is caused more by present events. Since, by definition, personality disorders are enduring patterns that affect a wide variety of activities and interactions since adolescence, it must be ascertained if the present personality difficulties are due to recent stressful events that have caused a change in a normal personality functioning or the continuation of a long-term personality disorder. Should the disordered behavior be a one-time occurrence resulting from a recent set of stressors, then it is probably more appropriately called an *adjustment reaction* (see Chapter 10). For instance, unless the person has shown a depressive reaction to others throughout life, then depression in response to beginning college is probably best seen as an adjustment reaction, not a personality disorder. As Frances concluded, to be a personality disorder, "the behavior in question would have to be general, longstanding, maladaptive, and not merely an isolated role response to one difficult situation" (p. 1051).

Though DSM-III presents 11 different personality disorders, there is little empirical or research basis for developing these classifications. Since the primary basis for making these diagnoses is often clinical intuition, they need to be applied carefully, until additional data supporting this classification are collected.

The 11 personality disorders can be placed into three clusters. The first "cluster" includes the *paranoid, schizoid, and schizotypal disorders* characterized by odd and/or eccentric behaviors. In contrast, the second "cluster" of *avoidant, dependent, compulsive, or passive-aggressive disorders* shows anxious or fearful behavior. The last cluster of *histrionic, narcissistic, antisocial, and borderline personality disorders* reflects dramatic, emotional, or erratic behavior. Of the four patterns in this last group, we will single out for special attention the antisocial disorder. This separate discussion reflects the special nature and potential dangerousness of this pattern and the greater amount of research and theory generated by it.

Odd and Eccentric Behaviors

Within the developmental context of behavior, many of the personality disorders may be seen as milder versions of more severe disturbances. This is especially true in the cluster associated with odd and eccentric behaviors which parallel quite clearly the paranoid and schizophrenic psychoses.

Paranoid Personality

To obtain the diagnosis of *paranoid personality disorder*, people must show an interpersonal style characterized by rigidity, unwarranted suspicion, jealousy, envy, hypersensitivity, and anger. Generally these people are argumentative and tend to blame others for their problems

To those diagnosed as paranoid personality disorder, other people are viewed with suspicion, fear, and anger. (*Zimbel/Monkmeyer*)

(Millon, 1981). However, in spite of the fact that they are usually loners, and have few if any close friends, Lion (1981) notes that they often have a recognizable sense of humor. This humor may be cutting, self-deprecating, and sardonic—a style that Lion feels characterizes some very successful comedians. Paranoid personality style also may be seen in some bigots or overly jealous spouses.

Weintraub (1981) describes the paranoid personality as more interested in mechanical devices than people, although sensitive to the power and rank of others. The paranoid personality's hypersensitivity to others can make interpersonal interaction tense and uneasy.

People with paranoid personality disorder are rarely treated in psychotherapy because they tend to avoid initiating interactions with mental health systems. Generally, they may be brought into psychotherapy by other family members but, characteristically, because they see others and not themselves as responsible for whatever problems are occurring, they may leave therapy early. These are cold, unpleasant people whose limited affect, suspiciousness, and lack of responsiveness drives others away, thus confirming their view of the world as made up of people who do not care.

Personal Experience: Paranoid Personality Style

When I moved into my new neighborhood, I was pleased to find that most of my neighbors were quite friendly. That is, all except the guy in the house on the right of ours. About a week after we moved in, I got up real early and went out to start work on a fence for the yard. It must have been about seven o'clock when I got out there and drove in the first fencepost. Well, I couldn't believe it but, about 10 minutes later, here comes this guy with a ball of string and some papers. And he tells me that he wants to help me not to violate the county ordinance about how fences have to be 6 inches on the land of the builder of the fence and that the lay of the land out back was such that it was hard to know the boundary without a line and survey drawings. He pulls out the survey drawings and shows me where our land meets and then goes about stretching a string from one corner of the property to the other. I just stood there . . . I actually felt a little afraid of him. . . . After he finished, he wished me luck and went back into his house. Later on he came out to check how I was doing, and he told me about the "hippies" that sometimes come through the neighborhood and he has guns in the house just in case they start doing damage or going wild on drugs. I smiled. . . . We still live there and I know that the guy is a little strange, but he keeps a high-level executive job and seems basically stable . . . he's just a little more suspicious than the rest of the world.

Schizoid Personality

Like paranoid personalities, schizoid personalities are associated with symptoms that parallel psychotic syndromes. Early mention of the schizoid personality disorders can be found in the writings of the European psychiatrists Bleuler, Kretschmer, and Kraepelin who believed there was a specific personality out of which schizophrenia developed. Later the term "schizoid" came to mean a personality profile that designated a more general population of people characterized by social withdrawal. Schizoid people appear to be aloof and reserved. They do not seem to need emotional ties with others, preferring to be quiet, distant, and seclusive. If they adjust, it appears they adjust on the periphery of society in lonely jobs that most others do not want. In some cases, they can show a great deal of interest in such projects as astronomy, philosophical movements, or health fads, but only as long as they involve minimal interaction with others.

People with schizoid personality disorder spend much of their time fantasizing about being powerful and overcoming others. They seem to have great difficulty expressing anger and usually channel such feelings through daydreaming and fantasy. However, even though they may appear sullen and hostile, they rarely act out their anger.

Personal Experience: Interviewing a Schizoid Personality

I saw Bill at 10:00 o'clock. He was dressed in an old flannel shirt and ill-fitting khaki pants. I shook his hand and said hello. His handshake was limp and he mumbled something in response to my salutation. He remained standing even though I had seen him numerous times before. I motioned for him to sit down and asked how things were going. He pushed out an "ok." I felt myself becoming irritated with his lack of response. I asked him about his health, his family, his job, and what seemed like 50 other things. All I received back were some short answers. He volunteered no information. It did not appear that he was hiding anything, he just seemed uninterested in interacting with me. The time with Bill went agonizingly slowly. I looked at my watch; 5 minutes had passed. They seemed like 5 hours. Bill had been referred by his employer because the people in the apartment house he janitored thought he was "odd." In five sessions with him, I don't think he ever made eye contact with me. I know what the people that complained about him referred to: he was "odd" and he made me uncomfortable. I never looked forward to meeting with him.

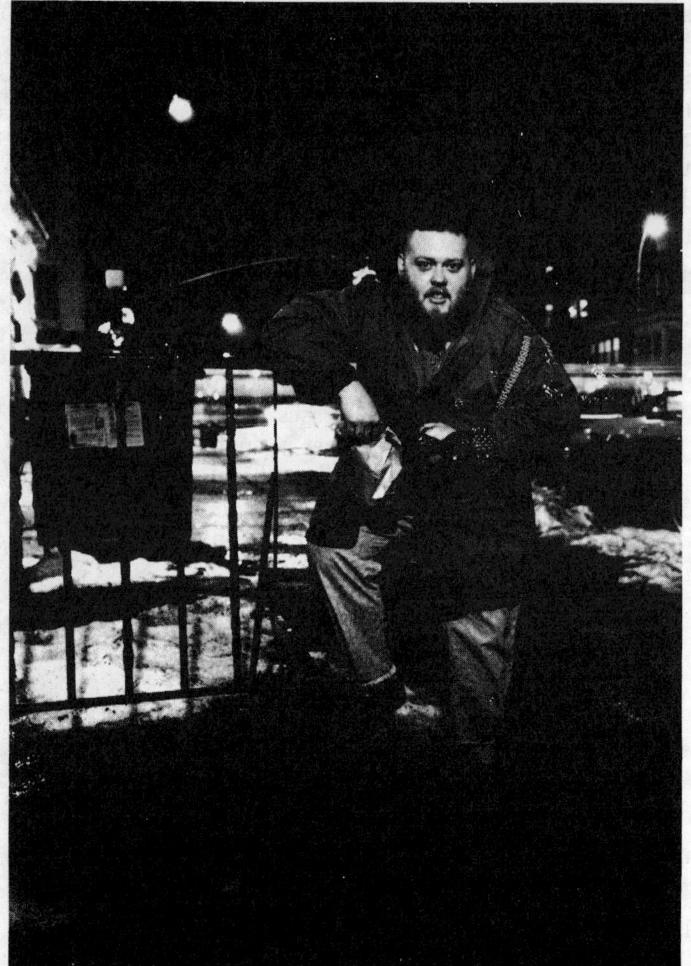

People diagnosed as schizotypal personality disorder often live on the fringe of society and are seen by others as "odd." (*Larry Racioppo*)

Schizotypal Personality

Sometimes referred to as simple or latent schizophrenia in the past, schizotypal disorders represent a connection between schizoid personality disorder and schizophrenia. Typically, their behavior is "odd" and they may claim clairvoyance or other special powers of thought. Like the schizoid personalities, schizotypal individuals are socially isolated, but in addition they manifest a marked tendency for loose thinking and communicating. Affective stimuli, be they positive or negative, can cause schizotypal individuals' speech to become digressive and incoherent. They seem to be on the verge of becoming schizophrenic should they experience even a moderate amount of stress. The authors of DSM-III appear to assume that there is some sort of biologically based genetic component in this disorder. One of the major criteria for inclusion in this diagnostic classification is a clear family history of schizophrenia—a criterion that is noticeably absent in diagnosing schizoid personality disorders.

Anxious or Fearful Behavior

Whereas the personality disorders described above were clustered around "odd" behaviors and behavioral parallels to psychosis could often be found, the personality disorders we will discuss next are grouped together by the common factor of anxiety. Though the anxiety may be expressed differently depending on the particular personality disorder, it is the single most salient symptom.

Avoidant Personality

The essential feature of the avoidant personality disorder is a "hypersensitivity to potential rejection, humiliation and shame" (DSM-III). While avoidant people may desire interpersonal contact, they will not enter into relationships unless they can be completely sure they will not be rejected by others. Interpersonally, avoidant personalities present themselves as tense, uncertain, and lacking in self-confidence. Vaillant and Perry (1980) describe avoidant personalities as having an "appealing waif-like" quality that attracts others to take care of them. Because of these personality traits, they rarely rise to places of power and authority. Millon (1981) believes that avoidant personalities "feel their loneliness deeply, experience being out of things and have a strong, though often repressed desire to be accepted" (p. 103). In other words, these are uncomfortable and needy people. Their apparent social detachment does not arise due to deficits in drives to approach people as may be the case in the paranoid and schizoid personality disorders, but more as a result of a set of self-protective maneuvers. These self-protective maneuvers are guided by a special ability to detect the feelings of others. However, they may spend so much time processing cues of possible rejection or disapproval that it interferes with the processing of other important information, especially in social situations.

The girl walking by herself away from the group characterizes the interpersonal style of the "avoidant" personality. (*Don Rutledge © 1981/Taurus Photos*)

Dependent Personality

New to DSM-III, dependent people are characterized by an ability to get others to assume responsibility for the major areas of their life, a marked lack of self-confidence, and a knack for subordinating their own needs to the needs of the person they are dependent on. As with the avoidant disorders, it appears that the people with dependent personality disorders have learned methods of making others respond in predictable ways. Anxious when alone, dependent individuals will be able to perform adequately if in the company of the people they depend on. They seem to be storing up their good deeds to use to buy "taking care of" from others. Once in a relationship with a dependent personality, it is very difficult to leave. Further, dependent people appear to be able to tolerate more than the average amount of unpleasant feelings in close relationships so that negative comments and behaviors from others do not drive them away.

Persons with dependent personality disorder often will come into psychotherapy when the people they depend on leave. They present special problems to therapists because, as they are prone to do outside of therapy, they become excessively dependent. This dependency often can stand in the way of therapeutic progress.

Compulsive Personality

Although compulsive people share anxious feelings with avoidant and dependent people, the compulsive personality has been studied longer and more intensively than these more recently delineated disorders. Vaillant and Perry (1980; 1985) listed nine traits from most to least important that describe the compulsive disorder: emotional constriction, orderliness, parsimony, rigidity, strict conscience, perseverance, obstinacy, indecisiveness, and a lack of sexual provocativeness. Above all, compulsive personalities are organized, thorough, serious, and slaves to their schedules. Should their schedules be disrupted, they become anxious and upset, as is shown in the following case history.

Case: Compulsive Personality Disorder

J., a 25-year-old corporation executive, came for psychiatric treatment after physically assaulting his girlfriend. He reported that this was the first time he had ever struck a woman and was afraid that he might completely lose control of himself. All his adult life, J. had led an extremely orderly existence, controlling to an incredible degree both his own behavior and that of people who came into contact with him. He refused to entertain in his apartment for fear that the precisely arranged furnishings might be moved out of place. When driving his car with his girlfriends, he wouldn't let them touch the glove compartment because its contents were meticulously arranged. Handsome and charming, he was attractive to many women, but he sooner or later found fault with them. The stress leading to his decompensation developed from an affair he was having with a psychiatric nurse. She reacted to his controlling behavior in the ways trained professionals often do with people close to them. In self-defense, she began to interpret J.'s behavior to him. She told him that he had no control over his orderly way of life, that he could not act differently even if he wished. This is a challenge few obsessional characters can resist. He tried to change his ways, to become more "flexible" but found instead that he was developing classic symptoms of an obsessive-compulsive neurosis. He became preoccupied with the thought that his anus was unclean and began to wash it repeatedly after defecation. He couldn't make decisions and was unable to use his beloved hi-fi system because he was convinced the arm was exerting too much pressure on the records and was damaging them. These symptoms were insufficient to deal with the rage that was building against his girlfriend who was continuing with her "wild analysis." When he lost control and struck her, he became alarmed and sought treatment. (Weintraub, 1981)

Unlike most other personality disorders, people with compulsive patterns are aware of their suffering and will seek treatment on their own (Salzman & Thaler, 1981). Psychotherapy with compulsive people may be characterized by a fight for control of the therapeutic relationship. The client may either be very compliant or may attack the therapist's intelligence and/or fairness. While difficult, therapy can be successful if the therapist can give support and not be drawn into the role of an adversary (Weintraub, 1981).

People with compulsive personality disorders are organized, thorough, overly serious, and slaves to their schedules. (*Michael Weisbrot and Family*)

Passive-Aggressive Personality

More than the other personality disorders in this section, passive-aggressive personalities tend to mix anger with their anxieties. DSM-III classification of passive-aggressive personality describes people who resist demands of others to perform certain tasks by procrastination, dawdling, stubbornness, intentional inefficiency, or forgetfulness. Although these people are not assertive, they can find fault in those who are in authority or on whom they are dependent. The following case describes a typical interaction between a passive-aggressive personality type and his parents.

Case: Passive-Aggressive Personality

James was 31 years old, single, and lived at home with his parents. Although he would have liked to have moved out and be on his own, his few attempts to go it on his own ended in disaster and he was forced to move back home. His parents, while verbally encouraging him to move out, nonverbally communicated that he stay home and keep them company. The tension created by this duplicitous communication could be felt often, especially when the parents wanted the son to do something for them. The sequence of demands by the parents–resistance by the son was repeated over and over. For example, when his mother asked James to shovel snow off the sidewalks he acted like he didn't hear her. When she repeated the request he replied, "Sure, sure." After she waited five minutes, James' mother repeated her request, but in a tone of voice that approximated a demand. At this point, James became angry and said he'd shovel the walk as soon as he was done eating. Mother again reminded James that if he didn't shovel the snow his father would have to and she intimated that this could cause him to have a heart attack. At this point James became sullen, ate very slowly . . . and eventually forgot to shovel the walk. This scenerio often was repeated with all parties threatening to leave one another, but rarely following through.

Generally, interacting with passive aggressive personalities can be an unnerving experience. Most people are unaware of the ability of passive-aggressive individuals to manipulate them into a hostile interaction. It is unsettling to find oneself becoming angry at someone and not be aware of why. Passive-aggressive personalities have a knack for drawing people close to them and then responding with anger-eliciting behaviors.

Psychotherapy with passive-aggressive personalities can be very complex. As Vaillant and Perry (1980; 1985) point out, to fulfill their demands supports their disordered way of interacting; to refuse their demands is tantamount to rejection. After rejection, passive-aggressive people have been known to choose suicide as a way of escaping their feelings of emptiness and abandonment.

Dramatic, Emotional, or Erratic Behavior

While fear and anxiety characterized the cluster of personality disorders just described, the next group we will discuss involves extremes of other emotions. Whereas anxious and fearful people shun attention, dramatic-emotional people often seek to be the center of attention.

Histrionic Personality

Histrionic personalities tend to behave in dramatic, excitable, and flamboyant ways in order to secure affection and approval from others. Millon (1981) refers to histrionic people as showing a "gregarious pattern." They share with dependent dis-

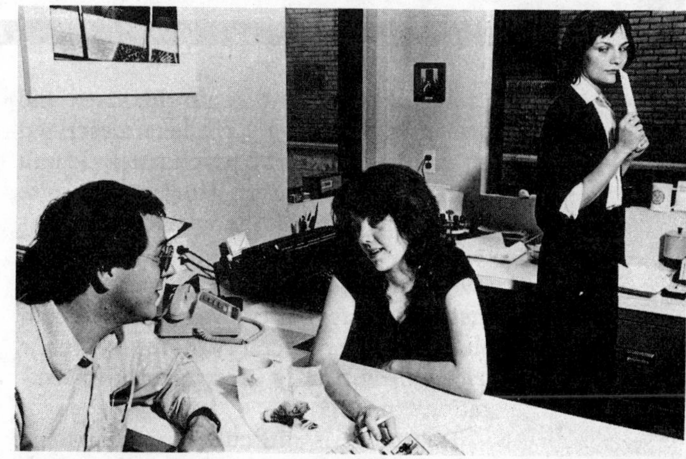

Passive-aggressive people often manipulate others into feeling irritated and angry. (*© 1982 Susan Rosenberg/Photo Researchers, Inc.*)

orders the need to be with and depend on others, but where dependent people quietly attempt to ingratiate themselves to a few others, the histrionic people put on a "show" often laced with sexual innuendo and ploys to please and manipulate others. The constant emotional displays, fickleness in feelings and relationships, sexual provocativeness, although at first interesting and exciting, soon wear thin and lead to disturbances in relationships. Histrionic people tend to be vain, egocentric, shallow, and inconsiderate of others' needs. Their inconsiderate behavior occurs in spite of the fact that histrionic individuals have what Millon calls "an exquisite sensitivity to the moods and thoughts of those they wish to please" (p. 131).

Personal Experience: Interviewing a Histrionic Person

I knew that Jill was very dramatic and seductive from the psychological report I had read, but it in no way prepared me for what came through the door for a meeting with me. What I thought would be a gaudy, "painted," and brassy woman was instead a very attractive, dark-haired woman in her early thirties. She walked slowly into the room and I couldn't help staring in spite of myself. Jill sat down and slowly crossed her legs and my eyes were drawn to that motion. In the first 30 seconds of the session she had gained the upper hand by sexualizing our interaction. "Well, doctor, what do you want to know about me," she asked. "I want to be as helpful as I can." She then moved to light a cigarette in another series of carefully orchestrated movements. After she lit her cigarette, Jill again spoke, "Doctor, you really look tired, I suppose dealing with crazy people all day takes it out of you." Of course, she was correct, I was tired and I was glad that someone had noticed. I then reviewed quickly what had happened and realized that the session was going to be very difficult; Jill was most adept at controlling interactions and was not going to give up that control easily.

The traits that make up the histrionic personality disorder have been described for many years in the psychoanalytic and psychological literature. However, in spite of the longevity of the concept, there is relatively little known about it. Pollak (1981), after reviewing 157 studies of the histrionic personality, was forced to conclude that "considerably more research is needed in virtually every area of investigation" (p. 98).

Treatment is difficult with histrionic individuals because they generally are unaware of their own feelings and have trouble expressing emotions honestly. Although infrequent, when they do seek therapy it is usually because they have experienced some sort of social disapproval or interpersonal deprivation. Their motivation for long-term therapy is usually low and environmental management, medication, and behavioral management appear to be minimally effective (Millon, 1981).

Narcissistic Personality

Another new addition to the DSM-III classification system, narcissistic personalities share with the histrionic person-

Histrionic people tend to behave in dramatic and flamboyant ways to obtain attention and affection from others. (*James Fitzgerald © 1985*)

ality a tendency to be demonstrative, dramatic, and at times seductive. However, where the histrionic person is playful and warm, the narcissistic person is haughty and cold (Akhtar & Thompson, 1982). To be diagnosed as a narcissistic personality, people must show a grandiose sense of self-importance, a preoccupation with fantasies of power and ideal love, demands for constant attention in the form of admiration, and a response of feelings of rage or emptiness to criticism. Further, in their interpersonal interactions with others these people show a remarkable inability to empathize. Although exploiting others is a common pattern, narcissistic people often are surprised and upset when others do not meet their wishes (Vaillant & Perry, 1980; 1985). In the following letter sent by a patient to her therapist, this narcissistic sense of injustice is shown.

Case: Narcissistic Personality Disorder

I hate myself after realizing in therapy today that I want you to love me, to make me feel important by treating me like you would treat a friend who is not a patient of yours. I know I shouldn't feel this way. When you are nice to me I want to have you stay near me and never leave me, and every time you say goodbye to me it tears me up inside. No, I don't want you to be angry with me—I just want you to understand why I sometimes want to turn up my anger on myself—it's because I want to punish myself for not adhering to what is best for me. . . . If I get too close to someone, I want to possess them completely. I want that special person to be with me all the time, and yet if he or she was with me all the time, I would feel very uncomfortable because of the fear of bringing about criticism and dislike of me from that person. If I like somebody very much, I want to do so much for that person and I'm afraid that whatever I do will never be enough. . . . I want you always to be by me and yet at the same time I know you cannot take care of me as you would your own child or wife. This is such a hard reality for me to face, but I face it every day and by facing it I feel bitter and rejected. (Hartocollis, 1980)

While the above letter demonstrates the DSM-III characteristics of the narcissistic personality, there is considerable disagreement among the major theorists about whether the pattern actually comprises a separate diagnostic entity. Kohut (1977) sees narcissistic personality as separate from other personality disorders, while Kernberg (1975) argues that it is a variant of borderline personality disorder. Others have attempted to resolve this apparent disagreement by offering other perspectives that describe narcissistic and borderline personality disorders as parts of the same dimension (Adler, 1981), but differing primarily in the way they present themselves to others (Rothstein, 1979). At this point, the eventual status of this "new entry" into the diagnostic system is unclear.

Borderline personality disorders include people who are lonely, bored, and unstable. (*Anthony A. Scaravilli*)

Borderline Personality

Although there is some limited disagreement over the existence of the narcissistic personality, perhaps no other personality disorder has created as much controversy as the borderline personality. Over the past three decades the category of "borderline" disorders has generated a significant flow of articles and books. What is presently referred to as borderline personality disorder, in the past has been called borderline schizophrenia, borderline state, and latent schizophrenia (Gallahorn, 1981). Even nationally organized workshops have been held in attempts to better understand what is meant by borderline disorders and how to treat them (e.g., Vail Conference, 1979). DSM-III attempted to derive concrete criteria to define the borderline personality and to separate it from the narcissistic personality we have just described. It is assumed that borderline people have contradictory images of themselves and others that lead them to show self-detrimental impulsivity in such areas as gambling, eating, or sex. Their relationships are unstable and show marked shifts from idealization to devaluation. One moment their partner is the best person in the world, while in the next moment this same person will be described as completely inadequate and selfish. During times of stress, borderline individuals show evidence of intense anger and problems in maintaining an independent self-identity. They are lonely, bored, and unstable people who seek to avoid loneliness by being with others, but have difficulty maintaining anything approaching a stable relationship as is shown in the following case history.

Case: Borderline Personality Disorder

Philip Berman, a 25-year-old, single, unemployed, former copy editor for a large publishing house, was referred for private outpatient therapy after he had signed out against medical advice following a two-week hospitalization. Mr. Berman had been hospitalized after a suicide attempt in which he deeply gashed his wrist with a razor blade. He described to the outpatient therapist how he had sat on the bathroom floor and watched the blood drip into the bathtub for some time before he telephoned his father at work for help. He and his father went to the hospital emergency room to have the gash stitched, but he convinced himself and the hospital physician that he did not need hospitalization. The next day when his father suggested he needed help, he knocked his dinner to the floor and angrily stormed to his room. When he was calm again he allowed his father to take him back to the hospital. The immediate precipitant for his suicide attempt was that he had run into one of his former girlfriends with her new boyfriend. The patient stated that they had a drink together, but all the while he was with them he could not help thinking that "they were dying to run off and jump in bed." He experienced jealous rage, got up from the table, and walked out of the restaurant. He began to think about how he could "pay her back."

Mr. Berman had felt frequently depressed for brief periods during the previous several years. He was especially critical of himself for his limited social life and his inability to have managed to have sexual intercourse with a woman even once in his life. As he related this to the therapist, he lifted his eyes from the floor and with a sarcastic smirk said, "I'm a 25-year-old virgin. Go ahead, you can laugh now." He has had several girlfriends to date, whom he described as very attractive, but who he said had lost interest in him. On further questioning, however, it became apparent that Mr. Berman soon became very critical of them and demanded that they always meet his every need, often to their own detriment. The women then found the relationship very unrewarding and would soon find someone else. (Spitzer et al., 1983)

Philip Berman shows the overwhelming anger characteristic of the borderline personality disorder in crisis. In contrast to the dependent personalities who also show a tendency to cling, borderline people can show intense anger at friends or colleagues when frustrated. However, they share with the dependent and histrionic personality types the ability to manipulate others into action. When these manipulations fail, however, the borderline person may feel empty and depressed. Although most writers have focused on the tendency of borderline individuals to become psychotic under stress, in actuality they seem to have short-lived psychotic episodes rather than full blown psychotic breaks (Vaillant & Perry, 1980).

Glazer (1979) has warned that the diagnosis of borderline personality disorder may be given too often or used as an excuse by therapists to maintain distance from a patient. Although more work needs to be done to see if DSM-III criteria can be applied reliably, early studies have shown high levels of reliability (e.g., Perry & Klerman, 1980).

Should psychotherapy based on the psychosocial paradigm be attempted with borderline personalities, the unpredictable and tumultuous interpersonal interactions characteristic of their day-to-day behavior is played out in the therapeutic relationship. Because borderline people can be overwhelmed by intimacy and affect, some therapists adopt an approach that is not confrontive, but supportive, and is directed toward attaining concrete goals. Such short-term approaches like crisis intervention, and brief intermittent supportive therapeutic contacts with or without medication have been applied successfully (Bauer, 1979; Leibovich, 1981).

Paradigmatic Perspectives on the Personality Disorders

It is hard to designate the particular paradigms that would adequately cover the varied personality disorders we have described. Genetic background (the biological paradigm) is a major criterion for diagnosing someone as schizotypal, and yet the biological approach is not mentioned in DSM-III for the other personality disorders. Only in the discussion of antisocial personality disorder that follows is the biological paradigm used once again. It seems that most of the explanations presently used to describe how personality disorders come about use the psychosocial paradigm. Overall, it may be said that the problems in defining personality disorders and the disagreements among "experts" about how to treat these difficulties may suggest some significant limits of present paradigms.

Deriving from the psychosocial paradigm, *psychoanalytic explanations* for personality disorders are based on the concept of developmental arrest at a psychosexual stage. Consistent with the view that personality disorders are less serious than psychotic syndromes, but more serious than "neurotic" disorders, the developmental arrest is earlier than that proposed to occur in neurosis but later than that for psychosis. Generally, it is assumed that the bulk of the libido remains fixated at the oral and anal stages with little movement toward phallic maturation. Parental behaviors at this stage of development can give impetus to the beginnings of particular types of personality disorders.

Shapiro (1965) also has offered a psychoanalytic explanation growing out of the psychosocial paradigm. According to Shapiro, the basic motivator for the development of different personality styles is the need to deal with, organize, and safely discharge "tension." The psychoanalytic perspective assumes that behavior is motivated by a need for tension reduction, regardless of whether the tension is biological (as in the case of hunger) or psychological (as in the case of interpersonal anxiety). To Shapiro, different psychological styles represent different *tension-organizing systems*. These systems develop to help individuals deal with what is going on around them. Thus, for example, some people may develop a *paranoid* style because dealing with others makes them anxious: If they keep their distance from others, they won't become anxious. Developing such a view of the world can help people to make sense of what happens to them and to deal effectively with daily tensions. However, if an unusual or severe kind of tension is experienced, the paranoid style may need to become a "defense" against ego deterioration. When this occurs, the paranoid personality style may deteriorate into a diagnosable psychotic paranoid reaction.

According to Shapiro, personality styles develop out of *innate organizational configurations* designed to process internal and external stimuli. These innate configurations are composed of the basic psychological (mental, perceptual, and physical) equipment with which each individual is born. From birth on, information from various sources and the tension resulting from too much conflicting information are dealt with in an individualistic way. Although the specific style of the adult isn't always clearly present in the child, even at early ages some children show the beginnings of a personality style by the manner in which they respond—or don't respond—to particular novel situations. Innate patterns result in each person's placing a unique "stamp" on all of his or her experiences. This "stamp" helps to shape the specific psychological personality style of the adult.

The nature of any person's reaction to events in the world should not be seen as independent of that person. Shapiro notes, in this regard, that people respond to the outcome of severe stress differently, depending on their previous styles of coping with stress. This same stress may produce a dependent personality disorder in one individual and a schizoid personality disorder in another. However, there is some reason to believe that the stress must be chronic to produce the consistent and rigid way of behaving that is characteristic of a personality disorder.

Antisocial Personality Disorder (Psychopathic Personality)

Personal Experience: Interviewing an Antisocial Personality

In the early 1950s, I interviewed a 20-year-old man on the prison ward at Bellevue Psychiatric Hospital who had planned, conspired, and helped commit a double murder with ruthless disregard for the consequences of his actions. In a very businesslike way he had persuaded a companion, a schizophrenic who was the only son of two physicians, to poison them by having them both drink champagne, which the instigator had filled with arsenic, on the parents' wedding anniversary night at a "celebration" by this foursome. The police listed their deaths as a double suicide for more than a year. Meanwhile, a life insurance policy of $150,000 was shared by the two youths. The reason for their eventual arrest was my patient's need to impress his girlfriend by constantly boasting of his role in killing his friend's parents; she eventually informed the police about the crime. As a result, both young men were placed on the prison ward for examination and observation. The couple's son was diagnosed as a schizophrenic and my patient as a "psychopathic personality."

During my psychiatric interviews with him, he neither showed conscious remorse, guilt, shame, nor anxiety, nor did he admit feeling any of these emotions. He admitted readily to his part in the murder which he said was, to him, an experience similar to Oscar Wilde's "In Search of a New Experience." He did not have any remorse about his actions, except for the regret he felt about being apprehended and imprisoned. He admitted seeing nothing wrong with murder, stealing, or any other immoral or amoral actions, provided he or anyone else could "get away with it." He showed no psychotic illness or symptoms. (Hott, 1979)

Although antisocial personality is grouped with the other personality disorders in DSM-III, it has been studied as a separate diagnostic category for many years. The authors of the DSM-III produced a very detailed set of criteria to use for diagnosing antisocial personality (also known as psychopathic personality or sociopathy). Generally, these criteria describe a variety of failures in adjusting to school, social, and work situations. In addition, as the above case presentation describes, antisocial personalities chronically violate the rights of others, with little or no guilt or remorse. In large measure, then, the diagnosis of antisocial personality depends primarily on past history.

The present DSM-III classification of antisocial personality is based, to a large part, on the work of Cleckley (1976). He reported his intensive study of the psychopathic personality in numerous edi-

Many of those diagnosed as antisocial personalities are involved in criminal activities that violate the rights of others. (*Larry Racioppo*)

tions of his book, *The Mask of Sanity*. The traits of antisocial personality describe a person who is characterized by superficial charm and intelligence; who fails to show any signs of irrational thinking, neurosis, or anxiety; who is insincere and unreliable; who is incapable of loving or relating to others or of learning from punishment; and who cannot develop a meaningful life plan. Apparently, antisocial personalities don't seem to be governed by such things as morality, guilt, or shame. They appear to be driven by the philosophy, "I want what I want when I want it and nothing and nobody better stand in my way."

Antisocial personality types often use their extraordinary insight into the workings of others to charm and manipulate them into doing what they want. They typically are likable at first meeting, and they will not hesitate to use this fact to manipulate others. However, because of their impulsiveness and low tolerance for tension, if their wit and charm don't succeed quickly enough, they may use violence.

An historically difficult aspect of diagnosing the antisocial personality is how to differentiate this pattern from a criminal one. However, in spite of the care used by those who developed the DSM-III definition of antisocial personality, there already is controversy regarding the relationship between this "clearer" classification and one describing a criminal (Frances, 1980). Using the present set of diagnostic criteria, a large number of criminals would fit in the antisocial classification (upwards of 80 percent). Some investigators have suggested additional differentiations that would be helpful. Schlesinger (1980) has offered a proposed classification in which the psychopath, antisocial personality, and sociopath are differentiated. Important to our present discussion is his assumption that the psychopath compared with the antisocial personality is smoother, more "finely honed," and less "crude." In a similar vein, Templeman and Wollersheim (1979) differentiate between "true" or *primary psychopaths* who are considered to be incapable of guilt and conscience, and *secondary psychopaths* who show some degree of guilt or remorse over their actions. Frances (1980) suggested that if many of the antisocial individuals are criminals, it would have been helpful for the DSM-III to include additional criteria to differentiate between those criminals who can show guilt and remorse and loyalty to others from those who cannot. Certainly this would help in developing appropriate interventions.

Personal Experience: Antisocial Personality

I have agreed to write this only because I am safe from any prosecution and cannot be harmed if this remains confidential. Anyway, most of what I will recount happened over 30 years ago. I am a professor of biology and have been for over 35 years. When I first began my teaching career, I had a great many things I wanted to do. I wanted to become a well-known and respected microbiologist; I wanted to attain a tenured faculty position at T__________ University; I wanted to be chairman of my department someday. Lots of things. But I had always wanted lots of things. As a child I can remember wanting a bullet that a friend of mine had brought in to show the class. I took it and put it into my school bag and when my friend noticed it was missing, I was the one who stayed after school with him and searched the room, and I was the one who sat with him and bitched about the other kids and how one of them took his bullet. I even went home with him to help him break the news to his uncle, who had brought it home from the war for him.

But that was petty compared to the stuff I did later. I wanted a Ph.D. very badly, but I didn't want to work very hard—just enough to get by. I never did the experiments I reported; hell, I was smart enough to make up the results. I knew enough about statistics to make anything look plausible. I got my master's degree without even spending one hour in a laboratory. I mean, the professors believed anything. I'd stay out all night drinking and being with my friends and then the next day I'd get in just before them and tell them I'd been in the lab all night. They'd actually feel sorry for me. I did my doctoral research the same way, except it got published and there was some excitement about my findings. The research helped me get my first college teaching job. There my goal was tenure.

The rules at my university were about the same as at any other. You had to publish and you had to be an effective teacher. "Gathering" data and publishing it was never any problem for me, so that part was fine. But teaching was evaluated on the basis of forms completed by students at the end of each semester. I'm a fair to good teacher, but I had to be sure that my record showed me as excellent. The task was simple. Each semester, I collected the evaluation forms, took out all the fair to bad ones and replaced them with doctored ones. It would take me a whole evening, but I'd sit down with a bunch of different-colored pens and pencils and would fill in as many as 300 of the forms. Needless to say, I was awarded tenure.

The difficulties inherent in the diagnosis of antisocial personality have not stopped researchers from studying this behavior pattern. Several paradigmatic perspectives, like the biological (genetic), the psychosocial, and the systems approaches, have contributed to a better understanding of its origins. Each paradigm, however, has fallen short in one way or another in clarifying how people develop antisocial personality.

From the biological perspective, Elliot (1978) has provided support for the conjecture by Cleckley (1976) that antisocial personalities have inherent neurological difficulties. However, while several studies have found that antisocial personalities show an excessive number of electroencephalographic abnormalities (Elliot, 1978; Hare, 1970), there are a number of

According to some estimates, up to 80 percent of criminals would fit the DSM-III classification of antisocial personality disorder. (*Sam Falk/Monkmeyer Press Photo Service*)

methodological difficulties that make these findings questionable (Vaillant and Perry, 1980; Reid, 1981). A recent study has found a functional similarity between the behavior of organisms with a lesion of the septum, hippocampus, and frontal cortex and the behavior of those with antisocial impulse control (Gorenstein, 1982). While there is a modest relationship between antisocial personality and "soft" neurological signs such as slower reaction times, studies that initially have found biochemical differences in the overproduction of phenylethylamine (Sandler et al., 1978) and underproduction of serum cholesterol (Vikkunen, 1979) have yet to be replicated. Further work may clarify how neurological difficulties are translated into the behavior shown by those with an antisocial personality disorder.

In addition to the neurological indications, there seems also to be evidence of a genetic component in antisocial personality. Slater and Cowie (1971), for example, have reported a higher-than-normal concordance rate for psychopathy when one member of a set of identical twins is psychopathic. Further, studies of adopted children in Denmark and the United States (Crowe, 1974; Schulsinger, 1972) indicate that adoptees isolated from biological parents who were diagnosed as psychopaths showed increased rates of criminality compared with adoptees whose biological parents were normal.

Counter to the biological theories, the psychosocial explanations hold that antisocial personality can best be seen as originating from some failure in socialization. From the psychoanalytic perspective, the antisocial personality is assumed never to have developed a superego. Without a superego a person has no conscience and thus can feel no guilt for his or her actions. Without a superego, id instincts can be satisfied by the antisocial individual's ego without regard to the ethical, moral, or cultural limitations felt by most people. It also has been proposed that antisocial personalities may fail to learn to experience resistance to temptation and guilt because they typically are disciplined for misbehavior long after undesirable behaviors have been emitted. This "delay of punishment" seems crucial to the development of the common antisocial behavior pattern in which the threat of punishment seems to have little or no effect (Leaff, 1978; Solomon et al., 1968).

Although the psychosocial explanations are intimately tied to family experiences such as child-rearing practices, the systems-paradigm-guided family-process theorists focus more on the adverse effects of a child's family experience as a whole rather than on any particular component of it (Reid, 1981). Hare (1970) noted that, "Perhaps the most popular generalization about psychopathy is that it is related to some form of early disturbance in family relationships, including parental loss, emotional deprivation (and) parental rejection" (p. 95). Rutter (1971), after reviewing the research results gathered on the effects of parental separation on children, concluded that parental separations due to psychiatric difficulties or marital problems are related to a higher rate of antisocial behavior in their children than separations for positive reasons such as vacation.

Robins (1966) has attempted to identify other family patterns in the childhood experiences of people with antisocial personality disorder. He followed 524 children referred to a child guidance clinic and found that sociopathic or alcoholic fathers were frequently associated with the development of antisocial personality disorders. Perhaps the fact that these kinds of disordered fathers are prone to abuse their children played a significant role in the development of antisocial behavior. For instance, Leaff (1978) found a pattern of overt paternal brutality toward children and maternal deprivation and tendency to cling associated with the development of antisocial behavior.

In spite of years of research guided by the biological, psychosocial, and systems paradigms, the origins of the antisocial personality disorder still remain largely unknown. Perhaps some newer integrative paradigm will bring the antisocial personality disorder into clearer relief. Both Reid (1980) and Guze (1976) note that substantial but diverse findings from the biological, psychosocial (psychoanalytic theory, in particular), and systems areas need to be combined in some meaningful way. The desirability for a new paradigm was hinted at by Reid (1981) when he concluded: "After all, information in each area is related to observation even more than to extrapolation and theorizing; it is unlikely that large groups of observers from different disciplines have misrepresented their data" (p. 154).

Given the lack of a strong paradigmatically guided understanding of antisocial personality, it may not be a surprise that little is known about effective ways to alter this pattern. Forms of intervention which are effective with other types of psychopathology often have limited utility in treating the antisocial personality. Both Hare (1970) and Cleckley (1976) have noted that traditional forms of psychotherapy are usually less effective with this group of disordered people.

The lack of success in treating antisocial personalities can be traced to several sources. First of all, antisocial personalities often see nothing wrong with themselves, since it usually is society that is uncomfortable, not them personally. Second, traditional psychotherapy tends to be based upon the relationship between the therapist and the client. The antisocial person who is unable to form *any* relationship easily certainly cannot easily form a strong therapeutic bond with a professional. Further, many people with antisocial personality can talk their way out of trouble or therapy by appearing to be normal and in control of themselves. Many therapists have been "fooled" into giving an antisocial personality a clean bill of health because the client "convinced" them that he or she had recovered and reformed. Finally, antisocial personalities may not be good candidates for group psychotherapy, because many of them cannot empathize with others and may say and do things that are actually harmful to fellow group members.

Others, however, are not so pessimistic about the chances of successfully treating antisocial personalities. Reid (1981) stated that "it is important to dispel the commonly held notion that antisocial syndromes—or antisocial personality—are untreatable" (p. 156). Such attitudes doom therapy to failure before it begins, because therapists believe they cannot be successful. Such expectations may be inappropriate. Lion (1981) has reported successfully treating antisocial personalities by breaking through their defenses and "making them" depressed. The occurrence of depression is taken as a positive sign to the therapist even though it may be frightening to the patient because it signals the development of realistic feelings needed to build a relationship. To deal with antisocial personalities in individual psychotherapy, Lion recommends that the therapist become "a real person" who consistently confronts the patient while being aware of the patient's fragility. Finally, Templeman and Wollersheim (1979) have offered a cognitive-behavioral approach that appeals to the self-interests of the antisocial personality to motivate him or her to change. In this treatment the patients are taught self-control and prosocial behavior. While Templeman and Wollersheim offer no research data to support their conclusions, the framework lends itself nicely to research testing.

Aside from incarceration in a prison, there are other systems paradigm–based group methods which can be used to treat the antisocial personality. These programs both in the United States and in Europe have used, with some success, a variety of institutional environments to change the behavior of antisocial personalities who are involved in criminal activities (Strupp & Reid, 1981). Generally these programs use structured environments with intensive individual and group psychotherapy to teach new ways of relating to others.

Concluding Comments

The personality disorders are the most common form of behavioral "disturbance" encountered in everyday life. There can be little question that, on a daily basis, most of us interact with people who would fit into one of the categories we have described in this chapter. The reason for this should be clear. In their milder forms, the personality disorders may be nothing more than personality *types*, characteristics which differentiate people from one another. Thus, a rather dramatic person's behaviors, in the extreme, might be considered signs of histrionic personality disorder. Similarly, the "careful" money counting of the conscientious bank teller might, in the extreme, be part of a compulsive personality disorder. Probably nowhere in our discussion of psychopathology is the line between normal and abnormal as unclear as in the case of personality disorders. In DSM-II, personality disorders were included among the categories of significant mental disturbances. It is a credit to the developers of DSM-III that they have deemed these patterns *not* to be instances of mental disorders in the same category as schizophrenia and affective psychosis and have chosen to code significant personality variations on Axis II.

With our discussion of the personality disorders we bring to a close our series of nine chapters dealing with the DSM-III classifications for abnormal behavior. Throughout these chapters, we have tried to apply, wherever possible, the three major paradigms. At times this has been possible and productive, at other times not. The limitations of the major paradigms may have become evident as we considered the varieties of psychopathology. Such limitations are the sources of the kind of tension that Kuhn described in his theories of science. It is this tension which leads to the emergence of new paradigms such as the developmental paradigm to which we shall now turn our attention.

Summary Chart

In Chapter 15 we discussed the personality disorders, a group of mild disturbances which are coded on Axis II of DSM-III. We divided these disorders into three major groups:

Odd and eccentric behaviors: Paranoid personality, schizoid personality, schizotypal personality
Anxious and fearful behaviors: Avoidant personality, dependent personality, compulsive personality, passive-aggressive personality
Dramatic and emotional behaviors: Histrionic personality, narcissistic personality, borderline personality

After examining several paradigmatic perspectives on the personality disorders, especially the psychosocial view of Shapiro, we turned to a more in-depth discussion of a most serious personality disorder, antisocial personality:

Diagnosis of antisocial personality—also termed psychopathy, sociopathy
Primary and secondary psychopathy
Biological, psychosocial, and systems explanations
Paradigmatically based interventions

III

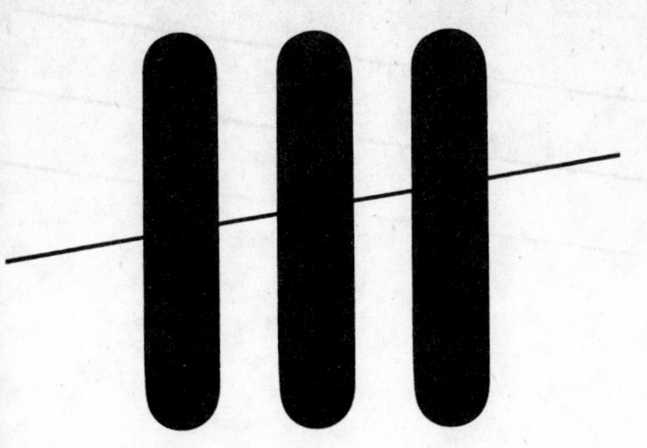

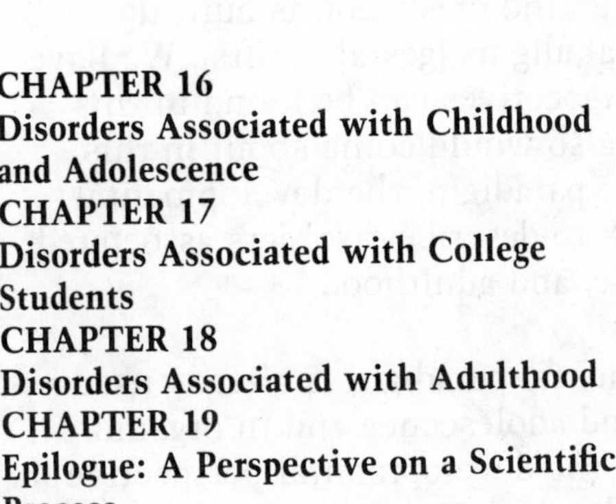

Application of the Developmental Paradigm:

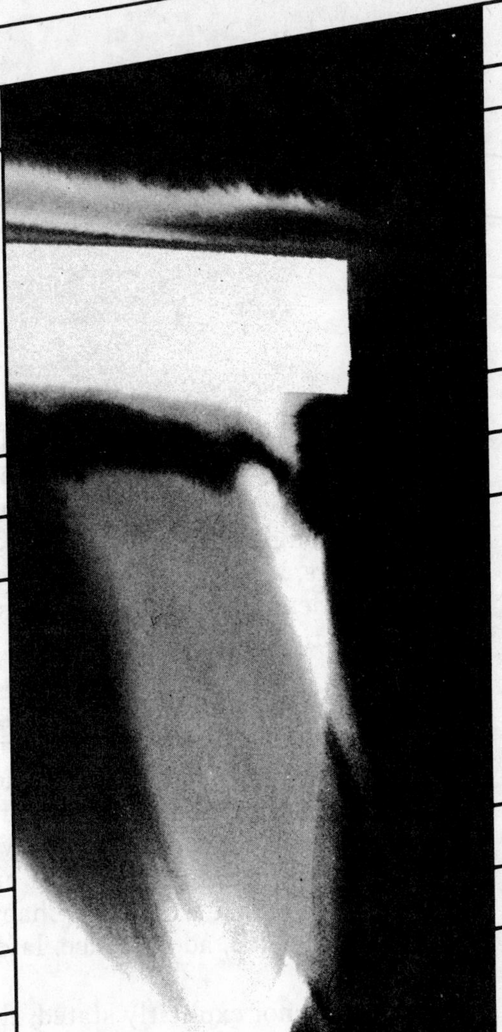

Disorders of Childhood, Adolescence, Late Adolescence (College Students), and Adulthood

To this point we have examined abnormal behavior primarily from the perspectives offered by the three major paradigms of the twentieth century. However, we have seen that application of these paradigms has not always led to completely satisfactory explanations or interventions for mental disorders. We have indicated where one, two, or even all three of the paradigms had difficulty with certain facets of disorders or in some instances an entire diagnostic category.

In our opening chapters, we suggested that when major paradigms encounter difficulties over an extended period of time, a kind of tension is built up that may eventuate in the creation of new paradigms (gestalt shifts). We have argued that the origins of the three major perspectives can be found in this process, and we believe that new paradigms also would come about in this same way. Such is the case for an alternative paradigm, the developmental perspective, that we use in Chapters 16 to 18 to describe disorders associated with childhood, adolescence, late adolescence, and adulthood.

Although not explicitly stated, the developmental paradigm is already used in DSM-III to describe disorders in childhood and adolescence and in organic disorders in the elderly. Therefore our use of the developmental perspective can be viewed as an expansion of an already beginning trend to find a more integrated approach to abnormal psychology. However, it is also true that the explicit application of the developmental paradigm to the entire age range has certain implications. Since all three forms of the Diagnostic and Statistical Manual have focused on children and adolescents and to a lesser extent, the elderly, there will be significantly more theoretical and research work to report for these age ranges than for the other significant life stages. For this reason, our discussion of the relatively underinvestigated late adolescent and early and middle adult life stages may be more speculative and less data-based than our presentations of the other, more frequently investigated developmental life periods.

An implication of the developmental perspective is that people continue to have an option to grow or regress at any age (Gutmann, 1980; Offer & Sabshin, 1984). Writers like Sheehy (1976) and Levinson (1978) have helped sensitize professionals and lay people alike to the particular challenges implicit throughout the life span. We begin our examination of maladaptive reactions to these challenges with a discussion of the disorders associated with childhood and adolescence.

CHAPTER 16

Disorders Associated with Childhood and Adolescence

Between birth and the teenage years, humans go through significant physical and psychological changes. They begin this sequence completely helpless and dependent and, if successful, they end it as independent self-directed individuals. However, the path is not an easy one and many children develop problems along the way.

Disorders Associated with Childhood

The disorders observed in children cover a broad spectrum varying in symptom content, severity, and duration. We focus first on the relatively less severe problems of childhood in the form of *developmental deviations*, *anxiety disorders*, and *hyperactivity*. We then turn our attention to a discussion of the relatively more severe *pervasive developmental disorders* (also called childhood schizophrenia and autism).

Developmental Deviations

Developmental deviations represent a wide variety of instances in which normal child development has temporarily or permanently jumped the track. Deviations from normal developmental progress often cause parents great concern. However, most of these problems will disappear with time and calm parental response. Since there is no one agreed upon set of paradigmatically based explanations or treatments for the developmental deviations, we will include relevant theories or therapies when available.

Disturbances Related to Bodily Functions

Children can develop problems in the areas of sleeping, eating, and elimination. All these functions, though necessary to life, must also conform to the rules of the family and society. Some parents may overreact to difficulties, unwittingly damaging the self esteem of their children in their attempts to help.

Sleeping Some children never want to see the day end and will attempt to stay awake long past the bedtime established by their parents. Sleep seems to mean the end of fun and separation from others. One 7-year-old child handled this problem in a unique way. When asked how long he slept, he informed us that he "never slept."

One way to minimize fears about bedtime is for parents to spend some quiet time with children when they are ready for bed. (*Gloria Karlson*)

He admitted to closing his eyes but explained he was merely resting them.

Because going to sleep usually involves a series of events over time, there is potential for children to develop bedtime *rituals.* A young boy required a certain pair of red and white striped socks on his feet, a bowl of peanuts in his bed, two small lights placed in specific positions in his room, a shade half drawn on his window, three poems read to him in the same order, and three kisses on each cheek. Any deviation from this order and he became quite agitated and needed the entire ritual repeated again. Although "cute" at first, his parents came to dislike this ritual intensely, but were forced to continue it to avoid a noisy confrontation.

Unlike bedtime rituals, *nightmares* and *night terrors* are rarely thought to be "cute" and can leave all involved quite upset. This can be seen in the following personal experience of an 8-year-old's reaction to night terrors.

Personal Experience: Night Terrors

I saw things . . . big scary things . . . they were after me (he stops and sobs, his mother hugs him and he clings to her). Are they gone? (Interviewer says, "yes.") They're mean, make them stop! Make them go away! They had teeth and big eyes and they're after me. Are you sure I was dreaming? Really? Mama, was I dreaming? (Mother answers "yes" and assures her son that everything is going to be all right.) I'm so cold, mama get me warm. I don't want to talk any more. (Child continues to alternately sob and look terrified for nearly 15 minutes.)

Nightmares and night terrors occur in normal as well as disturbed children, but they usually are more severe and frequent in the latter. Although sometimes seen as similar to one another, nightmares and night terrors are two separate events (see Table 16-1). Nightmares, for instance, are shorter in duration and take less time to recover from, compared with night terrors that can leave the child terrified and disoriented for hours.

Eating Like bedtime, mealtime has potential for creating ritual and conflict. It has been estimated that 25 percent of children have a recognized eating problem (Palmer & Horn, 1978). Some parents equate eating with affection. Children can learn that eating or not eating controls interactions with their parents and others.

While eating difficulties can occur in normal children as well as those who are disturbed, *pica* occurs primarily in children who have a more serious disturbance. In pica, children ingest inedible substances. Like a magpie (which, in Latin, is a pica), a bird reputed to eat anything, these children may eat paper, wool, plaster, paint chips, buttons, string, bugs, and pebbles (Kanner, 1972). In one study, it was found that 16 percent of a sample of children living in a rural area of Georgia ate clay or soil (Vermeer & Frate, 1979). As usual, developmental stage must be considered in diagnosing pica, for it is normal for very young children to place inedible materials in their mouths. However, children with pica don't seem to outgrow this pattern and continue this practice to an inappropriate age.

Disorders relating to reduced food intake (anorexia nervosa) and food binging and purging (bulimia) do not make frequent appearances until late adolescence.

Table 16-1 Differences between Nightmares and Night Terrors

Nightmares	*Night Terrors*
Fearful sleep experience followed by awakening.	Fearful experience occurs in sleep; awakening does not follow.
Slight moaning or movement are only noticeable signs.	Features are distorted; eyes wide open expressing terror; sits up or jumps from bed; cries out.
Child is awake when parents arrive and can tell what happened.	Child sleeps as parents watch child; cannot be awakened or attack shortened by parents.
After awakening, child recognizes parents and surrounding objects.	If child awakes, does not recognize parents or surroundings.
No hallucinations.	Child hallucinates actual dream objects.
No perspiration.	Profuse perspiration.
Long period of wakefulness and review of dream may follow.	Peaceful sleep instantly follows termination of terror.
Entire nightmare lasts no longer than 1 or 2 minutes.	Terror may last up to 20 minutes.
Contents are remembered fairly clearly.	Complete amnesia for contents of and occurrence of terror.

Source: From L. Kanner, *Child Psychiatry* (4th Ed.), Copyright 1972 by Charles C. Thomas, Springfield, Illinois.

Most children enjoy playing with mud or clay, but in "pica" children eat these materials. (© *Rhoda Galyn*)

They will be discussed in the sections on disorders of adolescents and college students.

Elimination When children past 3 years of age have bowel movements in their clothes the problem is called *encopresis*. About 3 percent of the general pediatric population is estimated to be encopretic (Levine, 1975). Sometimes the reasons for the encopresis are clearer than others. In one instance a boy had a 2-month history of soiling himself between 3 and 5 o'clock each school-day afternoon. Although his house was unlocked, he seemed to prefer to have a bowel movement in his pants rather than enter the house while his mother was still at work. He finally related that someone had told him that "creatures wait in empty houses to eat up little boys." At times, encopresis may be a sign of a more severe underlying disorder and this possibility should always be evaluated.

In *fecal retention*, children refuse to have regular bowel movements. Retention of feces is potentially dangerous and can lead to disorders of the colon. Any treatment response must be quick and effective to protect the children's health.

Encopresis and fecal retention, although disconcerting, are not as frequent as lack of bladder control, *enuresis*. Generally, attainment of bowel control precedes and is not as difficult to master as bladder control. For unknown reasons, bladder control seems to be more affected by emotional states in children than is bowel control. Enuresis can be *nocturnal* (occurs at night) or *diurnal* (occurs during the day). Nocturnal enuresis is more common and considered to be less serious than wetting during the day. To be classified as enuresis, wetting must occur more than once a week. The pattern is considered more serious when it occurs in older children. Although we do not know the true incidence of enuresis, it has been estimated that somewhere around 5 million children and adolescents are affected (Turner & Taylor, 1974). The incidence of enuresis decreases as children become older. At age 7 it is estimated that 21 percent of the boys and 15 percent of the girls are enuretic. This number decreases to 3 percent of the boys and 2 percent of the girls at age 14 (Bindelglas, 1975; Rutter et al., 1973).

Most enuretics are enuretic since birth (*primary enuresis*), while a lesser number of children may return to bed-wetting after having been dry for an extended period of time (*secondary enuresis*). Usually secondary enuresis is associated with emotional conflict within the child or within the family. It is not uncommon for a 3- to 5-year old to become temporarily enuretic when a sibling is born.

Fortunately, the treatment of bed-wetting is one of the earliest examples of the successful application of the psychosocial paradigm–based learning approach to the alteration of abnormal behavior. The procedure is based upon the idea that waking to go to the bathroom is a response that must be associated with the stimulus of bladder distention. To establish this association, Mowrer and Mowrer (1938) devised a system in which two copper screens separated by a cotton pad were laid on the child's bed. Each screen was connected to one pole of a buzzer attached to a battery source. The device was hardly noticeable in the child's bed and quite comfortable to sleep on when covered with an ordinary bed sheet. When a few drops of urine were passed, the cotton pad became wet and the salinity of the urine served as an electrical conductor completing the circuit between the copper screens. The completed circuit set off a loud buzzer that woke the child, who could then get up and go to the bathroom to urinate. In this way, waking was associated with bladder distention and the child could learn within a few weeks to get up and urinate before having to hear a noisy buzzer.

Researchers have found that this treatment eliminates enuresis in about three out of four cases within less than 12 weeks (DeLeon & Mandell, 1966; Doleys, 1977). However, about one out of two enuretic children will relapse and have to be treated again within a year (Taylor & Turner, 1975).

Biologically based interventions have generally involved the use of drugs. The most commonly used drug is imipramine (Tofranil), an antidepressant. About three-quarters of the children who take this drug show considerable or complete improvement (Perlmutter, 1976). The drug must be judiciously applied because it can have serious side effects (like liver damage) and should not be given to children younger than 6 years of age (Gaultieri, 1977).

Stuttering Unlike in the treatment of bladder control disorders, there has been no breakthrough for people who have the problem of *stuttering*. Of the 1 percent of the population who stutter, more than half are children. Eight times as many males as females stutter (Knopf, 1979). Most normal children exhibit *primary* or normal developmental stuttering between 2

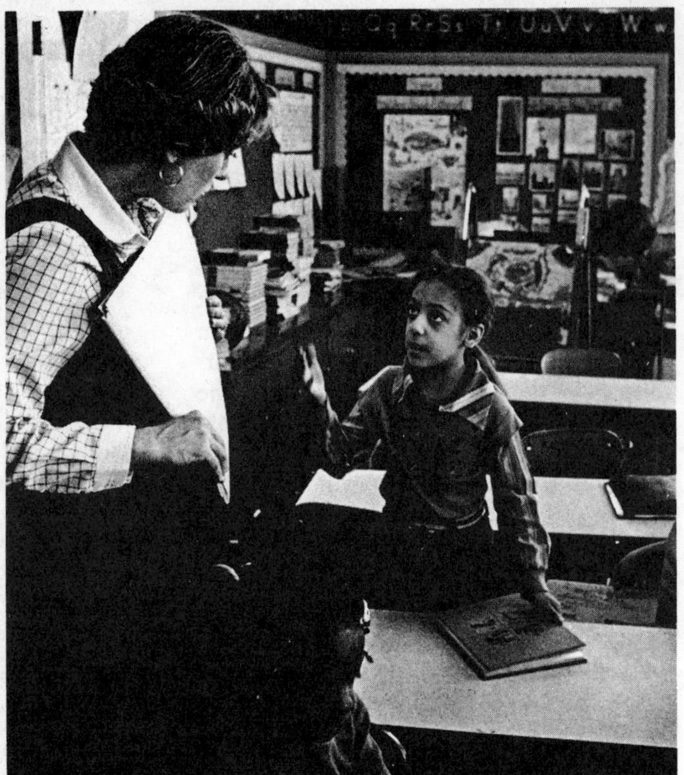

Stuttering is increased when children are in stressful situations where speech is important. (© *1979 Laimute E. Druskis/Taurus Photos*)

and 5 years of age. Rarely does the onset of stuttering come beyond the age of 10. Most primary stutterers are not self-conscious about their speaking difficulty, but there is some chance that if parents and others overreact to these early disfluencies,they can become *secondary*. In secondary stuttering, children are painfully aware of their speaking problem and, if their attempts at self-control of stuttering fail, they may become even more anxious and stutter more.

The cause of many cases of stuttering remains largely unknown. Some researchers guided by the biological paradigm (Sheehan & Costley, 1975) have proposed that there is a genetic basis for stuttering. They believe that stuttering results from *mixed cerebral dominance* (Orton, 1937; Travis, 1931) in which neither of the cerebral hemispheres is dominant. Neither side of the brain can attain the dominance necessary to synchronize the speech musculature.

Others have been guided by the psychosocial paradigm to explain how stuttering originates. Sheehan and Lyon (1974) suggest that early stutterers play a "false" role by attempting to cover up their speech problems. Eventually their concealment fails and they become increasingly stressed and stutter even more. Johnson (1955), on the other hand, believes that pathological stuttering is caused by parental overreaction to normal primary stuttering. That is, parents may become anxious about speech disfluencies and attempt to force their children to slow down, to repeat what they say, and to pay attention to their speech patterns. Contrary to their intent, overreacting parents may make their children more concerned about their stuttering and convince them that there is something different about them. A high level of anxiety about speaking may produce even more stuttering, and the children may find themselves in the middle of a process of ever spiraling stress. A list of possible threats to self esteem that may cause increased stuttering is presented in Table 16-2.

Disorders Associated with the Musculature

Movement requires the smooth interaction of many muscle groups. Any of the voluntary or involuntary muscle systems can be involved in the developmental deviations.

Tics Sudden, quick involuntary repetitive muscular movements reflected in blinking eyes, grimacing, sniffing, arm or leg jerking, and hiccuping are known as *tics*. In contrast to voluntary learned activities such as thumb-sucking, tics are involuntary and may increase in frequency with increasing anxiety levels.

As with stuttering, many children between the ages of 7 and 9 often develop ticlike behavior. The sudden occurrence of eye blinking or tongue clicking can be quite worrisome to others, but will usually disappear shortly if they are not overreacted to.

Should a tic establish itself and become a source of discomfort to child and parents alike, one effective intervention is a procedure called *negative practice*. The procedure is relatively simple: Each time the parents observe the tic, they calmly instruct the child to produce the behavior voluntarily for about a minute. After a short time, voluntary production of the tic typically becomes aversive and the involuntary tic decreases in frequency.

Table 16-2 Normal Stuttering-inducing Situations

Being overstimulated
Having to compete to speak
Expecting to be interrupted before finishing
Feeling that what he is saying is being disapproved
Feeling that he won't be believed
Admitting to bad behavior
Being unable to see his listeners
Feeling the listener is angry
Being tired
Expecting punishment
Feeling the listener is impatient
Being asked to "perform" for people
Being afraid of something
Using words he isn't sure of
Not being positive he is correct
Being upset because parents are fighting
Telling a lie
Being compared unfavorably with other children

Source: Based on Engel & Helfand, 1964.

Tourette's Syndrome

Personal Experience: Observing a Person with Gilles de la Tourette's Disease

There were four junior high school students gathered around the bulletin board. The school dance was scheduled in about 2 weeks and these students, as part of the decoration committee, were preparing the bulletin board to reflect the theme of the dance, winter wonderland. One student was cutting out snowflakes while another was putting them up. Two boys and two girls were taking turns cutting and the conversation was full of giggles and whispers. One of the girls reached down to pick up a paper snowflake. She smiled at one of the boys as she reached up to pin the snowflake decoration on the bulletin board. Suddenly, seemingly out of nowhere and for no reason she suddenly barked, a gutteral loud and abrasive bark. She barked again, this time with her head twisting about. In the next 5 or 10 seconds, she gave vent to vile curses. We all looked at her momentarily and then looked away because we knew she couldn't help herself and was embarassed by her own actions and we felt so sorry for her.

The child described in this personal experience was suffering from Tourette's disease, a disorder characterized by recurrent, involuntary, repetitive, rapid, purposeless motor movements (tics) and multiple vocal tics. The vocal tics may involve verbal utterances in the form of swearing, epithets, and obscenities. These verbalizations are at times accompanied by spitting, blowing, and barking sounds. Such behavior, termed *coprolalia* (feces-speech), is present in about 60 percent of all patients; it typically occurs without warning (Silver, 1980). Tourette's disease is very rare, occurring in about 1 out of every 12,500 cases presented in psychi-

DISORDER TAKES TOLL ON TWINS

BOX 16-1

By Toni Baker
Chronicle Staff Writer

A strange disorder has a lasting grip on Carla and Claudia Huntey.

"The noise and the fighting," that's the worst part, said Carla, half of a set of attractive, 18-year-old twins who share more than looks.

The Atlanta twins have Tourette's Syndrome, a neurological disorder that has been wrongly diagnosed in others as everything from mental illness to demonic possession.

Tourette's is a strange disorder.

Its victims are normal, intelligent people with no apparent physical problem, until a head twitches or an arm jerks out of control. Sometimes they will utter a noise that resembles a bark or let loose with profanity.

"They labeled us bad," said Carla of the years of struggling to control the odd behavior before the twins or Huntey family knew it had a name.

"We felt the kids were hyper or whatever," said father Robert Huntey. He recalled the trouble starting when the twins were about age 12.

"That's about when they started having problems in school . . . losing friends. They started arguing, bickering every day . . . making barking sounds and hand movements. We thought they were playing.

"We would punish the kids," Huntey said. "Then after we found out what they had . . . we would punish ourselves."

Public school was a nightmare for the twins. "The kids would be making fun of them, calling them the weird twins," Huntey said. So additional money was spent and the girls went to private schools.

This was just the beginning of the financial and emotional strain.

What followed was a series of doctor, hospitals, frustration and pain in the search for the cause of the strange behavior. Those bouts in the hospitals left the young twins feeling that they were being punished instead of helped.

Then in 1978, after a 600-mile trip to a clinic in Topeka, Kan., and shelling out a $10,000 fee per child, the diagnosis of the neurological disorder called Tourette's was made.

With that diagnosis came the promise of long-term hospitalization and the suggestion that the twins be separated.

"I was scared to death. I didn't want to do that," Carla said. But, she realizes the problem that prompted the suggested separation. "When she'd make a noise, I'd make one. It has to be as loud as hers," said Carla of times when she and her twin Claudia are together.

"I really don't know why I'd want to," she said. She feels she has some control over the noises. But she also realizes that much of it is out of her control.

While the twins were in Topeka, the father was transferred from Louisville, Ky., to Atlanta and the twins were referred to a private psychiatric facility in Atlanta for care.

At that hospital, the girls were separated; not allowed to talk, look at or touch one another. "It was miserable. I hated it. I cried and cried," Carla said.

The twins were to spend two 14-month stays in that hospital. The second trip, they were not separated, because separation had proved futile in efforts to curb their unusual behavior.

Now the twins have come to Augusta, Dr. Richard Borison and the movement disorder clinic at the Medical College of Georgia for help.

. . . the Hunteys still try to maintain an optimistic outlook for their future.

The twins next big hurdle is finishing up school and thinking about a future that they hope will find them independent.

"I just have to go out and meet people," said Carla, who has tired of her fears about meeting outsiders. "I get real self-conscious very easy. I don't know how I'm going to go about meeting new friends. It's going to be hard."

She says she is a social outcast. "I feel like I've made myself that way. I'm not going to put that on other people," she said.

"It has taken its toll," said her father. "My wife and I . . . we're together and we still love each other after 29 years." The family manages to live a comfortable lifestyle, despite the financial drain the disorder has imposed. There are three other children in the Huntey family. Everyone has done his part to keep the family together. "We used to say we hated them . . . We didn't think they loved us," Carla said of the parents who have shared the anguish of Tourette's. Now . . . "I know they love us a lot."

Source: *Augusta Chronicle*, June 15, 1982, Augusta, Ga.

atric clinics. Of the 250 cases of this disorder studied over the past decade, there are more females than males at a ratio of about 3 to 1 (Hajal & Leach, 1981). A rare case of Tourette's in twins is highlighted in Box 16-1.

Although the etiology of Tourette's remains unknown, the biological paradigm may be the best guide to its ultimate discovery. While not clear support for a biological cause, Tourette's has been found to be associated with a higher incidence of minimal brain dysfunction, abnormal electroencephalograms, and left-handedness (Silver, 1980). While there is no necessary connection between an effective physical treatment and a physical cause, it is at least consistent with biologically based paradigmatic explanations, that drug treatment, specifically haloperidol, significantly reduces Tourette's symptoms (Shapiro et al., 1978; Shapiro et al., 1973).

Anxiety Disorders

Children with a diagnosis of anxiety disorder are characterized by fear and apprehension associated with varying factors. Children with anxiety disorders are often unable to play, go to school, attend special events, or take part in many of the everyday activities of childhood.

Forms of Anxiety Disorders in Children

Childhood anxiety may manifest itself in several forms. Among these are separation anxiety, avoidant disorder, and overanxious disorder.

In *separation anxiety*, children show "exaggerated distress at the separation from parent, home, or familiar surroundings" (DSM-III). They may ruminate about their parents becoming ill, injured, or killed. In some cases these worries may include fantasies about being kidnapped or harmed when they are separated from their parents. Fears are shown by "expressing discomfort about leaving home, engaging in solitary activities and continuing to use the mothering figure as a helper in buying clothes and entering social and recreational activities" (Werkman, 1980, p. 931). Anxiety increases during transitions such as going to and from school, changing schools, or moving away from home.

As with most of the anxiety-related disorders, in *avoidant disorders* children also have difficulties making transitions. While usually fine at home, youngsters with avoidant disorders shrink from interaction and show embarrassment, timidity, and withdrawal when forced to come in contact with strangers. Timidity is a great roadblock to the building of normal peer relationships and to the experiencing of interpersonal activities necessary to growth and maturity. Avoidant youngsters, though not usually participating in many activities, do seem to want to be accepted by peers and to be competitive in academic and athletic situations. However, should their initial ef-

Though desiring to be a part of peer activities, avoidant disorder children shy away from others. (*Marion Bernstein*)

forts meet with failure, they typically stop trying and quickly withdraw from the activity.

While rumination can be part of all anxiety disorders, it is the major symptom in the *overanxious disorder*. These youths ruminate about things such as examinations, possible future events, and past difficulties. Interested in pleasing others and usually quite conforming, overanxious children also are prone to gain attention by exaggerating their pains or illnesses and having more than their share of accidents. Their sleep is often disturbed because nighttime appears to be an especially favorable time to ruminate about the past day's events as is shown in the following personal experience of an 11-year-old.

Personal Experience: Overanxious Disorder

I just can't help it. As soon as mom turns the light out I start thinking about stuff. Sometimes its good but a lot of the time its about things that worry me. Like last night I was worried that I didn't do all of my homework and that the teachers would be mad at me. Then I thought about that bully Bobby who picks on me. I wondered if he was mad at me because I wouldn't give him my cupcake at lunch. Then I had some scary thoughts about mommy getting sick and having to go to the hospital. You know she hasn't been feeling well. She's OK, isn't she?

Paradigmatic Perspectives on the Treatment of Anxiety Disorders

Most of the interventions for children with anxiety-related disorders have been derived from the psychosocial paradigm. They can be subsumed under the major headings of play therapy and behavioral therapy. While play therapy was devised specifically for children, the behavioral methods are a subset of the more general behavioral therapies applied to adults as well.

Play Therapy Play therapists take advantage of the fact that children often can express themselves better in play than in talking. The approach can be used to treat less severely disturbed children, but it is especially useful with children who have limited verbal ability.

In psychoanalytic play therapy, the therapist's role is to identify problems in psychosexual development and to attempt to understand the symbolic nature of the child's play behavior. Through "corrective" play and interpretation, insights and behavior change may occur as the child is placed back on the normal track of psychic development. By skillful interpretation of the use of play materials, the psychoanalytic therapist can gain an understanding of the child and can direct movement toward more developmentally appropriate play objects. If a child smears finger paints for a long time, a therapist may try to help the child to use crayons, a more controlled mode of emotional expression. It is assumed that this more controlled mode of expression will generalize to situations outside the playroom.

Instead of trying to redirect deviant psychosexual development, therapists espousing *nondirective play therapy* (Axline, 1964) provide an atmosphere of acceptance that will help the child work out problems with a minimum of direction and guidance. Axline defined the role of the therapist in nondirective play therapy:

1. The therapist must develop a warm, friendly relationship with the child as soon as possible.
2. The therapist accepts the child exactly as he or she is.
3. The therapist establishes a feeling of permissiveness in the relationship so that the child feels free to express his or her feelings completely.
4. The therapist is alert to recognize the feelings the child is expressing and reflects those feelings back in such a manner that the child can gain insight into his or her behavior.
5. The therapist maintains a deep respect for the child's ability to solve his or her own problems if given the opportunity.
6. The therapist does not attempt to direct the child's actions or conversations in any manner. The child leads the way; the therapist follows.
7. The therapist does not attempt to hurry the therapy along. It is a gradual process and is recognized as such.
8. The therapist establishes only those limitations that are necessary to anchor the therapy to the world of reality and to make the child aware of his or her responsibility in the relationship.

The last of Axline's guiding principles is perhaps the most important. Although

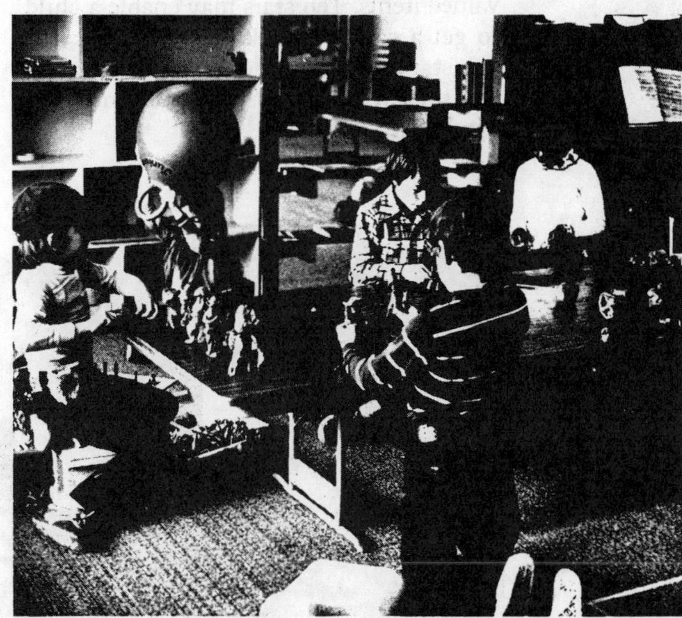

Play is an effective way to understand and correct some children's problems. (© *Miriam Reinhart, 1975/Photo Researchers, Inc.*)

the play-therapy relationship is a special one, children must learn to live with realistic expectations and limits if they are to transfer their progress in the playroom to their home environment. Some therapists consider limit setting to be the essence of play therapy and the main source of its effectiveness (Ginott, 1964).

Behavior Therapies Rather than focusing on the relationship between child and therapist, therapists using behavioral techniques emphasize procedures derived from learning theory. In *token-reinforcement* methods, tokens are given to children when they perform acceptable behavior. Teachers have long used "tokens" like stars and smiling face stickers to reward positive performance of their students. A token is any object that has acquired value because it can be traded for something else of value. For example, a nickle is a "token" that can be "traded" for some gum. In token-reinforcement systems, tokens are given for desirable behavior and can be used to obtain other valued items. Ten stars may enable a child to get a candy bar. Perhaps they receive one star every time they clean their room. Thus, each star represents one-tenth of a candy bar.

In a typical application of a token-reinforcement system, parents, child, and therapist all agree on *target behaviors*, or behaviors that need to be altered. Target behaviors may include "dos" like homework and cleaning up rooms, or "don'ts" like not poking baby brother or talking with a full mouth. There are various ways to keep track of the children's positive behavior. In one application (Figure 16-1), children are presented with a pictorial representation of a road that has 10 "toll booths" or "gates" with 10 stars or tokens required for passage through a gate. At the very end of the road is a representation of a previously agreed-upon reinforcer (a toy or a similar desirable object) that the child may obtain only by traversing the "road." Behaviors that will result in the awarding of a token are clearly set forth for the child. At each 10-token gate, a smaller reinforcer (a candy bar or comic book) may be given to the child. These *intermediate reinforcers* ensure the maintenance of behavior from the beginning of the program to the final reward which may be as many as 100 tokens down the road. Using the token-reinforcement star road, such behaviors as school avoidance, lying, irritating a younger sibling, and refusing to do homework may be effectively changed and

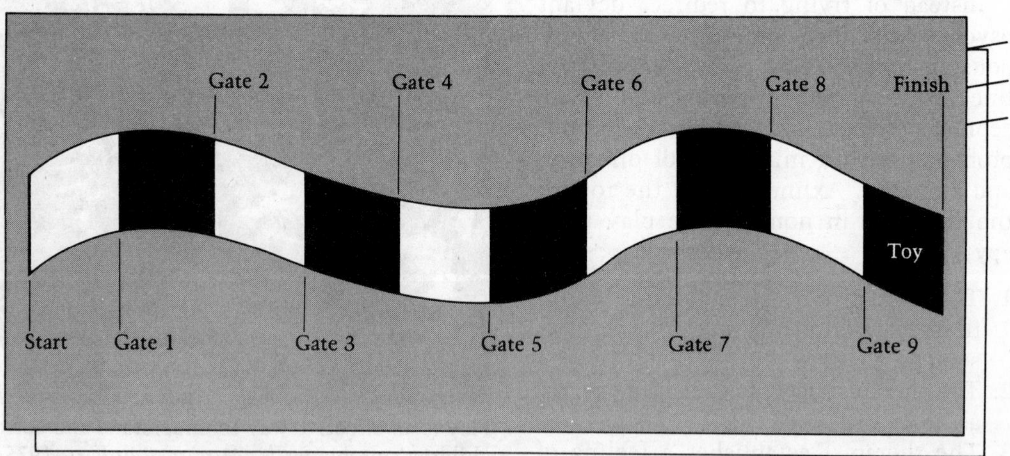

Figure 16-1 A Star Road.

replaced with more acceptable behaviors.

Some professionals have suggested using progressive relaxation training for children who have high levels of tension or identifiable fears (e.g., O'Bannon, 1981). Procedures may have to be modified for treating children. They need to be rewarded for complying with the instructions and their sessions should be much shorter, probably about 15 minutes in length. However, it appears that therapists may be too creative in adapting desensitization procedures for children (Hatzenbuehler & Schroeder, 1978) to the extent that there is little evidence for particular repeatable interventions (Rickard & Elkins, 1983).

Hyperactivity

Personal Experience: Observing a Child Who Is Hyperactive

Jim was a cute 7-year-old boy. He seemed to have mischief in his eyes as he came into the interview room. After shaking hands quickly, he moved over to where the coffee was kept and picked up a styrofoam cup. "Do you drink this coffee?" he asked. "My mother won't let me drink coffee at home." "Can I have a taste of your coffee?" After being told he could not have a "taste" of coffee, Jim moved over to the window and looked out. "There's my teacher," he said, "she's from California. I like her. She's pretty." I asked Jim to sit down at the table. He walked once around the table and pulled the chair out and sat on the arm of the chair. "How long have you been coming here? I've never seen you. I have talked with Dr. Smeltzer. He's funny. He wears bow ties." Again he was asked to sit down so that we could complete some tasks together. He sat down, but jumped up quickly and ran to the window in response to a noise from outside. When asked to come back to the table, he stayed at the window and explained, "I think that's my class outside. I thought that noise was my best friend Greg. I like Greg. He has a huge dog called Jumbo. We play with him after school sometimes." After more coaxing, Jim returned to the table. Though he stayed seated for a while, he fidgeted about in the chair. His eyes darted all over the room, he tapped his fingers and played with a piece of wood that stuck out from the table. Questions often had to be repeated. He would say "huh" after most every question, even when he did seem to understand. While Jim was of average intelligence, he was not passing in school, and in the first month of the school year had become well-known in the school as being "impossible."

The above interaction describes a child who would be placed within the DSM-III classification of *attention deficit disorder with hyperactivity*. Up to 40 percent of children referred to child guidance clinics and about 5 percent of all elementary school children are classified as hyperactive (Pelham, 1978; Safer, 1971). More often than not the hyperactive child is male. One estimate showed nine times as many males as female with this diagnostic label (Miller et al., 1973).

BOX 16-2

DISORDERS ASSOCIATED WITH SCHOOL AND LEARNING

In addition to the patterns of disturbance in children coded on Axis I of DSM-III, there is also a group of *specific developmental disorders* classified on Axis II. These disorders reflect specific difficulties in such school-related skills as reading, writing, paying attention, and speaking. These problems have also been classified as "learning disorders" or "specific learning disabilities."

According to Ross (1974), a child with a *learning disorder* is one whose basic ability to learn is not impaired, but who cannot learn because of "acquired, incompatible responses." For example, children who cannot sit still and attend to a written page will be unable to learn what is on the page because their incompatible behaviors prevent them from attending long enough to read the material. Further, children may have learned that certain aspects of the school situation are aversive (kids pick on them and so forth), and as a result, they avoid going to class or to school altogether. In the extreme learning disorder known as *school refusal* (Atkinson et al., 1985), children fail to learn not because they are incapable but because of their avoidance and fear of school. The following case history is an example of school refusal.

John M., a cute 7-year-old boy, was brought to a psychologist on the advice of his pediatrician. His mother reported that John had not attended school for the previous 2 weeks because of a stomach ailment and that, even though he had recovered, the child would not go back to school. For 3 days, his mother had taken John out to the bus stop, where John had begun to complain about going to school. Each day when the bus approached, the child became visibly fearful and began to gag and choke. The gagging was followed by his vomiting his breakfast and returning home. John's father had become angry about this at first, feeling that the boy was just making himself sick so he wouldn't have to go back to school. His mother felt differently, and a strong conflict arose between John's parents.

It was eventually determined that, on the day before he became ill with the original stomach ailment (which may or may not have been physiological), John had had a fight with a girl in the class—and had lost. In fact, he had been pinned to the ground by this girl, and she had spat on him while all the other children watched and laughed. As a final embarrassment, the boy had been forced to say numerous self-derogatory things before he was allowed to get up.

Atkinson et al. (1985) note that school refusal can be understood from many theoretical perspectives, but treatment for the problem seems to involve primarily the psychosocial and systems points of view. For example, Kennedy (1965) has presented a program of treatment for school refusal. He describes six essential aspects of the approach:

1. Early identification of the problem—within two or three days after onset
2. De-emphasis of somatic complaints (I'm sick or I don't feel well)
3. Insistence upon school attendance, including the use of force when necessary
4. Matter-of-fact approach to the problem on the part of parents and support for attending school under any conditions

5. Discussions with the child *after* school hours, further emphasizing the importance of facing fear and going to school
6. Informal telephone follow-up to the child

In addition to learning disorders, specific learning disabilities can also hamper the learning process. These problems have been formally defined as follows:

> A learning disability means a disorder in one or more of the basic psychological processes involved in understanding or in using language, spoken or written, which may manifest itself in an imperfect ability to listen, think, speak, read, write, spell, or do mathematical calculations. The term includes such conditions as perceptual handicaps, brain injury, minimal brain dysfunction, dyslexia, and developmental aphasia. The term does not include children who have problems which are primarily the result of visual, hearing or motor handicaps, of mental retardation or of environmental, cultural, or economic disadvantage. (*Federal Register*, 1976, p. 52, 404)

Children with specific learning disabilities manifest a large number of difficulties with concept formation, attention, perception, coordination, communication, and motor control. They may be hyperactive and distractible, and may manifest school-related problems in reading, spelling, arithmetic, and verbal or auditory reception, association, and expression. Treatment of such conditions often involves assessment by a specialist in learning dysfunctions or learning disabilities, and remedial training carried out in the home and classroom.

Hyperactive children seem to be driven, easily distractable, and readily excited. One moment they may be frustrated and tearful because they cannot find their pencil, while at the next moment they will be laughing loudly because one of the other children made a strange noise. They are described by their parents as frequent criers, very active and erratic eaters and sleepers (Laufer & Shetty, 1980).

Although attempts have been made, no paradigm has generated an acceptable theory for the origins of hyperactivity. Some investigators with biological perspectives have implicated defects in cortical arousal (Rosenthal & Allen, 1978; Hastings & Barkley, 1978), environmental toxins such as lead poisoning or food additives (Feingold, 1975), and minimal brain dysfunction (McGlannon, 1975) in causing hyperactivity. The wide variety of possible causes suggests that there may be more than one way to become hyperactive.

The proponents of psychosocial and biological paradigms have clashed over the correct ways to treat hyperactivity. For example, drugs that usually stimulate the brain and energize behavior, like amphetamines and caffeine, paradoxically calm hyperactive children (Goodman & Gilman, 1982; Safer & Allen, 1973). Others have pointed out that prolonged use of antiactivity drugs like Dexedrine and Ritalin may result in a number of serious side effects such as liver disorders and suppressed growth (Laufer & Shetty, 1980). However, those opposed to drug treatment for hyperactivity have suggested the use of psychosocially based programmed learning procedures and, in some instances, cognitive behavioral techniques that combine positive reinforcement with verbal self instructions (e.g., Kendall & Finch, 1978; Meichenbaum & Goodman, 1971).

Long-term follow-up of hyperactive children shows that they fall further and further behind their peers academically. The resulting loss of self-esteem compounds their personal problems and they may become isolated or delinquent in their later years (Minde et al., 1971; Pelham, 1978; Solomon, 1972).

Pervasive Developmental Disorders

Most children who show developmental deviations like anxiety disorders and patterns of hyperactivity are amenable to therapeutic interventions and may improve simply with the passage of time. In contrast, *pervasive developmental disorders* are more serious and resist most interventions. Although DSM-III has classified most forms of childhood psychoses under the rubric of pervasive developmental disorders, the theory, research, and therapy for severe disturbances of childhood continue to reflect the existence of two major patterns—*childhood schizophrenia* and *autism*.

Childhood Schizophrenia

Reviewers of the childhood-psychosis literature have noted that the term childhood schizophrenia often is used as a "semantic convenience," a label that may be applied to any or all of a broad variety of severe behavioral deviations in children (Laufer & Gair, 1969; Rutter & Schopler, 1978). However, there are those who believe that a specific disorder called *childhood schizophrenia* does exist and that it is clearly distinguishable from other disorders (Goldfarb, 1974b). Generally the symptoms of childhood schizophrenia include gross impairment of relationships, unawareness of personal identity, increased or decreased sensitivities to perceptual experiences, auditory and visual hallucinations, age-inappropriate speech, clumsy or rigid physical movements, and a history of serious psychological difficulties reaching a peak after 10 years of age.

It is very difficult to estimate the prevalence of childhood schizophrenia because of confusion with the classification of autism. However, Dawson and Mesibov (1983) conclude that the prevalence is less than 4 cases in 100,000 with about three times as many boys as girls. Most of the children did not manifest symptoms of childhood schizophrenia until age 7. Eggers (1978) found that children who showed signs of this disorder before the age of 10 tended to develop a chronic rather than an acute course.

Case: Childhood Schizophrenia

Gerald was an 11-year-old boy who had enjoyed a normal developmental history until the age of 6. He had learned to talk and walk at almost the same time as his peers, but had experienced a large number of minor physical ailments; he seemed pale and looked somewhat weak. Nevertheless, his parents reported that he played and romped with the other children in his neighborhood.

At the age of 6, upon entering school, Gerald began to change. His teacher reported that he would often sit in his seat and stare at the walls, apparently attending to things of which she was not aware. When she called on him, he often failed to respond. After one year in school, Gerald developed a host of other problems; his speech became noticeably hard to understand, and he had a number of aggressive and violent outbursts. Gerald became harder and harder to control in the classroom and he was often sent to the office. It was in the principal's office that Gerald first showed the "saliva-throwing" behavior that led to his expulsion from school. As children passed him, he would put his fingers in his mouth, wet the tips with some saliva and then flick the saliva at them. The victims complained and Gerald was expelled.

At his first meeting with a psychiatrist, Gerald said nothing; he sat and stared at the doctor and flicked saliva at him. No matter what the psychiatrist did, he could not change Gerald's behavior. Gerald had withdrawn almost completely, yet he wouldn't avoid company or ignore others—he would "relate" to them but only through his saliva flicking. Finding Gerald intractable at home, his parents finally agreed to hospitalize him when he was 7. He has remained withdrawn and unresponsive to treatment.

Autism

Personal Experience: Observing an Autistic Child

When I first saw Joey I was struck with how attractive he was. He was six years old and dressed in jeans and a western style shirt. His freckles, blue eyes, and sandy hair made him look like children who appear in television ads for cereals. That impression lasted only momentarily. He entered the room and acknowledged neither the person who brought him nor me. Instead he walked over to where a sink was and intently began fingering the spigot where the water was dripping out. He stayed there for nearly five minutes, paying no attention to my pleas for him to return to the table and sit with me. Finally, he abruptly turned away from the sink and came toward me. I thought he was going to relate to me in some way. Instead, as he reached me he began to climb up me as though I were an inanimate object that stood in his way. In fact, Joey wanted to get to a brightly colored car that was on a shelf behind me. The absence of any signs of acknowledgment of my "humaness" was disconcerting. I felt very "weird" and uncomfortable. Finally I was able to get Joey to the table by offering him some candy which he quickly ate and then got up and walked back over to the sink to watch the water drip from the spigot. At no time during this 30-minute interaction did Joey pay any attention to me or make any eye contact.

Joey is one of nearly 80,000 children who have the pervasive developmental disorder diagnosis of *autism* (Schreibman & Koegel, 1975). The worldwide prevalence rate is fairly constant across countries of the world at about 5 cases per 100,000 (Ritvo & Freeman, 1977; Rutter, 1978a, b). Autism is characterized by extreme withdrawal, unresponsiveness to social stimulation and absence of an ability to relate to others beginning at an early age. (For a comparison between autism and childhood schizophrenia, see Table 16-3.) Kanner (1943) noted that autistic children are usually males (4 to 1) who, during the first 10 weeks of life, are described as exceptionally healthy and precocious. The earliest a reliable sign of autism occurs is at 6 months of age when parents notice that the child doesn't make the typical anticipatory movements normal children do before they are picked up. Between 6 and 18 months of age, the additional signs of autism may appear: head-banging, apathy toward people and playthings, highly repetitive and situational play, unusual language patterns, and an insistence upon being left alone. What Kanner called *autistic aloneness*, the child's insistence on being left alone, leads the autistic child to withdraw into a world of inner fantasy, devoid of people, by the age of 2.

Although most symptoms of autism represent deficits, certain autistic children have specific abilities superior to those of normal children. Kanner (1972) believes that autistic children often have an uncanny ability to remember exactly situations and stimuli to which they have been exposed. Some autistic children have been found to have superior musical ability. Rimland (1969) reported that one autistic child was able to reproduce an operatic aria in a foreign language after having heard it only once. Sherman (1953) reported an autistic child who, by the age

Table 16-3 Comparison of Early Infantile Autism and Childhood Schizophrenia

Characteristics	*Autism*	*Schizophrenia*
Onset and course	Present from beginning of life	Disordered behavior follows period of normal development
Health and appearance	Excellent health, well formed, good-looking	Poor health from birth; somatic problems in all body systems
EEG	Normal	Over 80% have abnormal EEGs
Physical responsiveness	Do not adapt to being held; are stiff and unresponsive	"Mold" to parents—clinging
Aloneness	Withdrawn; demand isolation	Seem isolated, but wish contact and care
Preservation of sameness	Go to any length to keep things exactly as they are	Do not care about sameness; will throw things into disarray
Hallucinations	No hallucinations or delusions	Frequent delusions and visual and auditory experiences
Motor performance	Excellent	Poor coordination, balance, and locomotion
Language	Do not use the word *I* until age 7 or older; repetitious	Often incoherent, but use the words *I* and *yes* early in life
Personal orientation	*Un*oriented, detached, oblivious to environment; do not wish to relate	*Dis*oriented and confused; try to relate but can't
Conditionability	Difficult to condition classically	Easy to condition classically
Parents' background	Highly educated, higher class, intellectual	Poorly educated, lower class, non-intellectual
Family history of disturbance	Low incidence of disorders in relatives	Higher rate of disorders in families
Development	Arrested	Regressed
Fascination with mechanical objects	Fascinated by mechanical objects	Not fascinated by mechanical objects
Thoughts	Inhibition of thoughts	Confusion of thoughts
Spinning of objects	Deft spinning of objects	Clumsy spinning of objects

Source: From B. Rimland, 1964 (copyright 1964 by Appleton-Century-Crofts) and T. Tustin, *Autism and Childhood Psychosis* (copyright 1972 by Hogarth Press, Ltd.). Reprinted by permission of the publishers, Prentice-Hall, Inc. and Hogarth Press, Ltd.

Severely disturbed children need close and meaningful attention. (*Michael Weisbrot and Family*)

of 14 months, could reproduce the entire musical scale with perfect pitch and, by the age of 3, sang a remarkable repertoire of music, including themes from symphonies by Mozart and Haydn, songs by Schubert and Brahms, selections from Carmen, material from a Tchaikovsky piano concerto, "and diversified well-known songs" (p. 825).

Reports of special abilities among autistic children often receive widespread publicity. As a result, many people believe that some autistic children grow up to become noted artistic geniuses or that autistic children outgrow their autism and become creative and accepted people. Sadly, nothing could be further from the truth. In a follow-up study of his original sample of 11 autistic children, Kanner

(1963) reported that, at the ages of 30 to 40, the majority remained hospitalized or in some other way isolated from society. However, one had completed a bachelor's degree and was working as a bank teller. Upon considering the fate of most of his original subjects, Kanner said: "After its nearly 30 year history and many bona-fide efforts, no one as yet has succeeded in finding a therapeutic setting, drug method or technique that has yielded an amelioration and lasting results for all children" (pp. 186–187). His conclusion generally remains accurate today.

Sometimes objective data such as those reported by Kanner fail to adequately reflect the pain and stress of those who are charged with the responsibility of parenting autistic children. The reaction of a grandmother to her autistic granddaughter is presented next. It reveals what Bettelheim (1967) pointed out so well, that an autistic child fails ever to become part of the human world.

Personal Experience: Living with an Autistic Child

I awoke to a noise I couldn't mistake. I looked at the clock—5 A.M. Penny was flipping a shoelace on the cold air register—up and down, up and down. She had finally gotten to sleep at midnight the night before. Five hours is all she seems to need. I need twice that. I changed her diapers; she's 3 but not toilet trained yet. It is almost impossible to train her, although she is upset if I drop milk on her dress giving her a drink. She likes to be neat.

She amuses herself quietly—doesn't demand attention as long as she can find a shoelace, a drawer handle to flip, a piece of plastic to shake, paper that crackles. She'll hold the point of the shoelace between her fingers and run it up and down a cold air register, a window, legs of furniture, or even the shoe that holds the shoe lace. She loves our plastic tablecloth because it makes a noise when she shakes it up and down. Now she has found a small ball with a rattle in it. She jumps up and down, holding it in her hand and laughs as it rattles. Now she is on all fours, and each time she crawls forward the rattle makes a noise when her hand hits the floor. The faster she crawls, the more noise—and she laughs. She dropped it when she spotted a round plastic coffee lid and started biting it and letting it go—this amused her for a minute—but she started to flip at furniture with it, going from one piece to another, then bending down and stroking the floor with it. Now she has spotted her Raggedy Ann doll and sat on the floor with it in her arms, not moving, for 5 minutes. Looking at her sweet face with an expression of peace, contentment, a faint smile made her look like an angel—not a trace of a damaged child. She looks so perfect—how can anything be wrong? There should be some facial characteristic to show all this lack of normalcy. I can see none. Maybe it is self-willed rejection of our world. She moved, and I stopped my poor reasoning and watched as she wrapped the Raggedy Ann doll's dress around the finger of her left hand and used the other hand to pick at the covered finger. Her mouth moved in a sucking motion (mouth closed). Now she rubs her lips with the covered finger. This she does often. . . .

She will spread the fingers of her left hand and hold it about 3 inches from her left ear and make ah ah sounds. Sometimes loudly, sometimes not so loudly. Ah ha! I think, I bet there is something wrong with her left ear—maybe something bothers her and she is trying to clear her ear. I guess and guess and I am still puzzled with her.

Most of her day is spent flipping something onto some object. She'll flip a drawer pull if she hasn't a string, stick, spoon, pencil, or anything she can find like that. She seems fascinated with plastic garment bags. Often I find her in a closet shaking the bottom of a plastic garment bag. If I didn't get her she would spend hours doing that and be so content. . . .

The sound of water—in the sink or bathtub—draws her attention. She can hear that from a distance and runs to watch. If she has something in her hand, she will very quickly drop it in the sink or tub. I have to watch closely if she is in the bathroom, as she will walk into a filling tub with her shoes and clothes on. . . .

Her diet is milk and graham crackers. Peanut-butter on bread—very little—and lately babyfood, cottage cheese, and bananas, and if there isn't Heinz, she compresses her lips and refuses. Sometimes she'll take vitamins—sometimes no. Every kind of food has been offered. She climbs out of a high chair—if she eats, it is while she is walking around. . . .

I wonder how much she remembers, how far back it goes and just what she remembers. Is she storing it up and when the "bin" is full, it will all spill out and that is the "breakthrough" they talk about? I've heard of kids not talking until they were 4 years old and suddenly saying everything in sentences. Please God let that be your will! I'm sure she has a working mind. Why is she hiding it from us—or trying to? She has a lot of normal impulses, and every once in a while they sneak out, which gives me hope and assurance that one day she will be normal and perhaps exceptionally bright.

A sad follow-up note to this poignant description is that this writer's granddaughter, consistent with the research on what happens to autistic children as they grow older, has spent most of her life institutionalized. Though she is still very attractive, she has failed to develop speech or form any meaningful interpersonal relationships.

Paradigmatic Explanations and Treatments for Pervasive Developmental Disorders

Most of the developmental deviations, anxiety disorders, and patterns of hyperactivity seen among children may be conceptualized within a developmental perspective as temporary, age-related patterns and not permanent disturbances. However, the pervasive developmental disorders take in most of the personality and are largely unresponsive to therapeutic intervention. These unique disorders have drawn the interest of researchers and practitioners working within a combined psychosocial–systems paradigm as well as within the biological paradigm.

The Psychosocial–Systems Paradigm

The psychosocial–systems explanations of pervasive developmental disorders focus on the environment and parent-child interactions as causative factors. Kanner (1943) was among the first to suggest that without cold, unfeeling parents (he called them "refrigerator-type"), psychotic children probably could have grown up to be basically normal. While there was early acceptance of Kanner's view, recent work has failed to find any pertinent differences between parents of autistic children and parents of normal children (e.g., McAdoo & DeMyer, 1978).

To psychoanalysts, while adult psychosis represents a deterioration of the ego, child psychosis reflects the failure of the ego to develop very much or not at all (Alanen, 1965). According to theory, schizophrenic children make some minimal progress toward ego growth and then become abnormally "fixated" at early levels of development. In the autistic child, there is no ego development and normal development of the self through the process of primary to secondary thought may never occur.

Probably the best-known analytic–systems intervention was developed by Bettelheim (1974). He removes children from their parents and brings them into an insitutional therapeutic milieu. Within this milieu there is an attempt to build a positive relationship with the autistic child through play and interpretive discussions. Hopefully, such intensive work builds an ego and helps the child progress through psychosexual stages. While maintaining a group of faithful adherants, analytic approaches like Bettelheim's have fallen out of favor to be replaced by behaviorally oriented views (Ross, 1980).

Differing from psychoanalysts, behaviorists believe that learning principles rather than complex constructs like ego deterioration can more adequately explain how childhood psychoses develop. Ferster (1965) suggested that autistic behavior was partially the result of the parents' failure to use praise or attention to reinforce the child's appropriate behavior. Parents probably failed to reinforce their children, because they themselves were too involved in their own personal problems. Depressed or otherwise self-preoccupied parents might not respond to their child's request to play a game. If children's appropriate social behaviors are ignored by parents for very long, they eventually would extinguish for lack of reinforcement. After a period of time with this kind of experience, only behaviors will remain which are self-stimulatory, self reinforcing, or bizarre enough to get attention from the parents, like smearing feces and head banging. By their actions then, parents may unwittingly encourage the development of psychotic behaviors.

Building on behavioral approaches like Ferster's, professionals have taught autistic children to play appropriately with toys (Romancyzk et al., 1975), to control their aggressiveness (Carr et al., 1976) and to give friendly greetings (Lovaas et al., 1974). They also have been involved in teaching parents of autistic children how to manage them. Schopler and his colleagues (e.g., Schopler & Reichler, 1971) have developed a statewide program in North Carolina in which they teach parents of autistic children behavior management. The program has been in operation for over a decade and has managed to gain the support not only of parents but of teachers and school administrators as well (Short, 1980).

In a few extreme situations, punishment rather than reward may be more effective in changing children's behavior. Lovaas and his colleagues have instituted these procedures when children showed little social behavior and self-injurious actions like biting, hitting, and head banging (Lovaas, 1967; Lovaas & Koegel, 1973). In his somewhat controversial procedures, psychotic children were rewarded with food stuffs and personal contact when they behaved appropriately. However, when they behaved inappropriately, they received electric shock. In one example of this procedure, a child was placed on a shock platform that was surrounded by therapists. One of the therapists called to the child and if the child did not respond by approaching the therapist, he or she was shocked. Because of the discomfort, the child would run, often in tears to one of the therapists, who then hugged and kissed the child reinforcing "approaching people" behavior. Used only as a last resort, such punishment-oriented interventions were only turned to when other treatments failed.

The Biological Paradigm Instead of environmental or parental factors, the biological perspective leads researchers to seek the role of organic causes in the origins of pervasive developmental disorders. Unfortunately, biological theories have not been as helpful in producing viable explanations or treatments in childhood schizophrenia as they were in the adult disorders (Harris & Gottesman, 1976).

There is some support for a genetic predisposition for both autism and childhood schizophrenia. Rutter (1967) has reported a 2 percent rate of autism in siblings and a higher than expected rate of autism in monozygotic compared with dizygotic pairs of twins (Folstein & Rutter, 1977). There seems to be a higher than chance incidence of childhood schizophrenia in the siblings of the affected individuals (Gottesman & Shields, 1976).

For Bender (1971) childhood schizophrenia was not so much caused by direct genetic factors as by some "pre- or perinatal deficit, trauma, or damage, or a physiological crisis which is the stress that decompensates the genetically vulnerable child" (p. 667). This interactive model is probably accepted by most of those who favor a biological explanation of childhood schizophrenia.

On the other hand, Rimland (1969) saw the biological defect causing autism as residing in the neurological system that is responsible for "waking up" a person, the reticular activating system. Damage to this system results in an inability to attend to relevant stimuli long enough to relate one stimulus to another. Thus, the child may not be able to establish love for the mother because of an inability to associate her actions with relief of pain, satisfaction of hunger, and warmth.

Rather than the "waking system," Rutter (1978a) hypothesized that children's autistic behavior results from damage to the speech area of the brain. This kind of damage prevents autistic children from receiving spoken information accurately and expressing themselves effectively. Deficits like these can interfere with the children's ability to interact with their environment in order to meet their basic needs.

Unlike in adult psychoses, the search for biochemical bases for pervasive developmental disorders has generally been unproductive. Few researchers have reported biochemical abnormalities in autistic children. For example, blood levels of the neurotransmitters serotonin and L-Dopa have been studied in a number of investigations (e.g., Ritvo & Freeman, 1977; Campbell et al., 1976). However, even these findings have not been replicated and neither autism or childhood schizophrenia seems related to any particular biochemical abnormality (W. Goldfarb, 1974b, 1980).

The biological perspective has gained popularity over the past 10 years. Various biological treatments have been used with some success with autistic and schizophrenic children. Because of the high tendency of autistic children to develop seizures, anticonvulsant drugs have been used effectively (Deykin & MacMahon, 1979). Both phenothiazines and haloperidol have reduced the self-injurious and self-destructive behaviors of both autistic and schizophrenic children (Dalldorf & Schopler, 1981). Less well tested is the giving of megavitamins, large doses of standard vitamins, to reduce symptoms of pervasive developmental disorders. This approach seems to be gaining in popularity, although it lacks strong scientific support.

Disorders Associated with Adolescence

Along with the physiological changes of puberty, adolescents must contend with role changes forced by parents, teachers, and friends. Socially, adolescents must begin the interpersonal work that prepares them for adult tasks such as marriage and raising a family. Adolescents are caught between childhood and adulthood, and at times the added stress of this transition plays a part in the development of psychological problems and disorders. Because the transition between childhood and adolescence is not always clear, the disorders to follow may occur in both age groups. Generally, however, the *conduct disorders* and *runaway reactions* are more prevalent during the adolescent stage of development than during childhood.

Conduct Disorders

While 5 to 15 percent of all adolescents show "occasional" acts of antisocial behavior (Meeks, 1980), the conduct disorders are characterized by more persistent displays of antisocial activity. Four types of conduct disorders share the DSM-III core description of repetitive and persistent patterns of antisocial behavior that violate the rights of others, beyond the ordinary mischief and pranks of children and adolescents.

In the conduct disorder of the *aggressive and undersocialized type*, youths show a consistent disregard for the feelings of others, bully smaller children, have few, if any, same-age friends, and present serious school problems. They generally are hostile, verbally abusive, defiant, and negativistic.

Personal Experience: Observing an Aggressive and Undersocialized Conduct Disorder

Billy was an overweight, sloppily dressed 13-year-old boy. The teacher who brought him into the interview room looked harried and raised her eyebrows as if to say I was really in for it. I was! Billy fairly charged into the room. He knocked over a small lamp and let loose with a veritable stream of profanity that would have made a longshoreman blush. The "interview" went downhill from there. He told me he didn't want to speak to no f_______ shrink. I offered him some chocolate if he would sit down and talk with me. Even though he loved chocolate, he told me in no uncertain terms what I could do with it. After a number of other attempts to get Billy to talk with me it became apparent that I was getting nowhere. So I told him that it was time for him to go back to his classroom. He told me he was going home. I said that he would have to stay in school. I made the mistake of standing in front of the door to make my point. The next thing I knew Billy and I were on the floor. I had him under control but I also had a bloody nose. I was very glad to see the special education teacher and her aide arrive to take Billy back to the classroom.

Youths who are diagnosed as conduct disorders rarely have experienced consistent discipline or pleasantness. They usually do not have any feelings of responsibility or guilt for their misbehavior and tend to be uncooperative and provocative.

Though anger is also present to some degree, it is not as obvious in youngsters classified as *unaggressive conduct disorder, undersocialized type.* While these youths are adept at manipulating people for favors, they also share, with their aggressive counterparts, a lack of concern for the feelings of others. Generally, they show one of two patterns of behavior. In the first pattern they are timid, unassertive, and whiney, and often report feeling rejected and mistreated. At times they will be victimized, most often sexually. In a second pattern, the adolescents are less timid and more likely to exploit and manipulate others. Unlike their aggressive counterpart's response of uncontrolled anger when frustrated, these youths are more likely to react to pressure with deviousness and guile.

Adolescents designated as being *socialized conduct disorders* show an ability to make friends with some of their peers. In *aggressive conduct disorder, socialized type,* youths commit violations of the basic rights of others usually by some combination of physical violence or robbery. While they do not seem to have feelings of guilt or remorse for their illegal activities, socialized aggressive adolescents have an ability to develop friendships and maintain them for 6 months or more. They will extend themselves to help those they call friends, even to the point of taking punishment rather than informing on them.

Personal Experience: Observing an Aggressive Conduct Disorder, Socialized Type

Lance was dressed in fatigues. He was about 6 feet tall, with dark wavy hair. By any set of criteria, Lance was a good-looking young man of 16. He was in a program for severely disturbed adolescents and I was to evaluate his progress. He smiled broadly as he entered the room and warmly took my hand. "Hi doc. How have you been?" Lance took control of the session from the start. He was friendly up until the time I asked him about the drug-selling charge that was presently being drawn up against him. He hit the table hard and said "That b________ Phil he turned me in. I'm going to kick his a— when I see him." I pointed out that if he did that, he would violate his probation. His response was that he didn't care. I asked him who had given him the drugs to sell. He became sullen, "None of your dam–business." The rest of the interview was tense. When he was leaving he said to me, "I thought you were my friend, but you're not. You're just like all those others. I'd watch out for my car if I were you. It might have an accident or two." Lance greeted his classroom teacher with that same charming smile he had given me. "I enjoyed talking to Dr. ________, maybe we can get together again."

The final group of conduct disorders, the *unaggressive and socialized type,* is also marked by rebellion against authority, but lacks the physically aggressive quality of the aggressive and socialized pattern. Some of the behavior of the nonaggressive adolescents seems pranklike, but in actuality they often end up in serious trouble with school and community authorities.

Runaways

Though many children and adolescents remain at home and act out their frustrations and anxieties aggressively, nearly 1 million youngsters per year run away. Involving nearly equal numbers of boys and girls, runaways have been characterized as insecure, unhappy, and impulsive (Jenkins & Stahle, 1972), having low self-esteem (Beyer, 1974), and feeling out of control (Bartollas, 1975). The bulk of research on runaways shows them to be more disturbed than normal teenagers.

Why do over 1 million youngsters "run" each year? Disturbed parent-child relationships seem to be one of the most important reasons (e.g. Brandon, 1974; Gottlieb & Chafetz, 1977), but runaways also have problems in school (Walker, 1976), seem to need to search for adventure and meaning (Watternberg, 1956), and suffer from boredom (Tobias, 1970). Hoshino (1973) points out that the entire family of a runaway may be under stress and each family member would, if given the opportunity, choose to run to escape the difficulties within the home. Families of runaways more often appear to be organized around punishment and negativism and seem unable to support one another in crises.

Occasionally, runaways end up in serious trouble, but the great majority of them return home safely. Unfortunately, they often return to home situations that have not changed, and they may have to face the very same problems that pushed them to run away in the first place. Hopefully, time away from the stressful family situation may give runaways an opportunity to reassess who they are and find new ways to deal with their difficulties. The laws in some states make running away a crime. When runaways return, they may face incarceration or they may be forced to see a counselor. Should counseling take place, chances for success improve if the entire family can be involved.

Although they can develop close relationships with fellow gang members, socialized, aggressive conduct-disorder adolescents frequently use physical violence in their actions against society. (*Michael Weisbrot and Family*)

Over a million adolescents run away from home every year. (*Marion Bernstein © 1980*)

SUICIDE IN ADOLESCENCE

BOX 16-3

"I'm no use to anyone. I can't do anything right. I try but it just doesn't seem to make any difference. I love all of you but I just can't seem to do things right. It's not your fault. There's nothing you could do. Its me, only me. I love you."

This passage was taken from a suicide note written by a 13-year-old girl who committed suicide by taking a massive dose of sleeping capsules. Although it is not a behavior limited to adolescence, suicide makes its first significant appearance in this age group. For many years it was believed that children did not attempt suicide. However, we now know that suicide attempts and completions show a marked increase at age 14 (Whiting, 1981). The incidence of suicide continues to increase through 19 years of age, becoming the most frequent cause of death for the age group 14 through 19 (Haim, 1974; Remschmidt & Schwab, 1978). The three main causative factors identified for attempted suicide in 157 adolescents were family conflicts, difficulties with partners, and school problems. Since two of the major tasks facing adolescents are learning how to deal with independence from their families and developing adequate heterosexual relationships, it should come as no surprise that failure in these two important areas are related to suicidal attempts. Prevention programs might do well to focus on these two tasks as well as to alert the public that threats of suicide during the impulsive adolescent years should be taken seriously by parents, teachers, and peers.

Paradigmatic Perspectives on the Disorders of Adolescence

Arguably the most traumatic and intense phase of development, adolescence is characterized by an interplay of psychosocial, biological, and systems factors.

The psychosocial and biological paradigms have been especially helpful in understanding adolescent disorders, but for many researchers, the systems paradigm may hold the most promise.

The Psychosocial Paradigm and Adolescent Disorders

From the psychosocial perspective, deviant adolescent behavior is most frequently seen resulting from a failure to cope effectively with the special developmental problems associated with the transition between childhood and adulthood. Generally the psychosocial theory that captures what is involved in this difficult transition is that of Erik Erikson (1950, 1968). Erikson sees adolescence as the crucial period of life for the development of identity and sense of being (Gallatin, 1975; Guardo, 1975).

According to Erikson, an individual passes through a series of eight psychosocial developmental stages (see Chapter 5). At each stage there is a "crisis," or turning point, during which persons may choose adaptive or maladaptive behavioral solutions. Each stage presents a developmental task whose resolution is reflected in a balance between two opposing personality components (e.g., trust versus mistrust, autonomy versus shame and doubt). In the developmental stage called adolescence, the crisis is "identity versus identity confusion." Within this stage, Erikson describes seven major developmental subtasks. Each of these subtasks has to do with identity versus confusion, and each is tied, in some way, to past and present crisis resolutions. A description of these seven developmental subtasks may clarify how adjustment or maladjustment in adolescent identity can arise.

1. *Temporal perspective versus time confusion*. The earlier resolution of the trust-mistrust challenge leaves children predisposed to different reactions to adolescence. If they are trusting,

children usually enter adolescence with confidence in accepting the past and security in preparing for the future (good time perspective). If they are nontrusters, in adolescence they may be isolated and unable to view the past, present, or future in an integrated way.

2. *Self-certainty versus self-consciousness.* Autonomous children typically enter adolescence confident of their own abilities to face difficulties and accepting of themselves as good human beings. Shameful children often question their ability, may be self-conscious, and are probably not secure in their problem-solving ability.
3. *Role experimentation versus role fixation.* Children with initiative usually enter adolescence ready to experiment with new role identities and new experiences; they have the courage to face the task of seeking a new being. In contrast, guilt-ridden children may be "role-inhibited" and fearful of changing fixed patterns.
4. *Apprenticeship versus work paralysis.* Industrious children generally enter adolescence ready to master new tasks and to apply themselves to the problems of role identification. Children who feel inferior may see nothing worth trying, may feel frustrated, and may be unable to mobilize their energies to confront challenges.

Erikson suggested that one important subtask facing adolescents is overcoming self-doubt and self-consciousness in order to accept themselves as "good human beings." (*Michael Weisbrot and Family*)

A successful resolution of the adolescent stage can increase the chances of success in the three major life phases still to come. The three adolescent subtasks to follow lay the crucial foundations for later development.

5. *Sexual polarization versus bisexual confusion.* This subtask focuses on the attainment of a sex-appropriate identification. Sexually polarized adolescents usually are secure in their masculinity or femininity and thus ready for later intimate heterosexual relationships. However, sexually confused adolescents may be in store for later difficulty in establishing meaningful intimate relationships.
6. *Leadership and followership versus authority confusion.* Besides establishing their sexuality, adolescents must build the foundation for later professional, social, or familial productivity. To accomplish this goal, adolescents should develop an ability to see them-

selves alternately as leader and follower. Confusion about when to submit to authority may result in later difficulties in dealing with adult relationships.

7. *Ideological commitment versus confusion of values.* If the previous subgoals are resolved in the direction of ideological commitment, the final adolescent subtask usually results in an adult with a set of values that can serve as guides to life. In late adolescence, such values allow for a more positive review of one's life and a sense of integrity. If confusion of values is the result of this adolescent subtask, a weakened guiding philosophy emerges, and later life may be filled with self-doubt, a sense of wasted years, and despair.

For Erikson, adolescence is a socially authorized "delay of adulthood," a time when the limitations of childhood are lifted, but the responsibilities of adulthood are not yet imposed. Erikson sees this period of delay as a social moratorium in which adolescents may experiment with different values, attitudes, and patterns of behavior before committing themselves to an identity with which they may have to live for the rest of their lives. During this moratorium, the seven developmental subtasks must be successfully completed. If, because of fate, family needs, or other events, the moratorium ends too soon, adolescents may show identity confusion, feelings of failure, and fear of adulthood. Maladjustment in adolescence may reflect an inability to deal with the requirements of the moratorium. A failure to meet the requirements of adolescence may be due to a faulty resolution of preadolescent crises or an extreme lack of support and open rejection during the course of adolescence. According to Erikson, it is quite normal for adolescents to feel tumultuous and upset. Abnormality often appears when the adolescent chooses avoidance, denial, and aggression to deal with problems rather than coping with stresses by confronting and resolving crises.

The Biological Paradigm and Adolescent Disorders

In contrast to Erikson's popular psychosocial explanation, there are some who believe that genetic and neuropsychological perspectives may eventually lead to explanations for the occurrence of some disorders in adolescence, particularly the conduct disorders (e.g., Hutchin, 1973). For example, Berman and Siegel (1972) have shown that children diagnosed as conduct disorders show signs of neurological and cerebral dysfunction. These neurological findings lead some to conclude that conduct disorders are genetically based and are caused by neurological malfunctions (e.g., Douvan & Adelson, 1976). Voorhees (1981) examined the neuropsychological differences between those with conduct disorders and a comparable control group. He found that youths with conduct disorders did more poorly than their peers on those tasks requiring persistent levels of concentration and attention.

The Systems Paradigm and Adolescent Disorders

From the point of view of systems theorists, the problems of adolescence derive from much the same source as the normal behaviors of adolescence, that is, from the groups of which adolescents are a part. Lerner and Shea (1982) state:

> adolescents may be seen as inevitably embedded in a social context and as invariably being both products and producers of this context. . . . (p. 522).

> behavioral changes in adolescence involve reciprocal, multidirectional exchanges between the adolescent and his/her environment. The environment includes both other people and numerous societal institutions such as religion, education, and politics. Additional contextual variables such as the mass media, eco-

> nomic factors, and contemporary cultural and subcultural issues also undoubtedly influence and are influenced by adolescent development. (p. 504)

In addition to their belief that social factors affect adolescence, Lerner and Shea clearly reflect the systems paradigm when they note the reciprocity between person and system; among the systems studied by scientists are peer groups, the family, and society.

Peer groups have been defined as clusters of "associates who know each other and who serve as a source of reference or comparison for one another." (Newman, 1982, p. 526). Newman (1982) notes four main functions of such a system:

1. to be a setting in which adolescents can establish increased autonomy from parents or older siblings
2. to offer a place for experimenting with new values and to help in resisting established family or cultural views
3. to be a nonfamily group that allows for a sense of belonging or affection outside of the nuclear family
4. to be a source or regulation and direction of individual behavior

Within these four functions of the peer group system may be found the sources of both normal and abnormal behavior. For example, without the benefit of a peer group system, adolescents may become undersocialized. Without proper peer group pressure against it, aggression may come to characterize an adolescent's behavior. Further, through support, affection, and belongingness, peer groups can direct adolescents toward deviant and other culturally inappropriate behavior patterns. Sometimes termed *dyssocial* behavior, such peer group endorsed yet socially unacceptable patterns might include stealing by members of juvenile gangs or open aggression and destructiveness endorsed by some radical youth organizations.

While the peer group is often the most important system affecting adolescent behavior, the family system and the social-cultural system also play major roles. We focussed on the ways in which family structure can affect behavior in Chapter 6. We need to note here that the weaker the family structure, the more potent may be the effects of an adolescent's peer group. Adolescents especially need to feel they *belong* and are valued. Due to maladaptive family structure or other family system disturbances, if they do not feel they belong at home, they probably will find other systems to which they will attach themselves. If these alternate systems provide sound structure and direction, the adolescent can develop normally and adaptively; if these systems are also disturbed in structure or content, the adolescent is more likely to develop diagnosable behavior patterns.

In general, regardless of their differences, all peer groups and families are part of a larger system called "society" or "culture." As such, individual members of these smaller systems are continually in the process of being acculturated into the larger system. Those who learn culturally appropriate patterns are typically deemed normal; those who do not might be termed deviant or abnormal. Cultures differ in the degree to which they attempt to formalize the process of acculturation of adolescents. In the United States, for example, there is relatively little systematic attempt to guide the peer group subsystems and their effects on their members (Newman, 1982). By contrast, Bronfenbrenner (1970) has reported that in the Soviet Union both the family and the school are actively and directly used as socialization agents. Peer pressure is used to guide young people toward the desired sense of peer responsibility for group behavior. The success of the Soviet socialization process was demonstrated in a study by Bronfenbrenner (1970) in which he compared Soviet and Swiss children in terms of how they would handle 21 different examples of peer misconduct.

Bronfenbrenner found that 75 percent of the Soviet children would say something corrective to their peers, whereas only 33 percent of the Swiss children would. Further, while 20 percent of the Swiss children said they would do nothing, only 1 percent of the Soviet children felt they would not act at all.

Bronfenbrenner notes that such dramatic effects of the social system on its individual young members would not be possible in the United States, due to the strength of other important systems in our society. "The emphasis in the United States is on individual development. Argument, conflict and disagreement are what we agree to do . . . No one controls how people, family and friends treat a person. . . . There is no uniform code for expected or accepted behavior in American peer groups or families" (Newman, 1982, p. 534).

Paradigmatically Based Approaches to the Treatment of Adolescent Disorders

Although there is recent evidence of some biological involvement in the adolescent disorders, the major therapeutic efforts for this age group continue to be derived primarily from the psychosocial and systems paradigms. These approaches include individual and group psychotherapy and community intervention.

The Psychosocial and Systems Paradigms: Individual and Group Psychotherapy

While they are among the most widely used adolescent treatment approaches, individual and group psychotherapy with teenagers are especially difficult. Adolescents are notoriously uncooperative, especially if therapy is not their choice. Therapists must try to create trust and to convince young clients that they are out to help them. In our own work with adolescents, we have learned to apply seven guidelines.

1. I am here to help you, and not necessarily your parents.
2. I will not tell your parents or anyone else anything that goes on between us unless you and I both agree that I should do so.
3. I will tell your parents that they cannot tell me anything for my ears only. If they call me, I will tell them before they say anything to me that I will tell you everything they say to me when I report the call to you.
4. Even if it hurts or embarrasses me or you, I will always be straight with you and I will tell you what I am feeling.
5. I will try never to be late or miss appointments or not be ready to relate to you during our sessions (unless some personal emergency arises), and I expect the same commitment from you.
6. You can talk about terminating our relationship whenever you wish, but you must give me at least 1 week's notice. We must try to agree mutually as to when we stop seeing each other.
7. I am older than you and I realize it; don't let my age lead you to believe that I cannot understand any of your feelings.

Whenever any of these guidelines is violated, it should be discussed by therapist and client. The adolescent has the responsibility for bringing in topics to discuss. The therapist works to make sure that the client's confidence is never violated and supports the adolescent in trying new roles.

Those youngsters who are classified as socialized conduct disorders may not benefit optimally from passive permissive psychotherapeutic approaches like those described above. Rather what seems to work best for them are reality-based group procedures that use reformed conduct disorder youths to confront the client's style of denial, rationalization, and projection.

Personal Experience: Psychotherapy with a Youth Classified as a Conduct Disorder, Aggressive Unsocialized Type

I sat back with a bit of awe. I had seen Ethelia for a number of sessions, but with little success. She was a belligerent, bossy, 15-year-old girl who had been involved in a number of delinquent acts such as robbing smaller children and shoplifting. She saw her present difficulties as primarily due to others. The storekeeper who caught her was a "racist." Teachers in school were "out to get her." Ethelia in no way saw herself as being responsible for her present troubles. I attempted to break through her denial and anger by trying to be her friend. I let her talk about anything she wanted. If she verbally abused me, I took it, in an attempt to win her over. Facing failure, I had taken the chance of getting a reformed conduct disorder woman who was presently a vocational counselor to talk to Ethelia. Though only about 3 years older than Ethelia and about half her size, this woman seemed confident as she listened to Ethelia "rant on" about her problems. After about 5 minutes, the counselor raised her hand to stop Ethelia, but she continued on. "Girl! I don't want to hear no more about what a poor thing you are! I've been that way myself and it just don't work." Ethelia seemed stunned and stammered something about not liking to be talked to that way. The counselor pressed on and within 15 minutes actually had Ethelia listening to what she had to say.

I don't want to mislead you. This one interaction did not lead to a miracle cure, but it did set the stage for my using a different approach in my working with Ethelia. I can tell you that we did make some progress in her making a better and more effective adjustment.

In some instances, *group approaches* may be more appropriate than one-to-one counseling. Groups consist of anywhere from five to eight adolescents who meet with one or two counselors. Some clinicians believe that group therapy is to be preferred over individual therapy for several reasons (MacClennen & Felsenfeld, 1968; Rosenbaum, 1972). First, many of the problems of adolescents are centered upon or associated with peer relationships. Thus, learning to relate well to an adult professional may not be as much help to an adolescent as learning to relate to similarly troubled peers. A second reason for preferring groups is that many adolescents do not easily trust one-to-one relationships with adults. Often they feel the therapist may be an agent of their parents who will try to force them to comply with parental wishes. Also, as mentioned earlier, adolescents sometimes are late to or absent from individual therapy sessions. In group therapy, peer pressure can be brought to bear on such problems.

Adolescents with conduct disorders are especially difficult to treat because of their inability to form adequate relationships. To increase chances of success, therapists must attempt to involve the youngster's whole family. However, the family is often characterized by angry relationships and an intense resistance to outside influence. Therefore the task of the therapist is to help the family members, especially the parents, to communicate more positively with one another.

Adolescents can sometimes work their problems out in group therapy with peers. (*Michael Weisbrot and Family*)

Systems Paradigm-based Therapies for Adolescents

In addition to individual and group work with adolescents, there have been recent increases in what might be termed "community" interventions in schools and in neighborhoods. Disturbed adolescents have been helped through *psychoeducational* approaches in which they are taught both academic and social interpersonal skills by a highly trained professional staff of a special school program. Some of these intervention programs are behaviorally oriented (Levine et al., 1981), using primarily operant techniques to deal with profoundly behaviorally disordered adolescents. Other programs have used a more humanistic experiential approach that focuses on helping the disturbed adolescents to learn how to behave appropriately by attempting to build their own community among themselves (Carp, 1981). In both approaches, the mental health workers seek to deliver services outside a residential treatment facility, to keep the adolescents closer to the community in which they live.

The goal of most who espouse a community approach is to use the least restrictive means of helping disturbed youngsters. In some instances, however, adolescents must be institutionalized. When hospitalization is necessary, many programs are geared to help adolescents become stabilized enough to return quickly to their community. Dattilio (1981) believes that for the typical acting-out adolescent, consistency and structure are essential and can result in reintegration into the community after no more than 90 days in the hospital. In a follow-up evaluation of Dattilio's program, 12 of the 17 adolescents participating in the program's first year "graduated" and went on to live in less structured community environments. Six of the 12 were placed back in their own homes and were doing well after 6 months.

In one approach (Nowicki, 1983) the youngster spends weekdays in residential treatment and the weekend at home. Families are seen in ongoing family therapy. This kind of arrangement gives parents some relief from a troublesome child, but it does not allow them to abdicate total responsibility. The weekends at home allow the family to work on new ways of dealing with their old problems. Programs such as this one have obtained some significant success with youngsters for whom success is very rare.

Concluding Comments

The Romans had a unique way of handling the problems inherent in the transition from childhood to adulthood; when a Roman child became 12, he became an adult. While some present day people might like to take the same approach of ignoring the differences between childhood and adolescence, doing so makes the questions of etiology and intervention more difficult to answer. For example, in comparison with children, adolescents are probably more volatile and rebellious. However, Shopper (1975) points out that rebelliousness may be a necessary part of their achieving independence. Rather than trying not to have any conflicts, parents should strive to ensure that the results of these unavoidable conflicts are used to help both adolescents and parents form new and more positive relationships.

Conservative estimates of children and adolescents under the age of 18 who need "immediate" professional help is nearly 2 million. The number rises to nearly 10 million when we include those who need professional help but are not in crisis. Should these youngsters not receive the support and treatment to help them resolve their difficulties, the chances for them becoming troubled adults increases significantly.

Summary Chart

In Chapter 16, we began our look at the application of a developmental paradigm to the study of psychopathology with descriptions of special patterns associated with childhood and adolescence.

The disorders of childhood were examined first:

Developmental deviations: Disturbances of bodily functions (eating, sleeping, elimination, and speech), disturbances of musculature (tics, Tourette's disease)

Anxiety disorders: Separation anxiety, avoidant disorder, overanxious disorder

Hyperactivity: With attention deficits, without attention deficits

Pervasive developmental disorders: Psychoses, childhood schizophrenia, autism

Explanations and treatments for disorders of childhood have focused primarily on the most severe disorders:

The systems paradigm: Faulty parenting

The psychosocial paradigm: Faulty learning, inappropriate development

The biological paradigm: Heredity, central nervous system malfunctions

Treatments: Play therapies, behavioral therapies

We then turned to the disorders of adolescence:

Patterns of disturbances: Conduct disorders, runaway reactions

Explanations: Traumatic adolescent crisis, cerebral and neurological dysfunctions

Treatments: Individual therapy, group therapy, family therapy, psychoeducational approaches

CHAPTER 17

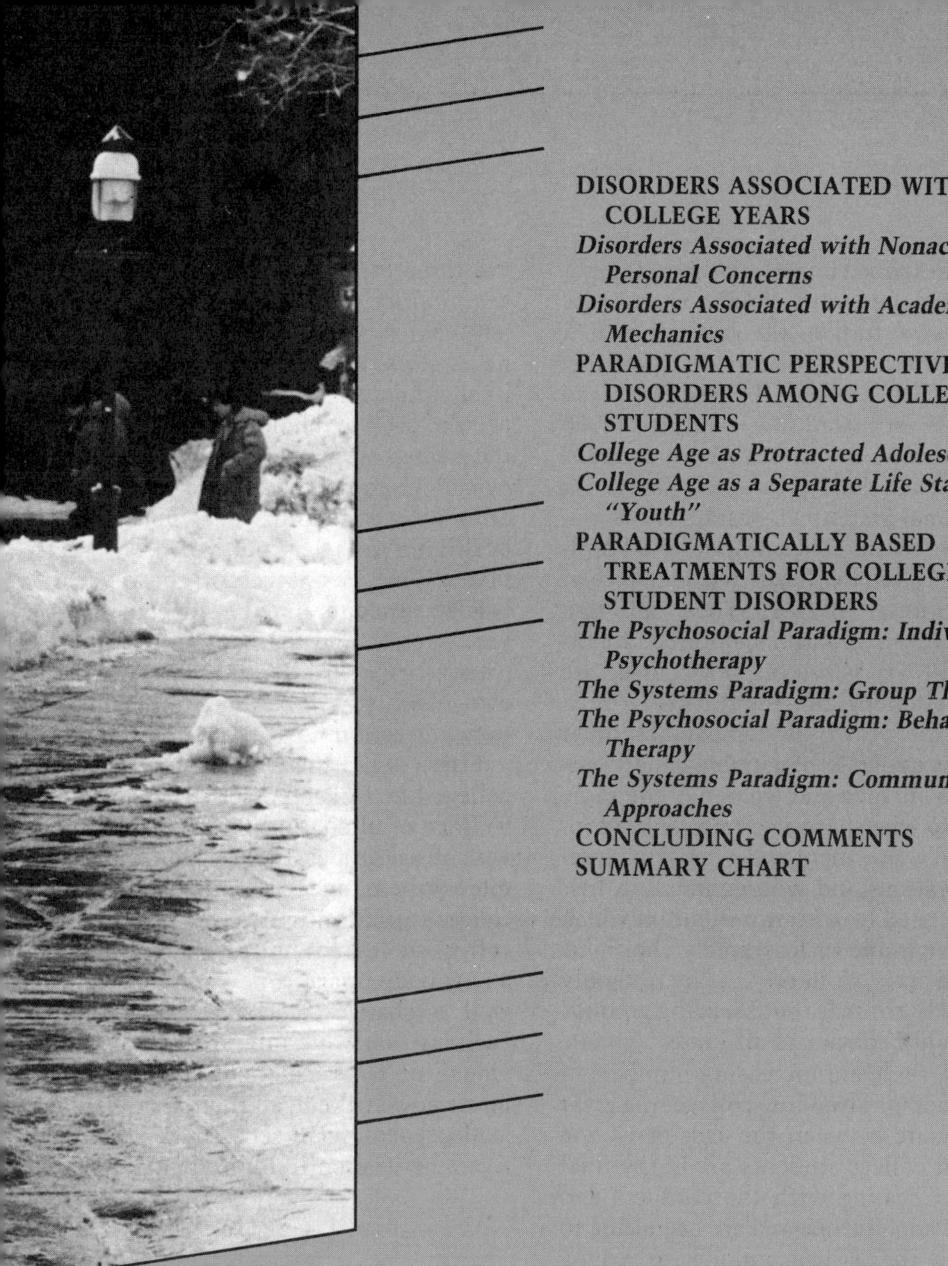

Disorders Associated with College Students

Having described for you the special problems associated with childhood and adolescence, we turn to the group to which most of the readers of this text probably belong, college students. Between 1975 and 1985, it is estimated that over 11,328,000 bachelor degrees will have been awarded (Sweat et al., 1981; National Center for Educational Statistics). Besides these students, there are at least another 11 million who attend colleges without receiving a formal degree. They all find themselves in situations described by Erikson (1971): "Colleges, of course, are foremost among the institutions which permit the study of comparable inner problems under demonstrable conditions. Students are men and women of the same age-group who share a certain range of intellectual endowment and a converging set of motivations and who compete in life-tasks dictated by a known tradition which they have (more or less) freely chosen as a trusted style. Colleges . . . [are not] only good study grounds, but breeding grounds for deviant behavior of all kinds" (p. xx).

While there are increasing numbers of older students attending college, the great majority are between the ages of 17 and 25. Most college students are in the final stages of dealing with the conflicts and crises of adolescence and are beginning to confront the issues unique to young adulthood. However, not all students can cope with these issues. It has been estimated that, during the undergraduate years, about 2 percent of college students will experience a psychotic disorder requiring hospitalization (Ryle, 1969). Further, an additional 15 percent of college students are likely to have an emotional disturbance sufficiently intense to warrant treatment by professionals. Another 20 percent may experience transitory symptoms as a result of one or more of the three major stressors of college life: *examinations, social interaction*, and *career choice*. Perhaps as a result of these major stressors, college students are more likely than their same-aged noncollege peers to seek psychological help. Whether the greater use of psychological assistance by college students is due to greater need or to wider availability of campus mental health services has not yet been ascertained. One fact is certain, however, in college, students may be subjected to severe stresses and many are often ill-prepared to cope with them in terms of their own identity, self-confidence, and vocational direction.

Stress is not the only unique aspect of college life. Erikson asserts that although feelings of alienation may be associated with all age groups, these feelings are rarely more salient and dramatic than among college students. Josselyn (1954) notes, "the college adolescent must learn to deal with a new body image, a new physical self as well as changes in body sensations. . . . Feelings that were unknown to the individual, or were experienced in modified forms now strike in all their rawness. The [college] adolescent senses he is different. Again he is alien to himself" (p. 223).

Disorders Associated with College Years

While most forms of disturbance can and do occur in college students, traditional classification systems are often difficult to apply. In trying to use the traditional diagnostic categorization system to classify college students, Blos (1946) was forced to conclude, "When I tried to classify 387 cases, I was appalled to find that classification would indeed be fitting them into a procrustean bed for the sake of typology. I began to realize that I was dealing with case material which was basically different from cases seen in a mental hygiene or child guidance clinic" (p. 571). His statement is four decades old, but it seems as relevant to today's DSM-III as it was to the traditional diagnostic system then. Reflecting the difficulty in classification, it is estimated that anywhere from 25 to 50 percent of college students with psychological difficulties coming to the attention of helping personnel are assigned to the "wastebasket" category of "problem diagnoses" (Blaine & McArthur, 1971).

In light of diagnostic problems, a number of investigators have attempted to reclassify college student disorders (Lucas, 1976; Veasey, 1977). For instance, Handforth (1981) has proposed a classification system based on study difficulties. In addition, an extensive survey of college student problems and emotional concerns was completed by Wechsler et al. (1981). They asked more than 7000 undergraduate students attending colleges in New England to respond to a list of "21 common concerns and feelings experienced by many college students" (p. 720). These 21 concerns were placed into four broad groups: *anxiety* (feeling tense, keyed up), *depressed affect* (feeling worthless, hopeless, depressed), *motivational problems* (feeling bored, having trouble concentrating), and *interpersonal problems* (feeling shy, lonely).

Wechsler et al. found that 47 percent of their respondents admitted to having at least one of the 21 concerns as a problem. Anxiety-related concerns were most frequently reported (33 percent), followed by interpersonal (23 percent), motivational problems (20 percent), and depressed affect (14 percent). Females reported more problems than males especially in the areas of anxiety and depression. Minority women showed a higher frequency of motivational problems than white women (31 to 20 percent).

Other data from Wechsler et al. showed that students who were overweight showed increased frequency of problem concerns. Control of weight was a problem for nearly one-quarter of the college women (23 percent) but only for 5 percent of the college males. About one half of the college women who reported themselves to be overweight also reported concerns in the area of anxiety and interpersonal relationships. Since these rates are much higher than the total group rates, they suggest that overweight students may be a particular population at risk.

Besides nontraditional classification for college student problems, DSM-III has also been applied. Stangler and Printz (1980) reported DSM-III diagnostic data gathered on 500 students who applied to their student health service. Since the researchers did not report who made the diagnosis or whether the diagnoses were reliable, the information gathered must be interpreted cautiously. However, depressive symptoms account for the majority of diagnoses. More prevalent among women, its frequency was disquieting because this diagnostic category assumes a criterion of at least 2 prior years of depressive symptomatology. Such chronic depression is frequently inappropriate for short-term interventions common in most student mental health facilities.

Other significant findings involved the greater frequency of women (64 percent) to men (36 percent) clients, the greater frequency of women students in the categories of *identity disorder*, *bulimia*, and *histrionic disorders*; and the greater frequency of men students in the *compulsive disorders* category. The authors were especially impressed by the frequency of bulimia in the college population.

The college student is indeed in a special situation that produces special problems. Erikson describes the college student as a "combination of explosive

Although all college students face a variety of stresses, only some will develop diagnosable disorders. (*P. Conklin/ Monkmeyer Press Photo Service*)

impulsivity and obsessive introspection," whose major problems appear to be motivation to stay in college and a great need for affection (in Blaine & McArthur, 1971). We agree, but we see college students as having other problems as well.

In a 2-year study of students applying for therapy at our university counseling service (Nowicki & Duke, 1978), we found that problems severe enough to merit students' coming for help other than vocational guidance could be placed into three categories. *Existential depression* manifested itself in problems like "I need to find out why I am not happy," or "Where am I headed in life?" *Social problems* were reflected in complaints such as "lack of social life," "using sex as a way of relating," and "difficulties in getting along with and establishing relations with members of the opposite sex." The last group, *parental problems,* was exemplified by questions like, "How do I get my mother off my back?" and "How do I make my parents proud of me?"

While most of the concerns of college students seem to fall into the three categories of existential, social, and parental problems, we have found that the effects of these problems upon the life of the college student can be varied. Symptoms may be manifested in studies, test performance, personal functioning, and career progress. Combining our own work with that of other researchers, we propose a two-part classification of college student disorders: *disorders associated with nonacademic personal concerns* and *disorders associated with academic mechanics.*

Disorders Associated with Nonacademic Personal Concerns

Although many of the problems faced by college students are involved in some way with the task of completing college and beginning a career, there are other types of college student disorders that seem to be more personal than academic. Among these disorders are *the identity crisis, suicide, eating disorders,* and *apathy reaction.*

The Identity Crisis

Many writers share the opinion that the most important task for college students is the formation of an identity (Bernard, 1981; Gould, 1978; Levinson, 1978). In fact, the process of searching for an identity probably had begun during the senior year in high school. Hayes (1981) sees the senior year in high school as a crucial preparatory time for the student to "grieve" the loss of childhood and the passing of the high school experience. He believes that many students may not complete the task during their high school senior year and may continue the process into their college years. Thus, we find students grappling with such questions as: "What am I on Earth for?" "What do I really believe in?" "Is there a God?" "Is all I really want material things?" The conflicts that often characterize the identity crisis are revealed in the account offered by a student in the following excerpt from White (1952):

Personal Experience: Identity Crisis

I began trying to fit a personality to my make-up. I began acting out personalities and tried observing people and copying them, but I realized what I was doing and so carried that "how'm I doing attitude," that is, continually looking at and thinking about what I'd said or done, what impression I had made. But these personalities were all short-lived because they pleased some and not others and because they didn't produce that underlying purpose of making people like me; and every time unconsciously I would resort to my childish attitude to make myself noticeable. Examples of these "personalities" are independence (but I couldn't keep it up); arrogance (but people were only arrogant back at me); big shot in sex (but people weren't so much in love with it as I thought); hatefulness (people paid no attention to me); extreme niceness (people took advantage of it, kidded me about it because I did it to an ultra degree); humorous nature (but I was only being childish, silly); quiet and studious (but people were only passing me by and I kept feeling I was missing something). I became a daydreamer so intensively that up to the present I find I'm daydreaming almost all the time. I became conscious of a person's approach and would become fluttered, flustered, would try to make a friend of him no matter who he was but I overdid it.

Source: From Robert W. White, *Lives in Progress: A Study of the Natural Growth of Personality,* p. 154. Copyright 1952 by Robert W. White. Reprinted by permission of Holt, Rinehart and Winston and Robert W. White.

Regardless of their age, most students are bothered by questions of "meaning" at one time or another during their college years. However, in some instances the identity crisis becomes so intense that it may incapacitate them. Students may stop doing course work or attending classes and, as a result, may find themselves in trouble with the administration. Because they aren't comfortable with themselves, students may withdraw from friends and organizational activities as they search for meaning in their own existence.

In our research (Nowicki & Duke, 1978), we reported that nearly one out of every three students coming for personal counseling had what could be classified as an identity problem. In the midst of such difficulties, these individuals tended also to show a great sensitivity to any occurrence that might reflect badly on their self-con-

One of the important tasks facing college students is developing a satisfactory identity. (*Rogers/Monkmeyer Press Photo Service*)

cept. Failure in either the social or academic realm was frequently magnified as the person searched for a sense of self.

Other professionals also see the formation of a satisfactory identity as an important goal. Bernard (1981) suggests that professionals can aid this identity development process by: (1) presenting courses on "identity formation" that include an emphasis on adult development; (2) making available consultation services that help to create a milieu that encourages self-exploration and support for the late adolescent as he or she goes through the process of forming an identity; and (3) helping expose students to adults in all of their complexity so that the adults can be effective role models for the choices the student is trying to make.

Suicide

Stress, anxiety, and failure are often associated with college life. At times the negative feelings may become so intense that students may contemplate suicide. Second only to accidents as a cause of death in college students, the suicide rate has been increasing to the point that it may be up to 50 percent higher in some college student groups than in the population as a whole (Nowicki & Duke, 1982; Stenzel, 1964). Ryle (1969) reported that the student suicide rate is approximately 4 out of 100,000 per year, but that the greater proportion of suicides occur in students who suffered in precollege years from severe depressive illnesses. In other words, rarely do student suicides occur in response to single psychologically disturbing events such as failure on a given test or lack of a date. Students who take their own life usually have had a history of difficulty in adjusting and may have experienced a long series of disappointments, failures, and other insidious stresses. Further, student suicides usually do not occur more frequently at any particular point in the four years of college (Ryle, 1969).

In addition to those who actually attempt suicide, many more students think about it. A survey done at the University of Cincinnati found that nearly 30 percent of the students sampled admitted thinking about their own suicide during the academic year. Approximately 1 out of every 10 of these students rated these suicidal thoughts as very serious (Craig & Senter, 1972). More recent data suggest that 30 percent may even be an underestimate of the frequency of suicidal thoughts. Domino et al., (1980) asked 800 students from nine colleges to complete a suicide attitude questionnaire. Of these students, 76 percent endorsed the statement that "almost everyone has at one time or another thought about suicide."

Student suicides affect other people as well as the individual involved. Seiden (1966), for example, points out that the shock of suicide is especially great on a college campus. "For here are a relatively privileged group of persons enjoying valued advantages of youth, intelligence and educational opportunity. Why should persons, seemingly so rewarded, seek to kill themselves?" (p. 389). Seiden found that students who later committed suicide could be differentiated from those who did not in a number of ways. A sample of 23 University of California at Berkeley students who committed suicide was compared with students in general. Generally, it was found that suicide was more frequent in older than in younger students, in males than in females (more than 3 to 1), in graduate students than in undergraduate students, in single students than in married students, in foreign students than in native, in language and literature than in other majors, in high-grade-point-average students than in low-grade-point-average students, and in those who came to a mental health facility than in those who did not. Further, it appears that the peak months for suicides were October and February. Surprisingly, only 1 of the 23 suicides occurred during the final exam period. In fact, most suicides occurred during the first 6 weeks of the quarter. The suicides were most likely to take place on a Monday or a Friday and at the residence of the student.

According to Seiden, most students gave some warning that they were going to attempt suicide. For example, in completing a medical-history form, one student crossed out the word "emergency" and wrote in the word "death" in the question, "Whom shall we notify in case of emergency?" Clues are not always this obvious, but Seiden reports that suicide victims often presented a similar symptom picture of "insomnia, anorexia, and extreme moodiness, especially moods of despondency" (p. 397). Among the particular crises precipitating suicides in college students were concern over grades, unusual somatic complaints, and difficulties with interpersonal relationships. This last precipitator usually involved students who were asocial and withdrawn.

Eating Disorders

Suicide is not the only pattern of behavior which threatens the lives and well-being of some college students. During the past decade there has been increasing interest in the eating disorders of *anorexia nervosa* and *bulimia.* Increasing numbers of college students have been identified as having one or the other eating difficulty. Although eating disorders are included within disorders of childhood and adolescence in DSM-III, there are relatively few reports of early adolescents who are anorexic or bulimic. Rather, most of the research and treatment has taken place with college students.

There is something intriguing to professionals and lay people alike as to why intelligent, attractive young people are driven to starve and/or overeat and then to purge themselves by vomiting. These are life-threatening disorders that have been occuring with greater frequency (Crisp, 1980).

Anorexia Nervosa According to DSM-III, anorexia nervosa is a disorder characterized by self induced starvation, a fear of being fat, and amenorrhea in women (or a lowered sex drive in men). Although it is estimated to be nine times as common in women, it does occur in males as shown in the following two cases.

Case: Male Anorexic

Patient 1 was the youngest of identical triplets. Unlike his two brothers, he had always been an underachiever, he was overweight premorbidly. He developed anorexia nervosa at the age of 18, shortly after the death of his mother. After the onset of his illness he had intensive psychotherapy and was admitted five times in 5 years to a university psychiatric unit for feeding until he reached his target weight. He remained ill and was admitted to our hospital. His stay was stormy; on one occasion he took an overdose of drugs. After 6 months, he was discharged weighing 70 kg, but he lost weight rapidly. At this point paradoxical intention technique was used. The patient was told (1) that he should keep his illness; (2) that he seemed to gain the following benefits through his illness—he could punish his family for keeping his mother's illness a secret from him and for blaming him later for her death and his slimness represented a radical break with his "bad" past and made him look more like his two slim brothers; and (3) that he did not have to agree with our understanding of such "benefits" and that he could continue to be seen by us, if he so wished, to explore other issues. In the following session he explored his guilt about his past "bad" behavior and about his anger and hatred of his family. For 6 months he attended these sessions, during which time he maintained his weight at 90% average weight (Hsu & Lieberman, 1982).

Case: Female Anorexic

Patient 2, a registered nurse, developed anorexia nervosa at the age of 20 when she came to London for training in nursing. She began mixing with many "trendy" people and felt exceedingly uncomfortable because of her lower class background, and so she started dieting. Soon she resorted to vomiting and laxative or amphetamine abuse to control her weight. After 4 years of illness she was admitted to our hospital but her stay was a problematic one, during which time she contracted gonorrhea and attempted suicide by taking an overdose of drugs. During her stay in the hospital she reached her target weight, but after her discharge she lost weight rapidly. Her bulimia/vomiting/purging was uncontrollable, and she was admitted to a local psychiatric hospital. After her discharge from the psychiatric hospital and another suicide attempt by drug overdose, paradoxical intention techniques were used. It was suggested to her (1) that she should keep her illness because attempts to make her gain weight seemed to make her even more unhappy; (2) that her thinness had won her admiration from all; and (3) that her bulimia/vomiting/purging/amphetamine abuse was the price she had to pay for wanting to be different.

After six weekly sessions her bulimia/vomiting/laxative and amphetamine abuse improved, and she gradually reached 45 kg in weight. She was seen at weekly intervals for another 9 months, during which time she discussed issues of differentiation from her family and other relationship problems. Her weight steadied at 50 kg, and she was engaged to be married. Her eating pattern became normal, but she was still taking 2 laxative tablets daily. At followup 3 years later she was at normal weight (50 kg); she was working, married and enjoying a full social life. However, she still took up to 10 laxative tablets daily and tended to overeat if she felt bored. (Hsu & Lieberman, 1982)

Estimates of the incidence of anorexia nervosa vary from 0.1 percent in the general population (Robins et al., 1984) to 1 percent and 3 percent in the college population (Stangler & Printz, 1980; Halmi et al., 1981). These surveys consistently report a 9 to 1 ratio for women as opposed to men. Although there is not substantial support for an anorexia nervosa personality, people with this pattern have been described as perfectionistic, rigid, and self-critical. They tend to begin dieting when they are in their early teens in order to lose somewhere up to 20 pounds. Generally, they come from middle to upper-middle-class families that are going through some kind of stress (Andersen, 1983).

A major psychosocial explanation for anorexia nervosa is psychoanalytic (Lawrence, 1984). Early proponents of this approach implicated the pre-Oedipal period, specifically the oral stage, in the origins of this disorder. Because the person is fixated at this level, there is confusion between oral and the more mature, genital sexuality. When the person enters puberty, she may develop symbolic fears of becoming pregnant by eating. The confusion of oral and genital sexuality becomes expressed in self-starvation which is a way of symbolically preventing becoming pregnant.

Bruch (1974), in her analytic view of eating disorders, emphasized the struggle for control and competence, rather than confused sexuality as central to anorexia nervosa. Based on this view, she implicates the early mother-daughter interaction as the source of disturbed eating behavior. In Bruch's studies she found that mothers described their anorexic daughters as being very "good" children who were cheerful, happy, and friendly prior to showing the eating dysfunction. On the other hand, mothers were characterized as being overanxious and oversolicitous to the point of anticipating every need of their daughters. It is Bruch's opinion that mothers of anorexics form a symbiotic re-

To those suffering from anorexia nervosa, loss of weight is equated with health and beauty, even when the weight loss is severe. (*© 1982 Susan Rosenberg/Photo Researchers, Inc.*)

lationship with their daughters and do not allow them to develop senses of autonomy and independence. The daughters' starvation behavior is a way of continuing to please their mothers. While plausible, there has been little verification of this explanation except for single case studies such as that reported by Rampling (1980).

Rather than early mother-child difficulties, the systems perspective implicates communication patterns among all family members. There are two systems-based explanations, family and cultural. In the strategic family therapy approach (Palazzoli, 1974), families of anorexics are seen to be more prone to reject the messages of one another, to avoid taking leadership roles, to avoid taking the blame, and to form alliances between two people against a third. The anorexic person is involved in the conflict and competiveness that goes on between the parents. In structural family therapy (Minuchin et al., 1978), families of anorexics are seen as having poorly differentiated boundaries (enmeshed) that lead to family members being overinvolved with one another. In families like these there is little privacy, extreme rigidity, and overprotectiveness. The anorexic person plays a major role in maintaining the homeostasis of the family by helping the parents avoid their open conflicts through attending to the "sick" child.

Another systems-derived explanation focuses on the impact of the culture rather than the family on the anorexic person. Hsu (1983) suggests that the importance of physical attractiveness in western cultures plays an important role in the development of anorexia nervosa. He quotes the work of Garner et al. (1980) who analyzed the data from *Playboy* centerfolds and Miss America Pageant contestants over the past 20 years and found that there was a significant drop in the average weight of both groups of women. This is true in spite of the fact that according to actuarial statistics, the average weight of women below the age of 30 has significantly increased over the same time span. Hsu (1983) feels there is increasing pressure on women, especially those in the middle and upper classes to appear slim. It appears that attempts to become slim are rewarded with approval by friends and relatives (Branch & Eurman, 1980). With demands and rewards so high, some women are driven to become anorexic in an attempt to maintain their slimness and their popularity.

Biological explanations have been less evident than psychosocial or systems ones. Primarily, the hypothalamus has been hypothesized to be involved in an anorexic disorder. The hypothalamus is known to play a part in the regulation of feeding and

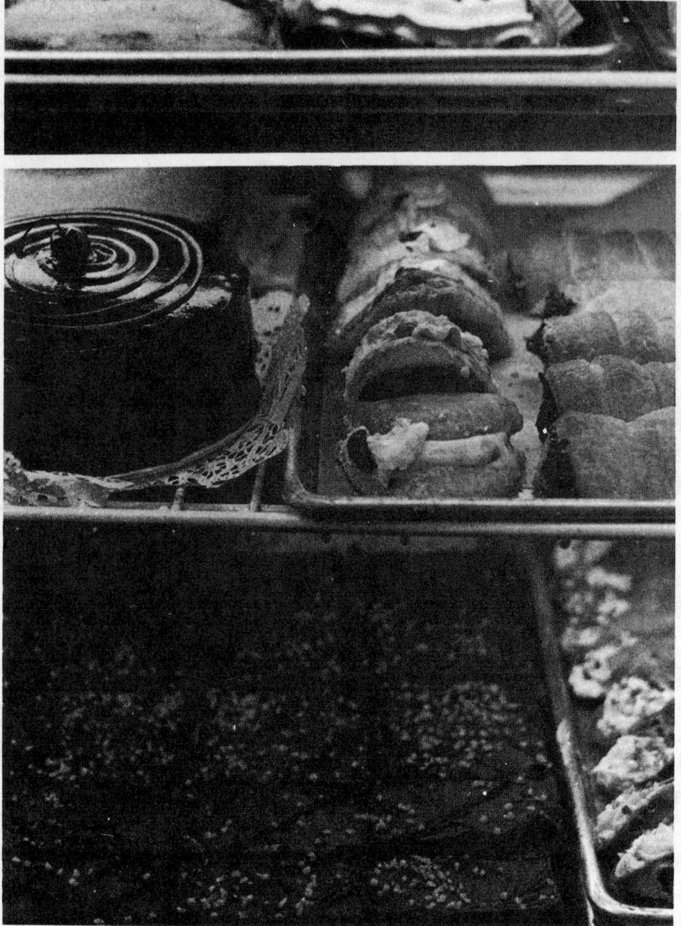

One of the foods most often binged on are pastries. (*Anthony A. Scaravilli*)

satiety. It is suggested that a hypothalamic dysfunction of unknown origin causes the disruption of eating behavior in anorexia nervosa (Russell, 1977). While it is possible that the hypothalamus may be involved in some significant way, convincing support has yet to be gathered.

Disagreements as to the causes of anorexia are reflected in disagreements about how best to treat the disorder. However, there seems to be consensus that because of the threat of serious illness, complications, or even death, hospitalization is often necessary (Lawrence, 1984). Professionals disagree about whether the patient should be forced to gain weight. Bruch (1974) feels that therapists should work with anorexics even if they have weight loss, whereas Crisp (1980) believes that weight gain is a prerequisite to other treatment.

Highest weight gain while hospitalized appears to result from a combination of drugs (chlorpromazine and insulin), bed rest, and a high calorie diet (Blinder et al., 1970). Lowest weight gain was found in hospital regimens that emphasized counseling and psychotherapy. At times operant techniques have been used to increase eating behavior in patients with some success (Brady & Brodie, 1978). However, there are others who believe that "... by adopting a stark, mechanistic and manipulative approach, one is often merely reconfirming for the anorectic her earlier experiences of life." (Crisp, 1980).

Family treatment approaches have also had some success with anorexics. Strategic family therapists reported that through the use of paradoxical prescription of symptoms they wanted to remove, 9 of 12 anorexics and their families showed significant improvement (Speed, 1984). Minuchin et al. (1978), on the other hand, seeks to change the interaction patterns in the family. If mealtime interactions are important to the maintenance of starving behavior, Minuchin may even have a family session during a lunchtime while the patient is hospitalized. Structural family therapists may also use intensive individual therapy in conjunction with family work to remove the anorexic's symptoms.

Regardless of approach, the symptoms of anorexia nervosa can be very difficult to change. Younger people who have had the symptoms for shorter durations have a better prognosis. Lawrence (1984) concluded that no more than 50 to 60 percent of the patients will ever make a complete recovery. For such a potentially dangerous disorder, this is a discouragingly low rate.

Bulimia Bulimia has only been officially viewed as a syndrome separate from anorexia nervosa since 1980. While bulimics share with anorexics an abnormal concern with being overweight, bulimics differ in that they may gain or lose weight and do not show amenorrhea. Bulimia is a disorder in which people lose control of the impulse to binge, ingest large amounts of food, and then use a variety of methods of purging so as to avoid weight gain. Binging may take place up to 12 times a week (Johnson & Larson, 1982), and each episode may involve up to 27 times the normal food intake (Abraham & Beumont, 1982). The foods most often binged upon are ice cream, bread toast, candy, doughnuts, soft drinks, salads, sandwiches, cookies, and popcorn (Mitchell et al., 1981). Usually binging is done alone and lasts about an hour.

Since binging is usually done in secret, it is difficult to obtain an accurate measure of its incidence. The few studies of its frequency have been done with college students. Stangler and Printz (1980) reviewed the diagnoses of 500 cases at the University of Washington Psychiatric Clinic and found that about 4.4 percent, or 22 cases had eating disorders; 19 of these 22 were bulimic. Another study showed that 13 percent of the students at a liberal arts college were bulimic. Occasional binging and purging were reported by 79 percent of females and 49 percent of males of varying weights surveyed in a large scale study (Hawkins & Clement, 1980). It appears that occasional binging and purging are very common in college students, and that binging and purging frequently enough to earn the classification of bulimia is relatively common in college females (9 to 1 compared with males).

Generally bulimia begins between the ages of 15 and 20, with a mean of about 18, usually following a period of voluntary dieting (Abraham & Beumont, 1982). The binging may be triggered by a variety of feelings such as depression, anger, or helplessness. If not treated, the disorder may last as long as 5 years (Johnson & Larson, 1982).

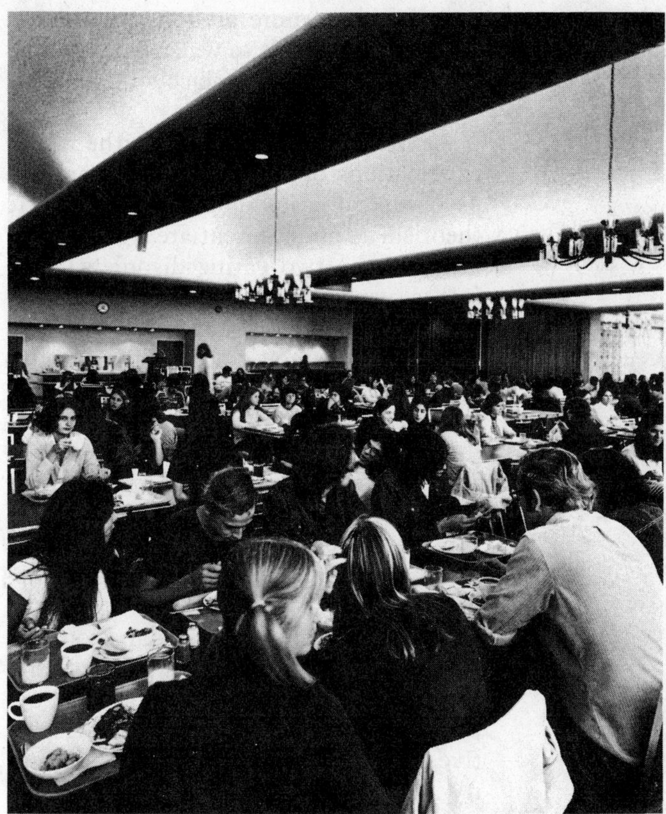

Eating usually fulfills social as well as physical needs. However, for those bulimics, binging and purging of food is done in secret. (*Hugh Rogers/Monkmeyer Press Photo Service*)

While not a necessary symptom, self-induced vomiting (purging) is frequently involved in bulimia. When it is a part of the disorder, it may lead to a variety of medical difficulties. The person may develop cavities and dental enamel erosion due to the intake of sweets and the acid in the vomitus. Continuous vomiting can also deplete the electrolyte balance which in turn can cause urinary infections and abdominal pain (Abraham & Beumont, 1982; Gandour, 1984).

Bulimics may be constantly preoccupied with thoughts of food. Retrospective studies suggest that bulimic people reported feeling more anxious, impulsive, alienated, and prone to wider mood swings than normal control subjects (Johnson & Larson, 1982).

As with anorexia nervosa, the major explanations of bulimia derive from the psychosocial paradigm. Psychoanalytic theorists do not differentiate significantly between the two eating disorders. Bulimia is seen to originate in pre-Oedipal rivalries and poor early object relationships that result in an overindentification with a passive father and hostility to an aggressive mother. This leads to sexual confusion in adolescence. Bulimics are seen as not as perfectionistic and rigid as anorexics. Gandour (1984) points out that this explanation does not explain bulimia in men and has yet to gather empirical support.

Another psychosocial explanation sees bulimia as arising from an extreme desire to attain some ideal of femininity. In opposition to the psychoanalytic perspective that assumes a rejection of femininity, this social learning explanation concludes that bulimics embrace femininity. Women learn early to adopt a passive approach to life that is reinforced by parents and friends. In adolescence, women have to deal with a desire for validation by men and a fear of men. From this perspective, binging takes on a sexual parallel in which overeating is seen as a sexual release. However, "like a good girl gone bad," feelings of guilt and shame follow the binging and lead to a resolve not to have food at all. While they are denying themselves food, bulimics feel in control of themselves and "good." Gandour (1984) criticizes this theory because like the psychoanalytic explanation it does not explain how bulimia develops in males nor does it account for the fact that some bulimic women have active and satisfying sex lives (Russell, 1979).

Gandour (1984) describes two explanations based on the biological perspective. In the first, hypothalamic malfunction is assumed based on abnormal EEGs reportedly found in a sample of bulimics (Green & Rau, 1975). However, the abnormal EEGs have failed to be replicated nor have bulimic people responded to anticonvulsive medication calculated to correct EEG-reflected brain dysfunction. In the second, it is proposed that binging is brought about because dieting has lowered weight to a "set point" below which the person becomes chronically hungry or produces a heightened salivary response to food (Klajner, et al., 1981). However, more research is needed to relate such physiological triggering mechanisms to binging episodes.

Since bulimia has been conceptualized as an independent disorder for a relatively short time, treatment approaches from any of the basic paradigms have been sparse and largely unsubstantiated. The psychosocial paradigm has given rise to a number of possible interventions. Psychoanalytic therapies have sometimes been applied strictly to bulimia, and behavioral interventions have been reported for single cases. For example, a female in her midtwenties who had been vomiting for 10 years was treated by (1) having herself monitor her food intake, vomiting behavior, and concurrent thoughts and feelings; (2) having her avoid foods and situations that were associated with vomiting; and (3) challenging her irrational beliefs about herself and her vomiting (Grinc, 1982). Through these procedures vomiting behavior was controlled within 10 months and had not reoccurred on 5-month follow-up. Other investigators have used cognitive-behavioral approaches to reduce bulimic behaviors by widening social activities (Long & Cordle, 1982).

Systems-based interventions have primarily been in the form of group psychotherapy. Boskind-Lodahl and White (1978) recruited people with binge-purge problems. Subjects were seen for 11 weekly group therapy sessions. They discussed topics such as hostility toward parents, independence, and fear and hatred of men. Group leaders attempted to make connections between feelings and eating and to help modify interactions with men and parents. A variety of therapy aids were used: role playing, diary keeping, and guided fantasy. Of the 12 participants, 4 stopped binging completely, 6 reduced their frequency of binging, and 2 showed no change. Long and Cordle (1982) pointed out that the approach may have been more successful if more attention had been paid to the eating patterns and subgroups of bulimics. It appears that group approaches are only moderately effective with bulimic subjects (Schlesier-Stropp, 1984).

When bulimic people show severely reduced weight, serious metabolic abnormalities, suicide intent, and failure in outpatient treatment programs they are candidates for hospitalization (Andersen, 1983). The goal of hospitalization is to break the bulimia-vomiting cycle through a variety of procedures. Behavioral techniques might be set up to control use of bathrooms after eating or to desensitize patients to foods that might make them anxious. If the patient shows depressive symptoms, antidepressant medication or electroconvulsive shock may be used. With the variety of treatments used in the hospital, it is nearly impossible to evaluate which are the critical elements in successful interventions.

Bulimia is recognized today as the complex disorder it truly is. There is a need for a multimodal research and treatment approach to identify those variables that are related to the origins and maintenance of this pattern of behavior and to reduce its impact on so many young people.

Apathy Reaction

We try to stop those who are suicidal or bulimic from acting on their impulses; with apathetic students, we might sometimes wonder if they have any impulses at all. Walters (1971) defines apathy in college students as "a state of reduced emotional lability, preoccupation with current work difficulties to the exclusion of past experiences and future expectations and an inability, in spite of constant effort, to study effectively" (p. 129).

Called erroneously *sophomore slump* by some, *apathy reaction* is much more than a drop in motivation and can affect the functioning of students regardless of their year of school. The apathetic student is more than merely uninterested, but "is reacting with profound, generalized disinterest over a longer period of time to less defined and often obscure circumstances (and) frequently hangs on to his disinterest until academic indolence results in his withdrawal or severance from college" (Walters, 1971, p. 145). Walters also points out that, unlike depressed people, apathetic students do not seem to be trying to obtain love and attention from the outside world; rather, they seem to have decided that the outside world does not have what they need. Because of this conclusion, their problem usually is not that they have the wrong educational or social goals, but that they have *no* goals. Apathetic students typically have spent little time thinking about or formulating goals and, as a result, they frequently are "committed to nothing."

We discovered in our own research (Nowicki & Duke, 1978) that all but one of our sample of apathetic students were male. They usually came to the attention of others during times of academic stress or decision and exhibited lack of interest in educational, social, and interpersonal matters. The most usual initial complaint involved the inability to concentrate on studies.

Walters (1971) concludes that apathy often may be used by the college student to anger and provoke others. He presents the following case history to show the characteristics of apathy and its provocative nature:

Case: Apathy Disorder

A 21-year-old college junior was referred for therapy because of the conviction that he was intellectually inferior to his friends because something (either heredity or a disease) had impaired his memory. He was a potentially bright, innately warm young man who had long substituted these gifts with uneven, mediocre performance and a defensively reserved manner. He was aggressive, but only in projects in gunsmithing and automobile mechanics where his considerable talents were well hidden from his outgoing and popular older brother and his eminently successful father with whom he was in passive competition. In therapy he soon worked through his feelings of intellectual inferiority and allowed himself academic success. His social defenses, however, proved more formidable. His innate warmth and compassion seemed to be sensed by fellow students and over his protests he was included in the usual social activities. In contrast his view of this was that his friends only felt sorry for him; and he could cite their inevitable exasperation that his passivity would ultimately produce as examples of their untrustworthiness. A turning point in therapy, however, began with his insight into the following incident: The patient was playing hockey with friends. The score was close and competitive spirit was high. The patient, however, reacted to this by a completely lackadaisical attitude. When the puck was passed to him, he would make a grossly ineffectual stab at it, miss it, and then slowly, even indolently, skate out of bounds to retrieve it. Quite naturally this soon reduced both sides into railing at the patient for his lack of spirit. The patient, quite predictably, assumed that they were angry and intolerant of his inadequacy. By clarifying this example, the therapist was able to point out how the patient had made both sides feel defeated, and thus was using "passive resistance" as a way of satisfying his own aggressive urges. By rationalizing this into inadequacy he protected himself from seeing the aggressive nature of his action (p. 139).

Disorders Associated with Academic Mechanics

Disorders associated with personal concerns affect personal functioning and are usually first detected by an individual's family, roommates, or friends. On the other hand, the problems of *academic mechanics*—difficulties associated with the technical tasks necessary for successful college-level work—are most likely to come to the attention of counselors, administrators, or faculty. Students may experience difficulties in studying or taking exams, either of which can be academically disastrous.

Daydreaming, inability to sit still for even short periods of time, inability to concentrate, memory impairment, lack of study skills, and the like can all be associated with difficulties in studying. Study disabilities can be either *general* (the student can study no subject at all) or *specific* (the student may do very well studying art, but has trouble with physics). Often referred to as a *mental block*, the inability to study may begin a vicious circle that produces more anxiety and more difficulty in studying. Students may find that they can not finish their assignments, so they fall behind and worry even more.

It has been our experience that the sudden onset of a general inability to study is often related to some transient life disturbance, such as family trouble or the breakup of a personal relationship. However, specific study disabilities are most frequently related to career-choice conflicts. For example, a premedical student who really wants to be an artist may find herself at the top of her art classes yet be unable to study organic chemistry. Inability to study often serves the purpose of calling parents' attention to the possibility that medicine or some other parentally approved career may no longer be the student's choice.

Unlike study difficulties, in which the student does not learn the required academic materials, in *test-taking difficulties* the student may know the material but be unable to show this knowledge. Also referred to as *test anxiety* (Mandler & Sarason, 1952), these difficulties are characterized by extreme incapacitating anxiety either during exams or just before them. The test-anxious student may miss the exam or take it and do poorly. Typically, test-anxious students study very hard for exams and believe that they "know their stuff." However, as the exam nears, these students usually experience a specific sequence of events (Wine, 1971). First, they begin to doubt their own knowledge—other students obviously know more than they do—they will never be able to pass. Second, the student tends to overvalue the importance of the test. That is, the test comes to be more than a measure of knowledge in a course; it becomes an indication of a student's self-worth. It appears that test-anxious people may "worry" too much (Wine, 1971). The worry may be associated with self-talk characterized by negative statements about themselves that interferes with their performance on the task at hand.

Besides worry (which is primarily cognitive), test anxiety also consists of a feeling component (which is primarily physiological). Recent work suggests that high and low test-anxious individuals do not differ in overall emotionality (physiological arousal) when at rest (Smith & Morris, 1976) or when taking examinations (Holroyd et al., 1978). Tryon (1980) concluded that worry and not physiological emotionality has a negative effect on performance. However, because questionnaires that attempt to separate the worry and emotionality components of test anxiety are easy to fake, Tryon cautions that a "treatment that results in a decrease in self-reported test anxiety may not result in an increase in grades" (p. 348). Therefore, the worth of any treatment intervention with test-anxious college students should be measured by improvement in grades and not by changes in self-reported test anxiety scores.

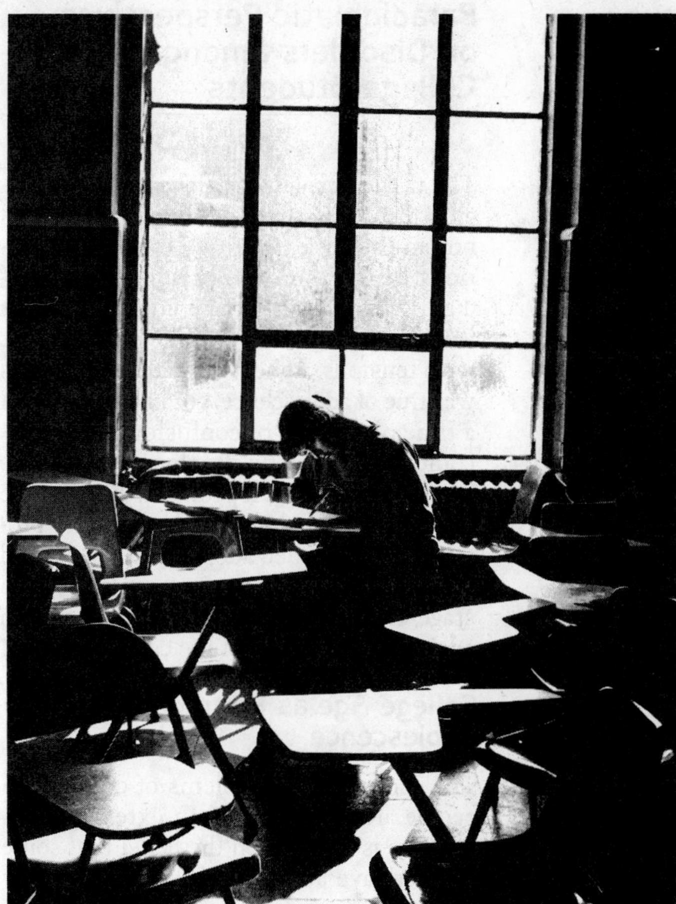
Even when they know the material, those who are test anxious suffer doubts about their abilities and worry to the point that it negatively affects their performance. (*Rogers/Monkmeyer Press Photo Service*)

What seems to differentiate treatments that change grade performance from those that do not is a focus on changing the thinking process. Treatment programs that help the college student to adopt better strategies of studying and to reduce the worry that interferes with processing of test information have been the most successful (see Holroyd, 1976; Allen, 1973).

Paradigmatic Perspectives on Disorders among College Students

The task of explaining the sources of specific disorders among college students is not an easy one. The two major explanations derive from the psychosocial paradigm. It is clear that the college student is living through a time of life often fraught with tensions, upheavals, and turmoil. As was true of adolescence, college age is often a time of growth, of confusion, and of accomplishing specific developmental tasks. We present two perspectives. First is the view that the college student is in a protracted or extended adolescence. A second theory is that college-age people are in a stage of life different and separable from adolescence—a stage of life called "youth."

College Age as Protracted Adolescence

The concept that problems of college age people are the result of an extended adolescence is based upon the belief that some people leave adolescence chronologically before they are ready psychologically. In other words, many people of college age have not completely resolved adolescent confusion, or established social, sexual, or personal identity. The result of these incomplete adolescent tasks can be that difficulties are carried over into the college years (Levinson, 1978; Ryle, 1969).

Entering college may be seen as a major transitional step toward adulthood, a step in which the authority of parents may be replaced in the student's mind by the less frequently used, yet nevertheless present, power of the college administration. Some people, therefore, view student unrest and rebellion as a continuation and displacement of incomplete adolescent rebellion. Problems among college students can then be seen as reflecting a lack of adequate role development in adolescence. According to the protracted-adolescence theory, when problems arise for the college student, the symptoms will "generally take the form of a re-enactment in the present situation of those conflicts not resolved in earlier stages" (Ryle, 1969, p.27). College age, then, may be a continuation of adolescence—a late adolescence, if you will. Those remaining out of the mainstream of adulthood, those who do not begin careers immediately after high school, those whom we call "college students" are—according to the protracted-adolescence theory—destined to continue their adolescence long after their peers have made the transition to adult productivity and adjustment.

College Age as a Separate Life Stage of "Youth"

Many people are not comfortable with the concept of a 22-year-old still being in a protracted adolescence. One such person is Keniston (1970, 1975), who has noted that, although many college-age people are indeed "victims of stretched adolescence, many others are less impelled by juvenile grandiosity than by a rather accurate analysis of the perils or injustices of the world in which they live" (1975, p. 304). For Keniston, modern society is markedly different from the one in which Hall (1904) first noted the emergence of adolescence as a separate stage of life. With the increased emphasis on advanced education, there is a delay of entry into adulthood for an increasingly large number of young people. Keniston notes that, whereas in the 1900s there were only 238,000 college students, in the 1990s an estimated 10 million people (8 million of them between the ages of 18 and 25) will be enrolled in U.S. colleges. According to Keniston, social change seems to have produced a new developmental period, a period he has named "youth."

Like adolescence, youth is a transitional stage (not an end point) that occurs between the end of adolescence and the beginning of adulthood. The college student, who apparently delays entry into adulthood by enrolling for advanced education, probably belongs to the youth stage. According to Keniston, the presence of 10 major themes determines youth, not necessarily college student status alone.

Keniston outlines the following defining characteristics of youth:

1. *Tension between self and society*. Whereas the adolescent typically is struggling to define who he or she is, the youth usually knows and often recognizes great disparity between his or her self and the larger society.
2. *Pervasive ambivalence*. Ambivalence may be felt toward self and society. Rejection of the adolescent self may result in efforts at transformation of the self through meditation, drugs, or religion. Ambivalence also occurs between the autonomous self and the socially involved self.
3. *The wary probe*. Serious forays into the adult world characterize youth. Adolescent probes or experimental youthful probes can lead to permanent commitment. Self-probes begin as well—"What are my strengths, weaknesses, and vulnerabilities?"
4. *Alternating estrangement and omnipotentiality*. Feelings of isolation, absurdity, or unreality in an interpersonal social and phenomenological world may occur. "Who am I?" "Why am I here?" Also common are feelings of omnipotentiality—of total freedom, of being able to change or do anything, of being able to change others' lives completely, to do the socially impossible.
5. *Refusal of socialization*. In youth, earlier socializations may be criticized and questioned; the conformity of adolescence may be rejected. Attempts may be made to probe new social rules and to resist "capitulating."

Keniston believes that youth is defined by a number of characteristics such as refusal of socialization and emergence of youth-specific identities. (*Anthony A. Scaravilli*)

6. *Emergence of youth-specific identities*. Youthful identities usually do not pass so quickly as those of adolescence or become so rigid as those of the adult. The identities may last from a few months to as many as ten years and include attachment to groups such as yuppies, radicals, Moon children. Some youth-specific identities may be maintained as foundations for later life, but most seem to be abandoned.
7. *Valuing of movement and change*. Youth requires change; staying in one place physically or psychologically for too long often results in tension and imbalance. There are needs to move the self (that is, to grow); needs to move others (for example, attempts at political change); and needs to move through the world (to travel with great restlessness). Stasis seems to produce terror.
8. *Halting of movement may be seen as "death."* The greatest fear of youth probably is being unable to change, to "lose one's essential vitality." In some cases, suicide may be preferable to loss

of movement potential or failure to effect desired changes.

9. *Adults may be viewed as "static" nonbeings*. Youths often see growing up as a cessation of living. The slower developmental changes of adulthood may be seen as complete stoppage; growing up may be a feared and avoided event.
10. *Emergence of youthful counterculture*. In hopes of staving off adulthood, solidarity with other youths is often established. Specific groups and entire youth culture may develop so that deliberate distance from the existing social order can be maintained.

Keniston notes that youths tend to view adulthood as marked by "stasis, decline, foreclosure and death." However, he also indicates that youth may anticipate adulthood eagerly, because in adulthood there usually are financial security, career productivity, and other indicators of success. Youth is thus a confusing time, a time that, according to Keniston, is a psychological stage not rigidly equated with any specific age range. It is a time of radicalism, of social action, a time when the themes of adolescent development may be outgrown, but the commitment to adulthood may not yet be made.

Paradigmatically Based Treatments for College Student Disorders

Interventions for college student disorders are found primarily in the psychosocial and systems paradigms. We have already mentioned specific treatments for the eating disorders, but the general interventions we are going to describe also can be applied to these as well.

The Psychosocial Paradigm: Individual Psychotherapy

Although most forms of traditional psychotherapy may be applicable to the college student, there are a number of differences between the college population and the general population that are worthy of mention. Not only are most college students in a specialized, highly structured, and scheduled environment, but, as a group, they tend to be more intelligent, more critical, more ready to change, and more difficult to impress with titles and complex terms. Based upon these and other special qualities of the college student, Whittington (1963) has described a number of general characteristics of college student therapy. First of all, change usually is more rapid among college students; the average number of therapy sessions is about five (Nowicki & Duke, 1978; Whittington, 1963). Further, rather than awaiting the establishment of trust and rapport, college students tend to be more open and self-disclosing earlier in therapy. Third, college students, with their youth, vitality, and frequent charm, can be quite distracting to therapists.

In addition to changing more quickly, being more open and more distracting, college students tend to experience more extreme reactions to their therapists than do people in the general population. Another difference is that therapy with college students may be especially difficult owing to the campus skepticism that often surrounds seeing therapists and to the fact that some college student clients may know a great deal about psychology, psychiatry, and personality theory as compared with their noncollege peers. A last difference is that there are many times in the college student's life when situational variables such as finals, midterms, and term papers may interfere with the smooth progress of therapy. This effect of scheduling upon psychotherapy can be critically felt when therapy may have to terminate prematurely due to the end of the school year or other cyclical breaks. Therapists working with people from other sectors of the population rarely have to stop therapy for a summer break.

In addition to the points made by Whittingon, the availability of psychological help to the college student is an important facet of college life. Most other people in the 18 to 29 age group do not have such easy access to facilities like college counseling centers and campus mental health centers. At these centers, college students usually can find immediate and competent help with any of the problems we described earlier. However, many centers do not offer treatment for psychotic disturbances, although they do help severely disturbed students find appropriate sources of care. Typical counseling centers may offer vocational guidance, group therapy, individual therapy, and testing for abilities, intelligence and personality. Center staffs usually are composed of professionally trained psychotherapists.

Individual therapy with college students usually involves a one-to-one relationship between a troubled student and a trained therapist. Meeting once or twice a week for an hour over a relatively brief period of time (usually 5 to 20 weeks), the therapist and client attempt to use their relationship to ease the problems for which the student first came for help. The therapist's intervention perspective can vary, but may include Gestalt, reality, or other kinds of generally humanistic-existential approaches. Therapy with college students is not always easy as is demonstrated in the following excerpt from the fourth meeting with an individual therapy client at a college counseling center.

Personal Experience: Individual Therapy with College Students

Therapist: OK, so how do you feel about what she said?

Client: I don't like it! I mean, she tells me that she loves me and then turns around and goes out with Bob!

Therapist: So, you are very angry about what she did?

Client: Wait a minute! Do you think I'm dumb or something? You sit there "reflecting my feelings." Christ, I know about Carl Rogers. "So you are very angry about what she did." Now I'm supposed to say, "Yes, I am." Then you empathize with me and show me you care about me and unconditionally accept me.

Therapist: What's this all about?

Client: You tell me that you sincerely care about me. I have trouble believing it. You have to see me. I don't believe you care about me—my case, maybe, but not me.

Therapist: You're really angry at me and I don't really know why. I wish you'd put aside all this about Rogers and cases and all and tell me what your real feelings are toward me.

Client: You're almost my same age. How can you help me? You're hung up on your own problems. How the hell can you help me?

Therapist: I can help if you let me try. If you would try to relate to me as a person. I think you relate to others in the same way you're relating to me now. You jump at their motives and don't look at them. Now you started the conversation with a gripe about Janet; how is your reaction to me similar to the reaction you had to Janet's going out with Bob?

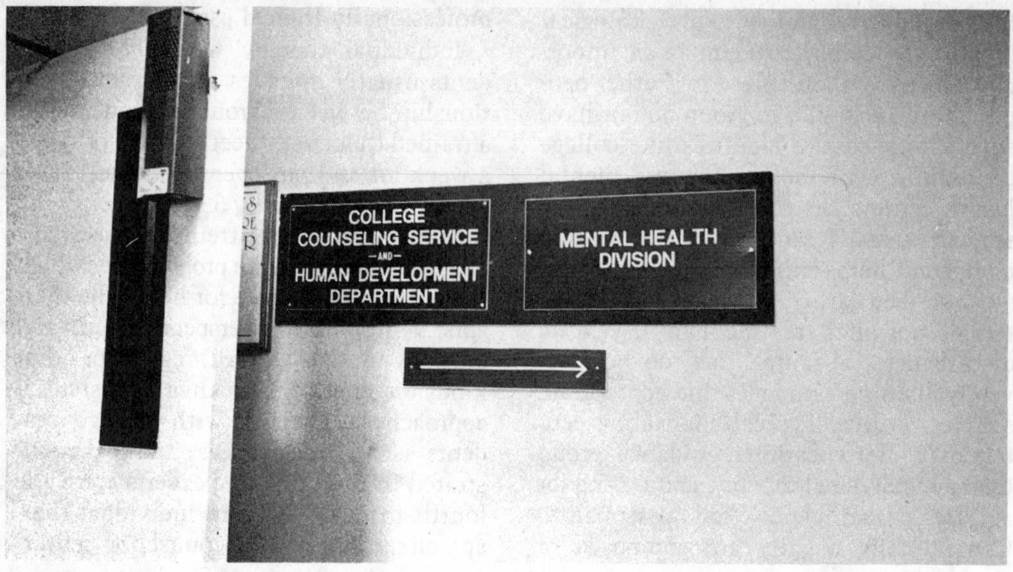

It's the rare college that does not have mental health professionals available to help students. (© *Beryl Goldberg*)

Individual therapy with college students can be very challenging. The student mentioned in the personal experience seemed to find it difficult to relate to the therapist because they were close in age. There are other difficulties facing the student seeking counseling help on a college campus. Possibly, the therapist will be known to the students and may interact with the student in other situations such as the classroom. There is a good chance that the therapist and client will run into each other in any number of other places on the campus or in the community. It is important for parties involved to discuss these possibilities and maintain confidentiality for what occurs in the therapy situation.

The Systems Paradigm: Group Therapy

With regard to the special nature of college student therapy groups, there are several things of note. For instance, many college students have been in groups before and may bring some positive and negative expectations with them to their present therapy groups; these expectations can be either helpful or destructive. In addition, many college students know about group therapy and may resist standard group techniques that are effective with others. One result of this resistance can be hostile, open challenges to the competence of the leader. A third characteristic of college student groups is that they are often marked by frequent early termination, and by additions of new members as the academic year progresses. Further, the fact that students, especially on small campuses, often see each other between group sessions can make it difficult to keep all group business confidential. Sometimes conflicts begun and not resolved in a group session will be resolved between sessions, cutting off the majority of members from being involved in important group interactions (Brandes & Gardner, 1973). Some of the special characteristics of college student groups may be seen in the following excerpt from a group held in a college counseling center.

Personal Experience: Group Therapy with College Students

Jim: I really like the way this group is run.
Therapist: Are you being sarcastic?
Jim: Of course!
Sue: You're always complaining. I think this is a good group.
Jim: Well, I've been in groups before and . . .
Art: There he goes, telling us how much better he is than we are—"I've been in groups before!"
Therapist: It seems that you use your being in groups before to keep yourself out of this one.
Jim: If it gets to be good, I'll expend my energy and take part. Right now I'm just watching.
Bob: Goddammit, Jim, you pompous ass, I get so mad at you. You sit there and watch us. Who the hell do you think you are?
Art: Ditto. You really have a lot of nerve. We sit here and expose ourselves. You sit smugly by.
Therapist: What does the group think we can do about Jim's feeling toward us?
Art: Ask him to leave.
Sue: But he's here for a reason. Maybe Jim can't admit he wants help.
Therapist: Jim?
Jim: I'm just listening.
Therapist: Let's let Jim listen for a while. When he feels he can share his real feelings with us we'll be ready to hear them. Bob, what's been going on with you?

The Psychosocial Paradigm: Behavior Therapy

In addition to individual and group "talk" therapies, behavior therapy is frequently used with college students. Behavior therapy differs from traditional individual and group therapies in its primary focus on behavior as opposed to feelings. By using systematic variation of reinforcement, punishment, and extinction, behavior therapists can increase or decrease the frequencies of many desirable or undesirable behaviors. Although a number of student problems are existential and therefore not easily treated by behavior therapy, some "habit" problems, such as test anxiety, may be altered by behavioral methods.

There are several approaches to the behavioral treatment of test anxiety. Kotska and Galassi (1974) have described two. In *systematic desensitization*, groups of 8 to 10 students usually meet weekly. Through the repeated pairing of physical relaxation with thoughts of taking exams, these subjects can learn to face tests much more calmly. *Covert reinforcement* (Cautela, 1970a), a second approach, involves the students' imagining that they are without anxiety during test situations and following these thoughts, "rewarding" themselves by imagining an especially pleasurable scene (natural, gastronomic, or sexual). Kotska and Galassi reported that both of these techniques were useful in reducing test anxiety.

In addition to desensitization and covert reinforcement, extinction of fear and establishment of an expectation of success in exams are used in the treatment of severe test anxiety, as illustrated by the following case history.

Case: Test Anxiety

The client was a fifth-year graduate student in history who had attempted three times to take and pass his Ph.D. qualifying exams. Each time, he had failed even to finish the timed test owing to his inability to be satisfied with any one particular answer. As a result of his dissatisfaction, he spent most of the exam time rewriting one or two questions and worrying about possible imperfections. He was told that he would be required to complete and pass the next exam he was given; if he didn't, he would be dropped from the Ph.D. program.

Treatment involved specific training in relaxation so that he could control his tension during exams. Next, a series of 10 Ph.D. qualifying exams was prepared with the help of the more than cooperative history department faculty. Each week for 10 weeks, this student came to the psychological center and took a 3-hour Ph.D. qualifying exam. During the exam, the therapist monitored his behavior, requiring the student to divide the test into time units and not to allow himself to work on an item for more than the allotted time. In this way, his finishing the exam was guaranteed, and he did so by the end of the fifth week. In addition, he learned to outline the answers to each question more efficiently before writing the full essay; using this method, he found he was quite satisfied with his work.

One week after the tenth practice exam, he took the "eleventh" exam. He passed quite easily and reported no difficulty with tension, problems in timing, or coming up with satisfactory answers. He had learned through his practice exams that he could easily schedule himself and finish, and that he could complete the essays satisfactorily within the time allotted to him.

The Systems Paradigm: Community Approaches

The treatment approaches we have discussed thus far focus on the problems of the individual alone or of the individual with a small group of peers. Community approaches, however, focus on the college community itself. Moreover, the individual, group, and behavioral treatment approaches primarily evolve from a basic therapeutic position of passivity toward the student. That is, the therapist usually waits in his or her office for the troubled student to come for help. In contrast, advocates of community approaches propose going out to offer help where the students are, on the student's home ground, at a time when students need it.

Surprisingly few satisfactory community programs are found on college campuses. It may be, as Brigante (1965) pointed out some time ago, that many members of the academic world have a negative view of community efforts. Most of the successful interventions have involved impacting on college residence halls. The manner in which students live can have significant effects on the development of disordered behavior. For example, while placing three students in a living unit may save the university money, recent work suggests that that particular arrangement may not be optimal for positive social interaction. Baum et al. (1979) investigated the impact of having two or three stu-

Community psychology interventions are characterized by going out to where the students are, working with groups and helping to build strength to combat the development of disordered behavior. (*Strickler/Monkmeyer Press Photo Service*)

dents in bedroom units on developing interpersonal relationships. They used a variety of means to gather information about the triads and concluded that the three-person group is inherently an unstable one that inevitably leads to one of the three students being left out. Most of the time two-person coalitions are formed with the third person being excluded from group activities. Not too surprisingly, it usually was the third student who ended up complaining to housing deans about the physical living arrangements and feeling crowded.

One example of a college community intervention program was developed at Emory University (Nowicki & Duke, 1982). As with most other programs (Bloom, 1977) the major emphasis was on prevention and early detection of disordered behavior (primary and secondary prevention). A major feature of this intervention is the freshmen residence program. Groups of freshmen met weekly with at least two faculty or staff members of the Emory community. At these weekly meetings a wide variety of topics was discussed. Group interactions were calculated to introduce these freshmen more easily into the Emory community and reduce the stress associated with beginning college. At various times during the year, personnel from the counseling center attended the meetings. At times they were there to answer questions should they come up or to participate in the discus-

Table 17-1 Types of Calls Received by a Campus Help line

Problem Area	*Number of Calls*	*Percentage*
Dating	66	29
Family	40	19
Loneliness	28	12
Pregnancy	22	9
Classes	21	9
Finances	8	3
Marriage	7	3
Drugs	6	2
Alcohol	5	2
Other*	28	12
Total	231	100

*Such as obesity, insomnia, selective service, employment, religion, housing.
Source: From B. J. Tucker, D. Megenity, and L. Virgil, "Anatomy of a Campus Crisis Center," *Personnel and Guidance Journal,* 1970, *48*(5), 343–348. Copyright 1970 by the American Personnel and Guidance Association. Reprinted by permission.

sion as a member of the group. Other times they might make a major presentation. Some sample topics were "anticipating crises during the freshmen year" and "learning how to relax."

The counseling center also was involved in the second focus of the community program, the residence halls. Center staff were assigned as consultants to residence advisors who lived in the residence halls. They met weekly with residence hall advisors to discuss difficulties certain students were having and the best way to respond to them. If a particular set of student problems repeated themselves, it might be addressed by a workshop presentation. For example, it became apparent that a number of students were having difficulties controlling their dieting and eating behaviors. In response to this problem, during the meeting with the counseling center staff person, the residence hall advisor suggested that a talk might be in order describing bulimia and other eating problems. While the staff person was not an expert in that area, she was able to contact another staff member who could set up a workshop on this problem area. As a direct result of this presentation, two of the residence hall students initiated counseling for their eating problems. Meetings were also held biweekly between the head of the counseling center and the head of residence life to discuss any system wide stressors that might be contributing to overall tension, and to find ways to make the campus a more positive place to be. A number of projects such as athletic events and concerts resulted from these and other meetings to help reduce stress and increase positive mental health on the campus.

In addition to programs initiated by professionals on college campuses, some community treatment interventions have been started by students themselves. Most of these student-initiated interventions involve the development of *hotlines*. These projects allow some students to help others who want someone to listen to them when they are troubled. Especially prevalent during the late 1960s, the number of student-intiated programs seems to have decreased, perhaps because, in response to the needs of students, professionals now often provide such crisis counseling.

Although the number of student-initiated interventions has decreased in recent years, the use of undergraduate and graduate students as helping agents by mental health professionals has increased. Usually in such programs, student volunteers are trained in telephone counseling and in role playing. Meetings are scheduled to discuss the kinds of problems being called in (see Table 17-1) and the methods for dealing with them. Telephone hotlines may be staffed at times such as late afternoons, evenings, and weekends, when other helping agencies are often closed. It is difficult to evaluate such programs formally, but hotline facilities seem to have been very helpful on campuses. Further, besides helping the troubled student, these programs give student volunteers positive experiences within the academic community.

In many community interventions, college students work with advisors to plan programs to reduce stress. (*Strickler/Monkmeyer Press Photo Service*)

Personal Experience: Working on a Help Line

I am finishing up my second and last year on the help line. This is a good chance to try and put the last 2 years into perspective. I remember starting. I was going to save the world. I expected that I would be glued to the phone for hours at a time in some life and death struggle to save someone's life. When I started training I couldn't wait to get on the phones. I didn't realize that not everyone can be a phone volunteer. I had to go through an initial interview, than a second and third one before I finally was allowed to "officially" begin my training. Training was hard. I had to learn to be caring without being sickly sweet. I had to learn some very important things about how I came across to others . . . some weren't so nice. I guess that's one of the best things about my experience; I grew up alot. I remember one day I got into an emotional role-playing situation with the instructor. The crux of it was that I got really angry at the role the instructor was playing. He wouldn't listen to me! In essence at the end of the role play, the man the instructor was role-playing chose to kill himself. And, I believe that if he were the real thing, he would have done the same thing. Because I was so selfish and thought I was so neat, I could have killed a person. That experience sobered me. I never realized how much of a little kid I still was. It was time to grow up. I made it through the rest of my training and I had my share of interesting phone calls to handle. Most of the time the callers were people from campus, but every once in a while I dealt with someone from the general community. I think I've helped a few people over the last 2 years, but I think that the experience has helped me more. I am now helping to train the new people this year and I try to give them what I've learned. It's nice to be a part of a college campus in this way.

Minority students are also a focus of community programs. At most campuses, although minority students are a population at risk and under considerable stress, they generally underuse counseling center services. To meet this problem, Wood (1980) developed a model for counseling minority students in which they are made aware of the counseling services via nontraditional means. For example, with the assistance of peer counselors, center staff go out on campus to meet with minority students and let them know about services. Counseling services are changed to be less formal and more group- than individual-oriented. The group sessions are closer to "rapping" than formal group therapy. Black, Asian-American, Mexican-American, and multiethnic "rap" groups have been employed. The program has been very effective in increasing the minority students' contacts with the counseling center.

Such community approaches may hold promise for dealing with problems on college campuses. If the college environment can be changed to make it less stressful and more liable to provide reinforcements, the pressures that play a role in the development of disordered behaviors may be reduced.

Concluding Comments

In this chapter we have examined some of the specific problems associated with the college experience. However, while we have described students primarily, it is also the responsibility of college counselors, deans, and faculty to make the college experience a positive one. More and more of such college personnel are realizing that the "mental health" of an elite group of young men and women is in their hands, and they need to exert all efforts to reduce psychological stress. The temporary or permanent loss of any of these young people because of psychological problems may reduce their potential to contribute to society as a whole and to themselves as individuals. Also, as we will see in the next chapter, difficulties unresolved at this point in development may predispose college students to develop psychological disorders later in their life. College students are among our brightest citizens, and we expect much from them. They deserve and will probably make good use of any help and support we can give them. We believe that, with reduced stresses and increased availability of help, more college students will be able to realize their potential and face the challenges of continuing life transitions with confidence.

Summary Chart

There are special benefits in being a college student—and special stresses and patterns of disturbance as well. In Chapter 17, we began with a look at some of the forms of these special problems:

Disorders associated with the college years: Specific risks for college students
Disorders associated with nonacademic personal concerns: Identity crisis, suicide, anorexia, bulimia, apathy reaction
Disorders associated with academic mechanics: Study blocks, test anxiety

Several paradigmatically based views of the college years have helped explain some of their special stresses:

College as protracted adolescence
College as a separate stage of life called "youth"

Both the psychosocial and the systems paradigms have been applied in the treatment of disorders among college students:

Individual therapy
Group therapy
Behavior therapy
Community approaches
Telephone hotlines

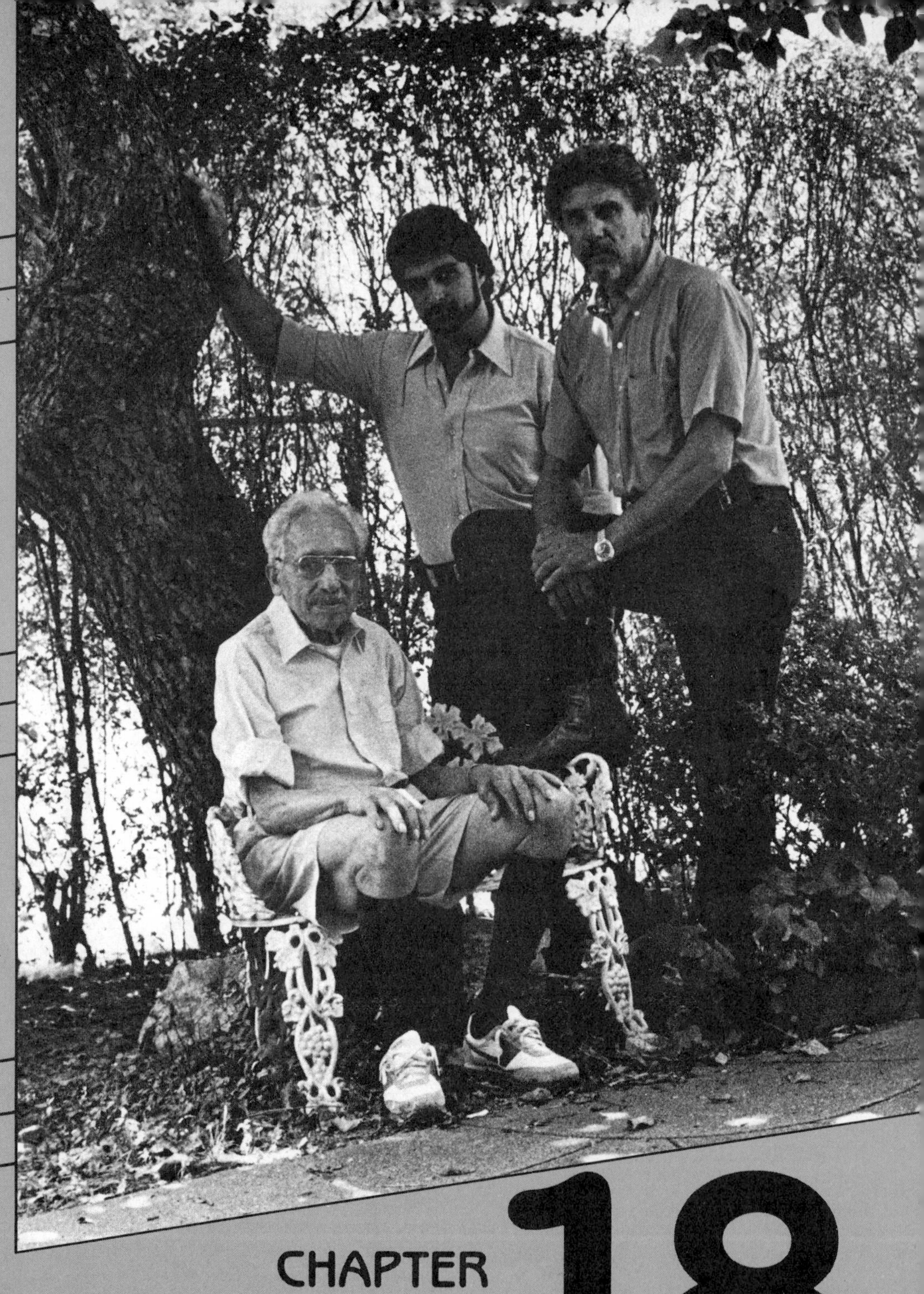

CHAPTER 18

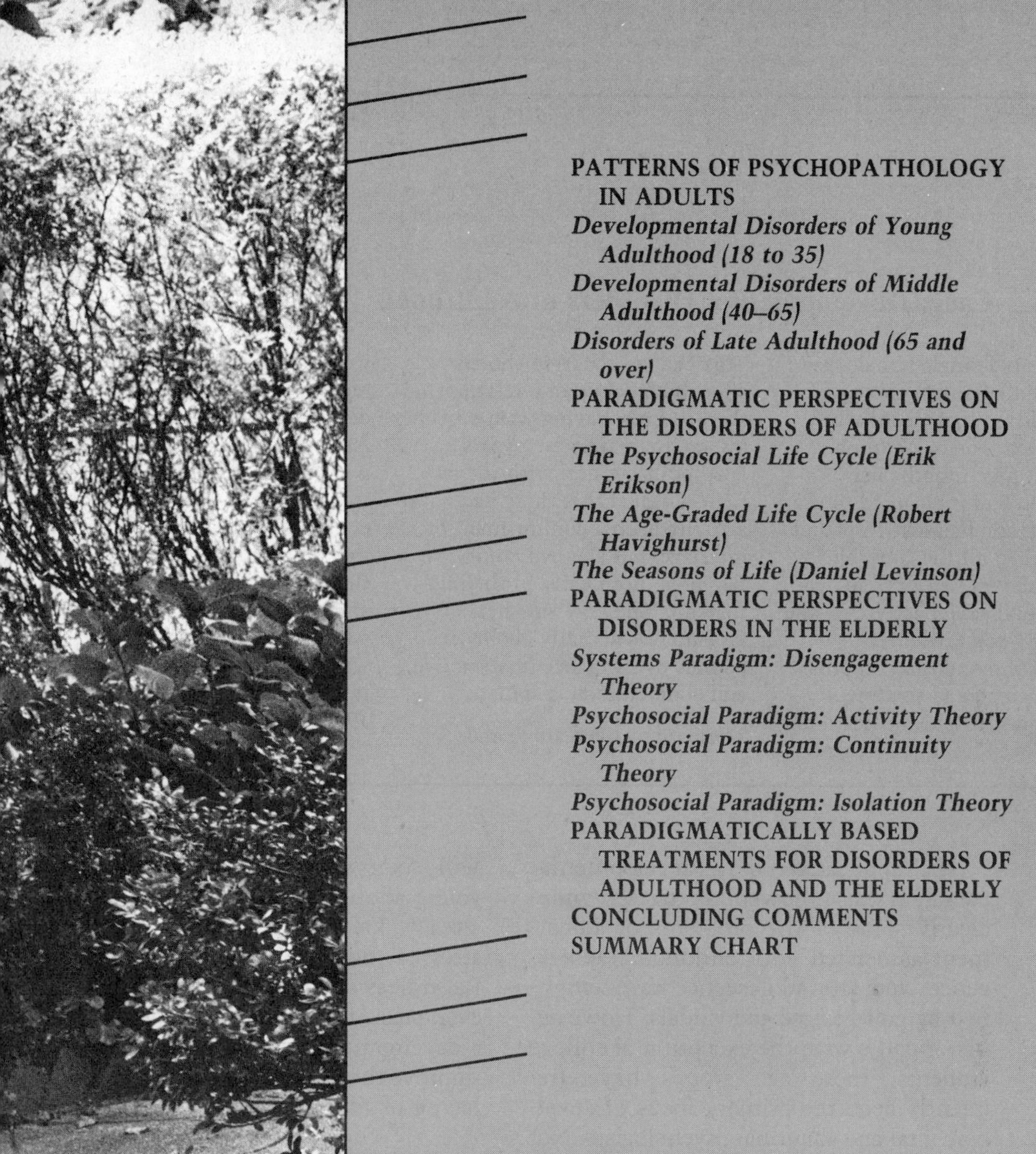

PATTERNS OF PSYCHOPATHOLOGY IN ADULTS
Developmental Disorders of Young Adulthood (18 to 35)
Developmental Disorders of Middle Adulthood (40–65)
Disorders of Late Adulthood (65 and over)
PARADIGMATIC PERSPECTIVES ON THE DISORDERS OF ADULTHOOD
The Psychosocial Life Cycle (Erik Erikson)
The Age-Graded Life Cycle (Robert Havighurst)
The Seasons of Life (Daniel Levinson)
PARADIGMATIC PERSPECTIVES ON DISORDERS IN THE ELDERLY
Systems Paradigm: Disengagement Theory
Psychosocial Paradigm: Activity Theory
Psychosocial Paradigm: Continuity Theory
Psychosocial Paradigm: Isolation Theory
PARADIGMATICALLY BASED TREATMENTS FOR DISORDERS OF ADULTHOOD AND THE ELDERLY
CONCLUDING COMMENTS
SUMMARY CHART

Disorders Associated with Adulthood and Aging

Case: Developmental Disorders of Adulthood

A 38-year-old single female was referred for cognitive therapy. . . . Her condition had recently become much worse. Within a period of three months her depression had intensified to the point that she had lost 15 pounds, she felt tired all the time, she had withdrawn herself from nearly all her usual social activities, and she openly acknowledged thoughts of overdosing on pills. Psychotherapy and treatment with antidepressant medication had produced no improvement. This change occurred shortly after the breakup of a relationship she had been having with a man for approximately two years. Further discussion with the patient revealed that there had never actually been a commitment of marriage, but she had clung to this hope from early in the relationship. She now saw herself as fat (she was actually about 10 pounds overweight), unattractive, and doomed to be a spinster.

The patient lived alone and worked full-time as a pediatric nurse while pursuing a master's degree in nursing part-time. Although she had never had a wide circle of friends, the past two years had seen her social contacts become even more limited. Other than the few evenings that she spent with her boyfriend, she had gradually managed to work herself into a life of all work and no play, and she was intensely lonely. (Spitzer et al., 1983, p. 127)

The application of a developmental paradigm has allowed us to see more clearly some of the problems of adjustment associated with childhood, adolescence, and late adolescence as exemplified by college-aged individuals. However, historically, with the exception of college students, these age groups have frequently been the primary focus of developmental and abnormal psychologists. Not until recently has there been a major concerted focus on the developmental problems of adults over the age of 21. The focus is especially timely since in the United States 45 percent of our population is now over 35 and 11 percent are 65 years of age or older. The life expectancy of individuals living in the United States in 1983 has risen from an average of 51.4 years in 1900 to 76.4 for women and from 48.2 years to 68.7 for men. In fact, presently over 100,000 Americans are 100 years of age or older.

Most readers of this textbook fall into the late adolescent, college aged group who will soon experience a transition into young adulthood. Readers who are older already know first hand some of the stresses that await their younger peers. Regardless of the age of the reader, however, presentation of adult disorders within a developmental framework may help to improve the understanding of unusual behavior of adults throughout the age span.

Patterns of Psychopathology in Adults

As people grow older, they are faced with a continuous series of developmental tasks. While some transitional tasks are defined by a marker age, like 65 for retirement, or biological events such as cessation of menses in women's menopause, others are not tied to any particular chronological age or event (Wortley and Amatea, 1982). However they occur, transitional tasks can cause significant stress that, if not handled correctly, can result in *transitional disorders*. While serious in themselves, over time adult transitional problems can also eventually turn into more traditional DSM-III disorders.

Developmental Disorders of Young Adulthood (18 to 35)

We begin the description of adult developmental disorders by focusing on two classes of problems associated with the early adult years. During this time the critical choices of mate and occupation must be made. Since about 97 percent of people in the United States marry, and nearly that many work, problems in either area can have farreaching consequences (Lidz, 1980). The pursuit of either a career or marriage can result in at least two identifiable transitional disorders: the *isolation disorder* in younger adults and the *thirties crisis* in somewhat older adults. The description of these entities derives from the work of various professionals like Levinson (1978) and Lidz (1980).

We are all part of a continual process of growth and change. (© *Richard Frieman/Photo Researchers, Inc.*)

Isolation Disorder

Similar to the identity disorders experienced by adolescents and college students, isolation disorders are characterized by intensive feelings of "aloneness" and "not belonging." The twenties is a time of adult beginnings, of becoming independent. Some view this decade as a "period of increasing stress . . . " and a "testing of self in employment and in social relationships" (Passages, 1981, p. 10).

If attempts to adjust to adult roles are unsuccessful, individuals may either withdraw from the adult world because they feel out of place in it or they may become completely enmeshed in the adult society in an attempt to "find" themselves. In the first instance, people cling to groups and places characterizing their adolescence in a vain attempt to maintain a safe but less mature life-style. They rigidly keep their adolescent relationships and become angry when others attempt to re-

The transition into adulthood can be difficult and leave some feeling isolated and alone. (*Falk/Monkmeyer Press Photo Service*)

late to them in a more appropriate adult manner. Their negative response to others causes them to become even more isolated and less able to form mature intimate relationships with their same-age peers.

Personal Experience: Observing an Isolation Disorder

I'll never forget Chaucey. We'd be playing basketball at the armory; five on five. We were all in high school at the time. Every time we'd get started in would come Chaucey. He played a little varsity basketball when he was in high school, but that was 10 years ago. He wasn't that good then, and well, he's older now and isn't very good now. But we all feel sorry for him. He's really a nice guy. He seems to love to talk to us guys. After we're done playing he likes to stand around for hours and talk about the old days in high school. How it used to be so much tougher and how the teachers all knew him. We've heard the stories many times but, like I said, he's a nice guy so we humor him. I know he's tried a few jobs, in fact he had a good job but it would have taken him out of town and he decided to stay near home. I think he has friends his own age but I never see him with them. I like him, but sometimes he makes me feel real uncomfortable.

While less outwardly distressed than their withdrawn peers, those who enmesh themselves into adult society also experience feelings of isolation and distress (Davidson, 1979). Their path toward isolation is different from those who cling to adolescent ways of interacting. They have attempted to move directly from adolescence to adulthood by conforming to what other adults expect of them. Rather than experiment with the rich variety of experiences available to them as they emerge into adulthood, they move directly into adult roles: they take the "right" kind of job, get married, and have children (Fischer & Oliver, 1983). Soon, however, they begin to feel dissatisfied with their lives and feel apart from the very relationships they were trying to obtain by conforming. The adult world that was to free them becomes more like their prison, a prison that holds them in solitary confinement.

The dynamics of an isolation disorder are complex. In order to make the transition from adolescence to adulthood, people must experience some sense of loss and sadness for things that once were. However, those with an isolation disorder attempt to avoid these feelings by maintaining a particular life-style. Yet such rigid attempts to ward off isolation eventuates in their feeling sad, lonely, and isolated—the very set of feelings they were trying to avoid. These people have a very gloomy view of the future and a very shaky picture of who they are and where they might be going.

The Thirties Crisis

While most of us will spend some time reconsidering and thinking about our lives and future when we reach our early thirties, some individuals reexamine themselves so intensely they have a difficult time making the transition from their early into their late thirties (Levinson, 1977;

Lidz, 1980). People who experience a thirties transitional disorder are dissatisfied with who they are and yet cannot bring themselves to make the necessary changes to improve matters. They may become unhappy with their spouses and often pursue extramarital relationships. However, rarely do sexual affairs solve their problems and thirties crisis individuals continue to experience intensive feelings of depression and anxiety. As the pressure builds on them, they may begin to "act out" against distressing feelings by taking drugs, frequently changing jobs, or finding new relationships. These are adults who cannot seem to find a comfortable place within the fabric of what was previously a satisfactory life situation. Without help and support, their feelings of agitation and dissatisfaction may soon become feelings of hopelessness and despair.

Women tend to experience the thirties crises during their early thirties while men seem to experience it later (Levinson, 1978). Some women who are childless at 30, may feel upset at the passing opportunity for having and raising children.

The thirtieth birthday is usually celebrated in a special manner because of its importance as a developmental marker. (© *Bill Bachman 1983/Photo Researchers, Inc.*)

Developmental Disorders of Middle Adulthood (40 to 65)

Between the years of 40 and 65, called middle adulthood, adults face a number of difficult transitions (Neugarten, 1968, 1979). Many experience success and become richer, more stable and more powerful in their communities. However, these gains are balanced against failing physical abilities and other losses. When losses outweigh the gains, disorders associated with transitions may develop: the *forties life crisis, midlife reaction to menopause in women*, and the *sixties transition*.

The Forties Life Crisis

The indications that one is getting older, subtle in the thirties, become clearer in the forties. Becoming 40 has had special meaning to scientists and lay people alike. Jung, for instance, differed with Freud's belief that the personality matured by age 20. In contrast, Jung saw age 40 as the "noon of life" and a time when significant changes and continued development can take place. For some, however, the changes can be negative and result in a *forties life crisis*.

People who experience a forties transition disorder are troubled, irritable, and unsure of themselves, in spite of seeming successful in most areas of their life. For the first time in perhaps a decade or more, they question who they are and what they want out of life (Perosa & Perosa, 1983). Many of the same questions of identity faced in adolescence seem to reemerge with renewed force at this time. In addition, more at this time than at any other, changes are more likely in family, work, and life-style (Notman, 1979).

Case: Forties Life Crisis

Mrs. C. was 45 when she was referred for treatment by her dentist, who was concerned about her inability to tolerate the necessary dental reconstruction. Mrs. C. was restless, short-tempered, and weepy. She could not make any decisions about her periodontal work and was suspicious about whether she was being overcharged and whether she was getting "the best". Mrs. C. was married to a man 20 years her senior who had recently been ill with prostate-gland pathology. She was afraid that he might develop cancer and die. They had no children. Mrs. C.'s background was a good one but her early family relationships had been chaotic and had included some incest. At age 26, she had become a successful interior designer and decorator, but her personal relationships had continued to be chaotic and promiscuous. She entered therapy at that time for a short period, married her husband as a resolution to her problems, and settled down very well with him until this midlife crises.

From the viewpoint of primary prevention, this woman, whose initial ego adjustment had been borderline, had settled and had been encouraged by her therapist to settle for too simple a goal at 26. It was foreseeable that marriage alone could not solve her problems. The two primary preventive tasks here were (1) more therapy and (2) pursuit and development of her career as well as marital goals. . . . Without either . . . she was a certain candidate for midlife depression when a series of inevitable losses was bound to occur. (Davidson, 1979, pp. 167–168)

In a forties crisis, people often report feeling torn between continuing to work toward traditional goals originating in their teens or twenties and trying to reorganize their priorities in order to pursue new goals and missed opportunities (Lidz, 1980).

Personal Experience: Forties Life Crisis

The thing that's distressing to me at the moment is the absence of a goal that I consider worthwhile. I have to couch it in the framework of science, because that's the only thing I'm really trained to do, but I think the problem is perfectly general. I don't in all honesty, see a goal that's worth having at the moment. . . . This is what really shakes me up. It worries me much more than what the hell I'm going to do in the next year or two in detail. Usually people say, well, you know, the preservation of the human race. Why? That's not a useful goal as far as I'm concerned, if that's all there is to it. (Levinson, 1978, pp. 274–275)

People suffering through the forties transition crisis report a number of fears, especially those regarding their loss of youth and the aging process. These changes help explain some of the psychological effects that occur during the middle and late years of adulthood. The decline in physical abilities that began in the early thirties becomes more obvious during the forties. Changes in energy levels and physiological functioning have significant impacts on what people do and how well they do it (see Table 18-1).

Midlife Reaction to Menopause in Women

Both women and men experience biological changes that signal loss of procrea-

Table 18-1 Important Changes after the Age of 40

Changes in sensory and perceptual capability: Beginning in the fourth decade there are changes in the structure of the eyes that diminish their ability to transmit and accommodate light. More light is needed to see clearly than was needed before. There also is an increasing tendency to retain the initial perception of stimuli and some difficulty in changing or reorganizing new stimuli coming in. More light is needed to increase contrasts among figure and background and make perception easier.

Auditory acuity: Significant hearing loss occurs as early as 32 years of age for men and 37 years of age for women (Lebo & Reddell, 1972). The physiological degeneration usually results first in losses in high-frequency tonal areas of acuity that in turn leads to difficulties in discrimination of phonetically similar words with the letters *s, t, g, f,* and *a.* Women's hearing losses are generally less severe than those of men. Such losses can make a person more open to misinterpreting what others are saying, perhaps even to the point of believing others may be talking about them.

Perceptual speed: People in their forties begin to have difficulty perceiving a visual or auditory stimulus if it is followed too quickly by a second stimulus. Likewise it also takes longer scanning times for them to pick up relevant stimuli from the environment (Walsh et al., 1978). However, if given a bit more time, people who are in their forties can process stimuli as well as younger adults.

Energy level: One of the most visible signs of aging involves the lowered energy level that is both an objective and subjective phenomenon. Lowered energy level may be attributable to a more sedentary life-style. Those with lowered energy levels may not be as able to process environmental information needed for adjusting.

Information acquisition: With aging come losses in long-term memory ability. Longer-term memory problems begin to show up in the forties and increase with age. They seem to be caused by less efficient encoding methods used by older people. However, the deficit is less pronounced when well-known and meaningful material is memorized.

Information retrieval: Older adults, compared with younger ones, have difficulty retrieving information. When the information is learned through more than one sensory modality, however, then it is more efficiently retrieved.

Changes in motivation: Beginning in the forties adults approach new situations with increasing cautiousness and a lowered expectancy of performance. There also is a tendency for aging adults to become more conforming in behavior, values, and goals and to gravitate toward situations that are common, don't include social interaction, and have positive outcomes.

Source: Schaie (1981).

tional abilities. However, the biological changes that take place in women between their late thirties and early fifties have been more carefully documented. Menopause is defined as the cessation of menses for 1 year (Notman, 1979). It has long been associated with a variety of behavioral difficulties ranging from depression and sleeplessness to dizzy spells, irritability, and headaches. The symptoms of hot flashes and night sweats appear to be the most general and may continue for years beyond the cessation of menses.

The age at which menopause occurs does not seem to be related to age of menarche or socioeconomic status (McKinlay et al., 1972). However, reaction to meno-

The forties can be a time of questioning, anxiety, and decline. (*Gloria Karlson*)

pause will probably parallel how women reacted to menarche and pregnancy. It also seems that when children of menopausal women leave home, it has as much impact on the response to menopause as biological factors. The fact that both environmental and biological events may occur simultaneously for many women may mask the independent impact of each set of factors on their behavior. Nowhere else is this confusion more prominent than in determining whether menopause significantly increases the likelihood of depression in women (Weissman & Klerman, 1977a).

Compared with lower-class women, it appears that women from the middle and upper social classes tend to minimize menopausal reactions (Neugarten & Kraines, 1965). Researchers have found it difficult to ascertain whether this is the result of a more active denial of the biological event on the part of middle-class women or not. In any case, menopause appears to have its greatest impact on women from the lower social class and on women who have no clearly delineated course for their lives. Menopause is a difficult event to ignore and may serve as a reminder to women that they have reached a certain place in the developmental process. Notman (1979) suggests that women experiencing psychological difficulties associated with menopause may need to "mourn" their past lives before they can move on to new styles of living. Without help and support, the symptoms of the midlife, menopausal reaction may be prolonged and set the stage for other severe developmental disorders at later ages.

Personal Experience: Menopause in Women

I was so frightened about what menopause would be like. When it finally started happening I thought I was in for the worst time of my life. I was closer than I thought to being right. I read all the books that said much of what happens is in your own head. I tried to keep reminding myself of that, but I was still behaving as though I was crazy. I had the sweats and nightmares, terrible nightmares about losing my teeth or being closed up in some small place and not being able to get out. I was a real bitch with my husband and my two children when they came to visit. Everything upset me. The television was too loud, my husband wanted to play too much tennis, the sun light looked wrong, my feet were sore. . . . The worst thing was that I thought I was enlightened and that menopause wouldn't be as bad as when I started my period. But it was.

The Sixties Transition

The loss of physiological powers and functions noticeable during the forties and continuing through the fifties accelerates as people approach 60. Not only are there objective markers in our society pertaining to the age of 60, but also there are a number of personal events that remind these people that they are moving out of middle age and toward old age. As Levinson (1978) has pointed out, even if they are in good health, people in their sixties have more aches and pains and probably have already experienced at least one major illness or difficulty such as heart attack, depression, or some loss of physical abilities. They realize that nothing now stands between themselves and old age.

One response to this set of realizations results in the *sixties transition disorder*, in which people overreact to their lowered abilities in a number of ways. They may become intensely involved in risky and youthful behaviors in an attempt to deny their declining abilities. In one extreme case, a 63-year-old man took up skydiving even though he was afraid of heights.

In an opposite, though equally unrealistic response to the roles and pressures of becoming 60, some individuals become too depressed in response to unpleasant events. Rather than denying them, they focus on their aches and pains, resulting in lowered activity level and greater numbers of visits to physicians. Both of these extreme reactions reflect inappropriate ways of responding to loss of youth. Unless an adequate adjustment can be made to the demands of this midlife developmental period, adults may develop DSM-III disorders and/or face greater difficulties meeting the tasks and goals of later adulthood.

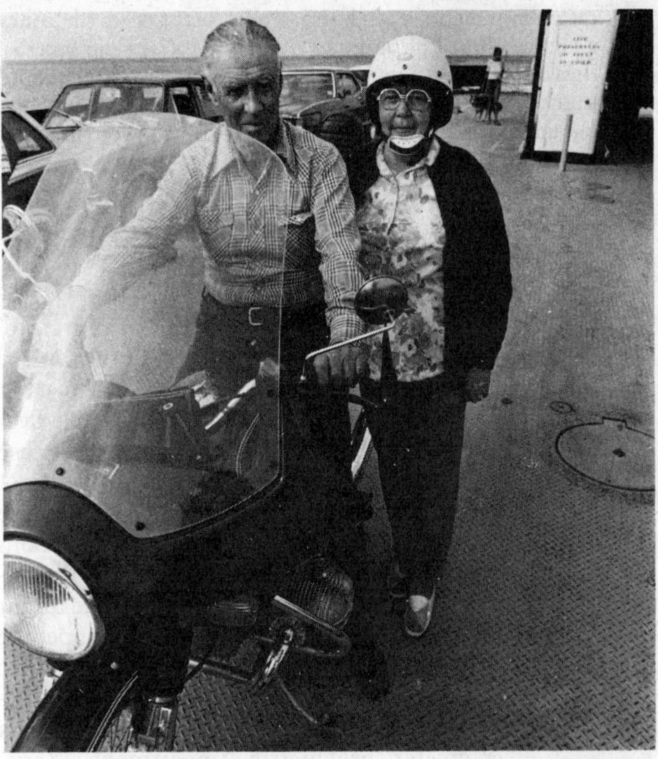

One reaction to the sixties transition is to become involved in youthful activities in an attempt to deny declining abilities. (*Michael Weisbrot and Family*)

Disorders of Late Adulthood (65 and over)

Case: Developmental Disorders of Late Adulthood

A 78-year-old woman came to an outpatient clinic demanding to see a psychiatrist. She had found herself getting increasingly angry and annoyed, and she felt it was time to do something about it. She had also experienced severe deterioration of vision over the past few years; the decline had not been halted despite extensive opthalmologic intervention, including surgery.

Not long into the initial interview the psychiatrist became the object of her anger. The patient said she doubted the psychiatrist could do anything about her state of mind, and that the doctor was probably incompetent anyway. It became apparent that the patient was repeating in this new relationship what had recently occurred in other relationships: she would approach persons for help, only to berate them and drive them away. Her severe visual impairment had placed her in the position of needing considerably more help from others than ever before, and stirred up long-standing conflicts about dependency. She had always seen herself "in the driver's seat," and would strive to turn a situation where she was passive into one where she could be active. She had several living siblings, many of whom had invited her to visit, but she consistently responded with "Who wants a blind lady?" and said she "was not accepting any invitations."

Despite her difficulties, she continued to display a tremendous degree of energy, initiative and resourcefulness. For example, this 78-year-old nearly blind woman on her own used public transpor tation two nights a week to attend a course offered by an inner city university. What was especially unusual was the course she selected to attend—"How to Become a Funeral Parlor Director." When asked by a psychiatrist why she was taking the course, she replied, "To perform your funeral!" Her actual loss of vision, "the lights going out," symbolized death to this woman, and as had been her pattern, she responded with an attempt at action, saying she was "going to get the upper hand on death, gain control over it, by learning how to be a funeral parlor director." (Committee on Aging, 1983, pp. 10–11)

As we mentioned at the beginning of this chapter, the population of the United States is getting older. One of the most rapidly expanding age groups is people over 65. Zarit (1980) believes that this increase in the number of people over 65 years of age will rise until the year 2010 when those born in the post-World War II baby boom will reach late adulthood. While the increase in the number of aged people might worry those who believe that older people have a greater frequency of psychiatric disorders, there is little support for a belief that advancing age necessarily means greater psychiatric impairment (Zarit, 1980).

The disorders of the elderly may be categorized as either functional or organic. *Functional disorders* are assumed to be caused by psychological stresses of aging. In contrast, *organic disorders* originate from physical damage caused by disease, injury, or natural deterioration.

Functional Disorders

The functional disorders in late adulthood can include all the disturbances found among people of any age. However, we must consider some of the special circumstances leading to the possible susceptibility of the elderly to psychological aberrations. In recent years, the study of the aging process has developed into a specific subdiscipline of psychology and psychiatry (Birren, 1964; Eisdorfer & Lawton, 1973; Howells, 1975; Verwoerdt, 1976). The knowledge resulting from the work of professionals in *geriatric psychology and psychiatry* has contributed to a more accurate perception of the elderly and their problems. Fozard and Thomas (1975) have reached several conclusions regarding the psychological characteristics of the elderly. Many of these conclusions can serve as guides to "normally occurring deviations" among the old. Among them are:

1. Mental abilities will deteriorate as a person passes 50, particularly to the extent that tasks are speeded.
2. Personality is remarkably stable over the adult years.
3. People tend to appear more rigid in thinking with age.
4. Older people are more likely to be introverted, controlled, less flexible, less energetic, lower in need to achieve and to socialize.
5. There is no such thing as the "old personality"; different people age in different ways.
6. Adaptation to current environment is usually fine; ability to adapt to new environments is impaired.
7. Age is not the crucial variable in aging.
8. The interdependence between a person and the environment increases with age.

When "normally occurring deviations" such as these result in significant emotional and personal stress, more severe disturbance can occur. Although all types of functional disorders are possible, the most frequent are the *paranoid*, *depressive*, and *confusional states*.

Paranoid States (Paraphrenia) in Old Age

When severe, the paranoid pattern may be classified as psychotic and called *paraphrenia*. Though those diagnosed as paraphrenic have few intellectual difficulties, their thinking usually is characterized by delusions and hallucinations (Weinberg, 1975). Persecutory ideas regarding the motives of family, friends, and hospital staff often play a large part in paraphrenic thought processes. The possibility of such persecutory ideas beginning and, once begun, sustaining themselves may be increased in the elderly because of normal losses in hearing and vision that tend to decrease the ability to monitor reliably what others are doing or saying.

Case: Disorders Associated with Late Adulthood—Paranoid State

A 66-year-old man was discussed in consultation with the resident manager of a senior citizens housing project. The man was described as bizarre and very provocative. The manager expressed the belief that it would perhaps be better for everyone if he no longer remained in the building. His behavior disturbed other residents. For example, when he walked through the building he would be seen sprinkling perfume on himself, taping pennies to his wrists, and touching a Bible and a bar of soap to his lips.

The psychiatric consultant explained to the manager that the bizarre traits of this man were symptoms, that symptoms are usually signals of underlying problems, and that people under stress sometimes indirectly give out messages seeking help in the form of symptoms. The psychiatrist further suggested that the next time the manager meets the man she should ask him how he is doing, and she might inform the man that she had been concerned about him and wondered if he would like to talk to a doctor who came to the clinic to help people with their worries and other problems. To her surprise, when she carried out the suggestion, the man accepted her recommendation to see a psychiatrist.

When interviewed, the man presented the previously described appearance and demeanor. Not long into the interview the meaning of some of his symptoms became clear. He described horrible hallucinations of smell which he attempted to dilute by sprinkling perfume on himself. He expressed considerable guilt about sexual fantasies he had about women other than his wife, who had become nearly bed-bound with illness and was physically unattractive to him. His bizarre way of dealing with this guilt was to attempt to control and cleanse his thoughts with the Bible and the bar of soap on his lips. Understanding the significance of the pennies taped to the man's wrist was considerably more difficult and challenging. The therapist began to see the association and to recognize the significance of this symptom; another name for a penny is a *cent* which in the primary process thinking to which he had regressed was equated to the homonym *scent*. The patient's primitive symbolic approach to gain control over his olfactory hallucinations was to smother these scents (cents) under tape on his wrists and use the perfume and soap. Meanwhile, comprehensive medical evaluation disclosed no organic basis for the symptoms.

While details of these therapeutic discussions were not shared with the manager of the building, she was told that this deeply troubled man was tormented by his terribly distressing hallucinations of smell which he tried to control in the ways described above. The manager's uneasiness about the man, largely due to her fear of the unknown, was replaced by compassion and concern. In further consultation sessions with her, such topics as the nature of chronic illness, including severe emotional and mental problems, were discussed. The manager was able to recognize her tenant's problem as a chronic psychosis and came to understand the implication of this diagnosis. (Committee on Aging, 1983, pp. 11–12).

Depressive States Whereas the major symptom continuum in paraphrenia is mild to intense suspiciousness, in the depressive states feelings can range from the relatively mild feelings of depression to nihilistic ideas and incapacitating sadness found in severe depression. Generally, older depressed adults, especially males, are greater suicide risks (Committee on Aging, 1983). In fact, the ratio of men to women who end their own lives rises to a high of 12 to 1 by age 85. Many suicides can be traced to the loss of a spouse. For the 4 years following the death of a spouse, the likelihood of death by suicide is greater in the elderly than is death by all other causes (Bunch, 1972). The loss of loved ones, coupled with reduced status, abilities, and security are especially devastating to elderly adults.

Case: Developmental Disorders of Late Adulthood-Depressive State

An 82-year-old woman was referred for an evaluation to consider a nursing home placement. Memory changes were described as being so severe she could not even recall the death of a daughter 2 months earlier. Constant fatigue and poor appetite were also described. Her "senility," as it was called, was getting worse.

The woman was evaluated initially in her apartment. When a family portrait was presented to her, she gave a fairly good history for each person in the photo except one—the recently deceased daughter—for whom she appeared to have no recall. Thirty minutes later, however, the woman broke into tears, explaining that her daughter had visited her daily for years until she had died suddenly and unexpectedly from a heart attack. Further discussions revealed that the patient had become extremely dependent on the daughter, whose death left her with mixed feelings of grief and anger. Unconsciously, she experienced her daughter's death as a form of abandonment. Unable to deal with the anger, she repressed the death of her daughter and became depressed.

Physical examination and laboratory studies revealed dehydration, an iron deficiency anemia, and a low grade duodenal peptic ulcer. The consultant considered that, in addition to her symptoms of depression, anemia was probably contributing to her fatigue, the ulcer to her appetite problem, and the dehydration with associated electrolyte imbalance, to an acute brain syndrome which aggravated her memory disturbance. A combination of medical care, social service involvement and psychotherapy brought significant improvement in her overall health and functioning over the next year and enabled her to remain in her apartment. (Committee on Aging, 1983, pp. 9–10)

Confusional States Besides suspiciousness and depression, a third frequent psychological difficulty encountered in late adulthood is the *confusional state* (Kral, 1975; Roth, 1955). Typically occurring in the absence of permanent organic damage, the confusional state usually follows an experience of acute stress, such as physical injury or death of a loved one. Symptoms of confusional states may include clouding of consciousness, lowered level of awareness of self and environment, and disorientation for time and place. As in brain disorders, short-term memory also may be impaired. In mild cases, the confusional state and memory difficulties usually remit in a few days or weeks. Although there is no verifiable organic basis, confusional states can resemble the delirium associated with acute brain syndromes.

Organic Disorders

Unlike the functional disorders we have described, the source of organic disorders can be traced to physical dysfunctions in the brain and nervous system. Interestingly, the severity of observed behavioral symptoms of many aged people is not directly related to the amount of actual brain deterioration. There are two major forms of organic brain disorders associated with aging, *senile dementia* and *arteriosclerotic dementia.*

Senile Dementia Among its symptoms, senile dementia includes all the characteristics of permanent mental deterioration described in Chapter 12. However, the irreversible mental deterioration seen in senile dementia is due primarily to insidious atrophy of the brain and nervous system as part of the aging process. Kolb and Brodie (1982) note that, at age 75, the brain may be only 55 percent of the size it was in young adulthood. In addition to the mental deterioration in senile dementia old age brings wrinkled skin, failing vision and hearing, loss of weight, flaccid muscles, slowed gait, and tremulous hands and legs. The physical and mental signs of aging combine to form the basis for the diagnosis of senile dementia.

Each subtype of senile dementia has a characteristic core symptom. In *paranoid senile dementia* people have delusions of persecution. In the *presbyophrenic type* of senile dementia, patients compensate for lack of memory with fantasies or fabricated stories (Korsakoff's syndrome). They are generally cheery and talkative and do not seem aware of their substituting fantasy for real memory. It seems more than likely that the specific subtype of senile dementia that develops depends on the premorbid personality.

Arteriosclerotic Dementia Commonly referred to as "hardening of the arteries," cerebral arteriosclerosis is a common adjunct of the aging process. Unlike senile dementia, which is characterized by a slow onset, *arteriosclerotic dementia* usually occurs quickly, over a few weeks' time. Symptoms may include loss of awareness, restlessness, and hallucinations. Often these symptoms abate after a short time, leaving the person intellectually impaired and in a state of progressive deterioration.

After a succession of losses, some elderly people may become confused and disoriented. (*Michael Heron/Monkmeyer Press Photo Service*)

Personality, emotional stability, problem-solving ability, and practical judgment can be adversely affected. It had long been assumed that arteriosclerosis caused many patterns of disordered behavior. However, recent evidence suggests that the relationship may not be as direct as previously thought. Goldfarb (1974a) concluded that arteriosclerosis is only infrequently the cause of psychotic disorders in the elderly. Investigators using data based on autopsies have shown that arteriosclerosis is not always found in people who were diagnosed as having arteriosclerotic dementia (Ernst et al., 1977; Ernst & Badash, 1977).

Moreover, evidence of arteriosclerosis is often found in the elderly who never showed any behavioral symptoms associated with that disorder. Based on these data, to suggest that all psychological disorders of the aged are physically based could lead to serious treatment errors.

Paradigmatic Perspectives on the Disorders of Adulthood

Most theories regarding the transition disorders of adulthood derive from a developmental or life-span perspective. However, the explanations vary in their paradigmatic roots and thus in the roles they ascribe to the innate personality and to the effects of the environment in determining how disordered behavior develops.

The Psychosocial Life Cycle (Erik Erikson)

As we presented in Chapter 5, Erikson described eight sequential stages or challenges for the developing person. While a person may be at any of these stages when reaching adulthood (as defined by chronological age), the final three stages, 6 to 8, are most often associated with adulthood.

Stage 6 is described as a struggle of *intimacy* versus *isolation*. Usually this struggle takes place during young adulthood, when people attempt to establish and experience intimacy with at least one other person. To attain intimacy, people must come to grips with their own finiteness and uniqueness. Only then, according to Erikson, can they allow another to come close enough to become intimate and experience love and belonging. However, should people fail to allow others their own uniqueness and instead use them to solve their own needs, they will experience feelings of isolation.

Once intimacy is achieved, adults then must face the basic struggle between *generativity* and *stagnation* (Stage 7). This usually takes place during middle age. To Erikson, generativity refers to a concern with future generations that is shown by helping younger people learn and develop so that they can carry on in leadership positions. Similar to parenting, generativity is not necessarily found in all people.

The successful accomplishment of the tasks of late adulthood leaves a person with a sense of "ego integrity," a sense of living a worthwhile life. (*Max Tharpe/Monkmeyer Press Photo Service*)

Those who develop generativity will be capable of caring and helping others grow while those who do not will experience feelings of stagnation and decay.

Should people accomplish intimacy and generativity during their young and middle adult years, they still must face the struggle of *ego integrity* versus *despair* in their late adult years. To Erikson, the major goal in old age is to develop a sense of ego integrity, that is, a strong belief that one's life has had meaning. Though not everything might have gone as wished, aged people need to feel that the energies and investments of their lifetime were worthwhile. Should people feel satisfied with their accomplishments, they will develop wisdom. However, should they feel as though they have missed significant opportunities, they will experience a sense of despair and loss.

Erikson believes that though these stages are universal, the exact timing of events is a function of a particular culture. However, he fails to define clearly many of the terms he uses. How do we measure "intimacy" and "wisdom," for example? The lack of clarity sometimes has led to misapplication in nonresearch contexts. However, within the field of psychology itself, scientists have attempted to gather evidence from adult populations to test Erikson's concepts.

Vaillant and Milofsky (1980) used a modified Eriksonian model to look at the adult development of 94 sophomore men selected and interviewed between 1940 and 1942. These men were reinterviewed at age 30 (1951) and at age 47 (1968). Another sample of 392 inner-city youths were followed and reinterviewed at ages 25 (1955), 32 (1962), and 47 (1977).

On the basis of test scores, interviews, and other sources of data, clinicians judged the life stages of these individuals. They found that, as Erikson suggested, the stages of a life cycle must be passed through sequentially. Moreover, if people fail at one of the stages they also seem to fail to progress through any of the higher stages. The actual age at which a stage is completed varied dramatically. For some men generativity was reached at age 32, for others at age 50, and for others, never. Lastly, these authors found that the stage attained in adulthood seemed to be independent of childhood education or social class.

While supportive of Erikson's basic concepts, Vaillant and Milofsky's data were gathered only from male subjects. Until there is additional evidence that Erikson's concepts generalize to women beyond the mostly anecdotal evidence provided by some (e.g., Sheehy, 1976), these research conclusions must be taken as tentative and only reflective of males.

The Age-Graded Life Cycle (Robert Havighurst)

Havighurst (1963) generally adopted Erikson's concepts of life stages. His unique contribution was the delineation of the specific concrete tasks that needed to be completed successfully for each age group before they can move on to the next set of tasks. Completion of age relevant tasks leads to feelings of satisfaction and even happiness while failure usually leads to feelings of unhappiness and low self-esteem. Failure at one group of age-related tasks also predisposes the person to greater chances of failure with the next group.

Unlike Erikson who often is vague about specific goals, Havighurst clearly delineates a variety of developmental tasks. He defines one type of task as universal and experienced by all members of a particular group. An example of this kind of task would be menarche in females. He defines a second type of task like retiring from the work force that varies from culture to culture. Some tasks occur only once, like learning how to walk, while some are recurrent such as forming relationships with same-age peers. The variety of tasks provides constant challenges to the developing person.

While Havighurst has had great impact on education in the United States and other countries, it should be kept in mind that he assumes that we all experience a common adulthood. In actuality his framework seems to hold best for white middle-class people who marry and raise families. It does not describe as well the sequence of developmental tasks that might be followed by a single or minority person.

The Seasons of Life (Daniel Levinson)

Levinson (1978) is one of the first theorists to focus primarily on the adult stages of human development. He based his model on data obtained via interviews,

According to Levinson, a positive resolution of mid-life crisis leads people to pass on their skills, or legacy, to others. (© *1983 L. Racioppo*)

autobiographies, and test information. One key concept introduced by Levinson and his colleagues is *life structure*, or a person's design for life. The life structure is revealed through the kinds of choices made in the areas of occupation, marriage and the family, friendship, and religion. People may choose to make one or more of these areas central to their lives.

Compared with Erikson's three adult stages, Levinson suggests five overlapping eras in adult life. Within each era there are stable phases that last about 7 years and transition periods of about 5 years in length. Levinson points out that each era has a different set of meanings that are developed primarily through the interactions people have with their environment.

The five eras overlap with one another: *preadulthood* from age 0 to age 22; *early adulthood* from age 17 to age 45; *middle adulthood* from age 40 to age 65; *late adulthood* from age 60 to age 85; and *late, late adulthood* from age 80. Although Levinson includes the entire age range in his theory, most of his data gathering has taken place with men from the early and middle adult eras. On the basis of his information, Levinson describes the progression through adulthood by men but not women. Generalizations to women would be very difficult if not impossible to make from the data gathered by Levinson and his colleagues. If generalization to women is to take place, it must include a study of the tasks of motherhood and employment. Until then the conclusions made by Levinson should pertain only to males.

Before middle adulthood, Levinson suggests that men are focused on creating a dream or vision of what they wish to build their life around. The building of a dream continues until the end of early adulthood, when men become aware of their own fallibility and death. Up to this point men were primarily intent on proving themselves, a process Levinson calls *BOOM* or *Becoming One's Own Man*.

In contrast to the intense struggle to Become One's Own Man which is characteristic of early adulthood, middle adulthood involves the development of mentor relationships with younger people and closer ties with the family. During this time, men come to grips with deciding what "legacy" they wish to pass on to others.

Levinson presents relatively little information about late adulthood. He does suggest that around age 60 there is a difficult transition to old age during which people must deal with their declining abilities. As Levinson's sample of men becomes older, we may find out more about exactly what happens in this late adulthood period. Other theorists, however have dealt more fully with what takes place in late adulthood and they will be presented next.

Paradigmatic Perspectives on Disorders in the Elderly

Although the life-span theories we have described previously can be applied to the elderly as well as to younger and middle-aged people, there are also a number of theories which are directed specifically at understanding the difficulties associated with advanced age. These explanations derive primarily from the systems and psychosocial paradigms.

Systems Paradigm: Disengagement Theory

The basis of disengagement theory (Cumming, 1964; Cumming & Henry, 1961) is that, due to the mortality of man and the relative permanence of society, there comes a time when society must disengage itself from specific members who no longer can contribute. Usually there are rules, such as mandatory retirement ages, that allow society to disengage itself effectively from its working members. Likewise, at some point in later life, individuals themselves also may choose to disengage from society. Older people manifesting signs of increasing disengagement from society typically cease attending meetings of organizations, reduce visits to friends, and stop going to movies and other social activities.

Disengagement from society frequently leads to an increase in preoccupation with the self and withdrawal into a more and more limited life space. The withdrawal often brings about fewer social interactions, decreasing feelings of self-worth, and difficulties in adjustment. However, Atchley (1972) points out that not all disengagement produces problems. If society and the individual agree on the time of disengagement, good postdisengagement adjustment can be expected. If, however, society is not ready to let go (forced engagement) or the person is not ready to retire (forced disengagement), psychological problems are more probable.

When older adults are forced to disengage from society, it may lead them to withdraw from active lives and become sedentary. (© *Rhoda Galyn*)

An example of the effects of forced disengagement may be seen in the following personal experience:

Personal Experience: Forced Disengagement

I worked for ______ for over 40 years. Never had more than one week out sick the whole time. But when I turned 65, I . . . and my friend Dan . . . had to retire—we had to. . .No ifs, ands, or buts—company rules. I had no financial worries, I was actually pretty excited at the thought of doing whatever I wanted whenever I wanted—no whistle, no fighting the traffic in ______ each morning. Mary and I made plans for a trip to Mexico. I always wanted to go there. . . .

After we got back from the trip, it hit me. God, I was restless. I couldn't sit at home. I had to get out. I decided to get a part-time job. No dice—"Too old"—"Sorry, we need a younger man"—"You're retired, enjoy it!" Crap! Enjoy it? It drove me nuts. As I look back on it, that was the worst few days I ever spent. I felt like crying, like hitting somebody. The company didn't help; they said my pension was all they owed me. I started having trouble sleeping. I couldn't eat, lost weight (for a while my wife didn't mind that because I lost a lot of my beer belly). I felt real bad. . . .

This part-time job is a godsend. I pump gas a few hours a day. I keep active. I talk to people. I don't care about the money, but I feel like I'm back in the world!

Psychosocial Paradigm: Activity Theory

Whereas disengagement theory emphasizes a certain time for middle-age activities to end, *activity theory* (Havighurst, 1963) generally asserts that behavioral norms and requirements for old age are the same as for middle age and that sound adjustment to aging may be measured in terms of how much of middle-age activity is maintained or lost in old age. To activity theorists, older people may be said to be poorly adjusted if they manifest significant amounts of behavior other than that appropriate to middle age, such as gainful employment, social interaction, travel, and other activities. Absence of these kinds of patterns can indicate old age and deterioration and is usually accompanied by depression or other symptoms.

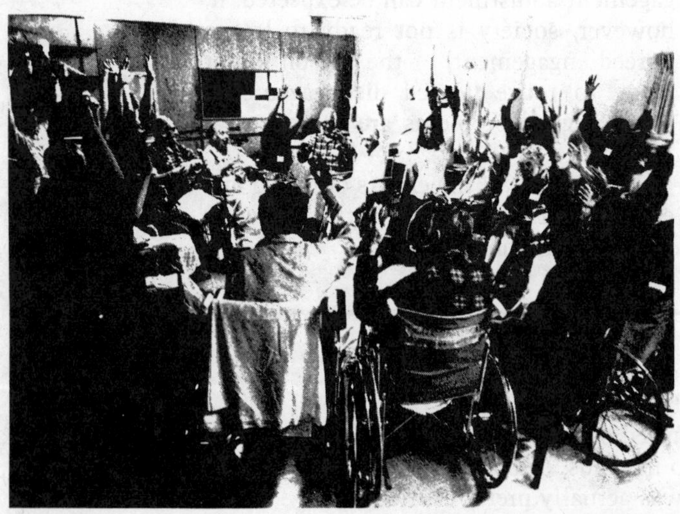

Physical activities can help overcome withdrawal and stimulate communication among older adults. (© *Karen R. Preuss 1978/ Taurus Photos*)

For many elderly people and their families, activity theory serves as a guide to late-life adjustment. Some older people try to maintain more youthful, middle-aged appearances through clothing, cosmetic surgery, and other means. According to activity theory, their attempts to "hold on" may be motivated by the social "requirement" to remain middle-aged.

Psychosocial Paradigm: Continuity Theory

Instead of engagement with society or activity, *continuity theory* (Neugarten, 1964, 1979; Rosow, 1963) proposes that successful coping with aging is reflected in the ability of the elderly adults to maintain continuity from adulthood to old age in habits, relationships, and activities. For example, if individuals have led an extremely sedentary life, onset of physical slowing and loss of energy may cause little stress. On the other hand, in people with a history of high levels of physical activity, loss of energy represents a discontinuity that could lead to poor adjustment and depression. Continuity theory can explain, therefore, why the same life experience can have such varying effects on different people. The theory also accounts nicely for the fact that no two people age in exactly the same way.

One continuity theorist (Rosow, 1963) proposes that certain crucial areas of change occur in the later years and that two specific factors determine how people adjust to these changes. The types of changes noted by Rosow include new occupations, changing relationships with others, and role conflicts. The first factor that determines how well a person adjusts to change is *continuity versus discontinuity*; that is, is the changed situation continuous with (not necessarily identical to) the old? A second factor deals with the *subjective feeling of loss or gain* resulting from the changes. For instance, if a person hates work, retirement probably will be a gain because it reduces negative stimulation. However, if a person's life is built around work, then retirement may be a traumatic event. Individual histories can lead two people to react quite differently to the change of occupational status. Its ability to explain individual differences in people's response to a similar event makes continuity theory potentially very useful.

Psychosocial Paradigm: Isolation Theory

Unlike the theories of aging we have already described, *isolation theory* attempts to identify the specific mechanism by which the deleterious effects of aging may occur. In brief, isolation theory holds that the elderly person experiences isolation as a result of factors such as disengagement, discontinuity, illness, death of friends, and lack of interest by family and others. Typically the person may be isolated from the sources of stimulation to which he or she was accustomed throughout adult life. As a result, psychological changes associated with sensory deprivation may begin to appear. These changes include loss of interest in surroundings, increased focus on internal physical and mental processes, loss of ability to concentrate, increased anxiety, and restlessness (Freedman et al., 1961).

Experimentally induced sensory deprivation can produce psychiatric symptoms in people of all ages, and isolation theorists propose that naturally occurring isolation is the chief source of deprivation in the old. For example, loss of hearing and vision can increase the chances of developing paranoid ideas. Hearing deficits often cause the elderly to feel isolated and frightened, and when questions such as "What did you say?" are met with "Oh, never mind, it's not important," fears and suspicions may be strengthened. So powerful can be the effects of isolation that some geriatric psychiatrists (Ernst & Badash, 1977) have concluded: "Isolation is the major cause of psychiatric disturbances in the aged. The frequency of organically based disturbances is small compared to those caused by loss of contact with the world and by stimulus deprivation" (p. 14).

Paradigmatically Based Treatments for Disorders of Adulthood and the Elderly

In that the traditional paradigms used to explain the transitional disorders of adults and the elderly are primarily psychosocial and systems-based, most of the forms of therapy described in Chapters 5 and 6 are applicable. In addition, the developmental paradigm also has guided some specific treatment efforts. While intensive long-term interventions such as psychoanalysis might be used, short-term interventions of 10 sessions or less may be

An effective way for older adults to deal with their feelings of isolation is to reach out to children. (*Michael Weisbrot and Family*)

The experience of increasing isolation and loneliness is a major problem of the aged in our society. (*Anthony A. Scaravilli*)

all that are needed to tip the scales in the direction of a positive resolution of an adult transitional life crisis.

Another developmental paradigm-generated therapeutic approach is *anticipatory guidance* (Bloom, 1977). In this approach people are educated about what to expect in the future so that they will be better able to deal with the difficulties when they occur. The writings of Sheehy (1976) and Levinson (1978) have done much to sensitize the public to the fact that there are certain life difficulties that result during normal adult development. With such knowledge, adults experiencing the anxiety and discomfort of normal development will be able to put these feelings in perspective rather than perhaps overreacting. Somehow just knowing that what you are going through is shared by others your age can be very helpful and supportive. Groups that seek to raise both female and male adult consciousness can be useful sources for dealing with present and future adult life crises and transitions.

The range of therapies for the elderly is limited. Older people tend to be less "attractive" patients to many professionals who believe that the elderly are too rigid and have organically based psychological problems (Blau & Berezin, 1975; Eisdorfer & Stotsky, 1977; Richards & Thorpe, 1978). The fragmentary state of the therapeutic approaches for the elderly has led, in some instances, to an emphasis on custodial care. Custodial care enforces a passive approach to solving problems (Gottesman & Boureston, 1974). However, as the field of *gerontology* expands, traditional as well as more innovative approaches are being explored and evaluated for their usefulness in treating the problems of the elderly. One recent application, for example, is teaching the elderly communication skills that would enable them to become peer counselors (Becker & Zarit, 1978; Alpaugh & Hickey-Haney, 1978). Zarit et al. (1980) used such peer group support techniques to aid elderly persons regain their memories.

Several other generalized therapeutic approaches also show promise of being effective. Sensory stimulation therapy is based upon the idea that the symptoms of aging can be counteracted if people are "energized" through stimulation. Stimulation includes group exercises to induce awareness of body parts, touching of objects, smelling of odors, attending to varying sounds, and concentrated "looking." Ernst and Badash (1977) report that among a group of women treated with this technique, level of awareness and ability increased from a low rating of 3 to a high rating of 8 on a scale of 10 over a 6-week treatment period.

Concluding Comments

The use of a developmental paradigm has resulted in a number of explanations and treatments for the special problems associated with mid- and later life. However, in addition to the positive effects of this alternative approach on these age groups per se, the paradigm also has led to an increasing awareness among all age groups of the expected patterns of maladjustment throughout the life cycle. After reading about disorders of adulthood, some young people might be prone to become melancholy about their own futures. While understandable, such a reaction probably is not realistic or adaptive. Problems associated with any developmental period need to be faced squarely; and the news is not all bad. Although older people suffer from a variety of psychological and physiological stresses, it should be remembered that only 5 percent of Americans over 65 are institutionalized in such settings as mental hospitals and homes for the aged (Kalish, 1975). The vast majority of older people live at home and, much like the rest of us, deal effectively with the stresses and strains of daily life. However, special stresses like those caused by fixed incomes, loss of some abilities, and the deaths of some friends and relatives need to considered. Many older people do not want more than their fair share, but rather the support, help, and guidance given to any group of people dealing with unavoidable stresses regardless of their age.

Summary Chart

In Chapter 18, we described special disorders observed in adulthood and old age. We began with an examination of some of the patterns seen as various age levels:

18 to 35 years: Isolation disorders, thirties crisis
40 to 65 years: Forties crisis, changes in physical, intellectual, and sexual capacity, sixties transition
Late adulthood (over 65): Functional disorders with paranoid, depressive, or confusional symptoms, organic disorders such as senile dementia and arteriosclerotic dementia

We then turned to some paradigmatic perspectives on adulthood and aging disorders:

The developmental paradigm-stage theories: Erikson's theory, age graded life cycle, seasons of life
The systems paradigm: Disengagement theory
The psychosocial paradigm: Activity theory, continuity theory, isolation theory

We closed the chapter with a presentation of some paradigmatically based treatments for the special problems of adulthood and aging:

Anticipatory guidance
Applied gerontology

CHAPTER 19

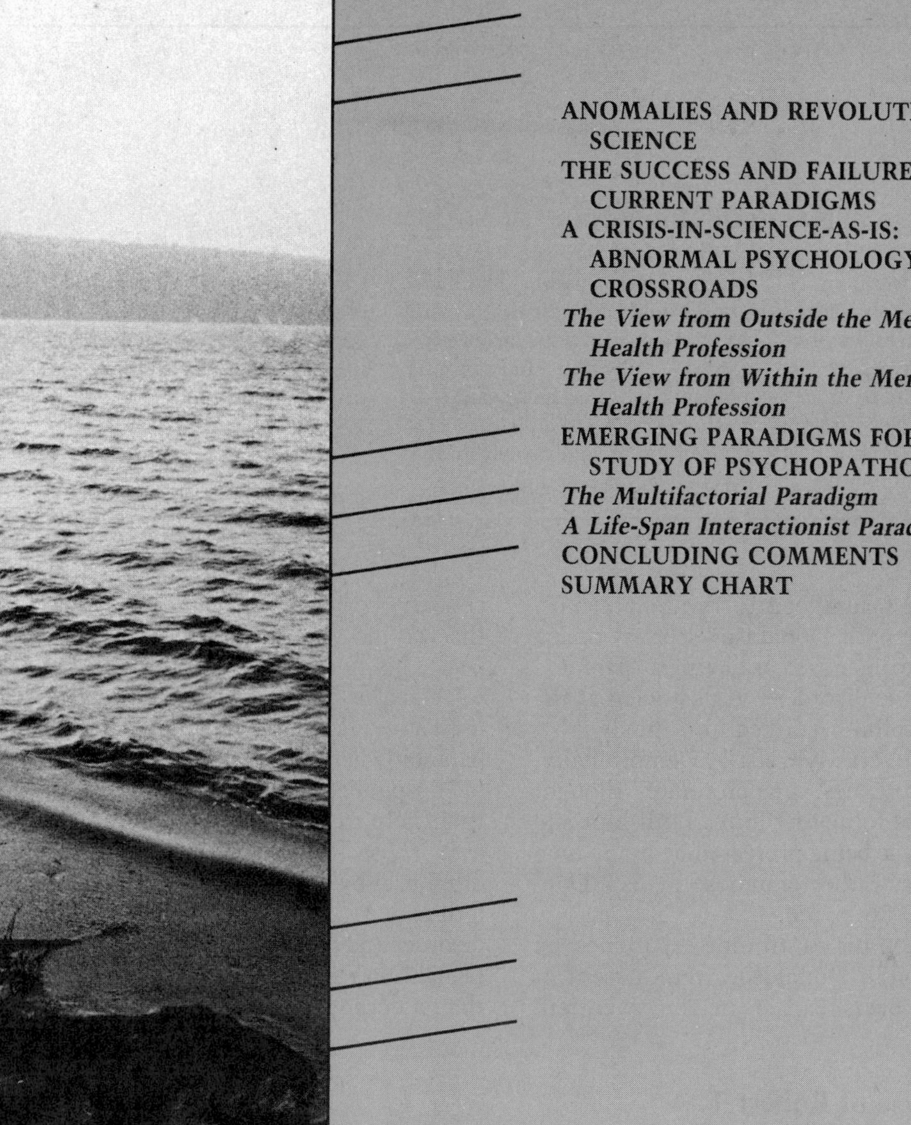

Epilogue: A Perspective on a Scientific Process

The Case of Kenneth Donaldson

On a dreary winter morning in 1943, I stood before an Onandega County judge in the stately courthouse of Syracuse, N.Y. before the regular session came to order. I was not a criminal. I was there to ask the judge's advice on a matter that had come up on my job at a defense plant. I had had some trouble and felt that I could not go back to work again. But the law said that I could not quit a defense job. The judge said it was a matter for the doctors. He advised me to sign myself in at a psychiatric observation center. On my decision voluntarily to place my fate in the hands of doctors lies the wreckage of my life, traumatizing everyone else in my family as well. (Donaldson, 1976, p. 55)

When first admitted to the mental hospital, Kenneth Donaldson's behavior led him to be diagnosed as having a "paranoid disturbance disorder". A physician at the state hospital described him thusly " . . . restless, overactive, shallow emotionally; affect, at times, inappropriate; thought men were following him to kill him and that he was being protected by many men . . . makes rather grandiose plans" (Donaldson, 1976, p. 65).

Based on his continuing experiences in the hospital, Donaldson, reminiscent of Clifford Beers earlier in the twentieth century, began writing a book critical of the way he was being treated. For many years, his book and his continual efforts to obtain his release from the hospital were used as evidence to confirm his diagnosed paranoid disturbance. Over the years of his hospitalization he wrote politicians for their help in obtaining his release. However, those responding to his pleas were often told by hospital authorities that the letters were part of Donaldson's paranoid disorder and that seemed to close matters. Donaldson remained incarcerated for more than a decade.

The Case of Robert T.

Robert T. was considered an "unusual" child since birth. Soon after starting kindergarten his behavior came to the attention of school psychologists. He acted like a "little teacher" shouting about rules and attempting to punish (quite severely) other children in his class. After having to be "pulled off" of another child in a completely uncontrollable state, Robert was referred to and eventually placed in a school for emotionally disturbed children. At age 7, Robert continued his "teacher" behavior but also began having difficulty with reality contact; he was convinced that he was a bird and that he was 17 years old. He remained at the special school until he was 19 years old with little or no change in the basic types of symptoms he showed. He was aggressive and tried to punish other children for breaking rules during every year of his schooling. Further, although he stopped believing he was a bird, he began thinking he was a car and was convinced of this for several years. During his 14 years at the special school, Robert received individual therapy, group therapy, medication, and family therapy; and behavior modification was used in all of his classrooms. In spite of these efforts by highly skilled professionals, Robert was hospitalized for several months on two occasions. When he left the school, he was preoccupied with death, fearful that he would be unable to support himself, and extremely paranoid with a tendency toward being violent. The final entry in Robert's chart at the school read, "He will probably always need help in the future."

Robert T. remained in a treatment setting for emotionally disturbed children from age 5 until age 19. He was then released to the care of his family. However, shortly after leaving the special school that had been the source of his stability for most of his life, Robert experienced a psychotic breakdown and was hospitalized. He is now 31 years old and a chronic patient at a large state hospital. The prognosis for Robert is poor.

Anomalies and Revolutions in Science

Much like Clifford Beers, whose case launched our study of abnormal psychology, Kenneth Donaldson, Robert T., and thousands of modern-day patients like them may be standing at a significant crossroads in the development of paradigms-as-sets-of-shared-beliefs in the study of disordered behavior. As Beers seems to have represented issues important in the transition from the supernatural paradigm to the current biological, psychosocial, and systems paradigms, Donaldson and Robert T. may be seen as symbolizing a bridge from these same modern-day paradigms to future ways of conceptualizing disordered behaviors. The difficulty faced by mental health professionals in their efforts to adequately treat large numbers of patients may be seen as reflecting a failure of modern paradigms to guide us toward effective interventions. Cases like Donaldson's and Robert's, therefore, may represent "anomalies" with which modern paradigms cannot adequately deal. From Kuhn's (1962, 1981) perspective, as anomalies increase, they create tension and a state of crisis out of which "paradigm switches" may occur.

In our examination of the three major paradigms-as-sets-of-shared-beliefs currently in use in the science of abnormal psychology, it has appeared that no one of them has been able to provide adequate treatment-generating explanations for the wide variety of patterns of psychopathology we have examined in this text. Rather, the picture over the years seems to have been one of a mixture of successes and failures. In this final chapter, we will examine some of these successes and fail-

In some institutions entrusted with the care for the mentally ill, patients may not even receive the simplest of treatment to which they are legally entitled. (© *Jerry Cooke/Photo Researchers, Inc.*)

ures. We then will propose that, in large measure due to the inadequacy of current paradigms (as reflected in legal and psychiatric-psychological dissatisfaction and concern), the discipline of abnormal psychology may be in a crisis-in-science-as-is. We will propose further that this crisis is similar to others that have occurred throughout history. This is to say that the crisis may be seen as a part of the natural progression of normal science, and that it may indicate the emergence of new paradigms which can deal with the anomalies increasingly beyond the reach of the current biological, psychosocial, and systems views. We will conclude the chapter by presenting several emerging possible alternative paradigms, one of which may become a set of shared beliefs which guides the science of abnormal psychology in the future.

The Success and Failure of Current Paradigms

According to Kuhn, even if they are imperfect, scientific paradigms continue to exist unless better paradigms are developed to replace them. Presently, with no clear acceptable alternative general paradigm available to those in the field of abnormal psychology, the somewhat flawed biological, psychosocial, and systems paradigms continue to be used to guide research, theory, and treatment development. As we have seen, each of these paradigms, in some way, fails to explain satisfactorily various aspects of disordered behavior. However, though imperfect, these modern paradigms continue to be used because each has been able to explain *some* significant aspects of abnormal behavior. Also, because each perspective is a paradigm-as-a-*shared*-set-of-beliefs, there are firmly established groups of influential scientists who adhere to each view and who encourage its continued use.

Each paradigm appears to have had differential success in dealing with varying types of disordered behaviors. For example, followers of the biological paradigm seem to have made significant progress in clarifying the mechanisms underlying schizophrenia, affective psychosis, psychophysiological disorders, and substance-use disorders, but have been far less successful in gathering useful information for patterns like anxiety disorders, personality disorders, sexual paraphilias, and paranoid conditions. On the other hand, the greatest success of the psychosocial paradigm appears to have been with anxiety and sexual disorders, certain paranoid conditions, and personality disturbances, but it has been of less value explaining the schizophrenias and affective psychoses. Lastly, the systems paradigm probably has had its greatest impact on the conceptualizations underlying substance use and traumatic stress disorders and certain types of schizophrenia, but has provided less clarification for sexual, anxiety, and personality disorders.

The inconsistent successes of modern-day paradigms suggest a careful reconsideration of their worth. As paradigms show decreasing ability to explain behavioral events, scientists are forced to face several important questions. Among the most pressing are: What should be done about the crisis-in-science-as-is? How long should imperfect paradigms be kept? Which imperfect paradigms should be kept? What alternative paradigms do we have?

A Crisis-in-Science-as-Is: Abnormal Psychology at a Crossroads

The three current major paradigms seem to have failed in various ways to produce effective explanations for all abnormal be-

The biological paradigm has been most effective in studying and treating disorders like schizophrenia, affective psychoses, and substance abuse. (© *1984 Martin M. Rotker/Taurus Photos*)

haviors. While this alone could signal that the science of abnormal psychology is a science-in-crisis, there seems to be other substantiating evidence. First, from *outside* the mental health profession, we have a growing amount of litigation involving the field's ability to treat and "cure" abnormality. Second, we have an increasing number of leaders *inside* the mental health fields who are concluding that our current sets of shared beliefs have not led us to our hoped-for understanding of psychopathology and that we must seek alternatives.

The View from Outside the Mental Health Profession

The case of Kenneth Donaldson is but one among many which have gained legal attention in recent years (see also *Wyatt vs Stickney*; *Wyatt vs Aderholt*, in Miller et al., 1976; see also Bazelon, 1979). Several high courts decided that Donaldson had been incarcerated without being offered adequate treatment for the disorder upon the basis of which he was hospitalized. In ruling on the case, a U.S. Court of Appeals judge concluded that Donaldson was not provided with even the "simplest" of therapeutic care such as grounds privileges, occupational therapy, and talks with a psychiatrist. It was noted that in 8½ years of hospitalization, Donaldson had been seen by his primary psychiatrist for "not more than a total of two hours—an average of about fourteen minutes a year" (Miller et al., 1976, p. 503). The court's ultimate decision was that Donaldson's *right to receive treatment* had been vio-

BOX 19-1

THE OBLIGATION TO WARN: A SIGN OF PARADIGMATIC CRISIS?

Although one of the traditional mainstays of psychotherapy, the concept of confidentiality of communication between client and therapist has recently come under scrutiny of the legal system. The reconsideration of confidentiality came about as a result of an increasing number of cases such as *Tarasoff vs The Regents of the State of California, et al.* Schwitzgebel and Schwitzgebel (1980) have described the case as follows:

> In the fall of 1968, Prosenjit Poddar, a graduate student from India studying at the University of California at Berkeley, met Tatiana (Tanya) Tarasoff at a folk dancing class. They saw each other weekly during the fall, and on New Year's Eve she kissed him. Poddar interpreted this act as a sign of formal engagement (as it might have been in India where he was a member of the Harijam or "untouchable" caste). Tanya told him that she was involved with other men, and indicated that she did not wish to have an intimate relationship with him.
>
> Poddar became depressed as a result of the rebuff, but he saw Tanya a few times during the spring (occasionally tape recording their conversations in an effort to understand why she did not love him). Tanya left for Brazil in the summer, and Poddar at the urging of a friend went to the student health facility where a psychiatrist referred him to a psychologist for psychotherapy. When Tanya returned in October, 1969, Poddar discontinued therapy. Based in part on Poddar's stated intention to purchase a gun, the psychologist notified the campus police, both orally and in writing, that Poddar was dangerous and should be taken to a community mental health center for psychiatric commitment.
>
> The campus police interviewed Poddar, who seemed rational and promised to stay away from Tanya. They released him, and notified the health service. No further efforts at commitment were made because apparently the supervising psychiatrist decided that such was not needed and, as a matter of confidentiality, requested that the letter to the police as well as certain therapy records be destroyed.
>
> On October 27th, Poddar went to Tanya's home armed with a pellet gun and a kitchen knife. She refused to speak to him. He shot her with the pellet gun. She ran from the house, was pursued, caught, and repeatedly and fatally stabbed. Poddar was found guilty of voluntary manslaughter rather than first or second degree murder. The defense established, with the aid of the expert testimony of three psychiatrists, that Poddar's diminished mental capacity (paranoid schizophrenia) precluded the malice necessary for first or second degree murder. After his prison term, he returned to India where, according to his own report, he is happily married. (Schwitzgebel and Schwitzgebel, 1980, p. 205)

One outcome of the litigation surrounding the Tarasoff case was a ruling that psychotherapists are responsible for determining whether or not their clients are dangerous and, having determined danger, are responsible for warning potential victims of client violence. Although the initial ruling was based upon a clear need to protect life and property of others, recent reports have suggested that the Tarasoff ruling may present special problems for the mental health professions (Appelbaum, 1985). For example, many therapists seem to believe that the obligation to warn and the potential for breaking confidence which it involves, jeopardizes their therapeutic relationship with clients and ultimately could reduce the effectiveness of treatment (Gurevitz, 1977). In spite of such concern, however, Beck (1982) reports that 50 percent of a group of therapists surveyed had at some point since the Tarasoff decision issued warnings to potential victims of client violence.

Appelbaum (1985) has proposed a three-phase model for application of the Tarasoff ruling. Each phase appears to be important not only in ensuring the safety of others but also in pointing out some paradigmatic problems being faced by modern abnormal psychology. In phase I, the therapist's task is to assess accurately the degree of client dangerousness. In this task, the limits of the current major paradigms seem to be pressed significantly. Although there are some rough guidelines for assessing dangerousness, some people believe that accurate prediction of dangerousness is "beyond the capacity of the mental health professions" (Appelbaum, 1985, p. 426). However, others believe that enough is known about the signs of dangerousness for professionals to agree on potential for violence (Monahan, 1981). Recognizing both views, Appelbaum still concludes, "Given our failure so far to demonstrate any significant predictive abilities, one can only note the difficulty that this . . . first stage represents" (p. 426). From the perspective of abnormal psychology as a science, it would seem that we are faced here with an anomaly, a situation which cannot adequately be handled within current paradigmatic perspectives.

In phase II of the Tarasoff process, there are also some difficulties which seem to illuminate the limits of our understanding. Here therapists must choose a course of action designed to protect potential victims of client violence. Once again, the need for effective paradigmatically derived views of behavior may be seen, for in their decisions about which paradigm to apply, therapists are placing people's emotional and physical well-being on the line. In addition to or in lieu of actual warning of potential victims, several different paradigmatic views may be applied, as described by Appelbaum (1985):

> Depending on the circumstances, one might choose to hospitalize the patient voluntarily or involuntarily, to transfer an already hospitalized patient to a more secure ward, or to maintain the outpatient status but begin medication, intensive individual therapy, family therapy, or other systems—oriented therapy. . . . (p. 426)

The final step in application of the Tarasoff decision is the *effective* use of the course of action chosen in phase II. Here, the skill of the therapist and the appropriateness of the chosen action are crucial factors. For example, if the potential violence is biologically based (as has been suggested in some studies of genetic variations among criminals) and a systems-based intervention is chosen, effective reduction of danger may not be realized. Similarly, improper dosage or selection of medication, even if a biological approach is warranted, may not protect potential victims.

In addition to decreasing the likelihood of harm coming to family, friends, or others who interact with dangerous disturbed persons, the Tarasoff decision is also important as an event in the ongoing history of the science of abnormal psychology. When looked at from the perspective of philosophy of science, several implications emerge. The need to warn, for example, seems to reflect a limited capacity to reliably *alter* dangerous behavior. Limited capacity to alter dangerous behavior may reflect a lack of clear understanding of its causes (remember Dearborn's Dictum—If you can't change something, then you don't understand it). The lack of clear understanding suggests that existing paradigms are faced with an anomaly and new paradigms may be needed. Although apparently a discouraging state of affairs, the obligation to warn and its implications for the mental health professions need to be seen as part of the natural and normal ongoing process of the science of abnormal psychology.

lated and he was ordered to be released from the hospital.

We do not contend that Donaldson's caretakers (nor the caretakers at Bryce Hospital in Alabama against whom the *Wyatt vs Stickney right to treatment* decisions were directed) were unwilling to help their patients. Rather, we suggest that there was not a sufficient amount of scientific knowledge of psychopathology available to allow these professionals to treat their patients effectively.

Bronfenbrenner (1977) has invoked a saying ascribed to one of his valued men-

One significant indication of the failure of our present day paradigms to deal adequately with disordered behavior is the increased involvement of the legal profession in determining how mental health treatment should be administered. (*©1981 Laimute E. Druskis/Taurus Photos*)

tors, Walter Dearborn. Dearborn's Dictum, as described by Bronfenbrenner, reads, "If you want to understand something, try to change it" (Bronfenbrenner, 1977, p. 517). We suggest that a corollary of Dearborn's Dictum might be stated, "If you can't change something, it may be that you do not understand it fully." The legal system appears to believe that psychiatry and clinical psychology do not fully understand abnormal behavior. In this light, Miller et al. (1976) note:

> Despite many recent advances in medical knowledge, it remains a stubborn fact that there are many forms of mental illness which are untreatable in the sense that no effective therapy has yet been discovered for them and that rates of "cure" are generally low. (p. 522)

Probably one of the best ways to measure how well we understand mental disorders is to assess the efficacy of our treatments. From the perspective of the legal profession, Miller et al. consider the mental health profession to be doing less than an adequate job of treating disordered behavior. Using as an indicator of treatment success the rate of patient *recidivism* (return to the hospital or recurrence of severe symptoms), they conclude:

1. Traditional methods . . . including individual therapy, group therapy, work therapy, and drug therapy do not affect differentially, discharged patients' community functioning as measured by recidivism and post-hospital employment.
2. Recidivism rate for a one-year period (post-hospitalization) is approximately 40–50%.

A disquieting upshot of legal disenchantment with psychiatric care and with abnormal psychology as a science is that the legal system has been "forced" to intervene and monitor the activities of many mental health care facilities. For example, rather than professional mental health workers determining proper therapeutic environment and regimen based on sound, paradigmatically derived, research-supported understanding of mental disorder, courts have sometimes "ordered" treatment facilities to follow specific guidelines based on litigated patient rights to receive and/or refuse treatment. (This was especially evident in the cases of Donaldson and *Wyatt vs Stickney*.) In many of these cases, mental health professionals have been cast as "the bad guys" who need to be controlled by outside forces rather than as the concerned professionals they typically are.

From the view of abnormal psychology as a science, the involvement of the legal system must be taken as an indicator of a crisis-in-science-as-is. It is a sign that our current modes of thinking about, studying, and treating abnormal behavior may not be working optimally, and that a paradigmatic shift to a new global view of abnormality may be in order.

The View from Within the Mental Health Profession

The legal system has been drawn into the crisis in abnormal psychology less out of inherent interest in the field as a paradigmatic science than out of the necessity of protecting people's constitutional rights. Within the mental health field, however, there are also a growing number of voices being raised which are reaching the same conclusion as the courts regarding the inadequacy of our current approaches to dealing with psychopathology. Proponents of all three major paradigms, in fact, appear to agree that we must alter our basic paradigmatic approach to psychopathology.

In one of the earliest statements from proponents of the psychosocial paradigm, Braginsky et al. (1964) paint a pessimistic picture of the chances of present-day paradigms and their derived methods, to adequately study the origins of, and interventions for, disordered behavior.

> Despite innumerable clinical observations recorded throughout history and thousands of empirical studies conducted within the last century our understanding of mental illness is still tragically inchoate. The history of the study of mental illness is littered with the debris of discarded conceptions of psychosis as well as now abandoned methods of treatment. This gloomy history is too well known for us to have to recapitulate it here. Today, too, we have our conceptions of mental illness and our preferred modes of treatment; what we do not have is any assurance that our present views and procedures are any more enlightened and efficacious than those that we now consider outmoded. Indeed there seems to be an increasingly uneasy feeling that we may be on the wrong track altogether, that our conception of mental illness is largely adventitious. (p. 11)

Twenty years after the Braginskys expressed their concerns, the efficacy of the systems perspective was questioned by Murphy et al. (1984). These investigators examined the prevalence rates for anxiety and depression in the same county where Leighton had studied them nearly 20 years

Although Murphy et al. would have expected deteriorated social conditions to be related to increased rates of disorder, he found they did not. (*Gloria Karlson*)

earlier. The expectation was that significant changes in the social, family, and work systems would result in greater rates of mental symptoms. Their finding was that the rates *had not changed significantly* in spite of all the increased complexities of life they observed. They concluded:

> Despite major social changes in Stirling County, we found that the prevalence of depression and anxiety remained at a strikingly constant level over an 18 year segment of the century's third quarter. Our purpose in this study was a descriptive one, focused on the question of whether prevalence increased, decreased, or remained stable. The findings, however, run counter to (our) theoretical expectations. . . . Many of the events that took place in Stirling County are similar to those that have been suggested as fostering depression and anxiety—weakening of community and religious ties, breakup of traditional patterns of work and family life, growing urbanism, exposure to mass media, etc.
>
> At the present time there is, however, an increasing amount of evidence that depression and anxiety are causally complex. It is likely, for example, that some depressions and some anxiety states are primarily biogenetic in origin, while others may be rooted in personality or psychosocial factors, and many may involve multiple interactive causes. The problem is that, thus far, ways have not been found for determining to any certain degree that one person's depression is genetic and another person's depression is social in nature. (Murphy et al., 1984, p. 996)

Finally, an adherent of the biological paradigm, Engel (1977) stated that the basic "fault in psychiatry" appears to be " . . . adherence to a model of disease no longer adequate for the scientific tasks and social responsibilities of either medicine or psychiatry" (p. 129). Engel stated further:

> . . . it serves little to be able to specify a biochemical defect in schizophrenia if one does not know how to relate this to particular psychological and behavioral experiences of the disorder. (p. 132)

While the views we have just described derive from different theoretical positions, they have been aptly summarized and reaffirmed by Marmor (1983), an internationally recognized figure in modern psychiatry and psychology. Marmor also believes that we are on the verge of a "paradigmatic shift" in the sciences of psychiatry and abnormal psychology. He contends that "unifactorial" adherence to what he calls the biological, psychological (psychosocial), and sociological (systems) paradigms has generated three major sources of scientific error in the study and treatment of abnormal behavior. The errors Marmor describes are in the form of *scientific reductionism,* that is, tendencies to reduce complex issues to more simplistic and probably less accurate levels of analysis.

> These fallacies fall into three categories: biological reductionism, psychological reductionism, and sociological reductionism. They all share a tendency to think of causation in linear, unifactorial terms, rather than in terms of the complex, pluralistic, multifactorial dynamics that are involved in all human psychopathology. (p. 835)

Much of Marmor's concern seems to be focused on the *unifactorial* views represented by the three major paradigms we have discussed throughout this text. With more specific reference to the simplistic use of the biological paradigm, Marmor states:

> . . . biological reductionism, in its crudest form, embraces the assumption that all mental illnesses are biological or biochemical in origin and that ultimately we shall be able to evolve an appropriate pill or pills that will "cure" all mental illness. . . . I am fully cognizant of the value of pharmacological agents in these various conditions, and I support their use. What I am concerned about is the tendency to approach many of these problems simply as biological ones, and in so doing, to ignore the other factors involved in such illnesses. (p. 835)

Marmor's concern about biological reductionism is matched by his apprehension that scientists will see everything as psychologically (psychosocially) determined. He traces psychological reductionism to the application of psychoanalytic theory (and we could probably add, behavioral theory) to almost all forms of psychopathology:

> Most of the emphasis was placed on the mothering relationship, and almost all forms of functional psychopathology were attributed to faulty parenting (or learning). . . . To this day there are still some individuals who treat the schizophrenic psychoses exclusively by long-term psychoanalytic techniques and oppose the use of antipsychotic medications. Many other illnesses such as the affective psychoses, infantile autism, Gilles de la Tourettes's syndrome, transsexualism, and some cases of homosexuality, in which genetic or biological components are now believed probably to be involved, were similarly explained on a purely psychogenic basis. . . . (p. 835)

Noting that many patterns of psychopathology seemingly arise more out of sociological (systems) than biological factors, Marmor also expresses concern about sociological reductionism. He warns that the unifactorial application of the systems paradigm represents an effort to:

> . . . "explain" problems of juvenile delinquency, violence, drug addiction and mental retardation wholly in terms of social, economic, or ethnic factors and to ignore relevant biological and psychodynamic factors that also may be involved. Although such sociological factors have some validity in terms of group trends, they fail entirely as explanations in any individual instance precisely because they assume a linear relationship between such external factors and the disordered behavior without considering the variety of (other) factors that also may be involved. (p. 835)

Having identified and expressed concern over the three forms of reductionism that hamper the study of abnormal behavior, Marmor calls for the development of alternative paradigms to more clearly reflect the multifactorial etiology of psychopathology. In our next section we will consider two such paradigms which have begun to emerge in response to the crisis-in-science affecting abnormal psychology.

Emerging Paradigms for the Study of Psychopathology

Throughout this text, we have examined the differential ability of what Marmor has termed the unifactorial paradigms to explain abnormal behavior patterns. In several instances where the unifactorial biological, psychosocial, and systems views have been inadequate, we have noted that integrations of these paradigms have been offered and in some cases seemed to result in better understanding of the disorders. In a sense, throughout the text we, ourselves, have been coming face to face with the crisis in abnormal psychology and with the problems of scientific reductionism described by Marmor; wherever this occurred, it seems, we were able to suggest evidence of emerging alternative paradigms such as the integrated approaches to schizophrenia, affective disturbances, and the substance-induced organic mental disorders. We have tried to present evidence that abnormal psychology is a science in search of new paradigms, that it is in the process of a paradigmatic shift. But where might such a shift lead? To some combination of all three existing paradigms? To a basically new way to explain human behavior? Or to some combination of these? While we do not know the forms future paradigms may take, there are possible alternatives beginning to emerge.

One alternative represents increasing usage of *multifactorial* combinations of the three existing paradigms. A second approach, the *interactionist* view, attempts to combine facets of heredity and environment within a developmental *life-span* framework. Each "new" paradigm is a possible successor to existing approaches and each could serve as a set-of-shared-beliefs to guide the work of significant groups of researchers and clinicians in the continuing process of the science of abnormal psychology.

The Multifactorial Paradigm

The multifactorial paradigm may best be described as an integration of the biological, psychosocial, and systems views. One of the major proponents of such a combination, which also has been called the *biopsychosocial paradigm,* is Engel (1977):

> The boundaries between health and illness are far from clear and never will be clear, for they are diffused by cultural, social, and psychological considerations. . . . By evaluating all the factors contributing to both illness and patienthood, rather than giving primacy to biological factors alone, a biopsychosocial model would make it possible to explain why some individuals experience as "illness" conditions which others regard merely as "problems in living." (pp. 132, 133)

In addition to Engel's call for a multifactorial paradigm, throughout this text we have seen other attempts to apply this emerging perspective. The final common pathway view of schizophrenia proposed by Cools (Chapter 8) and of depression offered by Akiskal and McKinney (Chapter 9), and the multiple viscious circles perspective on drug use (Chapter 13) are examples. In addition to its impact on theory, the multifactorial paradigm also can lead to the development of different research methods and topics for scientific investigations. For example, a study of the dopamine levels at the synapses of schizophrenics might not be seen as a useful endeavor unless these biochemical levels were tied in some way to things like the immediate psychological state of the subjects, their social class, or level of life stress.

A Lifespan Interactionist Paradigm

The *life-span interactionist paradigm* shares much with the multifactorial approach but adds to it a developmental component. As described by McCall (1977), this emerging paradigm "emphasizes a complex and interacting set of environmental and organismic determinants that *change over age.*" (p. 342). The determinants described by McCall refer to biological, psychosocial, and systems factors. However, interactional theorists seem to consider the multifactorial view by itself limited because:

> . . . it is insufficient to facilitate our understanding of the actual mechanisms leading to later outcomes. The major reason behind the inadequacy of this (the multifactorial) model is that neither constitution nor environment is necessarily constant over time. At each moment, month, or year the characteristics of both the child (or adult) and his environment change in important ways. Moreover, these differences are interdependent and change as a function of their mutual influence on one another. (Sameroff, 1975, p. 281)

The interactionist perspective includes a developmental view of behavior (Magnusson & Allen, 1983). According to this view, biological, psychosocial, and systems factors will differentially affect behavior as a function of age. Further, for different aged people, varying situational factors will result in greater or lesser abilities to cope and to behave in an adaptive fashion. Thomas and Chess (1980, 1984) have applied the interactionist paradigm in what they term the *goodness of fit—badness of fit* model of behavioral development and maladjustment. They state:

> Goodness of fit results when properties of the environment and its expectations and demands are in accord with the individual's own capacities. When this *consonance* between organism and environment is present, optimal development in a progressive direction is possible. Conversely, poorness of fit involves discrepancies and dissonances between the individual's capacities and environmental opportunities and demands, so that distorted development and maladaptive functioning occur. Goodness of fit is never an abstraction, but is always formulated in terms of the values, demands, and expectations of a given culture or socioeconomic group. (1980, p. 234)

From the view of researchers and clinicians, the interactionist paradigm suggests methods which emphasize the longitudinal aspects of the origins and maintenance of abnormal behavior. By studying infants, Thomas and Chess have identified three basic types of inborn *temperaments.* Depending on the family atmosphere, children with differing temperaments could experience either goodness or badness of fit. If they experience goodness of fit, their development may be optimized; if they face badness of fit, they may develop maladjustive patterns of behavior. The interactionist view is consistent with our presentation of developmental disorders in Chapters 16 to 18. These chapters demonstrated that the symptom patterns of psychopathology do in fact vary as a function of age and life situation. It would follow then that the causes, courses, and treatments of various patterns may also vary over the span of life.

Extending further the interactionist paradigm offered by Thomas and Chess, we have tried to emphasize the developmental aspects of the interaction among biological, psychosocial, and systems factors in the appearance of psychopathology (See also Magnusson & Allen, 1983). This extended perspective may be termed a *life-span interactionist paradigm.*

Based on our study of abnormal behavior and on research such as that reported by Thomas and Chess (1980, 1984), it appears that at least three things must be considered in order to understand disordered behavior: (1) the disorder in ques-

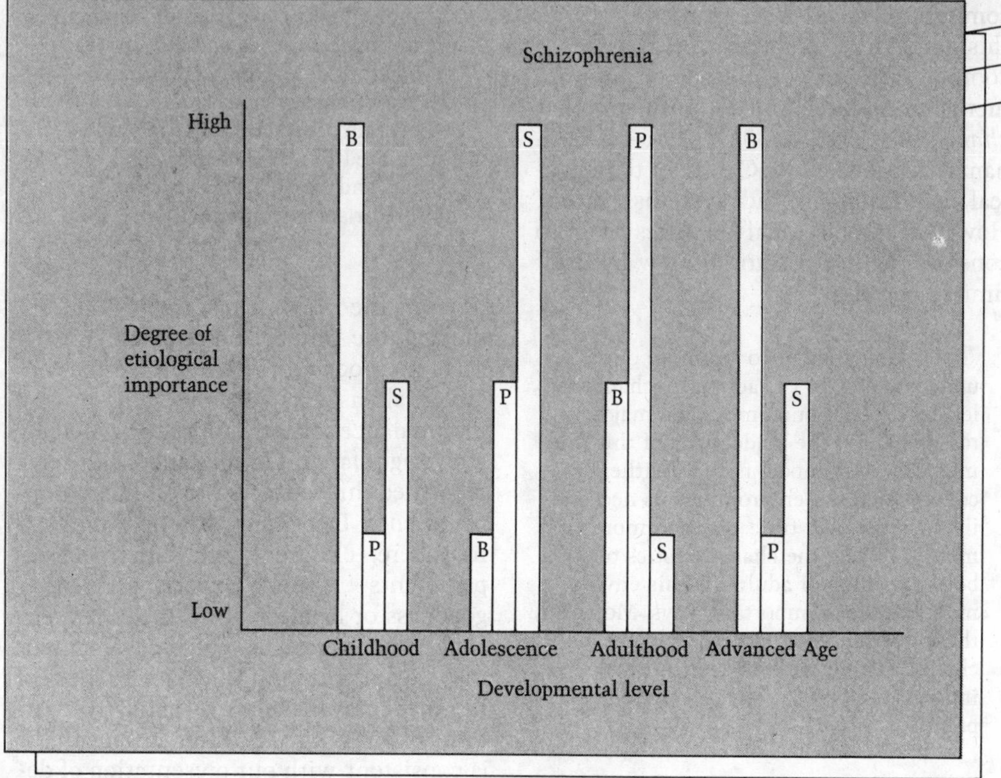

Figure 19-1 A Hypothetical Application of a Life-Span Interactional Paradigm to Schizophrenia: B—Biological Contribution; P—Psychosocial Contribution; S—Systems Contribution.

tion; (2) the *relative* importance or contribution to the disorder of biological, psychosocial, and systems factors; and (3) the age of the impacted individual. As depicted in Figure 19-1, the life-span interactionist view proposes that each specific disorder is affected differentially by biological, psychosocial, and systems factors as a function of an individual's developmental level.

Some examples may help show how applying the life-span interactionist paradigm can aid in explaining disordered behavior and directing intervention. In Figure 19-1 the application of this paradigm to schizophrenia is described. As shown, when schizophrenia occurs during the developmental stage of childhood, the biological components probably make the most significant contribution to the symptom pattern. However, in adolescence and young adulthood, most significant impact probably comes from systems sources such as family, social relationships, and social class. Figure 19-1 suggests further that psychosocial components may be most important in middle adulthood. Finally, in old age, as in childhood, schizophrenia may be determined primarily by biological components.

Treatment efforts based on the life-span interactionist paradigm also could be differentially applied. For example, because environmental manipulations are derived from the systems paradigm, they might

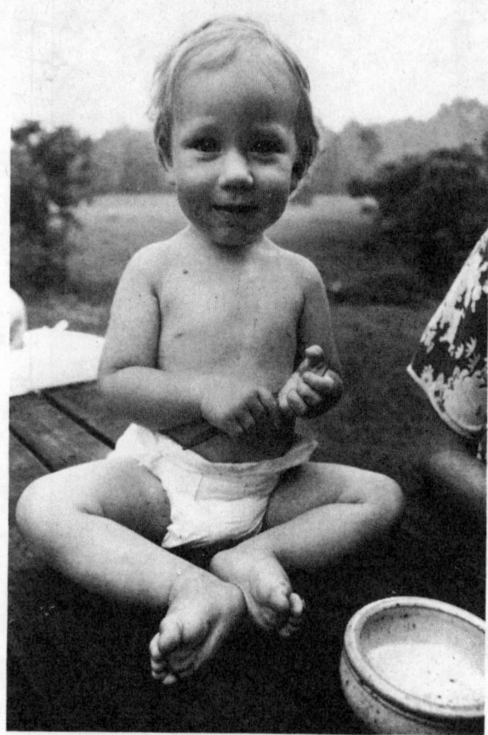

The relative importance of biological, psychosocial, and systems factors may differ considerably for the same disorder as a function of the age of the individual. (top left: *Michael Weisbrot and Family*; top right: *Laimute Druskis/Taurus*; bottom: © *Frank Siteman 1981/ Taurus*)

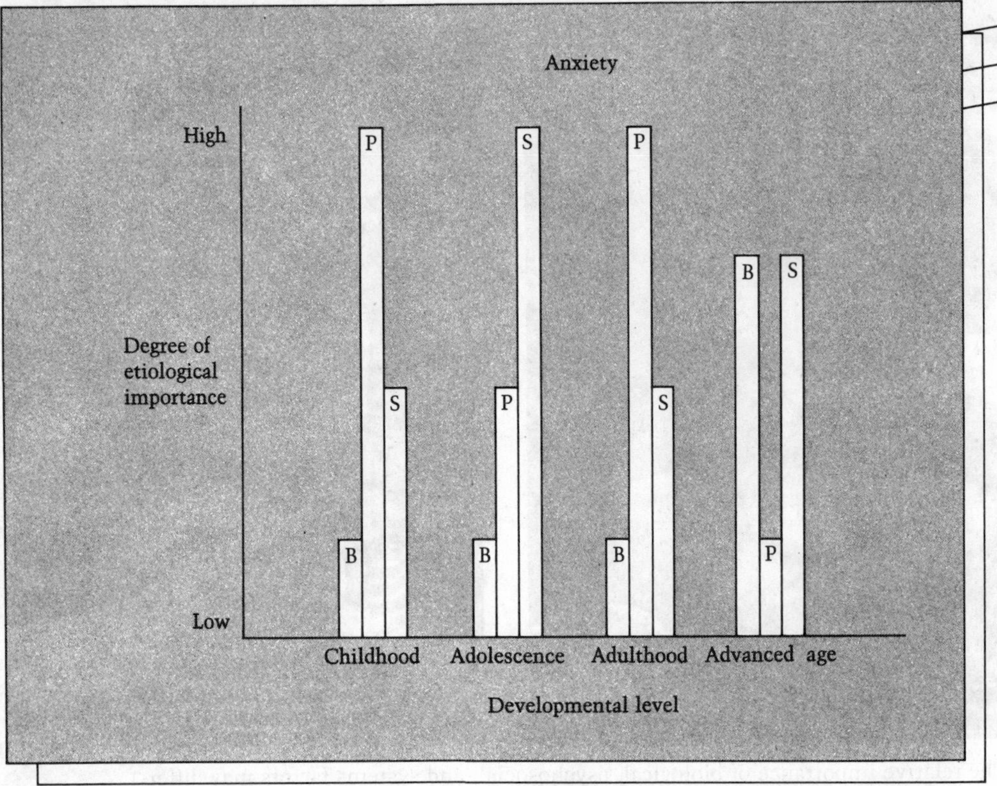

Figure 19-2 A Hypothetical Application of a Life-span Interactional Paradigm to Anxiety Disorders: B—Biological Contribution; P—Psychosocial Contribution; S—Systems Contribution.

be most effective for dealing with adolescents. On the other hand, for adults who probably are most affected by psychosocial factors, psychotherapy may be the preferred intervention. Finally, for children and the elderly, biologically based interventions might be most effective.

Another example may be helpful in clarifying how the life-span interactionist paradigm could be applied to conceptualizing psychopathology. In Figure 19-2, the paradigm is applied across age groups for anxiety disorders. Research evidence suggests that psychosocial factors would be most important for children and systems factors like peer and group pressures, for adolescents. Anxiety would be caused primarily by psychosocial factors again in adulthood, while factors like loss of sensory processing abilities and other faculties may make the biological paradigm the most appropriate perspective from which to view anxiety in the elderly. As in the example using the disorder of schizophrenia, primary interventions used would depend on the most important causative factor at a particular level of development.

Not only may the life-span interactionist paradigm yield new explanatory and therapeutic perspectives, but new research efforts as well. Research derived from this paradigm might focus on comparing children, adult, and elderly patterns of psychopathology and should involve approaches reflecting the combined efforts of scientists guided by the developmental, biological, psychosocial, and systems perspectives. One example is the work of D'Arcy (1982), who reported significant age variations in his study of symptomatology. D'Arcy reported higher rates of nonpsychotic symptoms in older and younger males and lower rates in middle-aged males. In women, on the other hand, severity of symptoms and rate of disorders seemed to increase with age in a more direct fashion.

Before concluding our description of the life-span interactionist paradigm, we will apply it to the case of Robert T. Were Robert to have been understood from this perspective we may have found his treatment to be much more biologically oriented when he was younger, perhaps involving genetic studies or efforts at biochemical adjustments. As he grew and more interpersonal demands were placed upon him, his treatment may have shifted significantly to helping him to learn verbal and nonverbal skills and improved ways of interacting with peers. In adolescence, Robert's treatment would have been focused on group functioning, fitting in, developing age-appropriate dress, and interest patterns. In young adulthood, despite the limited advances he had made to that point, major effort needed to be extended in teaching him basic skills so that he might be able to meet (even at the lowest levels) the age-related societal requirement to hold a job. As he grows older, he will need to face the changes brought about in his life by his parents' and his own aging. From the traditional paradigmatic perspectives, many of these life-span requirements also would be addressed, but many of them would probably not have been given the same level of emphasis.

The interactionist view is among several which are currently emerging. However, no one of these emerging views has, as yet, generated sufficient research and theory to render it a significant force when compared with the unifactorial biological, psychosocial, and systems paradigms. Future research and application of the new paradigms must be the determinants of their eventual usefulness as sets-of-shared-beliefs in the science of abnormal psychology.

Concluding Comments

Over the years, the major paradigms guiding the science of abnormal psychology have led to significant advances in our abilities to understand and treat psychopathology. However, as is true of any paradigmatic science, there comes a time when advances based upon existing paradigms become increasingly small and the limits of guiding global views become increasingly apparent. It is our belief that for abnormal psychology that time is now upon us. We believe that the science of abnormal psychology is at a crucial place, a growing "crisis" stage that Kuhn feels can precede a scientific "revolution." Out of this healthy and normal crisis stage, we believe the paradigms of the future will emerge to replace and/or supplement those that have directed the study of disordered behavior for over a century. Be the future paradigms unifactorial, multifactorial, interactionist, or some as-yet-unthought-of view, the paradigmatic shifts of the future will have as much impact as those which have in the past changed the course of abnormal psychology. Perhaps the scientific "tension" of the present may yield positive changes like the rise of humanistic treatment of the mentally ill brought about by Pinel; the focus on psychosocial factors brought about by Freud; the emergence of the systems view spurred by the work of Dix and other community-oriented thinkers; the hospital reforms in response to the historical work of Clifford

Beers; the reduction in hospitalization rates produced by the advent of drug treatments; and the recognition of the legal rights of mental patients gained through the case of Kenneth Donaldson. If Kuhn's description of the progress of science is at all correct, then whether we like it or not, we may be in the midst of a significant change process that can result in new, more effective ways of studying, understanding, and above all, helping disordered people.

Summary Chart

In this last chapter of our text, we first tried to provide a general overview of the major paradigms and their strengths and weaknesses.

Biological paradigm: Works well with schizophrenias, affective psychoses, some somatic disorders, and addictions

Psychosocial paradigm: Best with anxiety disorders, paranoid disturbances, dissociative disorders, and personality disturbances

Systems paradigm: Effective in explaining and treating substance-abuse disorders, stress disorders, and certain psychotic patterns

We noted that there seems to be growing concern about our understanding of abnormal behavior:

The legal perspective: Right to treatment cases, high rates of recidivism, legal intervention with psychiatric treatment

The mental health profession's perspective: Concerns from supporters of all three major paradigms

Out of the current concerns regarding the difficulties faced by the three major modern paradigms guiding abnormal psychology, some newer paradigms are beginning to emerge:

The multifactorial paradigm: A biopsychosocial view of psychopathology; applied to several disorders in the text

The life-span interactionist paradigm: Differential contribution of biological, psychosocial, and systems factors as functions of age of individual and disorder in question

We closed our text with a restatement of our belief that abnormal psychology is a vibrant, ongoing scientific process and that its successes and failures are parts of the normal progression of scientific inquiry.

Glossary

Abreaction: The reliving or reexperiencing of feelings about past events; catharsis

Academic-mechanics disorders: Patterns in college students in which specific academic skills, such as the ability to take tests, are either lacking or impaired

Accidental crisis: In community psychology, a crisis precipitated by a stressful and unpredictable life experience

Acetylcholine: A catecholamine serving as a neurotransmitter at many sites throughout the nervous system

Acquisition: The learning of a response in classical or operant conditioning

Action potential: The brief electrical impulse by which information is conducted along an axon

Activity theory: A theory stating that behavioral norms for old age are identical to those for middle age, and which measures adjustment to aging by the amount of middle-aged activity maintained or lost

Acute brain syndrome: A pattern of symptoms, including delirium, occurring as a result of some trauma, intoxication, or the like

Acute versus chronic schizophrenia: A dimensional representation of schizophrenia ranging from that with sudden onset (acute) to that associated with long-term symptomatology (chronic)

Addiction: A physiological dependence on a drug characterized by increased bodily tolerance and withdrawal symptoms

Addison's disease: An endocrine disorder caused by reduced levels of adrenal corticoids associated with psychological symptoms of fear, hallucinations, irrational beliefs, and depression and physical symptoms of muscular weakness, stomach upset, and skin discoloration

Adolescent crisis: An adjustment reaction of adolescence that can range from normal turmoil to severe disturbance

Adjustment reaction: A transient, acute psychopathological response to a situation without underlying personality disturbance

Adoption studies: A research method which estimates the heritability of a trait or disorder by comparing incidence rates in adoptive and biological families

Adrenaline: A hormone secreted by the adrenal glands; also called epinephrine

Affect: A term referring to the expression of emotions in general

Affective disorders: A group of psychotic disorders characterized by disturbance of mood

Affective personality: A personality disorder in which the primary personality style is marked by alternating and recurring episodes of depression and elation

Affective psychosis: See Affective disorders

Agitated depression: Feelings of sadness and dejection accompanied by an inability to stop moving about or talking rapidly

Agoraphobia: An anxiety disorder characterized by fear of open places

Alcoholics Anonymous: A self-help organization begun by recovered alcoholics to aid in the rehabilitation of other alcoholics through group meetings and mutual support

Alcoholism: Dependence on alcohol with increased bodily tolerance and the presence of withdrawal symptoms

Altruistic suicide: Durkheim's term for suicide performed as a sacrifice for the common good

Alzheimer's disease: Presenile dementia due to widespread degeneration of brain cells

Ambivalence: Often a primary sign of schizophrenia, this term describes the mixture of positive and negative feelings about a given thing, person, or situation

Amnesia: Disruption of memory processes associated with dissociative reactions, organic brain syndromes, or hypnosis

Amphetamines: A group of drugs that function as central nervous system stimulants

Anal stage: Freudian psychosexual stage in which satisfactions center about the retention or passage of feces

Analysand: A patient in psychoanalysis

Anhedonia: A defect in the capacity to feel pleasure

Anomic suicide: Durkheim's term for suicide that occurs after an unfavorable change in social or financial conditions, when a person believes his or her expected lifestyle is no longer possible

Anomie: Durkheim's term for the feelings surrounding social isolation and alienation

Anorexia nervosa: A psychophysiological disorder characterized by prolonged inability to eat or retain food

Anoxia: Lack of oxygen in the tissues

Antidepressant drugs: A group of chemicals, including tricyclics and monoamine oxidase inhibitors, that relieve the symptoms of depression

Antimanic drugs: A group of drugs, the most effective of which is lithium carbonate, that reduce the symptoms of manic disorders

Antipsychotic drugs: A group of chemicals known to reduce (not cure) many symptoms of severe psychosis

Antisocial personality disorder: A longstanding pattern of antisocial behavior, including at least four of the following manifestations: inability to work consistently; inability to function responsibly as a parent; repeated violations of the law; inability to maintain an enduring sexual relationship; frequent fighting; failure to repay debts and provide child support; travel from place to place without planning; repeated lying and conning; and extreme recklessness

Anxiety: An unrealistic and irrational fear of some thing or situation; the pattern has both psychological and physiological characteristics

Anxiety disorders: A group of disorders characterized by the predominance of anxiety, or the experience of anxiety when a dreaded object or situation is confronted or obsessions and compulsions are resisted

Anxiety states: A group of anxiety disorders marked by persistent feelings of apprehension and impending disaster, and "free-floating fear," accompanied by symptoms such as insomnia, difficulty making decisions, loss of appetite, and heart palpitations

Apathy reaction: A pattern often seen in college students in which malaise and boredom seem to overpower the motivation to study

Apraxia: An inability to perform a specific motor act

Arteriosclerosis: A disorder affecting blood flow in the blood vessels which is believed to be involved in the onset of some cases of senile dementia

Assertion training: A behavioral therapy technique in which people learn through behavioral rehearsal to defend their rights and assert themselves appropriately

Astasia-abasia: A motor conversion disorder marked by an inability to stand (astasia), or an inability to walk without a wobbly, staggering gait

Asthenic personality: A personality disorder in which the primary personality style is marked by fatigue and lack of energy

Asthma: A respiratory disorder characterized by difficulty in breathing sometimes brought about by stress

Attention deficit disorder: A childhood disorder marked by inattention and impulsivity, which may or may not be accompanied by hyperactivity

Attentional-interference theory: A psychosocial approach to schizophrenia which focuses on the role of attention and perception in etiology

Autism: A self-centered involvement in one's own feelings and thoughts, often to the exclusion of the rest of the world

Autonomic conversion disorder: A form of conversion disorder affecting the digestive, eliminative, or reproductive system

Autonomic conversion reaction: A nonorganic hysterical reaction resulting in impairment of some autonomic process

Autonomic nervous system: That part of the nervous system which controls "involuntary" processes like breathing, perspiration, digestion

Autoscopic experiences: Disorders in which people perceive themselves as being projected outside of their own bodies

Aversive conditioning: A behavioral therapy technique in which behavioral frequency is decreased by associating an undesirable behavior with an aversive consequence

Aversive therapy: A behavior therapy procedure in which punishment or aversive stimulation is used to eliminate undesired responses

Avoidance learning: A form of operant learning in which an organism learns to avoid aversive experiences and situations

Avoidant personality disorder: A long-standing personality pattern characterized by hypersensitivity to perceived rejection, a demand for uncritical acceptance, social withdrawal despite a desire for affection and acceptance, and low self-esteem

Axon: A fiber emanating from the cell body of a neuron that is primarily involved in carrying impulses to other cells

Barbiturates: Addictive sedatives that function as central nervous system depressants

Barnum effect: A magnification of the placebo effect in psychotherapy through the "selling" of a technique by a therapist

Basedow's disease: A condition caused by a hyperactive thyroid gland and marked by irritability and anxiety

Bedlam: The colloquial name for St. Mary's of Bethlehem, a mental hospital noted for its inhumane treatment of inmates

Behavioral psychotherapy: Psychotherapy derived from laboratory principles of learning and behavior change; also known as behavior modification or behavior therapy

Behavior modification: See Behavioral psychotherapy

Behavior modification groups: Group application of behavioral methods such as systematic desensitization or covert sensitization

Benzodiazepine: A class of minor tranquilizers, including diazepam (Valium). Widely prescribed in the United States, these drugs are effective in reducing anxiety

Bestiality: Sexual activity between humans and animals

Biochemical theory of schizophrenia: A general belief deriving from the biological paradigm that schizophrenia is caused by some chemical aberration in the body

Bioenergetic group therapy: Group treatment of psychological problems through involvement of the mind *and* body in the therapy process

Biofeedback: Presentation of physiological responses as a means of training an individual to gain conscious control over these responses

Biogenic: Physically caused or based

Biological paradigm: A paradigm that focuses on organic causes of abnormal behavior

Biopsychosocial paradigm: A paradigm which integrates biological, psychosocial, and systems approaches to the study of mental health and specific mental disorders

Bipolar disorder: An affective disorder in which the individual has experienced episodes of both mania and depression or of mania alone

Blunting of affect: A muffling of the intensity of expressed feelings often seen in schizophrenic people

Borderline personality disorder: A long-standing personality pattern characterized by extreme fluctuations in mood, interpersonal relationships, and self-image

Brain stem: The part of the brain containing the pons and medulla oblongata. It connects the spinal cord with the cerebrum and functions as a neural relay station

Brawner rule: A 1972 American court ruling that effectively reduced the power of expert witnesses in insanity defense cases by allowing them to be cross-examined and requiring them to provide objective support for their contentions

Brief reactive psychosis: A syndrome in which a period of stress leads to emotional turmoil and at least one psychotic symptom, such as loose associations, delusions, hallucinations, or catatonia

Bulimia: An eating disorder in which the individual repeatedly and uncontrollably consumes large quantities of food and drink in a short time. This binge eating is followed by depressed mood and self-deprecation, and often by attempts to lose weight by vomiting, dieting, or use of cathartics.

Butyrophenones: A category of antipsychotic drugs, including haloperidol

Campus crisis center: A location on many college campuses where, on a 24-hour basis, immediate help is available for emotional problems

Cannula: A small tube implanted in a specific site in the brain through which chemicals under study may be passed and their effects on behavior noted

Capgras' syndrome: A condition marked by the belief that familiar objects and persons are actually frauds or imposters

Cardiac arrhythmia: Irregular heartbeat

Cardiovascular disorder: Medical problems involving the heart and blood circulation system, such as hypertension and coronary heart disease

Castration anxiety: Fear of having the genitals removed or injured. According to psychoanalytic theory, this fear is associated with a boy's concern that his father might discover the sexual attraction he has for his mother.

Cataplexy: A sudden loss of muscle tone resulting in collapse of the entire body

Catatonia: A psychotic behavior pattern usually marked by mutism, waxy flexibility, automatic obedience, and withdrawal, but sometimes indicated by severe agitation and hyperactivity

Catecholamine hypothesis: The biological paradigm—based belief that deviations in certain neurotransmitters play a role in the development of the affective disorders

Catecholamines: A group of biochemicals, some of which (acetylcholine and norepinephrine, for example) are involved in neural transmission

Catharsis: Discharge of pent-up feelings; believed to be of therapeutic value

Cenesthetic hallucinations: Sensations experienced in bodily locations which are not neurologically "wired" to experience them

Central nervous system: Neural system composed of the brain and spinal cord

Cerebellum: A major structure of the hindbrain concerned with balance, posture, and motor coordination

Cerebral cortex: The highly convoluted surface layers of the cerebrum

Cerebrospinal fluid: The protective fluid that surrounds most of the central nervous system

Childhood depression: Depressive patterns in children through age 12

Childhood schizophrenia: A term applied to various symptoms of a schizophrenic nature appearing early in life, such as absence of emotional responsivity, disturbed language functions, failure to relate to others, distorted and autistic thinking, and disordered motor activity

Chlorpromazine: A phenothiazine derivative, one of the most commonly prescribed antipsychotic drugs

Chronic brain syndrome: A pattern of symptoms, including dementia, usually occurring as a result of some form of progressive brain disease

Circumscribed amnesia: A form of psychogenic amnesia involving loss of memory for a specified period of time

Circumscribed delusions: Unfounded beliefs that are limited in scope to a specific thing, person, or situation

Clang association: An association of words by similarity of sound instead of meaning

Classical conditioning: The association of a neutral stimulus (conditioned stimulus) with an unconditioned stimulus such that the neutral stimulus comes to bring about a conditioned response; also known as respondent conditioning

Client-centered therapy: A form of psychotherapy developed by Carl Rogers that emphasizes providing an atmosphere in which client's innate self-actualizing tendencies can produce positive growth

Clinical psychologist: A person holding a Ph.D. or Psy.D. degree in applied or clinical psychology who is trained in diagnostic testing, psychotherapy, and research methodology

Cocaine: A pain-reducing stimulant obtained from the leaves of the coca plant

Cognitive behavior modification: A treatment approach based on the assumption that clinical disorders are due to maladaptive thought patterns, and that the task of therapy is to identify these patterns and replace them with more adaptive cognitions

Cognitive dysfunctions: Thinking disorders

Colitis: A sometimes psychophysiologically based disorder in which intense abdominal pain, bleeding stools, and irritation of the colon are common symptoms

Community intervention: Organized efforts to deal actively with community problems

Community psychology: A systems-based approach to mental disturbances that focuses on prevention at the societal level rather than on treatment at the individual level

Compulsive personality disorder: A long-standing personality pattern characterized by perfectionism, preoccupation with details and schedules, stinginess, difficulty expressing warm emotions, emphasis on work rather than pleasure, and avoidance of decisions for fear of making a mistake

Compulsive reaction: A persistent, uncontrollable impulse to perform a stereotyped, repetitive action

Concordance rate: The percentage of twin pairs in which both members manifest the same disturbance under study

Concretization: A disturbance marked by overemphasis on detail and immediate experience

Conditioned emotional reaction: A learned fear to a once neutral and usually harmless situation

Conditioned response (CR): In classical conditioning, the response elicited by the conditioned stimulus

Conditioned stimulus (CS): In classical conditioning, the originally neutral stimulus which, through association with an unconditioned stimulus, comes to elicit a conditioned response

Conduct disorder: A disorder marked by repetitive, persistent conduct which violates the basic rights of others or major social norms and rules

Confusional psychosis: A psychosis in which behavior ranges from excited confusion to inhibited confusion

Congruence: In Rogers' client-centered approach, the need for the therapist to act in accordance with his true feelings

Conjoint family therapy: A method of therapy developed by Satir in which an entire family is seen in an attempt to help one of its members

Conscience: That part of the superego composed of thoughts and behaviors to be avoided; a listing of "don'ts"

Conscious: According to Freud, those needs, wishes, thoughts, memories, and motives of which a person is aware at any given time

Continuity theory: A theory stating that adjustment to old age should be measured by one's ability to maintain continuity in habits, relationships, and activities

Continuous amnesia: A form of psychogenic amnesia involving memory loss for events subsequent to a specific time up to and including the present

Continuous reinforcement: A schedule of reinforcement in which rewards are administered every time a response is emitted

Control group: A group of subjects exposed to all aspects of an experiment except for the experimental variable

Conversion disorder: A somatoform disorder characterized by the appearance of physical symptoms or malfunctions without actual physical bases; formerly termed conversion hysteria

Coprolalia: The use of obscene and lewd language, often in an impulsive and uncontrolled way

Coronary personality: A person whose life-style predisposes him or her to coronary heart disease; often referred to as type A personality

Correlate: A variable that is related to another variable

Correlation: Any relationship between two variables, especially a concomitant variation

Covert reinforcement: A method used in behavior therapy in which a person strengthens desirable behavior by imagining a pleasant event or situation as a reward

Covert sensitization: A behavioral-therapy technique in which, in the imagination, undesirable behaviors or thoughts are reduced in frequency by association with aversive thoughts and images

Cretinism: A condition caused by hypoactivity of the thyroid gland, marked by inhibited growth, bodily distortion, and retarded intellectual development

Crisis: A situation or event which produces stress and precipitates disorganization of behavior or affect

Crisis-intervention theory: The belief that people are most responsive to helping efforts when in a state of crisis, as when contemplating suicide or under other great stress

Cultural relativism: The idea that psychological theories and behavioral standards developed in one culture may not apply to another

Curative factors: Factors which are presumed to account for the efficacy of group therapy

Cushing's disease: An endocrine disorder caused by excess levels of adrenal corticoids and characterized by psychological symptoms of crying, jitteriness, agitation, and irritability

Cyclothymic disorder: An affective disorder characterized by chronic recurrent mood disturbance involving repetitive periods of moderate depression alternating with hypomania

Defense mechanism: A general name for a variety of methods through which a person protects the integrity of the ego

Delirious mania: A degree of manic excitement so severe that the individual becomes delirious and loses touch with the environment

Delirium: A set of symptoms usually caused by reversible and temporary cessation of brain function. Symptoms may vary but include clouding of thought, bewilderment, hallucinations, and the like.

Delirium tremens (DT's): Hallucinations, delusions, and other symptoms often accompanying withdrawal from alcohol addiction

Delusion: A belief or attitude system not shared by the majority of others and seemingly not based upon realistic assessment of events

Dementia: A progressive loss of brain function usually associated with chronic and irreversible brain disease

Dementia praecox: A little used term for schizophrenia meaning "early madness"

Demographic variables: Characteristics of people such as age, sex, marital status, and the like that are often related statistically to differential incidence or prevalence of disorders

Dendrites: Fibers emanating from a neuron cell body that are primarily involved in receiving impulses from other neurons

Denial: A defense mechanism that involves denying specific aspects of the internal or external environment

Dependent personality disorder: A long-standing personality pattern characterized by passively allowing others to take responsibility for major areas of life

Dependent variable: In a psychological experiment, the factor which the hypothesis predicts will vary with changes in the independent variable

Depersonalization: A state of mind in which the individual experiences oneself as unreal, and feels estranged from oneself and the external world; thoughts and experiences take on a distant, dreamlike quality

Depersonalization disorder: A dissociative disorder marked by one or more episodes in which the self appears unreal, the individual feels estranged from the outside world, and thoughts and experiences take on a distant, dreamlike quality

Depression: A type of disorder, of either neurotic or psychotic degree, characterized by sadness, apathy, and self-deprecation

Depressive neurosis: A neurotic disorder marked by excessive sadness usually precipitated by some specific environmental event

Depressive stupor: A degree of depression so severe that the person does not move, talk, or show many signs of responsivity

Dereism: A tendency toward fantasies and hallucinations

Developmental crisis: A crisis precipitated by

a transition from one developmental phase to another

Detachment level: The degree to which an immigrant group has been assimilated (or not) into a new culture

Dexamethasome suppression test (DST): A laboratory test for endogenous depression. Research has shown that depressed individuals tend not to process the drug dexamethasone in the same way as normals and thus manfest higher concentrations at intervals past administration.

Diabetes mellitus: A metabolic disorder caused by ineffective production or utilization of the hormone insulin, which is secreted by the pancreas

Diathesis: Predisposition toward a disease or abnormality

Diathesis-stress theory: The belief that schizophrenia and several other disturbances are the result of the interaction between some inherited predisposition and some adverse environmental circumstances

Direct analysis: A form of psychotherapy developed by John Rosen that is especially effective with psychotic people

Disengagement theory: A theory stating that retirement involves a concomitant sharp decline in social interaction, a reduced life space, and loss of social esteem and morale

Displacement: A defense mechanism characterized by a shift of feelings from an original thing, person, or situation to some less threatening thing, person, or situation

Dissociative disorders: A group of disorders in which separation of anxiety-producing thoughts or personality characteristics from awareness results in sudden, temporary alterations in consciousness, identity, or motor behavior

Dizygotic twins: Twins having different genetic makeup; fraternal twins

Dopamine hypothesis: The concept that schizophrenia is caused by excessive dopamine in the brain, due to either overproduction of dopamine or a deficiency in the enzyme which converts dopamine to norepinephrine

Double-bind communication: A type of communication in which the tone of the message and the verbal content of the message contradict or negate each other

Down's syndrome: A type of mental retardation caused by an extra chromosome, once termed mongolism because of the characteristic epicanthan fold about the eyes

Dream analysis: A key psychoanalytic technique involving interpretation of the patient's dreams

Drug abuse: Use of any drug in a manner for which it was not prescribed or developed

DSM-II: The second edition of the Diagnostic and Statistical Manual of Mental Disorders published by the American Psychiatric Association

DSM-III: The current diagnostic and statistical manual of the American Psychological Association

Durham rules: A 1954 American court decision which stated that defendents were not considered criminally responsible if their unlawful acts were a product of mental disease

Dysfunction: A malfunction of a behavioral system; a disorder or disturbance

Dysphoria: An unpleasant mood characterized by discontent, depression, anxiety, and restlessness

Dyspnea: A feeling of difficulty in getting sufficient air; difficulty in breathing

Dyspraxia: An inability to perform a specific motor act adequately

Dyssocial personality: A pattern of personality developed in and approved by a subculture but often rejected or condemned by the dominant culture

Dysthymic disorder: An affective disorder characterized by chronic mood disturbance involving persistent or recurrent periods in which relatively mild depressive symptoms predominate

Echolalia: A symptom characterized by mimicking the verbalizations of others

Echopraxia: A symptom characterized by mimicking the behaviors of others

Eclecticism: A theoretical and practical approach which combines diverse conceptual formulations or techniques into an integrated approach

Educable mentally retarded: Retarded people with IQs ranging from 50 to 75 who can be expected to achieve from a third- to a sixth-grade educational level

Ego: According to Freud, that part of the psychic triumvirate which mediates between id and superego requirements and the limits of reality

Ego-analysis: A modification of classical psychoanalysis, based on a conception of the human being as having a stronger, more autonomous ego with gratifications independent of id satisfactions

Ego boundary: A psychoanalytic term referring to the limits set by the ego between the self and the rest of the world

Ego disintegration: The loss of the ability of the ego to mediate between the demands of the id and superego and the outside world; personality breakdown

Ego-dystonic: A term which describes impulses or thoughts that are unacceptable to oneself

Ego ideal: That part of the superego which is composed of positive goals; a listing of "do's"

Egoistic suicide: Durkheim's term for individualistic suicide, not associated with a person's relationship to society

Electra phase: See Oedipal-Electra phase

Electroconvulsive therapy (ECT): Electrical induction of convulsive seizures that can be effective in the treatment of depression

Electroencephalogram (EEG): A recording of the electrical activity of the brain

Electromyograph: A device for recording the electrical activity of muscles

Emotive imagery: A therapeutic technique for children in which fears are countered with images of special relationships with heroes, valued objects, and the like

Empathy: The objective awareness of another person's thoughts and feelings and their possible meanings

Encephalitis: An inflammation of the brain, most often caused by a virus. Symptoms may be mild and resemble those of the flu, or may be very serious, with fever, delirium, convulsions, coma, and death

Encopresis: Weak or absent control over bowel movements in older children and adults

Encounter group: A form of group therapy emphasizing personal growth and improved interpersonal communications through direct confrontation and reduction of defenses

Endocrine system: The group of glands that secrete behavior-affecting chemical substances (hormones) directly into the bloodstream

Endogenous depression: Depression seemingly caused by internal processes of a chronic nature

Endogenous hallucinogens: Hallucinogenic chemicals produced within the body

Endorphins: Opiate-like substances produced in the brain and pituitary gland; neuropeptides

Enuresis: Weak or absent control over urination in older children and adults; bedwetting

Epidemiology: The study of the incidence of pathological conditions and their distribution.

Epilepsy: A chronic brain disorder characterized by some form of seizure, often accompanied by loss of consciousness

Erectile dysfunction: The inability of a male to achieve or maintain an erection sufficient for completion of intercourse

Erogotamine tartrate: A drug obtained from ergot, a plant fungus; which is used to treat migraine headaches

Eros: According to Freud, the innate life instinct

Essential hypertension: High blood pressure with no discernible physical basis

Etiology: Causative factors in a disease or disturbance

Eugenics: The application of genetics to the alteration of a species

Exhibitionism: Arousal related to the display of one's sexual organs in public

Existential anxiety: According to Sören Kierkegaard, a universal experience occurring when a person faces responsibility for his or her own fate

Existential therapy: A form of psychotherapy emphasizing a person's need to live within the "now" and to exercise free choice in life

Experimental group: A group of subjects exposed to one or more independent variables or to a set of treatment conditions for purposes of scientific inquiry

Experimenter bias: The ability of a researcher

to influence the behavior of a subject consistent with the researcher's beliefs

Exogenous depression: Depression seemingly caused by some external stressful life event

Exorcism: A method through which those believed to be possessed by demons are released through prayer, incantation, and sometimes physical abuse

Expectancies: Beliefs in the chance of occurrence of certain events based upon previous experiences in similar situations

Experimental neurosis: An abnormal behavior pattern produced in animals by specific classical or operant conditioning procedures

Explosive personality: A personality disorder in which the primary style is marked by dangerous episodic outbursts of physical aggression

Extinction: Reduction of the frequency of a response due to lack of reinforcement (operant conditioning) or to repeated presentation of a conditioned stimulus in the absence of an unconditioned stimulus (classical conditioning)

Family therapy: A method of treatment in which the family rather than one individual in the family is the target of therapeutic efforts

Fetishism: Sexual attraction to an inanimate object or specific body part

Final common pathway theory of affective disorders: The belief that symptoms of affective disorders may be the final pathway for a variety of disturbances based on social, psychological, biological, or genetic factors

Final common pathway theory of schizophrenia: The belief that schizophrenic behavior may be the end result of not one but a variety of problems, be they social, psychological, biological, or genetic

Fixations: According to Freud, an abnormal degree of psychological energy invested at some psychosexual stage

Fixed-interval schedule: A reinforcement schedule in which a reward is given after a specific amount of time has passed and responding has continued

Fixed-ratio schedule: A reinforcement schedule in which a reward is given after a specific number of responses

Flight of ideas: A thought disturbance consisting of a rapid succession of superficially related ideas

Flooding: A method of behavioral therapy in which a person is made to confront anxiety-arousing stimuli until irrational fear is extinguished

Folie á deux: A shared psychosis in which two or more people have the same delusional belief systems

Free association: A basic procedure in psychoanalysis in which the individual is asked to say, without censoring, all of the things that come to mind

Freshman adjustment reaction: Depression, severe homesickness, anxiety, and restlessness sometimes seen in college students during their freshman year

Frottage: Sexual arousal through rubbing against another person

Fugue state: A hysterical dissociative reaction marked by amnesia and running away, often resulting in the beginning of an entire new life elsewhere

Functional disorders: Disorders without organic or physical basis

Ganglion: A group of neurons clumped together

Ganser's syndrome: A disorder characterized by "passing beside the point," in which the person just misses the correct answers to questions. It is often mistaken for conscious malingering

General paresis: A chronic brain syndrome occurring in some cases of untreated syphilis

General systems theory: An approach which studies human behavior as a subsystem of an organized whole

Generalization: The application of a learned response to new but similar stimuli

Generalized amnesia: A form of psychogenic amnesia involving loss of memory for an individual's entire life

Generalized anxiety disorder: An anxiety state characterized by a generally anxious mood, motor tension, and apprehension, lasting at least 1 month

Genetic counseling: Counseling prospective parents concerning the probability of their having defective offspring as a result of genetic defects

Genital stage: Freudian psychosexual stage, considered to be the height of development and marked by mature heterosexual relationships

Geriatric psychology: The study of old age and psychological aspects of the aging process

Gestalt therapy: A method of psychotherapy developed by Frederick Perls that emphasizes the "here and now" in attempts to break down the deleterious effects of the past

Grand mal: A major form of epileptic seizure often accompanied by loss of consciousness

Group therapy: A treatment technique involving one or two therapists meeting regularly with a group of people (usually 7 to 10)

Habituation: A process whereby an individual's response to the same stimulus lessens with repeated presentations

Hallucination: Perception of a stimulus when there is no actual source for such a stimulus

Hemispheric dominance: The tendency for one brain hemisphere to be dominant over the other for most functions, leading to preferential use of one side of the body

Heritability: The statistical chance that a given relative of a proband will inherit a specific disorder

Heterosexuality: Sexual attraction towards members of the opposite sex

Higher-order conditioning: In classical conditioning, the establishment of a new conditioned stimulus through association with an established conditioned stimulus

Histrionic personality disorder: A long-standing personality pattern consisting of self-dramatization designed to draw attention to oneself, craving of activity and excitement, overreaction to minor events, and outbursts of anger

Homeostasis: A physiological and psychological process whereby an organism in a state of need or tension tends to be motivated to return to a state of neutrality or balance

Homosexuality: Sexual attraction towards members of the same sex

Hormones: Chemicals secreted by endocrine glands that regulate the development or function of various bodily organs

Huntington's chorea: A genetically based chronic brain syndrome of unknown origin

Hyperactive: More active than normal

Hyperendorphinemia theory: The belief that excess levels of endorphins may produce schizophrenic symptoms

Hyperesthesia: Extreme sensitivity to sensory stimuli, occuring as a symptom of conversion disorders

Hyperventilation: Rapid breathing often accompanying anxiety; can result in fainting

Hypnosis: A trancelike mental state induced in a cooperative subject by suggestion and characterized by increased suggestability

Hypnotics: Drugs that induce sleep, for example, barbiturates; also known as sedatives

Hypoactive: Less active than normal

Hypochondriasis: A somatoform disorder marked by an unrealistic fear or belief of having a disease, in the absence of indentifiable physical disorder, despite medical reassurance

Hypoendorphinemia theory: The contention that some forms of psychopathology (e.g., schizophrenia) are a result of abnormally low levels of endorphins

Hypomania: The mildest form of manic psychosis

Hypothesis: A testable proposition about behavior based on theory or observation and stating an expected outcome

Hysteria: A disorder, known even to the ancient Greeks and Romans, in which physical symptoms occur with no apparent physical cause (now known as conversion hysteria or conversion reaction)

Hysterical aphonia: A motor conversion disorder in which an individual cannot speak above a whisper

Hysterical neurosis: A neurotic disorder characterized by impaired functioning of some bodily system (conversion hysteria) or altered state of consciousness (dissociative reaction)

Hysterical personality: A personality disorder in which the primary style is marked by emotional instability, excess excitability, overreactivity, and a tendency to overdramatize

Id: In Freudian theory, the part of the psychic triumvirate in which instincts and psychic energy lie

Identification: The process of associating one's self closely with other persons and assuming their characteristics or views

Identification with the aggressor: An unconscious mechanism in which the individual identifies with an opponent he cannot master

Identity crisis: According to Erik Erikson, the stressful emergence of identity during adolescence

Idiopathic: Without known cause; usually used in reference to a disease

Implosive therapy: A behavioral therapy technique in which anxiety-arousing stimuli are presented intensively (in the imagination or in fact) and individuals are encouraged to experience and eventually extinguish the anxiety

Incest: Sexual activity between close relatives

Incidence rates: The number of new cases of a particular syndrome per a given number of people over a set period of time

In vivo desensitization: A technique used in behavior therapy in which a phobic individual is gradually exposed to anxiety-producing objects or situations in the real world

Independent variable: In a psychological experiment, the factor that is under the investigator's control and which is expected to have an effect on subjects as measured by changes in the dependent variable

Individual psychotherapy: Psychotherapy in which one therapist meets with one client on a regular basis

Indoleamines: Biochemical compounds formed by an indole molecule, some of which appear to act in neurotransmission, including serotonin and tryptamine

Indoleamine hypothesis: The belief that variations in certain biochemicals called indoleamines may play a role in the development of the affective disorders

Infantile autism: A childhood psychosis marked by extreme withdrawal, unresponsiveness to social stimuli, and absence of ability to relate to others

Inimicality: In assessment of suicide potential, the degree to which a person's general life-style predisposes them to suicide

Insight: The experience of self-understanding that often occurs in psychotherapy

Insomnia: Sleeplessness due to physical disorder or emotional and psychological conditions

Instrumental behavior: Behavior emitted in order to obtain a specific desired result

Insulin coma therapy: A type of "shock treatment" in which seizures and coma are produced chemically through the administration of insulin, rather than electrically as in electroconvulsive therapy

Integrative model of affective disorders: An approach that attempts to understand affective disorders in terms of the interaction of experiential, biochemical, and behavioral levels of function

Intellectualization: A defense mechanism in which emotion problems are attacked abstractly, or concealed by excessive intellectual activity.

Intelligence test: A standardized test composed of mental tasks of graded difficulty used to assess a person's intellectual abilities; for example, the Stanford Binet test and the Wechsler Adult Intelligence Scale

Interactional/interpersonal theory: Extending from Sullivan's interpersonal theory, a modern school of conceptual and therapeutic thought which views difficulties in interpersonal relationships as the primary source of emotional and behavioral problems

Interpersonal theory: Harry Stack Sullivan's conceptualizations, which emphasize that disordered behavior is usually brought about by some form of interpersonal frustration or conflicts

Intrapsychic censor: According to Freud, a mental process by which threatening ideas and feelings are repressed

Introjection: In psychoanalytic theory, the unconscious incorporation of qualities or values of another person or group into one's own ego structure

Involutional melancholia: A depressive psychosis appearing in older people and having no clear environmental precipitator

Involutional paraphrenia: Paranoid psychosis of old age

Isolation disorder: A disorder of young adulthood in which unsuccessful transition from adolescent to adult roles results in withdrawal from the adult world

Kaiserian psychotherapy: A treatment method developed by Helmuth Kaiser that focuses upon communication and relationship patterns in disturbed people

Korsakoff's syndrome: Pseudomemory in which a person reminisces about events that never happened and fills in memory gaps with fantasies

La belle indifference: A term originally used by Janet to characterize the unconcern manifested by many hysteric patients about their physical symptoms

Latency stage: Freudian psychosexual stage characterized by sexual dormancy prior to the onset of puberty

Latent schizophrenia: A psychotic condition in which a person functions at a very minimal level owing to an as yet undeveloped psychosis

Law of effect: The principle that responses that have rewarded consequences are strengthened and those that have aversive consequences are weakened or eliminated

Learned helplessness: An attitude resulting from repeated experiences of inescapable aversive stimulation; thought to play a role in the development of depression

Learning disability: A discrepancy between achievement level and general abilities caused by a specific expressive, associative, or receptive deficit

Lethality: The probability that an individual will attempt to commit suicide

Libido: According to Freud, the collective sexual instincts

Life prevalence: The number of people who will have a given disorder during their lifetimes

Life-span interactionist paradigm: A paradigm which integrates biological, psychosocial, and systems approaches to the study of mental health and disorder within a framework of developmental changes

Limbic system: A section of the brain below the cortex that is involved in regulating emotional reactions

Lithium carbonate: A drug used in the control and treatment of manic psychosis

Lobotomy: A surgical technique in which the neural pathways between the frontal lobes and thalamus are severed

Locus of control of reinforcement: The degree to which people perceive what happens to them to be the result of their own behavior (internal control) or uncontrollable factors such as fate or powerful others (external control)

Logorrhea: An endless stream of verbalization often seen as a symptom in psychosis

Lycanthropy: The belief, widespread in the Middle Ages, that one is a wolf

Lysergic acid diethylamide (LSD): A drug that produces hallucinations, delusions, and other schizophrenic-like symptoms

Magical thinking: A primitive cognitive process based on the illusion that thoughts can control events

Mainstreaming: Placement of mentally retarded or other "different" children in classrooms with normal children

Major depression: A severe affective disorder in which the individual has experienced episodes of depression, but not of mania; also called unipolar disorder

Malingering: Deliberate feigning of an illness or disability

Malleus malificarum: A manual written in the fifteenth century to classify abnormal behavior which was then considered linked to witchcraft

Major tranquilizers: A group of antipsychotic and antianxiety agents, including phenothiazine derivatives and butyrophenones

Mania: An affective psychosis marked by extreme elation and euphoria, grandiose thoughts, and excess activity

Manic-depressive psychosis: A severe psychological disturbance marked by either excess depression, excess mania, or a cycling between both moods

Manic episode: An affective disorder characterized by hyperactivity, pressure of speech, flight of ideas, inflated self-esteem, decreased need for sleep, distractibility, and excessive involvement in activities that have a potential for painful consequences

Marathon group therapy: A method of treatment in which group meetings last 24 hours or more. The resultant fatigue and weakening of defenses often allow for greater ease of insight and openness to change

Marital schism: A family situation thought by some to be conducive to schizophrenia in children; for example, the family may bicker constantly.

Marital skew: A family situation thought by some to be conducive to schizophrenia in children; the family's energies are inordinately focused on one of its members, but to outsiders the family appears harmonious

Masochism: Sexual arousal related to being subjected to pain

McNaughton rule: An 1843 British court decision stating that an insanity defense may be established by proving that a defendant did not know what he or she was doing or did not realize it was wrong

Meningitis: An inflammation of the meninges, the three-layered membranes that cover the brain and spinal cord

Mental retardation: Subaverage intellectual functioning combined with deficits in adaptive behavior; may be mild, moderate, severe, or profound

Mental-status examination: An evaluation of the psychological condition of an individual, usually involving assessment of orientation in time, place, person, and circumstance and of perceptual abilities

Mescaline: A psychedelic chemical that produces hallucinations, delusions, and other perceptual-cognitive distortions

Meta-analysis: A procedure for assessing experimental outcome by analyzing findings across similar studies

Methadone: An addictive synthetic narcotic that has been widely used as a substitute for heroin

Migraine headache: Intense psychophysiologically based headache due to dilation of arteries in the brain

Milieu therapy: A method of treatment in which the total environment of a disturbed individual is controlled and therapeutic

Minnesota Multiphasic Personality Inventory (MMPI): True-false questionnaire composed of 566 items used in the diagnosis of mental disturbance

Minor tranquilizer: Any of a variety of drugs used to reduce mild to moderate anxiety, agitation, and tension

Modeling: Learning by observing and imitating the behavior of others; observational learning

Monoamine oxidase hypothesis: A theory that abnormalities in the neural enzyme, monoamine oxidase, involved in metabolizing dopamine, can lead to various forms of psychopathology

Monoamine oxidase (MAO) inhibitors: A class of drugs especially useful in the treatment of certain depressions

Monozygotic twins: Identical twins having the same genetic makeup

Moral anxiety: Psychoanalytic term for the ego's fear of punishment for violating the constraints of the superego

Motility psychosis: An atypical cycloid psychosis in which behavior ranges from hyperkinetic to akinetic

Motor conversion disorder: A conversion disorder in which an individual experiences motor symptoms such as muscle contractions, tremors, or seizures without physical basis

Multiaxial: Having several dimensions, each of which is employed in categorizing. DSM-III is a multiaxial classification system.

Multiple-family therapy: Treatment in a large group composed of several entire families

Multiple-impact therapy: Method of treatment in which an entire set of professionals works with a disturbed family during an intensive, limited period of time

Multiple personality: A rare dissociative reaction in which a person has a number of distinct personalities

Muscle-contraction headache: A common headache due to nervous tension, fatigue, and the like

Mutism: Absence of speech secondary to physical or psychological disturbance

Myocardial infarction: Medical term for heart attack

Narcissistic personality disorder: A long-standing personality pattern consisting of a grandiose sense of self-importance and abilities

Narcolepsy: A disorder consisting of a sudden, irresistible urge to fall asleep. Some cases are due to organic causes, and others are presumed to be psychogenic in nature.

Nature-nurture controversy: The theoretical and experimental "battle" over whether heredity or environment is more important in the development of personality and abnormal behavior

Necrophilia: Sexual attraction toward dead bodies

Negative practice: A behavioral-therapy technique in which behavioral frequency is reduced by requiring a person to emit undesirable behaviors to such a degree that he or she wishes to stop them due to the buildup of an aversion to their expression

Neologisms: "New words" sometimes created by psychotic people

Neurological disorders: Disorders characterized by disruption of the nervous system as a result of injury, disease, drugs, or other toxins

Neuromuscular dysfunction approach: A biochemical approach to the study of schizophrenia which focuses on peripheral neuromuscular dysfunctions

Neuron: The primary cell of which the brain and nervous system are composed

Neuropeptides: See Endorphins

Neuropsychology: The study of the relation between brain function and behavior

Neurosis: See Psychoneurosis

Neurotic anxiety: Fear of dangers or threats not based on reality

Neurotransmitters: Chemical substances located near synapses that are involved in the chemical transmission of impulses from one neuron to another

Night terror: A sleep disorder in which the individual repeatedly awakens from sleep abruptly, with symptoms of extreme panic and intense anxiety

Norepinephrine: Also known as noradrenaline, this biochemical is important as a neurotransmitter; when present in abnormal amounts, it also seems to be related to the presence of certain forms of psychotic symptoms

Norms: Standards against which the performance of one person on a test may be compared with the performance of others

Observational learning: Learning of new behaviors by observing others responding and receiving some form of consequence

Obsessive-compulsive disorder: An anxiety disorder in which obsessions (persistence, recurrent thoughts, or impulses) or compulsions (repetitive, stereotyped actions) create distress and interfere with an individual's ability to function

Obsessive-compulsive personality: A personality disorder in which the primary style is marked by excessive concern with sameness and rigid thoughts and behavior

Oedipal-Electra phase: Stage of psychosexual development at which a child is sexually attracted to the parent of the opposite sex

Operant conditioning: A basic learning procedure in which a person or animal learns to respond in specific ways in order to obtain a specific reinforcement

Opiates: A class of highly addictive narcotics obtained from the poppy plant

Oral stage: The Freudian psychosexual stage in which satisfactions are centered about the mouth

Organic mental disorders: Mental disturbances due to either transient or permanent brain dysfunction caused by specific organic factors

Outcome studies: Investigations of psychotherapy focusing on different rates of success or improvement in different forms of treatment

Panic attack: An episode of acute anxiety and disorganization, usually lasting several minutes, accompanied by symptoms such as shortness of breath, palpitations, chest pain, dizziness, sweating, and fear of dying or going crazy

Paradigm: A set of basic assumptions that specify concepts considered legitimate and methods to be used in the collection and interpretation of data

Paradox: A self-contradictory statement based on a valid deduction from acceptable premises

Paralogical thinking: Illogical thinking and

verbalizations, found primarily in schizophrenics

Paranoia: A psychotic disorder characterized by a well-developed and wide-ranging delusional system

Paranoid disorders: A group of disorders characterized by persistent persecutory delusions or delusional jealousy

Paranoid eroticism: A condition in which, due to a delusional belief, a person feels some important other secretly is in love with him or her

Paranoid litigious state: A condition in which, due to a delusional system, a person continuously brings legal actions against others

Paranoid personality: A personality disorder in which the primary interpersonal style is marked by rigidity, suspiciousness, jealousy, envy, and a tendency to blame others

Paranoid pseudocommunity: A term proposed by Norman Cameron to describe the extensive delusional systems in which the paranoid person may live

Paranoid psychosis: A severe disturbance marked primarily by delusional beliefs of various kinds

Paranoid state: A circumscribed and transient condition marked by a specific delusional belief

Paraphilias: A group of psychosexual disorders in which unusual or bizarre images or acts are needed to experience sexual gratification

Paraphrenia: Paranoid psychosis in old age

Parasympathetic nervous system: That part of the autonomic nervous system concerned with the production and conservation of energy

Parkinson's disease: A progressive degenerative disease of the nervous system. Symptoms include hand and head tremors, increasing muscular rigidity, and slower voluntary movements.

Passive-aggressive personality disorder: A long-standing personality pattern in which the individual uses various maneuvers, such as forgetting, procrastination, and dawdling, to avoid adequate social and occupational performance

Partial reinforcement: In operant conditioning, a schedule of reinforcement in which rewards are not given every time a response is emitted; one result is increased resistance to extinction

Pastoral counselors: Clergymen who, in addition to their religious training, have been trained in certain forms of counseling and psychotherapy

Pathoplastic effect of age: The fact that the same disorder may be manifested in different ways among different age groups

Pedophilia: Sexual attraction toward young children

Penis envy: In psychoanalytic theory, the desire of the female to possess a male genital organ

Period prevalence: The number of cases of a disease existing in a given population during a specified time

Peripheral nervous system: All neural systems outside the brain and spinal cord

Permissive-amine hypothesis: The belief that reduced serotonin levels may permit other biochemicals to vary unchecked, thereby producing affective psychotic patterns of behavior

Perseveration: The pathological repetition of the same act, idea, word, or phrase; also an inability to interrupt a task or shift from one task or procedure to another

Personality: A collection of behaviors and response patterns that may be seen as characterizing a specific individual

Personality disorders: Patterns of disturbance characterized by a tendency to depend upon one specific style of responding to a wide variety of different situations

Perturbation: In assessment of suicide potential, the degree to which an individual is distressed, disturbed, or agitated

Pervasive developmental disorder: A group of disorders, appearing in childhood, involving extreme distortions in psychological functions such as language, perception, reality testing, attention, social skills, and movement

Petit mal: A mild form of epileptic seizure in which a person loses touch with the environment for a short time, but doesn't usually have a convulsive seizure

Phallic stage: Freudian psychosexual stage in which satisfaction centers in the genital area

Phenothiazine derivatives: A group of psychoactive drugs especially effective as antipsychotic agents

Phenylketonuria (PKU): A metabolic disorder that causes severe mental retardation unless controlled by a restricted diet

Phobic disorders: A group of disorders marked by persistent, irrational fear and avoidance of a specific object, activity, or situation

Pica: A symptom involving the eating of inedible materials such as dirt, plaster, and the like

Pick's disease: A rare degenerative disease of the brain. Symptoms include increased difficulty in thinking, concentrating, and dealing with new situations

Pituitary gland: The "master" endocrine gland which controls growth as well as the function of other endocrine glands

Placebo effect: Therapeutic progress based on the belief that a neutral therapeutic method will be beneficial

Play therapy: A therapeutic technique for children that uses play rather than verbal interaction as the major mode of communication

Point prevalence: The number of cases of a disease existing in a given population at a specific point in time

Positioning: A strategic therapy technique in which the therapist exaggerates the family's views

Positron Emission Transaxial Tomography (PETT): A technique using radioactive trace elements to evaluate cerebral metabolism

Postpartum depression: Depression in the mother following the birth of a child

Posttraumatic stress disorder: An anxiety disorder produced by an extremely stressful event, characterized by recurrent recollections or dreams of the event; reduced responsiveness to or involvement with the external world; and symptoms such as hyperalertness, sleep disturbance, guilt about surviving, impaired memory or concentration, and avoidance of activities reminiscent of the traumatic event

Postvention: Therapeutic intervention efforts aimed at helping those who survive the suicide or murder of a loved one

Preconscious: According to Freud, those needs, wishes, thoughts, memories, and motives which, although not in awareness at a given moment, can be brought into awareness quite easily

Presenile dementia: Chronic loss of brain function due to presenile conditions such as Alzheimer's disease or Pick's disease

Prescribing the symptom: A paradoxical technique which forces a client to either give up a symptom or admit that it is under voluntary control

Prevalence rate: The total number of cases of a type of disorder in existence at any one time

Primal therapy: A method of therapy devised by Arthur Janov that focuses on release of primal pains experienced in early childhood and infancy

Primary affective disorders: Affective disorders occurring in the absence of any other syndromes

Primary deviance: The violation of rules, laws, or mores of a group

Primary drives: Innate motivations for behavior that require satisfaction for survival and that do not weaken if unsatisfied—for example, hunger and thirst

Primary prevention: Altering of circumstances that might promote disordered behavior

Primary-process thought: According to Freud, the psychotic-like thinking characteristic of the id

Primary reinforcer: Stimuli that increase the probability of responses that they follow without prior learning (e.g. food)

Proband: In genetic studies, the person about whom hereditary information is sought

Process schizophrenia: A type of schizophrenia characterized by slow insidious onset, poor prognosis for recovery, and previous history of maladjustment

Process studies: Investigations of psychotherapy focusing on the characteristics of the therapeutic interaction that appear to be responsible for positive change

Prodromal phase: Early symptoms of an impending mental or physical disorder

Prognosis: Prediction of the probable course and outcome of a disorder

Projection: A defense mechanism in which an individual attributes his or her impulses or motives to someone else

Projective tests: Tests such as the Rorschach Inkblot Test and TAT in which people's responses to unstructured stimuli are assumed to reflect their basic needs and personality

Propanediol carbamates: A class of minor tranquilizers, including meprobamate

Propfhebephrenic psychosis: A psychotic behavior pattern superimposed upon or concomitant with mental retardation

Protracted-adolescence theory: A theory stating that college students, who do not begin careers immediately after high school, will continue their adolescence after their peers have made a transition to adult roles and responsibilities

Pseudocyesis: False pregnancy, a hysterical reaction with a symptom that closely resembles actual pregnancy

Pseudoneurotic schizophrenia: A special type of schizophrenia, the symptoms of which often lead to a misdiagnosis of neurosis

Psychasthenia: An obsolete term applied by Janet to a type of neurosis characteized by anxiety states, phobias, obsessions, and compulsions

Psyche: A term used by Freud to refer in general to the mental apparatus

Psychedelic drugs: Drugs that are capable of producing visual hallucinations and other psychotic-like experiences

Psychiatric nurse: A nurse specially trained in the care of psychologically disturbed hospital patients

Psychiatric social worker: A social worker specially trained in dealing with psychiatric problems of individuals and their families

Psychiatrist: A physician specializing in the diagnosis, treatment, and management of people with emotional and behavioral disorders

Psychic numbing: Constriction of emotional responsiveness, often occurring in reaction to extreme stress

Psychic triumvirate: According to Freud, the three-part governing system of the personality: the id, ego, and superego

Psychoanalysis: A special form of psychotherapy devised by Sigmund Freud. The term should not be used interchangeably with psychotherapy.

Psychoanalyst: A practitioner of psychoanalysis

Psychochemotherapy: The use of chemicals in the treatment of psychological disturbances

Psychodrama: A method of group treatment devised by Moreno in which individuals act out their conflicts and problems with the help of "actors" who are other members of the group

Psychogenetics: The study of the inheritance of emotional and behavioral characteristics

Psychogenic: Psychologically produced or caused

Psychogenic amnesia: A dissociative disorder marked by sudden inability to recall important personal information, without organic causes

Psychogenic pain disorder: A somatoform disorder marked by severe and prolonged pain, without apparent physical basis, and with evidence of a psychological etiology

Psychological autopsy: An attempt to understand the psychosocial components of suicide

Psychomotor epilepsy: A kind of epileptic seizure in which consciousness is disturbed and automatic involuntary behavior may occur in the absence of convulsions

Psychoneurosis: Also known as neurosis. A mild to moderately severe disturbance characterized by anxiety or self-defeating attempts to deal with anxiety

Psychopath (sociopath): See Antisocial personality disorder

Psychophysiological disorders: Patterns of psychological disturbance in which actual physical symptoms occur as a result of psychological factors. Not to be confused with conversion reactions, in which there is typically no real physical damage.

Psychosexual development: In Freudian theory, the process of passing through five basic stages with varying loci of need satisfaction: oral, anal, phallic, latency, and genital stages

Psychosis: A severe form of psychological disturbances typically characterized by loss of touch with reality and personality disintegration

Psychosocial paradigm: A perspective based on the belief that behavior is determined primarily by individual experiences, such as interpersonal relationships and learning

Psychosocial stages: Stages of development of the personality from the perspective of Erik Erikson; also known as the "eight stages of man"

Psychosurgery: Surgical manipulation of neural pathways to change behavior

Psychotherapy: A form of primarily verbal treatment for psychological disorders

Psychotic depressive reaction: A severe depression brought about by some highly stressful environmental event such as the death of a loved one

Psychotic mannerisms: Stereotypic behaviors associated with many types of psychoses; may include gestures, facial grimacing, repetitive body movements

Psychotomimetic drugs: Drugs that produce psychic and behavioral changes similar to psychosis

Rational-emotive therapy: A method of therapy devised by Albert Ellis that focuses on identifying irrational beliefs and altering cognitive styles

Rationalization: The defense mechanism in which questionable reasons are given to justify unacceptable behavior or personal shortcomings

Rauwolfia alkaloids: A group of antipsychotic drugs obtained from the Indian shrub *rauwolfia serpentina*

Reaction formation: A defense mechanism characterized by behaving in ways directly opposite of one's true desires

Reactive mania: An episode of manic excitement typically in response to the removal of some chronic emotional stress

Reactive schizophrenia: A type of schizophrenia characterized by abrupt onset, good prognosis for recovery, and little history of severe maladjustment

Realistic anxiety: Fear of dangers and threats that are based on reality

Reality principle: Awareness of the demands of the environment and adjustment of behavior to meet these demands

Reality therapy: A method of therapy devised by William Glasser that focuses on individual needs for love and acceptance of responsibility

Recidivism: Repetition of delinquent or criminal behavior

Reciprocal inhibition: A technique used in behavior therapy which pairs responses antagonistic to anxiety with anxiety-producing stimuli

Regression: According to Freud, the psychological return to some previous stage of psychosexual development. It often occurs in the face of severe stress.

Reinforcement schedule: A schedule according to which reinforcements are administered in classical and operant conditioning, either continuous or partial

Reinforcer: A stimulus that increases the probability of occurrence of a response that it follows (*See* Primary and secondary reinforcement)

Reliability: The degree to which an assessment procedure measures the same thing from one time to another

Remission: The disappearance of symptoms and the return to normality

Repression: A defense mechanism that involves the unconscious forgetting of threatening thoughts or memories

Residual phase: A period in which acute symptoms of disorder have subsided, but chronic or less severe symptoms remain

Residual rules: Unwritten rules that are not noticed until they are broken, such as standing too close to someone when conversing

Resistance: In psychoanalysis, an unconscious process that blocks an individual from gaining insight into conflicts and unconscious motives

Response prevention: A behavior therapy technique, used mainly for obsessive-compulsive behaviors, in which the individual is prevented from making the accustomed response

Respondent learning: *See* Classical conditioning

Restitutional symptoms: Symptoms observed in schizophrenic patients who are attempting to regain reality and mental processes lost by regression

Restraining: A strategic therapy technique for overcoming resistance by suggesting that a family not change, or change very slowly

Reticular activating system: A network of cell bodies and fibers in the lower and ventral portion of the brainstem, extending from the spinal cord to the thalmus, serving as an indirect route or transmission of sensory impulses to the cerebral cortex

Retrospective data: Data obtained by having the subject recollect a past event

Rorschach Inkblot Test: A series of 10 unstructured inkblots used to elicit responses that can help in psychological diagnosis (*See* Projective tests)

Rumination syndrome: An infant's bringing up of food without vomiting or retching; if uncontrolled it can lead to failure to thrive and death

Sadism: Sexual arousal derived from inflicting pain on another

Satiation: A condition of being satisfied or gratified regarding a need for food, fluid, sexual stimulation, or a psychic goal

Schemas: Ways of conceptualizing the world or of organizing perceptions

Schizoid personality: A personality disorder in which the primary style is marked by withdrawal from others, shyness, reticence to interact, and "eccentric" behavior

Schizoaffective disorder: A diagnostic category sometimes used when differential diagnosis between affective and schizophrenic disorder cannot be made

Schizophrenia: A form of psychosis involving disturbed thought processes and a variety of specific emotional and behavioral symptoms

Schizophrenia spectrum: A conceptualization of schizophrenic disorders such that they are seen as composing a range of patterns from some forms of mild neuroses and character disorders all the way to severe schizophrenic psychosis

Schizophrenic disorder, catatonic type: A type of schizophrenia involving marked psychomotor disturbance such as stupor, rigidity, purposeless motor activity

Schizophrenic disorder, disorganized type: A type of schizophrenia marked by incoherence, absence of systematized delusions and blunted, inappropriate, or silly affect

Schizophrenic disorder, paranoid type: A type of schizophrenia marked by delusions of persecution or grandeur, delusional jealousy, or persecutory or grandiose hallucinations

Schizophrenic disorder, residual type: A disorder in which the individual has experienced at least one acute episode of schizophrenia which has subsided

Schizophrenic disorder, undifferentiated type: A disorder involving prominent psychotic features which do not meet the criteria for other types of schizophrenia, or meets the criteria for more than one type

Schizophreniform disorder: A disorder meeting all the criteria for schizophrenia except for shorter duration and greater likelihood of emotional turmoil

Schizophrenogenic environment: An environment that may produce schizophrenia in those genetically predisposed to the disorder

Schizotaxia: An inherited predisposition to schizophrenia, according to Paul Meehl

Schizotypal personality disorder: A longstanding personality pattern involving a variety of oddities in speech, thought, perception, and behavior which are not sufficiently severe to warrant a diagnosis of schizophrenia

Secondary affective disorders: Affective disorders occurring simultaneously with other disorders

Secondary deviance: Being labeled as deviant for breaking the rules of a group and then becoming someone who fits the label applied by the group, such as "criminal" or "mental patient"

Secondary drives: Motives to emit certain behaviors developed out of associations with primary drives—for example, a need to have relationships

Secondary prevention: Efforts to reduce the rate or severity of existing disorders through early detection and intervention

Secondary-process thought: According to Freud, the rational thinking that is characteristic of the ego

Secondary reinforcers: Stimuli that are not innately rewarding, but that acquire reinforcing properties owing to their association with primary reinforcers

Security operations: Defense mechanisms within the theoretical framework of Harry Stack Sullivan

Sedatives: Substances which reduce excitement or irrtability by depressing the central nervous system; also known as hypnotics

Seizure: A sudden onset of symptoms including convulsions, palpitations, dizziness, or other disagreeable sensations; most often associated with epilepsy

Self-actualizing tendency: According to Carl

Rogers, an innate tendency toward positive self-growth

Self-labeling: The decision that something is deviant about oneself and the resultant changes in self-concept and behavior that may ensue

Self-report test: Any questionnaire, inventory, or other instrument on which a subject indicates personality characteristics and behavior that apply or do not apply to him

Senile dementia: A mental disturbance most likely caused by degeneration of nerve and brain tissue with advancing age

Senior anticipatory adulthood reaction: Anxiety sometimes seen in students leaving the "protection" of college and entering the "real world"

Sensory conversion disorder: A form of conversion disorder involving inability to receive or process sensory stimuli

Sensory conversion reaction: Hysterical reaction resulting in impairment of some sensory process

Sensory-stimulation therapy: A treatment for the elderly in which symptoms of senility are countered by increased activity

Serial compulsion: A ritualized series of compulsive behaviors

Serotonin: A neurotransmitter substance believed to be involved in some way in the development of certain psychotic disorders

Sexual dysfunction: Impairment or disturbance in the functioning of the sexual organ systems

Sexual-orientation disturbance: Term applied to ego-dystonic sexual and emotional attraction to members of the same sex

Shaping: An operant conditioning procedure in which successive approximations of a desired behavior are reinforced

Signal detection theory: A group of concepts relating to factors which influence the perception of signals on a background of noise

Simple phobia: An anxiety disorder characterized by persistent, irrational fear of a specific object, animal, or situation

Skin conductance: The level of resistance to an electric current passed through the skin.

Skin conductance orienting responses (SCOR's): Skin conductance responses observed when an organism is presented with a new stimulus

Social-network therapy: Therapy with a "tribe" of up to 40 people composing the "network" of relatives and friends surrounding a disturbed family or individual

Social phobia: An anxiety disorder characterized by a persistent, irrational fear of situations involving the scrutiny of others, such as speaking, eating, or writing in public, or using a public lavatory

Social stress hypothesis: A theory which posits that environmental stressors can produce schizophrenic symptomatology

Societal-reaction theory: The belief that the reaction of society to the deviant behavior of its members has much to do with the establishment of abnormal behavior patterns

Socioenvironmental theory: The belief that abnormality is caused by stresses brought about by significant life events

Sociopath: See Antisocial Personality Disorder

Soma: The cell body of a neuron.

Somatization disorder: A somatoform disorder marked by physical symptoms which appear to be unrelated to physical injury or disorder

Somatoform disorders: A group of disorders marked by physical symptoms, but for which there are no demonstrable organic bases

Somnambulism: An hysterical dissociative reaction that occurs in a sleeplike state; sleepwalking.

Somnolence: Pathological sleepiness or drowsiness

Spontaneous recovery: In conditioning, the increase in strength of an extinguished response following a period of time

Spontaneous remission: The disappearance of symptoms without formal treatment

Standardization: The process of ensuring that all materials and instructions given to test takers are identical so that administrations of an assessment procedure are the same for all subjects

Stereotyped behavior: Persistent and inappropriate repetition of words, gestures, and actions

Stimulus discrimination: The ability to distinguish different stimuli

Stimulus generalization: A learning phenomenon in which an individual responds to stimuli similar to those with which original learning took place even though no actual learning experience has been had with the similar stimulus

Strategic family therapy: A form of brief, systemic family therapy which focuses on problem solving and emphasizes method

Stressor: Any adjustment demand that requires coping behavior by an individual or group

Structural family therapy: A method of family therapy devised by Salvador Minuchin that emphasizes the need for certain types of healthy family structures and communications boundaries

Substance abuse: The daily, pathological use of alcohol or drugs, for more than 1 month, resulting in impaired social and occupational functioning

Substance dependence: Physiological dependence on alcohol or drugs resulting from a pattern of constant, pathological substance use

Substance tolerance: A physiological manifestation of substance dependence, in which increased amounts of drugs or alcohol are required to obtain the desired effect

Successive approximation: A method used in conditioning in which small steps toward the final behavior are reinforced in an effort to shape the final pattern of responding

Suicide-prevention center: Crisis-intervention program typically involving paraprofessional volunteers who answer hotline phones and meet with emergency walk-ins

Superego: According to Freud, that part of the psychic triumvirate which includes internalized cultural and parental values and mores; it is not in touch with reality

Survivor guilt: Feelings of guilt for having survived event, when others did not

Symbiotic psychosis: Extreme parent-child interdependency such that separation may result in severe psychotic disturbance in either one or both individuals

Symbolism: The representation of one object, person, or situation by some often unrelated object, person, or situation

Sympathetic chain: The interconnections among the ganglia of the sympathetic nervous system

Sympathetic nervous system: That part of the autonomic nervous system activated in emergency or stress situations

Symptom: A behavior or characteristic typically associated with a specific disorder

Synanon: A self-help organization begun by former drug addicts to help rehabilitate active drug addicts through residential treatment and group encounters

Synapse: The minute space between the fibers of adjoining neurons through which neurotransmitters travel during nerve transmission

Syndrome: A cluster of symptoms usually appearing together

Synesthesia: A condition often experienced under the influence of hallucinogens, in which stimulation of one sensory modality arouses sensations in another

Syphilis: A contagious venereal disease; usually, but not always, transmitted by sexual contact

System: A set of elements organized to work together to perform a function

Systematic desensitization: A behavioral therapy method in which counterconditioning is used to treat anxiety, phobias, and the like

Systems paradigm: A paradigm which explains behavior in terms of group, family, societal, and/or cultural systems

T-groups: Training (T) groups in which members learn about human interactions within a semistructured framework

Tactual anesthesia: The loss of the sense of touch in part of the body, which may occur as a symptom of sensory conversion disorders.

Tarantism: The dancing mania of the Middle Ages thought to be caused by the bite of a spider

Tardive dyskinesia: A long-term side effect of drug treatment characterized by oral and facial grimaces, tongue movements, and spasmodic contractions of the neck muscles

Target behavior: In behavior therapy, the behavior selected for modification

Teleology: The concept that all mental processes are purposive (goal-directed)

Tertiary prevention: Efforts to shorten or minimize the impact of disorders after they have appeared

Test anxiety: A condition in which extreme incapacitating anxiety during or immediately preceding examinations results in an inability to perform up to ability

Test reliability: The degree to which a test measures the same thing from one time to another

Test validity: The degree to which a test measures what it purports to measure.

Testosterone: A male sex hormone produced by the testes.

Thematic Apperception Test (TAT): A series of pictures about which people tell stories that can be used in the diagnosis of mental disturbance and the study of personality.

Therapeutic community: A setting in which disturbed people live and are cared for in a total and constant therapeutic atmosphere.

Thioxanthines: A group of antipsychotic drugs often used when treatment with the pharmacologically similar phenothiazines is not effective

Thirties crisis: A transitional disorder of young adulthood in which extreme confusion about social and occupational decisions is manifested by intense feelings of anxiety and depression and behaviors such as drug use, frequent job changes, and changes in interpersonal relationships

Thought-stopping: A behavioral-therapy technique in which obsessive thoughts or hallucinations may be stopped by repeated verbalizations of the word "stop"

Tic: A repeated, involuntary contraction of a small group of muscles, produced by either psychological or neurological disturbance

Token economy: A method of treating groups of people in which desired behaviors are emitted in return for tokens, which may then be used to "buy" privileges

Tourette's syndrome: A stereotyped movement disorder marked by repeated involuntary movements of various muscle groups, including vocal tics such as grunts, yelps, barks, and sniffs

Trainable mentally retarded: Retarded people with IQs ranging from 25 to 49 who cannot achieve useful academic skills but can learn basic self-care skills

Tranquilizers: Psychoactive drugs that relax and pacify, usually without interrupting consciousness.

Transference: In psychoanalysis, the projection onto the therapist of feelings and early attitudes toward parents and other significant figures in one's life

Transmethylation hypothesis: The belief that, through some metabolic defect, certain normal body chemicals are turned into schizophrenia-producing LSD-like chemicals in the brain.

Transsexualism: The belief that one's biological sex is incongruent with one's true gender. Such people may undergo surgery to change their physical sexual characteristics.

Transvestism: Sexual arousal related to dressing in the clothing of the opposite sex

Trephinization: Ancient "treatment" for the mentally disturbed in which a hole was chipped in the skull so that evil spirits could escape.

Tricyclic drugs: A class of antidepressant medications.

Triadic-based family therapy: A method of treatment that focuses on disordered triads within families

Trichotillomania: Hair-pulling behavior

Twin method: A research method which attempts to elucidate the differential contributions of heredity and environment by comparing concordance rates of monozygotic and dizygotic twins

Type A personality: A personality pattern used to identify a person whose life-style predisposes him or her to coronary heart disease. Such a person is highly competitive, suppresses fatigue, and shows hostility when efforts to meet deadlines are frustrated

Type B personality: A personality pattern used to identify a person who can relax without feeling guilty, and who can work without being easily frustrated. This personality is distinguishable from the type A personality or coronary prone personality.

Ulcer A painful sore on a mucous membrane, such as in the mouth or stomach

Unconditional positive regard: An attitude of concern, acceptance, and warmth, which is considered by humanistic therapists to be conducive to client self-awareness and personality growth

Unconditioned response (UCR): In classical conditioning, a response that occurs spontaneously to an unconditioned stimulus (UCS)

Unconditioned stimulus (UCS): In classical conditioning, a stimulus that, without special teaching of the trainee, is capable of producing a specific response (UCR)

Unconscious: According to Freud, those needs, wishes, thoughts, memories, and motives which motivate much behavior but of which one is not aware and cannot easily become aware.

Unipolar disorder: An affective disorder in which only depressive episodes occur, in contrast to a bipolar condition in which both manic and depressive processes are present.

Unipolar versus bipolar affective disorders: A dimension of affective disorders ranging from those in which only depression or mania occurs (unipolar) to those in which both occur (bipolar).

Universal magnetism theory: Mesmer's belief that the universe was made up of magnetic fluid and that abnormal behavior was a result of fluid imbalances within the body.

Vaginismus: A vaginal spasm occurring before or during sexual intercourse, making intercourse painful or impossible

Variable-interval schedule: A reinforcement schedule in which a reward is given after intervals of time that vary around a specific average

Variable-ratio schedule: A reinforcement schedule in which a reward is given after some average number of responses

Verbigeration: A symptom of schizophrenia in which repetitions of often long series of verbalizations emanate from a person over an extended period of time

Vicarious conditioning: Learning which results from indirect experience and observation

Viral hypothesis of schizophrenia: The belief that some types of schizophrenia may be caused by some prenatal or postnatal viral infection

Voyeurism: Sexual arousal related to watching others undress or engage in sexual activity; peeping Tomism

Vulnerability/stress model: An etiological model for schizophrenia which posits an interaction between vulnerability factors in the individual and environmental stressors in producing the disorder

Waxy flexibility: A symptom of stuporous catatonic schizophrenia in which a person's body or limbs will remain in positions in which they are placed for a period of time

Wechsler intelligence scales: A series of intelligence tests for varying age groups developed by David Wechsler. The series includes the Wechsler Adult Intelligence Scale (WAIS), the Wechsler Intelligence Scale for Children-Revised Form (WISC-R), and the Wechsler Preschool and Primary Scale of Intelligence (WPPSI).

References

Abraham, S., & Beumont, P. (1982) How patients describe bulimia or binge eating. *Psychological Medicine, 12,* 625.

Abramson, L., Seligman, M., & Teasdale, J. (1978) Learned helplessness in humans: Critique and reformulation. *Journal of Abnormal Psychology, 87,* 49.

Abramson, L., Garber, J., & Seligman, M. (1980) Learned helplessness: An attributional analysis. In J. Garber & M. Seligman (Eds.), *Human helplessness: Theory and application.* New York: Academic Press.

Abuclo, D. (1983) Genetic disorders. In J. Matson & J. Mulick (Eds.), *Handbook of mental retardation.* New York: Pergamon.

Ackerman, N. (1963) Family diagnosis and therapy. In J. Masserman (Ed.), *Current psychiatric therapies.* Vol. 3. New York: Grune & Stratton.

Ackerman, S., Manaker, S., & Cohen, M. (1981) Recent separation and the onset of peptic ulcer disease in older children and adolescents. *Psychosomatic Medicine, 43,* 305.

Adams, H., Feuerstein, M., & Fowler, J. (1980) Migraine headache: Review of parameters, etiology and intervention. *Psychological Bulletin, 87,* 217.

Adler, G. (1981) The borderline-narcissistic personality continuum. *American Journal of Psychiatry, 138,* 46.

Akhtar, S., & Thompson, A. (1982) Overview: Narcissistic personality disorder. *American Journal of Psychiatry, 139,* 12.

Akiskal, H., & McKinney, W. (1973) Depressive disorders: Toward a unified hypothesis. *Science, 182,* 20.

Akiskal, H., & McKinney, W. (1975) Overview of recent research in depression. *Archives of General Psychiatry, 32,* 285.

Akiskal, H., & Webb, W. (1983) Affective disorder: I. Recent advances in clinical conceptualization. *Hospital and Community Psychiatry, 34,* 695.

Alanen, A. (1965) A review of psychoanalytic theories of childhood psychoses. In J. Howells (Ed.), *Perspectives in child psychiatry.* Edinburgh: Oliver & Boyd.

Alapin, B. (1973) Trichloro-ethylene addiction and its effects. *British Journal of Addiction, 68,* 331.

Alexander, F. (1934) The influence of psychological factors upon gastrointestinal disturbances. *Psychoanalytic Quarterly, 3,* 501.

Alexander, F. (1952) *Psychosomatic medicine.* London: Allen & Unwin.

Alexander, B. (1975) Tension can be licked. *Los Angeles Times,* July 6, 1; 5.

Alksne, H. (1981) The social basis of substance abuse. In J. Lowinson & P. Ruiz (Eds.), *Substance abuse.* Baltimore: Williams & Wilkins, p. 78.

Allen, G. (1973) Treatment of test-anxiety by group-administered and self-administered relaxation and study counseling. *Behavior Therapy, 7,* 349.

Alpaugh, P., & Hickey-Haney, M. (1978) *Counseling older adults: A training manual for beginning counselors and paraprofessionals.* Los Angeles: Andrus Gerontology Center.

American Psychiatric Association. (1952) *Diagnostic and statistical manual of mental disorders (DSM-I).* Washington, D.C.: American Psychiatric Association.

American Psychiatric Association. (1968) *Diagnostic and statistical manual of mental disorders (2d ed.) (DSM-II).* Washington, D.C.: American Psychiatric Association.

American Psychiatric Association. (1980) *Diagnostic and statistical manual of mental disorders (3d ed.) (DSM-III).* Washington, D.C.: American Psychiatric Association.

Anastasi, A. (1982) *Psychological testing.* New York: Macmillan.

Anchin, J., & Kiesler, D. (1982) *Handbook of interactional psychotherapy.* New York: Pergamon.

Andersen, A. (1983) Anorexia nervosa and bulimia: A spectrum of eating disorders. *Journal of Adolescent Health Care, 4,* 15.

Andersen, N. B., & Beech, P. (1981) Characteristics of negative reinforcement in obsessive-compulsive behavior. *Scandinavian Journal of Behavior Therapy, 10,* 21.

Anderson, N., Lawrence, P., & Olson, T. (1981) Within subject analysis of autogenic training and cognitive coping training in the treatment of tension headache pain. *Journal of Behavior Therapy and Experimental Psychiatry, 12,* 219.

Andrasik, F., & Holroyd, K. (1980) A test of specific and non-specific effects in the biofeedback treatment of tension headache. *Journal of Consulting and Clinical Psychology, 48,* 575.

Andreasen, N. (1980) Adjustment disorders in adolescents and adults. *Archives of General Psychiatry, 37,* 1166.

Andrews, G., & Harvey, R. (1981) Does psychotherapy benefit neurotic patients? A reanalysis of the Smith, Glass and Miller data. *Archives of General Psychiatry, 38* 1203.

Anisman, H., & Zacharko, R. (1982) Depression: The predisposing influence of stress. *Behavioral and Brain Sciences, 5,* 89.

Applebaum, P. (1985) Tarasoff and the clinician: Problems in fulfilling the duty to protect. *American Journal of Psychiatry, 142,* 425.

Arieti, S. (1955) *Interpretation of schizophrenia.* New York: Grune & Stratton.

Arieti, S. (1966) Schizophrenic cognition. In P. Hoch & J. Zubin (Eds.) *Psychopathology of schizophrenia.* New York: Grune & Stratton.

Astin, A. (1977) *Four critical years.* San Francisco: Jossey-Bass.

Astrachan, B., Brauer, L., Harrow, M., & Schwartz, C. (1974) Symptomatic outcome in schizophrenia. *Archives of General Psychiatry, 31,* 155.

Atchley, R. (1972) *Social forces in later life.* Belmont, Calif.: Wadsworth.

Atkinson, L., Quarrington, B., & Cyr, J. (1985) School refusal: The heterogeneity of a concept. *American Journal of Orthopsychiatry, 55,* 83.

Avery, D., & Winokur, G. (1973) Mortality in depressed patients treated with ECT and anti-depressants. *Archives of General Psychiatry, 33,* 1029.

Axline, V. (1964) The eight basic principles. In M. Haworth (Ed.), *Child psychotherapy.* New York: Basic Books.

Ayllon, T., & Azrin, N. (1968) *The token economy: A motivational system for therapy and rehabilitation.* New York: Appleton-Century-Crofts.

Ayllon, T., & Michael, J. (1959) The psychiatric nurse as a behavioral engineer. *Behavior Research and Therapy, 2,* 323.

Ayd, F. (1975) *Rational psychopharmacology and the right to treatment.* Baltimore: Ayd Medical Communication.

Bagshaw, M., & Kimble, D. (1972) Bimodal EDR orienting response characteristics of limbic lesioned monkeys: Correlates with schizophrenic patients. Paper presented to Society for Psychophysiological Research, Boston, October.

Bagshaw, M., Kimble, D., & Pribram, K. (1965) The GSR of monkeys during orienting and habituation and after ablation of the amygdala, hippocampus and the inferotemporal cortex. *Neuropsychologia, 3,* 111.

Baird, P., & Sadovnick, A. (1985) Mental retardation in over half a million consecutive live births: An epidemiological study. *American Journal of Mental Deficiency, 89,* 323.

Baldessarini, R., Stramentinoli, G., & Lipinski, J. (1979) The methylation hypothesis. *Archives of General Psychiatry, 36,* 303.

Bandura, A. (1969) *Principles of behavior modification.* New York: Holt, Rinehart and Winston.

Bandura, A. (1977) *Social learning theory.* Englewood Cliffs, N.J.: Prentice Hall.

Bandura, A., Blanchard, E., & Ritter, B. (1968)

The relative efficacy of desensitization and modelling therapeutic approaches for inducing behavioral, affective and attitudinal changes. Unpublished manuscript. Palo Alto, Calif.: Stanford University Press.

Bandura, A., Ross, D., & Ross, S. (1961) Transmission of aggression through imitation of aggressive models. *Journal of Abnormal and Social Psychology, 63,* 575.

Barker, J., & Miller, M. (1973) Recent developments and some future trends in the applications of aversive conditioning. Unpublished manuscript. (Cited in J. Wolpe, *The practice of behavior therapy.* New York: Pergamon.)

Barlow, D., Mavissakalian, M., & Hay, L. (1981) Couples treatment of agoraphobia: Changes in marital satisfaction. *Behaviour Research and Therapy, 19,* 245.

Baron, M., Levitt, M., Gruen, R., Kane, J., & Asnis, L. (1984) Platelet MAO activity and genetic vulnerability to schizophrenia. *American Journal of Psychiatry, 141,* 836.

Bartollas, C. (1975) Runaways at the training institute in central Ohio. *Canadian Journal of Criminology and Corrections, 17,* 221.

Batchelor, I. (1957) Suicide and old age. In E. Shneidman & N. Farberow (Eds.), *Clues to suicide.* New York: McGraw-Hill.

Bateson, G., Jackson, D., Haley, J., & Weakland, J. (1956) Toward a theory of schizophrenia. *Behavioral Science, 1,* 241.

Bauer, M. (1972) *Health characteristics of low income persons.* (DHEW Pub. No. HSM 73-1500) Washington, D.C.: National Center for Health Statistics.

Bauer, R. (1979) The use of trance in working with the borderline personality. *Psychotherapy, Theory, Research and Practice, 16,* 371.

Baum, A., Shapiro, A., Murray, D., & Wideman, M. (1979) Interpersonal mediation of perceived crowding and control in residential dyads and triads. *Journal of Applied Social Psychology, 9,* 491.

Bazelon, C. (1979) Implementing the right to treatment. *University of Chicago Law Review, 36,* 742; 747.

Beach, F. (1948) *Hormones and behavior.* New York: Hoeber.

Beck, A. (1976) *Cognitive therapy and the emotional disorders.* New York: International Universities Press.

Beck, A. (1967) *Depression.* New York: Harper & Row.

Beck, A., & Rush, A. (1979) Cognitive approaches to depression and suicide. In G. Serban (Ed.), *Cognitive defects in the development of mental illness.* New York: Brunner/Mazel.

Beck, J. (1982) When the patient threatens violence: An empirical study of clinical practice after Tarasoff. *Bulletin of the American Academy of Psychiatry Law, 10,* 189.

Beck, J., Golden, S., & Arnold, F. (1981) An empirical investigation of psychotherapy with schizophrenic patients. *Schizophrenia Bulletin, 7,* 241.

Becker, F., & Zarit, S. (1978) Training older adults as peer counselors. *Educational Gerontology, 3,* 241.

Becker, H. (1963) *Outsiders.* New York: Free Press.

Beers, C. (1931) *A mind that found itself.* Garden City, N.Y.: Doubleday (a later edition of the 1908 book).

Bejerot, N. (1980) Addiction to pleasure—a biological and sociopsychological theory of addiction. In D. Lettieri, M. Sayer, & H. Pearson (Eds.), *Theories of drug use.* Washington, D.C.: NIDA Research Monograph 30, p. 246.

Bell, A., & Weinberg, M. (1978) *Homosexualities: A study of diversity among men and women.* New York: Simon & Schuster.

Bell, J. (1975) *Family therapy.* New York: Aronson.

Bell, L. (1981) *Treating the mentally ill from colonial times to the present.* New York: Praeger.

Bellman, M. (1966) Studies on encopresis. *Acta Pediatrica Scandinavica Suppl., 170,* 121.

Belmont, J. (1971) Medical behavioral research in retardation. In N. Ellis (Ed.) *International review of research in mental retardation.* Vol. 5. New York: Grune and Stratton.

Benda, C. (1946) *Mongolism and cretinism.* New York: Grune & Stratton.

Bender, L. (1938) A visual motor gestalt test and its clinical use. *American Orthopsychiatry Association Monographs, 3.*

Bender, L. (1971) The nature of childhood psychosis. In J. Howells (Ed.), *Modern perspectives in international child psychiatry.* New York: Brunner/Mazel.

Bendetti, G. (1980) Individual psychotherapy in schizophrenia. *Schizophrenia Bulletin, 6,* 633.

Benedict, R. (1934) Anthropology and the abnormal. *Journal of General Psychology, 10,* 59.

Benjamin, S., & Kincey, J. (1981) Evaluation of standardized behavior treatment for agoraphobic in-patients administered by untrained therapists. *British Journal of Psychiatry, 138,* 423.

Bennett, G., Vourakis, C., & Woolf, D. (1983) *Substance abuse: Pharmacological, developmental and clinical perspectives.* New York, Wiley.

Benson, H., Shapiro, D., Tursky, B., & Schwartz, G. (1971) Decreased systolic blood pressure through operant conditioning techniques in patients with essential hypertension. *Science, 173,* 740.

Benton, A. (1980) Psychological testing for brain damage. In H. Kaplan, A. Freedman, & B. Sadock (Eds.), *Comprehensive textbook of psychiatry/III.* Baltimore: Williams & Wilkins, 966.

Bergin, A. (1971) The evaluation of therapeutic outcomes. In A. Bergin & S. Garfield (Eds.) *Handbook of psychotherapy and behavior change.* New York: Wiley.

Bergin, A., & Suinn, R. (1975) Individual psychotherapy and behavior therapy. *Annual review of psychology.* Vol. 16. Palo Alto: Annual Reviews Press.

Berlin, F., & Meinecke, C. (1981) Treatment of sex offenders with antiandrogenic medication: Conceptualization, review of treatment modalities and preliminary findings. *American Journal of Psychiatry, 138,* 601.

Berman, H., & Siegel, G. (1972) Children who run. *American Academy of Child Psychiatry, 11,* 294.

Berman, J., & Ford, R. (1970) Intelligence quotients and intelligence loss in persons with PKU and some variant states. *Journal of Pediatrics, 77,* 764.

Bernard, H. (1981) Identity formation during late adolescence: A review of some empirical findings. *Adolescence, 62,* 349.

Bertalanffy, L. von. (1967) *Robots, men and minds.* New York: Brazeller.

Bertalanffy, L. von. (1975) *Perspectives on general systems theory.* New York: Brazeller.

Bertalanffy, L. von. (1981) *A systems view of man.* Boulder, Col.: Westview Press.

Bettelheim, B. (1967) *The empty fortress: Infantile autism and the birth of the self.* New York: The Free Press.

Bettelheim, B. (1974) *A home for the heart.* New York: Knopf.

Beyer, M. (1974) Psychosocial problems of adolescent runaways. Unpublished manuscript. Yale University.

Bibring, E. (1953) The mechanisms of depression. In P. Greenacre (Ed.), *Affective disorders.* New York: International Universities Press.

Bieber, I., Dain, H., Dince, P., Drellich, M., Grand, H., Gundlach, R., Kremer, M., Rifkin, A., Wilbur, C., & Bieber, T. (1962) *Homosexuality: A psychoanalytical study.* New York: Random House.

Billings, A., & Moos, R. (1982) Psychosocial theory and research on depression: An integrative framework and review. *Clinical Psychology Review, 2,* 213.

Bindelglas, P. (1975) The enuretic child. *The Journal of Family Practice,* October, 375.

Binswanger, L. (1963) *Being in the world.* New York: Basic Books.

Biran, M., Augusto, F., & Wilson, G. (1981) In vivo exposure versus cognitive restructuring in the treatment of scriptophobia. *Behaviour Research and Therapy, 19,* 525.

Bird, E., Spokes, E., & Iversen, L. (1979) Brain norepinephrine and dopamine in schizophrenia. *Science, 204,* 93.

Birren, J. (1964) *The psychology of aging.* Englewood Cliffs, N.J.: Prentice-Hall.

Bixler, R. (1981) The incest controversy. *Psychological Reports, 49,* 267.

Blaine, G., & McArthur, C. (Eds.). (1971) *Emotional problems of the college student.* New York: Appleton-Century-Crofts.

Blair, C., & Lanyon, R. (1981) Exhibitionism: Etiology and treatment. *Psychological Bulletin, 89,* 439.

Blanchard, E., & Young, L. (1974) Clinical applications of biofeedback training. *Archives of General Psychiatry, 30,* 573.

Blashfield, R. (1973) An evaluation of the DSM-II classification of schizophrenia as nomenclature. *Journal of Abnormal Psychology, 82,* 382.

Blashfield, R. (1982) Invisible colleges and the Matthew effect. *Schizophrenia Bulletin, 8,* 1.

Blau, D., & Berezin, M. (1975) Neurosis and character disorders. In J. Howells (Ed.) *Modern perspectives on the psychology of aging.* New York: Brunner/Mazel.

Bleuler, E. (1930) Primary and secondary symptoms in schizophrenia. *Zeitschrift fur generalische neurologische Psychiatrie, 124,* 607.

Blinder, B., Freeman, D., & Stunkard, A. (1970) Behavior therapy of anorexia nervosa: Effectiveness of activity as a reinforcer of weight gain. *American Journal of Psychiatry, 126,* 1093.

Bloom, B. (1977) *Community mental health: A general introduction.* Monterey, Calif.: Brooks/Cole.

Blos, P. (1946) Psychological counseling of college students. *American Journal of Orthopsychiatry, 16,* 571.

Boklage, C. (1977) Schizophrenia, brain asymmetry of development and twinning: Cellular relationships with etiology and possible prognostic implications. *Biological Psychology, 12,* 19.

Bootzin, R., & Accocella, J. (1984) *Abnormal Psychology: Current perspectives* (4th ed.). New York: Random House.

Bordin, E. (1974) *Research strategies in psychotherapy.* New York: Wiley.

Boskind-Lodahl, M., & White, W. (1978) The definition and treatment of bulimarexia in college women: A pilot study. *Journal of the American College Health Association, 97,* 84.

Boss, M. (1963) *Psychoanalysis and daseinanalysis.* New York: Basic Books.

Bourne, P., & Ekstrand, W. (1982) *Psychology: Its principles and meanings.* New York: Holt, Rinehart and Winston.

Bowden, C., & Sarabia, F. (1980) Diagnosing manic-depressive illness in adolescents. *Comprehensive Psychiatry, 21,* 263.

Bowen, M. Family therapy and family group therapy. (1971) In H. Kaplan & B. Sadock (Eds.), *Comprehensive group psychotherapy.* Baltimore: Williams & Wilkins.

Bowers, M. (1980) Biochemical processes in schizophrenia: An update. *Schizophrenia 1980.* Washington, D.C.: NIMH.

Boyd, J., & Weissman, M. (1981) Epidemiology of affective disorders. *Archives of General Psychiatry, 38,* 1039.

Brady, J. (1958) Ulcers in executive monkeys. *Scientific American, 199,* 95.

Brady, J., & Brodie, H. (1978) (Eds.) *Controversy in psychiatry.* Philadelphia: W. B. Saunders.

Braginsky, B., & Braginsky, D. (1967) Schizophrenic patients in the psychiatric interview: An experimental study of their effectiveness in manipulation. *Journal of Consulting and Clinical Psychology, 31,* 543.

Braginsky, B., Braginsky, D., & Ring, K. (1964) *Methods of madness.* New York: Holt, Rinehart and Winston.

Branch, D., & Eurman, L. (1980) Social attitudes towards patients with anorexia. *American Journal of Psychiatry, 137,* 632–633.

Brandes, N., & Gardner, M. (1973) *Group therapy for the adolescent.* New York: Jason Aronson.

Brandon, J. (1974) The relationship of runaway behavior in adolescence to the individual's perceptions of self, the environment and parental antecedents. Unpublished doctoral dissertation. University of Maryland.

Breggin, P. (1979) *Electroshock.* New York: Springer.

Brigante, T. (1965) Opportunities for community mental health training within a residential college campus context. *Community Mental Health Journal, 1,* 55.

Brockington, I., Kendall, R., & Leff, J. (1978) Definitions of schizophrenia: Concordance and prediction of outcome. *Psychological Medicine, 8,* 387.

Bronfenbrenner, U. (1970) *Two worlds of childhood: U.S. and U.S.S.R.* New York: Russell Sage Foundation.

Bronfenbrenner, U. (1977) Toward an experimental ecology of human development. *American Psychologist, 32,* 513.

Brooks, G., & Richardson, F. (1980) Emotional skills training: A treatment program for duodenal ulcer. *Behavior Therapy, 11.*

Brown, G., & Harris, T. (1978) *Social origins of depression.* London: Tavistock.

Brown, H. (1976) *Brain and behavior.* London: Oxford University Press.

Bruch, H. (1974) *Eating disorders: Obesity, anorexia nervosa and the person within.* London: Routledge and Kegan Paul.

Bunch, J. (1972) Recent bereavement and suicide. *Journal of Psychosomatic Research, 163,* 361.

Bunney, W. (1978) Drug therapy and psychobiological research advances in the psychoses in the past decade. *American Journal of Psychiatry, 135,* 8.

Burgess, A., & Holmstrom, L. (1979) Adaptive strategies and recovery from rape. *American Journal of Psychiatry, 136,* 1278.

Burgess, A., & Holmstrom, L. (1980) Rape typology and the coping behavior of rape victims. In S. L. McCombie (Ed.), *The rape crisis intervention handbook.* New York: Plenum Press.

Buros, O., (Ed.) (1979) *Seventh mental measurements yearbook.* Highland Park, N.J.: Gryphon Press.

Burton, T. (1974) Education for trainables: An impossible dream? *Mental Retardation, 12,* 45.

Byrne, D., & White, H. (1980) Life events and myocardial infarction revisited: The role of measures of individual impact. *Psychosomatic Medicine, 42,* 7.

Cadoret, R. (1978) Evidence for genetic inheritance of affective disorders in adoptees. *American Journal of Psychiatry, 135,* 463.

Call, P., & Bland, R. (1979) Manic depressive illness in adolescence and childhood. *Canadian Journal of Psychiatry, 24,* 255.

Callahan, E. (1980) Alternative strategies in the treatment of narcotic addiction. In W. Miller (Ed.), *The addictive behaviors.* New York: Pergamon, 143.

Cameron, N. (1947) *The psychology of behavior disorders.* Boston: Houghton Mifflin.

Campbell, M., Small, A., Collins, P., Friedman, E., David, R., & Genieser, N. (1976) Levodopa and levo-amphetamine: A crossover study in young schizophrenic children. *Current Therapeutic Research, 19,* 70.

Caplan, G. (1964) *Principles of preventive psychiatry.* New York: Basic Books.

Caplan, G. (1974) *Support systems and community mental health.* New York: Behavioral Publications.

Carey, G. (1982) Genetic influences of anxiety neurosis and agoraphobia. In R. J. Matthew (Ed.), *The Biology of Anxiety.* New York: Brunner/Mazel.

Carlsson, A. (1977) Does dopamine play a role in schizophrenia? *Psychological Medicine,* 7, 583.

Carlsson, A. (1978) Antipsychotic drugs, neurotransmitters, and schizophrenia. *Journal of Psychiatry, 135,* 164.

Carp, J. (1981) Youth's need for social competence and power: The community building model. *Adolescence, 64,* 935.

Carpenter, W., & Strauss, J. (1974) Cross-cultural evaluation of Schneider's first rank symptoms of schizophrenia: A report from the International Pilot Study of Schizophrenia. *American Journal of Psychiatry, 131,* 682.

Carpenter, W., & Strauss, J. (1973) Flexible system for the diagnosis of schizophrenia: Report from the WHO International study of schizophrenia. *Science, 182,* 1275.

Carr, E. G., Newsom, C. D., & Binkoff, J. A. (1976) Simultaneous control of self-destructive behavior in a psychotic child. *Journal of Abnormal Child Psychology, 4,* 139.

Carroll, B. (1979) Prediction of treatment outcome with lithium. *Archives of General Psychiatry, 36,* 870.

Carroll, B., Feinberg, M., Greden, J., Tarika, J., Albala, A., Haskett, R., James, N., Kronful, Z., Lohr, N., Steiner, M., deVigne, J., & Young, E. (1981) A specific laboratory test for the diagnosis of melancholia. *Archives of General Psychiatry, 38,* 15.

Carson, R. (1969) *Interaction concepts of personality.* Chicago: Aldine.

Carson, R. & Heine, R. (1962) Similarity and success in therapeutic dyads. *Journal of Consulting Psychology, 26,* 38.

Cashman, J. (1966) *The LSD story.* Greenwich, Conn.: Fawcett Publications.

Cassell, J. (1973) Planning for public health:

The case for prevention. Conference on education of nurses in public health, 1973. Cited in N. Robinson & H. Robinson (Eds.) (1976) *The mentally retarded child.* New York: McGraw-Hill.

Cautela, J. (1967) Covert sensitization. *Psychological Reports, 20,* 459.

Cautela, J. (1968) Personal communication.

Cautela, J. (1970a) Covert reinforcement. *Behavior Therapy, 1,* 33, (a).

Cautela, J. (1970b) Treatment of alcoholism by covert sensitization. *Psychotherapy: Theory, Research and Practice, 7,* 86.

Cerlitti, B., & Bini, L. (1938) L'elettroshock. *Archiva Generale Neurologia Psychiatria Psicoanalysia, 19,* 266.

Chamberlin, B. (1980) Mayo seminars in psychiatry: The psychological aftermath of disaster. *Journal of Clinical Psychiatry, 41,* 238.

Chapman, L. (1981) Recent advances in the study of schizophrenic cognition. *Special report: Schizophrenia 1980.* Rockville, Md.: U.S. Department of Health and Human Services.

Charney, D., Heninger, G., & Jatlow, B. (1985) Increased anxiogenic effects of caffeine in panic disorder. *Archives of General Psychiatry, 42,* 233.

Cheek, F., & Miller, M. (1981) The use of behavior modification techniques in developing socially appropriate behaviors in substance abusers. In J. Lowinson & P. Ruiz (Eds.), *Substance abuse.* Baltimore: Williams & Wilkins, p. 486.

Cheren, S., & Knapp, P. (1980) Gastrointestinal disorders. In H. Kaplan, A. Freedman, & B. Sadock (Eds.), *Comprehensive textbook of psychiatry/III.* Baltimore: Williams & Wilkins.

Chess, S., Korn, S., & Fernandez, P. (1971) *Psychiatric disorders of children with rubella.* New York: Brunner/Mazel.

Christian, S., Bennington, F., Morin, R., & Corbett, L. (1975) Gas-liquid chromatographic separation of biologically important indolealkylamines from human cerebrospinal fluid. *Biochemical Medicine, 14,* 191.

Ciesielski, K., Beech, H., & Gordon, P. (1981) Some electrophysiological observations in obsessional states. *British Journal of Psychiatry, 138,* 479.

Cleckley, H. (1976) *The mask of sanity* (5th ed.). St. Louis: Mosby.

Cohen, C., & Sokolovsky, J. (1978) Schizophrenia and social networks: Ex-patients in inner cities. *Schizophrenia Bulletin, 4,* 546.

Cohen, S. (1961) Future patterns of substance abuse. In J. Lowinson & P. Ruiz (Eds.), *Substance abuse.* Baltimore: Williams & Wilkins, p. 843.

Colasanti, B. (1982a) Anti-anxiety drugs. In C. Craig & R. Stitzel (Eds.), *Modern pharmacology.* Boston: Little, Brown, p. 493.

Colasanti, B. (1982b) Anti-psychotic drugs. In C. Craig & R. Stitzel (Eds.), *Modern pharmacology.* Boston: Little, Brown, p. 505.

Colasanti, B. (1982c) Anti-depressant therapy. In C. Craig & R. Stitzel (Eds.), *Modern pharmacology.* Boston: Little, Brown, 517.

Cole, J., & Davis, J. (1975) Anti-psychotic drugs; antidepressant drugs; minor tranquilizers, sedatives and hypnotics. In A. Freedman, H. Kaplan, & B. Sadock (Eds.), *Comprehensive textbook of psychiatry/II.* Baltimore: Williams & Wilkins.

Cole, J., Goldberg, S., & Davis, J. (1966) Drugs in the treatment of psychosis: Controlled studies. In P. Solomon (Ed.), *Psychiatric drugs.* New York: Grune & Stratton.

Cole, J., Goldberg, S. & Klerman, G. (1964) Phenothiazine treatment in acute schizophrenia. *Archives of General Psychiatry, 10,* 246.

Coleman, E. (1978) Toward a new model of treatment of homosexuality: A review. *Journal of Homosexuality, 3,* 345.

Collaborative study of children treated for PKU (1975) (Preliminary report No. 8). Presented to the Eleventh General Medical Conference, Stateline, Nev.

Committee on Aging of the Group for the Advancement of Psychiatry. Mental Health and Aging: Approaches to curriculum development. Vol. XI, Publication #114, April 1983. New York: Mental Health Materials Center.

Comstock, B. (1978) Psychological maladjustment in long term inhalant abusers. In C. Sharp & L. Carroll (Eds.), *Voluntary inhalation of industrial solvents.* Washington, D.C.: National Institute of Drug Abuse, 159.

Connoly, J. (1849) Quoted in J. Kolb & H. Brodie, *Modern clinical psychiatry* (10th ed.). Philadelphia: Saunders, 1982.

Cools, A. (1975) An integrated theory of the aetiology of schizophrenia. In H. Van Praag (Ed.) *On the origins of schizophrenia.* Amsterdam: De Erven Bohn.

Cooper, A. (1981) Short term treatment in sexual dysfunction: A review. *Comprehensive Psychiatry, 22,* 206.

Coppen, A. (1972) Indoleamines and affective disorders. *Journal of Psychiatric Research, 9,* 163.

Corey, G. (1977) *Theory and practice of counseling and psychotherapy.* Monterey, Calif.: Brooks/Cole.

Coursey, R. (1975) Electromyograph feedback as a relaxation technique. *Journal of Consulting and Clinical Psychology, 43,* 825.

Coyne, J., & Gotlib, I. (1983) The role of cognition in depression: A critical appraisal. *Psychological Bulletin, 94,* 472.

Craig, C. (1982) The CNS depressants. In C. Craig & R. Stitzel (Eds.), *Modern pharmacology.* Boston: Little, Brown, 473.

Craig, C., & Stitzel, R. (1982) *Modern pharmacology.* Boston: Little, Brown.

Craig, L., & Senter, R. (1972) Student thoughts about suicide. *Psychological Record, 22,* 355.

Cram, J. (1980) EMG biofeedback and the treatment of tension headaches: A systematic analysis of treatment components. *Behavior Therapy, 11,* 699.

Crawford, D. (1979) Modification of deviant sexual behavior: The need for a comprehensive approach. *British Journal of Medical Psychology, 52,* 151.

Crime in the United States. (1983) Uniform crime reports. Washington, D.C.: Federal Bureau of Investigation. U.S. Department of Justice.

Crisp, A. (1980) *Anorexia nervosa: Let me be.* London: Academic Press.

Cromwell, R., DeAmicis, L., Hayes, T., & Briggs, G. (1979) Reaction time crossover, a vulnerability index: Mean reaction time, a severity index. *Psychopharmacology Bulletin, 15,* 24.

Crowe, R. (1974) An adoption study of antisocial personality. *Archives of General Psychiatry, 31,* 785.

Crowe, R., & Johnstone, E. (1979) Electroshock in the treatment of affective disorders. In R. Crowe (Ed.), *Treatment of affective disorders.* London: Hogarth.

Crowe, R., Johnstone, E., Owens, D., Ferrier, I., MacMillan, J., Parry, R., & Tyrell, D. (1979) Characteristics of patients with schizophrenia or neurological disorders and virus-like agents in the cerebrospinal fluid. *Lancet, 11,* 842.

Crown, S., & D'Ardenne, P. (1982) Controversies, methods, results. *British Journal of Psychiatry, 140,* 70.

Cumming, E. (1964) New thoughts on the theory of disengagement. In R. Kastenbaum (Ed.), *New thoughts on old age.* New York: Springer.

Cumming, E. Primary prevention—more cost than benefit. (1976) In A. Dean, A. Kraft, & B. Pepper (Eds.), *The social setting of mental health.* New York: Basic Books, p. 328.

Cumming, E., & Henry, W. (1961) *Growing old: The process of disengagement.* New York: Basic Books.

Cutler, P., Aldredge, H., Fuller, D., & Siller, E. (1976) Migraine . . . and more: Treatment and prevention. *Current Prescribing, 2,* 46.

Dahlstrom, W., Welsh, G., & Dahlstrom, L. (1975) *An MMPI handbook. II: Research applications* (rev. ed.). Minneapolis: University of Minnesota Press.

Dalen, P. (1974) *Season of birth in schizophrenia and other disorders.* Goteborg: University of Goteborg.

Dalessio, D. (1972) *Wolff's headache and other head pain.* New York: Oxford University Press.

Dalldorf, J., & Schopler, E. (1981) Diagnosis and management of autism, *Comprehensive Therapy, 7,* 67.

D'Arcy, C. (1982) Prevalence and correlates of non-psychotic psychiatric symptoms in the general population. *Canadian Journal of Psychiatry, 27,* 316.

Dattilio, F. (1981) The Carkhuff systematic human relations training model in a short term treatment program for adolescent offenders. *Adolescence, 64,* 854.

Davidson, M. (1983) *Uncommon sense.* Los Angeles: Tarcher.

Davidson, L. (1979) Preventive attitudes toward midlife crisis. *American Journal of Psychoanalysis, 39,* 165.

Davies, M. (1970) Blood pressure and personality. *Journal of Psychosomatic Research. 14,* 89.

Davis, J., Nasi, S., Spira, N., & Vogel, C. (1981) Anxiety: Differential diagnosis and treatment from a biological perspective. *Journal of Clinical Psychiatry, 42,* 4.

Davis, J., Schaffer, C., Killian, G., Kincaid, C., & Chan, C. (1980) Important issues in the drug treatment of schizophrenia. *Schizophrenia 1980.* Washington, D.C.: NIMH.

Davison, G. (1978) Not can, but ought: The treatment of homosexuality. *Journal of Consulting and Clinical Psychology, 46,* 170.

Davison, G., & Neale, J. (1984) *Abnormal psychology: An experimental clinical approach.* New York: Wiley.

Dawson, G., & Mesibov, G. (1983) Childhood psychoses. In C. E. Walker & M. C. Roberts (Eds.), *Handbook of clinical psychology.* New York: Wiley.

Dawson, M., & Nuechterlein, K. (1984) Psychophysiological dysfunctions in the developmental course of schizophrenic disorder. *Schizophrenia Bulletin, 10,* 204:232.

Delozier, J., & Gagnon, R. (1974) *National ambulatory medical care survey.* Washington, D.C.: U.S. Government Printing Office, DHEW Publication No. HRA 76-1772.

DeLeon, G., & Mandell, W. (1966) A comparison of conditioning and psychotherapy in the treatment of functional enuresis. *Journal of Clinical Psychology, 22,* 326.

Delva, N., & Letmendin, F. (1982) Lithium therapy in schizophrenia and schizo-affective disorders. *British Journal of Psychiatry, 141,* 387.

Deneau, G., & Mule, S. (1981) Pharmacology of the opiates. In J. Lowinson & P. Ruiz (Eds.) *Substance abuse.* Baltimore: Williams & Wilkins, 129.

Deutsch, A. (1937) *The mentally ill in America.* Garden City, N.Y.: Doubleday.

de Wied, D. (1980) Hormonal influences on motivation. In D. Krieger & J. Hughes (Eds.), *Neuroendocrinology.* Sunderland, Mass.: Sinaud, p. 194.

Deykin, E., & MacMahon, B. (1979) The incidence of seizures among children with autistic symptoms. *American Journal of Psychiatry, 36,* 1310.

Dimond, R., Havens, R., & Jones, A. (1978) A conceptual framework for the practice of prescriptive eclecticism in psychotherapy. *American Psychologist, 33,* 239.

Dingemanse, E., & Freud, J. (1933) Identification of catatonine. *Acta Brevia Neerlandica Physiologica Microbiologica, 3,* 49.

Doane, J. (1978) Family interaction and communication deviance in disturbed and normal families: A review. *Family Process, 17,* 357.

Doerr, P., Pirke, K., Kockett, G., & Dittman, F. (1976) Further studies on sex hormones in male homosexuals. *Archives of General Psychiatry, 33,* 611.

Dohan, F., & Grasberger, J. (1973) Relapsed schizophrenics: Earlier discharge from the hospital after cereal-free, milk-free diet. *American Journal of Psychiatry, 130,* 685.

Dohrenwend, B. (1973) Social status and stressful life events. *Journal of Personality and Social Psychology, 28,* 228.

Dohrenwend, B. (1975) Socio-cultural and sociopsychological factors in the genesis of mental disorders. *Journal of Health and Social Behavior, 16,* 365.

Dohrenwend, B. (1976) Clues to the role of socioenvironmental factors. *Schizophrenia Bulletin, 2,* 440.

Dohrenwend, B., & Dohrenwend, B. (1974) Social and cultural influences on psychopathology. In *Annual Review of Psychology, Vol. 25.* Palo Alto, Calif.: Annual Reviews Press.

Dohrenwend, B., Dohrenwend, B., Gould, M., Link, B., Neugebauer, R., & Wunsch-Hitzig, R. (1980) *Mental illness in the United States: Epidemiological estimates.* New York: Praeger.

Dole, V., & Nyswander, M. (1965) A medical treatment for diacetylmorphine (heroin) addiction: A clinical trial with methadone hydrochloride. *Journal of the American Medical Association, 193,* 646.

Dole, V., & Nyswander, M. (1980) Methadone maintenance: A theoretical perspective. In D. Lettieri, M. Sayers, & H. Pearson (Eds.), *Theories of drug use.* Washington, D.C.: NIDA Research Monograph 30, p. 256.

Doleys, D. M. (1977) Behavioral treatments for nocturnal enuresis in children: A review of the recent literature. *Psychological Bulletin, 84,* 30.

Dollinger, S. J. (1983) A case report of dissociative neurosis (depersonalization disorder) in an adolescent treated with family therapy and behavior modification. *Journal of Consulting and Clinical Psychology, 51,* 479.

Domino, G., Gibson, L., Poling, S., & Westlake, L. (1980) Students' attitudes towards suicide. *Social Psychiatry, 15,* 127.

Donaldson, K. (1976) *Insanity inside out.* New York: Crown.

Donaldson, S., Gelenberg, A., & Baldessarini, R. (1983) The pharmacologic treatment of schizophrenia: Progress report. *Schizophrenia Bulletin, 9,* 504.

Donnelly, J. Psychosurgery. (1980) In H. Kaplan, A. Freedman & B. Sadock (Eds.), *Comprehensive textbook of psychiatry/III.* Baltimore: Williams & Wilkins, p. 2342.

Douvan, E., & Adelson, J. (1974) The adolescent experience. In A. Mussen, G. Conger, & J. Kagan (Eds.), *Child Development.* New York: Harper & Row.

Dowson, J. (1977) The phenomenology of severe obsessive-compulsive neurosis. *British Journal of Psychiatry, 13,* 75.

Drew, C., Logan, D., & Hardman, M. (1984) *Mental retardation: A life cycle approach* (3rd Ed.). St. Louis: Times Mirror/Mosby.

Dunn, L. (1968) Special education for the mildly retarded: Is much of it justified? *Exceptional Children, 35,* 5.

Dunn, L. (1973) Children with moderate and severe general learning disabilities. In L. Dunn (Ed.), *Exceptional children in schools* (2d Ed.). New York: Holt, Rinehart and Winston.

Durkheim, E. (1951) *Suicide.* New York: Free Press.

Durkheim, E. (1952) *Suicide.* London: Routledge and Kegan Paul.

Eckstein, G. (1970) *The body has a head.* New York: Harper & Row.

Edwards, D. (1983) Sexual behavior among college students. Emory University, Atlanta. Unpublished survey.

Eggers, C. (1978) Course and prognosis of childhood schizophrenia. *Journal of Autism and Childhood Schizophrenia, 8,* 21.

Eisdorfer, C., & Lawton, M. (Eds.) (1973) *The psychology of adult development and aging.* Washington, D.C.: American Psychological Association.

Eisdorfer, C., & Stotsky, B. (1977) Intervention, treatment and rehabilitation of psychiatric disorders. In J. Birren & K. Schaie (Eds.), *Handbook of the psychology of aging.* New York: Van Nostrand Reinhold.

Elliot, F. (1978) Neurological aspects of antisocial behavior. In W. Reid (Ed.), *The psychopath: A comprehensive study of antisocial disorders and behaviors.* New York: Brunner/Mazel.

Ellis, A. (1973) Rational-emotive therapy. In R. Corsini (Ed.), *Current psychotherapies.* Itasca, Ill.: Peacock.

Ellis, A. (1983) Must most psychotherapists remain as incompetent as they now are? *Journal of Contemporary Psychotherapy, 13,* 17.

Elms, A. (1975) The crisis of confidence in social psychology. *American Psychologist, 10,* 967.

Emmelkamp, P., & Kuypers, A. (1979) Agoraphobia: A follow-up study four years after treatment. *British Journal of Psychiatry, 134,* 352.

Endicott, J., & Spitzer, R. (1979) Use of the Research Diagnostic Criteria and the Schedule for Affective Disorders to study the affective disorders. *American Journal of Psychiatry, 136,* 52.

Engel, D. & Helfand, I. (1964) *Stuttering is a family affair.* Pamphlet published by Cleveland Speech and Hearing Center. Cleveland, Ohio.

Engel, G. (1975) Psychophysical gastrointestinal disorders. In A. Freedman, H. Kaplan, & B. Sadock (Eds.) *Comprehensive textbook of psychiatry/II.* Baltimore: Williams and Wilkins.

Engel, G. (1977) The need for a new medical model: A challenge for biomedicine. *Science, 196,* 129.

Engel, G. (1980) Psychophysical gastrointestinal disorders. In H. Kaplan, A. Freedman, & B. Sadock (Eds.) *Comprehensive textbook of psychiatry/III.* Baltimore: Williams & Wilkins.

Erikson, E. (1950) *Childhood and society.* New York: Norton.

Erikson, E. (1963) *Childhood and society* (2d ed.). New York: Norton.

Erikson, E. (1968) *Identity, youth and crisis.* New York: Norton.

Erikson, E. (1971) Introduction. In G. Blaine &

C. McArthur (Eds.), *Emotional problems of the student* (2d ed.). New York: Appleton-Century-Crofts.

Ernst, P., & Badash, D. (1977) Sensory stimulation in the elderly. *Annals of Israeli Psychiatry, 15*, 12.

Ernst, P., Beran, B., Badash, D., Kosovsky, R., & Kleinhauz, M. (1977) Treatment of the aged mentally ill: Further unmasking of the effects of a diagnosis of chronic brain syndrome. *Journal of American Geriatric Society, 10*, 466.

Erskine-Milliss, J., & Schonell, M. (1981) Relaxation therapy in asthma: A critical review. *Psychosomatic Medicine, 43*, 365.

Evans, M. (1978) *A ray of darkness*. London: B. J. Calder.

Evans, R. (1969) Childhood parental relationships of homosexual men. *Journal of Consulting and Clinical Psychology, 33*, 129.

Exner, J. (1976) Projective techniques. In I. Weiner (Ed.) *Clinical methods in psychology*. New York: Wiley.

Eysenck, H. (1952) The effects of psychotherapy: An evaluation. *Journal of Consulting Psychology, 16*, 319.

Eysenck, H. (1957) *Dynamics of anxiety and hysteria*. London: Routledge and Kegan Paul.

Eysenck, H. (1965) The effects of psychotherapy. *International Journal of Psychiatry, 1*, 97.

Eysenck, H. (1978) An exercise in mega-silliness. *American Psychologist, 33*, 519.

Eysenck, H., & Rachman, V. (1965) Cited by M. Gossop (1981), *Theories of neurosis*. New York: Springer Verlag.

Falloon, I., & Liberman, R. (1983) Interaction between drug and psychosocial therapy in schizophrenia. *Schizophrenia Bulletin, 9*, 543.

Farkas, T., Wolf, A., Jaeger, J., Brodie, J., Christman, D., & Fowler, J. (1984) Regional brain glucose metabolism in chronic schizophrenia. *Archives of General Psychiatry, 41*, 293.

Federal Register, Vol. 41, No. 23, Monday, November 29, 1976. Public Law 94–142, Section 5 (B).

Feighner, J., Robins, E., Guze, S., Woodruff, R., Winokur, G., & Munoz, R. (1972) Diagnostic criteria for use in psychiatric research. *Archives of General Psychiatry, 26*, 57.

Feingold, B. (1975) *Why your child is hyperactive*. New York: Random House.

Feldman-Summers, S., Gordon, P., & Meagher, J. (1979) The impact of rape on sexual satisfaction. *Journal of Abnormal Psychology, 88*, 101.

Ferster, C. (1965) Classification of behavior pathology. In L. Krasner & L. Ullman (Eds.), *Research in behavior modification*. New York: Holt, Rinehart and Winston.

Fenichel, O. (1945) *The psychoanalytic theory of neurosis*. New York: Norton.

Fenton, W., Mosher, L., & Matthews, S. (1981) Diagnosis of schizophrenia: A critical review of current diagnostic systems. *Schizophrenia Bulletin, 7*, 452.

Fieve, R. (1975) Lithium therapy. In A. Freedman, H. Kaplan, & B. Sadock (Eds.), *Comprehensive textbook of psychiatry/II*. Baltimore: Williams & Wilkins.

Fieve, R. (1973) Psychoanalysis. In R. Corsini (Ed.), *Current psychotherapies*. Itasca, Ill.: Peacock.

Fieve, R., Rosenthal, R., & Brill, H. (Eds.) (1975) *Genetic research in psychiatry*. Baltimore: Johns Hopkins Press.

Fine, R. (1973). Psychoanalysis. In R. Corsini (Ed.), *Current psychotherapies*. Itasca, Ill.: Peacock.

Fink, M. (1979) *Convulsive therapy*. New York: Raven Press.

Fink, M. (1984) Meduna and the origins of convulsive therapy. *American Journal of Psychiatry, 141*, 1034.

Fischer, C. S., & Oliver, S. J. (1983) A research note on friendship, gender, and the life cycle. *Social Forces, 62*, 124.

Fischer, M., Harvald, B., & Hauge, M. (1969) Danish twin study of schizophrenia. *British Journal of Psychiatry, 115*, 981.

Flor-Henry, P. (1974) Psychosis, neurosis and epilepsy. *British Journal of Psychiatry, 124*, 144.

Flor-Henry, P. (1976) Lateralized temporal-limbic system dysfunction and psychopathology. *Annals of the New York Academy of Science, 280*, 777.

Folstein, S., & Rutter, M. (1977) Genetic influences and infantile autism. *Nature, 265*, 726–728.

Forman, B. (1980) Psychotherapy with rape victims. *Psychotherapy, Theory, Research and Practice, 17*, 304.

Forrest, G. (1984) *Intensive psychotherapy of alcoholism.* Springfield, Ill.: Charles C. Thomas.

Fozard, J., & Thomas, J. (1975) Psychology of aging. In J. Howells (Ed.), *Modern perspectives on the psychology of aging.* New York: Brunner/Mazel.

Frances, A. (1980) The DSM-III personality disorders section: A commentary. *American Journal of Psychiatry, p. 137*, 1050.

Frederick, C. (1982) Drug use and learned behavior. In D. Lettieri, M. Sayer, & H. Pearson (Eds.) *Theories of drug use.* Washington, D.C.: NIDA Research Monograph 30, 191.

Freedman, D. (1984) Epidemiology counts. *Archives of General Psychiatry, 41*, 931.

Freedman, J. (1982) *Introductory psychology.* New York: Addison-Wesley.

Freedman, S., Grunebaum, H., & Greenblatt, M. (1961) Perceptual and cognitive changes in sensory deprivation. In P. Solomon (Ed.) *Sensory deprivation: A symposium.* Cambridge, Mass.: Harvard University Press.

Freeman, W., & Watts, J. (1950) *Psychosurgery* Springfield, Ill.: Charles C. Thomas.

Friedman, C., & Friedman, A. (1972) Sex concordance in psychogenic disorders: Psychosomatic disorders in mothers and schizophrenia in daughters. *Archives of General Psychiatry, 27*, 611.

Friedman, M., & Rosenman, R. (1959) Association of specific overt behavior patterns with blood and cardiovascular findings: Blood cholesterol level, clotting time, incidence of arcus semilis and clinical coronary artery disease. *Journal of the American Medical Association, 169*, 1286.

Friedman, M., & Rosenman, R. (1974) *Type A behavior and your heart.* Greenwich, Conn.: Fawcett.

Freud, J., & Dingemanse, E. (1932) Uber katatonin, einen giftigen stoff im lipoid ekstrakt von harm, gewirbsflussigkeiten und organen. *Biochemische Zeitschrift, 255*, 464.

Freud, S. (1936) *The problem of anxiety.* New York: Norton.

Freud, S. (1953) Three essays on the theory of sexuality. In J. Strachey (Ed.), *Standard edition of the complete works of Sigmund Freud.* Vol. 7. London: Hogarth Press, (Originally published, 1930).

Freud, S. (1957) Mourning and melancholia. In J. Strachey (Ed.), *Standard edition of the complete works of Sigmund Freud.* Vol. 14. London: Hogarth Press.

Fromm-Reichmann, F. (1948) Notes on the development of treatment for schizophrenia by psychoanalytic psychotherapy. *Psychiatry, 11*, 263.

Frutiger, A. (1981) Treatment of penetration phobia through the combined use of systematic desensitization and hypnosis: A case study. *American Journal of Clinical Hypnosis, 23*, 269.

Gallahorn, G. (1981) Borderline personality disorders. In J. Lion (Ed.), *Personality disorders: diagnosis and management.* Baltimore: Williams & Wilkins.

Gallatin, J. (1975) *Adolescence and individuality.* New York: Harper & Row.

Gandour, M. (1984) Bulimia: Clinical description, assessment, etiology and treatment. *International Journal of Eating Disorders, 3*, 3.

Gardner, D., Garfinkel, P., Schwartz, D., & Thompson, S. (1980) Cultural expectations of thinness in women. *Psychological Reports, 47*, 483.

Gardner, W. (1970) Use of behavior therapy with the severely retarded. In F. Menolascino (Ed.), *Psychiatric approaches to mental retardation.* New York: Basic Books.

Garfield, S., & Katz, R. (1976) Clinical psychologists in the 1970's. *American Psychologist, 31*, 1.

Gaultieri, C. T. (1977) Imipramine and children: A review of some speculations about the mechanism of drug action. *Diseases of the Nervous System, 38*, 368.

Gebhard, P., Gagnon, J., Pomeroy, W., & Christenson, C. (1965) *Sex offenders.* New York: Harper & Row.

Gentry, W., Harburg, E., & Havenstein, L. (1973) Effects of anger expression-inhibition and guilt on elevated diastolic blood pressure in high-low stress and black-white females. *Proceedings of the 81st Annual Convention of the American Psychological Association*, Montreal, Canada.

Gerard, J. (1973) Shifting attitudes toward criminal responsibility. *Medical World News: Psychiatry, 14,* 39.

Gershon, E. (1978) The search for genetic markers in affective disorders. In M. Lipton, A. Dimascio, & K. Killam (Eds.), *Psychopharmacology: A generation of progress.* New York: Raven Press, p. 1197.

Gershon, E., & Bunney, W. (1976) The question of X-linkage in bipolar manic-depressive illness. *Journal of Psychiatric Research, 13,* 99.

Gershon, E., Bunney, W., Lechman, J., van Eerdewagh, M., & Debauche, B. (1976) The inheritance of affective disorders: A review of data and hypotheses. *Behavior Genetics, 6,* 227.

Gershon, E., Targum, S., Kessler, L., Mazure, C., & Bunney, W. (1977) Genetic studies of biological strategies in the affective disorders. In A. Steinberg, A. Bearn, A. Motulsky, & B. Childs (Eds.), *Progress in medical genetics.* Philadelphia: Saunders, p. 103.

Gersten, J., Langner, J., Eisenberg, J., & Orzek, L. (1974) Child behavior and life events. In B. Dohrenwend & B. Dohrenwend (Eds.), *Stressful life events: Their nature and effects.* New York: Wiley.

Gilberstadt, H., & Duker, J. (1965) *A handbook for clinical and actuarial MMPI interpretation.* Philadelphia: Saunders.

Gillin, J., Kaplan, J., Stillman, R., & Wyatt, R. (1976) The psychedelic model of schizophrenia: The case of N,N-dimethyltryptamine. *American Journal of Psychiatry, 133,* 203.

Ginott, H. (1964) *Between parent and child.* New York: Macmillan.

Glatt, M. (1974) *A guide to addiction and its treatment.* New York: MTP Press (J. Wiley and Sons, Inc.).

Glazer, M. (1979) The borderline personality diagnosis: Some negative implications. *Psychotherapy: Theory, Research and Practice, 16,* 376.

Glover, H. (1984) Themes of mistrust and the post-traumatic stress disorder in Vietnam veterans. *Journal of Psychotherapy, 37,* 445.

Goddard, H. (1914) *Feeblemindedness—Its causes and consequences.* New York: Macmillan.

Goddard, H. (1919) *The Kallikak family.* New York: Macmillan.

Goffman, I. (1961) *Asylums.* New York: Anchor.

Golaan, S., & Fremouw, W. (Eds.) (1976) *The right to treatment for mental patients.* New York: Irvington Press.

Gold, M., Redmond, D., & Kleber, H. (1978) Clonidine blocks acute opiate withdrawal symptoms. *Lancet,* September 16, 559.

Goldenberg, I. (1971) *Build me a mountain: Youth, poverty and the creation of new settings.* Cambridge: MIT Press.

Goldfarb, A. (1974a) *Aging and organic brain syndromes.* Fort Washington, Pa.: McNeill Labs.

Goldfarb, W. (1974b) *Growth and change of schizophrenic children: A longitudinal study.* New York: Wiley.

Goldfarb, W. (1980) Pervasive developmental disorders of childhood. In H. Kaplan, A. Freedman, & B. Sadock (Eds.), *Comprehensive textbook of psychiatry/III.* Baltimore: Williams & Wilkins, p. 2527.

Goldfried, M., & Davison, G. (1976) *Clinical behavior therapy.* New York: Holt, Rinehart and Winston.

Goldman, H., Goldman, J., Kaufman, I., & Liebman, O. (1974) Later effects of early dietary protein intake on low birth weight infants. *Journal of Pediatrics, 85,* 764.

Goldstein, G., & Halperin, K. (1977) Neuropsychological differences among subtypes of schizophrenics. *Journal of Abnormal Psychology, 86,* 34.

Goldstein, M., Rodnick, E., Evans, J., May, P., & Steinberg, M. (1978) Drug and family therapy in the aftercare of acute schizophrenics. *Archives of General Psychiatry, 35,* 1169.

Gomberg, E. (1979) Problems with alcohol and other drugs. In E. Gomberg & V. Franks (Eds.), *Gender and disordered behavior.* New York: Brunner/Mazel, p. 204.

Goodman, L., & Gilman, A. (Eds.) (1980) *The pharmacological basis of therapeutics* (6th ed.). London: Collier-Macmillan.

Goodman, L., & Gilman, A. (Eds.) (1982) *The pharmacological basis of therapeutics* (7th ed.). London: Collier-Macmillan.

Goodman, S. (1982) Project PACT: The identification of and intervention with children at risk for schizophrenia. NIMH project report draft. Atlanta: Emory University.

Goodwin, D. (1979) Alcoholism and heredity. *Archives of General Psychiatry, 36,* 57.

Goodwin, D. (1985) Alcoholism and genetics. *Archives of General Psychiatry, 42,* 171.

Goodwin, D., Schulsinger, F., Knop, J., Mednick, S., & Guze, S. (1977a). Alcoholism and depression in adopted-out daughters of alcoholics. *Archives of General Psychiatry, 34,* 751.

Goodwin, D., Schulsinger, F., Knop, J., Mednick, S., & Guze, S. (1977b). Psychopathology in adopted and non-adopted daughters of alcoholics. *Archives of General Psychiatry, 34,* 1005.

Goodwin, F., Cowdry, R., & Webster, M. (1978) Prediction of drug response in the affective disorders. In M. Lipton, A. Dimascio, & K. Killam (Eds.), *Psychopharmacology: A generation of progress.* New York: Raven Press, p. 1277.

Gordon, B. (1980) *I'm dancing as fast as I can.* New York: Harper & Row.

Gordon, D., Terdal, L., & Sterling, E. (1974) The use of modeling and desensitization in the treatment of a phobic dental patient. *Journal of Dentistry for Children, 41,* 102.

Gorenstein, E. (1982) Frontal lobe functions in psychopaths. *Journal of Abnormal Psychology, 91,* 368.

Gossop, M. (1981) *Theories of neurosis.* New York: Springer-Verlag.

Gottesman, L., & Boureston, N. (1974) Why nursing homes do what they do. *Gerontologist, 14,* 501.

Gottesman, I., & Shields, J. (1976) A critical review of recent adoption, twin, and family studies of schizophrenia: Behavioral genetic perspectives. *Schizophrenia Bulletin, 3,* 360.

Gottesman, I., & Shields, J. (1972) *Schizophrenia and genetics: A twin study vantage point.* New York: Academic Press.

Gottlieb, D., & Chafetz, J. (1977) Dynamics of familial generational conflict and reconciliation: A research note. *Youth and Society, 9,* 283.

Gottlieb, J., Alter, M., & Gottlieb, B. (1983) Mainstreaming mentally retarded children. In J. Matson & J. Mulick (Eds.), *Handbook of mental retardation.* New York: Pergamon, p. 67.

Gould, R. (1978) *Transformations.* New York: Simon & Schuster.

Gove, W., & Howell, P. (1974) Individual resources and mental hospitalization: A comparison and evaluation of societal reaction and psychiatric perspectives. *American Sociological Review, 39,* 86.

Graber, B. (1981) Demystifying "sex therapy." *American Journal of Psychotherapy, 35,* 481.

Graham, E., Ernhart, C., Craft, M., & Berman, P. (1963) Brain injury in the preschool child. *Psychological Monographs, 77,* 573.

Graham, P., Rutter, M., Yule, N., & Pless, I. (1967) Childhood asthma: A psychosomatic disorder? *British Journal of Preventive Social Medicine, 21,* 78.

Greden, J. (1981) Caffeinism and caffeine withdrawal. In J. Lowinson & P. Ruiz (Eds.), *Substance abuse.* Baltimore: Williams & Wilkins, p. 274.

Green, R. (1980) Homosexuality. In H. Kaplan, A. Freedman, & B. Sadock (Eds.) *Comprehensive textbook of psychiatry/III.* Baltimore: Williams & Wilkins, p. 1762.

Green, R. & Rau, J. (1975) Compulsive eating: Neurologic approaches to certain eating disorders. *Comparative Psychiatry, 16,* 223.

Greenberg, E. (1982) A cure for suicide? *NIMH Bulletin, 2.*

Grier, W., & Cobbs, P. (1968) *Black rage.* New York: Basic Books.

Grinc, G. (1982) A cognitive behavioral model for the treatment of chronic vomiting. *Journal of behavioral medicine, 5,* 135.

Grinker, R. (1975) The relevance of general systems theory to psychiatry. In S. Arieti (Ed.), *American handbook of psychiatry.* Vol. 6. New York: Basic Books, p. 650.

Grinspoon, L., & Bakalar, J. (1981) Marijuana. In J. Lowinson & P. Ruiz (Eds.), *Substance abuse.* Baltimore: Williams & Wilkins, p. 140.

Grossman, H. (Ed.) (1973) *Classification in mental retardation.* Washington, D.C.: AAMD.

Grossman, H. (Ed.) (1983) *Classification in mental retardation.* Washington, D.C.: AAMD.

Groth, N. A., & Birnbaum, H. J. (1980) The rapist: Motivations for sexual violence. In S. L. McCombie (Ed.), *The rape crisis intervention handbook.* New York, Plenum Press.

Gruzelier, J., & Venables, P. (1975) Evidence of high and low levels of arousal in schizophrenics. *Psychophysiology, 12,* 66.

Guardo, C. (1975) *The adolescent as individual.* New York: Harper & Row.

Guillemin, R. (1980) Beta-lipotropins and endorphins: Implications of current knowledge. In D. Krieger & J. Hughes (Eds.), *Neuroendocrinology.* Sunderland, Mass.: Sinauer, p. 67.

Gunderson, J., Frank, A., Katz, H., Vannicelli, M., Frosch, J., & Knapp, P. (1984) Effects of psychotherapy in schizophrenia: II. Comparative outcomes of two forms of treatment. *Schizophrenia Bulletin, 10,* 564.

Gurevitz, H. (1977) Tarasoff: Protective privilege versus public peril. *American Journal of Psychiatry, 134,* 289.

Gurman, A. (1972) Therapist mood pattern and therapeutic facilitativeness. *Journal of Counseling Psychology, 19,* 169.

Gurman, A. (1973) Effects of therapist and patient mood on the therapeutic functioning of high and low facilitative therapists. *Journal of Consulting and Clinical Psychology, 40,* 48.

Gutting, G. (Ed.) (1980) *Paradigms and revolutions.* Notre Dame, Ind.: Notre Dame Press.

Guttmann, D. (1980) The post-parental years: Clinical problems and developmental possibilities. In W. Norman & T. Scaramella (Ed.), *Mid-life: Developmental and clinical issues.* New York: Brunner/Mazel.

Guze, S. (1976) *Criminality and psychiatric disorders.* New York: Oxford University Press.

Hacking, I. (1981) *Scientific revolutions.* New York: Oxford University Press.

Hafner, R., Gilchrist, P., Bowling, J., & Kalucy, R. (1981) The treatment of obsessional neurosis in a family setting. *Australian and New Zealand Journal of Psychiatry, 15,* 145.

Haier, R., Murphy, D., & Buchsbaum, M. (1979) Paranoia and platelet MAO in normals and non-schizophrenic psychiatric groups. *American Journal of Psychiatry, 136,* 308.

Haim, A. (1974) *Adolescent suicide.* Paris: Tavistock Publications.

Hajal, F., & Leach, A. (1981) Familial aspects of Gilles de la Tourette's syndrome. *American Journal of Psychiatry, 138,* 90.

Haley, J. (1973) *Uncommon therapy.* New York: Norton.

Haley, J. (1976) *Problem solving therapy.* San Francisco: Jossey-Bass.

Hall, C. (1934) Emotional behavior in the rat. I: Defecation and urination as measures of individual differences in emotionality. *Journal of Comparative Psychology, 18,* 385.

Hall, G. (1904) *Adolescence.* New York: Appleton.

Hall, H. (1983) Hypnosis and the immune system: A review with implications for cancer and the psychology of healing. *Journal of Experimental Hypnosis, 12,* 92.

Halleck, S. (1976) Another response to "Homosexuality: The ethical challenge." *Journal of Consulting and Clinical Psychology, 44,* 167.

Handforth, J. (1981) Study difficulty: Psychiatric and psychological aspects. *Canadian Psychiatric Association Journal, 23,* 549.

Hare, E. (1970) *Psychopathy.* New York: Wiley.

Hare, E., Price, J., & Slater, E. (1974) Mental disorders and season of birth. *British Journal of Psychiatry, 124,* 81.

Harper, R. (1975) *The new psychotherapies.* Englewood Cliffs, N.J.: Prentice Hall.

Harris, T., & Gottesman, I. (1976) A critical review of recent adoption, twin and family studies of schizophrenia: Behavioral genetics perspectives. *Schizophrenia Bulletin, 3,* 360.

Harrison, R. (1974) Psychological testing in headache: A review. *Headache, 15,* 177.

Harrow, M., Lanin-Kettering, I., Prosen, M., & Miller, J. (1983) Disordered thinking in schizophrenia: Intermingling and loss of set. *Schizophrenia Bulletin, 9,* 354.

Hart, M. (1978) Psychological adjustment of non-patient homosexuals: Critical review of recent literature. *Journal of Clinical Psychiatry, 39*, 604.

Hartocollis, P. (1980) Long-term hospital treatment for adult patients with borderline and narcissistic disorders. *Bulletin of the Menninger Clinic, 44*, 213.

Haskett, R., & Rose, R. (1981) Neuroendocrine disorders and psychopathology. *Psychiatric Clinics of North America, 4*, 239.

Hastings, J., & Barkley, P. (1978) Patterns of hyperactivity. *Youth/Society, 10*, 217.

Hatch, J. (1981) Voluntary control of sexual responding in men and women: Implications for the etiology and treatment of sexual dysfunctions. *Biofeedback and Self-Regulation, 6*, 191.

Hathaway, S., & McKinley, J. (1943) *Minnesota multiphasic personality inventory: Manual.* New York: The Psychological Corporation.

Hatzenbuehler, L. C., & Schroeder, H. E. (1978) Desensitization procedures in the treatment of childhood disorders. *Psychological Bulletin, 85*, 831.

Hauber, F., Bruininks, R., Hill, B., Lakin, K., Scheerenberger, R., & White, C. (1984) National census of retardation facilities: A 1982 profile. *American Journal of Mental Deficiency, 84*, 236.

Havighurst, R. (1963) Successful aging. In R. Williams, C. Tibbitts, & W. Donahue (Eds.), *Process of aging.* New York: Atherton.

Hawkins, R. & Clement, P. (1980) Development and construct validation of a self-report measure of binge eating tendencies. *Addictive Behaviors, 5*, 219.

Hayes, R. (1981) High school graduation: The case for identity loss. *Personnel and Guidance Journal, 59*, 369.

Heilman, K., & Valenstein, E. (1985) *Clinical neuropsychology* (2d ed.). New York: Oxford Press.

Heim, N., & Hursch, C. (1979) Castration of sex offenders: Treatment or punishment? A review and critique of recent European literature. *Archives of Sexual Behavior, 8*, 281.

Hellman, L., & Pritchard, J. (1971) *Williams obstetrics* (14th Ed.) New York: Appleton, Century, Crofts.

Henryk-Gutt, R., & Rees, W. (1973) Psychological aspects of migraine. *Journal of Psychosomatic Research, 17*, 141.

Heston, L. (1966) Psychiatric disorders in foster-home reared children of schizophrenic mothers. *British Journal of Psychiatry, 112*, 819.

Hirst, W. (1982) The amnesic syndrome: Descriptions and explanations. *Psychological Bulletin, 91*, 435.

Hobbs, N. (1964) Mental health's third revolution. *American Journal of Orthpsychiatry, 34*, 822.

Hocking, F. (1970) Extreme environmental stress and its significance for psychopathology. *American Journal of Psychotherapy, 24*, 4.

Hodapp, V., Weyer, G., & Becker, J. (1975) Situational stereotypy in essential hypertension patients. *Journal of Psychosomatic Research, 19*, 113.

Hoehn-Savic, R., Merchant, A. F., Keyser, M. L., & Smith, V. K. (1981) Effects of clonidine on anxiety disorders. *Archives of General Psychiatry, 38*, 1278.

Hoffman, E., & Grande, P. (1979) Academic advising: Matching student's career skills and interests. In E. Watkins (Ed.), *Preparing liberal arts students for careers.* Los Angeles: Jossey-Bass, p. 35.

Hoffman, M. (1977) Homosexuality. In F. Beach (Ed.), *Human sexuality in four perspectives.* Baltimore: Hopkins University Press.

Hokanson, J., & Burgess, M. (1962) The effects of three types of aggression on vascular processes. *Journal of Abnormal Psychology, 65*, 446.

Hokanson, J., DeGood, D., Forrest, M., & Brittain, T. (1971) Availability of avoidance behaviors for modulating vascular stress responses. *Journal of Personality and Social Psychology, 19*, 60.

Holinger, P. (1980) Violent deaths as a leading cause of mortality. *Journal of American Psychiatry, 137*, 472.

Hollister, L., Davis, K., & Davis, B. (1980) Hormones in the treatment of psychiatric disorders. In D. Krieger & J. Hughes (Eds.), *Neuroendocrinology.* Sunderland, Mass.: Sinauer.

Holmes, T., & Rahe, R. (1967) The social readjustment rating scale. *Journal of Psychosomatic Research, 11,* 213.

Holmstrom, L., & Burgess, A. (1979) Rape: The husband's and boyfriend's initial reactions. *Family Coordinators, 28,* 321.

Holroyd, D. (1976) Cognition and desensitization in group treatment of test anxiety. *Journal of Consulting and Clinical Psychology, 44,* 991.

Holroyd, D., Westbrook, T., Wolf, M., & Badhorn, E. (1978). Performance, cognition and physiological responding in test anxiety. *Journal of Abnormal Psychology, 87,* 442.

Holroyd, K., Andrasik, F., & Noble, J. (1980) A comparison of EMG biofeedback and a credible psychotherapy in treating tension headache. *Journal of Behavioral Medicine, 3,* 29.

Holtzman, P., Proctor, L., & Hughes, D. (1973) Eye-tracking patterns in schizophrenics. *Science, 181,* 179.

Holtzman, P., Proctor, L., Levy, D., Yasillo, N., Meltzer, R., & Hurt, S. (1974) Eyetracking dysfunctions in schizophrenic patients and their relatives. *Archives of General Psychiatry, 31,* 143.

Hoshino, K. (1973) Causal factors and patterns of behavior in running away from home. *Report of the National Research Institute of Police Science, 14,* 39.

Hott, L. (1979) The antisocial character. *American Journal of Psychoanalysis, 39,* 235–249.

Howard, K., & Orlinsky, D. (1972) Psychotherapeutic practices. In *Annual Review of Psychology.* Vol. 23. Palo Alto: Annual Reviews Press.

Howells, J. (Ed.) (1975) *Modern perspectives on the psychology of aging.* New York: Brunner/Mazel.

Hsu, L. (1983) The aetiology of anorexia nervosa. *Psychological Medicine, 13,* 231.

Hsu, L., & Lieberman, S. (1982) Paradoxical intention in the treatment of chronic anorexia nervosa. *American Journal of Psychiatry, 139,* 650.

Huber, G., Gross, G., Schuttler, R., & Linz, M. (1980) Longitudinal studies of schizophrenic patients. *Schizophrenia Bulletin, 6,* 592.

Humphreys, L. (1970) *Tearoom trade: Impersonal sex in public places.* Chicago: Aldine.

Hutchin, J. (1973) Dynamics and correlates of runaway behavior. *Crime and Delinquency, 19,* 101.

Huyck, M., & Hoyer, W. (1982) *Adult development and aging.* Belmont, Calif.: Wadsworth.

Isaacs, W., Thomas, F., & Goldiamond, I. (1960) Application of operant conditioning to reinstate verbal behavior in psychotics. *Journal of Speech and Hearing Disorders, 25,* 8.

Iversen, S. (1980) Brain chemistry and behavior. *Psychological Medicine, 10,* 527.

Jacobs, L. (1980) The ambivalent copulator: Ejaculatory incompetence and identity diffusion. *International Journal of Social Psychiatry, 26,* 179.

Jacobson, E. (1953) Contributions to the metapsychology of cyclothymic depression. In P. Greenacre (Ed.), *Affective disorders.* New York: International Universities Press.

Jacobson, E. (1938) *Progressive relaxation.* Chicago: University of Chicago Press.

Jaffe, J., & Kanzler, M. (1981) Nicotine. In J. Lowinson & P. Ruiz (Eds.), *Substance abuse.* Baltimore: Williams & Wilkins, p. 256.

Janet, P. (1925) *Psychological healing: A historical and clinical study* (E. & C. Paul, Trans.). London: George Allen and Unwin.

Jarvik, M. (1970) Drugs in the treatment of psychiatric disorders. In L. Goodman & A. Gilman (Eds.), *The pharmacological basis of therapeutics* (4th ed.). London: Collier-Macmillan.

Jarvis, E. (1971) *Insanity and idiocy in Massachusetts: Report of the Cambridge commission, 1855.* Cambridge, Mass.: Harvard University Press.

Jellinek, E. (1960) *The disease concept of alcoholism.* New Haven, Conn.: Hillhouse Press.

Jenkins, R., & Stahle, G. (1972) The runaway reaction: A case study. *Journal of the American Academy of Child Psychiatry, 11,* 294.

Jenni, M., & Wollersheim, J. (1979) Cognitive therapy stress management training and the type A behavior pattern. *Cognitive Therapy and Research, 3,* 61.

Jeri, F., Sanches, C., Del Pozo, L., & Fernandez, M. (1978) El sindrome de la pasta de coca. *Rev. Sanid. Ministerio Interior, 39,* 1.

Jerremalm, A., Johansson, J., & Ost, L. (1980)

Applied relaxation as a self-control technique for social phobias. *Scandinavian Journal of Behavior Therapy, 9,* 35.

Johnson, C., & Larson, R. (1982) Bulimia: An analysis of moods and behavior. *Psychosomatic Medicine, 44,* 341.

Johnson, G., & Leeman, M. (1977) Analysis of familial factors in bipolar affective disorders. *Archives of General Psychiatry, 34,* 1074.

Johnson, R. (1981) Psychodynamic and developmental considerations of the childless older woman. Unpublished doctoral dissertation, Northwestern University.

Johnson, W. (1955) *Stuttering in children and adults.* Minneapolis: University of Minnesota Press.

Johnston, L., Bachman, J., & O'Malley, E. (1982) *Student drug use in America 1975–1981.* Washington, D.C., DHHS Publ. No. ADM(82-1221-1982).

Jonas, D., & Jonas, D. (1980) A bio-anthropological view of addiction. In D. Lettieri, M. Sayer, & H. Pearson (Eds.). *Theories of drug use.* Washington, D.C.: NIDA Research Monograph 30, p. 269.

Jones, K., Smith, D., Streissguth, A., & Myrianthropoulos, N. (1974) Outcome in offspring of chronic alcoholic women. *Lancet, i,* 1076.

Jones, M. (1953) *The therapeutic community.* New York: Basic Books.

Jones, M. (1968) *Beyond the therapeutic community.* New Haven: Yale University Press.

Jones, M. C. (1924) A behavior study of fear: The case of Peter. *Journal of Genetic Psychology, 31,* 508.

Jorgensen, R., Houston, B., & Zurawski, R. (1981) Anxiety management training in the treatment of essential hypertension. *Behavior Research and Therapy, 19,* 467.

Josselyn, I. (1954) The ego in adolescence. *American Journal of Orthopsychiatry, 24,* 223.

Joynt, R., & Shoulson, I. (1985) Dementia. In K. Heilman & E. Valenstein (Eds.), *Clinical neuropsychology* (2d ed.). New York: Oxford Press, p. 453.

Julien, R. (1981) *A primer of drug action.* San Francisco: Freeman.

Jung, C. (1964) The development of personality. In *Collected works.* Vol. 17. Bollingen Series (Vol. 20). Princeton: Princeton University Press, (Originally published 1954).

Jung, C. (1976) The stages of life. In J. Campbell (Ed.), *The Portable Jung.* New York: Viking.

Kalinowsky, L. (1975a) The convulsive therapies. In A. Freedman, H. Kaplan, & B. Sadock (Eds.), *Comprehensive textbook of psychiatry/II.* Baltimore: Williams & Wilkins.

Kalinowsky, L. (1975b) Psychosurgery. In A. Freedman, H. Kaplan, & B. Sadock (Eds.), *Comprehensive textbook of psychiatry/II.* Baltimore: Williams & Wilkins.

Kalinowsky, L. (1980) Convulsive therapies. In H. Kaplan, A. Freedman & B. Sadock (Eds.), *Comprehensive textbook of psychiatry/III.* Baltimore: Williams & Wilkins.

Kalj, L. (1960) *Studies on the etiology and sequels of the abuse of alcohol.* Lund: University of Lund Press.

Kalish, R. (1975) *Late adulthood: Perspectives on human development.* Monterey, Calif.: Brooks/Cole.

Kallmann, F. (1938) *The genetics of schizophrenia.* New York: Augustin.

Kallmann, F. (1946) The genetic theory of schizophrenia. *American Journal of Psychiatry, 103,* 309.

Kallmann, F. (1952) Comparative twin study in the genetic aspects of male homosexuality. *Journal of Nervous and Mental Diseases, 115,* 283.

Kallmann, F. (1953) *Heredity in health and mental disorder.* New York: Norton.

Kanner, L. (1943) Autistic disturbances of affective contact. *Nervous Child, 2,* 217.

Kanner, L. (1972) *Child psychiatry* (4th ed.). Springfield, Ill.: Charles C. Thomas.

Kanner, L. (1973) *Childhood psychoses: Initial studies and new insights.* Washington, D.C.: Winston.

Kaplan, H. Freedman, H. & Sadock, B. (1980) Classification in psychiatry. In H. Kaplan, A. Freedman, & B. Sadock (Eds.), *Comprehensive textbook of psychiatry* (III). Baltimore: Williams & Wilkins, p. 273.

Kaplan, H., & Sadock, B. (Eds.) (1981a) *Modern synopsis of comprehensive textbook of psychiatry/III.* Baltimore: Williams & Wilkins.

Kaplan, H., & Sadock, B. (1981b) Theories of personality and psychopathology: Schools derived from psychology and philosophy. In H. Kaplan & B. Sadock (Eds.) *Modern synopsis of comprehensive textbook of psychiatry/III.* Baltimore: Williams & Wilkins.

Kaplan, H., & Sadock, B. (1985) *Comprehensive textbook of psychiatry* IV. Baltimore, Md.: Williams and Wilkins.

Kaplan, H. (1974) *The new sex therapy.* New York: Brunner/Mazel.

Kaplan, H. (1975) *The illustrated manual of sex therapy.* New York: Quadrangle.

Kaplan, H. (1979) *Disorders of sexual desire.* New York: Brunner/Mazel.

Kaplan, M. (1983) A woman's view of DSM-III. *American Psychologist, 83,* 786.

Kaplan, R., & Saccuzzo, D. (1982) *Psychological testing. Principles, applications and issues.* Belmont, Calif.: Wadsworth.

Karush, A., Daniels, G., Flood, C., & O'Connor, J. (1977) *Psychotherapy in chronic ulcerative colitis.* Philadelphia: Saunders.

Katschnig, K., & Shepherd, M. (1978) Neurosis: The epidemiological perspective. In H. M. van Praag, (Ed.), *Research in neurosis.* New York: Spectrum Publications.

Keith, S., Gunderson, J., Reifman, R., Buchsbaum, S., & Mosher, L. (1976) Special report: Schizophrenia. *Schizophrenia Bulletin, 2,* 510.

Keller, A., Althof, S., & Lothstein, L. (1981) Group therapy with gender identity patients—A four year study. *American Journal of Psychotherapy, 36,* 223.

Kellner, R. (1982) Psychotherapeutic strategies in hypochondriasis: A clinical study. *American Journal of Psychotherapy, 36,* 146.

Kempler, W. (1973) Gestalt therapy. In R. Corsini (Ed.), *Current psychotherapies.* Itasca, Ill.: Peacock.

Kendall, R. (1973) Relationship between agression and depression. *Archives of General Psychiatry, 22,* 308.

Kendall, P., & Finch, A. (1978) A cognitive-behavioral treatment for impulsivity: A group comparison study. *Journal of Consulting and Clinical Psychology, 46,* 110.

Keniston, K. (1970) *Youth and dissent: The rise of a new opposition.* New York: Harcourt Brace Jovanovich.

Keniston, K. (1975) Youth as a stage of life. In C. Guardo (Ed.), *The adolescent as individual.* New York: Harper & Row.

Kennedy, W. (1965) School phobia: Rapid treatment of 50 cases. *Journal of Abnormal Psychology, 70,* 285.

Kenyon, K. (1980) Cited in H. Kaplan, A. Freedman, & B. Sadock (Eds.), *Modern synopsis of comprehensive textbook of psychiatry/III.* Baltimore: Williams & Wilkins.

Kernberg, O. (1975) *Borderline conditions and pathological narcissism,* New York: Jason Aronson.

Kesey, K. (1962) *One flew over the cuckoo's nest.* New York: Viking.

Kessler, R. (1982) A disaggregation of the relationship between socioeconomic status and psychological distress. *American Sociological Review, 47,* 752.

Kessler, R., & Cleary, P. (1980) Social class and psychological distress. *American Sociological Review, 45,* 463.

Kessler, R., & McRae, J. (1981) Trends in the relationship between sex and psychological distress. *American Sociological Review, 46,* 443.

Kessler, S. (1980a) The genetics of schizophrenia: A review. *Schizophrenia Bulletin, 6,* 404.

Kessler, S. (1980b) The genetics of schizophrenia. In *Schizophrenia 1980.* Washington, D.C.: NIMH.

Kety, S. (1975) Biochemistry of the major psychoses. In A. Freedman, H. Kaplan, & B. Sadock (Eds.), *Comprehensive textbook of psychiatry/II.* Baltimore: Williams & Wilkins.

Kety, S., Rosenthal, D., Wender, P., & Schulsinger, F. (1968) The types and prevalence of mental illness in the biological families of adopted schizophrenics. In D. Rosenthal & S. Kety (Eds.), *The transmission of schizophrenia.* London: Pergamon.

Kierkegaard, S. (1946) *A Kierkegaard anthology* (R. Bretall, Ed.). Princeton: Princeton University Press.

Kiesler, D. (1966) Some myths of psychotherapy and the search for a paradigm. *Psychological Bulletin, 65,* 110.

Kiesler, D. (1979) An interpersonal communications analysis of relationship in psychotherapy. *Psychiatry, 42,* 299.

Kiesler, D. (1973) *The process of psychotherapy.* Chicago: Aldine.

Kilman, P. (1978) The treatment of primary and secondary orgasmic dysfunction: A methodological review of the literature since 1970. *Journal of Sex and Marital Therapy, 4,* 155.

Kilpatrick, D., Veroneu, L., & Resnick, P. (1979) The aftermath of rape: Recent empirical findings. *American Journal of Orthopsychiatry, 49,* 658.

King, N. (1980) The behavioral management of asthma and asthma-related problems in children: A critical review of the literature. *Journal of Behavioral Medicine, 2,* 169.

Kinsey, A., Pomeroy, W., & Martin, C. (1948) *Sexual behavior in the human male.* Philadelphia: Saunders.

Kinsey, A., Pomeroy, W., Martin, C., & Gebhard, P. (1953) *Sexual behavior in the human female.* Philadelphia: Saunders.

Kirk, S. (1972) *Educating exceptional children.* Boston: Houghton-Mifflin.

Kittrie, N. (1971) *The right to be different.* Baltimore: Johns Hopkins Press.

Klajner, F., Herman, C., Polivy, J., & Chabra, R. (1981) Human obesity, dieting, and anticipatory salivation to food. *Physiology and Behavior, 27,* 195.

Klerman, G. (1984) Ideology and science in the individual psychotherapy of schizophrenia. *Schizophrenia Bulletin, 10,* 608.

Kline, N., Li, C., Lehmann, H., Lajtha, A., Laski, E., & Cooper, T. (1977) Beta-endorphin induced changes in schizophrenic and depressed patients. *Archives of General Psychiatry, 34,* 1111.

Knapp, P., Mushatt, C., Nemetz, S., Constantine, H., & Friedman, S. (1970) The context of reported asthma during psychoanalysis. *Psychosomatic Medicine, 32,* 167.

Knopf, I. (1979) *Childhood psychopathology: A developmental approach.* Englewood Cliffs, N.J.: Prentice-Hall.

Koh, S. (1978) Remembering of verbal materials by schizophrenic young adults. In S. Schwartz (Ed.), *Language and cognition in schizophrenia.* Hillsdale, N.J.: Erlbaum and Associates.

Kohn, M. (1972) Class, family and schizophrenia: A reformulation. *Social Forces, 50,* 295.

Kohut, H. (1977) *The restoration of the self.* New York: International Universities Press.

Kolb, L. (1963a) Therapy of homosexuality. In J. Masserman (Ed.), *Current psychiatric therapies.* New York: Grune & Stratton.

Kolb, L. (1963b) Psychiatric aspects of the treatment of migraine. *Neurology, 13,* 34.

Kolb, L., & Brodie, H. (1982) *Modern clinical psychiatry* (10th ed.). Philadelphia: Saunders.

Kolodny, R. (1981) Evaluating sex therapy: Process and outcome at the Masters and Johnson Institute. *The Journal of Sex Research. 17,* 301.

Kolodny, R., Masters, W., Hendrys, J., & Toro, G. (1971) Plasma testosterone and the semen analysis of male homosexuals. *New England Journal of Medicine, 285,* 1170.

Koppitz, E. (1975) *The Bender Gestalt test for young children: Research and application.* New York: Grune & Stratton.

Koslow, S., Maas, J., Bowden, C., Davis, J., Hanin, I., & Javaid, J. (1983) CSF and urinary biogenic amines and metabolites in depression and mania. *Archives of General Psychiatry, 40,* 999.

Kotses, H., Glaus, K., Crawford, P., Edwards, J., & Scherr, M. (1976) Operant reduction of frontalis EMG activity in the treatment of asthma in children. *Journal of Psychosomatic Research, 20,* 453.

Kotska, M., & Galassi, J. (1974) Group desensitization versus covert positive reinforcement in the reduction of test anxiety. *Journal of Counseling Psychology, 21,* 464.

Kraepelin, E. (1896) *Lehrbuch der psychiatrie* (5th ed.). Leipzig: Barth.

Kraepelin, E. (1918) *Dementia praecox.* London: E. & S. Livingstone.

Kraft, A. (1976) Milieu therapy. In A. Dean, A. Kraft, & B. Pepper (Eds.), *The social setting of mental health.* New York: Basic Books.

Kral, V. (1975) Confusional states. In J. Howells (Ed.), *Modern perspectives on the psychology of aging.* New York: Brunner/Mazel.

Krieger, D., & Hughes, J. (Eds.). (1980) *Neuroendocrinology,* Sunderland, Mass.: Sinauer.

Kringlen, E. (1967) Heredity and social factors in schizophrenic twins: An epidemiological clinical study. In J. Romano (Ed.), *The origins of schizophrenia.* Amsterdam: Excerpta Medica.

Kringlen, E. (1976) Twins—Still our best method. *Schizophrenia Bulletin, 2,* 429.

Krohn, A. (1978) Hysteria: The elusive neurosis. *Psychological Issues, 12,* 45.

Krupnick, J., & Horowitz, M. (1981) Stress response syndromes. *Archives of General Psychiatry, 38,* 428.

Kuhn, T. (1962) *The structure of scientific revolution.* Chicago: University of Chicago Press.

Kuhn, T. (1970) *The structure of scientific revolution.* (2d Ed.). Chicago: University of Chicago Press.

Kuhn, T. (1981) Problems of scientific revolution. In I. Hacking (Ed.), *Scientific revolutions.* Oxford: Oxford University Press.

Labbe, R., Firl, A., Mufson, E., & Stein, D. (1983) Fetal brain transplants. *Science, 221,* 470.

LaBouvie, E. (1982) Issues in life span development. In B. Wolman (Ed.). *Handbook of developmental psychology.* Englewood Cliffs, N.J.: Prentice-Hall, p. 54.

Lacey, J. (1966) Somatic response patterning and stress: Some revisions of activation theory. In M. Appley & R. Trumball (Eds.), *Psychological stress.* New York: McGraw-Hill.

Lacey, J., & Lacey, B. (1958) Verification and extension of the principle of automatic response stereotype. *American Journal of Psychology, 71,* 56.

Lamb, H. (1979) The new asylums in the community. *Archives of General Psychiatry, 36,* 129.

Lamb, H. (1980) Board and care wanderers. *Archives of General Psychiatry, 37,* 135.

Langer, D., Brown, G., & Docherty, J. (1981) Dopamine receptor supersensitivity and schizophrenia: A review. *Schizophrenia Bulletin, 7,* 273.

Laqueur, H. (1972) Mechanisms of change in multiple family therapy. In C. Sager & H. Kaplan (Eds.), *Progress in group and family therapy.* New York: Brunner/Mazel.

Laufer, M., & Gair, D. (1969) Childhood schizophrenia. In L. Bellak & L. Loeb (Eds.) *The schizophrenia syndrome.* New York: Grune & Stratton.

Laufer, M., & Shetty, T. (1980) Attention deficit disorders. In H. Kaplan, A. Freedman, & B. Sadock (Eds.), *Comprehensive textbook of psychiatry/III.* Baltimore: Williams & Wilkins, p. 2538.

Laughlin, H. (1956) *The neurosis in clinical practice.* Philadelphia: Saunders.

Lawrence, M. (1984) Anorexia nervosa: An "update." *Association for Child Psychology and Psychiatry Newsletter, 6,* 2.

Leaff, L. (1978) The antisocial personality: Psychodynamic implications. In W. Reid (Ed.), *The psychopath: A comprehensive study of antisocial disorders and behaviors.* New York: Brunner/Mazel.

Leary, T. (1957) *Interpersonal diagnosis of personality.* New York: Ronald Press.

Lebo, C., & Reddell, R. (1972) The presbycusis component in occupational hearing loss. *Laryngoscope, 82,* 1399.

Lefrancois, G. (1980) *Introduction to Psychology.* Belmont, Calif.: Wadsworth.

Lehmann, H. (1980) Schizophrenic disorders. In H. Kaplan, A. Freedman, & B. Sadock (Eds.), *Comprehensive textbook of psychiatry/III.* Baltimore: Williams & Wilkins, p. 1104.

Lehne, G. (1978) Gay male fantasies and realities. *Journal of Social Issues, 34,* 28.

Leibovich, M. (1981) Short term psychotherapy for the borderline personality disorder. *Psychotherapy and Psychosomatics, 35,* 257.

Leonard, W. (1927) *The locomotive God.* New York: Century.

Liebowitz, M., & Klein, D. (1979) Assessment and treatment of phobic anxiety. *Journal of Clinical Psychiatry, 40,* 486.

Leland, H., & Smith, D. (1965) *Play therapy with mentally subnormal children.* New York: Grune & Stratton.

Leland, H., & Smith, D. (1972) Psychotherapeutic considerations with mentally retarded and developmentally disabled children. In I. Katz (Ed.), *Mental health services for the mentally retarded.* Springfield, Ill.: Charles C. Thomas.

Lerner, R. & Shea, J. (1982) Social behavior in adolescence. In B. Wolman (Ed.) *Handbook of developmental psychology.* Englewood Cliffs, N.J.: Prentice-Hall, p. 503.

Lettieri, D., Sayers, M., & Pearson, H. (Eds.). (1980) *Theories of drug use.* Washington, D.C.: NIDA Research Monograph 30.

Levine, D., & Levine, D. (1976) *The cost of mental illness—1974.* Washington, D.C.: NIMH DHEW Pub No 76-265.

Levine, D., Rittengouse, M., Smith, G., & Thompson, T. (1981) A conjoint operant model for assessing profoundly behaviorally disordered adolescents. *Adolescence, 62,* 299.

Levine, M. D. (1975) Children with encopresis: A descriptive analysis. *Pediatrics, 56,* 412, 416.

Levine, S., & Lothstein, L. (1981) Transsexualism or the gender dysphoria syndromes. *Journal of Sex and Marital Therapy, 7,* 85.

Levinson, D. (1977) The mid-life transition: A period in adult psycho-social development, *Psychiatry, 40, 99.*

Levinson, D. (1978) *The seasons of a man's life.* New York: Knopf.

Levy, L. (1970) *Conceptions of personality.* New York: Random House.

Lewine, R., Watt, N., & Grubb, T. (1981) High-risk-for-schizophrenia research: Sampling bias and its implications. *Schizophrenia Bulletin, 7,* 273.

Lewinsohn, P., & Atwood, G. (1969) Depression: A chemical approach. *Psychotherapy: Theory, Research and Practice, 6,* 166.

Liberman, R. (1972) *A guide to behavioral analysis and therapy.* New York: Pergamon.

Lidz, T. (1976) Commentary on "A critical review of recent adoption, twin and family studies of schizophrenia: Behavioral genetic perspective." *Schizophrenia Bulletin,* 2, 404–412.

Lidz, T. (1977) Reply to Kety et al. *Schizophrenia Bulletin, 3,* 522.

Lidz, T. (1980) Phases of adult life: An overview. In W. H. Norman and T. J. Scaramella (Eds.), *Mid-life, developmental and clinical issues.* Brunner/Mazel, New York.

Lidz, T., & Blatt, S. (1983) Critique of the Danish-American studies of the biological and adoptive relatives of adoptees who became schizophrenic. *American Journal of Psychiatry, 140,* 426.

Liem, J. (1980) Family studies in schizophrenia: An update and commentary. *Schizophrenia 1980.* Washington, D.C.: NIMH.

Lindemann, E. (1944) Symptomatology and management of acute grief. *American Journal of Psychiatry, 101,* 141.

Linden, W. (1981) Exposure treatments for focal phobias: A review. *Archives of General Psychiatry, 38,* 769.

Lindstrom, L., Widerlov, E., Gunne, L., Wahlstrom, A., & Terenius, L. (1978) Endorphins in human cerebrospinal fluid: Clinical correlations to some psychotic states. *Psychiatrica Scandinavica, 57,* 153.

Lion, J. (1981) *Personality disorders: Diagnosis and management.* Baltimore: Williams & Wilkins.

Lipowski, Z. (1975) Psychophysiological cardiovascular disorders. In A. Freedman, H. Kaplan, & B. Sadock (Eds.), *Comprehensive textbook of psychiatry/II.* Baltimore: Williams & Wilkins.

Lipowski, Z. (1979) *Delirium: Acute brain failure in man.* Springfield, Ill.: Charles C. Thomas.

Lipowski, Z. (1980a) Cardiovascular disorders. In H. Kaplan, A. Freedman, & B. Sadock (Eds.), *Comprehensive textbook of psychiatry/III.* Baltimore: Williams & Wilkins, p. 1891.

Lipowski, Z. (1980b) Organic mental disorders. In H. Kaplan, A. Freedman, & B. Sadock (Eds.), *Comprehensive textbook of psychiatry/III.* Baltimore: Williams & Wilkins, p. 1359.

Lipscomb, P., & Parker, G. (1979) Parental overprotection and asthma. *Journal of Psychosomatic Research, 23,* 295.

Litman, R. (1967) Sigmund Freud on suicide. In E. Shneidman (Ed.), *Essays in self destruction.* New York: Science House.

Litman, R. (1965) When patients commit suicide. *American Journal of Psychotherapy, 19,* 570.

Lloyd, C. (1980a) Life events and depressive disorders reviewed: I. Events as predisposing factors. *Archives of General Psychiatry, 37,* 529.

Lloyd, C. (1980b) Life events and depressive disorders reviewed: II. Events as precipitating factors. *Archives of General Psychiatry, 37,* 541.

Loftus, E., & Wortman, C. (1981) *Psychology.* New York: Knopf.

Lohr, J. (1985) Transient grasp reflexes in

schizophrenia. *Biological Psychiatry, 20,* 172.

Long, C., & Cordle, C. (1982) Psychological treatment of binge eating and self-induced vomiting. *British Journal of Medical Psychology, 55,* 139.

LoPiccolo, J. (1978) Direct treatment of sexual dysfunction. In J. LoPiccolo (Ed.), *Handbook of sex therapy.* New York: Plenum Press.

Loraine, J., Ismael, A., Adamopoulos, P., & Dove, G. (1970) Endocrine function in male and female homosexuals. *British Medical Journal, 4,* 406.

Lothstein, M. (1982) Sex reassignment surgery: Historical, bioethical and theoretical issues. *American Journal of Psychiatry, 139,* 417.

Lott, I. (1983) Perinatal factors in mental retardation. In J. Matson & J. Mulick (Eds.), *Handbook of mental retardation,* New York: Pergamon, p. 97.

Lovaas, O. I. (1967) Behavior therapy in treating childhood schizophrenia. In J. Hill (Ed.), *Minnesota symposium on child development.* Minneapolis: University of Minnesota Press.

Lovaas, O. I., & Koegel, R. (1973) Behavior therapy with autistic children. In C. Thoreson (Ed.), *Behavior modification and education.* Chicago: University of Chicago Press.

Lovaas, O. I., Schreibman, L., & Koegel, R. L. (1974) A behavior modification approach to the treatment of autistic children. *Journal of Autism and Childhood Schizophrenia, 4,* 111–129.

Lowinson, J. (1981) Methadone maintenance in perspective. In J. Lowinson & P. Ruiz (Eds.), *Substance abuse.* Baltimore: Williams & Wilkins, p. 344.

Lubin, B., Larsen, R., & Matarazzo, J. (1985) Patterns of psychological test usage in the United States: 1935–1982. *American Psychologist, 40,* 90.

Lucas, G. (1976) Psychological problems of students. *British Medical Journal, 2,* 1431.

Lukoff, I. (1980) Toward a sociology of drug use. In D. Lettieri, M. Sayers, & H. Pearson (Eds.), *Theories of drug use.* Washington, D.C.: NIDA Research Monograph 30, p. 201.

Lukoff, I., & Brook, J. (1974) A sociocultural exploration of reported heroin use. In C. Winick (Ed.), *Social aspects of drug dependence.* Cleveland: CRC Press, p. 35.

Lukoff, D., Snyder, K., Ventura, J., & Nuechterlein, K. (1984) Information processing and attentional functioning in the developmental course of schizophrenic disorders. *Schizophrenia Bulletin, 10,* 160.

Luisada, P. (1981) Phencyclidine. In J. Lowinson & P. Ruiz (Eds.), *Substance abuse.* Baltimore: Williams & Wilkins, p. 209.

Maas, J., Fawcett, J., & Dekirmenjian, W. (1972) Catecholamine metabolism, depressive illness and drug response. *Archives of General Psychiatry, 26,* 252.

MacCulloch, M., & Waddington, J. (1981) Neuroendocrine mechanisms and the aetiology of male and female homosexuality. *British Journal of Psychiatry, 139,* 341.

MacClennen, B., & Felsenfeld, N. (1968) *Group psychotherapy and counseling with adolescents.* New York: Columbia University Press.

MacMillan, D., Jones, R., & Meyers, C. (1976) Mainstreaming the mentally retarded: Some questions, cautions and guidelines. *Mental Retardation, 14,* 3.

Madanes, C. (1981) *Strategic family therapy.* San Francisco: Jossey Bass.

Magnusson, D., & Allen, V. (1983) *Human development: An interactional perspective.* New York: Academic Press.

Mahoney, M. (1974) *Cognition and behavior modification.* Cambridge, Mass.: Ballinger.

Mandler, G., & Sarason, S. (1952) A study of anxiety and learning. *Journal of Abnormal and Social Psychology, 47,* 166.

Margolis, G. (1981) Moving away: Perspectives on counseling anxious freshmen. *Adolescence, 16,* 633.

Marks, I. (1981) Review of behavioral psychotherapy: II. Sexual disorders. *American Journal of Psychiatry, 138,* 750.

Markush, R., & Favero, R. (1974) Epidemiologic assessment of stressful life events. In B. Dohrenwend & B. Dohrenwend (Eds.), *Stressful life events: Their nature and effects.* New York: Wiley.

Marlatt, G., & Donovan, D. (1982) Behavioral psychology approaches to alcoholism. In E. Pattison & E. Kaufman (Eds.), *Encyclopedic handbook of alcoholism.* New York: Gardner Press, p. 560.

Marmor, J. (1983) Systems thinking in psychiatry: Some theoretical and clinical implications. *American Journal of Psychiatry, 140,* 833.

Maser, J., & Seligman, M. (1977) *Psychopathology: Experimental methods.* San Francisco: Freeman.

Maslow, A. (1968) *Toward a psychology of being* (2d ed.). New York: Van Nostrand.

Maslow, A. (1971) *The farther reaches of human nature.* New York: Viking.

Masters, W., & Johnson, V. (1970) *Human sexual inadequacy,* Boston: Little, Brown.

Matarazzo, J. (1980) Psychological assessment of intelligence. In H. Kaplan, A. Freedman, & B. Sadock (Eds.), *Comprehensive textbook of psychiatry/III.* Baltimore: Williams & Wilkins, p. 926.

Matte-Blanco, I. (1959) A study of schizophrenic thinking. *International Congress of Psychiatry—Congress Report, 1,* 254.

May, R. (1967) *Psychology and the human dilemma.* Princeton: Van Nostrand.

May, P. (1984) A step forward in research on psychotherapy of schizophrenia. *Schizophrenia Bulletin, 10,* 604.

May, P., Tuma, A., Yale, C., Potepan, P., & Dixon, W. (1976) Schizophrenia—A follow-up study of results of treatment. II. Hospital stay over two to five years. *Archives of General Psychiatry, 33,* 481.

McAdoo, W., & DeMyer, M. (1978) Personality characteristics of parents. In M. Rutter & E. Schopler (Eds.), *Autism: A reappraisal of concepts and treatment.* New York: Plenum.

McCall, R. (1977) Challenge to a science of developmental psychology. *Child Development, 48,* 333.

McClelland, D. (1975) Sources of hypertension in the drive for power. Paper presented at the Kittay Scientific Foundation Symposium, "Psychopathology and Human Adaptation," New York.

McClelland, D. (1979) Inhibited power motivation and high blood pressure in men. *Journal of Abnormal Psychology, 88,* 182.

McGhee, A., & Chapman, L. (1961) Disorders of attention in early schizophrenia. *Journal of Medical Psychology, 34,* 103.

McGlannon, F. (1975) Learning disabilities: The decade ahead. *Journal of Learning Disabilities, 8,* 56.

McGuffin, P., & Mawson, D. (1980) Obsessive compulsive neurosis: Two identical twin pairs. *British Journal of Psychiatry, 137,* 285.

McKean, K. (1982) A picture of Hinckley's brain. *Discover, 3,* 78.

McKegney, F., Gordon, R., & Levine, S. (1970) A psychosomatic comparison of patients with ulcerative colitis and Crohn's disease. *Psychosomatic Medicine, 32,* 153.

McKinlay, S., Jeffreys, M., & Thompson, B. (1972) An investigation of the age of menopause. *Biosocial Science, 4,* 161.

McLean, P. (1976) Therapeutic decision making in the behavioral treatment of depression. In P. Davidson (Ed.), *Behavioral management of anxiety, depression and pain.* New York: Brunner/Mazel, p. 54.

McLean, P., & Hamstian, A. (1979) Clinical depression: Comparative efficacy of outpatient treatment. *Journal of Consulting and Clinical Psychology, 47,* 818.

McLemore, C., & Benjamin, L. (1979) Whatever happened to interpersonal diagnosis? A psychosocial alternative to DSM-III. *American Psychologist, 34,* 17.

Medina, J., & Diamond, S. (1977) Drug dependency in patients with chronic headaches. *Headache, 17,* 12.

Mednick, S. (1958) A learning theory approach to schizophrenia. *Psychological Bulletin, 55,* 316.

Mednick, S., & McNeil, T. (1968) Current methodology in research on the etiology of schizophrenia. *Psychological Bulletin, 70,* 681.

Mednick, S., Schulsinger, F., Teasdale, T., Schulsinger, H., Venables, P., & Rock, D. (1978) Schizophrenia in high risk children. In G. Serban (Ed.), *Cognitive dysfunction in the development of mental illness.* New York: Brunner/Mazel, p. 169.

Meehl, P. (1962) Schizotaxy, schizotypy and schizophrenia. *American Psychologist, 17,* 827.

Meehl, P., & Rosen, A. (1955) Antecedent probability and the efficiency of psychometric signs, patterns or cutting scores. *Psychological Bulletin, 52,* 194.

Meeks, J. (1980) Conduct disorders. In H. Kaplan, A. Freedman, & B. Sadock (Eds.), *Comprehensive textbook of psychiatry/III.* Baltimore: Williams & Wilkins, p. 2631.

Meichenbaum, D. (1977) *Cognitive behavior modification.* New York: Plenum.

Meichenbaum, D., & Goodman, J. (1971) Training impulsive children to talk to themselves: A means of developing self control. *Journal of Abnormal Psychology, 77,* 115.

Meissner, W. (1980) Classical psychoanalysis. In H. Kaplan, A. Freedman, & B. Sadock (Eds.), *Comprehensive textbook of psychiatry/III.* Baltimore: Williams & Wilkins.

Meltzer, H. (1976a) Serum creatine phosphokinase in schizophrenia. *American Journal of Psychiatry, 133,* 192.

Meltzer, H. (1976b) Neuromuscular dysfunction in schizophrenia. *Schizophrenia Bulletin, 2,* 106.

Meltzer, H. (1984) Schizoaffective disorders: Is news of its nonexistence premature? Editor's introduction. *Schizophrenia Bulletin, 10,* 11.

Mendlewicz, J., & Rainer, J. (1977) An adoptive study supporting genetic transmission in manic-depressive illness. *Nature, 268,* 327.

Menninger, K. (1938) *Man against himself.* New York: Harcourt & Brace.

Menninger, K. (1945) *The human mind* (3d ed.). New York: Knopf.

Menninger, K. (1963) *The vital balance.* New York: Viking Press.

Mental health and aging: Approaches to curriculum development. (1983) *Mental Health Materials Center, Vol. XI, Publication number 114.* New York.

Mercer, J. (1979) *Labelling the mentally retarded: Clinical and social perspectives on mental retardation.* Berkeley, Calif.: University of California Press.

Meredith, R., & Riester, R. (1980) Psychotherapy, homosexuality and responsiblity: Clinical examination of socially deviant behavior. *Professional Psychology, 11,* 174.

Merton, R. (1949) *Social theory and social structure.* New York: Free Press.

Mesibov, G. (1976) Implications of the normalization principle for psychotic children. *Journal of Autism and Childhood Schizophrenia, 6,* 360.

Meyer-Bahlburg, H. (1979) Sex hormones and female homosexuality: A critical examination. *Archives of Sexual Behavior, 8,* 101.

Meyers, J. (1980) Paraphilias. In H. Kaplan, A. Freedman, & B. Sadock (Eds.), *Comprehensive textbook of psychiatry/III.* Baltimore: Williams & Wilkins, p. 1770.

Meyers, J., Lindenthal, J., & Pepper, M. (1971) Life events and psychiatric impairment. *Journal of Nervous and Mental Disease, 152,* 149.

Meyers, J., Lindenthal, J., & Pepper, M. (1974) Life events and psychiatric symptomatology. In D. Ricks, A. Thomas, & M. Roff (Eds.), *Life history research in psychopathology.* Vol. 3. Minneapolis: University of Minnesota Press.

Meyers, J., Lindenthal, J., & Pepper, M. (1975) Life events, social integration, and psychiatric symptomatology. *Journal of Health and Social Behavior, 16,* 421.

Meyers, J., & Reter, D. (1979) Sex reassignment: Follow-up. *Archives of General Psychiatry, 36,* 1010.

Meyers, J. Weissman, M., Tischler, G., Holzer, C., Leaf, P., Orvaschel, H., Anthony, J., Boyd, J., Burke, J., Kramer, M., & Stoltzman, R. (1984) Six-month prevalence of psychiatric disorders in three communities. *Archives of General Psychiatry, 41,* 959.

Miles, A. (1981) *The mentally ill in contemporary society.* New York: St. Martins Press.

Miles, C. (1977) Conditions predisposing to suicide. *Journal of Nervous and Mental Disease, 164,* 231.

Milkovich, L., & Vandenberg, B. (1974) Effects of prenatal meprobamate and chlordiazepoxide hydrochloride on human embryonic and fetal development. *New England Journal of Medicine, 291,* 1268.

Miller, F., Dawson, J., Dix, G., & Parnas, R. (Eds.), (1976) *The mental health process* (2d ed.). Mineola, N.Y.: The Foundation Press.

Miller, J. G., & Miller, J. L. (1985) General living systems theory. In H. Kaplan & B. Sadock (Eds.), *Comprehensive textbook of psychiatry/IV.* Baltimore, Md.: Williams & Wilkins, p. 13.

Miller, L., Bergstrom, D., Cross, H., & Grube, J. (1981) Use of the DSM-III system. *Professional Psychology, 12,* 385.

Miller, N. (1980) Application of learning and

biofeedback in psychiatry and medicine. In H. Kaplan, A. Freedman, & B. Sadock (Eds.) *Comprehensive textbook of psychiatry/III.* Baltimore: Williams & Wilkins, p. 468.

Miller, N. (1976) Clinical applications of biofeedback. In T. Barber, D. Shapiro, & J. Stoyva (Eds.), *Biofeedback and self control; 1975/1976.* Chicago: Aldine.

Miller, R., Palkes, H., & Stewart, M. (1973) Hyperactive children in suburban elementary schools. *Child Psychiatry and Human Development, 4,* 121.

Miller, W., Williams, M., & Bernstein, M. (1982) The effects of rape on marital and sexual adjustment. *American Journal of Family Therapy, 10,* 51.

Millon, T. (1981) *Disorders of personality: DSM-III, Axis II.* New York: Wiley.

Millon, T. (1983) The DSM-III: An insider's perspective. *American Psychologist, 38,* 804.

Minde, K., Lewin, D., Weiss, G., Laiquer, H., Douglas, V., & Sykes, R. (1971) The hyperactive child in elementary school: A five year controlled follow-up. *Exceptional Children, 38,* 215.

Minuchin, S. (1974) *Families and family therapy.* Cambridge, Mass.: Harvard University Press.

Minuchin, S., & Fishman, H. (1981) *Family therapy techniques.* Cambridge, Mass.: Harvard University Press.

Minuchin, S., Rosman, B., & Baker, L. (1978) *Psychosomatic families: Anorexia in context.* Cambridge, Mass.: Harvard University Press.

Mischel, W. (1976) *Introduction to personality* (2d ed.). New York: Holt, Rinehart and Winston.

Mitchell, K., & Mitchell, D. (1973) An exploratory treatment application of programmed behavior therapy techniques. *Behavior Research and Therapy, 72,* 137.

Mitchell, J., & Popkin, M. (1982) Antipsychotic drug therapy and sexual dysfunction in men. *American Journal of Psychiatry, 139,* 633.

Mitchell, J., Pyle, R., & Eckert, E. (1981) Frequency and duration of binge eating episodes in patients with bulimia. *American Journal of Psychiatry, 138,* 835.

Moller, H., vonZerssen, D., Werner-Eilert, K., & Wuscher-Stockheim, M. (1982) Outcome in schizophrenia and similar paranoid psychoses. *Schizophrenia Bulletin, 8,* 99.

Monahan, J. (1981) *The clinical prediction of violent behavior.* Rockville, Md.: NIMH.

Money, J., & Ehrhardt, A. (1972) *Man and woman, boy and girl: Differentiation and dimorphism of gender identity.* Baltimore: Johns Hopkins Press.

Money, J., Wiederking, C., Walker, P., & Gain, D. (1976) Combined antiandrogenic and counseling program for the treatment of sex offenders. In E. Sacher (Ed.), *Hormones, behavior and psychopathology.* New York: Raven Press.

Money, J., Wiederking, C., Walker, P., Migeon, C., Meyer, W., & Borganonker, D. (1975) 47,XYY and 46,XY males with antisocial and/or sex offending behavior. *Psychoneuroendocrinology, 1,* 165.

Monteflores, C. de, & Schultz, S. (1978) Coming out: Similarities and differences for lesbians and gay men. *Journal of Social Issues, 34,* 59.

Morey, L., Skinner, H., & Blashfield, R. (1984) A typology of alcohol abusers: Correlates and implications. *Journal of Abnormal Psychology, 93,* 408.

Morgan, R. (1981) Amphetamines. In J. Lowinson & P. Ruiz (Eds.), *Substance Abuse.* Baltimore: Williams & Wilkins, p. 158.

Morrisey, J., Burton, N., & Steadman, H. (1977) *Developing an empirical basis for psycholegal policy analysis of ACT: A New York State survey.* New York: Dept. of Mental Hygiene.

Mosher, L., & Keith, S. (1980) Psychosocial treatment: Individual, group, family and community support approaches. *Schizophrenia 1980.* Washington, D.C.: NIMH.

Mostow, E., & Newberry, P. (1975) Work role and depression in women. *American Journal of Orthopsychiatry, 45,* 538.

Mowrer, O., & Mowrer, W. (1938) Enuresis—A method for its study and treatment. *American Journal of Orthopsychiatry, 8,* 436.

Mullahy, P. (1980) Harry Stack Sullivan. In H. Kaplan, A. Freedman, & B. Sadock (Eds.), *Comprehensive textbook of psychiatry/III.* Baltimore: Williams & Wilkins.

Munby, M., & Johnston, D. (1980) Agoraphobia: The long term follow-up of behavioral treatment. *British Journal of Psychiatry, 137,* 418.

Murdock, B. (1975) *The other children.* New York: Harper & Row.

Murphy, P. J. (1980) The police investigation. In S. L. McCombie (Ed.). *The rape crisis intervention handbook.* New York, Plenum Press.

Murphy, J., Sobol, A., Neff, R., Olivier, D., & Leighton, A. (1984) Stability of prevalence. *Archives of General Psychiatry, 41,* 990.

Murray, H. (1938) *Explorations in personality.* New York: Oxford University Press.

Murray, R. (1981) Lesbians in therapy: An examination of some issues in theory and practice. *Comprehensive Psychotherapy, 3,* 141.

Murray, R., Oon, M., Rodnight., R., Birley, J., & Smith, A. (1979) Increased excretion of dimethyltryptamine and certain features of psychosis. *Archives of General Psychiatry, 36,* 644.

Murray, R., & Stabeneau, J. (1982) Genetic factors in alcoholism predisposition. In E. Pattison & E. Kaufman (Eds.), *Encyclopedic handbook of alcoholism.* New York: Gardner Press, p. 135.

Nathan, P., & Hay, W. (1984) Alcoholism. In H. Adams & P. Sutker (Eds.), *Comprehensive handbook of psychopathology.* New York: Plenum, p. 623.

Nathanson, C. (1975) Illness and the feminine role: A theoretical review. *Social Science and Medicine, 9,* 57.

National Migraine Foundation report. (1980) Cited in H. Adams, M. Feurstein, & J. Fowler. Migraine headache: Review of parameters, etiology and intervention. *Psychological Bulletin, 87,* 217.

Nelson, J., & Charney, D. (1981) The symptoms of major depressive illness. *American Journal of Psychiatry, 138,* 1.

Nemiah, J. (1975a) Obsessive compulsive neurosis. In A. Freedman, H. Kaplan, & B. Sadock (Eds.), *Comprehensive textbook of psychiatry/II.* Baltimore: Williams & Wilkins.

Nemiah, J. (1975b) Phobic neurosis. In A. Freedman, H. Kaplan, & B. Sadock (Eds.), *Comprehensive textbook of psychiatry/II.* Baltimore: Williams & Wilkins.

Nemiah, J. (1975c) Depressive neurosis. In A. Freedman, H. Kaplan, & B. Sadock (Eds.), *Comprehensive textbook of psychiatry/II.* Baltimore: Williams & Wilkins.

Nemiah, J. (1980) Obsessive-compulsive disorder. In H. Kaplan, A. Freedman, & B. Sadock (Eds.), *Comprehensive textbook of psychiatry/III.* Baltimore: Williams & Wilkins, p. 1504.

Nemiah, J. (1981) A psychoanalytic view of phobias. *American Journal of Psychoanalysis, 41,* 115.

Neugarten, B. (1968) *Middle age and aging.* Chicago: University of Chicago Press.

Neugarten, B. (1964) *Personality in middle and later life.* New York: Atherton.

Neugarten, B. (1979) Time, age and life cycle. *American Journal of Psychiatry, 136,* 887.

Neugarten, B., & Kraines, R. (1965) Menopausal symptoms in women of various ages. *Psychosomatic Medicine, 27,* 266.

Newsweek Magazine (1984) Days in the life. December 3, pp. 26–27.

Newman, P. (1982) The peer group. In B. Wolman (Ed.), *Handbook of developmental psychology.* Englewood Cliffs, N.J.: Prentice-Hall.

Nichols, J., & Hsiao, S. (1967) Addiction liability of albino rats: Breeding for quantitative differences in morphine drinking. *Science, 157,* 561.

Nichols, M. (1984) *Family Therapy.* New York: Gardner Press.

Nichols, M., & Zax, M. (1977) *Catharsis in psychotherapy.* New York: Gardner.

Nihira, K., Foster, R., Shellhaas, N., & Leland, H. (1974) *AAMD adaptive behavior scale, Manual.* Washington, D.C.: American Association on Mental Deficiency.

Nilsson, A. (1982) Application of perceptogenetic approach to separation and Oedipal conflict problems in primitive-hysteria and obsessive compulsive neurosis. *Psychological Research Bulletin, 22,* 1.

Niswander, K., & Gordon, M. (1972) *Women and their pregnancies (Vol. 1)* Philadelphia: Saunders.

Norcross, J., & Prochaska, J. (1982) National survey of clinical psychologists: Characteristics and activities. *Clinical Psychologist, 35,* 1.

Norris, J., & Feldman-Summers, S. (1981) Factors related to the psychological impacts of rape on the victim. *Journal of Abnormal Psychology, 90,* 562.

Notman, M. (1979) Midlife concerns of women: Implications of the menopause. *American Journal of Psychiatry, 136,* 1270.

Nowicki, S. (1983) Village of St. Joseph: An integrative approach. Atlanta: Emory University.

Nowicki, S., & Duke, M. (1978) An examination of counseling variables within a social learning framework. *Journal of Counseling Psychology, 25,* 1.

Nowicki, S., & Duke, M. (1982) Integrating counseling center services within a community psychology framework. Atlanta: Emory University.

Noyes, R., Clancy, J., Crowe, R., Hoenk, P., & Slymen, D. (1978) The familial prevalence of anxiety neurosis. *Archives of General Psychiatry, 35, 1057.*

Nuechterlein, K., & Dawson, M. (1984a) A heuristic vulnerability/stress model of schizophrenic episodes. *Schizophrenia Bulletin, 10,* 300.

Nuechterlein, K., & Dawson, M. (1984b) Information processing and attentional functioning in the developmental course of schizophrenic disorder. *Schizophrenia Bulletin, 10,* 160.

Nuffield, E. (1983) Psychotherapy. In J. Matson & J. Mulick (Eds.), *Handbook of mental retardation.* New York: Pergamon, p. 351.

O'Bannon, R. M. (1981) The effectiveness of brief progressive relaxation training as a function of procedural variation and anxiety level. Unpublished doctoral dissertation, University of Alabama.

Offer, D., & Sabshin, M. (1984) *Normality and the life cycle.* New York: Basic Books.

O'Hara, M., Rehm, L., & Campbell, S. (1982) Predicting depressive symptomatology: Cognitive-behavioral models and postpartum depression. *Journal of Abnormal Psychology, 91,* 457.

Oltmanns, T., & Neale, J. (1978) Distractability in relation to other aspects of schizophrenic disorder. In S. Schwartz (Ed.), *Language and cognition in schizophrenia.* Hillsdale, N.J.: Erlbaum Associates.

Oltmanns, T., Ohayon, J., & Neale, J. (1978) The effects of antipsychotic medication and diagnostic criteria on distractability in schizophrenia. In L. Wynne, R. Cromwell, & S. Matthyse (Eds.), *The nature of schizophrenia: New approaches to research and treatment.* New York: Wiley.

O'Neal, J. (1984) First person account: Finding myself and loving it. *Schizophrenia Bulletin, 10,* 109.

Orlinsky, D., & Howard, K. (1967) The good therapy hour. *Archives of General Psychiatry, 16,* 621.

Orlinsky, D., & Howard, K. (1975) *Varieties of psychotherapeutic experience.* New York: Teachers College Press.

Orsulak, P., Schildkraut, J., Schatzberg, A., & Herzog, J. (1978) Differences in platelet MAO activity in subgroups of schizophrenias and depressive disorders. *Biological Psychiatry, 13,* 637.

Orton, S. (1937) *Reading, writing and speech disorders in children.* New York: Norton.

Osmond, H., & Smythies, J. (1952) Schizophrenia: A new approach. *Journal of Mental Science, 98,* 304.

Ost, L., & Hugsdahl, K. (1981) Acquisition of phobias and anxiety response patterns in clinical patients. *Behavior Research and Therapy, 19,* 439.

Overall, J., & Hollister, L. (1979) Comparative evaluation of Research Diagnostic Criteria for schizophrenia. *Archives of General Psychiatry, 36,* 1198.

Palazzoli, M. (1974) *Self starvation.* London: Chaucer Press.

Palmer, S., & Horn, S. (1978) Feeding problems in children. In S. Palmer & S. Ekvall (Eds.)., *Pediatric nutrition in developmental disorders.* Springfield, Ill.: Charles C. Thomas.

Papez, J. (1937) A proposed mechanism of emotion. *AMA Archives of Neurology and Psychiatry, 38,* 725.

Parenteau, P., & Lamontagne, Y. (1981) The thought stopping technique: A treatment for different types of ruminations. *Canadian Journal of Psychiatry, 26,* 192.

Parloff, M. B. (1982) Psychotherapy research evidence and reimbursement decisions: Bambi meets Godzilla. *American Journal of Psychiatry, 139,* 718.

Parloff, M. B. (1984) Psychotherapy research and its incredible credibility crisis. *Clinical Psychology Review, 4,* 95.

Parloff, M. B., Waskow, I. E., & Wolfe, B. E. (1983) Research on therapist variables in relation to process and outcome. In S. L. Garfield and A. E. Bergin (Eds.), *Handbook of psychotherapy and behavior change.* New York: Wiley.

Parsons, O., & Hart, R. (1984) Behavioral disorders associated with central nervous system dysfunction. In H. Adams & P. Sutker (Eds.), *Comprehensive handbook* of *psychopathology.* New York: Plenum, p. 841.

Pascal, G., & Suttell, B. (1951) *The Bender Gestalt test: Identification and validity for adults.* New York: Grune & Stratton.

Passages. (1981) Predictable mortality through the life stages. A digest. Division of Public Health. Georgia Department of Human Resources.

Pastorelli, F. (1936) *The glorious bondage of illness.* London: Allen & Unwin.

Pattison, E., Brissenden, A., & Wohl, T. (1967) Assessing specific effects of inpatient group psychotherapy. *International Journal of Group Psychotherapy, 17,* 283.

Pattison, E., & Kaufman, E. (Eds.) (1982) *Encyclopedic handbook of alcoholism.* New York: Gardner Press.

Pauly, I. (1981) Outcome of sex reassignment surgery for transsexuals. *Australia and New Zealand Journal of Psychiatry, 15,* 45.

Pavlov, I. (1927) *Conditioned reflexes.* New York: Oxford University Press.

Payne, R. (1962) An object classification test as a measure of overinclusive thinking in schizophrenic patients. *British Journal of Social Psychology, 7,* 213.

Peele, S. (1981) Reductionism in the eighties. *American Psychologist, 36,* 807.

Pelham, W. (1978) Hyperactive children. *Psychiatric Clinics of North America, 1,* 227.

Penfold, P. (1981) Women and depression. *Canadian Journal of Psychiatry, 26,* 24.

Penn, H., Lacy, J., Lapham, L., Mandel, M., & Sandt, J. (1972) Catatonic behavior, viral encephalopathy and death: The problem of fatal catatonia. *Archives of General Psychiatry, 27,* 758.

Peplau, L., Cochran, S., Rook, K., & Padesky, J. (1978) Loving women: Attachment and autonomy in lesbian relationships. *Journal of Social Issues. 34,* 7.

Perlmutter, A. D. (1976) Enuresis. In T. P. Kelalis and L. R. King (Eds.), *Clinical pediatric urology.* Philadelphia: Saunders.

Perls, F. (1969a). *Gestalt therapy verbatim.* Lafayette, Calif.: Real People Press.

Perls, F. (1969b). *In and out the garbage can.* Lafayette, Calif.: Real People Press.

Perls, F., Hefferline, R., & Goodman, P. (1958) *Gestalt therapy.* New York: Julian.

Perosa, S., & Perosa, L. (1983) The mid-career crisis: A description of the psychological dynamics of transition and adaption. *Vocational Guidance Quarterly, 32,* 69.

Perry, J., & Klerman, G. (1980) Clinical features of the borderline personality disorder. *American Journal of Psychiatry, 137,* 165.

Perry, W. (1980) *Forms of intellectual and ethical development in the college years.* New York: Holt, Rinehart and Winston.

Person, E., & Ovesey, L. (1978) Transvestism: New perspectives. *Journal of the American Academy of Psychoanalysis, 6,* 301.

Peterson, G. (1980) Organic brain syndromes associated with brain trauma. In H. Kaplan, B. Friedman, & B. Sadock (Eds.), *Comprehensive textbook of psychiatry/III.* Baltimore: Williams & Wilkins, p. 1422.

Petho, B. (1984) Hourglass model of psychiatric disease: The endogenous psychoses. *Schizophrenia Bulletin, 10,* 509.

Pevnick, J., Jasinski, D., & Haertzen, C. (1978) Abrupt withdrawal from therapeutically administered diazepam: Report of a case. *Archives of General Psychiatry, 35,* 995.

Phares, E. (1979) *Clinical psychology: Concepts, methods and profession.* Homewood, Ill.: Dorsey Press.

Philips, C., & Hunter, M. (1981) The treatment of tension headache. I: Muscular abnormality and biofeedback. *Behavior Research and Therapy, 19,* 485.

Phillip, R., Wilde, G., & Day, J. (1971) Suggestion and relaxation in asthmatics. *Journal of Psychosomatic Research, 16,* 193.

Physician's Desk Reference (1982). (36th ed.) Oradell, N.J.: Medical Economics.

Pollak, J. (1981) Hysterical personality: An appraisal in light of empirical research. *Genetic Psychology Monographs, 104,* 71.

Prange, A., Wilson, I., & Lynn, C. (1974) L-tryptophan in mania: Contributions to a permissive amine hypothesis of affective disorders. *Archives of General Psychiatry, 30,* 56.

Pratt, J. (1906) The "home sanitorium" treatment of consumption. Paper presented to Johns Hopkins Medical Society, January.

Prentky, R., Lewine, R., Watt, N., & Fryer, J. (1980) A longitudinal study of psychiatric outcome. *Schizophrenia Bulletin, 6,* 139.

President's Commission on Mental Health, 1978. (1980) Cited in B. Dohrenwend et al. (Eds.), *Mental illness in the United States.* New York: Praeger.

Prioleau, L., Murdock, M., & Brody, N. (1983) An analysis of psychotherapy versus placebo studies. *The Behavioral and Brain Sciences, 6,* 275.

Quinsey, V. L., Chaplin, T. C., & Upfold, D. (1984) Sexual arousal to nonsexual violence and sadomasochism themes among rapist and non-sex-offenders. *Journal of Consulting and Clinical Psychology, 52,* 651.

Rabkin, J. (1977) *Strategic psychotherapy.* New York: Basic Books.

Rachman, S. (1966) Sexual fetishism: An experimental analogue. *Psychological Record, 16,* 293.

Rachman, S., & Wilson, G. T. (1980) *The effects of psychological therapy.* New York: Pergamon.

Rahe, R., & Lind, E. (1971) Psychosocial factors and sudden cardiac death: A pilot study. *Journal of Psychosomatic Research, 15,* 19.

Rainwater, N., & Alexander, A. (1982) Respiratory disorders: Asthma. In D. Doleys, R. Meredith, & A. Ciminero (Eds.), *Behavioral medicine.* New York: Plenum Press, p. 435.

Rampling, D. (1980) Abnormal mothering in the genesis of anorexia nervosa. *Journal of Nervous and Mental Disease, 168,* 501.

Ramsey, J. (1974) Guide to recognizing and handling mental illness. *Family Circle Magazine,* October pp. 163–170.

Ray, W., Raczynski, I., Rogers, T., & Kimball, W. (1979) *Evaluation of clinical biofeedback.* New York: Plenum Press.

Rees, L. (1964) The significance of parental attitudes in childhood asthma. *Journal of Psychosomatic Research, 7,* 253.

Rees, L. (1980) Etiological factors in asthma. *Psychiatric Journal of the University of Ottowa, 5,* 250.

Regier, D., Myers, J., Kramer, M., Robins, L., Blazer, D., Hough, R., Eaton, W., & Locke, B. (1984) The NIMH epidemiologic catchment area program. *Archives of General Psychiatry, 41,* 934–941.

Reid, W. (1981) *The treatment of antisocial syndromes.* New York: Van Nostrand Reinhold.

Reiss, D. (1976) The family and schizophrenia. *American Journal of Psychiatry, 133,* 181.

Reivich, M., Alavi, A., Greenberg, J., Farkas, T., & Wolf, A. (1981) 18-F fluorodeoxyglucolase method for measuring local cerebral glucose metabolism in man: Technique and results. *Progress in Nuclear Medicine, 7,* 138.

Remschmidt, H., & Schwab, T. (1978) Attempted suicide in children and young people. *Acta Paedopsychiatrica, 43,* 197.

Report of the President's Commission on Mental Health (1978) Washington, D.C.: U.S. Government Printing Office, 4, 1962.

Rich, A. (1981). Of woman born. Cited in S. Penfold. Women and depression. *Canadian Journal of Psychiatry, 26,* 24.

Richards, W., & Thorpe, G. (1978) Behavioral approaches to the problems of later life. In M. Storandt, I. Siegler, & M. Elias (Eds.), *The clinical psychology of aging.* New York: Plenum Press.

Rickard, H. D., & Elkins, P. D. (1983) Behavior therapy with children. In C. E. Walker and M. C. Roberts (Eds.), *Handbook of clinical child psychology.* New York, Wiley.

Riddle, D., & Sang, B. (1978) Psychotherapy with lesbians. *Journal of Social Issues, 34,* 84.

Rimland, B. (1964) *Infantile autism.* New York: Appleton-Century-Crofts.

Rimland, B. (1969) Psychogenesis versus biogenesis: The issues and the evidence. In S. Plog & R. Edgerton (Eds.), *Changing perspectives in mental illness.* New York: Holt, Rinehart and Winston.

Rist, K. (1979) Incest: Theoretical and clinical views. *American Journal of Orthopsychiatry, 49,* 680.

Ritvo, E. R., & Freeman, B. J. (1977) National society for autistic children's definition of the syndrome of autism. *Journal of Pediatric Psychology, 2,* 146.

Ritzler, B. (1977) Proprioception in schizophrenia. *Journal of Abnormal Psychology, 86,* 501.

Robertson, B. (1979a) The psychoanalytic theory of depression. I: The major contributors. *Canadian Journal of Psychiatry, 24,* 341.

Robertson, B. (1979b) The pysychoanalytic theory of depression. II: The major theories. *Canadian Journal of Psychiatry, 24,* 557.

Robins, L. (1966) *Deviant children grow up.* Baltimore: Williams & Wilkins.

Robins, L. (1982) The diagnosis of alcoholism after DSM-III. In E. Pattison & E. Kaufman (Eds.), *Encyclopedic handbook of alcoholism.* New York: Gardner Press, p. 40.

Robins, L., Helzer, J., & Davis, D. (1975) Narcotic use in Southeast Asia and afterward. *Archives of General Psychiatry, 32,* 955.

Robins, L., Helzer, J., Weissman, M., Orvaschel, H., Gruenberg, E., Burke, J., & Regier, D. (1984) Lifetime prevalence of specific psychiatric disorders in three sites. *Archives of General Psychiatry, 41,* 949.

Robinson, N., & Robinson, H. (1976) *The mentally retarded child.* New York: McGraw Hill.

Rodgon, M. (1984) Emotional and behavioral pathology in mentally retarded individuals. In H. Adams & P. Sutker (Eds.), *Comprehensive handbook of psychopathology.* New York: Plenum, p. 1001.

Roffe, M., & Britt, B. (1981) A typology of marital interaction for sexually dysfunctional couples. *Journal of Sex and Marital Therapy, 7,* 207.

Rogers, C. (1980) Client centered therapy. In H. Kaplan, A. Freedman, & B. Sadock (Eds.), *Comprehensive textbook of psychiatry/III.* Baltimore: Williams & Wilkins, p. 2153.

Rogers, C. (1942) *Counseling and psychotherapy.* Boston: Houghton Mifflin.

Rohrabough, M., Tennen, H., Press, S., White, L., Raskin, P., & Pickering, M. (1977) Paradoxical strategies in psychotherapy. Symposium presented at the American Psychological Association convention, San Francisco.

Roman, P. (1982) Sociological factors. In E. Pattison & E. Kaufman (Eds.), *Encyclopedic handbook of alcoholism.* New York: Gardner Press, p. 367.

Romancyzk, R. G., Diament, C., Coren, E. R., Trunell, G., & Harris, S. L. (1975) Increasing isolate and social play in severely disturbed children: Intervention and post-intervention effectiveness. *Journal of Autism and Childhood Schizophrenia, 5,* 57.

Romano, J. (1979) On the nature of schizophrenia: Changes in the observer as well as the observed. *Schizophrenia Bulletin, 3,* 532.

Romney, D., & LeBlanc, E. (1975) Relationship between formal thought disorder and retardation in schizophrenia. *Journal of Consulting and Clinical Psychology, 43,* 217.

Rooth, G. (1974) Exhibitionists around the world. *Human Behavior, 3,* 61.

Rorschach, H. (1942) *Psychodiagnostics* (P. Lemkau & B. Kronenberg, Trans.). Berne: Huber Verlag.

Rose, R., Jenkins, C., & Hurst, M. (1978) *Air traffic controller health change study.* Washington, D.C.: Federal Aviation Administration.

Rosen, J. (1953) *Direct analysis.* New York: Grune & Stratton.

Rosenbaum, M. (1972) Group therapy with adolescents. In B. Wolman (Ed.), *Manual of child psychopathology.* New York: McGraw-Hill.

Rosenberg, C. (1982) The paraprofessionals in alcoholism treatment. In E. Pattison & E. Kaufman (Eds.), *Encyclopedic handbook of alcoholism.* New York: Gardner Press, p. 802.

Rosengarten, H., & Friedhoff, A. (1976) A review of recent studies of the biosynthesis and excretion of hallucinogens formed by the methylation of neurotransmitters or related substances. *Schizophrenia Bulletin, 2,* 90.

Rosenhan, D. (1973) On being sane in insane places. *Science, 179,* 250.

Rosenman, R., Brand, R., Jenkins, C., Friedman, M., Strauss, R., & Wurm, M. (1975)

Coronary heart disease in the Western Collaborative Group Study: Final follow-up experiences of 8½ years. *Journal of the American Medical Association, 233,* 872.

Rosenthal, D. (1971) *Genetics of schizophrenia.* New York: McGraw-Hill.

Rosenthal, D. (1977) Searches for the mode of genetic transmission in schizophrenia: Reflections and loose ends. *Schizophrenia Bulletin, 3,* 268.

Rosenthal, D., & Kety, S. (1968) *The transmission of schizophrenia.* London: Pergamon.

Rosenthal, D., Wender, P., Kety, S., Welner, J., & Schulsinger, F. (1971) The adopted away offspring of schizophrenics. *American Journal of Psychiatry, 128,* 307.

Rosenthal, N., Sack, D., Carpenter, C., Parry, B., Mendelson, W., & Wehr, T. (1985) Antidepressant effects of light. *American Journal of Psychiatry, 142,* 163.

Rosenthal, R., & Allen, T. (1979) An examination of attention, arousal and learning dysfunctions of hyperkinetic children. *Psychological Bulletin, 85,* 689.

Rosow, I. (1963) Adjustment of the normal age: Concept and measurement. In R. Williams, C. Tibbitts, & W. Donahue (Eds.), *Process of aging.* New York: Atherton.

Ross, A. (1980) *Psychological disorders of children.* New York: McGraw-Hill.

Ross, M., Rogers, L., & McCulloch, H. (1978) Stigma, sex and society: A new look at gender identification and sexual variation. *Journal of Homosexuality, 3,* 315.

Ross, A. (1979) *Psychological disorders of children: A behavioral approach to theory, research, and therapy.* New York: McGraw-Hill.

Roth, M. (1955) The natural history of mental disorders in old age. *Journal of Mental Science, 101,* 281.

Rothstein, A. (1979) An exploration of the diagnostic term "narcissistic personality disorder." *Journal of the American Psychoanalytic Association, 27,* 893.

Ro-Trock, G., Wellisch, D., & Schooler, J. (1977) A family therapy outcome study in an inpatient setting. *American Journal of Orthopsychiatry, 47,* 514.

Rotter, J. (1966) Generalized expectancies for internal versus external control of reinforcements. *Psychological Monographs, 80* (Whole no. 609).

Rotter, J. (1975) Some problems and misconceptions related to the construct of internal vs. external locus of control of reinforcement. *Journal of Consulting and Clinical Psychology, 43,* 56.

Rowbotham, S. (1981) Woman's consciousness, Man's world. Cited in S. Penfold, Women and depression. *Canadian Journal of Psychiatry, 26,* 24.

Rudin, D. (1979) Covert transport dysfunction in the choroid plexus as a possible cause of schizophrenia. *Schizophrenia Bulletin, 5,* 623.

Rush, A., & Beck, A. (1978) Cognitive therapy of depression and suicide. *American Journal of Psychotherapy, 32,* 201.

Russell, G. (1979) The present status of anorexia nervosa. *Psychological Medicine, 7,* 353–367.

Rutter, M. (1967) Psychiatric disorders in early childhood. In A. Copper and A. Walk (Eds.), *Recent developments in schizophrenia* (British Journal of Psychiatry-special publication). Ashford, Kent: Headley.

Rutter, M. (1971) Parent-Child separation: Psychological effects on children. *Journal of Child Psychology and Psychiatry, 12,* 233.

Rutter, M. (1978a) Diagnosis and definition. In M. Rutter & E. Schopler (Eds.), *Autism: A reappraisal of concepts and treatment.* New York: Plenum Press.

Rutter, M. (1978b) On confusion in the diagnosis of autism. *Journal of Autism and Childhood Schizophrenia, 8,* 137.

Rutter, M., & Schopler, E. (Eds.), (1978) *Autism: A reappraisal of concepts and treatment.* New York: Plenum Press.

Rutter, M., Yule, W., & Graham, P. (1973) Enuresis and behavioral deviance: Some epidemiologic considerations. In I. Kolvin, R. MacKeith, & S. Meadow (Eds.), *Bladder control and enuresis.* Philadelphia: Lippincott.

Ryle, A. (1969) *Student casualties.* London: Penguin.

Sadava, S. (1984) Other drug abuse and dependence disorders. In H. Adams & P. Sutker (Eds.), *Comprehensive handbook of psychopathology*. New York: Plenum Press, p. 623.

Sadock, V. (1980) Special areas of interest. In H. Kaplan, A. Freedman, & B. Sadock (Eds.), *Comprehensive textbook of psychiatry/III*. Baltimore: Williams & Wilkins.

Saenger, G. (1960) *Factors influencing the institutionalization of mentally retarded individuals in New York City*. Albany: Interdepartmental Health Resource Board.

Safer, D. (1971) Drugs for problem school children. *Journal of School Health, 41*, 491.

Safer, D., & Allen, R. (1973) Stimulant drugs said to suppress weight and height. *Psychiatric News, 8*, 9.

Saghir, M., & Robins, E. (1973) *Male and female homosexuality*. Baltimore: Williams & Wilkins.

Sainsbury, P., & Barraclough, B. (1968) Differences between suicide rates. *Nature, 220*, 1252.

Salama, A. (1980) The multiple personality: A case study. *Canadian Journal of Psychiatry, 25*, 569.

Salter, A. (1949) *Conditioned reflex therapy*. New York: Creative Age Press.

Salzman, L., & Thaler, F. (1981) Obsessive-compulsive disorders: A review of the literature. *American Journal of Psychiatry, 138*, 286.

Sameroff, J. (1975) Early influences on development. Fact or fancy? *Merrill-Palmer Quarterly, 20*, 275.

Sanders, R. (1967) New manpower for mental hospital service. In E. Cowen, E. Gardner, & M. Zax (Eds.), *Emergent approaches to mental health problems*. New York: Appleton-Century-Crofts.

Sandler, M., Ruthven, C., Goodwin, B., Field, H., & Matthews, R. (1978) Phenylethylamine overproduction in aggressive psychopaths. *Lancet, 103*, 1269.

Sankar, D., Cates, N., Broer, P., & Sankar, B. (1963) Biochemical parameters in childhood schizophrenia (autism) and growth. *Recent Advances in Biological Psychiatry, 5*, 76.

Sarnoff, I. (1962) *Personality dynamics and development*. New York: Wiley.

Satir, V. (1964) *Conjoint family therapy*. Palo Alto: Science and Behavior Books.

Sawrey, W. (1961) Conditioned responses to fear in relationship to ulceration. *Comparative and Physiological Psychology, 54*, 347.

Schaie, K. (1981) Psychological changes from midlife to early old age: Implications for the maintenance of mental health. *American Journal of Orthopsychiatry, 51*, 199.

Scheff, T. (1966) *Being mentally ill*. Chicago: Aldine.

Scheff, T. (1970) Schizophrenia as ideology. *Schizophrenia Bulletin, 2*, 15.

Scheff, T. (1975) *Labelling madness*. Englewood Cliffs, N.J.: Prentice-Hall.

Scheflen, H. (1961) *Psychotherapy of schizophrenia: Direct analysis*. Springfield, Ill.: Charles C. Thomas.

Schildkraut, J. (1970) *Neuropsychopharmacology of the affective disorders*. Boston: Little, Brown.

Schildkraut, J., Herzog, J., & Orsulak, P. (1976) Reduced platelet MAO activity in a subgroup of schizophrenic patients. *American Journal of Psychiatry, 133*, 438.

Schlesier-Stropp, B. (1984) Bulimia: A review of the literature. *Psychological Bulletin, 95*, 247–257.

Schlesinger, L. (1980) Distinctions between psychopathic, sociopathic and antisocial personality disorders. *Psychological Reports, 47*, 15.

Schneider, K. (1959) *Clinical psychopathology* (M. Hamilton, Trans.). New York: Grune & Stratton.

Schopler, D., & Reichler, R. J. (1971) Parents as co-therapists in the treatment of psychotic children. *Journal of Autism and Childhood Schizophrenia, 1*, 87–102.

Schramski, T. G. (1984) Factors that contribute to post therapy persistence of therapeutic change. *Journal of Clinical Psychology, 40*, 78–85.

Schreiber, F. (1974) *Sybil*. New York: Warner.

Schreibman, L., & Koegel, R. (1975) Autism: A defeatable behavior. *Psychology Today, 8*, 61.

Schuckit, M. (1980) A theory of drug abuse—a genetic approach. In D. Lettieri, M. Sayer, & H. Pearson (Eds.), *Theories of drug use*. Washington, D.C.: NIDA Research, Monograph 30, p. 297.

Schuckit, M., Goodwin, D., & Winokur, G. (1972) A study of alcoholism in half-siblings. *American Journal of Psychiatry, 128,* 1132.

Schulsinger, F. (1980) Biological psychopathology. *Annual Review of Psychology, 31,* 583.

Schulsinger, F. (1972) Psychopathy, heredity and environment. *International Journal of Mental Health, 1,* 190.

Schulsinger, F., Kety, S., Rosenthal, D., & Wender, P. (1979) A family study of suicide. In M. Schous & E. Stromgren (Eds.), *Origins, prevention, and treatment of affective disorders.* London: Academic Press, p. 276.

Schultz, L. (1979) The sexual abuse of children and minors: A bibliography. *Child Welfare, 58,* 147.

Schwab, J., & Schwab, M. (1978) *The sociocultural roots of mental illness.* New York: Plenum Press.

Schwartz, G., & Beatty, J. (Eds.). (1977) *Biofeedback: Theory and research.* New York: Academic Press.

Schwitzgebel, R. L., & Schwitzgebel, R. K. (1980) *Law and psychological practice.* New York: Wiley.

Seiden, R. (1966) Campus tragedy: A study of student suicide. *Journal of Abnormal Psychology, 71,* 389.

Seiden, R., & Freitas, R. (1980) Shifting patterns of deadly violence. *Suicide and Life-Threatening Behavior, 10,* 195.

Seidensticker, J., & Tzagournis, M. (1968) Anorexia nervosa: Clinical features and long-term follow-up. *Journal of Chronic Diseases, 21,* 361.

Seligman, M. (1975) *Helplessness.* San Francisco: Freeman.

Sellers, E., & Kalant, H. (1981) Alcohol withdrawal and DT's. In J. Lowinson & P. Ruiz (Eds.), *Substance abuse.* Baltimore: Williams & Wilkins, p. 147.

Selvini-Palazzoli, M., Boscolo, L., Cecchin, G., & Prata, G. (1978) *Paradox and counterparadox.* New York: Jason Aronson.

Selzer, M. (1980) Alcoholism and alcohol psychoses. In H. Kaplan, A. Freedman, & B. Sadock (Eds.), *Comprehensive textbook of psychiatry/III.* Baltimore: Williams & Wilkins, p. 1629.

Seixas, F. (1981) Alcohol. In J. Lowinson & P. Ruiz (Eds.), *Substance abuse.* Baltimore: Williams & Wilkins, p. 191.

Shakow, D. (1962) Segmental set. *Archives of General Psychiatry, 6,* 1.

Shapiro, A. (1971) Placebo effects in medicine, psychotherapy, and psychoanalysis. In A. Bergin & S. Garfield (Eds.), *Handbook of psychotherapy and behavior change.* New York: Wiley.

Shapiro, A., Shapiro, E., & Wayne, H. (1973) Treatment of Tourette's syndrome. *Archives of General Psychiatry, 28,* 92.

Shapiro, D. (1965) *Neurotic styles.* New York: Basic Books.

Shapiro, D. A., & Shapiro, D. (1982) Meta-analysis of comparative therapy outcome research: A critical appraisal. *Behavioural Psychotherapy, 10,* 4–25.

Shapiro, K., Shapiro, E., Brunn, R., & Sweet, R. (1978) *Gilles de la Tourette's syndrome.* New York: Raven Press.

Shapiro, S., Skinner, E., Kessler, L., Von Korff, M., German, P., Tischler, G., Leaf, P., Benham, L., Cottler, L., & Regier, D. (1984) Utilization of health and mental health services: Three epidemiological catchment area studies. *Archives of General Psychiatry, 41,* 971–978.

Sharp, C., & Korman, M. (1981) Volatile substances. In J. Lowinson & P. Ruiz (Eds.), *Substance abuse.* Baltimore: Williams & Wilkins, p. 19.

Shaw, D., Camps, F., & Eccleston, F. (1967) 5-Hydroxtryptamine in the hindbrain of depressive suicides. *British Journal of Psychiatry, 113,* 1407.

Shean, G. (1978) *Schizophrenia: An introduction to research and theory.* Cambridge, Mass.: Winthrop Publishers.

Sheehan, D. (1983) *The anxiety disease.* New York: Charles Scribner's Sons.

Sheehan, J., & Costley, M. (1975) A re-examination of the role of heredity in stuttering. *Journal of Speech and Hearing Disorders, 40,* 27.

Sheehan, J., & Lyon, M. (1974) Role perception in stuttering. *Journal of Communication Disorders, 7,* 113.

Sheehy, G. (1976) *Passages.* New York: E. P. Dutton.

Shepard, T. (1974) Teratogenicity from drugs: An increasing problem. In *Disease-a-month.* Chicago: Yearbook Medical Publishers, June.

Sherman, A. (1953) Reactions to music of autistic (schizophrenic) children. *American Journal of Psychology, 109,* 823.

Sherman, M. (1979) *Personality.* New York: Pergamon.

Shields, J. (1978) Genetic factors in neurosis. In H. M. van Praag (Ed.), *Research in neurosis.* New York: Spectrum Publications.

Shields, J. (1973) Heredity and psychological abnormality. In H. Eysenck (Ed.), *Handbook of abnormal psychology* (2d ed.). New York: Knapp.

Shields, J., & Slater, E. (1961) Heredity and psychological abnormality. In H. Eysenck (Ed.), *Handbook of abnormal psychology.* New York: Basic Books.

Shneidman, E. (1969) Suicide, lethality and the psychological autopsy. In E. Shneidman & M. Ortega (Eds.), *Aspects of depression.* Boston: Little, Brown.

Shneidman, E. (1971) Prevention, intervention and postvention. *Annals of Internal Medicine, 75,* 453.

Shneidman, E. (1973) *Deaths of man.* New York: Quadrangle.

Shneidman, E. (1975) Suicide. In A. Freedman, H. Kaplan, & B. Sadock (Eds.), *Comprehensive textbook of psychiatry/II.* Baltimore: Williams & Wilkins.

Shneidman, E., & Farberow, N. (1961) *Some facts about suicide.* Washington, D.C.: U.S. Government Printing Office.

Short, A. (1980) Evaluation of short-term outcome using parents as co-therapists for their own psychotic children. Unpublished doctoral dissertation, University of North Carolina at Chapel Hill, 1980.

Shopper, M. (1975) Interview: The challenge of adolescence, by Don Crinklaw. *Marriage and Family Living,* July, 5.

Sigerist, H. (1943) *Civilization and disease.* Ithaca, N.Y.: Cornell University Press.

Silver, L. (1980) Stereotyped movement disorders. In H. Kaplan, A. Freedman, & B. Sadock (Eds.), *Comprehensive textbook of Psychiatry/III.* Baltimore: Williams & Wilkins, p. 2571.

Simari, C., & Baskin, D. (1980) Incest: No longer a family affair. *Child Psychiatry Quarterly, 13,* 36.

Simon, E. (1980) Opiate receptors and their implications for drug addiction. In D. Lettieri, M. Sayers, & H. Pearson (Eds.), *Theories of drug use.* Washington, D.C.: NIDA Research Monograph 30, p. 303.

Simon, E. (1981) Recent developments in the biology of the opiates: Possible relevance for addictions. In J. Lowinson & P. Ruiz (Eds.), *Substance abuse.* Baltimore: Williams & Wilkins, p. 45.

Singer, M., & Wynne, L. (1965) Thought disorders and family relations of schizophrenics. III: Methodology using projective techniques. *Archives of General Psychiatry, 12,* 187.

Singh, M., & Kay, S. (1976) Wheat gluten as a pathogenic factor in schizophrenia. *Science, 191,* 401.

Skinner, B. (1938) *The behavior of organisms.* New York: Appleton.

Skinner, B. (1959) *The behavior of organisms* (2d ed.). New York: Appleton.

Slater, E., & Cowie, V. (1971) *The genetics of mental disorders.* London: Oxford University Press.

Slater, E., & Shields, J. (1982) Reported by G. Carey, Genetic influences in anxiety neurosis and agoraphobia. In R. Matthew (Ed.), *The biology of anxiety.* New York: Brunner/Mazel.

Smith, C., & Morris, L. (1976) Effects of stimulative and sedative music on cognitive and emotional components of anxiety. *Psychological Reports, 38,* 1187.

Smith, D., & Kraft, W. (1983) Do psychologists really want an alternative? *American Psychologist, 38,* 777.

Smith, J. (1980) Ego-dystonic homosexuality. *Comprehensive Psychiatry, 21,* 119.

Smith, M. (1973) Is psychology relevant to new priorities? *American Psychologist, 28,* 463.

Smith, M. L., & Glass, G. V. (1977) Meta-analysis of psychotherapy outcome studies. *American Psychologist, 32,* 752–760.

Smith, M. L., Glass, G. V., & Miller, T. I. (1980) *The benefits of psychotherapy.* Baltimore: Johns Hopkins University Press.

Smythies, J. (1976) Recent progress in schizophrenia research. *Lancet, 11,* 136.

Snyder, S. (1975) Biology. In S. Perlin (Ed.), *A handbook for the study of suicide.* New York: Oxford University Press.

Snyder, S. (1978) The opiate receptors and morphine-like peptides in the brain. *American Journal of Psychiatry, 135,* 645.

Solomon, J. (1972) Why gamble? A psychological profile of pathology. *The Sciences, 12,* 20.

Solomon, R., Turner, L., & Lessac, M. (1968) Some effects of delay of punishment on resistance to temptation in dogs. *Journal of Personality and Social Psychology, 8,* 233.

Solomon, R., & Wynne, L. (1954) Traumatic avoidance learning: The principles of anxiety conservation and partial irreversibility. *Psychological Review, 61,* 353.

Speck, R., & Attneave, C. (1972) Social network intervention. In C. Sager & H. Kaplan (Eds.), *Progress in group and family therapy.* New York: Brunner/Mazel.

Speed, B. (1984) Family therapy: An update. *Association for Child Psychology and Psychiatry Newsletter, 6,* 2.

Spiegel, D., Frischolz, E., Maruffi, B. & Spiegel, H. (1981) Hypnotic responsivity and the treatment of flying phobia. *American Journal of Clinical Hypnosis, 23,* 239.

Spitzer, R. (1976) More on pseudoscience in science and the case for psychiatric diagnosis: A critique of D. Rosenham's "On being sane in insane places" and "The contextual nature of psychiatric diagnosis." *Archives of General Psychiatry, 33,* 459.

Spitzer, R., Endicott, J., & Robins, E. (1978) Research diagnostic criteria: Rationale and reliability. *Archives of General Psychiatry, 35,* 773.

Spitzer, R., Forman, J., & Nee, J. (1979) DSM-III field trials. I: Initial interrater diagnostic reliability. *American Journal of Psychiatry, 136,* 815.

Spitzer, R., Skodol, A., Gibbon, M., & Williams, J. (1981) *DSM-III casebook.* Washington, D.C.: American Psychiatric Association.

Spitzer, R., Skodol, A., Gibbon, M., & Williams, J. (1983) *Psychopathology: A case book.* New York: McGraw-Hill.

Spitzer, R., Williams, J., & Skodol, A. (1980) DSM-III: The major achievements and an overview. *American Journal of Psychiatry, 137,* 151.

Spitzer, R., & Wilson, P. (1975) Nosology and the official psychiatric nomenclature. In A. Freedman, H. Kaplan, & B. Sadock (Eds.), *Comprehensive textbook of psychiatry/II.* Baltimore: Williams & Wilkins.

Spohn, H., & Patterson, T. (1980) Recent studies of psychophysiology in schizophrenia. *Schizophrenia—1980.* Washington, D.C.: NIMH.

Srole, L., & Fischer, A. (Eds.). (1978) *Mental health in the metropolis. The Midtown Manhattan Study* (rev. ed.). New York: New York University Press.

Srole, L., Langner, T., Michael, S., Opler, M., & Rennie, T. (1975) *Mental health in the metropolis* (2d ed.). New York: Harper & Row.

Stampfl, T., & Levis, D. (1967) Essentials of implosive therapy: A learning based psychodynamic behavioral therapy. *Journal of Abnormal Psychology, 72,* 496.

Stangler, R., & Printz, A. (1980) DSM-III: Psychiatric diagnosis in a university population. *American Journal of Psychiatry, 137,* 937.

Stanton, A., Gunderson, J., Knapp, P., Frank, A., Vannicelli, M., Schnitzer, R., & Rosenthal, R. (1984) Effects of psychotherapy in schizophrenia: Design and implementation of a controlled study. *Schizophrenia Bulletin, 10,* 520.

Stanton, M., & Todd, T. (1979) Structural family therapy with drug addicts. In E. Kaufman & P. Kaufman (Eds.), *The family therapy of drug and alcohol abuse.* New York: Gardner Press.

Stauder, K. (1934) Lethal catatonia. *Archives fur Psychiatrische und Nervenkrankheiten, 102,* 614.

Stenzel, E. (1964) *Suicide and attempted suicide.* London: Penguin.

Stephan, C., Stephano, S., & Talkington, L. (1973) Use of modelling in survival skill training with educable mentally retarded. *The Training School Bulletin, 70,* 63.

Stevenson, J. (1971) *The diagnostic interview.* New York: Harper & Row.

Stickney, S. (1976) Wyatt v. Stickney-Background and postscript. In S. Golaan & W.

Fremouw (Eds.), *The right to treatment for mental patients.* New York: Irvington.

Stoller, R. (1977) Sexual deviation. In F. Beach (Ed.), *Human sexuality in four perspectives.* Baltimore: Johns Hopkins Press.

Storms, S. (1981) A theory of erotic orientation development. *Psychological Review, 88,* 340.

Storr, A. (1964) *Sexual deviation.* Baltimore: Penguin.

Strauss, J., & Gift, T. (1977) Choosing an approach for diagnosing schizophrenia. *Archives of General Psychiatry, 34,* 1248.

Strub, R., & Black, F. (1981) *Organic brain syndromes.* Philadelphia: Davis Co.

Strupp, G., & Reid, W. (1981) An historical view of institutional treatment. In W. Reid (Ed.), *Treatment of antisocial syndromes.* New York: Van Nostrand.

Su, C., Lin, S., Wang, Y., Li, C., Hung, L., Lin, C., & Lin, B. (1978) Effects of beta-endorphin on narcotic abstinence in men. *Journal of the Formosan Medical Association, 77,* 133.

Suinn, R. (1978) The coronary behavior pattern: A behavioral approach to intervention. In T. Dembrowski (Ed.), *Coronary prone behavior.* New York: Springer.

Sullivan, H. (1953) *The interpersonal theory of psychiatry.* New York: Norton.

Sullivan, S., Stanfield, C., Schanberg, S., & Cavenar, J. (1978) Platelet MAO and serum DBH activity in chronic alcoholics. *Archives of General Psychiatry, 35,* 1209.

Summit, R., & Kryso, J. (1978) Sexual abuse of children: A clinical spectrum. *American Journal of Orthopsychiatry, 48,* 237.

Sutherland, E. (1939) *Principles of criminology.* Philadelphia: Lippincott.

Sutker, P., & Archer, R. (1984) Opiate abuse and dependence disorders. In H. Adams & P. Sutker (Eds.), *Comprehensive handbook of psychopathology.* New York: Plenum, p. 585.

Sweat, S., Kelley, E., Blovin, K. & Glee, R. (1981) Career appearance perceptions of selected university students. *Adolescence, 16,* 359.

Switzky, H., & Haywood, H. (1984) A biosocial ecological perspective on mental retardation. In N. Endler & J. Hunt (Eds.), *Personality and the behavioral disorders.* New York: Wiley, p. 851.

Szasz, T. (1961) *The myth of mental illness: Foundation of a theory of personal conduct.* New York: Harper & Row.

Szasz, T. (1976) *Schizophrenia: The sacred symbol of psychiatry.* New York: Basic Books.

Szasz, T. (1980) *Sex by prescription.* New York: Anchor Press/Doubleday.

Szasz, T. (1982) The psychiatric will. *American Psychologist, 37,* 762.

Talkington, L., Hall, S., & Altman, R. (1973) Use of peer modelling procedure with severely retarded subjects as a basic communication response skill. *Training School Bulletin, 69,* 145.

Tamarin, G. (1963) Observations on asthma and psoriasis patients: Brief remarks on the clinical aspects of psychosomatic diseases. *Zeitschrift Psychosomatic Medicine, 9,* 26.

Tarasoff vs. the Regents of the University of California et al. 131 CAL RPTR 14, 551 P2d 334 (Cal 1976).

Taylor, P. D., & Turner, R. K. (1975) A clinical trial of continuous, intermittent and overlearning "bell and pad" treatments for nocturnal enuresis. *Behaviour Research and Therapy, 3,* 281.

Taylor, R. (1975) Electroconvulsive treatment (ECT): The control of therapeutic power. *exChange,* May/June, 32.

Teirmea, E. (1979) Psychosocial and psychic factors and age at onset of asthma. *Journal of Psychosomatic Research, 23,* 27.

Templeman, T., & Wollersheim, J. (1979) A cognitive-behavioral approach to the treatment of psychopathy. *Psychotherapy: Theory, Research and Practice, 16,* 132.

Teuting, P., Rosen, S., & Hirschfeld, R. (1981) *Special report on depression research.* Washington, D.C.: NIMH-DHHS Public No. (ADM) 81-1085.

Thomas, A., & Chess, S. (1980) *The dynamics of psychological development.* New York: Brunner/Mazel.

Thomas, A., & Chess, S. (1984) Genesis and evolution of behavior disorders: From infancy to early adult life. *American Journal of Psychiatry, 141,* 1.

Thorndike, E. (1913) *The psychology of learning.* New York: Teachers College.

Tienari, P. (1971) Schizophrenia and monozygotic twins. *Psychiatrica Finnica, 97,* 104.

Time Magazine, April 25, 1983, "Sexology on the defense," p. 55.

Tobias, J. (1970) The affluent male suburban delinquent. *Crime and Delinquency, 16,* 273.

Toolan, J. (1981) Depression and suicide in children: A review. *American Journal of Psychotherapy, 35,* 311.

Torgerson, S. (1979) The nature and origin of common phobic fears. *British Journal of Psychiatry, 134,* 343.

Torrey, E. (1983) *Surviving schizophrenia: A family manual.* New York: Harper & Row.

Torrey, E. & Peterson, M. (1976) The viral hypothesis of schizophrenia. *Schizophrenia Bulletin, 2,* 136.

Torrey, E., Peterson, M., Brannon, W., Carpenter, W., Post, R., & Van Kammen, D. (1978) Immunoglobins and viral antibodies in schizophrenic patients. *British Journal of Psychiatry, 132,* 342.

Toynbee, A. (1968) *A man's concern with death.* New York: McGraw-Hill.

Travis, L. (1931) *Speech pathology.* New York: Appleton-Century-Crofts.

Truax, C., & Carkhuff, R. (1967) *Counseling and psychotherapy: Training and practice.* Chicago: Aldine.

Tryon, G. (1980) The measurement and treatment of test anxiety. *Review of Educational Research, 50,* 343.

Tsuang, M. (1978a) Familial subtyping of schizophrenia and affective disorders. In R. Spitzer & D. Klein (Eds.), *Critical issues in psychiatric diagnosis.* New York: Raven Press, p. 203.

Tsuang, M. (1978b) Genetic counseling for psychiatric patients and their families. *American Journal of Psychiatry, 135,* 1465.

Tsuang, M., & Simpson, J. (1984) Schizoaffective disorder: Concept and reality. *Schizophrenia Bulletin, 10,* 14.

Turner, R., & Taylor, P. (1974) Conditioning treatment of nocturnal enuresis in adults: Preliminary findings. *Behavior Research and Therapy, 12,* 41.

Tustin, F. (1972) *Autism and childhood psychosis.* London: Hogarth Press.

Tyrell, D., Crowe, T., Parry, R., Johnstone, E., & Ferrier, I. (1979) Possible viruses in schizophrenia and some neurological disorders. *Lancet, 14,* 839.

Uhlenhuth, E. H. (1981) Specific anxiety syndromes: Current therapeutic options. *Journal of Clinical Psychiatry, 42,* 27.

Underwood, M. M., & Fiedler, N. (1983) The crisis of rape: A community response. *Community Mental Health Journal, 19,* 227.

Ullmann, L., & Krasner, L. (1969) *A psychological approach to abnormal behavior.* Englewood Cliffs, N.J.: Prentice-Hall.

Ullmann, L., & Krasner, L. (1975) *A psychological approach to abnormal behavior* (2d ed.). Englewood Cliffs, N.J.: Prentice-Hall.

Ungerleider, J., & DeAngelis, J. (1981) Hallucinogens. In J. Lowinson & P. Ruiz (Eds.), *Substance abuse.* Baltimore: Williams & Wilkins, p. 148.

Uniform Crime Reports—Federal Bureau of Investigation. (1978). Washington, D.C.: U.S. Department of Justice.

Uniform Crime Reports—Federal Bureau of Investigation. (1983) Washington, D.C.: U.S. Department of Justice.

Vahlquist, B. (1977) Migraine in children. *International Archives of Allergy, 7,* 348.

Vahlquist, B. (1955) Migraine in children. *International Archives of Allergy, 7,* 348.

Vail Conference: Borderline and narcissistic disorders. (1979) *Proceedings of the Vail Workshop,* March 3–10.

Vaillant, G., & Milofsky, E. (1980) Natural history of male psychological health. IX: Empirical evidence for Erikson's model of the life cycle. *American Journal of Psychiatry, 137,* 1348.

Vaillant, G., & Perry, J. (1980) Personality disorder. In H. Kaplan, A. Freedman, & B. Sadock (Eds.), *Comprehensive textbook of psychiatry/III.* Baltimore: Williams & Wilkins.

Vaillant, G., & Perry, J. (1985) Personality disorders. In H. Kaplan & B. Sadock (Eds.), *Comprehensive textbook of psychiatry/IV.* Baltimore: Williams and Wilkins, p. 958.

Valenstein, F. (1973) *Brain control.* New York: Wiley.

Van der Valk, J. (1960) Comparison of the social setting and behavior of patients with bronchial asthma, coronary occlusions, and healthy subjects. *Fortschrift Psychosomatic Medicinem, 1,* 284.

Van Dijk, W. (1971) Complexity of the dependence problem: Interaction of biological, psychogenic and sociogenic factors. In H. Van Praag (Ed.), *Biochemical and pharmacological aspects of dependence.* Haarlem, Netherlands: Bohm, p. 6.

Van Dijk, W. (1980) Biological, psychogenic, and sociogenic factors in drug dependence. In D. Lettieri, M. Sayers, & H. Pearson (Eds.), *Theories of drug use.* Washington, D.C.: NIDA Research Monograph 30, p. 164.

Van Dyke, J. (1981) Cocaine. In J. Lowinson & P. Ruiz (Eds.), *Substance abuse.* Baltimore: Williams & Wilkins, p. 158.

Van Osdol, W., & Shane, D. (1977) *An introduction to exceptional children.* Dubuque, Iowa: Wm. C. Brown.

Van Praag, H. (1980) Central monoamine metabolism in depression. II: Catecholamines and related compounds. *Comprehensive Psychiatry, 21,* 44.

Van Praag, H. (1981) Management of depression with serotonin precursors. *Biological Psychiatry, 16,* 291.

Van Praag, H., Korf, J., & Schut, D. (1973) Cerebral monoamines and depression: An investigation with the probenacid techniques. *Archives of General Psychiatry, 28,* 827.

Veasey, H. (1977) Aspects of student health: Specific psychological problems. *British Medical Journal, 7,* 26.

Venables, P. (1977) The electrodermal psychophysiology of schizophrenics and children at risk for schizophrenia: Current controversies and developments. *Schizophrenia Bulletin, 3,* 28.

Venables, P., & Christie, M. (1974) Mechanisms, instrumentation, recording techniques and quantification of response. In W. Prokasy & D. Raskin (Eds.), *Electrodermal activity in psychological research.* New York: Academic Press.

Venables, P., & Wing, J. (1962) Level of arousal and the subclassification of schizophrenia. *Archives of General Psychiatry, 7,* 114.

Verhoeven, W., van Praag, H., van Ree, J., & deWied, D. (1979) Improvements in schizophrenic patients treated with (des-Tyri)-gamma-endorphin. *Archives of General Psychiatry, 36,* 294.

Vermeer, D. E., & Frate, D. A. (1979) Geophagia in rural Mississippi: Environmental and cultural contexts and nutritional implications. *The American Journal of Clinical Nutrition, 32,* 2129.

Verwoerdt, A. (1976) *Clinical geropsychiatry.* Baltimore: Williams & Wilkins.

Vestergaard, P. (1980) Renal side effects in lithium. In F. Johnson (Ed.), *Handbook of lithium therapy.* Baltimore: University Park Press, p. 126.

Vikkunen, M. (1979) Serum cholesterol in antisocial personality. *Neuropsychobiology, 5,* 27.

Vital Statistics Report. (1981) Advance report of final mortality statistics, 1981. National Center for Health Statistics. Vol. 31, No. 9. U.S. Dept. of Health and Human Services.

Vitalo, R. (1971) Teaching improved interpersonal functioning as a preferred mode of treatment. *Journal of Clinical Psychology, 27,* 166.

Vogt, D. (1973) *Literacy among youths 12–17 years* (DHEW Pub. No. HRA 74-1613). Washington, D.C.: U.S. Government Printing Office.

Voorhees, J. (1981) Neuropsychological differences between juvenile delinquents and functional adolescents: A preliminary study. *Adolescence, 61,* 57.

Wagemaker, H., & Cade, R. (1977) The use of hemodialysis in chronic schizophrenia. *American Journal of Psychiatry, 134,* 684.

Wagner, G., & Metz, P. (1980) Impotence due to vascular disorders: An overview. *Journal of Sex and Marital Therapy, 6,* 223.

Wald, E., MacKinnon, J., & Desiderto, O. (1973) Production of gastric ulcers in the unrestrained rat. *Journal of Physiology and Behavior, 10,* 825.

Waldorf, D., & Daily, D. (1975) Debunking popular myths about addicts and addiction. In R. Coombs (Ed.), *Junkies and straights.* Lexington, Mass.: D. C. Heath.

Walinder, J., Skott, A., Carlsson, A., & Roos, B. (1976) Potentiation by metyrosine of thioridazine effects in chronic schizophrenics. *American Journal of Psychiatry, 133,* 501.

Walinder, J., & Thurne, I. (1975) *A social-psychiatric follow-up study of 24 sex reassigned transsexuals.* Copenhagen: Scandinavian University Books.

Walker, C. E. (1982) Sexual disorders in behavioral medicine. Assessment and treatment strategies. In D. M. Doleys, R. L. Meredith, and A. R. Ciminero (Eds.), *Behavioral medicine: Assessment and treatment strategies* New York, Plenum Press.

Walker, D. (1976) Suburban runaway youth of the 70's. Paper presented at the meetings of the American Psychological Association, Washington, D.C.

Walker, P. (1977) Medroxyprogesterone acetate as an antiandrogen for the rehabilitation of sex offenders. In R. Gemme & C. Wheeler (Eds.), *Progress in sexology: Selected proceedings of the 1976 international congress of sexology.* New York: Plenum Press.

Wallace, C. (1984) Community and interpersonal functioning in the course of schizophrenic disorder. *Schizophrenia Bulletin, 10,* 133.

Wallace, S. (1973) *After suicide.* New York: Wiley.

Walsh, D., Till, R., & Williams, M. (1978) Age and differences in peripheral perceptual processing: A monoptic backward masking investigation. *Journal of Experimental Psychology: Human Perception and Performance, 4,* 232.

Walters, P. (1971) Student apathy. In G. Blaine & C. McArthur (Eds.), *Emotional problems of the student* (2d ed.). New York: Appleton-Century-Crofts.

Watson, J., & Rayner, R. (1920) Conditioned emotional reactions. *Journal of Experimental Psychology, 3,* 1.

Watternberg, W. (1956) Boys who run away from, home. *Journal of Educational Psychology, 47,* 335.

Watzlawick, P., Weakland, J., & Fisch, R. (1974) *Change: Principles of problem formation and problem resolution.* New York: Norton.

Weakland, J., Fisch, R., Watzlawick, P., & Bodin, A. (1974) Brief therapy: Focused problem resolution. *Family Process, 13,* 141.

Webb, C., Gold, R., Johnstone, E., & Di-Clemente, C. (1981) Accuracy of DSM-III diagnoses following a training program. *American Journal of Psychiatry, 138,* 376.

Wechsler, D. (1980a) Psychological assessment of intelligence. In H. Kaplan, A. Freedman, & B. Sadock (Eds.), *Comprehensive textbook of psychiatry/III.* Baltimore: Williams & Wilkins, p. 926.

Wechsler, D. (1980b) *Manual for the WAIS-R.* New York: Psychological Corporation.

Wechsler, D. (1981) *Wechsler Adult Intelligence Scale-Revised.* New York: Psychological Corporation.

Wechsler, H., Rohman, M., & Solomon, R. (1981) Emotional problems and concerns of New England college students. *American Journal of Orthopsychiatry, 51,* 719.

Weinberg, J. (1975) Psychopathology. In J. Howells (Ed.), *Modern perspectives on the psychology of aging.* New York: Brunner/Mazel.

Weinberg, M., & Williams, C. (1974) *Male homosexuals: Their problems and adaptations.* New York: Oxford University Press.

Weiner, H. (1977) *Psychobiology and human disease.* New York: Elsevier, North Holland.

Weiner, H. (1980) Respiratory disorders. In H. Kaplan, A. Freedman, & B. Sadock (Eds.), *Comprehensive textbook of psychiatry/III.* Baltimore: Williams & Wilkins.

Weiner, I. (1969) The effectiveness of a suicide prevention program. *Mental Hygiene, 53,* 357.

Weintraub, W. (1981) Compulsive and paranoid personalities. In J. Lion (Ed.), *Personality disorders: Diagnosis and management* (Revised for DSM-III) (2d ed.). Baltimore: Williams & Wilkins.

Weiss, J. (1977) Psychological and behavioral influences on gastrointestinal lesions in animal models. In J. Maser & M. Seligman (Eds.), *Psychopathology: Experimental models.* San Francisco: Freeman.

Weissman, J., & Klerman, G. (1977a) Sex differences and epidemiology of depression. *Archives of General Psychiatry, 34,* 98.

Weissman, J., & Klerman, G. (1977b) The epidemiology of mental disorders. *Archives of General Psychiatry, 35,* 705.

Wells, L. (1981) Family pathology and father-daughter incest: Restricted pathology. *Journal of Clinical Psychology, 42,* 197.

Werkman, S. (1980) Anxiety disorders. In H. Kaplan, A. Freedman, & B. Sadock (eds.), *Comprehensive textbook of psychiatry/III.* Baltimore: Williams & Wilkins, 2620.

Werner, D. (1979) A cross-cultural perspective on theory and research on male homosexuality. *Journal of Homosexuality, 4,* 345.

Wheaton, B. (1978) The sociogenesis of psychological disorder: Re-examining the causal issues with longitudinal data. *American Sociological Review, 43,* 383.

White, R. (1952) *Lives in progress.* New York: Dryden Press.

Whiting, S. (1981) The problem of depression in adolescence. *Adolescence, 61,* 67.

Whittington, H. (1963) *Psychiatry on the college campus.* New York: International Universities Press.

Williams, J. (1985a) The multi-axial system of DSM-III: Where did it come from and where should it go? I: Its origins and critiques. *Archives of General Psychiatry, 42,* 175.

Williams, J. (1985b) The multi-axial system of DSM-III: Where did it come from and where is it going? II: Empirical studies, innovations, and recommendations. *Archives of General Psychiatry, 42,* 181.

Williams, J., & Spitzer, R. (1983) The issue of sex bias in DSM-III: A critique of "A woman's view of DSM-III" by Marcie Kaplan. *American Psychologist, 38,* 793.

Wilson, P. (1974) *Oscar: An inquiry into the nature of sanity.* New York: Random House.

Wine, J. (1971) Test anxiety and direction of attention. *Psychological Bulletin, 76,* 92.

Winick, M., & Russo, P. (1973) Effects of malnutrition on brain development. *Biology of Brain Dysfunction, 1,* 301.

Winokur, G., Clayton, P., & Reich, T. (1969) *Manic-depressive illness.* St. Louis: C. V. Mosby.

Wise, T., & Meyer, J. (1980) Transvestism: Previous findings and new areas of inquiry. *Journal of Sex and Marital Therapy, 6,* 116.

Wolf, S., & Wolff, H. (1947) *Human gastric function.* New York: Oxford University Press.

Wolpe, J. (1981) The dichotomy between clinical conditioning and cognitively learned anxiety. *Journal of Behavior Therapy and Experimental Psychiatry, 12,* 35.

Wolpe, J. (1973) *The practice of behavior therapy* (2nd ed.). New York: Pergamon.

Wolpe, J. (1958) *Psychotherapy by reciprocal inhibition.* Stanford: Stanford University Press.

Wood, E. (1980) Counseling minority students: A program model. *Personnel and Guidance Journal, 55,* 416.

World Health Organization (WHO). (1939) *Manual of the international statistical classification of diseases, injuries and causes of death.* Geneva: WHO.

World Health Organization (WHO). (1948) *Manual of the international statistical classification of diseases, injuries and causes of death.* Geneva: WHO.

World Health Organization (WHO). (1978) *Manual of the international statistical classification of diseases, injuries and causes of death.* Geneva: WHO.

Wortley, D. B., & Amatea, D. (1982) Mapping adult life changes: A conceptual framework for organizing adult developmental theory. *Personnel and Guidance Journal, 60,* 476.

Wortman, C., & Loftus, E. (1981) *Psychology.* New York: Knopf.

Wurmser, L. (1981) Psychodynamics of substance abuse. In J. Lowinson & P. Ruiz (Eds.), *Substance abuse.* Baltimore: Williams & Wilkins, p. 63.

Wyatt v. Aderholt. (1974) *U.S. Court of Appeals for the Fifth Circuit, 503,* F.2d, 1305.

Wyatt v. Stickney. (1972) U.S. District Court for the Middle District of Alabama, 344 F. Supp. aff'd, 503 F.2d, 1305 (5th Cir, 1974).

Wyatt, R., Potkin, S., & Murphy, D. (1979) Platelet MAO activity in schizophrenia: A review of the data. *American Journal of Psychiatry, 136,* 377.

Wynne, L., & Singer, M. (1963) Thought disorder and family relations of schizophrenics. II: A classification of forms of thinking. *Archives of General Psychiatry, 9,* 199.

Yager, J. (1974) Personal communication.

Yalom, I. (1980) *Existential Psychotherapy.* New York: Basic Books.

Yalom, I. (1970) *Theory and practice of group psychotherapy.* New York: Basic Books.

Yudovsky, S. (1982) Electroconvulsive therapy in the eighties: Techniques and technologies. *American Journal of Psychotherapy, 36,* 391.

Zahn, T. (1975) Psychophysiological concommitants of task performance in schizophrenia. In M. Kietzman, S. Sutton, & J. Zubin (Eds.), *Experimental approaches to psychopathology.* New York: Academic Press.

Zahn, T., Carpenter, W., & McGlashan, T. (1978) Short term outcome, clinical improvement and reaction time performance in acute schizophrenia. In L. Wynne, R. Cromwell, & S. Matthysse (Eds.), *The nature of schizophrenia: New approaches to research and treatment.* New York: Wiley.

Zarit, H. (1980) *Aging and mental disorders.* New York: Free Press.

Zarit, H., Gallagher, D., & Kramer, N. (1980) Memory training in the community aged: Effects of depression, memory complaints and memory performance. *Educational Gerontology, 5,* 238.

Zax, M., & Specter, G. (1974) *An introduction to community psychology.* New York: Wiley.

Zigler, E., & Balla, D. (1982) *Mental retardation: The development-difference controversy.* New Jersey: Erlbaum Associates.

Zigler, E., Balla, D., & Hodapp. R. (1984) On the definition and classification of mental retardation. *American Journal of Mental Deficiency, 89,* 215.

Zilboorg, G., & Henry, G. (1941) *A history of medical psychology.* New York: Norton.

Zillbergeld, H., & Evans, W. (1981) Cited in R. Kolodny. Evaluating sex therapy: Process and outcome at the Masters and Johnson Institute. *The Journal of Sex Research, 17,* 301.

Zubin, J., & Spring, B. (1977) Vulnerability—A new view of schizophrenia. *Journal of Abnormal Psychology, 86,* 103.

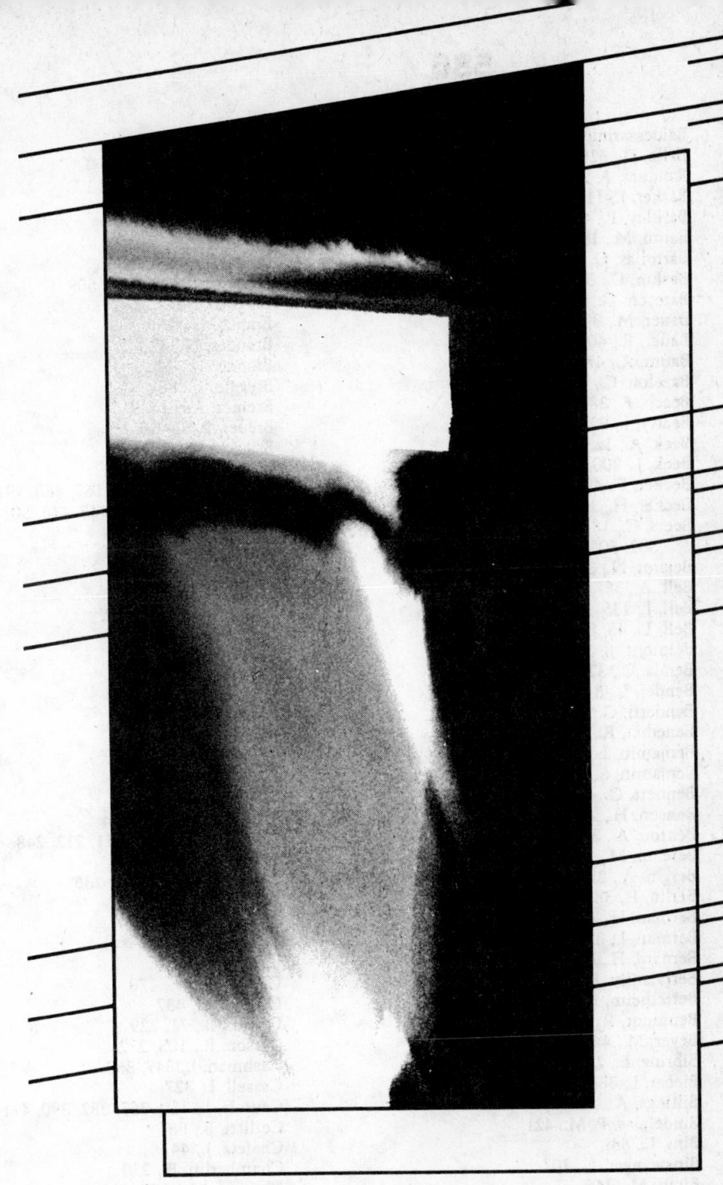

Name Index

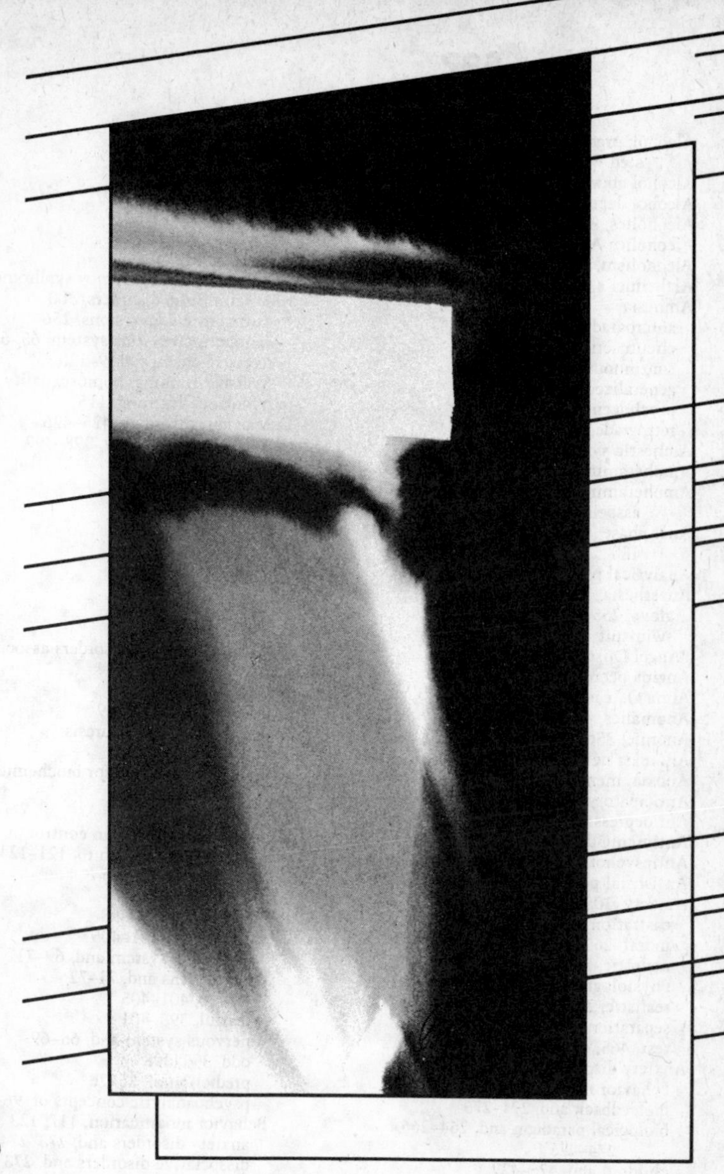

Subject Index